T0185783

Pro Power BI Desktop

Self-Service Analytics and Data Visualization for the Power User

Third Edition

Adam Aspin

Apress®

Pro Power BI Desktop: Self-Service Analytics and Data Visualization for the Power User

Adam Aspin
Stoke-on-Trent, Staffordshire, UK

ISBN-13 (pbk): 978-1-4842-5762-3   ISBN-13 (electronic): 978-1-4842-5763-0
https://doi.org/10.1007/978-1-4842-5763-0

Copyright © 2020 by Adam Aspin

This work is subject to copyright. All rights are reserved by the Publisher, whether the whole or part of the material is concerned, specifically the rights of translation, reprinting, reuse of illustrations, recitation, broadcasting, reproduction on microfilms or in any other physical way, and transmission or information storage and retrieval, electronic adaptation, computer software, or by similar or dissimilar methodology now known or hereafter developed.

Trademarked names, logos, and images may appear in this book. Rather than use a trademark symbol with every occurrence of a trademarked name, logo, or image we use the names, logos, and images only in an editorial fashion and to the benefit of the trademark owner, with no intention of infringement of the trademark.

The use in this publication of trade names, trademarks, service marks, and similar terms, even if they are not identified as such, is not to be taken as an expression of opinion as to whether or not they are subject to proprietary rights.

While the advice and information in this book are believed to be true and accurate at the date of publication, neither the authors nor the editors nor the publisher can accept any legal responsibility for any errors or omissions that may be made. The publisher makes no warranty, express or implied, with respect to the material contained herein.

Managing Director, Apress Media LLC: Welmoed Spahr
Acquisitions Editor: Jonathan Gennick
Development Editor: Laura Berendson
Coordinating Editor: Jill Balzano

Cover image designed by Freepik (www.freepik.com)

Distributed to the book trade worldwide by Springer Science+Business Media New York, 233 Spring Street, 6th Floor, New York, NY 10013. Phone 1-800-SPRINGER, fax (201) 348-4505, e-mail orders-ny@springer-sbm.com, or visit www.springeronline.com. Apress Media, LLC is a California LLC and the sole member (owner) is Springer Science + Business Media Finance Inc (SSBM Finance Inc). SSBM Finance Inc is a **Delaware** corporation.

For information on translations, please e-mail rights@apress.com, or visit http://www.apress.com/rights-permissions.

Apress titles may be purchased in bulk for academic, corporate, or promotional use. eBook versions and licenses are also available for most titles. For more information, reference our Print and eBook Bulk Sales web page at http://www.apress.com/bulk-sales.

Any source code or other supplementary material referenced by the author in this book is available to readers on GitHub via the book's product page, located at www.apress.com/9781484257623. For more detailed information, please visit http://www.apress.com/source-code.

Printed on acid-free paper

To Karine. For everything.

Table of Contents

About the Author

Adam Aspin is an independent business intelligence (BI) consultant based in the UK. He has worked with SQL Server for more than 25 years. During this time, he has developed several dozen reporting and analytical systems using Microsoft analytics.

A graduate of Oxford University, Adam began his career in publishing before moving into IT. Databases soon became a passion, and his experience in this arena ranges from Access to Oracle and MySQL, with occasional sorties into the world of DB2. He is, however, most at home in the Microsoft universe using SQL Server, SQL Server Analysis Services, SQL Server Reporting Services, SQL Server Integration Services, and Power BI, both on-premises and in Azure.

Business intelligence has been Adam's principal focus for the last 25 years. He has applied his skills for a range of clients in industry sectors such as finance, utilities, telecommunications, insurance, manufacturing, and banking.

Adam is a frequent contributor to SQLServerCentral.com and Simple Talk. He has written numerous articles for various French IT publications. A fluent French speaker, Adam has worked in France and Switzerland for many years. He speaks regularly at events such as SQLBits, SQL Saturdays, and local SQL Server user groups.

Adam is the author of *SQL Server 2012 Data Integration Recipes* (Apress), *High Impact Data Visualization with Power View, Power Map, and Power BI* (Apress), *Business Intelligence with SQL Server Reporting Services* (Apress), and *Data Mashup with Microsoft Excel* (Apress).

About the Technical Reviewer

Diana Gangan is a data analyst with extensive Power BI experience; she has supervised the adoption and implementation of Power BI reporting while consulting for some of the leading automotive and food and beverage companies in the world. Besides data analysis and Power BI, Diana specializes in the DAX, M Query, and Python languages, as well as data modeling, machine learning and mathematics for machine learning, and natural language processing.

Acknowledgments

Writing a technical book can be a lonely occupation. So I am all the more grateful for all the help and encouragement that I have received from so many fabulous friends and colleagues.

First, my considerable thanks go to Jonathan Gennick, the commissioning editor of this book. Throughout the publication process, Jonathan has been both a tower of strength and an exemplary mentor. He has always been available to share his vast experience selflessly and courteously.

Heartfelt thanks go to Jill Balzano, the Apress coordinating editor, for calmly managing this book through the production process. She succeeded—once again—in the well-nigh impossible task of making a potentially stress-filled trek into a pleasant journey filled with light and humor. Her team also deserves much praise for their efficiency under pressure.

I also owe a debt of gratitude to Diana Gangan for her time and effort spent reviewing this book. Being a technical reviewer is a thankless task, but I want to say a heartfelt "thank you" to Diana for the range and depth of her comments and for picking up so much that otherwise would have gone unnoticed. The book is a better one thanks to her.

My thanks also go to Ann Gemer Tuballa for her tireless and subtle work editing and polishing the prose and to the layout and production staff for the hours spent preparing the book for publishing.

Once again my deepest gratitude is reserved for the two people who have given the most to this book. They are my wife and son who have provided continual encouragement to persevere. Karine has not only given me the support and encouragement but also the love without which nothing would be worth any effort. I am a very lucky man to have both of them.

Introduction

Business intelligence (BI) has become one of the buzzwords that defines an age. Its younger sibling, self-service BI, has attained the status of a holy grail for businesses. Managers want their staff to deliver insight in seconds; users just want to do their jobs quickly. Everyone wants to produce clear, telling, and accurate analysis with tools that are intuitive and easy to use.

Microsoft recognized these trends and needs a few short years ago when they produced the first version of Power BI Desktop. Since its launch, the product has grown beyond recognition. It now allows any user to take data from virtually any source and use it to produce stunning dashboards and compelling reports in record time that will seize their audience's attention. Using this rapidly evolving tool, any user can slice and dice the data with remarkable ease and then add metrics, instant analyses, and key performance indicators (KPIs) to project their insights. Ultimately, they can use it to weave a data narrative that delivers a real competitive advantage.

This book shows how to deliver eye-catching business intelligence with Microsoft Power BI Desktop. It teaches you how to make raw data into clear, accurate, and interactive information. The aim of this book is to help you to push your BI delivery to the next level. In 24 chapters, you will learn to create great-looking visualizations and inspire your audience as they interact with the elegant and eloquent output that you can now deliver. You will see how to choose from a wide range of built-in and third-party visualization types so that your message is always enhanced. You'll discover ways to deliver those results on the PC, on tablets, and on smartphones. Finally, this book helps you save time by sourcing and preparing the underlying data without needing an IT department to cleanse and structure it for you.

Power BI Desktop will let your analyses speak for themselves. This book will help you learn how to unleash its vast resources.

If you wish, you can read this book from start to finish as it is designed to be a progressive tutorial that will help you to learn Power BI Desktop. However, as Power BI Desktop is composed of several interdependent BI functions, this book is broken down into groups of chapters that focus on the various areas of the product. It follows that you can, if you prefer, focus on individual areas of Power BI Desktop without having to take a linear approach to reading this book.

- Chapters 1 through 6 show you how to connect to a range of varied data sources and bring this data into Power BI Desktop.

- Chapters 7 through 12 explain how to transform and clean data so that you can use it for analysis.

- Chapter 13 introduces you to the art of creating a data model on which you can base your interactive dashboards and reports.

- Chapters 14 through 24 take you through the myriad possibilities that Power BI Desktop offers to help you create stunning reports and dashboards. This covers tables, charts, maps, KPIs, and many other types of visuals.

This is the third edition of *Pro Power BI Desktop*. In the course of a couple of years since the second edition, Power BI Desktop has evolved magisterially. So a new edition of the book was necessary to update the original with all the new and exciting changes and extensions that have been added to the product. Indeed, the monthly release cycle that Microsoft has maintained—and is still maintaining—is proof of the company's dedication to improving an already outstanding product. The book includes the latest updates added in April 2020.

This book comes with a small set of sample data that are used to create the examples that are used throughout the book. I realize that it may seem paradoxical to use a tiny dataset for a product that can handle tens of millions of rows of data, but I prefer to use a comprehensible set of source data so that the reader can concentrate on what is being learned, rather than the data itself.

It is inevitable that not every question can be anticipated and answered in one book. Nonetheless I hope that I have answered many of the self-service BI questions that you might encounter and—more importantly—have given you the approaches and the confidence to resolve most of the Power BI Desktop challenges that you might encounter when applying this product to solve real-world problems.

I wish you good luck in using Power BI Desktop, and I sincerely hope that you have as much fun using it as I did in writing this book.

CHAPTER 1

Discovering and Loading Data with Power BI Desktop

Before you can use Power BI Desktop to present any analysis or discover new insights, you need data. Your sources could be in many places and in many formats. Nonetheless, you need to access them, look at them, select them, and quite possibly restructure them or clean them up to some extent. You may also need to join many separate data sources before you shape the data into a coherent model that you can use as the foundation for your dashboards and reports. The amazing thing is that you can do all of this using Power BI Desktop without needing any other tools or utilities.

Discovering, loading, cleaning, and modifying source data are some of the many areas where Power BI Desktop really shines. It allows you to accomplish the following:

- *Data discovery*: Find and connect to a myriad of data sources containing potentially useful data. This can be from both public and private data sources. This is the subject of Chapters 1 through 6.

- *Data loading*: Select the data you have examined and load it into Power BI Desktop for shaping.

- *Data modification*: Modify the structure of each dataset that you have imported, then filter and clean the data itself (we will look at this in detail in Chapters 7 through 10).

- *Data shaping*: Join datasets to create a clear, unified, and accessible data model. You will learn how to do this in Chapter 13.

© Adam Aspin 2020
A. Aspin, *Pro Power BI Desktop*, https://doi.org/10.1007/978-1-4842-5763-0_1

Although I have outlined these four steps as if they are completely separate and sequential, the reality is that they often blend into a single process. Indeed, there could be many occasions when you will examine the data *after* it has been loaded into Power BI Desktop—or clean datasets *before* you load them. The core objective will, however, always remain the same: find some data and then load it into Power BI Desktop where you can tweak, clean, and shape it.

This process could be described simplistically as "First, catch your data." In the world of data warehousing, the specialists call it ETL, which is short for **E**xtract, **T**ransform, and **L**oad. Despite the reassuring confidence that the acronym brings, this process is rarely a smooth, logical progression through a clear-cut series of steps. The reality is often far messier. You may often find yourself importing some data, cleaning it, importing some more data from another source, combining the second dataset with the first one, removing some rows and columns, and then repeating these operations, as well as many others, several times over.

In this and the following few chapters, I will try to show you how the process can work in practice using Power BI Desktop. I hope that this will make the various steps that comprise an ETL process clearer. All I am asking is that you remain aware that the range of options that Power BI Desktop includes make it a multifaceted and tremendously capable tool. The science is to know *which* options to use. The art is to know *when* to use them.

The Data Load Process

Let's begin with a rapid overview of what you need to do to get some data into Power BI Desktop. Once you have launched Power BI Desktop, you are faced with the splash screen that you can see in Figure 1-1.

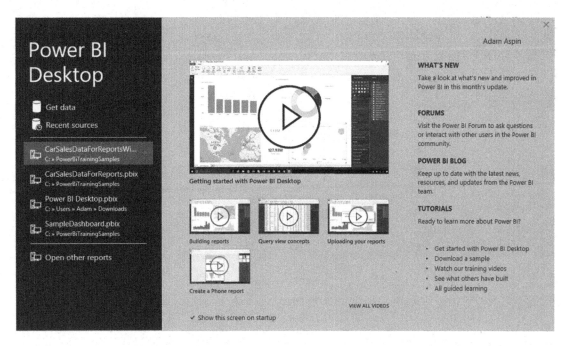

Figure 1-1. *The splash screen*

Given that you are working with an application that lives and breathes data, it is not really surprising that the first step in a new analytical challenge is to find and load some data. So the following explains what you have to do (assuming that you have downloaded the sample data that accompanies this book from the Apress website—this is explained in Appendix A):

1. Click Get Data in the splash screen. The Get Data dialog will appear, as shown in Figure 1-2.

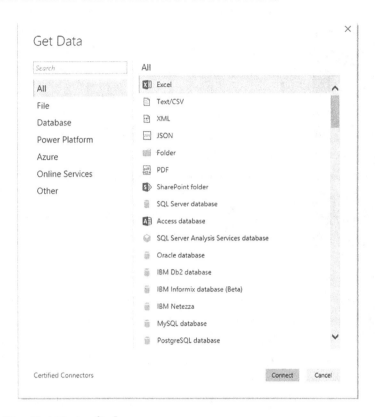

Figure 1-2. *The Get Data dialog*

2. In the list of all the possible data sources on the right of this dialog, click Excel, and then click Connect. The Windows Open File dialog will appear.

3. Click the file C:\PowerBiDesktopSamples\BrilliantBritishCars.xlsx. The Windows Open dialog will look like the one in Figure 1-3.

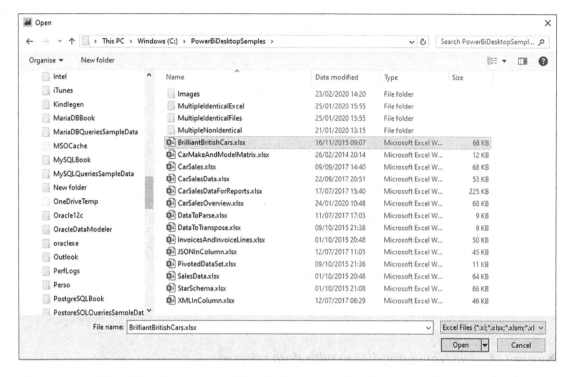

Figure 1-3. *The Windows Open File dialog when loading data from a file source*

4. Click the Open button. The Connecting dialog will appear for a second or two and then the Navigator dialog will appear.

5. You will see that the BrilliantBritishCars.xlsx file appears on the left of the Navigator dialog and that any workbooks, named ranges, or data tables that it contains are also listed. Click the BaseData worksheet name that is on the left. The contents of this workbook will appear in the data pane on the right of the Navigator dialog.

6. Click the check box for the BaseData worksheet on the left. The Load and Transform Data buttons will be activated. The Navigator dialog should look like Figure 1-4.

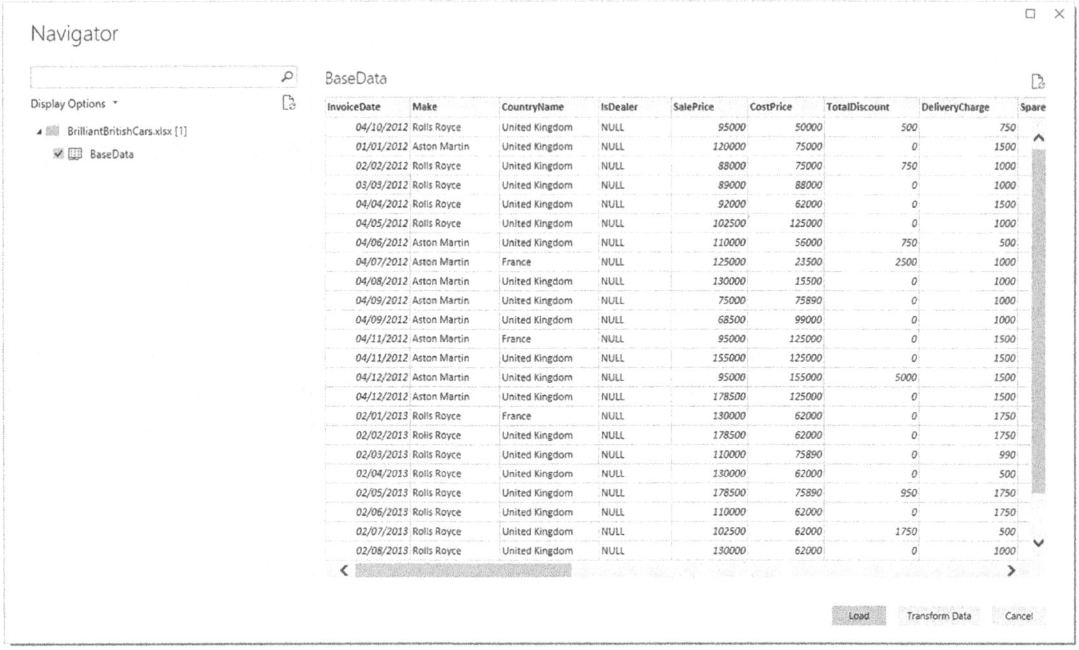

Figure 1-4. *The Navigator dialog with data selected*

7. Click Load. The data will be loaded from the Excel file into Power BI Desktop.

You will see the Power BI Desktop report window, like the one shown in Figure 1-5. This is the canvas where you will add visuals to create dashboards. You can see all the columns from the Excel worksheet are now fields in the Fields pane on the right of the Power BI Desktop application.

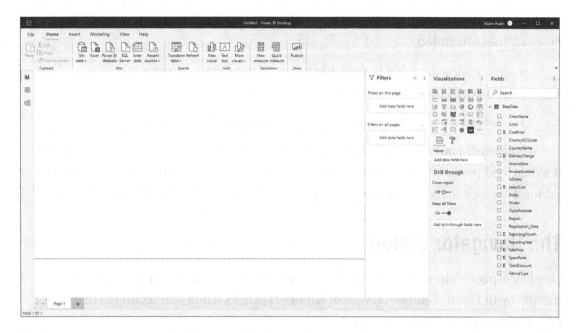

Figure 1-5. *Data available in Power BI Desktop*

I imagine that loading this data took under a minute. Yet you now have a fully operational data model in Power BI Desktop that is ready to feed data into your dashboard. However, as creating dashboards is explained later in this book, I would like to pause for an instant and explain exactly what you have seen so far. Of course, if you are itching to race ahead and actually create a couple of tables and charts, then you can always jump ahead to Chapters 14–24.

Note   The Get Data dialog contained a reference to certified connectors. These are developed by third parties but certified and distributed by Microsoft.

Understanding Data Load

What you have seen so far is an extremely rapid dash through a Power BI Desktop data load scenario. In reality, this process can range from the blindingly simple (as you just saw) to the more complex where you join, filter, and modify multiple datasets from different sources (as you will discover in Chapters 7 through 10). However, loading data will always be the first step in any data analysis scenario when you are using Power BI Desktop.

In this short example, you nonetheless saw many of the key elements of the data load process. These included

- Accessing data that is available in any of the source formats that Power BI Desktop can read

- Taking a first look at the data before loading it into Power BI Desktop

What you did not see here is how Power BI Desktop can add an intermediate step to the data load process that allows you to edit the source data in Power BI Desktop Query Editor. This aspect of data manipulation is covered extensively in Chapters 7 through 12.

The Navigator Dialog

One key aspect of the data load process is using the Navigator dialog correctly. You saw this dialog in Figure 1-4. The Navigator window appears when connecting to many, but not all, data sources. It allows you to

- Take a quick look at the available data tables in the data source

- Filter multiple data elements that are available in a single data source

- Look at the data in individual tables

- Select one or more data tables to load into Power BI Desktop

Depending on the data source to which you have connected, you might see only a few data tables in the Navigator window, or hundreds of them. In any case, what you can see are the structured datasets that Power BI Desktop can recognize and is confident that it can import. Equally dependent on the data source is the level of complexity of what you will see in the Navigator window. If you are looking at a database server, for instance, then you may start out with a list of databases and you may need to dig deeper into the arborescence of the data by expanding databases to list the available data tables and views.

The more you work with Power BI Desktop, the more you will use the Navigator dialog. So it seems appropriate to explain at this early juncture some of the tricks and techniques that you can apply to make your life easier when delving into potential sources of data.

Let's start by taking a closer look at the available options. These are highlighted in Figure 1-6.

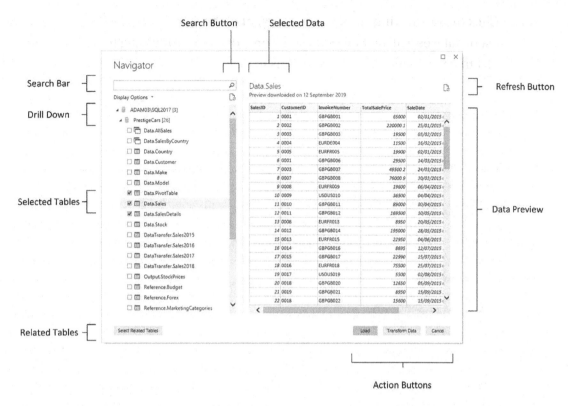

Figure 1-6. *The Navigator dialog*

The Navigator dialog is essentially in two parts:

- *On the left*: The hierarchy of available data sources. These can consist of a single dataset or multiple datasets, possibly organized into one or many folders.

- *On the right*: A preview of the data in the selected element.

The various Navigator dialog options are explained in the following sections.

Searching for Datasets

You will, inevitably, come across cases where the data source that you are connecting to will contain hundreds of datasets. This is especially true for databases. Fortunately, Power BI Desktop lets you filter the datasets that are displayed extremely easily.

1. In the Navigator dialog, click inside the Search box.

2. Enter a part of a dataset name that you want to isolate.

3. Click the magnifying glass icon at the right of the Search box. The
    list of datasets will be filtered to show only datasets containing the
    text that you entered. You can see this in Figure 1-7.

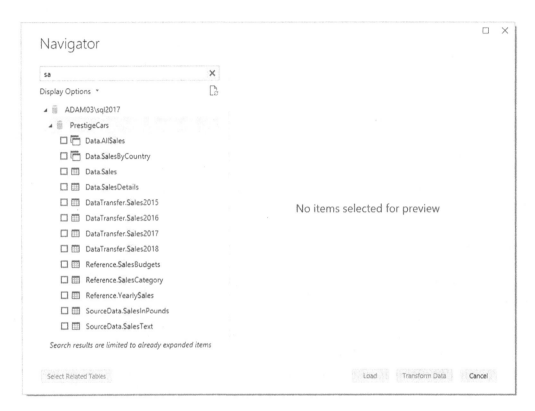

Figure 1-7. *Dataset search in the Navigator dialog*

Once you have previewed and selected the datasets that you want to use, simply click
the cross at the right of the Search box. Navigator will clear the filter and display all the
datasets in the data source.

Display Options

Clicking Display Options in the Navigator dialog will show a popup menu with two
options:

- Only selected items

- Enable data previews

Only Selected Items

Selecting this option will prevent any datasets that you have not selected from appearing in the data source pane.

Enable Data Previews

Selecting this option will show a small subset of the data available in the selected dataset. You could choose to disable data previews if the connection to the source data is slow.

Refresh

If you need to, you can refresh either or both of the following:

- The source data
- The data preview

Source Data Refresh

Clicking the preview button under the search bar will refresh the source data in the source data pane.

Data Preview Refresh

Clicking the preview button on the top right of the Navigator dialog will refresh the preview data visible on the right.

Select Related Tables

Clicking the Select Related Tables button is only valid for database sources, such as Microsoft SQL Server or Oracle. If the source database has been designed correctly to include joins between tables, then this option will automatically select all tables that are linked to any tables that you have already selected.

Note   In a database source, some tables can be related to other tables that are, themselves, related to other tables. This hierarchy of connections is not discovered in its entirety when you click Select Related Tables. In other words, you might have to select several tables and click this button repeatedly to select all the tables that you need.

You will see much, much more of the Navigator window in the following three chapters.

The Navigator Data Preview

The Navigator Data Preview pane (on the right) is, as its name implies, a preview of the data in a data source. It provides

- A brief overview of the *top few records* in any of the datasets that you want to look at. Given that the data you are previewing could be hundreds of columns wide and hundreds of rows deep, there could be scroll bars for the data table visible inside the Navigator Data Preview. Remember, however, that you are not examining *all* the available data and are only seeing a *small sample of the available records*.

- A list of the available columns in the data table.

Power BI Desktop can preview and load data from several different sources. Indeed (as you can see from the list of possible data sources in the Get Data dialog), it can read most of the commonly available enterprise data sources as well as many, many others. What is important to appreciate is that Power BI Desktop applies a common interface to the art and science of loading data, whatever the source. So whether you are examining a SQL Server or an Oracle database, an XML file or a text file, a web page or a big data source, you will always be using a standardized approach to examining and loading the data. This makes the Power BI Desktop data experience infinitely simpler—and extremely reassuring. It means that you spend less time worrying about technical aspects of data sources and you are free to focus on the data itself.

Note   The Navigator Data Preview is a brilliant data discovery tool. Without having to load any data, you can take a quick look at the data source and any data that it contains that can (probably) be loaded by Power BI Desktop. You can then decide if it is worth loading. This way you do not waste time on a data load that could be superfluous to your needs.

Modifying Data

Once you have one or more queries in Power BI Desktop that can connect to data sources and bring the data into this environment, you can start thinking about the next step—transforming the data so that it is ready for use. Depending on the number of data sources that you are handling and the extent of any modifications that are required, this could vary from the simple to the complex. To give a process some structure, I advise that you try to break down any steps into the following main threads:

- *Shape the dataset*: This covers filtering out records to reduce the size of the dataset, as well as removing any extraneous columns. It may also involve adding columns that you create by splitting existing columns, creating calculated columns, or even joining queries.

- *Cleanse and modify the data*: This is also known as *data transformation* (the *T* in ETL). It encompasses the process of converting text data to uppercase and lowercase, as well as (for instance) removing nonprinting characters. Rounding numbers and extracting date parts from date data are also possible (among the many dozens of other available transformations).

For the moment, however, it is only important to understand that Power BI Desktop can do all of this if you need it to. Transforming data is explained in detail in Chapters 7 through 12.

Data Sources

Previously in this chapter, you saw how quickly and easily you can load data into Power BI Desktop. It is now time to take a wider look at the *types* of data that Power BI Desktop can ingest and manipulate.

As the sheer wealth of possible data sources can seem overwhelming at first, Power BI Desktop groups potential data sources into the following categories:

- *File*: Includes Excel files, CSV (comma-separated values) files, text files, JSON files, and XML files. Power BI Desktop can even load entire folders full of files. You will discover many of these in the following chapter.

- *Database*: A comprehensive collection of relational databases that are currently in the workplace and in the cloud, including (among others) MS Access, SQL Server, and Oracle. The full list of those available when this book went to press is given in Chapter 3.

- *Power Platform*: These sources cover data that is made available in the Azure Power Platform and the Power BI Service in Azure. You can see how these are used with Power BI Desktop in Chapter 6.

- *Azure*: This option lets you see an immense range of data types that is hosted in the Microsoft cloud. This covers data formats from SQL Server through to big data sources. You can see how a few of these are used with Power BI Desktop in Chapter 5.

- *Online services*: These sources range from SharePoint lists to Salesforce, Dynamics 365 to Facebook—and many, many others. Some of these are examined in Chapter 5.

- *Other*: A considerable and ever-growing range of data sources, from Facebook to Microsoft Exchange. Some of these will be touched on in the course of the first six chapters in this book that cover accessing data in Power BI Desktop.

The list of possible data sources is changing all the time, and you need to be aware that you have to look at the version of Power BI Desktop that you are using if you want an exhaustive list of all the available data sources that you can use. Indeed, I expect that several more will have been added by the time that you read this book.

You can also list the contents of folders on any available local disk, network share, or even in the cloud and then leverage this to import several files at once. Similarly (if you have the necessary permissions), you can list the databases and data available on the database servers you connect to. This way, Power BI Desktop can provide not only the data but also the *metadata*—or data about data—that can help you to take a quick look at potential sources of data and only choose those that you really need.

Unfortunately, the sheer range of data sources from which Power BI Desktop can read data is such that we do not have space in a few chapters to examine the minutiae of every one. Consequently, we will take a rapid tour of *some* of the most frequently used data sources in this and the next few chapters. Fortunately, most of the data sources that Power BI Desktop can read are used in a similar way. This is because the Power BI Desktop interface does a wonderful job of making the arcane connection details as unobtrusive as possible. So even if you are faced with a data source that is not described in these chapters, you will nonetheless see a variety of techniques that can be applied to virtually any of the data sources that Power BI Desktop can connect to.

Note   The list of data sources that Power BI Desktop can access is growing all the time. Consequently, when you read this book, you will probably find even more sources than those described in this and the next few chapters.

Conclusion

In this chapter, you have seen how Power BI Desktop can connect to any of a wide range of data sources. You have seen that as long as you know what kind of data you want to load—and that Power BI Desktop has an available connector to this data—you can preview and load the data.

Now it is time to delve deeper into the details of some of the various data sources that you can use with Power BI Desktop. The next chapter will start on your journey by introducing many of the file-based data types that you can use to create analytical dashboards.

CHAPTER 2

Discovering and Loading File-Based Data with Power BI Desktop

File Sources

Sending files across networks and over the Internet or via email has become second nature to most of us. As long as the files that you have obtained conform to some of the widely recognized standards currently in use (of which you will learn more later), you should have little difficulty loading them into Power BI Desktop.

As the first part of your journey through the data mashup process, this chapter will show you how to find and load data from a variety of file-based sources. These kinds of data are typically those that you can either locate on a shared network drive, download from the Internet, receive as an email attachment, or copy to your computer's local drive. The files that are used in the examples in this chapter are available on the Apress website. If you have followed the download instructions in Appendix A, then these files will be in the C:\PowerBIDesktopSamples folder.

The file sources that Power BI Desktop can currently read and from which it can load data are given in Table 2-1.

© Adam Aspin 2020
A. Aspin, *Pro Power BI Desktop*, https://doi.org/10.1007/978-1-4842-5763-0_2

Table 2-1. *File Sources*

File Source	Comments
Excel	Allows you to read Microsoft Excel files (versions 97 to 2019) and load worksheets, named ranges, and tables.
CSV	Lets you load text files that conform to the CSV (comma-separated values) format.
XML	Allows you to load data from XML files.
Text	Lets you load text files using a variety of column separators.
Folder	Lets you load the information about all the files in a folder.
SharePoint folder	Allows you to list the files in a SharePoint folder.
Access database	Lets you connect to a Microsoft Access file on your network and load queries and tables.
JSON	Helps you to load data from JSON files.
PDF	Allows you to preview PDF files and load data from any tables that are in the document.

In this chapter we will be looking at how to import data from

- CSV files

- Text files

- XML files

- Excel files

- Power View, Power Query, and Power Pivot elements from Excel

- Access databases

- PDF files

More advanced techniques (such as importing the contents of entire folders of text or Excel files or importing complex XML files and JSON files) are described in Chapter 10. I prefer to handle these separately as they require more advanced knowledge of data transformation techniques—and you need to learn these first.

Note   I realize that Power BI Desktop considers MS Access to be a database and not a "file" data type. While I completely agree with this classification, I prefer nonetheless to treat Access as if it were a file-based data source, given that all the data resides in a single file that can be copied and emailed, and not in a database on a distant server. For this reason, we will look at MS Access in this chapter, and not the next one that deals with corporate data sources.

Loading Data from Files

It is time to start looking at the heavy-lifting aspect of Power BI Desktop and how you can use it to load data from a variety of different sources. I will begin on the bunny slopes (or "nursery" slopes as we say in the UK) with a simple example of loading data from a text file. Then, given the plethora of available data sources, and to give the process a clearer structure, we will load data from several of the ubiquitous file-based data sources that are found in most workplaces. These data sources are the basis of the data that you will learn to tweak and "mash up" in Chapters 7 through 10. This data could also become the basis of many of the dashboard elements that you will create in Chapters 14–24.

CSV Files

The scenario is as follows: you have been given a CSV file containing a list of data. You now want to load this into Power BI Desktop so that you can look at the data and consider what needs to be done (if anything) to make it usable.

First, you need an idea of the data that you want to load. If you open the source file `C:\PowerBIDesktopSamples\Countries.csv` with a text editor, such as Notepad, you can view its contents. This is what you can see in Figure 2-1.

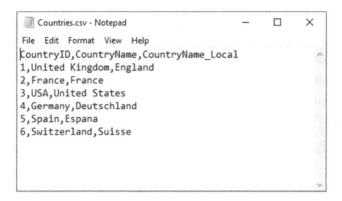

Figure 2-1. *The contents of the Countries.csv file*

The following steps explain what you have to do to load the contents of this file into Power BI Desktop:

1. Open Power BI Desktop and close the splash screen.

2. In the Power BI Desktop Home ribbon, click the Get Data button (and not the small triangle that displays menu options).

3. Click File on the left. You will see something like Figure 2-2 (the Get Data dialog).

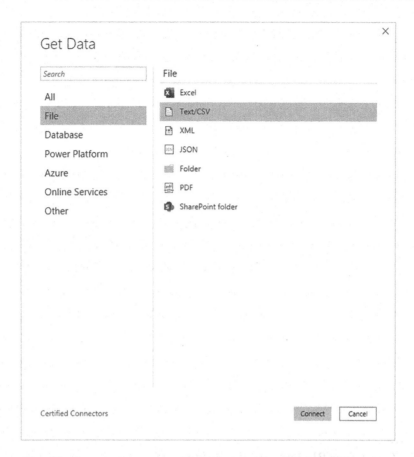

Figure 2-2. *The file data connectors in Power BI Desktop*

4.   Click Text/CSV on the right of the dialog.

5.   Click Connect. The Open dialog will appear.

6.   Navigate to the folder containing the file that you want to load
     and select it (C:\PowerBIDesktopSamples\Countries.csv, in this
     example).

7.   Click Open. A dialog will display the initial contents of the file, as
     shown in Figure 2-3.

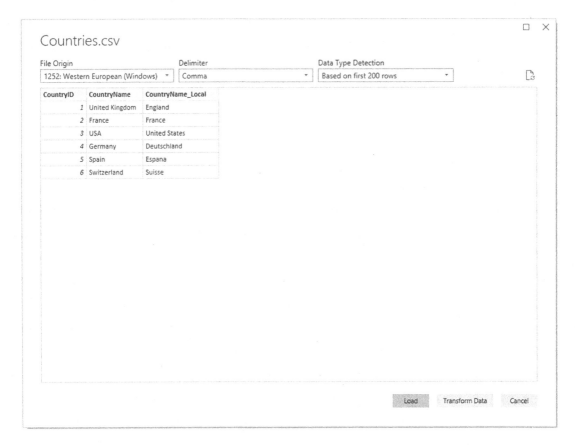

Figure 2-3. *The Power BI Desktop file dialog*

8. Click the Transform Data button. The Power BI Desktop Query
    window appears; it contains a sample of the contents of the CSV
    file—or possibly the entire file if it is not too large. You can see this
    in Figure 2-4.

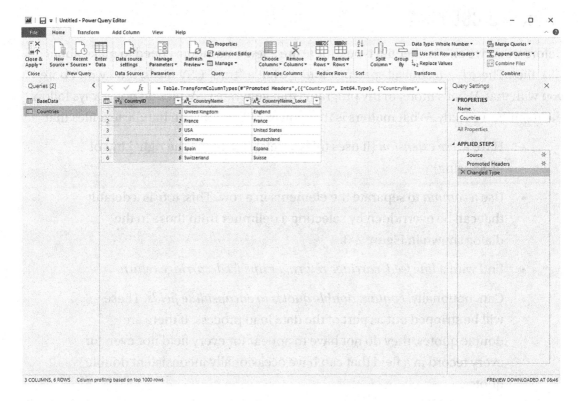

Figure 2-4. *The Power BI Desktop Query window with the contents of a CSV file loaded*

9. Click the Close & Apply button in the Power BI Desktop Query window (you can see this at the top left of Figure 2-4). The Power BI Desktop Query Editor will close and return the focus to the Power BI Desktop window, where you can see that the Countries dataset appears in the Fields list on the right of the screen.

And that, for the moment, is that. You have loaded the file into Power BI Desktop in a matter of a few clicks, and it is ready for use in dashboards and reports. In later chapters, you will learn how to shape this data. For the moment, however, let's continue looking at some other file-based data sources.

What Is a CSV File?

Before we move on to other file types, there are a few comments I need to make about CSV files. There is a technical specification of what a "true" CSV file is, but I won't bore you with that. What's more, many programs that generate CSV files do not always follow the definition exactly. What matters is that Power BI Desktop can handle text files that

- Have a *.csv extension* (it uses this by default to apply the right kind of processing).

- Use a *comma* to separate the elements in a row. This, too, is a default that can be overridden by selecting a delimiter from those in the dialog shown in Figure 2-3.

- End with a *line feed, carriage return, or line feed/carriage return.*

- Can, optionally, *contain double quotes to encapsulate fields.* These will be stripped out as part of the data load process. If there are double quotes, they do not have to appear for every field nor even for every record in a field that can have occasionally inconsistent double quotes.

- Can contain "irregular" records, that is, rows that do not have every element found in a standard record. However, the first row (whether or not it contains titles) must cover every element found in all the remaining records in the list. Put simply, any other record can be shorter than the first one but cannot be longer.

- Do not contain anything other than the data itself. If the file contains header rows or footer rows that are not part of the data, then Power BI Desktop cannot load the dataset without further work. There are workarounds to this all-too-frequent problem; one is given in Chapter 8.

Note   Another way of accessing CSV files is to click Get Data ➤ File and select Text/CSV in the Get Data dialog.

Text Files

If you followed the process for loading a CSV file in the previous section, then you will find that loading a text file is virtually identical. This is not surprising. Both are text files and both should contain a single list of data. The following are the core differences:

- A text file can have something *other* than a comma to separate the elements in a list. You can specify the delimiter when defining the load step.

- A text file should normally have the extension .txt (though this, too, can be overridden).

- A text file *must* be perfectly formed; that is, every record (row) must have the same number of elements as every other record.

- A text file, too, *must not* contain anything other than the dataset if you want a flawless data load the first time.

- If a text file encounters difficulties, it should import the data as a single column that you can then try and split up into multiple columns, as described in Chapter 8.

Here, then, is how to load a text file into Power BI Desktop:

- In the Power BI Desktop ribbon, click Get Data ➤ Text/CSV. The Open dialog will be displayed.

- Navigate to the folder containing the file and select the file (C:\PowerBIDesktopSamples\CountryList.txt, in this example).

- Click Open. A dialog will display the initial contents of the file (this dialog is essentially identical to the one that you saw for CSV files in Figure 2-3). You can, of course, double-click the file name rather than click Open.

- Click the Cancel button (because after a quick look at the contents of the file, you have decided that you do not really need it).

Note   As text-based files (which include CSV files) are such a frequent source of data, you will nearly always see the Text/CSV option directly accessible in the popup menu that you access by clicking the small triangle in the Get Data button in the Home ribbon. If this option is not visible, you can instead select Get Data ➤ File and select Text/CSV, as you did previously.

Where Power BI Desktop is really clever is that it can make a very educated guess as to how the text file is structured; that is, it can nearly always guess the field separator (the character that isolates each element in a list from the other elements). And so not only will it break the list into columns, but it will also avoid importing the column separator. If it does not guess correctly, then don't despair. You will learn how to correct this in Chapter 8.

Looking at the contents of a file and then deciding not to use it is part and parcel of the *data discovery* process that you will find yourself using when you work with Power BI Desktop. The point of this exercise is to show you how easy it is to glance inside potential data sources and then decide whether to import them into the data model or not. Moreover, it can be easier to see the first few rows of large text or CSV files directly in the Load dialog of Power BI Desktop than it is to open the whole file in a text editor.

Tip   At the risk of stating the obvious, you can press Enter to accept a default choice in a dialog and press Esc to cancel out of the dialog.

Text and CSV Options

You can see in Figure 2-3 that there are few options available that you can tweak when loading text or CSV files. Most of the time, Power BI Desktop will guess the correct settings for you. However, there could be times when you will need to adjust these parameters slightly. The potential options that you can modify are

- File origin

- Delimiter

- Data type detection

File Origin

This option defines the character encoding in which the file is stored. Different character sets can handle differing ranges of characters, such as accents and other diacritics. Normally this information is correctly interpreted by Power BI Desktop, and you should only need to select a different character set (file origin) on very rare occasions.

Delimiter

Power BI Desktop will try and guess the special character that is used in a text or CSV file to separate the "columns" of data. Should you wish to override the chosen delimiter, you have the choice of

- Colon
- Comma
- Equals sign
- Semicolon
- Space
- Tab character

You can also decide to enter a custom delimiter such as the pipe (|) character or even specify that every field has a fixed width. Choosing either of these options will display another entry field where you can type in the required delimiter—or the fixed length that you require.

Data Type Detection

Power BI Desktop will make an educated guess at the data encoding and data type that is used in a text or CSV file. By default, to save time, it will only read the first 200 records. However, you can choose from any of the following three options:

- Read the first 200 rows
- Read the entire file
- No data type detection

Note   Be warned that reading a large file in its entirety can take quite a while. However, without accurate data type detection, you risk seeing some weird characters in the data that you load.

Simple XML Files

XML, or Extensible Markup Language, is a standard means of sending data between IT systems. Consequently, you likely will load an XML file one day. Although an XML file is just text, it is text that has been formatted in a very specific way, as you can see if you ever open an XML file in a text editor such as Notepad. Do the following to load an XML file:

1. In the Power BI Desktop ribbon, click the small triangle on the Get Data button, and then click More in the menu that appears. Next, in the Get Data dialog, select File and XML.

2. Click Connect. The Open dialog will appear.

3. Navigate to the folder containing the file and select the file (C:\PowerBIDesktopSamples\ColoursTable.xml, in this example).

4. Click Open. The Navigator dialog will open.

5. Click the Colours dataset in the left-hand pane of the Navigator dialog. The contents of this part of the XML file will be displayed on the right of the Navigator dialog, as shown in Figure 2-5.

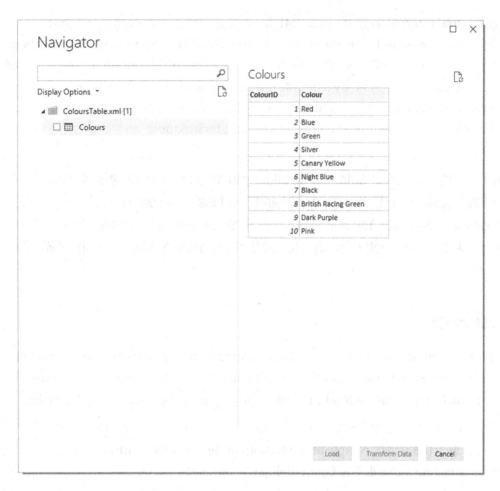

Figure 2-5. *The Navigator dialog before loading an XML file*

6. Click the check box to the left of the Colours dataset on the left. The Load and Edit buttons will be enabled.

7. Click the Transform Data button. The Power BI Desktop Data window will display the contents of the XML file.

8. Click the Close & Apply button in the Power BI Desktop Data window. You will see that the Colours dataset appears in the Fields list on the right of the screen.

The actual internal format of an XML file can get extremely complex. Sometimes an XML file will contain only one dataset; sometimes it will contain many separate datasets. On other occasions, it will contain one dataset whose records contain nested levels of data that you need to handle by expanding a hierarchy of elements. You will see how the Navigator dialog handles nested hierarchies of XML data in Chapter 10—once you have learned some of the required data transformation techniques.

Note   Certain types of data source allow you to load multiple sets of data simultaneously. XML files (unlike CSV and text files) can contain multiple independent datasets. You can load several datasets simultaneously by selecting the check box to the left of each dataset that you want to load from the XML file.

Excel Files

You are probably already a major Excel user and have many, many spreadsheets full of data that you want to rationalize and use for analysis and presentation in Power BI Desktop. So, let's see how to load a couple of worksheets at once from an Excel file.

1. In the Power BI Desktop Home ribbon, click Excel. Alternatively, click the small triangle at the bottom of the Get Data button and then click Excel. The Open dialog will appear.

2. Navigate to the directory containing the file that you want to look at (C:\PowerBIDesktopSamples, in this example).

3. Select the source file (InvoicesAndInvoiceLines.xlsx, in this example) and click Open. The Navigator dialog will appear, showing the worksheets, tables, and ranges in the workbook file.

4. Click one of the datasets listed on the left of the Navigator dialog. The top few rows of the selected spreadsheet will appear on the right of the dialog to show you what the data in the chosen dataset looks like.

5. Click the check boxes to the left of the Invoices and InvoiceLines datasets on the left. The Navigator dialog will look like the one shown in Figure 2-6.

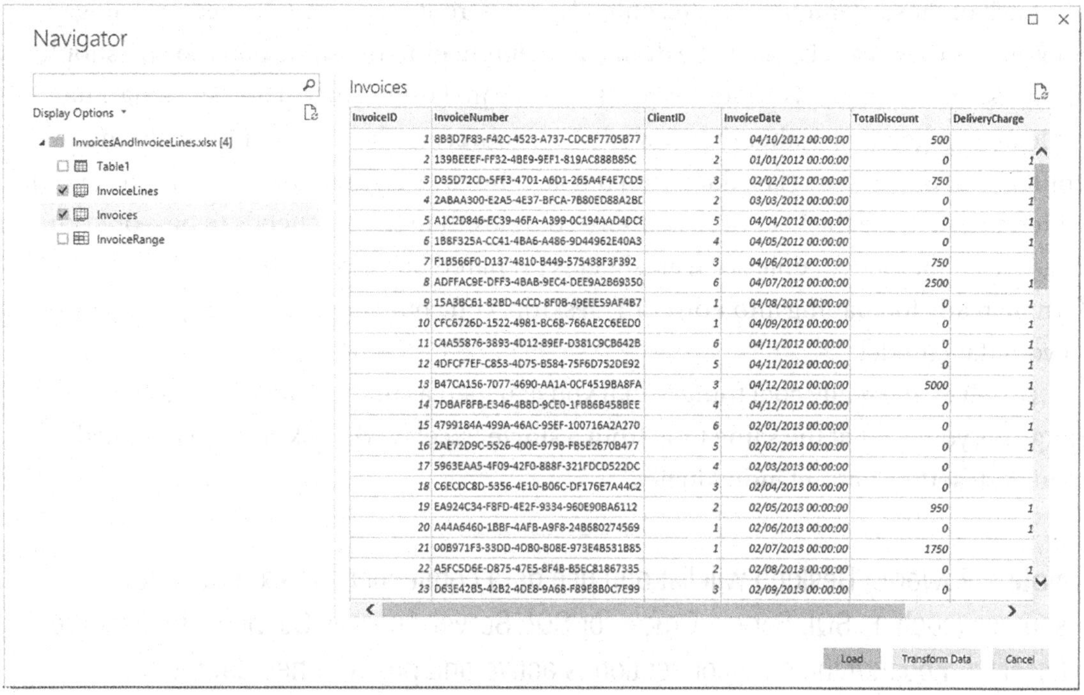

Figure 2-6. *The Navigator dialog before loading data from an Excel workbook*

6.   Click Load. The selected worksheets will be loaded into the Power
      BI Desktop data model and will appear in the Fields list in the
      Report window.

As you can see from this simple example, having Power BI Desktop read Excel data
is really not difficult. You could have edited this data in Power BI Desktop Query Editor
before loading it, but as the data seemed clean and ready to use, I preferred to load it
straight into Power BI Desktop (or rather the Power BI Desktop data model). As well,
you saw that Power BI Desktop can load multiple datasets at the same time from a single
data source. However, you might still be wondering about a couple of things that you saw
during this process, so here are some anticipatory comments:

The Navigator dialog displays

- Worksheets (Invoices and InvoiceLines in Figure 2-6)

- Named ranges (InvoiceRange in Figure 2-6)

- Named tables (Table1 in Figure 2-6)

Each of these elements is represented by a different icon in the Navigator dialog. Sometimes these can, in effect, be duplicate references to the same data, so you should really use the most precise data source that you can. For instance, I advise using a named table or a range name rather than a worksheet source, as the latter could easily end up containing "noise" data (i.e., data from outside the rows and columns that interest you), which would make the load process more complex than it really needs to be—or even cause it to fail. Indeed, unless a worksheet is prepared and structured in a simple tabular format, ready for loading into Power BI Desktop, you could end up with superfluous data in your data model.

However, the really cool thing is that you can load as many worksheets, tables, or ranges as you want at the same time from a single Excel workbook. You do not need to load each source dataset individually.

Note   Power BI Desktop will list and use data connections to external data sources (such as SQL Server, Oracle, or SQL Server Analysis Services) in a source Excel workbook *if* the data connection is active and has returned data to the workbook. Once a link to Power BI Desktop has been established, you can delete the data table itself in the source Excel workbook—and still load the data over the data connection in the source workbook into Power BI Desktop.

Power BI Desktop will *not* take into account any data filters on an Excel data table, but will load all the data that is in the source table. Consequently, you will have to reapply any filters (of which you'll learn more in Chapter 6) in Power BI Desktop if you want to subset the source data.

There are a couple of important points that you need to be aware of at this juncture:

- Multiple worksheets, tables, or named ranges can all be imported from the same workbook (i.e., Excel file) in a single load operation. However, you need to define a separate load operation for each individual Excel file.

- It is possible to load multiple identically structured Excel files simultaneously. This is explained in Chapter 10.

Importing Excel and Power View Items

Power BI Desktop is not, in truth, the first incarnation of Power BI; the data model that it uses has been around for some years now, and an early version of the visualization canvas existed as an Excel add-in named Power View. So, you may already be an accomplished Power View expert using Power View for Excel and not want to lose this work—or you may have existing data models that you have built using Power Pivot in Excel that you want to transfer into Power BI Desktop.

Fortunately, the team at Microsoft has thought of this, and the result is that you can transfer all your effort from Excel (Power View dashboards, Power Pivot data models, and DAX metrics) into Power BI Desktop with remarkable ease. Here is how:

1. Open a new, blank Power BI Desktop file.

2. In the File menu, select Import ➤ Power Query, Power Pivot, Power View, as shown in Figure 2-7.

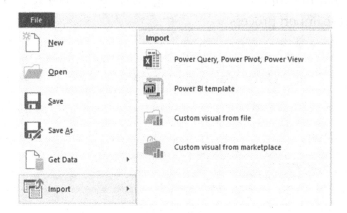

Figure 2-7. *Importing existing Power View or Power Pivot items from Excel*

3. The Windows Open dialog appears, from which you can select an existing Excel file containing Power View or Power Pivot items. In this example, you can use the file CarSalesForPowerBI.xlsx from the sample files for this chapter.

4. Click Open. The warning dialog that you can see in Figure 2-8 appears.

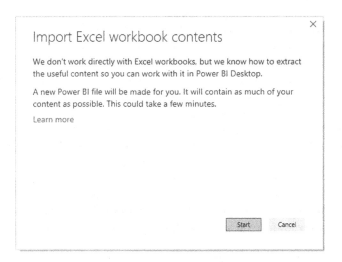

Figure 2-8. *Importing Power View and Power Pivot elements from Excel*

5. Click Start. Power BI Desktop will import any compatible items and display the import progress dialog (as shown in Figure 2-9) during the import process.

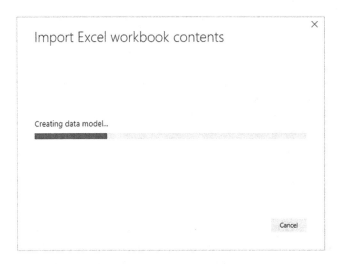

Figure 2-9. *Importing Power View and Power Pivot elements from Excel*

6. Once the import process has successfully finished, Power BI Desktop will display the summary dialog that you see in Figure 2-10.

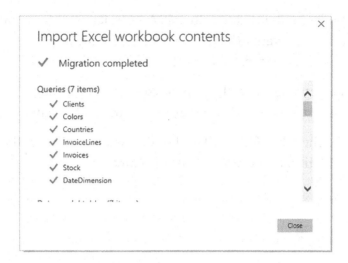

Figure 2-10. *The import summary dialog*

7.   Click Close. The items become a Power BI Desktop report.

As this book went to press, there were a few aspects of some Power View visualizations that were not imported perfectly into the Power BI Desktop data model. However, as this technology is currently developing at a rapid pace, you could well find that these minor limitations have been resolved by the time that you read this book. In any case, I advise you to consult the Power BI website (`https://powerbi.microsoft.com`) for up-to-date details on any remaining limitations concerning the conversion of Excel objects to Power BI Desktop reports.

Microsoft Access Databases

Another widely used data repository that proliferates in many corporations today is Microsoft Access. It is a powerful desktop relational database and can contain hundreds of tables, each containing millions of records. So we need to see how to load data from this particular source. Moreover, Power BI Desktop can be particularly useful when handling Access data because it allows you to see the contents of Access databases without even having to install Access itself.

1.   In the Power BI Desktop ribbon, click Get Data ➤ Database and select Access database in the Get Data dialog.

2.   Click Connect and navigate to the MS Access database containing the data that you want to load (C:\PowerBIDesktopSamples\ ClientsDatabase.accdb, in this example).

3.   Select the Access file and click Open. The Navigator dialog appears; it lists all the tables and queries in the Access database.

4.   Check the check box for the ClientList dataset. This displays the contents of the table, as you can see in Figure 2-11.

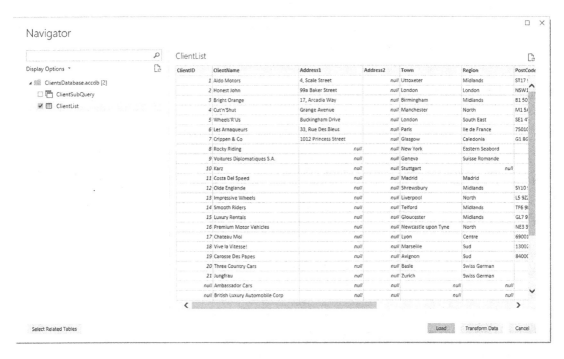

Figure 2-11.   *The Navigator dialog before loading data from an Access database*

5.   Click Load. The Power BI Desktop window opens and displays the table in the Fields list in the Report window.

If you look closely at the left of the Navigator dialog in Figure 2-11, you can see that it displays two different icons for Access objects:

•   A table for Access data tables

•   Two small windows for Access queries

This can help you to understand the type of data that you are looking at inside the Access database.

Note   Power BI Desktop *cannot* see linked tables in Access, only imported tables or tables that are actually in the Access database. It can, however, read queries overlaid upon native, linked, or imported data.

PDF Files

Power BI Desktop can also import tabular data from PDF files. This is really amazingly simple to do.

1. In the Power BI Desktop ribbon, click Get Data ➤ File and select PDF in the Get Data dialog.

2. Click Connect and navigate to the PDF document containing the data that you want to load (a Microsoft document about machine learning, in this example).

3. Select the PDF file and click OK. The Navigator dialog appears; it lists all the tables in the PDF document.

4. Check the check box(es) for the table(s) that you want to import into Power BI Desktop. This displays the contents of the selected table, as you can see in Figure 2-12.

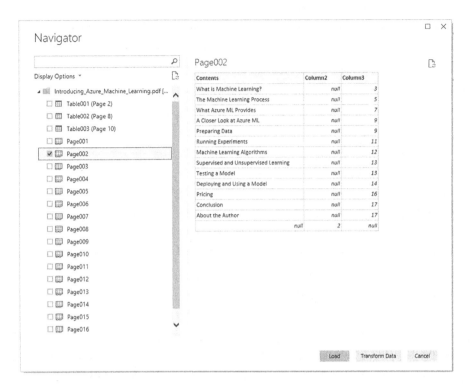

Figure 2-12. *Displaying the tables in a PDF document*

5. Click Load. The Power BI Desktop window opens and displays the table(s)—and their columns as fields—in the Fields list in the Report window.

Note   You can only see and consequently import tables from PDF documents. You cannot import paragraphs of text.

I am sure that you can see a pattern emerging in the course of this chapter. Indeed, this pattern will continue as you progress to loading tables from relational databases in Chapter 3. The process is nearly always

1. Know the type of source data that you want to look at

2. Find the source file that lets you access the data

3. Examine the data and select the elements that you want to load

Note   You need to be aware that Power BI Desktop can take quite a while to read a PDF file. So be patient when waiting for the Navigator dialog to appear once you have selected the PDF document that you want to load data from.

JSON Files

JSON files are, like XML, a file format that allows users (and computers) to send complex data structures between systems. Generally, JSON files require a little tweaking for them to be loaded in a state that is usable by Power BI Desktop. So we will be looking at how to load and prepare JSON files in Chapter 10, once you have assimilated the necessary data transformation techniques in Chapters 7 through 9.

Conclusion

In this chapter, you have seen how this powerful addition to the Microsoft business intelligence toolset, Power BI Desktop, can help you find and load data from a variety of file-based data sources. These sources can be Access, Excel (including Power View, Power Query, and Power Pivot elements), CSV, XML, PDF, or text/CSV files.

You have seen that Power BI Desktop will let you see a sample of the contents of the data sources that it can read without needing any other application. This makes it a superb tool for peeking into data sources and deciding if a file actually contains the data that you need. Indeed, Power BI Desktop's Navigator can help you filter multiple datasets in Excel or XML files or Access databases, preview each dataset, and only select the ones that you want to load. Of course, it can also load dozens of datasets at once if they all are stored in the same source.

This chapter is not a complete overview of how to load file-based sources. So if you need to load complex XML files or JSON files or need to understand how to load the contents of entire folders—or all the worksheets in an Excel file, for instance—then you can skip straight to Chapter 10 to learn these techniques.

However, file-based data sources are only a small part of the picture. Power BI Desktop can also load data from a wide range of relational databases and data warehouses. We will take a look at some of these in the next chapter.

CHAPTER 3

Loading Data from Databases and Data Warehouses

Much of the world's corporate data currently resides in relational databases, data warehouses, and data warehouse appliances either on-premises or in the cloud. Power BI Desktop can connect to most of the world's leading databases and data warehouses. Not only that, but it can also connect to many of the lesser-known or more niche data sources that are currently available. This chapter will show you how to extract data from several of these data sources to power your analytics using Power BI Desktop. Indeed, you will discover that once you have learned how to connect to one or two databases, you have learned how to use nearly all of them, thanks to the standardized interface and approach that Power BI Desktop brings to data extraction.

You need to be aware, however, that the examples in this chapter do not use sample data that is available on the Apress website. In this chapter I will let you load your own data or use the sample data that can be installed with the databases themselves.

Note It may be stating the obvious, but connecting to a database means that the database must be installed and running correctly and you already have to have access to it. Indeed, you may also need specific client software installed on the PC that is running Power BI Desktop. This chapter will not explain how to install or use any of the databases (or the client software) that are referenced. For this, you will have to consult the relevant database documentation.

© Adam Aspin 2020
A. Aspin, *Pro Power BI Desktop*, https://doi.org/10.1007/978-1-4842-5763-0_3

Relational Databases

Being able to access the data stored in relational databases is essential for much of today's business intelligence. As enterprise-grade relational databases still hold much of the world's data, you really need to know how to tap into the vast mines of information that they contain. The bad news is that there are many, many databases out there, each with its own intricacies and quirks. The good news is that once you have learned to load data from *one* of them, you can reasonably expect to be able to use *any* of them.

In the real world, connecting to corporate data could require you to have a logon name and usually a password that will let you connect (unless the database can recognize your Windows login or a single sign-on solution has been implemented). I imagine that you will also require permissions to read the tables and views that contain the data. So the techniques described here are probably the easy bit. The hard part is convincing the guardians of corporate data that you actually *need* the data and you should be allowed to see it.

The databases that Power BI Desktop can currently connect to, and can preview and load data from, are given in Table 3-1.

Table 3-1. *Database Sources*

Database	Comments
SQL Server database	Lets you connect to a Microsoft SQL Server on-premises database and import records from all the data tables and views that you are authorized to access.
Access database	Lets you connect to a Microsoft Access file on your network and load queries and tables (which we explored in the previous chapter).
SQL Server Analysis Services database	Lets you connect to a SQL Server Analysis Services (SSAS) data warehouse. This can be either an online analytical processing (OLAP) cube or an in-memory tabular data warehouse.
Oracle database	Lets you connect to an Oracle database and import records from all the data tables and views that you are authorized to access. This will likely require client software to be installed.

(continued)

Table 3-1. (*continued*)

Database	Comments
IBM DB2 database	Lets you connect to an IBM DB2 database and import records from all the data tables and views that you are authorized to access. This will likely require additional software to be installed.
IBM Informix database	Lets you connect to an IBM Informix database and import records from all the data tables and views that you are authorized to access. This will likely require additional software to be installed.
IBM Netezza	Lets you connect to an IBM Netezza data warehouse appliance and import records from all the data tables that you are authorized to access. This will likely require additional software to be installed.
MySQL database	Lets you connect to a MySQL database and import records from all the data tables and views that you are authorized to access.
PostgreSQL database	Lets you connect to a PostgreSQL database and import records from all the data tables and views that you are authorized to access. This will likely require additional software to be installed.
Sybase database	Lets you connect to a Sybase database and import records from all the data tables and views that you are authorized to access.
Teradata database	Lets you connect to a Teradata database and import records from all the data tables and views that you are authorized to access. This will likely require additional software to be installed.
SAP HANA database	Lets you connect to a SAP HANA in-memory database and import records from all the objects that you have permission to access. This will likely require additional software to be installed.
SAP Business Warehouse Application Server	Allows you to connect to a SAP Business Warehouse. This will likely require client software to be installed.
SAP Business Warehouse Message Server	Allows you to connect to a SAP Business Warehouse. This will likely require client software to be installed.
Amazon Redshift	Lets you connect to an Amazon Redshift database and import records from all the data tables and views that you are authorized to access.

(*continued*)

Table 3-1. (*continued*)

Database	Comments
Impala	Lets you connect to an Impala database and import records from all the data tables and views that you are authorized to access.
Google Big Query	Lets you access Google Big Query data repositories.
Essbase	Allows you to connect to Essbase cubes.
Snowflake	Lets you connect to Snowflake data warehouses in the cloud.
Exasol	Lets you connect to Exasol data repositories.

There are many other database connectors that are currently available. As a complete list would take several pages, I advise you to scroll down through the list in the Get Data dialog to see if the database that you are using has a connector to Power BI.

Note As the list of database and data warehouse sources that you can connect to from Power BI Desktop continues to evolve, this list could likely be extended to include several new items by the time that you read this book.

As well as connections for specific databases, Power BI Desktop contains generic connectors that can help you to read data from databases that are not specifically in the list of available databases. These generic connectors are explained in Table 3-2.

Table 3-2. *Generic Database Access*

Source	Comments
ODBC data source	Lets you connect over Open Database Connectivity to a database or data source.
OLE DB data source	Lets you connect over Object Linking and Embedding, Database to a database or data source.

Be warned that these generic connectors will not work with any database. However, they should work with a database for which you have procured, installed, and configured a valid ODBC or OLE DB driver. You can learn more about this in Chapter 6.

Note Although Power BI Desktop classifies Microsoft Access as a relational database, I prefer to handle it as a file-based source. For this reason, MS Access data was discussed in the previous chapter.

SQL Server

Here I will use the Microsoft enterprise relational database—SQL Server—as an example to show you how to load data from a database into Power BI Desktop. The first advantage of this setup is that you probably do not need to install any software to enable access to SQL Server (although this is not always the case, so talk this through with your IT department). A second advantage is that the techniques are pretty similar to those used and applied by Oracle, DB2, and the other databases to which Power BI Desktop can connect. Furthermore, you can load multiple tables or views from a database at once. To see this in action (on your SQL Server database), take the following steps:

1. Open a new Power BI Desktop application.

2. In the Power BI Desktop Home ribbon, click SQL Server. Alternatively, click the small triangle at the bottom of the Get Data button and then click SQL Server. The SQL Server database dialog will appear.

3. Enter the server name in the Server text box. This will be the name of your SQL Server or one of the SQL Server resources used by your organization.

4. Enter the database name.

5. Click the Import button. The dialog will look like Figure 3-1 (but with your server and database names, of course).

***Figure 3-1.** The Microsoft SQL Server database dialog*

6. Click OK. The SQL Server database dialog will appear. Assuming
    that you are authorized to use your Windows login to connect
    to the database, leave "Use my current credentials" selected, as
    shown in Figure 3-2.

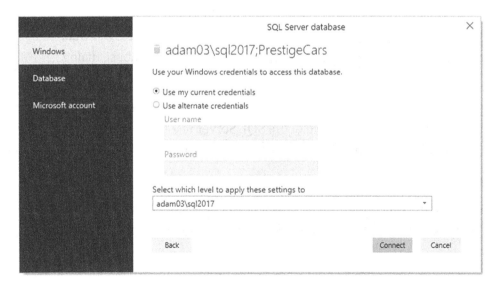

***Figure 3-2.** The credentials Database dialog*

7. Click Connect. The Encryption Support dialog may appear to warn
    you that the connection is not encrypted, as shown in Figure 3-3.

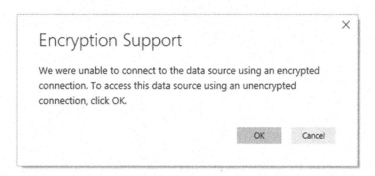

Figure 3-3. *The Encryption Support dialog*

8. Click OK. Power BI Desktop will connect to the server and display
    the Navigator dialog containing all the tables and views in the
    database that you have permission to see on the server you
    selected. In some cases, you could see a dialog saying that the
    data source does not support encryption. If you feel happy with an
    unencrypted connection, then click the OK button for this dialog.

9. Click the check boxes for the tables that you want to load. The data
    for the most recently selected dataset appears on the right of the
    Navigator dialog, as shown in Figure 3-4.

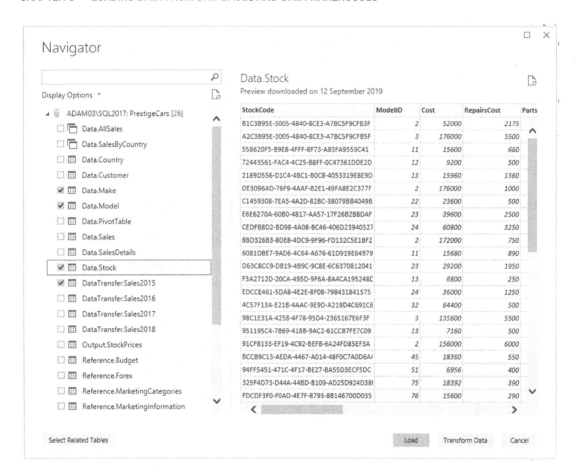

Figure 3-4. *The Navigator dialog when selecting multiple items*

10. Click Load.

11. While the data is being loaded, Power BI Desktop will display the Load dialog and show the load progress for each selected table. You can see this in Figure 3-5.

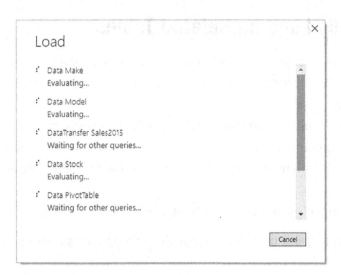

Figure 3-5. *The Load dialog displaying data load progress*

12.   The Power BI Desktop window will open and display the tables
       that you selected in the Fields list in the Report window when you
       click OK.

Tip   When selecting multiple tables or views, you will only ever see the contents
of a single data source in the Navigator dialog. However, you can preview the
contents of any of the selected data sources (or even any that are not selected)
simply by clicking the table or view name. This will not affect the choice of selected
tables and views that you want to load into Power BI Desktop.

Since this is very similar to the way in which you loaded data from Access in the
previous chapter, I imagine that you are getting the hang of how to use database sources
by now. Once again the Navigator dialog is a simple and efficient way to select the
datasets that you want to use in your reports and dashboards.

Note   You can enter the server IP address instead of the server name if you
prefer. If there are several SQL Server instances on the same server, you will need
to add a backslash and the instance name. This kind of detailed information can be
obtained from corporate database administrators (DBAs).

Automatically Loading Related Tables

Relational databases are nearly always intricate structures composed of many interdependent tables. Indeed, you will frequently need to load several tables to obtain all the data that you need.

Knowing which tables to select is not always easy. Power BI Desktop tries to help you by automatically detecting the links that exist in the source database between tables; this way, you can rapidly isolate the collections of tables that have been designed to work together.

Do the following to see a related group of tables:

1. Connect to the source database as described in the previous section.

2. In the Navigator dialog, click a table that contains data that you need.

3. Click the "Select related tables" button.

Any tables in the database that are linked to the tables that you selected in the Navigator dialog are selected. You can deselect any tables that you do not want, of course. More importantly, you can click the names of the selected tables to see their contents.

Note   Sometimes you have to select several tables in turn and click "Select related tables" to ensure that Power BI Desktop will select all the tables that are necessary to underpin your analysis.

Database Options

The world of relational databases is—fortunately or unfortunately—a little more complex than the world of files or MS Access. Consequently, there are a few comments to make about using databases as a data source—specifically, how to connect to them.

First, let's cover the initial connection to the server. The options are explained in Table 3-3.

Table 3-3. *Database Connection Options*

Option	Comments
Server	You cannot browse to find the server and you need to type or paste the server name. If the server has an instance name, you need to enter the server and the instance. Your IT department will be able to supply this if you are working in a corporate environment.
Database	If you know the database, then you can enter (or paste) it here. This restricts the number of available tables in the Navigator dialog and makes finding the correct table or view easier.
SQL statement	You can enter a valid snippet of T-SQL (or a stored procedure or a table-valued function) that returns data from the database.

These options probably require a little more explanation. So let's look at each one in turn.

Server Connection

It is fundamental that you know the exact connection string for the database that you want to connect to. This could be the following:

- The database server name.

- The database server name, a backslash, and an instance name (if there is one).

- The database server IP address.

- The database server IP address, a backslash, and an instance name (if there is one).

- If the SQL Server instance is using a custom port, you must end the server name with a comma followed by the port number. This is, inevitably, a question for corporate DBAs.

- If you are running a single SQL Server instance on your own PC, then you can use the name *localhost* (or a period) to refer to the local server.

Note   A database instance is a separate SQL Server service running alongside others on the same physical or virtual server. You will always need both the server and this instance name (if there is one) to successfully connect. You can also specify a timeout period if you wish.

Most SQL Server instances host many, many databases. Sometimes these can number in the hundreds. Sometimes, inevitably, you cannot remember which database you want to connect to. Fortunately, Power BI Desktop can let you browse the databases on a server that you are authorized to access. To do this, do the following:

1. In the Power BI Desktop ribbon, click the small triangle at the bottom of the Get Data button and then click SQL Server. The SQL Server database dialog will appear.

2. Enter the server name in the Server text box and click OK. Do *not* enter a database name. The Navigator window opens and displays all the available databases, as shown in Figure 3-6. Of course, the actual contents depend on the server that you are connecting to.

Figure 3-6. *The Navigator dialog when selecting databases*

You can see from Figure 3-6 that if you click the small triangle to the left of a database, then you are able to see all the tables and views that are accessible to you in this database. Although this can mean an overabundance of possible choices when looking for the table(s) or view(s) that you want, it is nonetheless a convenient way of reminding you of the name of the dataset that you require.

Tip   The actual databases that you will be able to see on a corporate server will depend on the permissions that you have been given. If you cannot see a database, then you will have to talk to the database administrators to sort out any permissions issues.

Searching for Databases, Tables, and Views in Navigator

If you are overwhelmed by the sheer volume of table(s) and view(s) that appear in the left panel of the Navigator dialog, then you can use Navigator's built-in search facility to help you to narrow down the set of potential data sources.

Searching for Databases

To isolate specific databases, do the following:

1. Carry out steps 1 and 2 in the earlier "SQL Server" section to connect to a SQL Server instance *without* specifying a database.

2. In the Search box of the Navigator dialog, enter a few characters that you know are contained in the name of the table or view that you are looking for. Entering, for example, **US** on my server gives the result that you see in Figure 3-7.

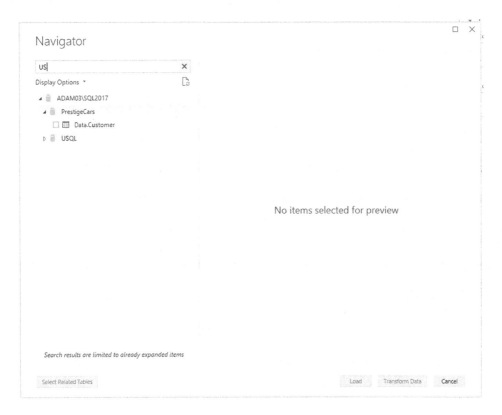

Figure 3-7. *Using Search with Navigator to find databases*

Searching for Tables

If you are searching for tables, do the following:

1. Expand any databases that you want to search for specific tables.

2. In the Search box of the Navigator dialog, enter a few characters that you know are contained in the name of the table or view that you are looking for. Entering, for example, **cust** on my server gives the result that you see in Figure 3-8.

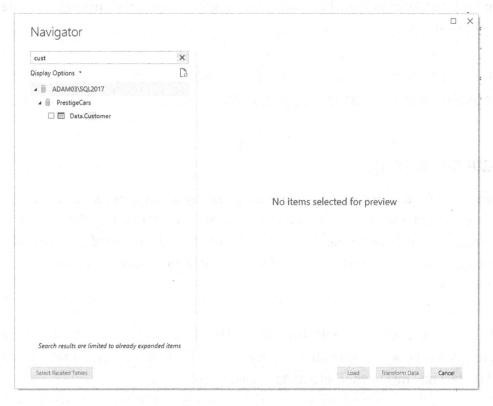

Figure 3-8. *Using Search with Navigator to find tables*

When searching for objects, you can enter the text in uppercase or lowercase (with most SQL Server installations), and the text can appear anywhere in the names of the tables or views—not just at the start of the name. With every character that you type, the list of potential matches gets shorter and shorter. Once you have found the dataset that you are looking for, simply proceed as described earlier to load the data into Power BI Desktop.

If your search does not return the subset of tables in any views that you were expecting, all you have to do is click the cross at the right of the Search box. This cancels the search and displays all the available tables, as well as clears the Search box.

If you are not convinced that you are seeing all the tables and views that are in the database, then click the small icon at the bottom right of the Search box (it looks like a small page with two green circular arrows). This is the Refresh button, which refreshes the connection to the database and displays all the tables and views that you have permission to see. Finally, it is worth noting that filtering tables can also be applied to Excel tables, worksheets, and named ranges. This is another example of how the unified Navigator interface can help minimize the learning curve when it comes to mastering Power BI Desktop.

Note   SQL Server databases can also be accessed using the DirectQuery option. This technique is explained in the next chapter.

Database Security

Remember that databases are designed to be extremely secure. Consequently, you only see servers, databases, tables, and views if you are authorized to access them. You might have to talk to your IT department to ensure that you have the required permissions; otherwise, the table that you are looking for could be in the database, but remain invisible to you.

Tip   If you experience a connection error when first attempting to connect to SQL Server, simply click the Edit button to return to the Microsoft SQL Database dialog and correct any mistakes. This avoids having to start over.

Using a SQL Statement

If there is a downside to using a relational database such as SQL Server as a data source, it is that the sheer amount of data that the database stores—even in a single table—can be dauntingly huge. Fortunately, all the resources of SQL Server can be used to filter the data that is used by Power BI Desktop before you even load the data. This way, you do not have to load entire tables of data at the risk of drowning in information before you have even started to analyze it.

The following are SQL Server techniques that you can use to extend the partnership between SQL Server and Power BI Desktop:

- SQL SELECT statements

- Stored procedures

- Table-valued functions

These are, admittedly, fairly technical solutions. Indeed, if you are not a database specialist, you could well require the services of your IT department to use these options to access data in the server. Nonetheless, it is worth taking a quick look at these techniques in case they are useful now or in the future.

Any of these options can be applied from the SQL Server database dialog. Here is an example of how to filter data from a database table using a SELECT statement:

1. In the Power BI Desktop ribbon, click the small triangle at the bottom of the Get Data button and then click SQL Server. The SQL Server database dialog will appear.

2. Enter the server name and the database.

3. Click the triangle to the left of Advanced options. This opens a box where you can enter a SQL command.

4. Enter the SQL command that you want to apply. In this case, it is `SELECT CountryName, MakeName, ModelName, Cost FROM Data.AllSales ORDER BY CountryName`. The dialog will look like Figure 3-9.

Figure 3-9. *Using SQL to select database data*

5. Click OK. You may get the Credentials and Encryption dialogs appearing. A sample of the corresponding data is eventually displayed in a dialog like the one shown in Figure 3-10.

CountryName	MakeName	ModelName	Cost
Belgium	Aston Martin	Vantage	100000
Belgium	Triumph	TR6	10000
Belgium	Aston Martin	Rapide	69200
Belgium	Peugeot	205	3160
Belgium	Noble	M600	23600
Belgium	Alfa Romeo	Spider	10000
Belgium	Triumph	Roadster	18800
Belgium	Alfa Romeo	Giulia	8400
Belgium	Peugeot	205	760
Belgium	Triumph	TR4	5560
France	Bugatti	57C	276000
France	Ferrari	F40	215600
France	Porsche	959	71600
France	Jaguar	XK120	17240
France	Bugatti	57C	284000
France	Rolls Royce	Silver Seraph	96000
France	Porsche	924	6040
France	Peugeot	203	1560
France	Triumph	TR7	7912
France	BMW	Alpina	17200

ⓘ The data in the preview has been truncated due to size limits.

Figure 3-10. *Database data selected using the SQL Statement option*

6. Click Load or Transform Data to continue with the data load process. Alternatively, you can click Cancel and start a different data load.

Tip   When entering custom SQL (or when using stored procedures, as is explained in the following section), you should, preferably, specify the database name in step 3. If you do not give the database name, you will have to use a three-part notation in your SQL query. That is, you must add the database name and a period before the schema and table name of *every* table name used in the query.

Stored Procedures in SQL Server

The same principles apply when using stored procedures of functions to return data from SQL Server. You will always use the SQL Statement option to enter the command that will return the data. Just remember that to call a SQL Server stored procedure or function, you would enter the following elements into the Microsoft SQL Database dialog:

- *Server*: <your server name>

- *Database*: <the database name>

- *SQL Statement*: EXECUTE (or EXEC) <enter the schema (if there is one, followed by a period) and the stored procedure name, followed by any parameters>

This way, either you or your IT department can create complex and secure ways to allow data from the corporate databases to be read into Power BI Desktop from databases.

To see this in practice, here is an example of using a SQL Server stored procedure to return only a subset of the available data. The stored procedure is called pr_DisplayUKClientData, and you apply it like this:

1. In the Power BI Desktop ribbon, click the small triangle at the bottom of the Get Data button and then click SQL Server. The SQL Server database dialog will appear.

2. Enter the server name and the database.

3. Click the triangle to the left of Advanced options. This opens a box where you can enter a SQL command.

4. Enter the SQL command that you want to apply. In this case, it is EXECUTE `dbo.pr_DisplayUKClientData`. The dialog will look like Figure 3-11.

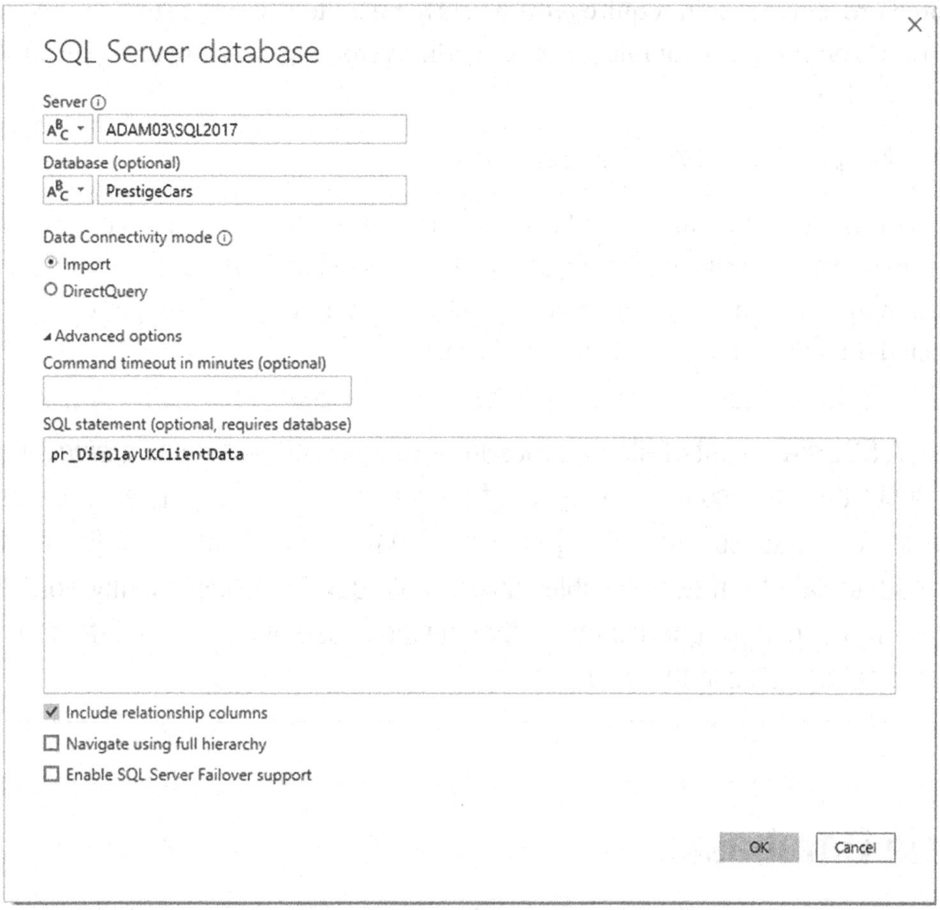

Figure 3-11. *Using SQL to select database data*

5.   Click OK. A sample of the corresponding data is returned to the Navigator.

6.   Click Load or Edit to continue with the data load process. Alternatively, you can click Cancel and start a different data load.

The data that is returned in this example is only a subset of the available data that has been selected by the stored procedure. You need to be aware that stored procedures can perform a multitude of tasks on the source data. These can include selecting, sorting, and cleansing the data.

Stored procedures often require *parameters* to be added after the stored procedure name. This is perfectly acceptable when executing a stored procedure in Power BI. An example would be

```
EXECUTE dbo.pr_DisplayUKClientData 2020
```

The key thing to remember—and to convey to your IT department—is that the SQL that Power BI expects is the flavor of SQL that the source database uses. So, for SQL Server, that means using T-SQL. In fact, this SQL becomes a "pass-through" query that is interpreted directly by the underlying database.

Note   A SQL statement or stored procedure will only return data as a *single table*. Admittedly, this table could contain data from several underlying tables or views in the source database, but filtering the source data will prevent Power BI Desktop from loading data from several tables as separate queries. Consequently, you could have to create multiple queries rather than a single load query to get data from a coherent set of tables in the data source.

Oracle Databases

There are many, many database vendors active in the corporate marketplace today. Arguably the most dominant of them is currently Oracle. While I have used Microsoft data sources to begin the journey into an understanding of how to use databases with Power BI Desktop, it would be remiss of me not to explain how to access databases from other suppliers.

So now is the time to show you just how open-minded Power BI Desktop really is. It does not limit you to Microsoft data sources—far from it. Indeed, it is every bit as easy to use databases from other vendors as the source of your analytical reports. As an example of this, let's take a look at loading Oracle data into Power BI Desktop.

Installing and configuring an Oracle database is a nontrivial task. Consequently, I am not providing an Oracle sample database, but will leave you either to discover a corporate database that you can connect to or, preferably, consult the many excellent resources available that do an excellent job of explaining how to set up your own Oracle database and install the sample data that is available.

Be aware that connecting to Oracle will require installing Oracle client software on the computer where you are running Power BI Desktop. This, too, can be complex to set up. So you might need some help from a corporate resource if you are planning to use Oracle data with Power BI Desktop.

Should you be feeling brave, you can use the following URLs to find the Oracle client software. For 32-bit versions of Power BI Desktop, you could try using the following link to download and install the 32-bit Oracle client:

`www.oracle.com/technetwork/topics/dotnet/utilsoft-086879.html`

For 64-bit versions of Power BI Desktop, use the following link to download and install the 64-bit Oracle client:

`www.oracle.com/technetwork/database/windows/downloads/index-090165.html`

Both these links were active as this book went to press.

If you need to check which version of Power BI Desktop you are using (32 bit or 64 bit), click File ➤ Help ➤ About. You will see a dialog that tells you which version you are using.

So, assuming that you have an Oracle database available (and that you know the server name or SID as well as a valid username and password), the following steps show how you can load data from this particular source into Power BI Desktop. I will be using standard Oracle sample data that is often installed with sample databases in this example.

1. Open a new Power BI Desktop application.

2. In the Power BI Desktop Home ribbon, click Get Data.

3. In the Get Data dialog, click Database on the left.

4. Click Oracle database on the right. The dialog will look like Figure 3-12.

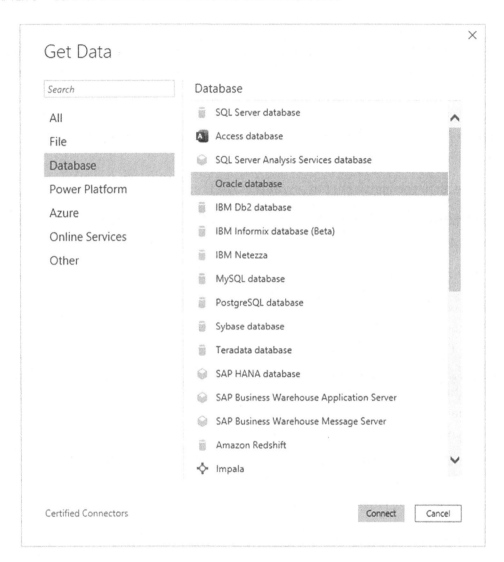

Figure 3-12. *Connecting to an Oracle database*

5. Click Connect. The Oracle database dialog will appear.

6. Enter the server name in the Server text box. This will be the name of your Oracle server or one of the Oracle server resources used by your organization.

7. Click the Import button. The dialog will look like Figure 3-13.

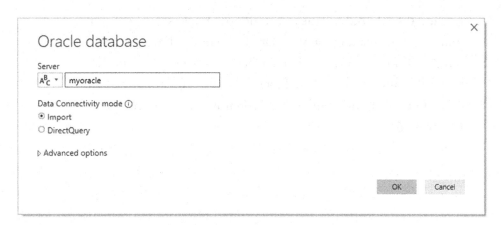

Figure 3-13. *The Oracle database dialog*

8. Click OK. The Oracle database security dialog will appear.
    Assuming that you are not authorized to use your Windows login
    to connect to the database, click Database on the left of the dialog.

9. Enter the username and password that allow you to log in to
    Oracle. You can see this dialog in Figure 3-14.

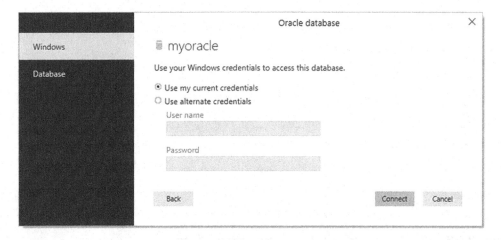

Figure 3-14. *The Oracle database security dialog*

10. Click Connect. Power BI Desktop will connect to the server and
    display the Navigator dialog containing all the tables and views
    in the database that you have permission to see on the server you
    selected. In some cases, you could see a dialog saying that the
    data source does not support encryption. If you feel happy with an
    unencrypted connection, then click the OK button for this dialog.

11.   Expand the HR folder. This is a standard Oracle sample schema
that could be installed on your Oracle instance. If not, you will
have to choose another schema. Click the check boxes for the
tables that interest you. The data for the most recently selected
data appears on the right of the Navigator dialog, as shown in
Figure 3-15.

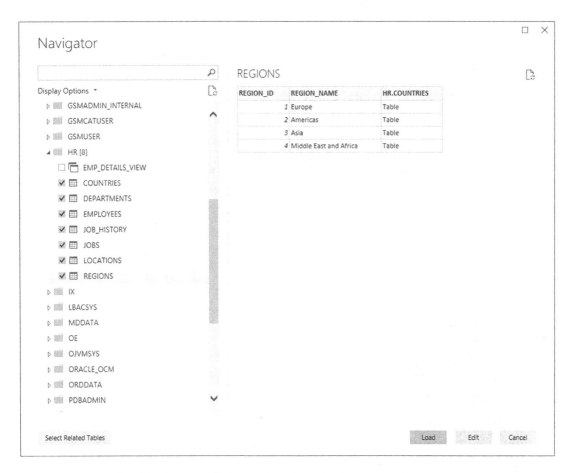

Figure 3-15. *The Navigator dialog using Oracle data*

12.   Click Load. The Power BI Desktop window will open and display
the tables that you selected in the Fields list in the Report window
when you click OK. If you have already followed the example earlier
in this chapter to load data from SQL Server, you will probably
appreciate how much the two techniques have in common.

Indeed, one of the great advantages of using Power BI Desktop is that loading data from different data sources follows a largely similar approach and uses many of the same steps and dialogs. This is especially true of databases, where the steps are virtually identical—whatever the database.

Of course, no two databases are alike. Consequently, you connect to an Oracle instance (or server) but cannot choose a database as you can in SQL Server (or Sybase, for instance). Similarly, where Oracle has schemas to segregate and organize data tables, SQL Server has databases. Nonetheless, the Power BI Desktop Navigator will always organize data into a hierarchy of folders so that you can visualize the data structures in a clear, simple, and intuitive manner, whatever the underlying database.

Note   Oracle databases can also be accessed using the DirectQuery option. This technique is explained in the next chapter.

Other Relational Databases

Table 3-1 at the start of this chapter contains the list of relational databases that Power BI Desktop could connect to as this book went to press. I imagine that the list has grown since this book was published. However, the good news is that you probably do not need much more information to connect to any of the databases that are available for you to use as data sources. Simply put, if you know how to connect to one of them, you can probably connect to any of them.

So I am not going to fill out reams of pages with virtually identical explanations of how to get data from a dozen or more relational databases. Instead I suggest that you simply try to connect, using the techniques that you have learned in this chapter for Oracle and SQL Server.

Be warned, though, that to connect to a relational database, you will inevitably need to know the following details:

- The server name

- A database name (possibly)

- A valid username (depending on the security that has been implemented)

- A valid password for the user that you are connecting as (this, too, will depend on the security in place)

However, if you have these elements, then nothing should stop you from using a range of corporate data sources as the basis for your analysis with Power BI Desktop. You will, of course, need all the necessary permissions to access the database and the data that it contains.

It is also worth knowing that connecting to DB2, MySQL, PostgreSQL, Sybase, IBM Informix, IBM Netezza, SAP HANA, or Teradata can require not only that the database administrator has given you the necessary permissions but also that connection software (known as *drivers* or *providers*) has been installed on your PC. Given the "corporate" nature of the requirements, it may help if you talk directly to your IT department to get this set up in your enterprise IT landscape.

One way to find out if the software that is required to enable a connection to a specific database has been installed is to select the database from the list available in the Get Data dialog. If the drivers have not been installed, you will see a warning similar to the one in Figure 3-16.

Figure 3-16. *The missing driver alert*

Clicking the "Learn more" link will take you to the download page for the missing drivers. Be warned, however, that configuring data providers can, in some cases, require specialist knowledge as well as access rights on the computer where the drivers have to be installed.

Microsoft SQL Server Analysis Services Data Sources

An Analysis Services database is a data warehouse technology that can contain vast amounts of data that has been optimized to enable decision making. *SSAS cubes* (as these databases are also called) are composed of facts (measures or values) and dimensions (descriptive attributes).

In fact—and with apologies to data warehouse purists—an SSAS cube is, essentially, a gigantic pivot table. So, if you have used pivot tables in Excel, you are ready to use data warehouse sources in Power BI Desktop.

Note   In this section I will be explaining access to *dimensional* (disk-based) SSAS data warehouses. I explain *tabular* SSAS in the next section.

If your workspace uses Analysis Services databases, you can access them by doing the following steps:

1. In the Power BI Desktop ribbon, click Get Data ➤ More. Click Database on the left of the Get Data dialog and select SQL Server Analysis Services database in the Get Data dialog.

2. Click Connect. The SQL Server Analysis Services database dialog will appear.

3. Enter the Analysis Services server name and the database (or "cube") name. The database I am using here is called CarSalesOLAP; you will have to specify your own SSAS database name. In any case you will need to use the name of your own SSAS server. The dialog will look something like the one shown Figure 3-17.

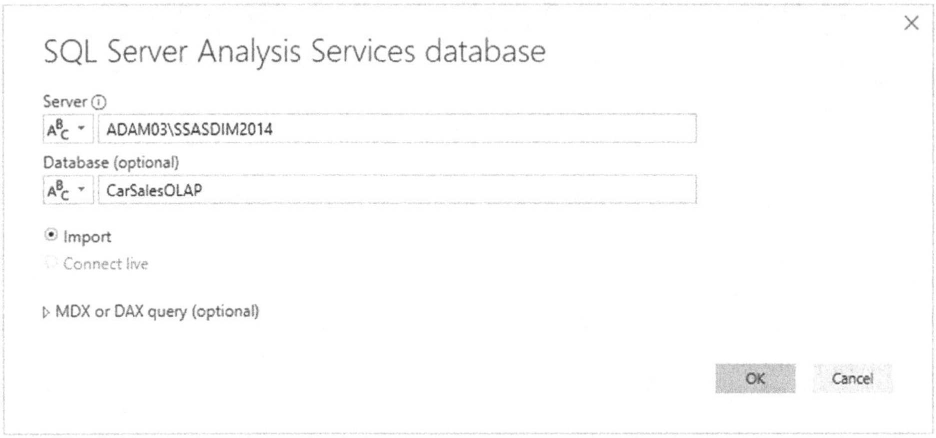

Figure 3-17. *Connecting to an SSAS (multidimensional) database*

4. Click OK. If this is the first time that you are connecting to the cube, then the Access SQL Server Analysis Services dialog will appear so that you can define the credentials that you are using to connect to the Analysis Services database, as shown in Figure 3-18.

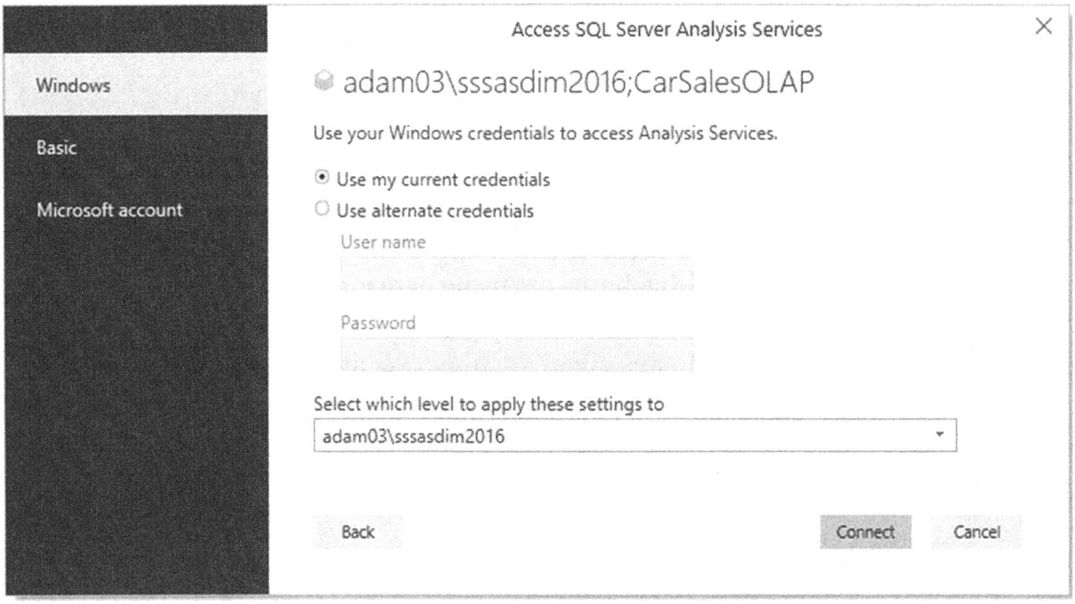

Figure 3-18. *SQL Server Analysis Services credentials dialog*

5. Accept or alter the credentials and click Connect. The Navigator dialog will appear.

6. Expand the folders in the left pane of the dialog. This way, you can see all the fact tables and dimensions contained in the data warehouse.

7. Select the fact tables, dimensions, or even only the dimension elements and measures that you want to load. The dialog will look something like Figure 3-19.

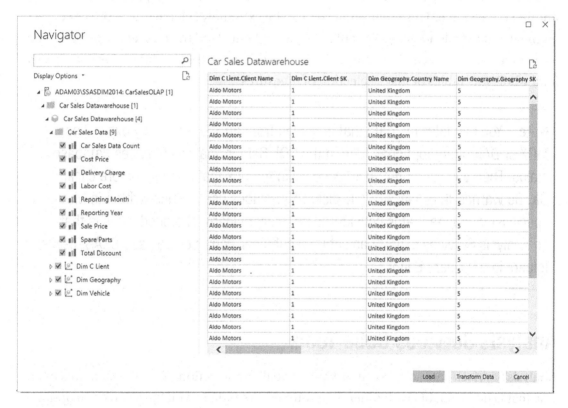

Figure 3-19. *Selecting attributes and measures from an SSAS cube*

8. Click Load. The Power BI Desktop window will open and display the measures and attributes that you selected in the Fields list in the Report window.

> **Note**   If you did not enter the cube (database) name in step 3, then the Navigator dialog will display all the available cubes on the SSAS server. From here you can drill down into the cube that interests you to query the data you require.

SSAS cubes are potentially huge. They can contain dozens of dimensions, many fact tables, and literally thousands of measures and attributes. Understanding multidimensional cubes and how they work is beyond the scope of this book. Nonetheless, it is important to understand that for Power BI Desktop, a cube is just another data source. This means that you can be extremely selective as to the cube elements that you load into Power BI Desktop and only load the elements that you need for your analysis. You can load entire dimensions or just a few attributes, just like you can load whole fact tables or just a selection of measures.

> **Note**   You can filter the data that is loaded from an SSAS cube by expanding the MDX or DAX query (optional) item in the SQL Server Analysis Services database dialog. Then you can enter an MDX query in the box that appears before clicking OK. Be warned that "classic" (on-disk) SSAS cubes use queries written in MDX—a specialist language that is considered not easy to learn. The good news is that if an Analysis Services expert has set up a cube correctly, you can see SSAS display folders in the Query Editor.

Analysis Services Cube Tools

Analysis Services data sources allow you to tweak the selection of source elements in a way that is not available with other data sources. Essentially, you have two extra options:

- Add Items
- Collapse Columns

Add Items

When using an SSAS data source, you can at any time add any attributes or measures that you either forgot or thought that you would not need when setting up the initial connection.

1. In Power BI Desktop, click the Edit Queries button. The Power BI Desktop Query Editor window will be displayed. Assuming that there is only one query, the Manage ribbon will appear, as shown in Figure 3-20. Otherwise, click the SSAS query that you have previously established.

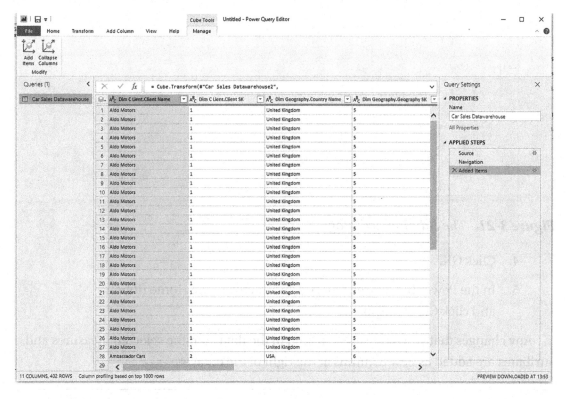

Figure 3-20. *Cube Tools*

2. In the Manage ribbon, click the Add Items button. The Add Items dialog will appear.

3. Expand any measure groups and select all the measures and attributes that you want to add, as shown in Figure 3-21.

73

Figure 3-21. *The Add Items dialog*

4. Click OK.

5. In the Power BI Desktop Query Editor, activate the Home ribbon
    and click Close & Apply.

Any changes that you made are reflected in the data, and the selected measures and
attributes are added as new columns at the right of the dataset.

Note   Power BI Desktop Query will not detect if any new measures and attributes
that you add are already in the dataset. So if you add an element a second time, it
will appear *twice* in the query.

Collapse Columns

Do the following to remove any columns that you no longer require from the data source (which can accelerate data refresh):

1. In the Query pane, click the SSAS query that you have previously established. (The sample data for this connection will be displayed in the center of the Query window—this is yet another term for the Query Editor window.) The Manage ribbon will appear.

2. In the Manage ribbon, click the Collapse Columns button.

The columns are removed from the connection to the SSAS cube and, consequently, from the Fields list at the right of the Power BI Desktop window. They are also removed from any visualizations that use them.

Note   Removing columns from Power BI Desktop Query can have a serious domino effect on reports and dashboards. Consequently, you need to be very careful when removing them.

SSAS Tabular Data Warehouses

The previous section showed you how to connect to a "classic" SQL Server Analysis Services cube. However, there are now two types of SQL Server Analysis Services data warehouses:

- The "traditional" dimensional cube

- The "newer" tabular data warehouse

As more and more data warehouses (at least the ones that are based on Microsoft technologies) are being built using the newer, tabular technology, it is probably worth your while to see how quickly and easily you can use these data sources with Power BI Desktop. Indeed, the steps that you follow to connect to either of these data warehouse sources are virtually identical. However, as Power BI is rapidly becoming the tool of choice to query tabular data warehouses, it is certainly worth a few minutes to learn how to connect to SSAS tabular (as it is often called, for short).

1. In the Power BI Desktop ribbon, click Get Data ➤ More ➤ Database and select SQL Server Analysis Services database in the Get Data dialog.

2. Click Connect. The SQL Server Analysis Services database dialog will appear.

3. Enter the Analysis Services server name and the tabular database name (we don't tend to call these cubes). Here, the database is CarSalesTabular on my PC; you will have to specify your own tabular database name. In any case you will need to use the name of your own SSAS server.

4. Click Import.

5. The dialog will look like Figure 3-22.

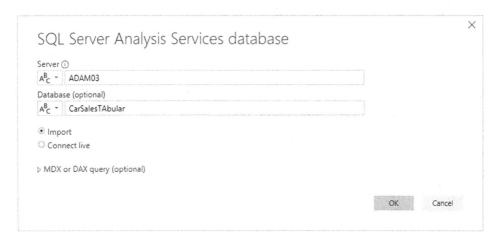

Figure 3-22. *Connecting to an SSAS (multidimensional) database*

6. Click OK. If this is the first time that you are connecting to the tabular warehouse, then the Access SQL Server Analysis Services dialog will appear so that you can define the credentials that you are using to connect to the Analysis Services database, where you will have to accept or alter the credentials and click Connect. The Navigator dialog will appear.

7. Expand the folders in the left pane of the dialog. This way, you can see all the tables contained in the data warehouse. These may—or may not—be structured as facts and dimensions as was the case with a "classic" SSAS data warehouse.

8. Select the tables that you want to load. The dialog will look something like Figure 3-23.

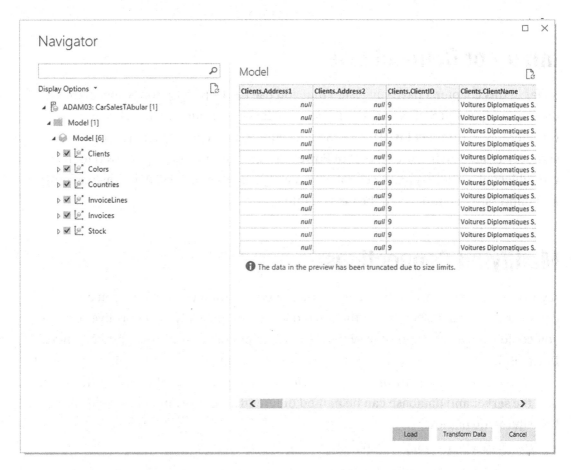

Figure 3-23. *Selecting attributes and measures from an SSAS tabular data source*

9. Click Load. The Power BI Desktop window will open and display the measures and attributes that you selected in the Fields list in the Report window.

Tip   You can filter the data that is loaded from an SSAS tabular database by expanding the MDX or DAX query (optional) item in the SQL Server Analysis Services database dialog. Then you can enter a DAX query in the box that appears before clicking OK. SSAS tabular databases use queries written in DAX, which is the language that Power BI itself uses to filter and calculate data.

Import or Connect Live

So far in this chapter, I have suggested that you use the Import option when sourcing data from Microsoft SQL Server databases and data warehouses. This is because the alternative, Connect Live (for SSAS data sources) and DirectQuery (for database sources), is such an important part of Power BI Desktop that I have preferred to make it the subject of a whole separate chapter. You will discover how to use this far-reaching and impressive technology in the next chapter.

Modifying Connections

If you are working in a structured development environment—or even if you are testing dashboards on a dataset that is either an old version or possibly on a non-live server—you could want at some point to switch from a current data source to another source. Power BI Desktop will let you do this. However, switching data sources will only work if the *structures of the source and the destination data are identical*. Practically, this means that the server and database can be named differently, but the tables and fields must have the same names.

To see this in action, you can do the following:

1. In an existing Power BI Desktop file, click the small triangle at the bottom right of the Edit Queries button in the Home ribbon, and select Data source settings. The Data source settings dialog will be displayed. Figure 3-24 shows you this dialog for the SQL Server connection that you saw at the start of this chapter.

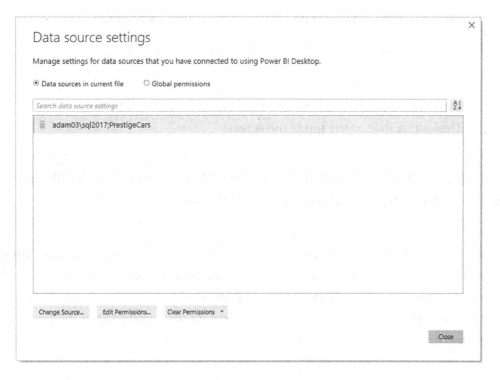

Figure 3-24. *The Data source settings dialog*

2. Click the connection that you want to modify.

3. Click Change Source. The dialog that originally allowed you to specify the data source (in this example that is the SQL Server database connection dialog) will appear. You can see this in Figure 3-25.

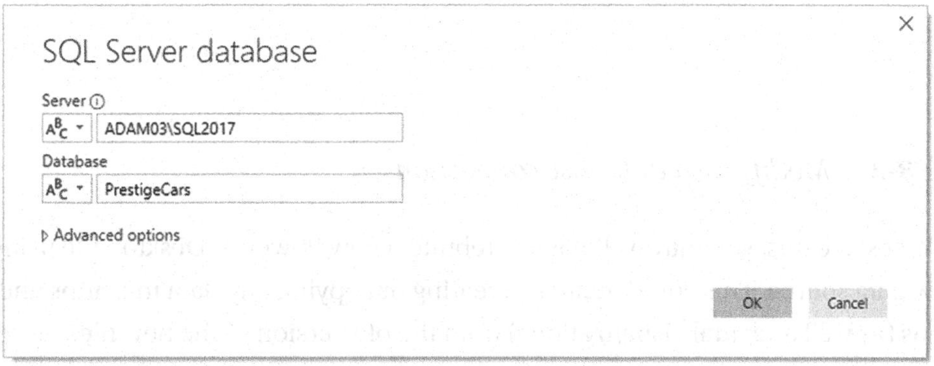

Figure 3-25. *The connection dialog*

4. Specify a different server and/or database as the data source.

5. Click OK. You will return to the Data source settings dialog.

6. Click Close.

7. Click the Apply Changes button that appears under the Power BI
    Desktop ribbon at the top of the screen.

Note   If this is the first time that you are establishing a connection to this new
server and database, you will have to specify the credentials to use.

Assuming that the new data source contains the same table names and structures,
the existing data will be replaced with the data from the new source that you specified.

I have to stress again that this technique will only work if the underlying database
metadata is *identical* across the two servers. If the data structures are not the same, you
will see an error dialog similar to that shown in Figure 3-26.

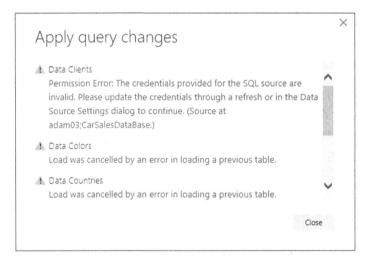

Figure 3-26.   Modifying a database connection

In cases like this, you may well have to rebuild a new Power BI Desktop file using
the new data source. This could mean re-creating or copying any data mashups and
formulas (as well as actual visualizations) from the old version to the new file.

Changing Permissions

It is all too frequent when working with databases and data warehouses to encounter permissions problems. It could be that you set up a connection to a database which required you to change the password at a later date. Meanwhile, the password stored in Power BI Desktop is the old version. So when you try to update your dashboard, you hit a blocker.

Fortunately (assuming, at least, that you know the new password), you can update your stored credentials in Power BI Desktop. As an example, let's suppose that you want to update your Oracle password. Here is how:

1. In an existing Power BI Desktop file, click the small triangle at the bottom right of the Edit Queries button in the Home ribbon, and select Data source settings.

2. Click the Global permissions radio button at the top of the dialog. The Data source settings dialog will be displayed. Figure 3-27 shows you this dialog for the current Power BI Desktop connections on my PC.

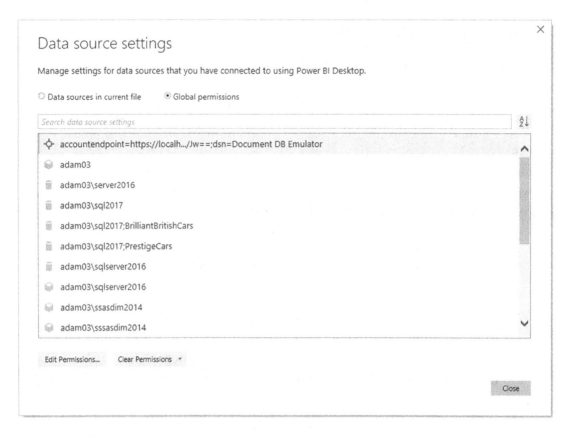

Figure 3-27. *Permissions for current connections*

3. Click the name of the connection that you want to change (ADAM03\SQLSERVER2016 in this example).

4. Click the Edit Permissions button. The Edit Permissions dialog will be displayed, as shown in Figure 3-28.

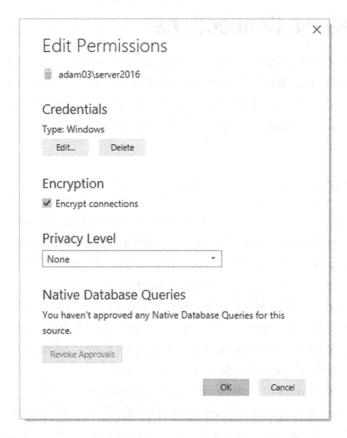

Figure 3-28. *The Edit Permissions dialog*

5. Click Edit. The connection permissions dialog will be displayed (shown earlier in Figure 3-14 in the section that explains how to connect to an Oracle database).

6. Modify the password (or even the username if this is required).

7. Click Save. This returns you to the Edit Permissions dialog.

8. Click OK. You will return to the Data source settings dialog.

9. Click Close to return to Power BI Desktop.

You can now refresh the data using the new permissions that you have just entered.

Other Database Connections

Power BI Desktop does not limit you to a predefined set of available data sources. Provided that your source database comes complete with one of the generic data providers—ODBC or OLE DB—then Power BI Desktop can, in all probability, access these sources too. You will learn about these in Chapter 5.

Conclusion

In this chapter, you have seen how to connect Power BI Desktop to some of the plethora of databases and data warehouses that currently exist. Moreover, you have seen that Power BI Desktop comes equipped "out of the box" with connections to most of the databases that currently exist in a corporate environment.

Moreover, corporate data sources can evolve and change. You also saw how Power BI Desktop allows you to update the permissions that you originally specified for a connection with the latest access details. You even saw how to switch between data sources and update the data both selectively and globally.

Despite their usefulness in storing and structuring large quantities of information, corporate databases can present one small drawback: the time that it can take to load the data from the database into Power BI Desktop's in-memory data model. The development team at Microsoft is clearly aware of this potential shortcoming and has come up with a solution, called DirectQuery (or Connect Live), which you can discover how to implement in the next chapter.

CHAPTER 4

DirectQuery and Connect Live

The previous chapter showed you how to access data from a range of database and data warehouse sources. This process is both simple and efficient, as you saw. However, there is one stage in the process of fetching data that can take a little time, especially if you are dealing with large datasets. This is the "load" phase where the data from the source system is transferred into the Power BI Desktop in-memory model and compressed.

The Power BI development team have clearly looked hard at this question and have come up with a potentially far-reaching solution: connect directly to the data source and avoid having to download the data. This technique is called DirectQuery. It is worth noting that Microsoft now calls the direct data connection to SQL Server Analysis Services "Connect Live." However, I will consider this to be, nevertheless, part of the DirectQuery technological approach.

In this chapter we will take a look at when you can use DirectQuery in Power BI Desktop and what the advantages (and, of course, any drawbacks) are to using these data connection methods.

DirectQuery and Connect Live

To begin with, you need to know that DirectQuery (and Connect Live) currently only works with a few of the available data sources that Power BI Desktop can connect to. At the time of writing, these are

- SQL Server database

- SQL Server Analysis Services ("classic" SSAS and tabular)

- Oracle database

© Adam Aspin 2020
A. Aspin, *Pro Power BI Desktop*, https://doi.org/10.1007/978-1-4842-5763-0_4

- Teradata database

- PostgreSQL

- SAP HANA

- SAP Business Warehouse Message Server

- SAP Business Warehouse Server

- Azure SQL Database

- Azure SQL Data Warehouse (now called Azure Synapse Analytics)

- Amazon Redshift

- AtScale cubes

- Azure HDInsight Spark

- Denodo

- Exasol

- Essbase

- HDInsight Interactive Query

- Impala

- Snowflake

- Spark

DirectQuery is different from the more traditional data load methods for the following reasons:

- You do not load the data into Power BI Desktop. Instead, you use the data directly from the database server.

- Because you are not loading a copy of the data into Power BI Desktop, you *cannot* work offline. You need to be able to connect to the source database or data warehouse to use the data.

- The connection to the source database or data warehouse—and the consequent availability of the data for analysis—is usually extremely fast, if not instantaneous.

- The data is fetched specifically for the requirements of each new visual that you create.

- You have all the data that is in the source database or data warehouse available.

- Data is refreshed every time you apply a slicer or a filter.

- You can (now) connect to any other data source if you are using DirectQuery. This means that you can mix data from direct query sources and those loaded into Power BI Desktop.

- It lets you build visualizations over very large datasets, where it would otherwise be unfeasible to first import all of the data.

There are several very valid reasons why you might want to use DirectQuery:

- It allows for enhanced security as data only transits through the cloud and is not stored outside the enterprise.

- You are sure of seeing the latest data always.

- It enables near real-time reporting.

- As there is no extensive refresh, it avoids loading very large datasets.

- Security rules are defined in the underlying source that connects to the data source using the current user's credentials or the defined user in the gateway.

- Data sovereignty can be respected.

- It applies data warehouse (SSAS/SAP) measures at the correct granularity.

Microsoft SQL Server Data

As a first example of DirectQuery at work, I will use a Microsoft SQL Server database as the data source. The steps are as follows:

1. Open a new Power BI Desktop application.

2. In the Power BI Desktop ribbon, click the small triangle at the bottom of the Get Data button and then click SQL Server. The SQL Server database dialog will appear.

3. Enter the server name in the Server text box. This will be the name of your SQL Server or one of the SQL Server resources used by your organization.

4. Enter the database name; if you are using the sample data, it will be CarSalesData.

5. Select the DirectQuery button. The dialog will look like Figure 4-1.

Figure 4-1. *The Microsoft SQL Server database dialog*

6. Click OK. The credentials dialog will appear. Define the type of credentials that you want to use, as you did in Chapter 3.

7. Click Connect. Power BI Desktop will connect to the server and display the Navigator dialog containing all the tables and views in the database that you have permission to see on the server you selected. In some cases, you could see a dialog saying that the data source does not support encryption. If you feel happy with an unencrypted connection, then click the OK button for this dialog.

8. Click the check boxes for the Clients, Colors, Countries, Invoices, InvoiceLines, and Stock tables. The data for the most recently selected data appears on the right of the Navigator dialog.

9. Click Load. Power BI Desktop will display the list of source tables
    for which it is establishing a connection. You can see this in
    Figure 4-2.

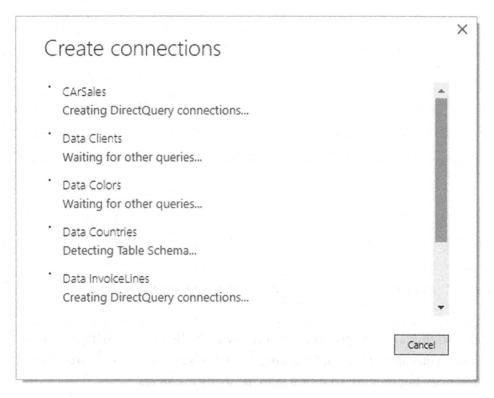

Figure 4-2. *Creating DirectQuery connections*

10. The Power BI Desktop window will open and display the tables
    that you selected in the Fields list in the Report window. You can
    see this in Figure 4-3.

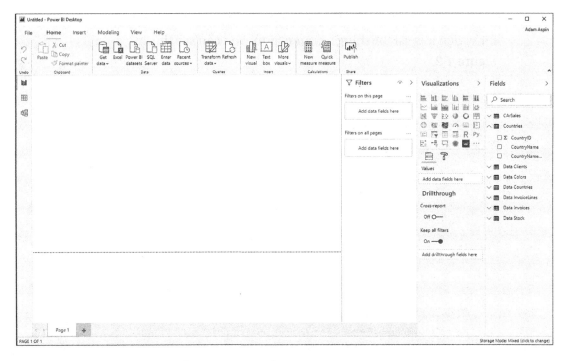

Figure 4-3. *Power BI Desktop using a direct connection*

This is so similar to the process that you saw as the first section of the previous chapter that you can be forgiven for asking, "So what's the difference?" Well there are a few differences, but they are so subtle as to be nearly invisible:

- There was no data load phase. When you clicked Load in step 9, the Power BI Desktop window appeared almost instantaneously. This is why the dialog that appeared briefly in step 9 says "Create Connections" instead of "Load Data."

- When you create Power BI Desktop visuals, they take a fraction longer to populate with data and display.

- To be slightly technical, what Power BI Desktop has done here is to query only the *metadata* from the source system. As metadata is nothing more than the description of the data and the data structures (or "data about data"), the process is extremely rapid as very little information is sent back from the server to Power BI Desktop. This is why establishing a DirectQuery connection is so fast, initially.

By deciding to use DirectQuery, you have adopted a different logic to how the data is stored. Instead of copying all the selected source data into Power BI Desktop, you are leaving the data where it is (in SQL Server in this example) and only importing the data that describes the data—the metadata. So instead of needing all the data in Power BI Desktop before you can do any analysis, you can access only the data that you need, as and when you need it. Nevertheless, you can use this data as a basis for the data mashup and modeling that are described in Chapters 7–12. So you can add calculations and tweak the data (with a few limitations, at least) just as you can if you have loaded all the source data into Power BI Desktop before you begin your analysis.

In deciding to use DirectQuery, you have, in essence, accepted a trade-off. Using DirectQuery implies that

- You will gain time through *not* loading the data into the Power BI Desktop in-memory model.

- Opening the report in Power BI Desktop, and choosing Refresh, will update the fields in the model to reflect metadata changes.

- You will query the data source every time that you create, modify, or filter a Power BI Desktop visual—but *only* for the subset of the data that is required for the specific visual that you are creating or modifying.

- When you refresh the data, you will *not* reload all the data into memory as is the case when importing data. Power BI Desktop will only query the database for the *data that is actually required* to display the visuals that you have created.

- Slicing data can take longer when using DirectQuery because all the Power BI Desktop visuals are re-queried.

- Some of the data mashup techniques that you will discover in Chapters 7–12 cannot be used. Fortunately, these are fairly rate occurrences.

- When the data necessary to service the request has recently been requested, Power BI Desktop uses recent data to reduce the time required to display the visualization. However, selecting Refresh from the Home ribbon will ensure all visualizations are refreshed with current data

However, if you have a largely clean and coherent set of source data—such as data from a corporate data warehouse, where the "heavy lifting" required to make the data reliable and usable has already been carried out—then DirectQuery can really accelerate your data analysis. And you are absolutely certain to be seeing the current data, as well.

Note   You can equally well use a T-SQL query or a SQL Server stored procedure to return data over a DirectQuery connection. Simply expand the Advanced Options section of the connection dialog in step 5 (see Figure 4-1) and enter or copy the SQL text to execute as described in the previous chapter for loading data from SQL Server.

To give a balanced picture (and despite a heartfelt appreciation of the usefulness of DirectQuery), I have to admit that there are a few drawbacks to this connection type that you have to be aware of:

- You cannot (for the moment at least) specify a stored procedure in the Advanced Options as the data source.

- All tables must come from a single database, unless you are using composite models (that mix DirectQuery and data loaded into memory) which were introduced in July 2019 to Power BI Desktop.

- The time required to refresh a visual is dependent on how long the data source takes to respond and return the results from the query.

- You can only return a maximum of one million records to Power BI Desktop when using DirectQuery. Fortunately this threshold is a row limit, and not a limit on the source data. So, if you are aggregating a billion-record data source but only returning 999,999 summary records, then the query will work.

- Relationship filtering (you will see this in Chapter 13) will only work in a single direction.

- Really complex DAX queries simply will not work when using DirectQuery. The only solution to force complex queries to work is to switch back to loading the source data into the in-memory data model.

- Selecting File ➤ Options and Settings ➤ Options ➤ DirectQuery and then "Allow unrestricted measures in DirectQuery mode" will prevent Power BI Desktop from applying built-in limitations to DAX expressions. However, this can make some queries extremely slow, as the conversion from DAX to SQL is not always efficient.

- DAX Time Intelligence is not available with DirectQuery.

- Some capabilities in the Power BI Service (such as Quick Insights) are not available for datasets using DirectQuery.

- There is limited complexity available for SQL queries.

- Date/time support is only to one second accuracy.

- Calculated columns are limited to being intra-row, as in, they can only refer to values of other columns of the same table, without the use of any aggregate functions.

- Calculated tables are not supported.

- It is not possible to use the clustering capability to automatically find groups.

To end on a positive note, DirectQuery does come with the following advantages:

- Reports created using DirectQuery can, of course, be published to the Power BI Service.

- The 1GB limit on the dataset size in Power BI Desktop does not apply to DirectQuery connections.

Note   If Power BI Desktop has recently requested the data from the server that is required for a visualization, then it will use the existing data that has been cached to avoid placing undue stress on the source server as well as to enhance the user experience. Consequently, you need to refresh the data if you want to be sure that you are looking at the most up-to-date information and you suspect that the data in the source has been updated recently.

SQL Server Analysis Services Dimensional Data

Another data source that can use DirectQuery (which uses the variant that Microsoft calls "Connect Live") is the SQL Server Analysis Services dimensional data warehouse—or "classic SSAS" as it is also known. Although a Live Connection to a classic SSAS dimensional data warehouse is very similar to loading data from SSAS into Power BI Desktop, there are a few differences that might make you prefer this method.

Note   Live Connection to a tabular data warehouse will only work if you are using SQL Server 2012 SP1 CU4 or greater. In this case you have to have an Enterprise or Business Intelligence Edition unless you are using SQL Server 2016, in which case standard edition may be used.

Setting up a Live Connection to classic SSAS requires the following steps:

1. In the Power BI Desktop ribbon, click Get Data ➤ More ➤ Database and select SQL Server Analysis Services database in the Get Data dialog.

2. Click Connect. The SQL Server Analysis Services database dialog will appear.

3. Enter the Analysis Services server name and the database (or "cube") name, if you know it. In this example, the database is named CarSalesOLAP; of course, you will have to specify your own SSAS database name. In all cases, you will need to use the name of your own SSAS server.

4. Select the Connect live button.

5. Click OK. If this is the first time that you are connecting to the cube, then the Access SQL Server Analysis Services dialog will appear so that you can define the credentials that you are using to connect to the Analysis Services database.

6. Accept or alter the credentials and click Connect. The Navigator dialog will appear.

7. Click the cube that you want to connect to from the SSAS
    database, drill into the cube elements, and select the metrics and
    dimensions that interest you. The dialog will look something like
    Figure 4-4.

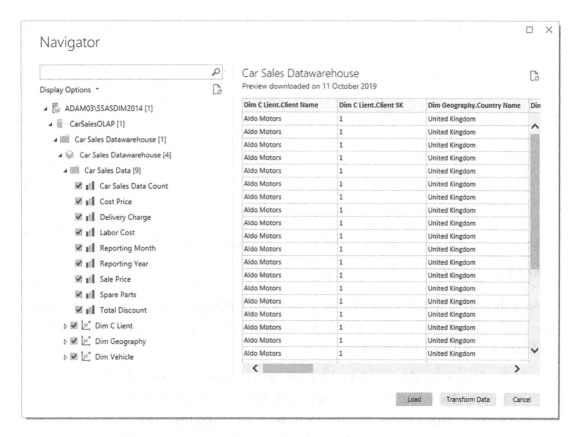

Figure 4-4. *Live Connect to a tabular database*

8. Click OK. The Power BI Desktop window will open and display the
    fact tables and dimensions that you selected in the Fields list in
    the Report window. It could look something like Figure 4-5.

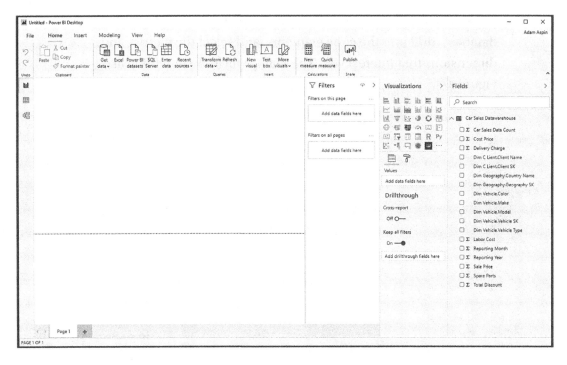

Figure 4-5. *Power BI Desktop using a Live Connection*

So, although generally similar to the process for loading data from classic SSAS into Power BI Desktop that you saw in the previous chapter, this approach does, nonetheless, manifest one fundamental difference:

- You were not able to select the tables to use from the tabular data source. However, the underlying structure of the Analysis Services cube is visible just as it would be from, say, Excel. This includes visibility of the folder hierarchy for data that is present in the SSAS cube.

So, overall, a Live Connection implies that the source data *must* be ready to use and correctly structured for you to base your Power BI Desktop analytical reports on it. You *cannot* make changes to the data or the data structures or add any calculations in Power BI Desktop.

There are a couple of other points that you might need to take into account if you are hesitating between a Live Connection and loading data into Power BI Desktop:

- None of the data mashup possibilities that you will learn in Chapters 7–12 are available.

- You cannot use MDX to select the data that you want to use in Power BI Desktop. So a Live Connection is an "all or nothing" option.

- Certain features in your cube are either not supported fully or not supported at all with Live Connections from Power BI Desktop.

Yet, once again, a direct connection brings one crucial factor into the mix, and that is sheer speed. As SSAS data warehouses can be huge, the fact that you are not loading massive amounts of data into Power BI Desktop can save an immense amount of time. Not only that, a data warehouse that was too large to load into Power BI Desktop could now become accessible over a direct connection. Moreover, your Power BI Desktop visuals will only return the exact data that they need from the SSAS data source, as was the case for the SQL Server database in the previous section. All the hard work is carried out by the server, leaving Power BI Desktop (and you) free to concentrate on analysis and presentation.

Microsoft SQL Server Analysis Services Tabular Data Sources

Now let's see how to use a Microsoft SQL Server Analysis Services tabular data warehouse as the data source for a Live Connection. A SQL Server Analysis Services tabular database is another technology that is used for data warehousing. It is different from the more traditional dimensional data warehouse in that it is entirely stored in the server memory and, consequently, is usually very much faster to use.

To establish a Live Connection to an SSAS tabular data source:

1. In the Power BI Desktop ribbon, click Get Data ➤ More ➤ Database and select SQL Server Analysis Services database in the Get Data dialog.

2. Click Connect. The SQL Server Analysis Services database dialog will appear.

3. Enter the Analysis Services server name and the tabular database name (I don't tend to call these cubes). The database I am using is CarSalesTabular; you must specify your own tabular database name and the name of your own SSAS server.

4. Select the Connect live button. The dialog will look like Figure 4-6.

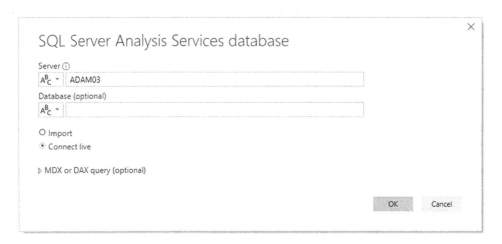

Figure 4-6. *Connecting to an SSAS (multidimensional) database*

5. Click OK. If this is the first time that you are connecting to the
    tabular data source, then the Access SQL Server Analysis Services
    dialog will appear so that you can define the credentials that you
    are using to connect to the Analysis Services database, where you
    will have to accept or alter the credentials and click Connect. The
    Navigator dialog will appear.

6. Click the perspective (Model in this example) that you wish to
    connect to. The dialog will look something like Figure 4-7.

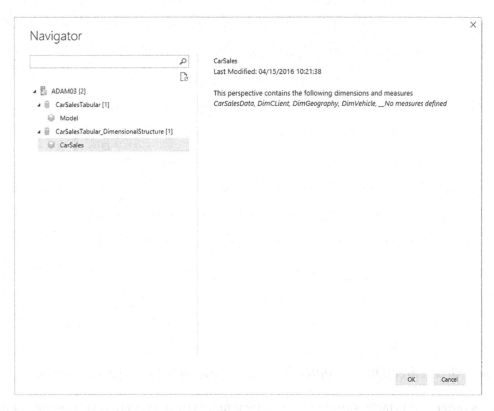

Figure 4-7. *Selecting attributes and measures from an SSAS tabular source*

7. Click OK. The Power BI Desktop window will open and display
    the tables that you selected in the Fields list in the Report window.
    You can see this in Figure 4-8.

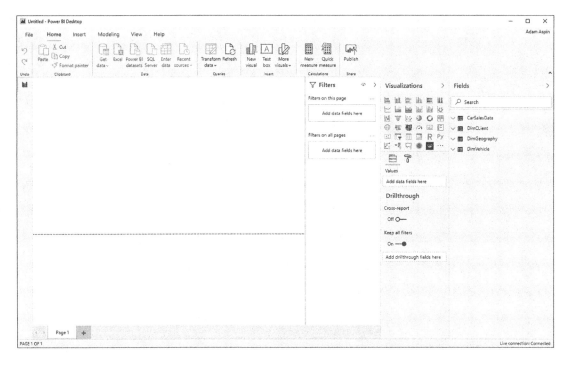

Figure 4-8. *A DirectQuery connection to an SSAS tabular data warehouse*

This process was fairly similar to the DirectQuery connection that you established in the previous section. There are, nonetheless, a couple of further differences:

- The Relationships icon is no longer available on the top left of the Power BI Desktop window.

- None of the data mashup possibilities that you will learn in Chapters 6–12 are available.

- You were not able to select the tables to use from the tabular data source.

These three points actually imply the even deeper trade-off that you have accepted when you clicked Connect live in step 4. What you have agreed to is using the data source as the *complete and final model* for the data. You are, in effect, using Power BI Desktop as the front end for the data "as is."

This trade-off, however, is bursting with positives for you, the data analyst and dashboard creator. You can now

- See all the data in the data warehouse (or at least the data that you are authorized to see) without a complex process where you have to select dozens of tables (and risk overlooking a few vital sources of data).

- Access the data model as it has been designed by an expert with all the relationships between the tables defined at source.

- Get the latest data—what you see in Power BI Desktop is the current data in the tabular data warehouse. You only need to refresh Power BI Desktop if the data is refreshed at source.

- Use predefined hierarchies and calculations from the tabular data warehouse.

- *Access the data at lightning speed, because the source data is stored in the host server's memory*, and not on disk (as is the case with classic relational databases).

This last point is the one that really needs emphasizing. Not only are you gaining time through not loading a copy of the data into the Power BI Desktop in-memory data model, you are *accessing in-memory data on the server itself*, avoiding the need for slow searches for data on disk. The overall result is unbelievably fast access to huge amounts of clean, structured, and aggregated data. All in all, the combination of a SQL Server tabular data warehouse and Power BI Desktop is designed to make data analysis considerably faster and easier.

It is worth noting that there is no real Power BI Desktop Query Editor access for a Live Connection to an Analysis Services tabular data warehouse. If you click the Edit Queries button, all you will see is the connection dialog for the Analysis Services database.

Note   When you set up a Live Connection to a tabular data source, you *cannot* filter the data that is loaded from an SSAS cube by expanding the MDX or DAX query (optional) item in the SQL Server Analysis Services database dialog and entering a DAX query.

DirectQuery with Non-Microsoft Databases

So far in this chapter, we have focused on using Microsoft data sources to establish DirectQuery connections to the source data. Fortunately, Microsoft has extended this technology to several other sources of corporate data.

Equally fortunate is the fact that connecting to (say) an Oracle database or a SAP HANA data warehouse using DirectQuery is every bit as simple as loading the data into Power BI Desktop from these (or indeed other) database and data warehouse sources. So I will not waste pages here in re-explaining the technique. If the source is a database, then you select DirectQuery; if the source is a data warehouse, then you can select Live Connection. A DirectQuery will allow you to specify a SQL statement to select data, and a Live Connection will display all the objects in the data warehouse. It really is that simple.

DirectQuery and In-Memory Tables

A recent addition to the Microsoft SQL Server database has been in-memory tables. These are perceived by tools like Power BI Desktop as standard tables, yet they exist in the server's memory (as opposed to storing the data on disk). This makes accessing data from in-memory tables extremely fast. When you add to this the fact that these tables can, in many cases, also use the compression technology that SSAS tabular data warehouses use, then you have pretty nearly the best of both worlds as far as analytics is concerned:

- Data stored in classic relational structures that is updated instantly

- Optimized structures for analytics (data is stored by column, rather than by row, and is both compressed and in-memory)

Here is not the place to expose all that this technology can bring to the table. However, as it is a potential game-changer, it is worth showing you how you can use the latest versions of SQL Server (i.e., 2016 and up) as a direct source of analytical data. As this is essentially a rerun of the initial section of this chapter, I will not show here, again, the same screenshots of the process.

1. Open a new Power BI Desktop application.

2. In the Power BI Desktop ribbon, click the small triangle at the bottom of the Get Data button and then click SQL Server. The SQL Server database dialog will appear.

3. Enter the server name in the Server text box. This will be the name of your SQL Server or one of the SQL Server resources used by your organization.

4. Enter the database name; on my PC it is CarSalesMemoryBased.

5. Select the DirectQuery button.

6. Click OK. The Access a SQL Server database dialog will appear. Define the type of credentials that you want to use, as you did in the previous chapter.

7. Click Connect. Power BI Desktop will connect to the server and display the Navigator dialog containing all the tables and views in the database that you have permission to see on the server you selected.

8. Click the check boxes for the Clients, Colors, Countries, Invoices, InvoiceLines, and Stock tables. The data for the most recently selected data appears on the right of the Navigator dialog.

9. Click Load. The Power BI Desktop window will open and display the tables that you selected in the Fields list in the Report window.

Yes, the process is identical to a "normal" DirectQuery connection. You will only return data when creating or modifying visuals. Yet here too, the data is stored in memory on the server, and all the heavy lifting is carried out by the server. However (and unlike when using a Live Connection to a tabular data warehouse), you can extend the data model, hide or add further columns, and create complex calculations. In many cases, this can be, quite simply, the best of all possible worlds.

DirectQuery and Refreshing the Data

You saw how to refresh data from databases and data warehouses in the previous chapter. If you are using DirectQuery, refreshing the data will likely only be necessary if the source data has changed. This is because every time that you create or modify a visual, or when you filter reports, pages, or visuals (or if you apply slicers), the data for any visual affected by the change is refreshed.

Consequently, you only have to click the Refresh button if you know that the source data has been updated. It could be, for instance, that the underlying database or data warehouse is reprocessed overnight—or even on an hourly basis. In cases like these, you should click the Refresh button once you know that the data has been updated on the server so that you can be absolutely sure that you are using the latest available data in your reports.

In the case of a DirectQuery connection to a database, you could wish only to refresh selected tables. In this case, all you have to do is to right-click the table name in the Fields list and select Refresh for each table that you want to update.

Microsoft provides the following tips when using DirectQuery that you need to be aware of. Fortunately they will probably not affect most standard use cases of DirectQuery:

- Avoid complex queries in Query Editor.

- Limit measures to simple aggregates.

- Avoid relationships on calculated columns.

- Avoid relationships on uniqueidentifier columns (there is no uniqueidentifier data type in Power BI Desktop), so this avoids a data type cast.

- Avoid calculated columns and data type changes.

- Assume referential integrity—to get inner joins.

- Do not use the relative data filtering in Query Editor.

Conclusion

This short chapter extended your abilities to use databases and data warehouses as the data source for your Power BI analysis. You saw that you can choose not to load data into the Power BI Desktop in-memory data model, but can, instead, connect directly to the source data repository. Moreover, you saw that the approach to setting up a direct connection is virtually identical to the way that you set up a standard data load into Power BI Desktop.

DirectQuery allows you to avoid a potentially massive data transfer. This can save you a large amount of time and also guarantees that you are looking at the latest data. So, while it can take a little longer to design and filter your visuals, you are only using the precise data that you need on each and every occasion. Sometimes this can be the only feasible way to analyze data from terabyte-sized data warehouses.

When combined with in-memory data storage on the server (in in-memory tables or tabular data warehouses), this technique can make Power BI Desktop into a near-perfect front end for the analysis of huge and complex corporate data sources.

However, corporate databases and data warehouses are not the only sources of large-scale data that exist. More and more data is now stored in the cloud. Accessing cloud and web-based data will be the subject of the next chapter.

CHAPTER 5

Loading Data from the Web and the Cloud

In this chapter we will take a look at a subset of the fast-growing and wide-ranging set of data sources available over the Internet that you can use as a source of analytical data for Power BI Desktop. While the data sources that you will see in the following pages may be extremely diverse, they all have one thing in common: they are stored outside the enterprise and are available using an Internet connection.

The ever-increasing range of data sources that are available are provided by a multitude of suppliers. Looking at all the current sources would take up an entire book, so I will show you how to access some of the mainstream services that are currently on offer. Once you have learned how to access a few of them, you should be able to extend the basic techniques to access just about any of the web and cloud services that can currently be used by Power BI Desktop.

Power BI Desktop is now firmly entrenched as a fundamental part of the Microsoft universe. As PowerBI.com (the cloud service that you can use to store and share dashboards) is part of Microsoft Azure—the Microsoft cloud—it is perhaps inevitable that the Power BI Desktop developers have gone out of their way to ensure that Power BI has become the analytical tool of choice for solutions that are hosted in Azure. For this reason, I will explain quite a few of the core services that host data in Azure.

Nearly all of the data connections outlined in this chapter require access to a specific online source. Most of these sources are industrial strength—and not free. However, if your enterprise is not a subscriber to these services, and you wish, nevertheless, to experiment with them, it could be worth taking a look at the free trial offers available from many (if not all) of the service providers whose offerings are outlined in this chapter.

© Adam Aspin 2020
A. Aspin, *Pro Power BI Desktop*, https://doi.org/10.1007/978-1-4842-5763-0_5

Web and Cloud Services

Before delving into the details of some of the web and cloud services that are available, let's take an initial high-level look at what these really are. These data sources include (among many others)

- Web pages

- Online services, such as Google Analytics, Salesforce, or MS Dynamics 365

- Microsoft Azure, which covers hosting files in Azure Blob services, storing data in an Azure SQL database, or storing data in an Azure Synapse Analytics (or even reading big data in Azure HDInsight)

- OData, a generic method of accessing data on the Internet

Web Pages

If you need to collect some data that you can see as a table in a web browser, you can use Power BI Desktop to connect to the URL for the page in question and then load all the data from any table on the page.

Online Services

Online services is a catch-all phrase used to describe data that you can access using the Internet. Most of the online services available to Power BI Desktop are what are called "platforms." These are (often huge) software and data resources that either are only available online or were once housed in corporate systems but are now available as services on the Internet. There are currently dozens of online services that are available to connect to using Power BI Desktop. Indeed, the number of available services is growing at a startling pace. Some of the more frequently used include those listed in Table 5-1.

Table 5-1. *Online Services Currently Available to Power BI Desktop*

Source	Comments
Azure DevOps	Accesses Azure DevOps data entities.
Salesforce Objects	Lets you access data in Salesforce.
Salesforce Reports	Lets you access the prestructured data objects (both native and custom) that underlies built-in Salesforce reports.
Google Analytics	Lets you access the data managed by Google to track website traffic.
Adobe Analytics	Lets you access the data tracked in Adobe Analytics.
Facebook	Accesses Facebook data.
SharePoint Online	Connects to the cloud-hosted version of Microsoft SharePoint.
Microsoft Exchange Online	Connects to the cloud-hosted version of Microsoft Exchange.
Dynamics 365 Online	Connects to the cloud-hosted version of Microsoft Dynamics 365—the MS CRM and ERP solution.
Dynamics 365 Business Central	Connects to Dynamics 365 Business Central (online and on-premises).
Dynamics NAV	Connects to Microsoft Dynamics NAV.
OData	Although OData is not, technically, an online platform, it is certainly an online source of data. This is a standardized method for connecting to different data structures using a URL as a starting point.
GitHub	Connects to GitHub.
MailChimp	Connects to MailChimp.

These are only some of the many available online services that you can connect to in Power BI Desktop. I advise you to examine the list and see if the service that you require is currently available.

Note   As the number of available online services is increasing at an ever-increasing rate, you will probably find many more than those that I have listed here by the time that this book is published. Moreover, there are currently a number of online services that are available as beta versions. This means that you can test them, but they are not yet finalized and supported.

Microsoft Azure

Azure is the Microsoft cloud. The Azure data sources that Power BI Desktop can currently connect to, and can preview and load data from, are given in Table 5-2.

Table 5-2. *Azure Sources*

Source	Comments
Microsoft Azure SQL database	Lets you connect to a Microsoft SQL Server cloud-based database and import records from all the data tables and views that you are authorized to access.
Microsoft Azure SQL Data Warehouse (now rebranded as Azure Synapse Analytics)	Lets you connect to Microsoft's cloud-based, elastic, enterprise data warehouse.
Azure Analysis Services database	Connects to an Azure Analysis Services database.
Microsoft Azure Blob Storage	Reads from a cloud-based unstructured data store.
Microsoft Azure Table Storage	Reads from Microsoft Azure tables.
Microsoft Azure Cosmos DB (formerly called DocumentDB)	Lets you connect to Microsoft's Azure-hosted NoSQL database.
Microsoft Azure Data Lake Storage (Gen1 and Gen2)	Lets you connect to Microsoft's raw data cloud storage.
Microsoft Azure HDInsight	Reads cloud-based Hadoop files in the Microsoft Azure environment.
Azure HDInsight Spark	Lets you connect to Microsoft's parallel processing framework in Microsoft cloud.
HDInsight Interactive Query	Runs interactive queries over HDInsight.

Obviously, more Azure connection options are being added to Power BI Desktop by Microsoft as the Azure offering is extended.

Web Pages

As a first and extremely simple example, let's grab some data from a web page. Since I want to concentrate on the method rather than the data, I will use a web page that has nothing to do with the sample data in the book. I will not be using this other than as a simple introduction to the process of loading data from web pages using Power BI Desktop.

Assuming that you have launched Power BI Desktop and closed the splash screen

1. Click the small triangle at the bottom of the Get Data button in the Home ribbon.

2. Select Web from the menu that appears, as shown in Figure 5-1.

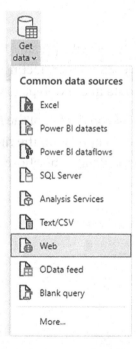

Figure 5-1. *The Get Data menu*

3. Enter the following URL (it is a Microsoft help page for Power
    BI Desktop that contains a few tables of data): `http://office.`
    `microsoft.com/en-gb/excel-help/guide-to-the-power-`
    `query-ribbon-HA103993930.aspx`. I am, of course, hoping that it
    is still available when you read this book. Of course, if you have a
    URL that you want to try out, then feel free! The dialog will look
    something like Figure 5-2.

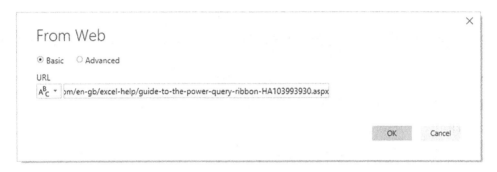

Figure 5-2. *The From Web dialog*

4. Click OK. The Navigator dialog will appear. After a few seconds,
    during which Power BI Desktop is connecting to the web page, the
    list of available tables of data in the web page will be displayed.

5. Click one of the table names on the left of the Navigator dialog.
    The contents of the table will appear on the right of the Navigator
    dialog to show you what the data in the chosen table looks like, as
    shown in Figure 5-3.

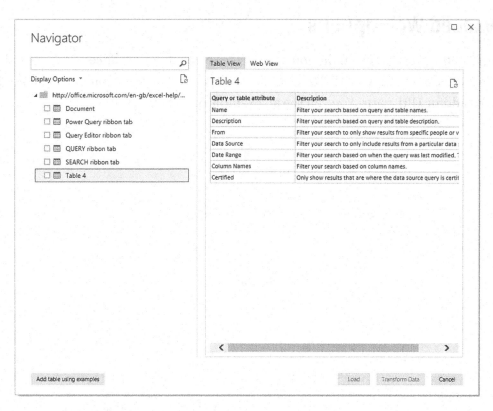

Figure 5-3. *The Navigator dialog previewing the contents of a table on a web page*

6. Select the check box in the Navigator dialog (shown to the left of Table 4 in Figure 5-3).

7. Click Load at the bottom of the window.

Tip Another way of accessing web pages is to click Get Data ➤ Other. You can then select Web in the list on the right of the Get Data dialog.

This simple example showed how you can load tables of data from a web page and load it into Power BI Desktop.

Advanced Web Options

In step 3 of the previous example, you could have selected the Advanced button. Had you done this, the From Web dialog would have expanded to allow you to build complex URLs by adding URL parts. You can see an example of this in Figure 5-4.

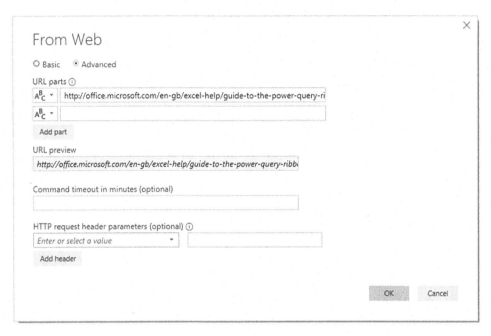

Figure 5-4. *The Advanced options in the From Web dialog*

Clicking the Add part button allows you to define multiple URL parts.

If necessary, you can also specify HTTP request header parameters that will be used when submitting the URL. These could be required by certain web pages. A discussion of these is outside the scope of this book.

Table View or Web View

Looking at the tables that a web page contains is not always the most natural way of finding the right data. This is because you are looking at the data tables out of context. By this I mean that you cannot see where they are on the web page. After all, the Web is a very visual medium.

To help you find the correct data table on a web page, the Query Editor lets you switch between two views of the web source:

- Table view (which you saw in Figure 5-3)

- Web view (which you can see in Figure 5-5)

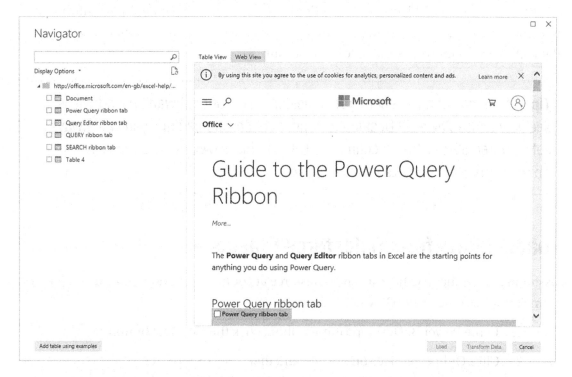

Figure 5-5. *Web View in the Navigator dialog*

You alternate between these ways of visualizing the web page by clicking the Table View and Web View buttons that are at the top center of the Navigator dialog. The same web page that you saw previously looks like Figure 5-5 when you switch to Web View.

Salesforce

One of the pioneers in the Software as a Service (SaaS) space—and now, indisputably, one of the leaders—is Salesforce. So it is perhaps inevitable that Power BI Desktop will allow you to connect to Salesforce and load any data that you have permission to view using your Salesforce account.

Indeed, Salesforce is such a wide-ranging and complete service that you have two possible methods of accessing your data:

- Objects

- Reports

Briefly, Salesforce objects are the underlying data tables that contain the information that you want to access. Salesforce reports are the data that has been collated from the data tables into a more accessible form of output.

Tip   If you do not have a corporate Salesforce account but want, nevertheless, to see how to use Power BI Desktop to connect to Salesforce data, you can always set up a free 30-day trial account. The URL for this is `www.salesforce.com/form/signup/freetrial-sales.jsp`.

Loading Data from Salesforce Objects

Assuming, then, that you have a valid Salesforce account, here is how you can load data from Salesforce objects into Power BI Desktop:

1. In the Power BI Desktop Home ribbon, click the Get Data button.

2. Click Online Services on the left, and then select Salesforce Objects on the right. The Get Data dialog will look like Figure 5-6.

Figure 5-6. *The Get Data dialog for online services*

3. Click Connect. The Salesforce Objects dialog will appear. It should
    look like the one shown in Figure 5-7.

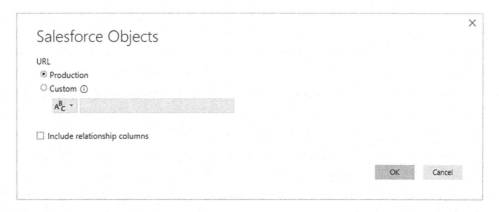

Figure 5-7. *The Salesforce Objects dialog*

4. Select the Production button and click OK. The Access Salesforce login dialog will appear. It should look like the one shown in Figure 5-8.

Figure 5-8. *The Access Salesforce login dialog*

5. Unless you are already signed in, click Sign in. The Salesforce sign-in dialog will appear.

6. Enter your Salesforce login and password. The dialog should look something like the one shown in Figure 5-9.

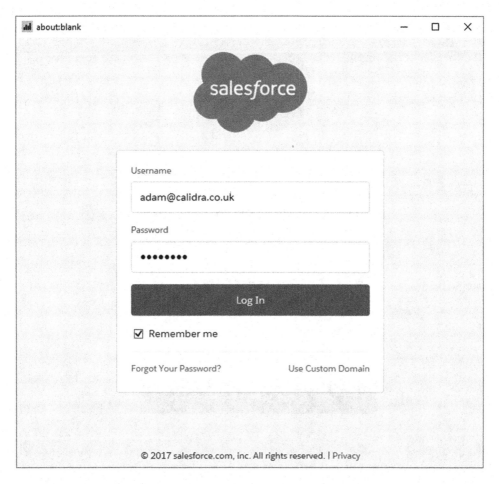

Figure 5-9. *The Salesforce sign-in dialog*

7.   If this is the first time that you are connecting to Salesforce from
     Power BI Desktop (or if you have requested that Salesforce request
     confirmation each time that you log in), you will be asked to
     verify your identity. The Salesforce Verify Your Identity dialog will
     appear, as shown in Figure 5-10.

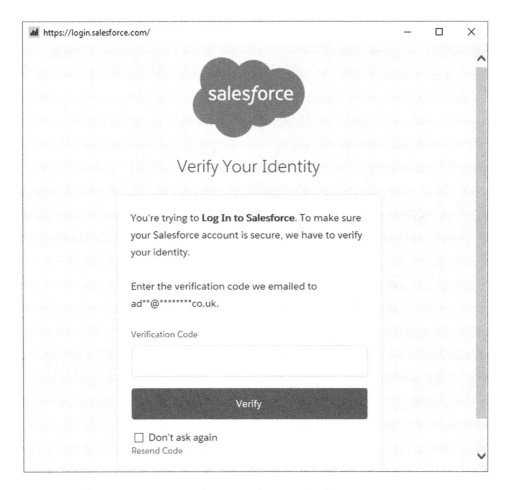

Figure 5-10. *The Salesforce Verify Your Identity dialog*

8. Click Verify. Salesforce will send a verification code to the email account that you are using to log in to Salesforce.

9. Enter the code in the Verification Code field and click OK. You will see the Allow Access dialog, as in Figure 5-11.

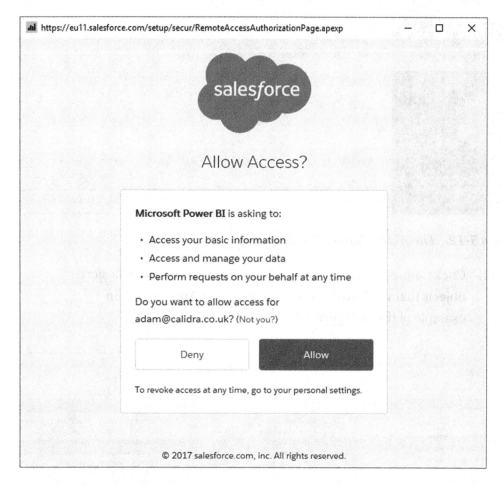

Figure 5-11. *The Salesforce Allow Access dialog*

   10.   Click Allow. You will return to the Access Salesforce dialog, only
         now you are logged in. You can see this in Figure 5-12.

Figure 5-12. *The Access Salesforce dialog*

11. Click Connect. The Navigator will appear, showing the Salesforce objects that you have permissions to access. You can see an example of this in Figure 5-13.

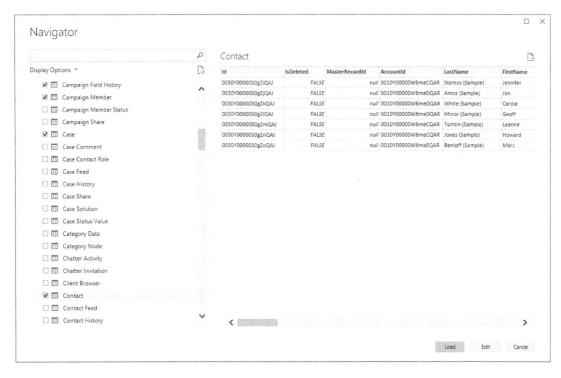

Figure 5-13. *Salesforce objects viewed in the Navigator*

12. Select the objects whose data you wish to load into Power BI
     Desktop and click Load. The data will be loaded into Power BI
     Desktop ready for you to create dashboards and reports based on
     your Salesforce data.

Tip   To avoid having to confirm your identity to Salesforce every time that you
create a new suite of Power BI Desktop reports using Salesforce data, you can
check "Remember me" in the Salesforce sign-in dialog and "Don't ask again" in
the Salesforce Verify Your Identity dialog.

Salesforce objects contain a vast amount of data. However, from the point of view of
Power BI Desktop, this is similar to accessing a database structure. This means that you
have to have some understanding of how the underlying data is stored. Should you wish
to learn about the way that Salesforce data is structured, then I suggest that you start with
the Salesforce documentation currently available at `https://trailhead.salesforce.`
`com/en/modules/data_modeling/units/objects_intro`.

Salesforce Reports

If you find that you are simply submerged by the amount of data that is available in
Salesforce, you can, instead, go directly to the data that underlies standard Salesforce
reports. This will avoid your having to learn about the underlying data structures. The
downside is that you cannot easily extend these datasets.

To access Salesforce report data, simply follow the steps outlined in the previous
section. However, instead of choosing Salesforce Objects in step 2, select Salesforce
Reports instead. The Navigator dialog will, in this case, look something like the one
shown in Figure 5-14.

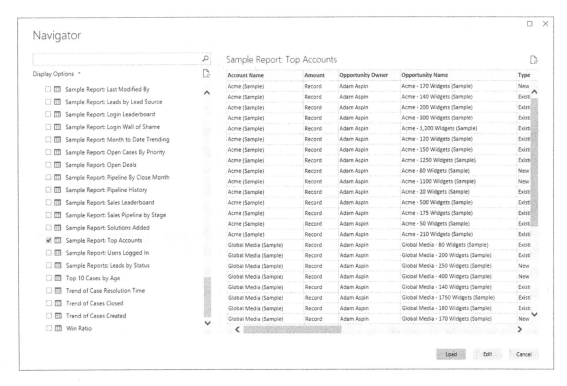

Figure 5-14. *The Navigator dialog showing the data for Salesforce Reports*

From here you can select and load the reports data from Salesforce that you want to use to create your own dashboards.

Microsoft Dynamics 365

Another online service that contains much valuable enterprise data is Microsoft Dynamics 365. As you would probably expect, Power BI Desktop can connect easily to Microsoft online sources such as Dynamics. Here is how to do this:

Tip   If you do not have a corporate Microsoft Dynamics 365 online account but want, nevertheless, to see how to use Power BI Desktop to connect to Microsoft Dynamics 365 data, you can always set up a free 30-day trial account. The URL for this is currently `https://trials.dynamics.com/CustomerEngagement/ChangeSignup/`. Indeed, this example is from using a free 30-day trial account (that will likely have expired long before this book is in print).

---

1. In the Power BI Desktop Home ribbon, click the Get Data button.

2. Click Online Services on the left, and then select Dynamics 365 (online) on the right. The Get Data dialog will look like Figure 5-15.

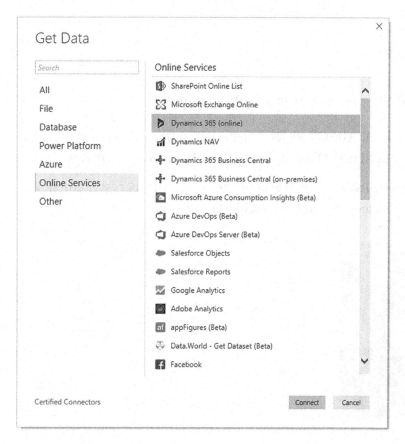

Figure 5-15. *The Get Data dialog for Dynamics 365*

3. Click Connect. The Dynamics 365 (online) dialog will appear.

4. Enter the URL that you use to connect to Dynamics 365 and add `/api/data/v8.1` (at least, this was the case as this book went to press). It could look like the one shown in Figure 5-16. Note, however, that this URL will vary depending on where you are in the world.

Figure 5-16. *The Dynamics 365 (online) dialog*

5.   Click OK. The OData feed dialog will appear. This is because
     Power BI uses OData to connect to Dynamics 365 Online.

6.   Select Organizational account as the security access method. The
     OData feed dialog will look like Figure 5-17.

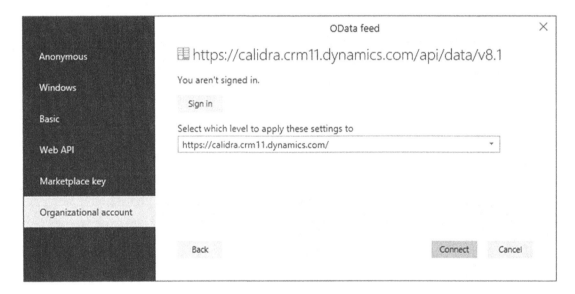

Figure 5-17. *The OData feed dialog for Dynamics 365*

7.   Click Sign in to sign in to your Dynamics 365 account and follow
     the Microsoft sign-in process. Once completed, the OData feed
     dialog will look something like the one in Figure 5-18.

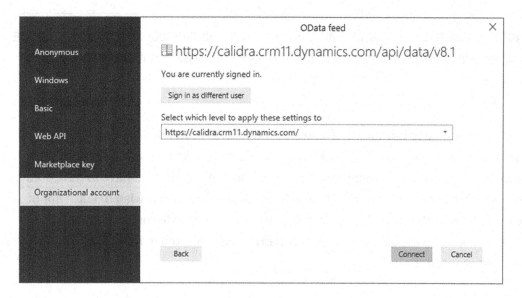

Figure 5-18. *The OData feed dialog after sign-in*

8.   Click Connect. The Navigator dialog will appear showing all the
Dynamics objects that you have permissions to connect to. You
can see an example of this in Figure 5-19.

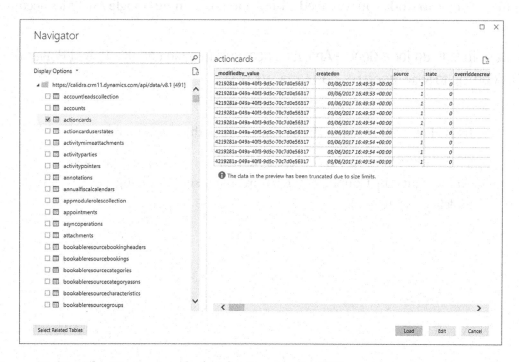

Figure 5-19. *The Navigator dialog for Dynamics 365*

Note   In step 6 you saw that an MS Dynamics 365 connection is really an OData connection. OData is explained in more detail in a subsequent section of this chapter.

There are a huge number of Dynamics 365 tables—and this number will vary depending on the subscription that your organization has taken out. However, you are, in reality, accessing a database structure. This means that you have to have some understanding of how the underlying data is stored. Should you wish to learn about Dynamics 365 tables, then I suggest that you start with the Microsoft online help at `https://docs.microsoft.com/en-us/dynamics365/unified-operations/dev-itpro/data-entities/data-entities`.

Google Analytics

Assuming that you have a valid Google Analytics account set up, you can use Power BI Desktop to connect to the Google Analytics data that you have permissions to access. For this example to work, you will need a valid and functioning Google Analytics account.

Note   To sign up for a Google Analytics account that you can use to test Power BI Desktop, go to `www.google.com/analytics`.

1. In the Power BI Desktop Home ribbon, click the Get Data button.

2. Click Online Services on the left, and then select Google Analytics on the right. The Connecting to a third-party service dialog will look like Figure 5-20.

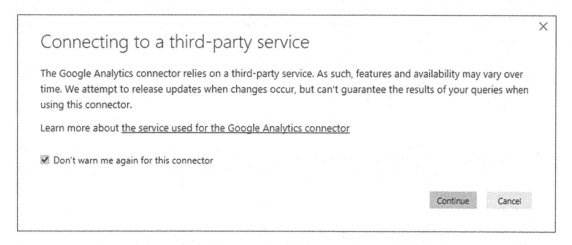

Figure 5-20. *The third-party service connector alert*

3.   Click Continue. The Google Account dialog will appear. This
      currently looks like the one in Figure 5-21.

Figure 5-21. *The Google Analytics connection dialog*

4.   Click Sign in. The Google Choose an account dialog will be
      displayed. This currently looks like the image in Figure 5-22.

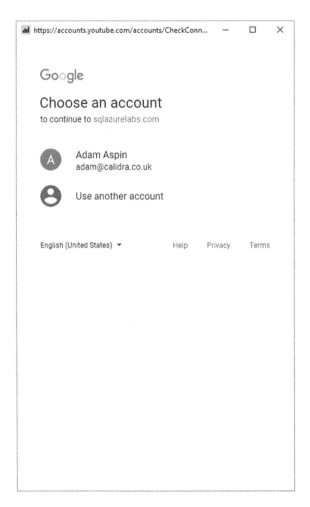

Figure 5-22. *The Google Analytics login dialog*

5. Click the existing account to use for Google Analytics. The Google
   Analytics permissions dialog will appear. This currently looks like
   the one in Figure 5-23.

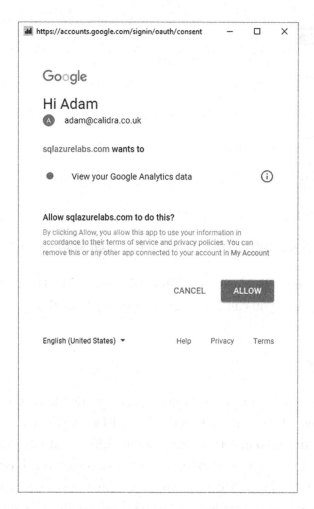

Figure 5-23. *The Google Analytics permissions dialog*

6. Click Allow. You will return to the Google Account dialog, but logged in this time. You can see this in Figure 5-24.

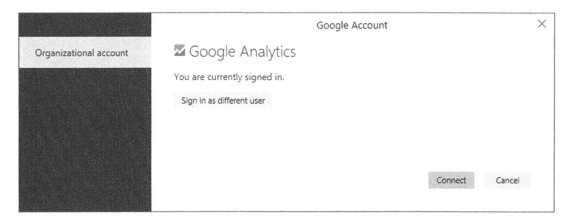

Figure 5-24. *The Google Analytics dialog when signed in*

7. Click Connect. The Navigator dialog will appear, displaying the data tables that you can connect to in Google Analytics.

OData Feeds

OData is a short way of referring to the Open Data Protocol. This protocol allows web clients to publish and edit resources, identified as URLs. The data that you connect to using OData can be in a tabular format or indeed in different structures.

OData is something of a generic method of connecting to web-based data. Consequently each OData source could differ from others that you may have used previously. Indeed, you have already seen OData when connecting to Dynamics 365.

However, there are a multitude of OData sources that are available. Some are public, some are only accessible if you have appropriate permissions. However, the access method will always be broadly similar. Here, then, is an example of how to connect to an OData sample source that Microsoft has made freely available (at least when this book went to press):

1. In the Power BI Desktop Home ribbon, click the small triangle at the bottom of the Get Data button. Alternatively, click the Get Data button and select Other from the left pane of the Get Data dialog.

2. Select OData feed from the menu. The OData feed dialog will appear.

3. Enter the URL that you are using to connect to the OData source. In this example I will use a Microsoft sample OData feed that you can find at `http://services.odata.org/northwind/northwind.svc`. The dialog should look like Figure 5-25.

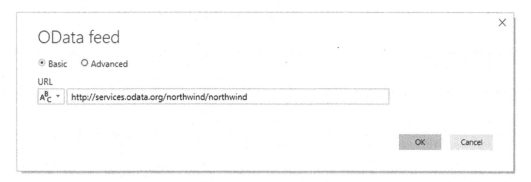

Figure 5-25. *The OData feed dialog*

4. Click OK. The Navigator dialog will be displayed and will show the data available using the specified URL.

OData Options

The OData feed dialog (rather like the From Web dialog that you saw earlier in this chapter) also contains an Advanced button. Selecting this will expand the dialog to allow you to add one or more URL parts to the URL. You can see this in Figure 5-26.

Figure 5-26. *The OData feed dialog Advanced options*

Note   URL parts can be parameterized in the Power BI Desktop Query Editor. I will explain parameterization in Chapter 11.

Azure SQL Database

SQL Server does not only exist as an on-premises database. It is also available as a "Platform as a Service" (also known as PaaS). Simply put, this lets you apply a pay-as-you-go model to your database requirements where you can fire up a database server in the cloud in a few minutes and then scale it to suit your requirements, rather than buying hardware and software and having to maintain them.

Connecting to Microsoft's PaaS offering, called Azure SQL database, is truly simple. If you have the details of a corporate Azure SQL database, you can use this to connect to. If you do not, and nonetheless want to experiment with connecting Power BI Desktop to Azure SQL database, you can always request a free trial account from Microsoft and set up an Azure SQL database in a few minutes. If this is the path that you are taking, then you can find instructions on how to do this (including loading the sample data that you will connect to later in this section) at the following URL: `https://docs.microsoft.com/en-gb/azure/sql-database/sql-database-get-started-portal`.

Tip   When you are creating an Azure SQL database for test purposes, be sure to define the source to be *Sample*. This will ensure that the MS sample data is loaded into your test database.

To connect from Power BI Desktop to an Azure SQL database:

1. Open a new Power BI Desktop application.

2. In the Power BI Desktop ribbon, click the small triangle at the bottom of the Get Data button and then click More.

3. Click Azure in the list on the left, and then Azure SQL database on the right. The Get Data dialog will look like the one in Figure 5-27.

Figure 5-27. *Azure data sources in the Get Data dialog*

4. Click Connect. The SQL Server database dialog will appear (after all, an Azure SQL database is a SQL Server database—but in the cloud).

5. Enter the Azure SQL database server name that you obtained from the Microsoft Azure management portal (or that was given to you by a corporate DBA). The SQL Server database dialog will look like the one shown in Figure 5-28.

Figure 5-28. *The SQL Server database dialog for an Azure SQL database connection*

6. Click OK. The credentials dialog will appear.

7. Click Database on the left and enter a valid username and password. The credentials dialog will look like the one shown in Figure 5-29.

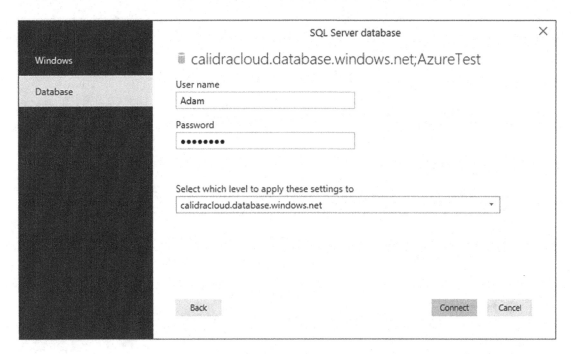

Figure 5-29. *The SQL Server credentials dialog for an Azure SQL database connection*

8. Click Connect. The Navigator dialog will appear showing the database(s) that you have permission to access in the Azure SQL Server database. This dialog will look like the one shown in Figure 5-30 if you are using the test data supplied by Microsoft for a default Azure SQL database.

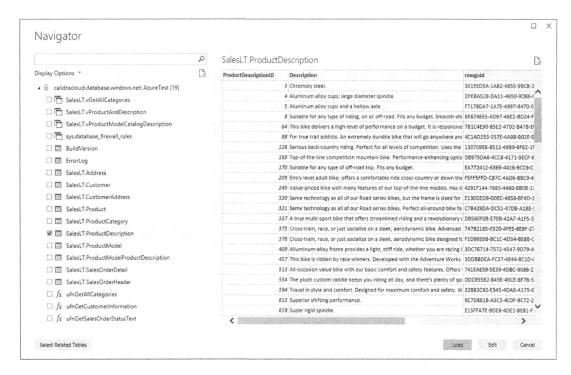

Figure 5-30. *The Navigator dialog for an Azure SQL database connection showing sample data*

Note   If you are setting up an Azure SQL database, make sure that you include firewall rules to allow connection from the computer where you are running Power BI Desktop to the Azure SQL database.

If you followed the steps to connect to an on-premises SQL Server database in Chapter 3, then you are probably feeling that the approach used here is virtually identical. Fortunately, the Power BI development team has worked hard to make the two processes as similar as possible. This extends to

- Ensuring that the DataSource settings are stored by Power BI Desktop and can be updated just as you can for an on-premises database connection

- Allowing you either to use DirectQuery (that you learned about in Chapter 4) or to import data into the Power BI Desktop in-memory data model

- Using the same Advanced options (writing your own SELECT queries or using stored procedures) that you can use with an on-premises SQL Server

Azure SQL Data Warehouse (Azure Synapse Analytics)

Azure has many available platforms to store data. One that is particularly well adapted to Power BI Desktop is the Azure SQL Data Warehouse—now known as Azure Synapse Analytics. This is an MPP (massively parallel processing) data warehouse that is hosted in Azure.

Once again I will presume that, unless you have a corporate Azure Synapse Analytics instance at hand, you will be using a trial Azure account and that you have provisioned Azure Synapse Analytics using the sample data that Microsoft provides. Setting up a test data warehouse is very similar to preparing a database, as described at the URL at the start of the previous section. Here, too, you need firewall rules to be set up correctly (although this may not be strictly necessary if you have previously set up firewall rules for, say, Azure SQL database).

Assuming that you have access to an Azure Synapse Analytics instance:

1. Open a new Power BI Desktop application.

2. In the Power BI Desktop ribbon, click the small triangle at the bottom of the Get Data button and then click More.

3. Click Azure in the list on the left and then Azure SQL Data Warehouse on the right.

4. Click Connect. The SQL Server database dialog will appear.

   Enter the Azure SQL Data Warehouse server name that you obtained from the Microsoft Azure management portal (or that was given to you by a corporate DBA). The SQL Server database dialog will look like the one shown in Figure 5-31. This is because Azure Synapse Analytics is, essentially, a SQL Server database.

Figure 5-31. *The SQL Server database dialog for an Azure Synapse Analytics connection*

5. Select the Import button and then click OK. The credentials dialog will appear.

6. Click Database on the left and enter a valid username and password.

7. Click Connect. The Navigator dialog will appear showing the database(s) that you have permission to access in the Azure SQL Server database. This dialog will look like the one shown in Figure 5-32 if you are using the test data supplied by Microsoft.

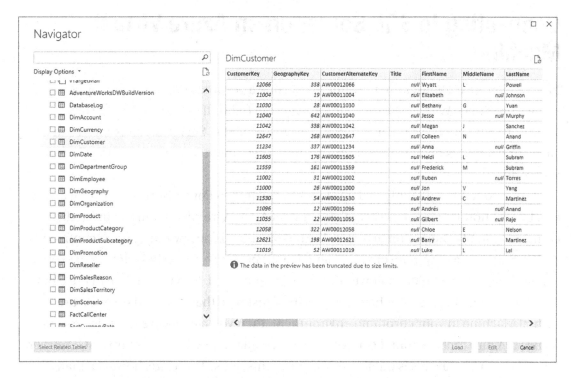

Figure 5-32. *The Navigator dialog for an Azure Synapse Analytics connection showing sample data*

8. Select the tables that you need and click Load or Edit to return to Power BI Desktop and begin adding visuals to your report.

Note   Do not be phased by the fact that the title for the dialog where you specify the server and database says "SQL Server database." This will connect you to the Azure Data Warehouse correctly.

As was the case for an on-premises connection, you can choose a Live Connection (even if the dialog calls it DirectQuery) and can expand the Advanced options field to enter a specific SQL query if you are loading data.

Connecting to SQL Server on an Azure Virtual Machine

More and more databases are now hosted outside a corporate environment by cloud service providers. With a provider such as Amazon (with RDS for SQL Server) or Microsoft (who offers virtual machines—or VMs—for SQL Server in Azure), you can now site your databases outside the enterprise and access them from virtually anywhere in the world.

So, to extend the panoply of data sources available to Power BI Desktop, we will now see, briefly, how to connect to SQL Server on an Azure Virtual Machine. Admittedly, connecting to SQL Server on an Azure Virtual Machine is nearly the same as connecting to SQL Server in a corporate environment. However, it is worth a short detour to explain, briefly, how to return data to Power BI Desktop from a SQL Server instance in the cloud.

Once again, if you do not have a SQL Server instance that is hosted on an Azure Virtual Machine in your corporate environment, then you can always test this process using an Azure trial account. I cannot, however, explain here how to set up a SQL Server instance on a VM, as this is outside the scope of this book. There are, however, many resources available that can explain how to do this should you need them.

To connect to SQL Server on a Virtual Machine:

1. Open a new Power BI Desktop application.

2. In the Power BI Desktop ribbon, click the small triangle at the bottom of the Get Data button and then click SQL Server. The SQL Server database dialog will appear.

3. Enter the full string that describes the server in the Server text box. Either this will be given to you by a corporate DBA or, if you are using your own Azure account, you can find it in the Azure Management Portal.

4. Enter the database name; if you have loaded the sample data that accompanies this book into a SQL Server instance in a VM, it will be CarSalesData. The dialog will look like Figure 5-33.

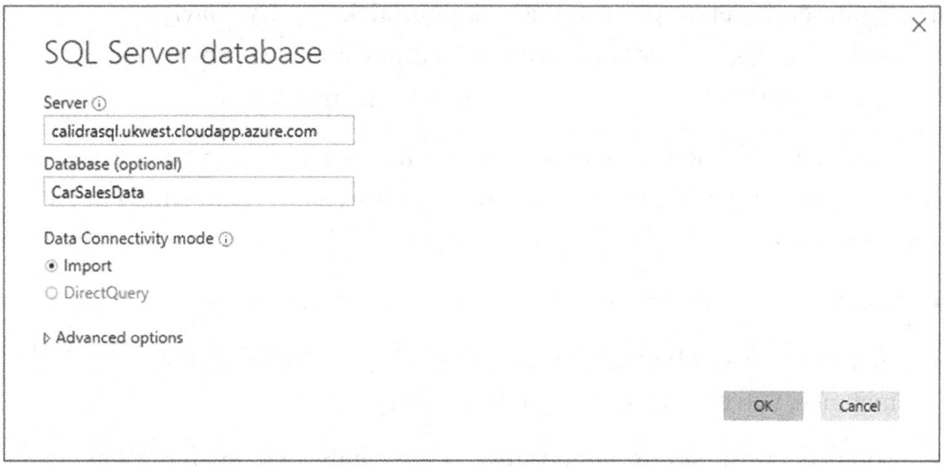

Figure 5-33. *The Microsoft SQL Server database dialog for an Azure VM*

5. Click OK. The Access a SQL Server database dialog will appear.
    Select Database as the security mode and enter the username
    and password, as shown in Figure 5-34. If you are using your own
    Azure account, these can be the username and password that you
    specified when setting up the virtual machine.

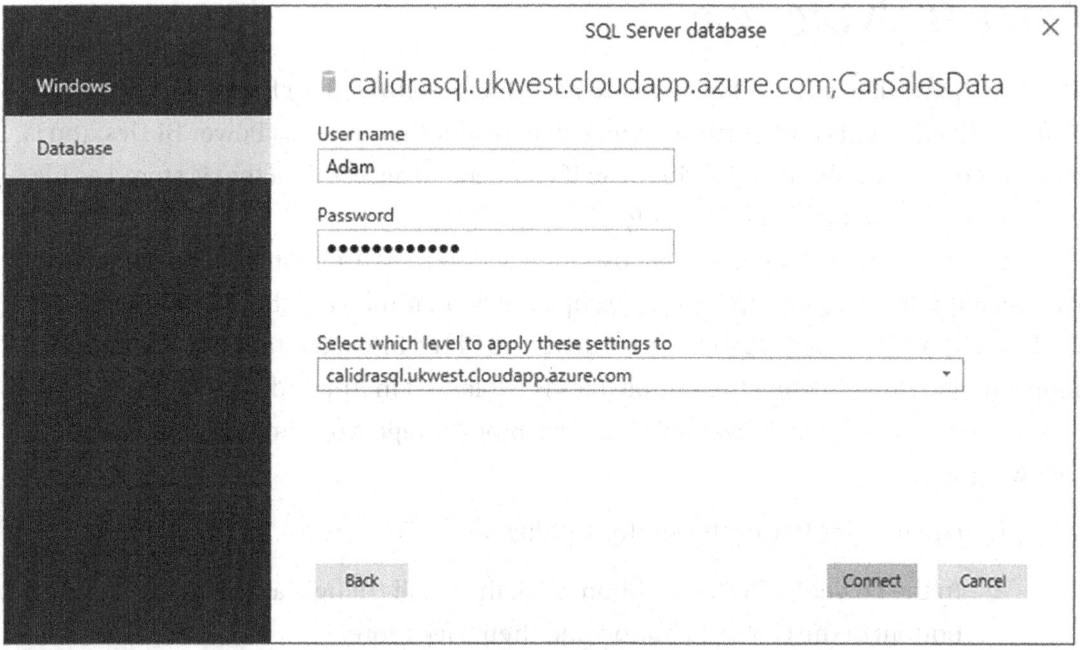

Figure 5-34. *The SQL Server database dialog when connecting to a virtual machine*

6. If you see the encryption support dialog, click OK. The Navigator dialog will appear, listing all the tables that you have permissions to see on the SQL Server hosted by the virtual machine.

As you can see, the process is virtually identical to the one that you followed to connect to SQL Server in Chapter 3. I have, nonetheless, a few points that I need to bring to your attention:

- You use the Azure VM multipart name as the server name.

- As was the case when connecting to an on-premises SQL Server instance, you can select the database if required.

- You can use the server's IP address as the database name if the VM has specified a public IP address.

- Security is a big and separate question. In a corporate environment, you *might* be able to use Windows security to connect. You will almost certainly have to use database security for a test VM.

- As is always the case in Azure, firewalls must be set up correctly.

Azure Blob Storage

The final Azure data source that I want to introduce you to in this chapter is Azure Blob Storage. To all intents and purposes, you can consider this, as far as Power BI Desktop is concerned, as a file share in the cloud. So if you need to access data that is stored as files, you can connect to them via Azure Blob Storage.

Once again, you will need either corporate access to Azure Blob Storage or an Azure trial account. In either case you need to copy the two sample files that are in the folder `C:\PowerBiDesktopSamples\MultipleIdenticalFiles` into a container in your Azure Blob Storage. Downloading the sample files is explained in Appendix A.

Once the source data is available in Azure Blob Storage, you can carry out the following steps:

1. Open a new Power BI Desktop application.

2. In the Power BI Desktop ribbon, click the small triangle at the bottom of the Get Data button and then click More.

3. Click Azure in the list on the left and then Azure Blob Storage on the right. The Azure Blob Storage connection dialog will be displayed.

4. Enter the account name that you are using to connect to Azure Blob Storage. The Azure Blob Storage dialog will look like the one shown in Figure 5-35. If you are using a corporate Azure Blob Storage account, then your system administrator will provide this. In a test scenario, you can find this in the Azure Management Portal by opening the Storage Account blade and copying the Blob Service Endpoint.

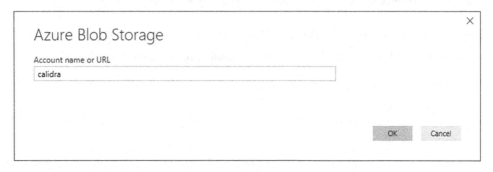

Figure 5-35. *The Azure Blob Storage connection dialog*

5. Click OK. The Azure Blob Storage Account key dialog will appear.

6. In the Azure Management Portal, copy an account key. These can be found in the Azure Management Portal by clicking the Storage Account blade and then clicking Access Keys. If you have been sent an account key by a system administrator, then use that instead.

7. Paste the account key into the Azure Blob Storage Account key dialog. The dialog will look like the one in Figure 5-36.

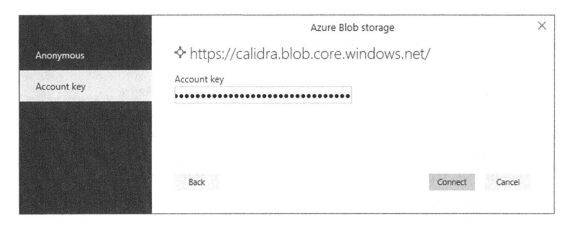

Figure 5-36. *The Azure Blob Storage Account key dialog*

8. Click Connect. The Navigator will appear, showing the list of files in the selected container. You can see an example of this in Figure 5-37.

Figure 5-37. *The Navigator dialog showing available containers in Azure Blob Storage*

9. Click Load. The list of files stored in Azure will appear in Power BI Desktop.

Note   It is important to note that, for the moment at least, what you have returned from Azure is a list of available files. Chapter 10 explains how to select and load data from some or all of the available files into Power BI Desktop, where they can be used as a basis for analytics.

Azure Security

All cloud service providers take security extremely seriously. As you have seen in this chapter, you will always be obliged to enter some form of security token and/or specify a valid username and password to connect to cloud-based data.

All the security information that you entered is stored in the Power BI Desktop Storage Settings. This can be removed or modified in the same way that you learned to update or remove database security information in Chapter 3.

Conclusion

In this chapter you saw an overview of how to retrieve data that you access using the Internet. This can range from a table of data on a web page to a massive Azure Synapse Analytics. Alternatively, perhaps you need to create dashboards based on your Salesforce, Google Analytics, or MS Dynamics 365 data. Maybe your organization has decided to move its data centers to the cloud and is using SQL Server in Azure or Amazon Redshift. In any case, Power BI Desktop can connect and access the data available in these services and repositories. It can even access big data in Hadoop.

Given the vast number of online sources, this chapter could only scratch the surface of this huge range of potential data repositories. However, as Power BI Desktop is rigorous about standardizing access to data, you should be able to apply the approaches you have learned in this chapter to many other data services, both current and future.

CHAPTER 6

Loading Data from Other Data Sources

Other Sources

There are currently many dozens of data sources for which Power BI connectors are available. Clearly it would be impossible to explain how to use all of them. In any case, the list of available sources is growing by the month—so this would be a fruitless task. To conclude our whistle-stop tour of available source data, this chapter will introduce you to

- Power BI datasets

- Power BI dataflows

- R transformations

- Python transformations

- Common Data Model

- ODBC data

- OLE DB data

- Adding your own free-form tables

If you have followed the download instructions in Appendix A, then any files used in this chapter will be in the `C:\PowerBIDesktopSamples` folder.

149

© Adam Aspin 2020
A. Aspin, *Pro Power BI Desktop*, https://doi.org/10.1007/978-1-4842-5763-0_6

Power BI Datasets

Power BI datasets are complete data models that have been designed for end users and made available in the Power BI Service—a Microsoft cloud-based platform. Usually Power BI datasets have been carefully designed to include only the data that you will need. They are nearly always tightly controlled by corporate data guardians.

Note   You can only access Power BI datasets if you have a Power BI account and have been given permissions by the dataset creator to access the dataset. If in doubt, consult your organization's IT department.

If you have been made aware of available Power BI datasets in your organization, you can connect to them and use them as the basis for your dashboards and reports like this:

1. In the Power BI Desktop Home ribbon, click the Get Data button.

2. Click Power Platform on the left, and then select Power BI datasets on the right. The Get Data dialog will look like Figure 6-1.

Figure 6-1.   *The Get Data dialog for Power BI datasets*

3. Sign in to the Power BI Service (unless you are already signed in). You can see the prompt to sign in in Figure 6-2.

Power BI dataflows
Organizational account
Power BI dataflows
You aren't signed in.
Sign in
Connect
Cancel

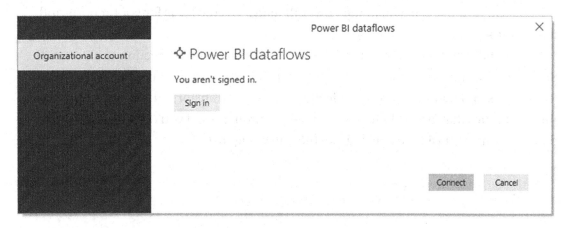

Figure 6-2. *The connection dialog for Power BI dataflows and datasets*

4. Once signed in, click Connect. You will see a list of all currently available datasets, as shown in Figure 6-3. Of course, you will only see the datasets that have been made available specifically for you.

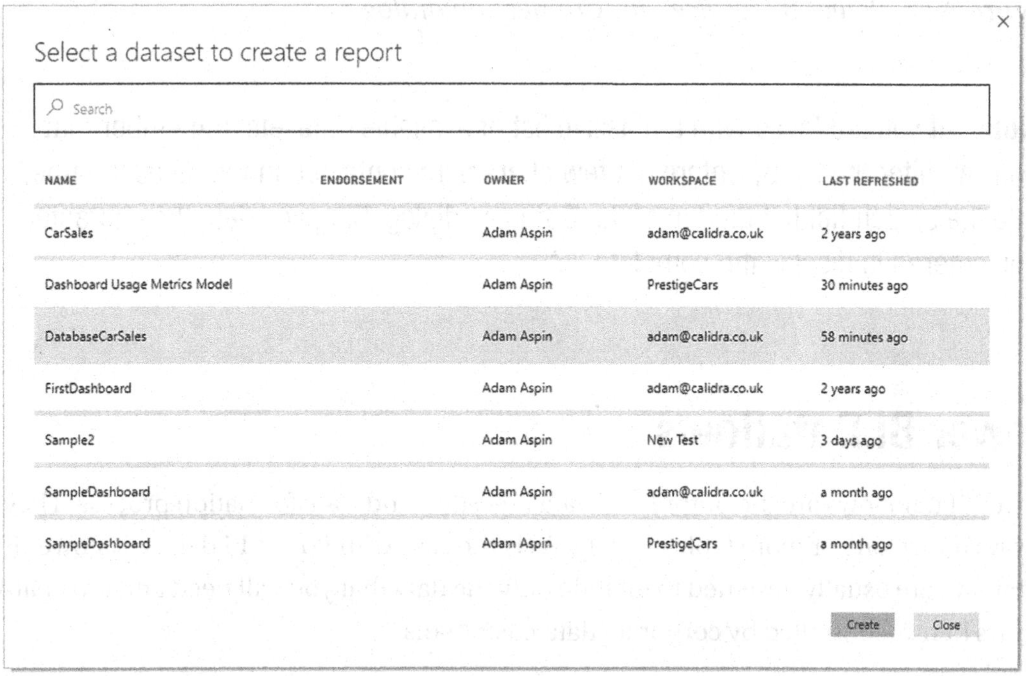

Select a dataset to create a report
Search
NAME
ENDORSEMENT
OWNER
WORKSPACE
LAST REFRESHED
CarSales
Adam Aspin
adam@calidra.co.uk
2 years ago
Dashboard Usage Metrics Model
Adam Aspin
PrestigeCars
30 minutes ago
DatabaseCarSales
Adam Aspin
adam@calidra.co.uk
58 minutes ago
FirstDashboard
Adam Aspin
adam@calidra.co.uk
2 years ago
Sample2
Adam Aspin
New Test
3 days ago
SampleDashboard
Adam Aspin
adam@calidra.co.uk
a month ago
SampleDashboard
Adam Aspin
PrestigeCars
a month ago
Create
Close

Figure 6-3. *Available datasets in the Power BI Service*

5. Click Create. The tables and fields that are in the dataset will appear in the Fields pane in Power BI Desktop.

You can now use the data in the Power BI dataset as the basis for your reports and dashboards.

You need to be aware that once you have established the connection to a Power BI Service Live Connection, there is very little that you can do except use the data to build dashboards and reports. More specifically, you cannot transform the data using any of the techniques that are explained in Chapters 7 through 10. If you try and modify the data structure, you will see a dialog like the one in Figure 6-4.

Figure 6-4. *Power BI Service Live Connection dialog*

Note   If you are faced with a massive list of available datasets, remember that you can filter the list by entering a few characters contained in the dataset name into the search field at the top of the Datasets dialog. Simply delete the characters you entered to display the complete list.

Power BI Dataflows

Power BI dataflows are the output of a data ingestion and transformation process. They always return one or more tables of data. As is the case with Power BI datasets, Power BI dataflows are usually designed to include only the data that you will need and are nearly always tightly controlled by corporate data custodians.

Should you have been given permission to use the data in a Power BI dataflow, this is how you can connect:

1. In the Power BI Desktop Home ribbon, click the Get Data button.

2. Click Power Platform on the left, and then select Power BI dataflows on the right. The Get Data dialog will look like Figure 6-5.

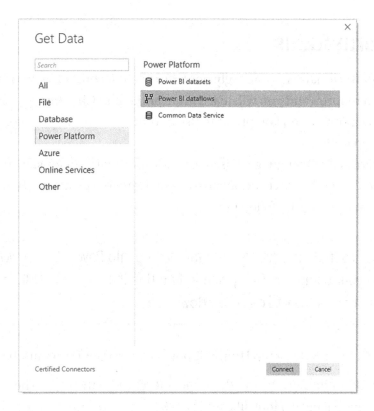

Figure 6-5. *The Get Data dialog for Power BI datasets*

3. Sign in to the Power BI Service (unless you are already signed in).

4. Click Connect. You will see a list of all currently available dataflows in the Navigator. Of course, you will see the dataflows that have been made available specifically for you.

5. Expand the dataset folder containing the dataset elements that you want to connect to.

6. Select the dataflow(s) that you require.

7. Click Load. The tables and fields that are in the dataflow(s) will
    appear in the Fields pane in Power BI Desktop.

You can now use the data in the Power BI dataflow as the basis for your reports and
dashboards.

R Transformations

Although Power BI Desktop is amazingly powerful when it comes to preparing data for
dashboards and reports (and you will learn more about it in Chapters 7 through 10),
there may be occasions when you prefer to use another tool to carry out some highly
specific data preparation.

One such tool is the R language. R is an open source platform for statistical analysis
and data science. If you have R experience that you want to use in conjunction with
Power BI, then you can try the following:

Note   To use R scripts to prepare data for loading into Power BI, you will first need
to install R on your computer. One place to find R is the following URL: `https://
mran.revolutionanalytics.com/download`.

---

1. In the Power BI Desktop Home ribbon, click the Get Data button.

2. Click Other on the left, and then select R script on the right. The
    Get Data dialog will look like Figure 6-6.

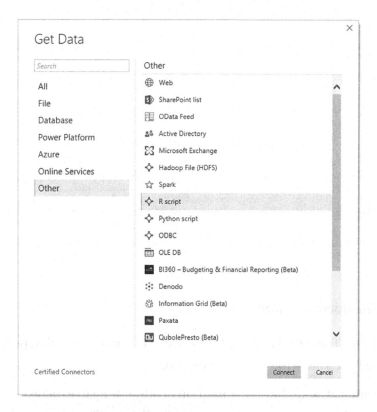

Figure 6-6. *The Get Data dialog when opting to use an R script*

3.   Click Connect. The R script dialog will appear, where you can paste in the script that connects to your data and preprocesses it. You can see this dialog in Figure 6-7.

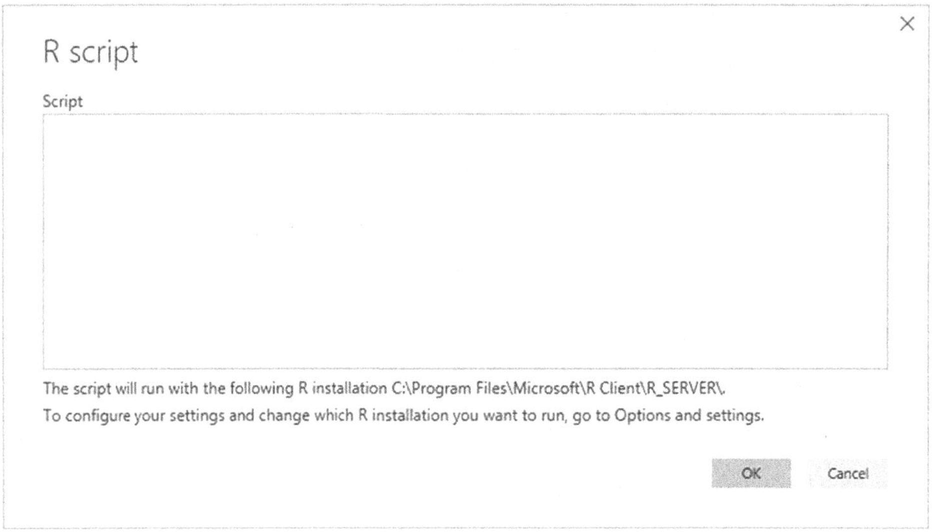

Figure 6-7. *The R script dialog*

4. Click OK. The tables and fields that are in the dataflow will appear
    in the Fields pane in Power BI Desktop.

R is a huge subject, and I have no intention of attempting to explain even a small part
of how to use it in this book. I merely want to make R practitioners aware that they can
harness their existing knowledge and put it to the service of Power BI.

Note   The R script dialog is most emphatically *not* an R IDE (development interface).
So you will probably need an R IDE to prepare and test the script that you then
paste into the R script dialog.

Python Transformations

- If Python is your preferred language for analytics, data
  transformation, and artificial intelligence, then you can also apply
  your existing Python knowledge to preparing data for Power BI
  dashboards.

Note   To use Python in conjunction with Power BI, you will need to install your preferred Python version and IDE on your computer.

1. In the Power BI Desktop Home ribbon, click the Get Data button.

2. Click Other on the left, and then select Python script on the right. The Get Data dialog will look like Figure 6-8.

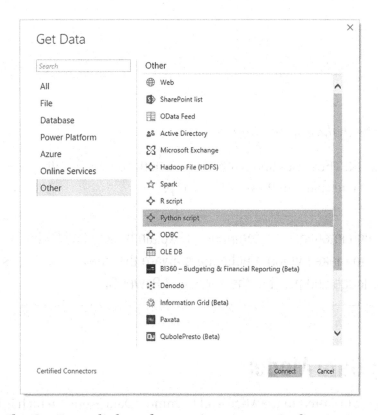

Figure 6-8. *The Get Data dialog when opting to use a Python script*

3. Click Connect. The Python script dialog will appear, where you can paste in the script you previously prepared in a Python IDE that connects to your data and preprocesses it. You can see this dialog in Figure 6-9.

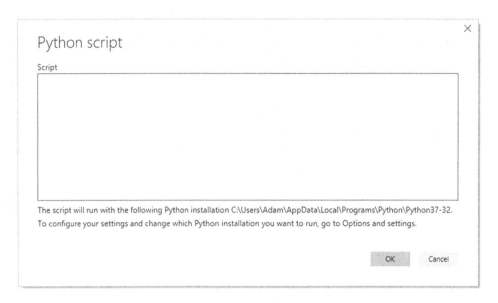

Figure 6-9. *The Python script dialog*

4. Click OK. The tables and fields that are in the dataflow will appear in the Fields pane in Power BI Desktop.

Note   I have no intention of attempting to explain how to use Python in this book. I merely want to make Python practitioners aware that they can harness their existing knowledge and put it to the service of Power BI.

Common Data Model

If you are using data stored in the Microsoft Common Data Model (which is part of the Common Data Service), then you can connect to this extremely easily—as you would probably expect.

1. In the Home ribbon, click Get Data ➤ More.

2. Select Power Platform on the left and Common Data Service on the right. The dialog should look like Figure 6-10.

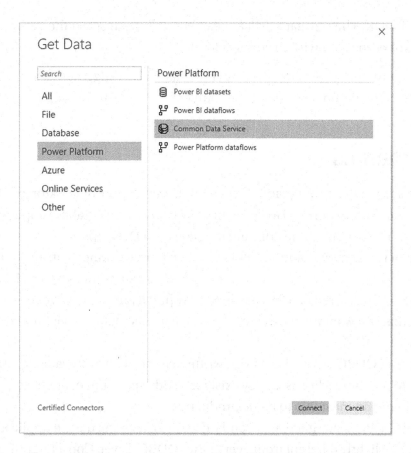

***Figure 6-10.** Connecting to the Common Data Service*

3. Click Connect, and enter your server URL in the Common Data
    Service dialog. This dialog should look something like Figure 6-11.

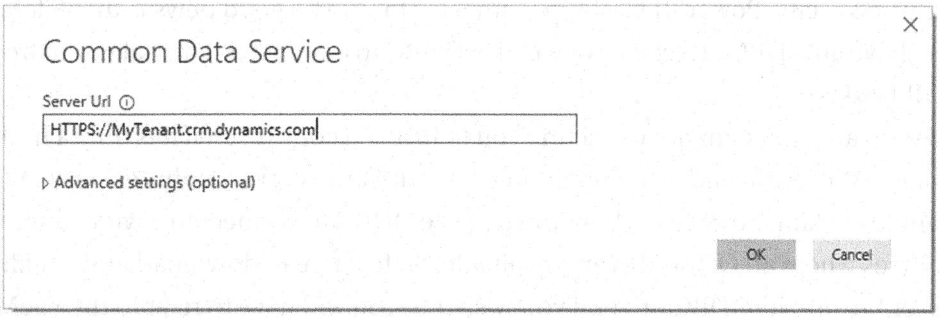

***Figure 6-11.** The Common Data Service dialog*

4. Click OK. The Navigator will appear where you can select the data
    entities that you wish to connect to.

As the Common Data Service is essentially a database, I suggest that you refer back
to Chapter 3 for details on using database sources for Power BI Desktop.

ODBC Sources

As you have seen in this chapter and the preceding one, Power BI Desktop can connect
to a wide range of data sources. However, there will always be database applications for
which there is no specific connector built into Power BI Desktop.

This is where a generic solution called Open Database Connectivity (or ODBC)
comes into play. ODBC is a standard way to connect to data sources, most of which
are databases or structured like databases. Simply put, if an ODBC driver exists for the
application that you want to connect to, then you can load data from it into Power BI
Desktop.

Hundreds of ODBC drivers have been written. Some are freely available, others
require you to purchase a license. They exist for a wide spectrum of applications ranging
from those found on most PCs to niche products.

Although ODBC is designed as a standard way of accessing data in applications, each
ODBC driver is slightly different from every other ODBC driver. Consequently, you might
have to spend a little time learning the quirks of the interface for the driver that comes
with the application that you want to connect to.

In this section we will use FileMaker Pro as a data source. This product is a desktop
and server database system that has been around for quite some time. However, there is
currently no specific Power BI Desktop connector for it. The good news is that FileMaker
Pro *does* have an ODBC driver. So we will use ODBC to connect to FileMaker Pro from
Power BI Desktop.

I have to add that I am not expecting you to install a copy (even if it is only a trial
copy) of FileMaker Pro and its companion ODBC driver to carry out this exercise. What
I do want to explain, however, is how you can use ODBC to connect to a wide range of
data sources where an ODBC driver is available. So feel free to download and install
FileMaker Pro and its ODBC driver if you wish, but you will have to refer to the FileMaker
Pro documentation for an explanation of how to do this.

Assuming that you have an ODBC-compliant data source and a working ODBC driver for this data source, here is how to load data into Power BI Desktop using ODBC:

1. Run the ODBC Data Source Administrator app. This is normally in the folder C:\ProgramData\Microsoft\Windows\Start Menu\ Programs\Administrative Tools. Be sure to use the 64-bit version if you are using 64-bit Power BI Desktop or the 32-bit version if you are using 32-bit Power BI Desktop.

2. Click the System DSN tab. You should see the dialog shown in Figure 6-12.

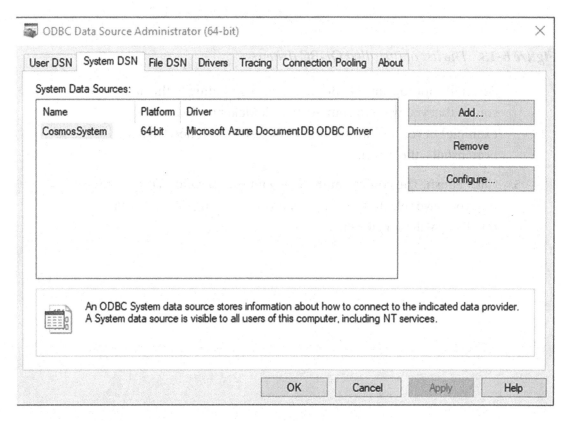

Figure 6-12. *The ODBC Data Source Administrator*

3. Click Add. You will see the list of all currently installed ODBC drivers on your computer. This should look something like the dialog shown in Figure 6-13.

161

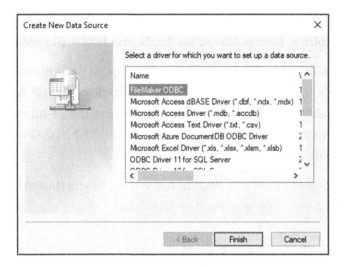

Figure 6-13. *The list of installed ODBC drivers*

4. Select the appropriate ODBC driver corresponding to the data
    source that you want to connect to (FileMaker ODBC in this
    example). If you cannot see the ODBC driver, you need to install—
    or reinstall—the driver.

5. Click Finish. The configuration dialog for the specific ODBC driver
    that you have selected will appear. If you are using FileMaker Pro,
    the dialog will look like Figure 6-14.

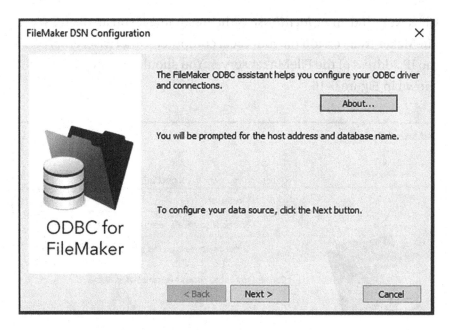

Figure 6-14. *The FileMaker Pro ODBC configuration assistant*

6. Click Next, and enter a name and a description for this particular
    ODBC connection. This should look something like the dialog
    shown in Figure 6-15.

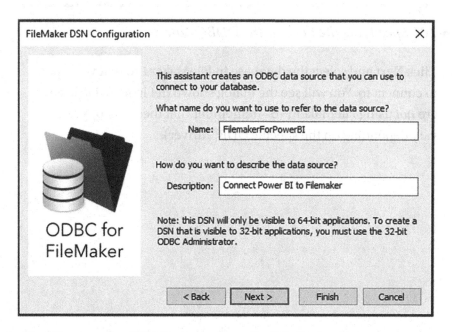

Figure 6-15. *Naming the ODBC connection for FileMaker Pro*

7. Click Next and enter **localhost** as the hostname if you are using a FileMaker trial version on your local computer. Otherwise, enter the IP address of the FileMaker server. You should see the dialog shown in Figure 6-16.

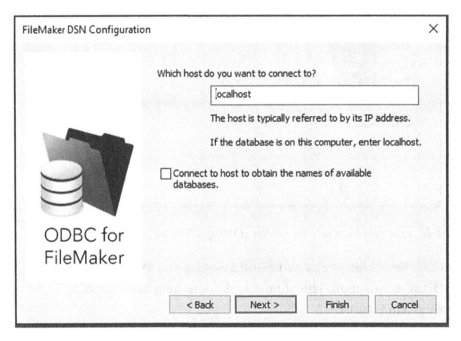

Figure 6-16. *Specifying the host for the ODBC data*

8. Click Next and select the database in FileMaker Pro that you want to connect to. You will see the dialog shown in Figure 6-17 (if you are *not* using FileMaker Pro—remember that these dialogs can vary depending on the specific ODBC driver).

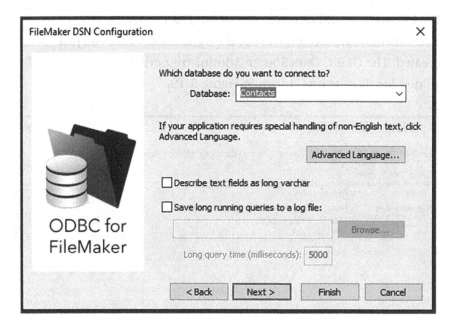

Figure 6-17. *Specifying the database for the ODBC data*

9. Click Next. The ODBC configuration dialog will resume the specifications for the connection. This could look something like the one shown in Figure 6-18.

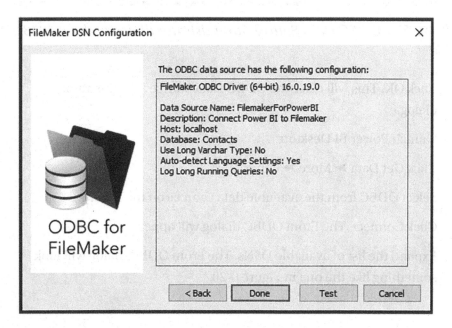

Figure 6-18. *The ODBC connection confirmation dialog*

10.   Click Done. You will return to the ODBC Data Source
       Administrator, where you will see the System DSN that you just
       created. The ODBC Data Source Administrator dialog should look
       something like the one shown in Figure 6-19.

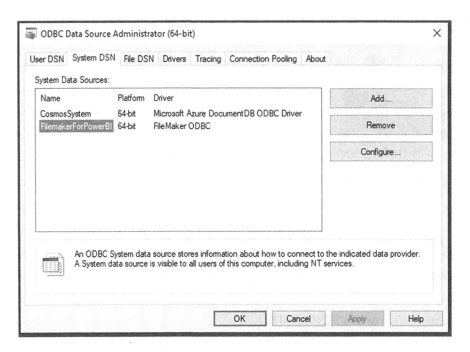

Figure 6-19. *The ODBC Data Source Administrator dialog with an ODBC driver*
configured

11.   Click OK. This will close the ODBC Data Source Administrator
       dialog.

12.   Launch Power BI Desktop.

13.   Click Get Data ➤ More ➤ Other.

14.   Select ODBC from the available data sources on the right.

15.   Click Connect. The From ODBC dialog will appear.

16.   Expand the list of available DSNs. The From ODBC dialog will look
       something like the one in Figure 6-20.

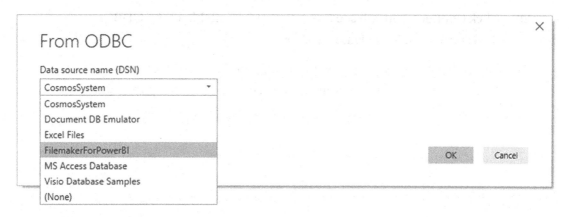

Figure 6-20. *The Power BI Desktop From ODBC dialog to select an ODBC data source*

17. Select the DSN that you created previously (FilemakerForPowerBI in this example).

18. Click OK. The credentials dialog will appear.

19. Choose Windows integrated security or click Database on the left and enter the username that has permissions to connect using the ODBC driver. The credentials dialog will look something like the one in Figure 6-21.

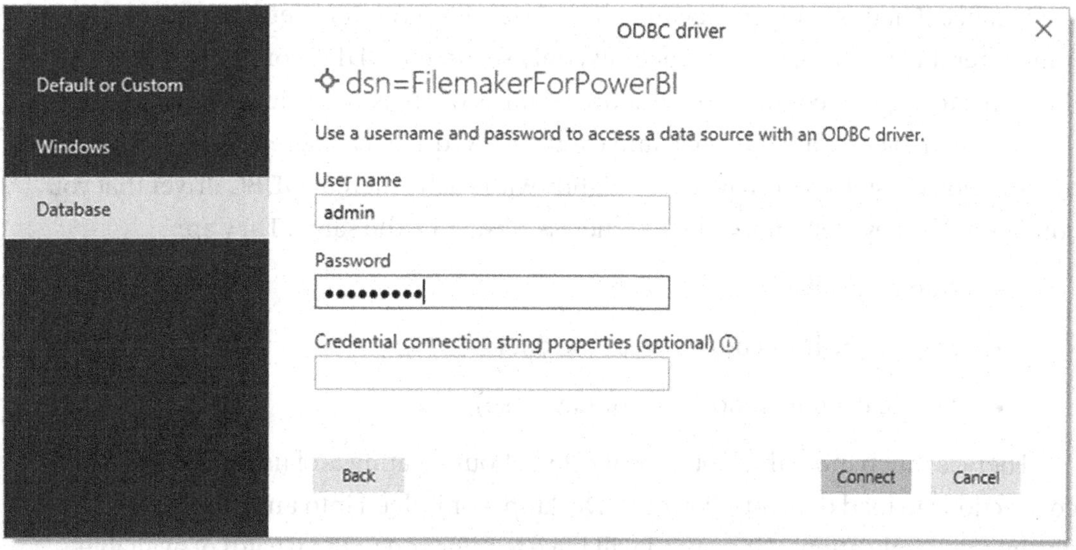

Figure 6-21. *The ODBC driver security dialog*

20. Click Connect. You will see the data that is available in the ODBC data source in the Navigator window.

21. Select the table(s) that you want to load into Power BI Desktop. You can see the data contained in the selected table in Figure 6-22.

Figure 6-22. *The Navigator dialog when using an ODBC source dialog*

22. Click Load to load the data from the ODBC source into Power BI Desktop.

I realize that this process may seem a little laborious at first. Yet you have to remember that you will, in all probability, only set up the ODBC connection once. After that you can use it to connect to the source data as often as you want.

You need to be aware that each and every ODBC driver is different. So the appearance of the dialogs in steps 5 to 10 will vary slightly with each different ODBC driver that you configure. The key elements will, nonetheless, always be the same. They are

- Name the DSN

- Specify the host computer for the data

- Define the data repository (or database)

There is much more that could be written about creating and using ODBC connections to load data into Power BI Desktop—or indeed into any number of destination applications. However, I will have to refer you to the wealth of available resources both in print and online if you need to learn more about this particular technology. A good starting point is the Microsoft documentation that explains the difference between system, user, and file DSNs and describes many of the key elements that you might need to know.

Note   FileMaker Pro must be open and/or running for an ODBC connection to work. Other ODBC sources could have their own specific quirks.

As a final point, I can only urge you to procure all the relevant documentation for the ODBC driver that you intend to use with Power BI Desktop. Indeed, if you are using an enterprise data source that uses ODBC drivers, you may have corporate resources who can configure ODBC for you.

OLE DB Data Sources

OLE DB (short for Object Linking and Embedding, Database) is technically what is known as an application programming interface (API). Less technically it is a technique for connecting to database sources in a generic manner.

So, in a somewhat similar fashion to ODBC, you can use OLE DB to connect to data sources (which are often databases, although they can be other sources of data). Indeed, you may find that OLE DB is a useful way to connect to a database even if another method exists.

So, whatever the use that you find for OLE DB, it is well worth getting to know how it works. In this example I will use OLE DB to connect to SQL Server and the sample database that you first saw at the start of this chapter.

1.   Open a new Power BI Desktop application.

2.   In the Power BI Desktop ribbon, click the Get Data button.

3.   Click Other on the left, then click OLE DB on the right. The dialog will look like Figure 6-23.

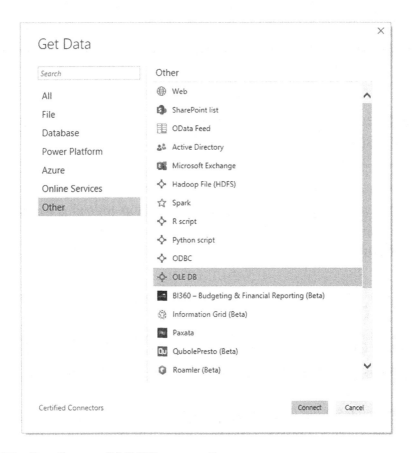

Figure 6-23. *Starting an OLE DB connection*

4. Click Connect. The From OLE DB dialog will appear. It should
    look like Figure 6-24.

Figure 6-24. *The From OLE DB dialog*

5. If you have a fully working connection string, enter it in the Connection string text box.

6. If you do not have a connection string, click the Build button. The OLE DB Data Link Properties dialog will be displayed, as shown in Figure 6-25.

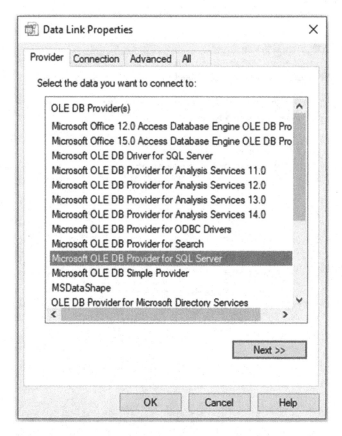

Figure 6-25. *The OLE DB Data Link Properties dialog*

7. Select the OLE DB data provider that you want to use. In this example, it will be Microsoft OLE DB Provider for SQL Server.

8. Click Next. The Connection properties pane of the OLE DB Data Link Properties dialog will appear.

9. Select an available SQL Server (or enter its name) from the "Select or enter a server name" popup.

10. Select the type of security, and enter a username and password if you have selected to use a specific username instead of using Windows NT Integrated security.

11. Select the source database from the "Select the database on the server" popup. The dialog will look something like the one shown in Figure 6-26.

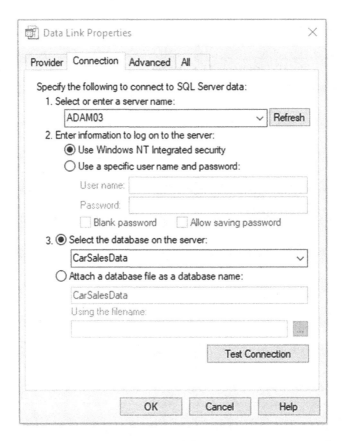

Figure 6-26. *The Connection properties of the OLE DB Data Link Properties dialog*

12. Click the Test Connection button to ensure that the connection is valid. You should see the message in Figure 6-27.

Figure 6-27. *The test connection alert*

13. Click OK. Power BI Desktop will build the connection string and insert it into the From OLE DB dialog, as shown in Figure 6-28.

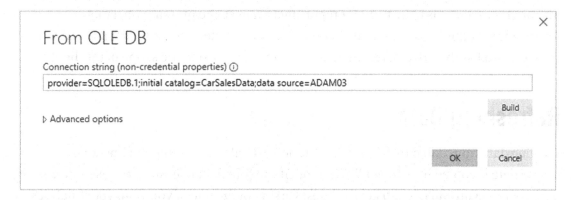

Figure 6-28. *The From OLE DB dialog with a valid connection string*

14. Click OK. The Navigator window will appear with the appropriate data displayed.

15. Select the source tables and click Load to load the data into Power BI Desktop.

Note   If this is a first connection to an OLE DB source, you may be asked for a username and password, as was the case with earlier examples in this chapter.

You need to be aware that an OLE DB connection requires that the OLE DB driver (or "provider") is installed on the computer where you are running Power BI Desktop. However, what is really interesting is that an OLE DB connection can be reduced to a simple connection string. So if you need to share the connection with other users, you can simply email the connection string to them in many cases. Your colleagues can then simply paste the connection string into the From OLE DB dialog in Power BI Desktop. In other words (and using this example as a model), you can simply send the following text to a coworker:

```
provider=SQLOLEDB.1;initial catalog=CarSalesData;data source=ADAMO3\
SQLSERVER2016
```

They can use this string to connect to a specified database by pasting it into the From OLE DB dialog.

There are other advantages to using OLE DB connections too. Specifically, you (or your IT department) can provide a high level of configuration in the connection string to speed up or otherwise ameliorate the access to the data. This could be by specifying a mirrored server that is to be used for reporting to relieve the pressure on a main server, for instance. At this level the technical ramifications will depend on the OLE DB data source as well as the driver used and consequently are outside the scope of this book.

Refreshing Data

Loading data from databases and data warehouses only means that a snapshot of the source data is copied into Power BI Desktop. If the source data is updated, extended, or deleted, then you will need to get the latest version of the data if you want your analyses to reflect the current state of the data.

Essentially you have two options to do this:

- Refresh all the source data from all the data sources that you have defined.

- Refresh one or more tables individually.

Refreshing the Entire Data in the Power BI Desktop In-Memory Model

There is only one way to be certain that all your data is up to date. Refreshing the entire data may take longer, but you will be sure that your Power BI Desktop file contains the latest available data from all the sources that you have connected to.

To carry out a complete refresh:

1. In the Home ribbon, click the Refresh button. The Refresh dialog will appear, showing all the data sources that are currently being refreshed. This dialog will look like the one in Figure 6-29.

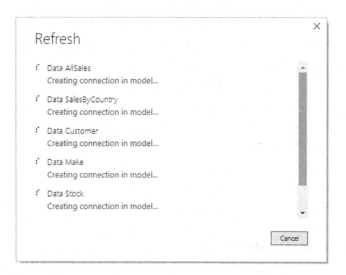

Figure 6-29. *The Refresh dialog*

Note   A full data refresh can take quite a while if the source data is voluminous or if the network connection is slow.

Refreshing an Individual Table

If you are certain that only one or more tables need to be refreshed in your Power BI Desktop data model, then you can choose to refresh tables individually. To do this:

1. In the Fields pane, right-click the table that you want to refresh.

2. Select Refresh data in the context menu. This is illustrated in Figure 6-30.

Figure 6-30. *Refreshing a single table*

The Refresh dialog will appear (possibly only briefly), and the existing data for this table will be replaced with the latest data.

Adding Your Own Data

All the data you need may not be always available. You might find yourself needing to add a list of products, a group of people, or, indeed, any kind of data to the datasets that you have loaded into Power BI Desktop.

The development team at Microsoft has recognized this need and offers a simple solution: you can create your own tables of data to complete the collection of datasets in a Power BI in-memory data model. Then you can enter any extra data that you need, on the fly.

1. In the Power BI Desktop Home ribbon, click Enter Data. The Create Table dialog will appear.

2. Click the asterisk to the right of Column1 to add a column.

3. Double-click any column name and enter a new name to rename the column.

4. Enter or paste in the data that you need. The dialog will look like
    the one shown in Figure 6-31.

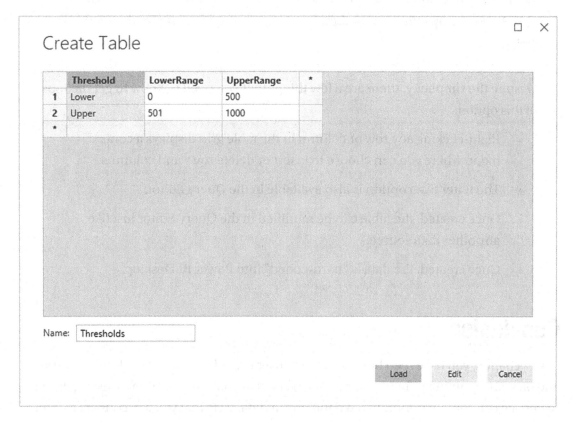

Figure 6-31. *The Create Table dialog*

5. Enter a name for the table in the Name field at the bottom of the
    dialog.

6. Click Load to load the data into the Power BI in-memory data
    model. The newly created table will appear in the Fields pane.

Editing facilities in the Create Table dialog are extremely simplistic. You can delete,
cut, copy, and paste data and columns, but that is about all that you can do. However,
this option can, nonetheless, be extremely useful when you need to add some last-
minute data to a model.

> **Note**   This is an extremely simple process that is designed for small amounts of data. If you need more than just a handful of rows and columns, you could be better served by creating the data in Excel and then loading it into Power BI Desktop.

Despite the simplicity, there are a few things that you need to know to get the most out of this option:

- Right-clicking any row or column in the table grid displays a context menu where you can choose to insert or delete rows and columns.

- The Enter Data option is also available in the Query Editor.

- Once created, the table can be modified in the Query Editor just like any other data source.

- Once created, the data is "hard-coded" into Power BI Desktop.

Conclusion

In this chapter, you have seen how to connect to a range of data sources—both in Azure and on your computer or network. You have seen that your organization's existing Power BI Service can contain pre-prepared dataflows and datasets that you can connect to. You have also learned that you can use the Microsoft Common Data Model as the basis for your Power BI reports and dashboards. You then learned that you can capitalize on your R and Python knowledge and use these two languages to prepare data for use by Power BI.

Finally, you saw that you can use a couple of the standard data access connectors—ODBC and OLE DB—to connect to sources of data for which there is not (yet) a built-in Power BI connector. Then, if all else fails, you can create your own table of data should you need to.

This chapter concludes the set of six chapters that introduced you to some of the many and varied data sources that you can use with Power BI Desktop. In the course of these chapters, you have seen how to load data from a selection of the more frequently used available sources. The good news is that Power BI Desktop can read data from dozens more sources. The bad news is that it would take a whole book to go into all of them in detail.

So I will not be describing any other data sources in this book. This is because now that you have come to appreciate the core techniques that make up the extremely standardized approach that Power BI Desktop takes to loading data, you can probably load any possible data type without needing much more information from me. Should you need any specific information on other data sources, then your best port of call is the Microsoft Power BI website. This is currently at `https://powerbi.microsoft.com/`.

Now that you can find, access, and load the data you need into Power BI Desktop, it is time to move on to the next step. This means cleansing and restructuring the datasets so that they suit your analytical requirements. Handling these challenges is the subject of the next six chapters.

CHAPTER 7

Structuring Imported Data

In the previous six chapters, you saw some of the ways in which you can find and load (or connect to) data into the Power BI Desktop data model. Inevitably, this is the first part of any process that you follow to extract, transform, and load data. Yet it is quite definitely only a first step. Once the data is in Power BI Desktop, you need to know how to adapt it to suit your requirements in a multitude of ways. This is because not all data is ready to be used immediately. Quite often, you have to do some initial work on the data to make it more easily usable in Power BI Desktop. Tweaking source data is generally referred to as *data transformation*, which is the subject of this chapter as well as the next three.

The range of transformations that Power BI Desktop offers is extensive and varied. Learning to apply the techniques that Power BI Desktop makes available enables you to take data as you find it, then cleanse it and push it back into the Power BI Desktop data model as a series of coherent and structured data tables. Only then is it ready to be used to create compelling dashboards and reports.

As it is all too easy to be overwhelmed (at least initially) by the extent of the data transformation options that Power BI Desktop has to offer, I have grouped the possible modifications into four categories. These categories are my own and are merely a suggestion to facilitate understanding:

- *Data transformation*: This includes removing columns and rows, renaming columns, as well as filtering data.

- *Data modification*: This covers altering the actual data in the rows and columns of a dataset.

- *Extending datasets*: This encompasses adding further columns, possibly expanding existing columns into more columns or rows, and adding calculations.

- *Joining datasets*: This involves combining multiple separate datasets—possibly from different data sources—into a single dataset.

© Adam Aspin 2020
A. Aspin, *Pro Power BI Desktop*, https://doi.org/10.1007/978-1-4842-5763-0_7

This chapter introduces you to the core data transformation techniques that you can apply to shape each individual dataset that you have loaded. These transformations include

- Renaming, removing, and reordering columns

- Removing groups or sets of rows

- Deduplicating datasets

- Sorting the data

- Excluding records by filtering the data

- Grouping records

In the next chapter, you learn how to cleanse and modify data. In Chapter 9, you see how to subset columns to extract part of the available data in a column, calculate columns, merge data from separate queries, and add further columns containing different types of calculations, and you learn about pivoting and unpivoting data. Chapter 10 explains how to handle complex source structures. So, if you cannot find what you are looking for in this chapter, there is a good chance that the answer is in the following three chapters.

In this chapter, I will also use a set of example files that you can find on the Apress website. If you have followed the instructions in Appendix A, then these files are in the `C:\PowerBiDesktopSamples` folder.

Power BI Desktop Queries

In Chapter 1, you saw how to load source data directly into Power BI Desktop from where you can use it immediately to create dashboards. Clearly, this approach presumes that the data that you are using is perfectly structured, clean, and error-free. Source data is nearly always correct and ready to use in reports and dashboards when it comes from "corporate" data sources such as data warehouses (held in relational, dimensional, or tabular databases). This is not always the case when you are faced with multiple disparate sources of data that have not been precleansed and prepared by an IT department. The everyday reality is that you could have to cleanse and transform much of the source data that you will use for your Power BI Desktop dashboards.

The really good news is that the kind of data transformation that used to require expensive servers and industrial-strength software is now available for free. Yes, Power BI Desktop comes with an awesome ETL (Extract, Transform, and Load) tool that can rival many applications that cost hundreds of thousands of dollars.

Power BI Desktop data transformation is carried out using *queries*. As you saw in previous chapters, you do not have to modify source data. You can load it directly if it is ready for use. Yet if you need to cleanse the data, you add an intermediate step between connecting the data and loading it into the Power BI Desktop data model. This intermediate step uses the Power BI Desktop Query Editor to tweak the source data.

So how do you apply queries to transform your data? You have two choices:

- Load the data first from one or more sources, and then transform it later.

- Edit each source data element in a query before loading it.

Power BI Desktop is extremely forgiving. It does not force you to select one or the other method and then lock you into the consequences of your decision. You can load data first and then realize that it needs some adjustment, switch to the Query Editor and make changes, and then return to creating your dashboard. Or you can first focus on the data and try to get it as polished and perfect as possible before you start building reports. The choice is entirely up to you.

To make this point, let's take a look at both of these ways of working.

Note   At risk of seeming pedantic and old-fashioned, I would advise you to make notes when creating really complex transformations, because going back to a solution and trying to make adjustments later can be painful when they are not documented at all.

Editing Data After a Data Load

In Chapter 1, you saw how to load the Excel workbook CarSales.xlsx directly into the Power BI Desktop data model to use it to create a starter dashboard. Now let's presume that you want to make some changes to the data structure of the data that you have already loaded. Specifically, you want to rename the CostPrice column. The file that you want to modify is CH07Example1.pbix file in the C:\PowerBiDesktopSamples directory.

1. Launch Power BI Desktop.

2. Open the sample file C:\PowerBiDesktopSamples\Example1. pbix. Note that in this example you are taking an existing Power BI Desktop file and modifying the existing data input process and *not* ingesting data. Take a look at the Fields list and note that there is a field named CostPrice.

3. In the Power BI Desktop Home ribbon, click the Transform Data button. The Power BI Desktop Query Editor will open and display the source data as a table. The window will look like Figure 7-1.

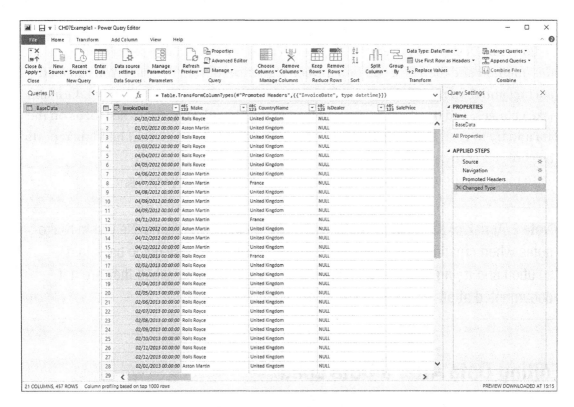

Figure 7-1. *The Power BI Desktop Query Editor*

4. Right-click the title of the CostPrice column. The column will be selected and the title will appear in yellow.

5. Select Rename from the context menu. You can see the context menu in Figure 7-2.

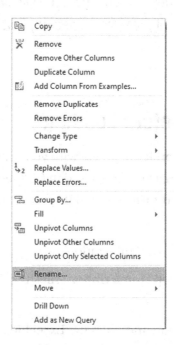

Figure 7-2. The column context menu in the Query Editor

6. Type **VehicleCost** and press Enter. The column title will change to VehicleCost.

7. In the Power BI Desktop Query Editor Home ribbon, click the Close & Apply button. The Power BI Desktop Query Editor will close and return you to the Power BI Desktop window. VehicleCost has replaced CostPrice anywhere that it was used in the dashboard. This is visible in the Fields list and all visuals that used this field.

I hope that this simple example makes it clear that transforming the source data is a quick and painless process. The technique that you applied—renaming a column—is only one of many dozens of possible techniques that you can apply to transform your data. However, it is not the specific transformation that is the core idea to take away here. What you need to remember is that the data that underpins your dashboard is always present and it is only a single click away. At any time, you can "flip" to the data and make changes, simply by clicking the Transform Data button in the Power BI Desktop window. Any changes that you make and confirm will update your dashboards and reports instantaneously.

Note   Alternatively, if you want you can edit the query behind any table that is visible in the Report or Data Views simply by right-clicking the table name in the Queries pane (or clicking the ellipses) and selecting Edit Query from the context menu.

Transforming Data Before Loading

On some occasions, you might prefer to juggle with your data before you load it. This is a variation on the approach that you have used in Chapter 1 when creating a simple dashboard. Do the following to transform the data you are ingesting *before* it appears in the Power BI Desktop window:

1. Open a new Power BI Desktop window.

2. In the Power BI Desktop Home ribbon, click the tiny triangle in the Get Data button.

3. Select Excel in the menu and open the Excel file
    C:\PowerBiDesktopSamples\CarSales.xlsx.

4. In the Navigator window, select the BaseData worksheet.

5. Click the Transform Data button (*not* the Load button).

6. The Power BI Desktop Query Editor will open and display the source data as a table.

7. Carry out steps 4 through 6 from the previous example to rename the CostPrice column.

8. In the Power BI Desktop Query Editor Home ribbon, click the Close & Apply button. The Power BI Desktop Query Editor will close and return you to the Power BI Desktop window. You will see the Apply query changes dialog while the data is loaded, like the one that you can see in Figure 7-3.

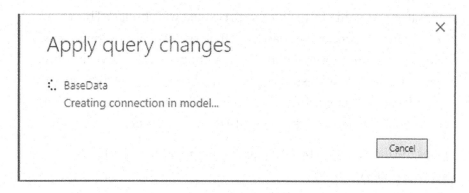

Figure 7-3. *The Apply query changes dialog*

This time, you have made a simple modification to the data *before* loading the dataset into the Power BI Desktop data model. The data modification technique was exactly the same. The only difference between loading the data directly and taking a detour via the Query window was clicking Edit instead of Load in the Navigator dialog. This means that the data was only loaded once you had finished making any modifications to the source data in the Power BI Desktop Query Editor.

Query or Load?

Power BI Desktop always gives you the choice of loading data directly into its data model or taking a constructive detour via Power BI Desktop Query. The path that you follow is entirely up to you and clearly depends on each set of circumstances. Nonetheless, you might want to consider the following basic principles when faced with a new dashboarding challenge using unfamiliar data:

- Are you convinced that the data is ready to use? That is, is it clean and well structured? If so, then you can try loading it directly into the Power BI Desktop data model.

- Are you faced with multiple data sources that need to be combined and molded into a coherent structure? If this is the case, then you really need to transform the data using the Power BI Desktop Query Editor.

- Does the data come from an enterprise data warehouse? This could be held in a relational database, a SQL Server Analysis Services cube, or even an in-memory tabular data warehouse. As these data sources are nearly always the result of many hundreds—or even thousands— of hours of work cleansing, preparing, and structuring the data, you can probably load these straight into the data model.

- Does the data need to be preaggregated and filtered? Think Power BI Desktop Query Editor.

- Are you likely to need to change the field names to make the data more manageable? It could be simpler to load the data directly into the data model and change them there.

- Are you faced with lots of lookup tables that need to be added to a "core" data table? Then Power BI Desktop Query Editor is your friend.

- Does the data contain many superfluous or erroneous elements? Then use Power BI Desktop Query Editor to remove these as a first step.

- Does the data need to be rationalized and standardized to make it easier to handle? In this case, the path to success is via the Power BI Desktop Query Editor.

- Is the data source enormous? If this is the case, you could save time by editing and filtering the data first in the Query Editor. This is because the Query Editor only loads a *sample* of the data for you to tweak. The entire dataset will only be loaded when you confirm all your modifications and close the Query Editor.

These kinds of questions are only rough guidelines. Yet they can help to point you in the right direction when you are working with Power BI Desktop. Inevitably, the more that you work with this application, the more you will develop the reflexes and intuition that will help you make the correct decisions. Remember, however, that Power BI Desktop is there to help and that even a directly loaded dataset is based on a query. So you can always load data and then decide to tweak the query structure later if you need to. Alternatively, editing data in a Query window can be a great opportunity to take a closer look at your data before loading it into the data model—and it only adds a couple of clicks.

So feel free to adopt a way of working that you feel happy with. Power BI Desktop will adapt to your style easily and almost invisibly, letting you switch from data to dashboards so fluidly that it will likely become second nature.

The remainder of this chapter will take you through some of the core techniques that you need to know to cleanse and shape your data. However, before getting into all the detail, let's take a quick, high-level look at the Power BI Desktop Query Editor and the way that it is laid out.

The Power BI Desktop Query Editor

All of your data transformation will take place in the Power BI Desktop Query Editor. It is a separate window from the one where you create your dashboards, and it has a slightly different layout.

The Power BI Desktop Query Editor consists of six main elements:

- The four ribbons: Home, Transform, Add Column, and View. Other ribbons are available when carrying out specific types of data transformations.

- The Query list pane containing all the queries that have been added to a Power BI Desktop file.

- The Data window, where you can see a sample of the data for a selected query.

- The Query Settings pane that contains the list of steps used to transform data.

- The formula bar above the data that shows the code (written in the Power BI "M" language that you will see in greater detail in Chapter 12) that performs the selected transformation step.

- The status bar (at the bottom of the window) that indicates useful information, such as the number of rows and columns in a query table, and the date when the dataset was downloaded.

The callouts for these elements are shown in Figure 7-4.

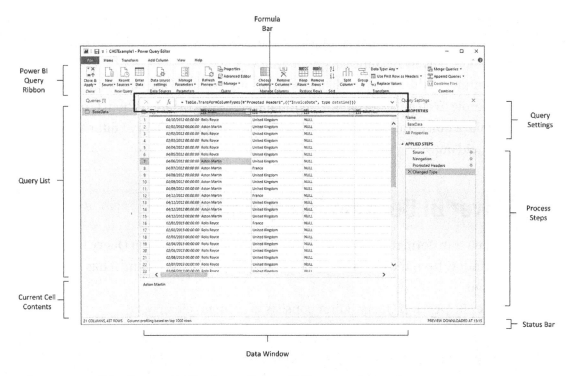

Figure 7-4. *The Power BI Desktop Query Editor, explained*

The Applied Steps List

Data transformation is by its very nature a sequential process. So the Query window stores each modification that you make when you are cleansing and shaping source data. The various elements that make up a data transformation process are listed in the Applied Steps list of the Query Settings pane in the Query Editor.

The Power BI Desktop Query Editor does not number the steps in a data transformation process, but it certainly remembers each one. They start at the top of the Applied Steps list (nearly always with the Source step) and can extend to dozens of individual steps that trace the evolution of your data until you load it into the data model. You can, if you want, consider the Query Editor as a kind of "macro recorder."

Moreover, as you click each step in the Applied Steps list, the data in the Data window changes to reflect the results of each transformation, giving you a complete and visible trail of all the modifications that you have applied to the dataset.

The Applied Steps list gives a distinct name to the step for each and every data modification option that you cover in this chapter and the next. As it can be important to understand exactly what each function actually achieves, I will always draw to your attention the standard name that Power BI Desktop Query applies.

The Power BI Desktop Query Editor Ribbons

Power BI Desktop Query Editor uses (in the February 2020 version, at least) four core ribbons. They are fundamental to what you learn in the course of this chapter. They are as follows:

- The Home ribbon

- The Transform ribbon

- The Add Column ribbon

- The View ribbon

I am not suggesting for a second that you need to memorize what all the buttons in these ribbons do. What I hope is that you are able to use the following brief descriptions of the Query Editor ribbon buttons to get an idea of the amazing power of Power BI Desktop in the field of data transformation. So if you have an initial dataset that is not quite as you need it, you can take a look at the resources that Power BI Desktop has to offer and how they can help. Once you find the function that does what you are looking for, you can jump to the relevant section for the full details on how to apply it.

The Home Ribbon

Since we will be making intense use of the Power BI Desktop Query Editor Home ribbon to transform data, it is important to have an idea of what it can do. I explain the various options in Figure 7-5 and in Table 7-1.

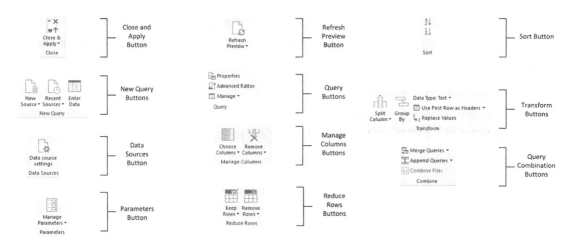

Figure 7-5. *The Query Editor Home ribbon*

Table 7-1. *Query Editor Home Ribbon Options*

Option	Description
Close & Apply	Finishes the processing steps; saves and closes the query.
New Source	Lets you discover and add a new data source to the existing query set.
Recent Sources	Lists all the recent data sources that you have used.
Enter Data	Lets you add your own specific data in a custom table.
Data Source Settings	Allows you to manage and edit settings for data sources that you have already connected to.
Manage Parameters	Lets you view and modify any parameters defined for this Power BI Desktop file. These are explained in Chapter 11.
Refresh Preview	Refreshes the preview data.
Properties	Displays the core query properties.
Advanced Editor	Displays the "M" language editor. This is explained in Chapter 12.
Manage	Lets you delete, duplicate, or reference a query.
Choose Columns	Lets you select the columns to retain from all the columns available in the source data.

(continued)

Table 7-1. (*continued*)

Option	Description
Remove Columns	Lets you remove one or more columns.
Keep Rows	Keeps the specified number of rows at the top of the table.
Remove Rows	Removes a specified number of rows from the top of the data table.
Sort	Sorts the table using the selected column as the sort key.
Split Column	Splits a column into one or many columns at a specified delimiter or after a specified number of characters.
Group By	Groups the table using a specified set of columns and aggregates any numeric columns for this grouping.
Data Type	Applies the chosen data type to the column.
Use First Row as Headers	Uses the first row as the column titles.
Replace Values	Carries out a search-and-replace operation on the data in a column or columns. This only affects the complete data in a column.
Merge Queries	Joins a second query table to the current query results and either aggregates or adds data from the second to the first. This is explained in Chapter 9.
Append Queries	Adds the data from another query to the current query in the current Power BI Desktop file. This is explained in Chapter 12.
Combine Files	Adds the data from a series of similarly structured text files into a single table. This is explained in Chapter 10.

The Transform Ribbon

The Transform ribbon, as its name implies, contains a wealth of functions that can help you to transform your data. The various options it contains are explained in Figure 7-6 and Table 7-2.

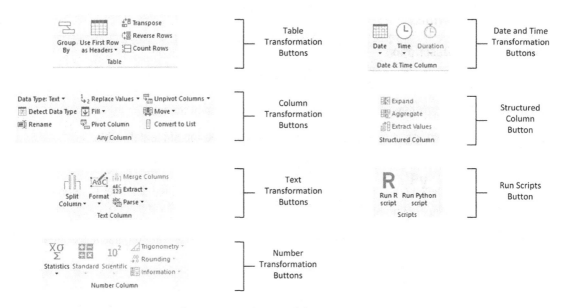

Figure 7-6. *The Query Editor Transform ribbon*

Table 7-2. *Query Editor Transform Ribbon Options*

Option	Description
Group By	Groups the table using a specified set of columns; aggregates any numeric columns for this grouping.
Use First Row as Headers	Uses the first row as the column titles.
Transpose	Transforms the columns into rows and the rows into columns.
Reverse Rows	Displays the source data in reverse order, showing the final rows at the top of the window.
Count Rows	Counts the rows in the table and replaces the data with the row count.
Data Type	Applies the chosen data type to the column.
Detect Data Type	Detects the correct data type to apply to multiple columns.
Rename	Renames a column.
Replace Values	Carries out a search-and-replace operation inside a column, replacing a specified value with another value.

(continued)

Table 7-2. (*continued*)

Option	Description
Fill	Copies the data from cells above or below into empty cells in the column.
Pivot Column	Creates a new set of columns using the data in the selected column as the column titles.
Unpivot Columns	Takes the values in a set of columns and unpivots the data, creating new columns using the column headers as the descriptive elements.
Move	Moves a column.
Convert to List	Converts the contents of a column to a list. This can be used, for instance, as query parameters. You will learn this in Chapter 11.
Split Column	Splits a column into one or many columns at a specified delimiter or after a specified number of characters.
Format	Modifies the text format of data in a column (uppercase, lowercase, capitalization) or removes trailing spaces.
Merge Columns	Takes the data from several columns and places it in a single column, adding an optional separator character.
Extract	Replaces the data in a column using a defined subset of the current data. You can specify a number of characters to keep from the start or end of the column, set a range of characters beginning at a specified character, or even list the number of characters in the column.
Parse	Creates an XML or JSON document from the contents of an element in a column.
Statistics	Returns the Sum, Average, Maximum, Minimum, Median, Standard Deviation, Count, or Distinct Value Count for all the values in the column.
Standard	Carries out a basic mathematical calculation (add, subtract, divide, multiply, integer-divide, or return the remainder) using a value that you specify applied to each cell in the column.
Scientific	Carries out a basic scientific calculation (square, cube, power of n, square root, exponent, logarithm, or factorial) for each cell in the column.

(*continued*)

Table 7-2. (*continued*)

Option	Description
Trigonometry	Carries out a basic trigonometric calculation (Sine, Cosine, Tangent, ArcSine, ArcCosine, or ArcTangent) using a value that you specify applied to each cell in the column.
Rounding	Rounds the values in the column either to the next integer (up or down) or to a specified factor.
Information	Replaces the value in the column with simple information: Is Odd, Is Even, or Positive/Negative.
Date	Isolates an element (day, month, year, etc.) from a date value in a column.
Time	Isolates an element (hour, minute, second, etc.) from a date/time or time value in a column.
Duration	Calculates the duration from a value that can be interpreted as a duration in days, hours, minutes, and so forth.
Expand	Adds the (identically structured) data from another query to the current query.
Aggregate	Calculates the sum or product of numeric columns from another query and adds the result to the current query.
Extract Values	Extracts the values of the contents of a column as a single text value.
Scripts	Runs scripts from languages such as "R" or Python.

The Add Column Ribbon

The Add Column ribbon does a lot more than just add columns. It also contains functions to break columns down into multiple columns and to add columns containing dates and calculations based on existing columns. The various options it contains are explained in Figure 7-7 and Table 7-3.

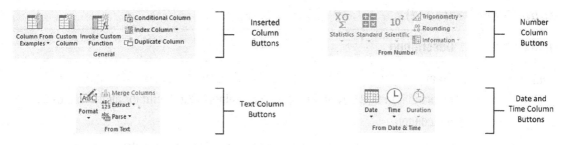

Figure 7-7. *The Query Editor Add Column ribbon*

Table 7-3. *Query Editor Add Column Ribbon Options*

Option	Description
Column From Examples	Lets you use one or more columns as examples to create a new column.
Custom Column	Adds a new column using a formula to create the column's contents.
Invoke Custom Function	Applies an "M" language function to every row.
Conditional Column	Adds a new column that conditionally adds the values from the selected column.
Index Column	Adds a sequential number in a new column to uniquely identify each row.
Duplicate Column	Creates a copy of the current column.
Format	Modifies the text format of data in a new column (uppercase, lowercase, capitalization) or removes trailing spaces.
Merge Columns	Takes the data from several columns and places it in a single column, adding an optional separator character.
Extract	Creates a new column using a defined subset of the current data. You can specify a number of characters to keep from the start or end of the column, set a range of characters beginning at a specified character, or even list the number of characters in the column.
Parse	Creates a new column based on the XML or JSON in a column.

(continued)

197

Table 7-3. (*continued*)

Option	Description
Statistics	Creates a new column that returns the Sum, Average, Maximum, Minimum, Median, Standard Deviation, Count, or Distinct Value Count for all the values in the column.
Standard	Creates a new column that returns a basic mathematical calculation (add, subtract, divide, multiply, integer-divide, or return the remainder) using a value that you specify applied to each cell in the column.
Scientific	Creates a new column that returns a basic scientific calculation (square, cube, power of n, square root, exponent, logarithm, or factorial) for each cell in the column.
Trigonometry	Creates a new column that returns a basic trigonometric calculation (Sine, Cosine, Tangent, ArcSine, ArcCosine, or ArcTangent) using a value that you specify applied to each cell in the column.
Rounding	Rounds the values in a new column either to the next integer (up or down) or to a specified factor.
Information	Replaces the value in the column with simple information: Is Odd, Is Even, or Positive/Negative.
Date	Isolates an element (day, month, year, etc.) from a date value in a new column.
Time	Isolates an element (hour, minute, second, etc.) from a date/time or time value in a new column.
Duration	Calculates the duration from a value that can be interpreted as a duration in days, hours, minutes, and seconds in a new column.

The View Ribbon

The View ribbon lets you alter some of the Query Editor settings and see the underlying data transformation code. The various options that it contains are explained in the next chapter.

Dataset Shaping

So you are now looking at a data table that you have loaded into Power BI Desktop. For argument's sake, let's assume that it is the `C:\PowerBiDesktopSamples\Example1.pbix` file from the sample data directory and that you have clicked the Transform Data button to display the Power BI Desktop Query Editor. What can you do to the BaseData dataset that is now visible? It is time to take a look at some of the core techniques that you can apply to shape the initial dataset. These include the following:

- Renaming columns

- Reordering columns

- Removing columns

- Merging columns

- Removing records

- Removing duplicate records

- Filtering the dataset

I have grouped these techniques together as they affect the initial size and shape of the data. Also, it is generally not only good practice but also easier for you, the data modeler, if you begin by excluding any rows and columns that you do not need. I also find it easier to understand datasets if the columns are logically laid out and given comprehensible names from the start. All in all, this makes working with the data easier in the long run.

Renaming Columns

Although we took a quick look at renaming columns in the first pages of this chapter, let's look at this technique again in more detail. I admit that renaming columns is not actually modifying the form of the data table. However, when dealing with data, I consider it vital to have all data clearly identifiable. This implies meaningful column names being applied to each column. Consequently, I consider this modification to be fundamental to the shape of the data and also as an essential best practice when importing source data.

To rename a column:

1. Click inside the column that you want to rename.

2. Click Transform to activate the Transform ribbon.

3. Click the Rename button. The column name will be highlighted.

4. Enter the new name or edit the existing name.

5. Press Enter or click outside the column title.

The column will now have a new title. The Applied Steps list on the right will now contain another element, Renamed Columns. This step will be highlighted.

Note   As an alternative to using the Transform ribbon, you can right-click the column title and select Rename.

Reordering Columns

Power BI Desktop will load data as it is defined in the data source. Consequently, the column sequence will be entirely dependent on the source data (or by a SQL query if you used a source database, as described in Chapter 3). This column order need not be definitive, however, and you can reorder the columns if that helps you understand and deal with the data. Do the following to change column order:

1. Click the header of the column you want to move.

2. Drag the column left or right to its new position. You will see the column title slide laterally through the column titles as you do this, and a thicker gray line will indicate where the column will be placed once you release the mouse button. Reordered Columns will appear in the Applied Steps list.

Figure 7-8 shows this operation.

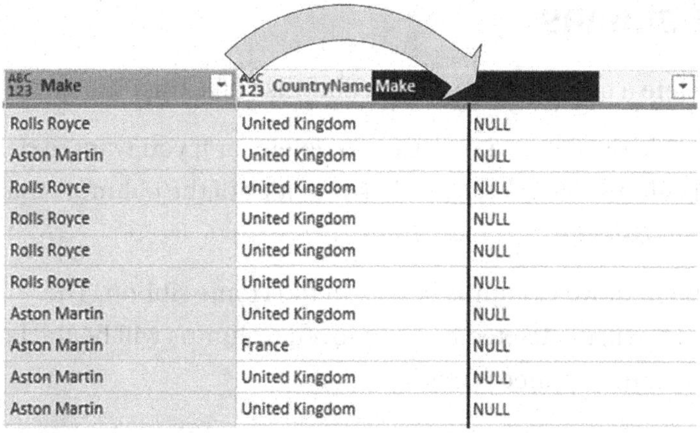

Figure 7-8. *Reordering columns*

If your query contains dozens—or even hundreds—of columns, you may find that dragging a column around can be slow and laborious. Equally, if columns are extremely wide, it can be difficult to "nudge" a column left or right. Power BI Desktop can come to your aid in these circumstances with the Move button in the Transform ribbon. Clicking this button gives you the menu options that are outlined in Table 7-4.

Table 7-4. *Move Button Options*

Option	Description
Left	Moves the currently selected column to the left of the column on its immediate left.
Right	Moves the currently selected column to the right of the column on its immediate right.
To Beginning	Moves the currently selected column to the left of all the columns in the query.
To End	Moves the currently selected column to the right of all the columns in the query.

The Move command also works on a set of columns that you have selected by Ctrl-clicking and/or Shift-clicking. Indeed, you can move a selection of columns that is not contiguous if you need to.

Note   You need to select a column (or a set of columns) before clicking the Move button. If you do not, then the first time that you use Move, Power BI Desktop Query selects the column(s) but does not move it.

Removing Columns

So how do you delete a column or series of columns? Like this:

1. Click inside the column you want to delete, or if you want to delete several columns at once, Ctrl-click the titles of the columns that you want to delete.

2. Click the Remove Columns button in the Home ribbon. The column(s) will be deleted and Removed Columns will be the latest element in the Applied Steps list.

When working with imported datasets over which you have had no control, you may frequently find that you only need a few columns of a large data table. If this is the case, you will soon get tired of Ctrl-clicking numerous columns to select those you want to remove. Power BI Desktop has an alternative method. Just select the columns you want to keep and delete the others. To do this:

1. Ctrl-click the titles of the columns that you want to keep.

2. Click the small triangle in the Remove Columns button in the Home ribbon. Select Remove Other Columns from the menu. All unselected columns will be deleted and Removed Other Columns will be added to the Applied Steps list.

When selecting a contiguous range of columns to remove or keep, you can use the standard Windows Shift-click technique to select from the first to the last column in the block of columns that you want to select.

Note   Both of these options for removing columns are also available from the context menu, if you prefer. It shows Remove (or Remove Columns, if there are several columns selected) when deleting columns, as well as Remove Other Columns if you right-click a column title.

Choosing Columns

If you prefer not to scroll through a wide dataset, yet still need to select a subset of columns as the basis for your reports, then there is another way to define the collection of fields that you want to use. You can choose the columns that you want to keep (and, by definition, those that you want to exclude) like this:

1. Open the sample file CH07Example1.pbix in the folder `C:\ PowerBiDesktopSamples` unless it is already open.

2. In the Home ribbon, click the Transform Data button. The Query Editor will open.

3. In the Home ribbon of the Query Editor, click the Choose Columns button.

4. Click (Select All Columns) to deselect the entire collection of columns in the dataset.

5. Select the columns Make, Color, and SalePrice. The Choose Columns dialog will look like the one in Figure 7-9.

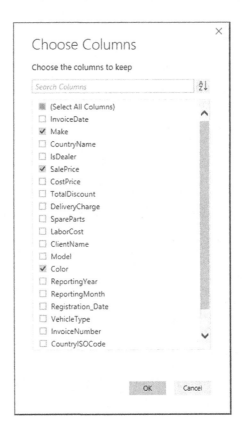

Figure 7-9. *The Choose Columns dialog*

6.   Click OK. The Query Editor will only display the columns that you
     selected.

The Choose Columns dialog comes with a couple of extra functions that you might
find useful when choosing the set of columns that you want to work with:

- You can sort the column list in alphabetical order (or, indeed, revert
  to the original order) by clicking the Sort icon (the small A-Z) at the
  top right of the Choose Columns dialog and selecting the required
  option.

- You can filter the list of columns that is displayed simply by entering
  a few characters in the Search Columns field at the top of the dialog
  and then pressing Enter.

- The (Select All Columns) option switches between selecting and
  deselecting all the columns in the list.

Merging Columns

Source data is not always exactly as you wish it could be (and that is sometimes a massive understatement). Certain data sources could have data spread over many columns that could equally well be merged into a single column. So it probably comes as no surprise to discover that Power BI Desktop Query can carry out this kind of operation too. Here is how to do it:

1. Ctrl-click the headers of the columns that you want to merge (Make and Model in the BaseData dataset in this example).

2. In the Transform ribbon, click the Merge Columns button. The Merge Columns dialog will be displayed.

3. From the Separator popup menu, select one of the available separator elements. I chose Colon in this example.

4. Enter a name for the column that will be created from the two original columns (I am calling it MakeAndModel). The dialog should look like Figure 7-10.

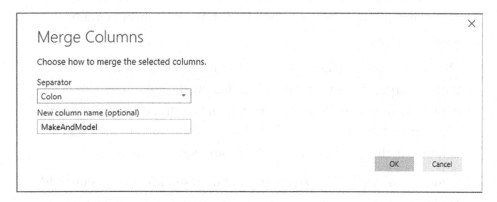

Figure 7-10. *The Merge Columns dialog*

5. Click OK. The columns that you selected will be replaced by the data from all the columns, as shown in Figure 7-11.

```
fx    = Table.CombineColumns(#"Changed Type",{"Make", "Model"},Combiner.CombineTextByDelimiter(":", QuoteStyle.None),"MakeAndModel")
```

	ClientName	MakeAndModel	Color	ReportingYear	ReportingMonth	Registration_Date
1	Aldo Motors	Rolls Royce:Camargue	Red	2012	10	08/01/1985
2	Honest John	Aston Martin:DBS	Blue	2012	1	09/05/2007
3	Bright Orange	Rolls Royce:Silver Ghost	Green	2012	2	08/09/2006
4	Honest John	Rolls Royce:Silver Ghost	Blue	2012	3	05/01/1987
5	Wheels'R'Us	Rolls Royce:Camargue	Canary Yellow	2012	4	08/01/1985
6	Cut'n'Shut	Rolls Royce:Camargue	British Racing Green	2012	5	06/05/1986
7	Bright Orange	Aston Martin:DBS	Dark Purple	2012	6	09/08/1991
8	Les Arnaqueurs	Aston Martin:DB7	Red	2012	7	08/05/1992
9	Aldo Motors	Aston Martin:DB9	Blue	2012	8	08/09/2005
10	Aldo Motors	Aston Martin:DB9	Silver	2012	9	08/05/1993
11	Aldo Motors	Aston Martin:DB4	Night Blue	2012	9	06/05/1975
12	Les Arnaqueurs	Aston Martin:Vantage	Canary Yellow	2012	11	15/01/1985
13	Wheels'R'Us	Aston Martin:Vanquish	Night Blue	2012	11	29/03/1979
14	Bright Orange	Aston Martin:Rapide	Black	2012	12	08/09/2004
15	Cut'n'Shut	Aston Martin:Zagato	British Racing Green	2012	12	04/06/1994
16	Les Arnaqueurs	Rolls Royce:Silver Ghost	Canary Yellow	2013	1	08/09/2006
17	Wheels'R'Us	Rolls Royce:Wraith	Silver	2013	2	01/09/2000
18	Cut'n'Shut	Rolls Royce:Silver Ghost	Green	2013	3	10/05/1997
19	Bright Orange	Rolls Royce:Camargue	Blue	2013	4	01/09/2001

Figure 7-11. *The result of merging columns*

I need to make a few comments about this process:

- You can select as many columns as you want when merging columns.

- If you do not give the resulting column a name in the Merge Columns dialog, it will simply be renamed Merged. You can always rename it later if you want.

- The order in which you select the columns affects the way that the data is merged. So, always begin by selecting the column whose data must appear at the left of the merged column, then the column whose data should be next, and so forth. You do not have to select columns in the order that they initially appeared in the dataset.

- If you do not want to use any of the standard separators that Power BI Desktop Query suggests, you can always define your own. Just select --Custom-- in the popup menu in the Merge Columns dialog. A new box will appear in the dialog, in which you can enter your choice of separator. This can be composed of several characters if you really want.

- Merging columns from the Transform ribbon removes all the selected columns and replaces them with a single column. The same option is also available from the Add Column ribbon—only in this case, this operation *adds* a new column and leaves the original columns in the dataset.

Note This option is also available from the context menu if you right-click a column title.

The available merge separators are described in Table 7-5.

Table 7-5. *Merge Separators*

Option	Description
Colon	Uses the colon (:) as the separator.
Comma	Uses the comma (,) as the separator.
Equals Sign	Uses the equals sign (=) as the separator.
Semi-Colon	Uses the semicolon (;) as the separator.
Space	Uses the space ( ) as the separator.
Tab	Uses the tab character as the separator.
Custom	Lets you enter a custom separator.

Tip You can split, remove, and duplicate columns using the context menu if you prefer. Just remember to right-click the column title to display the correct context menu.

Going to a Specific Column

Power BI Desktop can load datasets that contain hundreds of columns. As scrolling left and right across dozens of columns can be more than a little frustrating, you can always jump to a specific column at any time.

1. In the Home ribbon of the Query Editor, click the small triangle at
    the bottom of the Choose Columns button. Select Go to Column.
    The Go to Column dialog will appear.

2. Select the column you want to move to. The dialog will look like
    Figure 7-12.

Figure 7-12. *The Go to Column dialog*

3. Click OK. Power BI Desktop will select the chosen column.

Tip   If you prefer, you can double-click a column name in the Go to Column dialog
to move to the chosen column.

Removing Records

You may not always need *all* the data that you have loaded into a Power BI Desktop query. There could be several possible reasons for this:

- You are taking a first look at the data and you only need a sample to get an idea of what the data is like.

- The data contains records that you clearly do not need and that you can easily identify from the start.

- You are testing data cleansing and you want a smaller dataset to really speed up the development of a complex data extraction and transformation process.

- You want to analyze a reduced dataset to extrapolate theses and inferences, and to save analysis on a full dataset for later, or even use a more industrial-strength toolset such as SQL Server Integration Services.

To allow you to reduce the size of the dataset, Power BI Desktop proposes two basic approaches out of the box:

- Keep certain rows

- Remove certain rows

Inevitably, the technique that you adopt will depend on the circumstances. If it is easier to specify the rows to sample by inclusion, then the keep certain rows approach is the best option to take. Inversely, if you want to proceed by exclusion, then the remove certain rows technique is best. Let's look at each of these in turn.

Keeping Rows

This approach lets you specify the rows that you want to continue using. It is based on the application of one of the following three choices:

- Keep the top *n* records.

- Keep the bottom *n* records.

- Keep a specified range of records—that is, keep *n* records every *y* records.

Most of these techniques are very similar, so let's start by imagining that you want to keep the top 50 records in the sample `C:\PowerBiDesktopSamples\Example1.pbix` file.

1. In the Home ribbon of the Power BI Query Editor, click the Keep Rows button. The menu will appear.

2. Select Keep Top Rows. The Keep Top Rows dialog will appear.

3. Enter **50** in the "Number of rows" box, as shown in Figure 7-13.

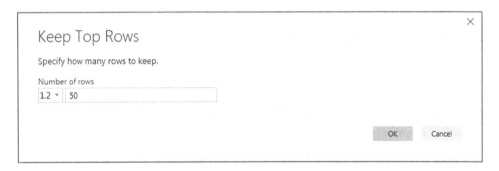

Figure 7-13. *The Keep Top Rows dialog*

4. Click OK. All but the first 50 records are deleted, and Kept First Rows is added to the Applied Steps list.

To keep the bottom *n* rows, the technique is virtually identical. Follow the steps in the previous example, but select *Keep Bottom Rows* in step 2. In this case, the Applied Steps list displays Kept Last Rows.

To keep a range of records, you need to specify a starting record and the number of records to keep from then on. For instance, suppose that you wish to lose the first 10 records but keep the following 25. This is how to go about it:

1. In the Home ribbon, click the Keep Rows button.

2. Select Keep Range of Rows. The Keep Range of Rows dialog will appear.

3. Enter **11** in the "First row" box.

4. Enter **25** in the "Number of rows" box, as shown in Figure 7-14.

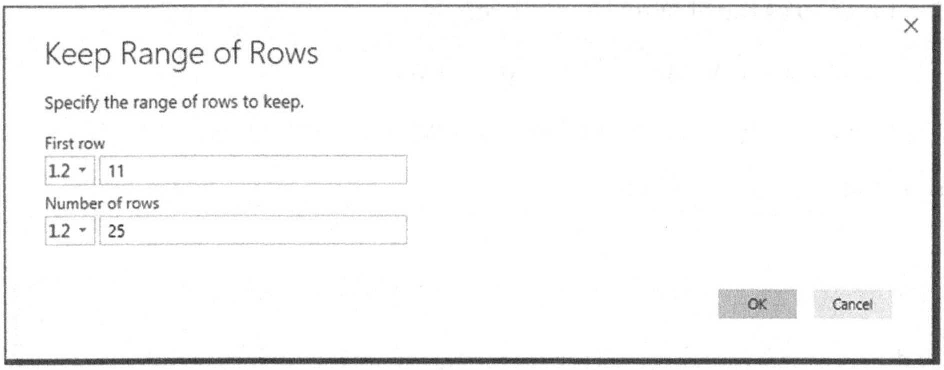

Keep Range of Rows

Specify the range of rows to keep.

First row

1.2 ▾ | 11

Number of rows

1.2 ▾ | 25

OK   Cancel

Figure 7-14. The Keep Range of Rows dialog

5.   Click OK. All but records 1–10 and 36 to the end are deleted, and
      Kept Range of Rows is added to the Applied Steps list.

Note   You may have noticed that this dialog—like many others—contains a
popup menu to the left of the fields where you enter values. This popup menu
allows you to *parameterize* the value. Parameters are explained in Chapter 11.

Removing Rows

Removing rows is a nearly identical process to the one you just used to keep rows. As
removing the top or bottom *n* rows is highly similar, I will not go through it in detail.
All you have to do is click the Remove Rows button in the Home ribbon and follow the
process as if you were keeping rows. The Applied Steps list will read Removed Top Rows
or Removed Bottom Rows in this case, and rows will be removed instead of being kept in
the dataset, of course.

The remove rows approach does have one very useful option that can be applied as
a sampling technique. It allows you to remove one or more records every few records to
produce a subset of the source data. To do this, you need to do the following:

1.   Click the Remove Rows button in the Query window Home
      ribbon. The menu will appear.

2.   Select Remove Alternate Rows. The Remove Alternate Rows dialog
      will appear.

3. Enter **10** as the First row to remove.

4. Enter **2** as the Number of rows to remove.

5. Enter **10** as the Number of rows to keep.

The dialog will look like Figure 7-15.

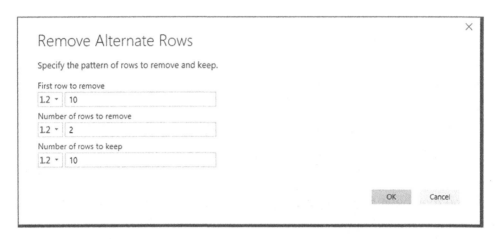

Figure 7-15. *The Remove Alternate Rows dialog*

6. Click OK. All but the records matching the pattern you entered in
    the dialog are removed. Removed Alternate Rows is then added to
    the Applied Steps list.

Note   If you are really determined to extract a sample that you consider to
be representative of the key data, then you can always filter the data before
subsetting it to exclude any outliers. Filtering data is explained later in this chapter.

Removing Blank Rows

If your source data contains completely blank (empty) rows, you can delete these as
follows:

1. Click the Remove Rows button in the Query window Home
    ribbon. The menu will appear.

2. Select Remove Blank Rows.

This results in empty rows being deleted. Removed Blank Rows is then added to the Applied Steps list.

Removing Duplicate Records

An external source of data might not be quite as perfect as you might hope. One of the most annoying features of poor data is the presence of duplicates. These are insidious since they falsify results and are not always visible. If you suspect that the data table contains *strict* duplicates (i.e., where every field is identical in two or more records), then you can remove the duplicates like this:

1. Click the Remove Duplicates in the popup menu for the table (this is at the top left of the table grid). All duplicate records are deleted and Removed Duplicates is added to the Applied Steps list.

Note   I must stress that this approach will only remove *completely* identical records where every element of every column is strictly identical in the duplicate rows. If two records have just one different character or a number but everything else is identical, then they are *not* considered duplicates by the Power BI Desktop Query Editor. Alternatively, if you want to isolate and examine the duplicate records, then you can display only completely identical records by selecting Keep Duplicates from the popup menu for the table.

So if you suspect or are sure that the data table you are dealing with contains duplicates, what are the practical solutions? This can be a real conundrum, but there are some basic techniques that you can apply:

- Remove all columns that you are sure you will not be using later in the data-handling process. This way, Power BI Desktop will only be asked to compare essential data across potentially duplicate records.

- Group the data on the core columns (this is explained later in this chapter).

Note   As you have seen, Power BI Desktop Query can help you to home in on the essential elements in a dataset in just a few clicks. If anything, you need to be careful that you are *not removing* valuable data—and consequently skewing your analysis—when excluding data from the query.

Sorting Data

Although not strictly a data modification step, sorting an imported table will probably be something that you want to do at some stage, if only to get a clearer idea of the data that you are dealing with. Do the following to sort the data:

1. Close the file CH07Example1.pbix (if, indeed, you have been using it to test the techniques explained so far in this chapter) without saving it.

2. Open the file `C:\PowerBiDesktopSamples\Example1.pbix`. Note that you are opening an existing Power BI desktop file and *not* loading data.

3. Click Transform Data to open the Query Editor.

4. Click inside the column you wish to sort by.

5. Click Sort Ascending (the A/Z icon) or Sort Descending (the Z/A icon) in the Home ribbon.

The data is sorted in either alphabetical (smallest to largest) or reverse alphabetical (largest to smallest) order. If you want to carry out a complex sort operation (i.e., first by one column and then by another if the first column contains the same element over several rows), you do this simply by sorting the columns one after another. Power BI Desktop Query Editor adds a tiny 1, 2, 3, and so on to the right of the column title to indicate the sort sequence. You can see this in Figure 7-16, where I sorted *first* on the column Make, and *finally* on the column Model.

Figure 7-16. *Sorting multiple columns*

As sorting data is considered part of the data modification process, it also appears in the Applied Steps list as Sorted Rows. If you look closely at the column headings, you will see a small "1" and "2" that indicate the sort priority as well as the arrows that indicate that the columns are sorted in ascending order.

Note   An alternative technique for sorting data is to click the popup menu for a column (the downward-facing triangle at the right of a column title) and select Sort Ascending or Sort Descending from the popup menu.

Reversing the Row Order

If you find that the data that you are looking at seems upside down (i.e., with the bottom rows at the top and vice versa), you can reverse the row order in a single click, if you want. To do this, do the following:

In the Transform ribbon, click the Reverse Rows button.

The entire dataset will be reversed and the bottom row will now be the top row.

Undoing a Sort Operation

If you subsequently decide that you do not want to keep your data sorted, you can undo the sort operation at any time, as follows:

1. Click the sort icon at the right of the name of the column that you used as the basis for the sort operation. The context menu will appear, as you can see in Figure 7-17.

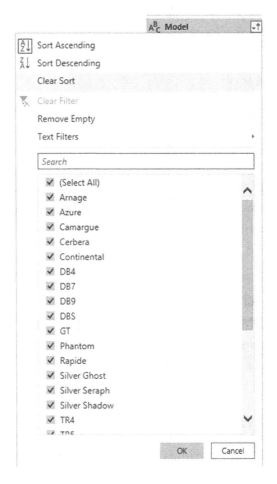

Figure 7-17. *Removing a sort operation*

2. Click Clear Sort.

The sort order that you applied will be removed, and the data will revert to its original row order.

Note   If you sorted the dataset on several columns, you can choose either to remove all the sort order that you applied by clicking the *first* column that you used to sort the data. This will remove the sort order that you applied to *all* the columns that you used to define the sort criteria. If all you want to do is undo the sort on the final column in a set of columns used to sort the recordset, then you can clear only the sort operation on this column.

Filtering Data

The most frequently used way of limiting a dataset is, in my experience, the use of filters on the table that you have loaded. Now, I realize that you may be coming to Power BI Desktop after years with Excel, or after some time using Power Pivot, and that the filtering techniques that you are about to see probably look much like the ones you have used in those two tools. However, because it is fundamental to include and exclude appropriate records when loading source data, I prefer to explain Power Query filters in detail, even if this means that certain readers will experience a strong sense of déjà vu.

Here are two basic approaches for filtering data in Power BI Desktop:

- Select one or more specific values from the unique list of elements in the chosen column.

- Define a range of data to include or exclude.

The first option is common to all data types, whether they are text, number, or date/time. The second approach varies according to the data type of the column that you are using to filter data.

Selecting Specific Values

Selecting one or more values present in a column of data is as easy as this (assuming that you are still using the Power BI Desktop file Example1.pbix and are in the Query Editor):

1. Click a column's popup menu. (I used Make in the sample dataset in this example.) The filter menu appears.

2. Check all elements that you want to retain and uncheck all elements that you wish to exclude. In this example, I kept Bentley and Rolls Royce, as shown in Figure 7-18.

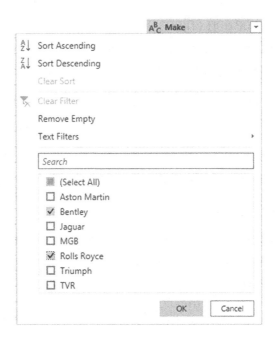

Figure 7-18. *A filter menu*

3. Click OK. The Applied Steps list adds Filtered Rows.

Note   You can deselect all items by clicking the (Select All) check box; reselect all the items by selecting this box again. It follows that, if you want to keep only a few elements, it may be faster to unselect all of them first and then only select the ones that you want to keep. If you want to exclude any records without a value in the column that you are filtering on, then select Remove Empty from the filter menu.

Finding Elements in the Filter List

Scrolling up and down in a filter list can get extremely laborious. A fast way of limiting the list to a subset of available elements is to do the following:

1. Click the popup menu for a column. (I use Model in the sample dataset in this example.) The filter menu appears.

2. Enter a letter or a few letters in the Search box. The list shortens with every letter or number that you enter. If you enter **ar**, then the filter popup will look like Figure 7-19.

Figure 7-19. *Searching the filter menu*

To remove a filter, all that you have to do is click the cross that appears at the right of the Search box.

Filtering Text Ranges

If a column contains text, then you can apply specific options to filter the data. These elements are found in the filter popup of any text-based column in the Text Filters submenu. The choices are given in Table 7-6.

Table 7-6. *Text Filter Options*

Filter Option	Description
Equals	Sets the text that must match the cell contents.
Does Not Equal	Sets the text that must *not* match the cell contents.
Begins With	Sets the text at the left of the cell contents.
Does Not Begin With	Sets the text that must *not* appear at the left of the cell contents.
Ends With	Sets the text at the right of the cell contents.
Does Not End With	Sets the text that must *not* appear at the right of the cell contents.
Contains	Lets you enter a text that will be part of the cell contents.
Does Not Contain	Lets you enter a text that will *not* be part of the cell contents.

Filtering Numeric Ranges

If a column contains numbers, then there are also specific options that you can apply to filter the data. You'll find these elements in the filter popup of any text-based column in the Number Filters submenu. The choices are given in Table 7-7.

Table 7-7. *Numeric Filter Options*

Filter Option	Description
Equals	Sets the number that must match the cell contents.
Does Not Equal	Sets the number that must not match the cell contents.
Greater Than	Cell contents must be greater than this number.
Greater Than Or Equal To	Cell contents must be greater than or equal to this number.
Lesser Than	Cell contents must be less than this number.
Lesser Than Or Equal To	Cell contents must be less than or equal to this number.
Between	Cell contents must be between the two numbers that you specify.

Filtering Date and Time Ranges

If a column contains dates or times (or both), then specific options can also be applied to filter the data. These elements are found in the filter popup of any text-based column in the Date/Time Filters submenu. The choices are given in Table 7-8.

Table 7-8. *Date and Time Filter Options*

Filter Element	Description
Equals	Filters data to include only records for the selected date.
Before	Filters data to include only records up to the selected date.
After	Filters data to include only records after the selected date.
Between	Lets you set an upper and a lower date limit to exclude records outside that range.
In the Next	Lets you specify a number of days, weeks, months, quarters, or years to come.
In the Previous	Lets you specify a number of days, weeks, months, quarters, or years up to the date.
Is Earliest	Filters data to include only records for the earliest date.
Is Latest	Filters data to include only records for the latest date.
Is Not Earliest	Filters data to include only records for dates not including the earliest date.
Is Not Latest	Filters data to include only records for dates not including the latest date.
Day ➤ Tomorrow	Filters data to include only records for the day after the current system date.
Day ➤ Today	Filters data to include only records for the current system date.
Day ➤ Yesterday	Filters data to include only records for the day before the current system date.
Week ➤ Next Week	Filters data to include only records for the next calendar week.

(*continued*)

Table 7-8. (*continued*)

Filter Element	Description
Week ➤ This Week	Filters data to include only records for the current calendar week.
Week ➤ Last Week	Filters data to include only records for the previous calendar week.
Month ➤ Next Month	Filters data to include only records for the next calendar month.
Month ➤ This Month	Filters data to include only records for the current calendar month.
Month ➤ Last Month	Filters data to include only records for the previous calendar month.
Month ➤ Month Name	Filters data to include only records for the specified calendar month.
Quarter ➤ Next Quarter	Filters data to include only records for the next quarter.
Quarter ➤ This Quarter	Filters data to include only records for the current quarter.
Quarter ➤ Last Quarter	Filters data to include only records for the previous quarter.
Quarter ➤ Quarter Name	Filters data to include only records for the specified quarter.
Year ➤ Next Year	Filters data to include only records for the next year.
Year ➤ This Year	Filters data to include only records for the current year.
Year ➤ Last Year	Filters data to include only records for the previous year.
Year ➤ Year To Date	Filters data to include only records for the calendar year to date.
Custom Filter	Lets you set up a specific filter for a chosen date range.

Filtering Data

Filtering data uses a very similar approach, whatever the type of filter that is applied. As a simple example, here is how to apply a number filter to the sale price to find vehicles that sold for less than £5,000.00:

1. Click the popup menu for the SalePrice column.

2. Click Number Filters. The submenu will appear.

3. Select Less Than. The Filter Rows dialog will be displayed.

4. Enter **5000** in the box next to the "is less than" box, as shown in Figure 7-20.

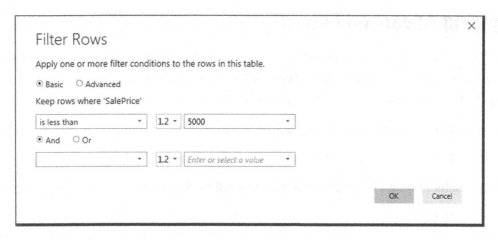

Figure 7-20. *The Filter Rows dialog*

5. Click OK. The dataset only displays rows that conform to the filter that you have defined.

Although extremely simple to apply, filters do require a few comments:

*   You can combine up to two elements in a basic filter. These can be mutually inclusive (an AND filter) or they can be an alternative (an OR filter).

*   You can combine several elements in an advanced filter—as you will learn in the next section.

*   You should *not* apply any formatting when entering numbers.

*   Any text that you filter on is not case-sensitive.

*   If you choose the wrong filter, you do not have to cancel and start over. Simply select the correct filter type from the popup in the left-hand boxes in the Filter Rows dialog.

Tip   If you set a filter value that excludes all the records in the table, Power BI Desktop displays an empty table except for the words "This table is empty." You can always remove the filter by clicking the cross to the left of Filtered Rows in the Applied Steps list. This will remove the step and revert the data to its previous state.

Applying Advanced Filters

Should you ever need to be extremely specific when filtering data, you can always use Power BI Desktop's advanced filters. These let you extend the filter elements so that you can include or exclude records to a high level of detail. Here is the procedure:

1. Click the popup menu for the SalePrice column.

2. Click Number Filters. The submenu will appear.

3. Select Equals. The Filter Rows dialog will be displayed.

4. Click Advanced.

5. Enter **5000** as the value for the first filter element in the dialog.

6. Select Or from the popup as the filter type for the second filter element.

7. Select Equals as the operator.

8. Enter **89000** as the value for the second filter in the dialog.

9. Click Add clause. A new filter element will be added to the dialog under the existing elements.

10. Select Equals as the operator.

11. Enter **178500** as the value for the third filter element in the dialog. The Filter dialog will look like the one shown in Figure 7-21.

Filter Rows

Apply one or more filter conditions to the rows in this table.

○ Basic   ⦿ Advanced

Keep rows where

And/Or	Column	Operator	Value
	SalePrice ▾	equals ▾	1.2 ▾	5000 ▾
Or ▾	SalePrice ▾	equals ▾	1.2 ▾	89000 ▾
Or ▾	SalePrice ▾	equals ▾	1.2 ▾	178500 ▾	•••

Add Clause

OK   Cancel

Figure 7-21. *Advanced filters*

12. Click OK. Only records containing the figures that you entered in the Filter dialog will be displayed in the Power BI Desktop Query Editor.

I would like to finish on the subject of filters with a few comments:

- In the Advanced Filter dialog, you can "mix and match" columns and operators to achieve the filter result that you are looking for.

- You can also order the sequence of filters if you ever need to. To do this, simply click inside a filter row and it will appear with a gray background (like the third filter in Figure 7-21). Then click the ellipses at the right of the filter row and select Move Up or Move Down from the popup menu. You can see this in Figure 7-22.

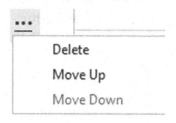

Figure 7-22. *Ordering filters*

- To delete a filter, click the ellipses at the right of the filter row and select Delete.

Note   When you are dealing with really large datasets, you may find that a filter does not always show all the available values from the source data. This is because Power BI Query Editor has loaded only a sample subset of the data. In cases like these, you will see an alert in the filter popup menu and a "Load more" link. Clicking this link will force Power BI to reload a larger sample set of data. However, memory restrictions may prevent it from loading all the data that you need. In cases like this, you should consider modifying the source query if possible so that it brings back a representative dataset that can fit into memory.

Grouping Records

At times, you will need to transform your original data in an extreme way—by grouping the data. This is very different from filtering data, removing duplicates, or cleansing the contents of columns. When you group data, you are altering the structure of the dataset to "roll up" records where you do the following:

- Define the attribute columns that will become the unique elements in the grouped data table.

- Specify which aggregations are applied to any numeric columns included in the grouped table.

Grouping is frequently an extremely selective operation. This is inevitable, since the fewer attribute (i.e., non-numeric) columns you choose to group on, the fewer records you are likely to include in the grouped table. However, this will always depend on the particular dataset you are dealing with, and grouping data efficiently is always a matter of flair, practice, and good, old-fashioned trial and error.

Simple Groups

To understand how grouping works—and how it can radically alter the structure of your dataset—let's see a simple example of row grouping in action:

1. In the sample file CH07Example1.pbix (in the Query Editor), click inside the Make column.

2. In either the Home ribbon or Transform ribbon, click the Group By button. The Group By dialog will appear, looking like the one in Figure 7-23.

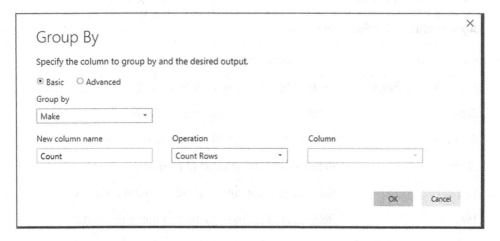

Figure 7-23. *Simple grouping*

3. Click OK. The dataset will now only contain the list of makes of vehicle and the number of records for each make. You can see this in Figure 7-24.

ABC 123 Make	1.2 Count
1 Rolls Royce	63
2 Aston Martin	110
3 Jaguar	129
4 Bentley	71
5 TVR	14
6 MGB	36
7 Triumph	34

Figure 7-24. *Simple grouping output*

Power BI Desktop will add a step named Grouped Rows to the Applied Steps list
when you apply grouping to a dataset.

Note   The best way to cancel a grouping operation is to delete the Grouped Rows
step in the Applied Steps list.

Although Power BI Desktop defaults to counting rows, there are several other
operations that you can apply when grouping data. These are outlined in Table 7-9.

Table 7-9. *Aggregation Operations When Grouping*

Aggregation Operation	Description
Count Rows	Counts the number of records.
Count Distinct Rows	Counts the number of unique records.
Sum	Returns the total for a numeric column.
Average	Returns the average for a numeric column.
Median	Returns the median value of a numeric column.
Min	Returns the minimum value of a numeric column.
Max	Returns the maximum value of a numeric column.
All Rows	Creates a table of records for each grouped element.

Complex Groups

Power BI Desktop can help you shape your datasets in more advanced ways by creating
more complex data groupings. As an example, you could try out the following to group
by make and model and add columns showing the total sales value and the average cost:

1. Open the sample file `C:\PowerBiDesktopSamples\Example1.pbix`.

2. Click Transform Data to open the Query Editor.

3. Select the following columns (by Ctrl-clicking the column headers):

   a. Make

   b. Model

4. In either the Home ribbon or Transform ribbon, click Group By.

5. In the New Column Name box, enter **TotalSales**.

6. Select Sum as the operation.

7. Choose SalePrice as the source column in the Column popup list.

8. Click the Add Aggregation button and repeat the operation, only this time, use the following:

   a. *New Column Name*: **AverageCost**

   b. *Operation*: Average

   c. *Column*: CostPrice

The Group By dialog should look like the one in Figure 7-25.

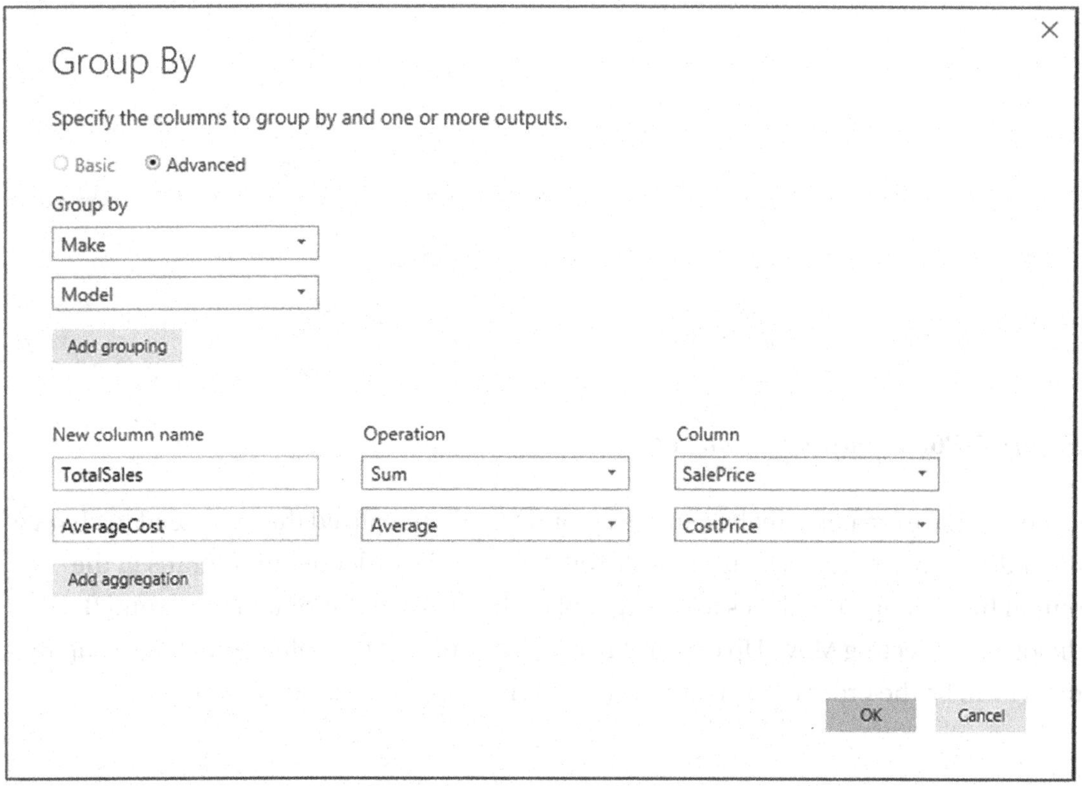

Figure 7-25. *The Group By dialog*

9. Click OK. All columns, other than those that you specified in the Group By dialog, are removed, and the table is grouped and aggregated, as shown in Figure 7-26. Grouped Rows will be added to the Applied Steps list. I have also sorted the table by the Make and Model columns to make the grouping easier to comprehend.

	Make	Model	TotalSales	AverageCost
1	Rolls Royce	Camargue	4116900	61002.69231
2	Aston Martin	DBS	465500	68000
3	Rolls Royce	Silver Ghost	1315500	75630
4	Aston Martin	DB7	1023480	23703.125
5	Aston Martin	DB9	5423860	59132.96296
6	Aston Martin	DB4	793000	84167.5
7	Aston Martin	Vantage	658200	38750
8	Aston Martin	Vanquish	1506750	89700
9	Aston Martin	Rapide	455500	142500
10	Aston Martin	Zagato	359750	127500
11	Rolls Royce	Wraith	359750	64500
12	Rolls Royce	Silver Shadow	622500	71445
13	Rolls Royce	Silver Seraph	582500	71445
14	Rolls Royce	Phantom	359750	64500
15	Jaguar	XK	4461250	39803.15789
16	Jaguar	XJ6	1239750	32630.76923
17	Jaguar	XJ12	618000	33750
18	Bentley	Continental	3662250	49256.86275
19	Bentley	Arnage	90750	28200
20	Bentley	Azure	489500	28200

Figure 7-26. *Grouping a dataset*

If you have created a really complex group and then realized that you need to change the order of the columns, all is not lost. You can alter the order of the columns in the output by clicking the ellipses to the right of each column definition in the Group By dialog and selecting Move Up or Move Down. The order of the columns in the Group By dialog will be the order of the columns (left to right) in the resulting dataset.

Note   You do not have to Ctrl-click to select the grouping columns. You can add them one by one to the Group By dialog by clicking the Add Aggregation button. Equally, you can remove grouping columns (or added and aggregated columns) by clicking the ellipses to the right of a column name and selecting Delete from the popup menu.

Saving Changes in the Query Editor

As you would expect, you can save any changes that you have made when using the Power BI Desktop Query Editor at any time. However, you need to be aware that when you click the Save icon above the ribbon (or if you click File ➤ Save), you will be presented with a choice in the dialog that you can see in Figure 7-27.

Figure 7-27. Applying pending changes before saving in the Query Editor

At this point you have to decide if you want only to save the work that you have done using the Query Editor, or if you want not only to save your work but also update the data in the data model with the latest version of the data that results from the data transformation that you have carried out.

Consequently, you have to choose between

- *Apply*: Apply the changes and load the data to the data model.

- *Apply later*: Save your modifications but leave the data as it is currently—and potentially update the data later.

Exiting the Query Editor

In a similar vein to the Save options just described, you can choose how to exit the Query Editor and return to your reports and dashboards in Power BI Desktop. The default option (when you click the Close & Apply button) is to apply all the changes that you have made to the data, update the data model with the new data, and return to Power BI Desktop.

However, you have two other options that may prove useful. These appear in the menu for the Close & Apply button:

- *Apply*: Apply the changes that you have made to the data model. This may involve changes to the fields in the Fields list.

- *Close*: Close the Query Editor but do not apply any changes.

If you choose not to apply the changes that you have made, then you will see the alert that is displayed in Figure 7-28. At some point you will have to update the data model to ensure that you are using the correct data for your reports by clicking the Apply Changes button in the alert that appears above the report canvas.

⚠ There are pending changes in your queries that haven't been applied.   Apply changes   ✕

Figure 7-28. The pending changes alert

Conclusion

This chapter started you on the road to transforming datasets with Power BI Desktop. You saw how to trim datasets by removing rows and columns. You also learned how to subset a sample of data from a data source by selecting alternating groups of rows.

You also saw how to choose the columns that you want to use in reports, how to move columns around in the dataset, and how to rename columns so that your data is easily comprehensible when you use it later in dashboards and reports. Then, you saw how to filter and sort data, as well as how to remove duplicates to ensure that your dataset only contains the precise rows that you need for your upcoming visualizations. Finally, you learned how to group and aggregate data.

It has to be admitted, nonetheless, that preparing raw data for use in dashboards and reports is not always easy and can take a while to get right. However, Power BI Desktop Query can make this task really easy with a little practice. So now that you have grasped the basics, it is time to move on and discover some further data transformation techniques. Specifically, you will see how to transform and potentially cleanse the data that you have imported. This is the subject of the next chapter.

CHAPTER 8

Data Transformation and Cleansing

Once a dataset has been shaped and filtered (as covered in the previous chapter), it probably still needs a good few modifications to make it ready for consumption. Many of these modifications are, at their heart, a selection of fairly simple yet necessary techniques that you apply to make the data cleaner and more standardized. I have chosen to group these approaches under the heading *data transformation and cleansing*.

The sort of things that you may be looking to do before finally loading source data into the data model normally cover a range of processes that *finalize* the data so that it is usable in the data model. They can include the following:

- Change the data type for a column—by telling Power BI Desktop that the column contains numbers, for example.

- Ensure that the first row is used as headers (if this is required).

- Remove part of a column's contents.

- Replace the values in a cell with other values.

- Transform the column contents—by making the text uppercase, for instance, or by removing decimals from numbers.

- Fill data down or up over empty cells to ensure that records are complete.

- Apply math or statistical (or even trigonometric) functions to columns of numbers.

- Convert date or time data into date elements such as days, months, quarters, years, hours, or minutes.

© Adam Aspin 2020
A. Aspin, *Pro Power BI Desktop*, https://doi.org/10.1007/978-1-4842-5763-0_8

Transforming data does not only consist of reducing it. Sometimes you may have to *extend* the data to make it usable. This normally means adding further columns to a data table. The techniques to do this include

- Duplicating column and possibly altering the format of the data in the copied column

- Extracting part of the data in a column into a new column

- Separating all the data in a column so that each data element appears in a separate column

- Merging columns into a new column

- Adding custom columns that possibly contain calculations or extract part of a column's data into a new column or even concatenate columns

- Adding "index" columns to ensure uniqueness or memorize a sort order

This chapter will take you on a tour of these kinds of essential data transformations. Once you have finished reading it, you should be confident that you can take a rough and ready data source as a starting point and convert it into a polished and coherent data table that is ready to become a pivotal part of your Power BI Desktop data model. Not only that, but you will have carried out really heavy lifting much faster and more easily than you could have done using enterprise-level tools.

The sample data that you will need to follow the exercises in this chapter is in the folder C:\PowerBiDesktopSamples. Please note that all the examples in this chapter presume that you have opened the Query Editor.

Viewing a Full Record

Before even starting to cleanse data, you probably need to take a good look at it. While the Power BI Desktop Query Editor is great for scrolling up and down columns to see how data compares for a single field, it is often less easy to appreciate the entire contents of a single record.

So to avoid having to scroll frenetically left and right across rows of data, the Query Editor has another brilliantly simple solution. If you click a row (or more specifically, the number of a row in the grid on the left), the Power BI Desktop Query Editor will display the contents of an entire record in a single window under the dataset. You can see an example of this in Figure 8-1, which uses the Power BI Desktop file CH08Example1.pbix.

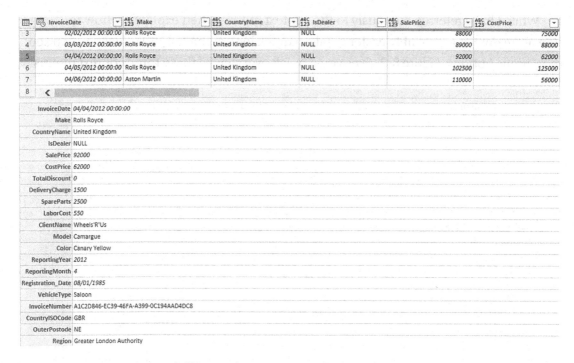

InvoiceDate	Make	CountryName	IsDealer	SalePrice	CostPrice
02/02/2012 00:00:00	Rolls Royce	United Kingdom	NULL	88000	75000
03/03/2012 00:00:00	Rolls Royce	United Kingdom	NULL	89000	88000
04/04/2012 00:00:00	Rolls Royce	United Kingdom	NULL	92000	62000
04/05/2012 00:00:00	Rolls Royce	United Kingdom	NULL	102500	125000
04/06/2012 00:00:00	Aston Martin	United Kingdom	NULL	110000	56000

InvoiceDate	04/04/2012 00:00:00
Make	Rolls Royce
CountryName	United Kingdom
IsDealer	NULL
SalePrice	92000
CostPrice	62000
TotalDiscount	0
DeliveryCharge	1500
SpareParts	2500
LaborCost	550
ClientName	Wheels'R'Us
Model	Camargue
Color	Canary Yellow
ReportingYear	2012
ReportingMonth	4
Registration_Date	08/01/1985
VehicleType	Saloon
InvoiceNumber	A1C2D846-EC39-46FA-A399-0C194AAD4DC8
CountryISOCode	GBR
OuterPostode	NE
Region	Greater London Authority

Figure 8-1. *Viewing a full record*

Note   You can alter the relative height of the recordset and dataset windows simply by dragging the gray separator line between the upper and lower windows up or down.

Power BI Desktop Query Editor Context Menus

As is normal for Windows programs, Power BI Desktop Query Editor makes full use of context (or "right-click") menus as an alternative to using the ribbons. When transforming datasets, there are three main context menus that you will probably find yourself using:

- *Table menu*: This menu appears when you right-click the top corner of the grid containing the data.

- *Column menu*: This menu appears when you right-click a column title.

- *Cell menu*: This menu appears when you right-click a data cell.

While I have referred copiously to the context menus when explaining how to transform data, it is probably easier to take a quick look at them now so that you can see the various options. Figure 8-2 gives you a quick overview of these three context menus.

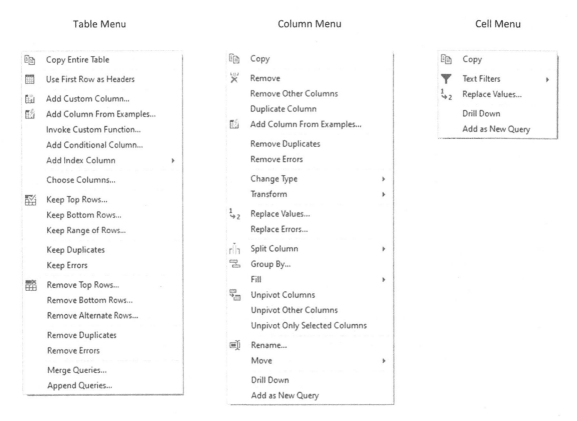

Figure 8-2. *The Power BI Desktop Query Editor context menus*

Because the options that are available in the context menus are explained throughout this, the previous, and the following four chapters, I will not explain them all in detail here.

Note   The cell context menu will reflect the data type of the cell in the filter option. So a numeric cell will have the option "Number filters."

Using the First Row as Headers

Power BI Desktop is very good at guessing if it needs to take the first record of a source dataset and have it function as the column headers. This is fundamental for two reasons:

- You avoid leaving the columns named Column1, Column2, and so on. Leaving them named generically like this would make it needlessly difficult for a user (or even yourself) to understand the data.

- You avoid having a text element (which should be the column title) in a column of figures, which can cause problems later on. This is because a whole column needs to have the same data type for another data type to be applied. Having a header text in the first row prevents this for numeric and date/time data types, for instance. This could be because the header is a text whereas the remainder of the column contains numbers or dates.

Yet there could be—albeit rare—occasions when Power BI Desktop guesses incorrectly and assumes that the first record in a dataset is data when it is really the header information. So instead of headers, you have a set of generic column titles such as Column1, Column2, and so forth. Fortunately, correcting this and using the first row as headers is a simple task:

> Click Use First Row as Headers in the Transform ribbon of the Power BI Desktop Query window.

After a few seconds, the first record disappears and the column titles become the elements that were in the first record. The Applied Steps list on the right now contains a Promoted Headers element, indicating which process has taken place. This step is highlighted.

Note   Power BI Desktop is often able to apply this step automatically when the source is a database. It can often correctly guess when the source is a file. However, it cannot always guess accurately, so sometimes you have to intervene. You can see if Power BI Desktop has had to guess this if it has added a Promoted Headers step to the Applied Steps list.

In the rare event that Power BI Desktop gets this operation wrong and presumes that a first row is column titles when it is not, you can reset the titles to be the first row by clicking the tiny triangle to the right of the Use First Row as Headers button. This displays a short menu where you can click the Use Headers as First Row option. The Applied Steps list on the right now contains a Demoted Headers element and the column titles are Column1, Column2, and so forth. You can subsequently rename the columns as you see fit.

Changing Data Type

A truly fundamental aspect of data modification is ensuring that the data is of the appropriate type; that is, if you have a column of numbers that are to be calculated at some point, then the column should be a numeric column. If it contains dates, then it should be set to one of the date or time data types. I realize that this can seem arduous and even superfluous; however, *if you want to be sure that your data can be sliced and diced correctly further down the line*, then setting the right data types at the outset is *vital*. An added bonus is that if you validate the data types early on in the process of loading data, you can see from the start if the data has any potential issues—dates that cannot be read as dates, for instance. This allows you to decide what to do with poor or unreliable data early in your work with a dataset.

The good news here is that for many data sources, Power BI Desktop applies an appropriate data type. Specifically, if you have loaded data from a database, then Power BI Desktop will recognize the data type for each column and apply a suitable native data type. Unfortunately, things can get a little more painful with file sources, specifically CSV, text, and (occasionally) Excel files, as well as some XML files. In the case of these file types, Power BI Desktop often tries to guess the data type, but there are times when it does not succeed. If it has made a stab at deducing data types, then you see a Changed Type step in the Applied Steps list. Consequently, if you are obtaining your data from these sources, then you could well be obliged to apply data types to many of the columns manually.

Note   In some cases, numbers are not meant to be interpreted as numerical data. For instance, a French postal code is five numbers, but it will never be calculated in any way. So it is good practice to let Power BI Desktop know this by changing the data type to text in cases when a numeric data type is inappropriate.

Do the following to change data type for a column or a group of columns:

1. Open the Power BI Desktop sample file
    C:\PowerBiDesktopSamples\CH08Example1.pbix.

2. Click the Transform Data button in the Home ribbon. The Query
    Editor will open.

3. Click inside the column whose data type you wish to change. If
    you want to modify several columns, then Ctrl-click the requisite
    column titles. In this example, you could select the CostPrice and
    TotalDiscount columns.

4. Click the Data Type button in the Transform ribbon. A popup
    menu of potential data types will appear.

5. Select an appropriate data type. If you have selected the CostPrice
    and TotalDiscount columns, then Whole Number is the type to
    choose.

After a few seconds, the data type will be applied. Changed Type will appear in the
Applied Steps list. The data types that you can apply are outlined in Table 8-1.

Table 8-1. *Data Types in Power BI Desktop*

Data Type	Description
Decimal Number	Converts the data to a decimal number.
Fixed Decimal Number	Converts the data to a decimal number with a fixed number of decimals.
Whole Number	Converts the data to a whole (integer) number.
Date/Time	Converts to a date and time data type.
Date	Converts to a date data type.
Time	Converts to a time data type.
Duration	Sets the data as being a duration. These are used for date and time calculations.
Text	Sets to a text data type.
True/False	Sets the data type to Boolean (true or false).
Binary	Defines the data as binary, and consequently, it is not directly visible.

Note   The Data Type button is also available in the Home ribbon. Equally, you can right-click a column header and select Change Type to select a different data type.

Inevitably, there will be times when you try to apply a data type that simply cannot be used with a certain column of data. Converting a text column (such as Make in this sample data table) into dates will simply not work. If you do this, then Power BI Desktop Query Editor will replace the column contents with Error. This is not definitive or dangerous, and all you have to do to return the data to its previous state is to delete the Changed Type step in the Applied Steps list using the technique described in the previous chapter.

Sometimes you could try and change a data type when the data type has already been changed. In this case you will get an alert like the one shown in Figure 8-3.

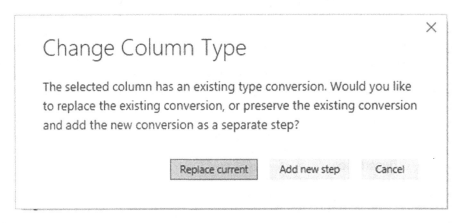

Figure 8-3. *The Change Column Type alert*

If this occurs, you can do one of two things:

- Let Power BI Desktop update the existing conversion step with the data type that you just selected.

- Add a new conversion step.

Your choice will depend on exactly what type of transformation you are applying to the underlying dataset.

It can help to alter data types at the same time for a *set* of columns where you think that this operation is necessary. There are a couple of good reasons for this approach:

- You can concentrate on getting data types right, and if you are working methodically, you are less likely to forget to set a data type.

- Applying data types for many columns (even if you are doing this in several operations, to single or multiple columns) will only add a single step to the Applied Steps list.

Note   Don't look for any data *formatting* options in Power BI Desktop Query; there aren't any. This is deliberate since this tool is designed to structure, load, and cleanse data, but not to present it. You carry out the formatting in the Power BI Desktop Data View, as you will see in Chapter 13.

Detecting Data Types

Applying the correct data type to dozens of columns can be more than a little time-consuming. Fortunately, Power BI Desktop now contains an option to apply data types automatically to a whole table:

1. In the Transform ribbon, click the Detect Data Type button.

2. Changed Type will appear in the Applied Steps list. Most of the columns will have the correct data type applied.

This technique does not always give perfect results, and there will be times when you want to override the choice of data type that Power BI Desktop has applied. Yet it is nonetheless a welcome addition to the data preparation toolset that can save you considerable time when preparing a dataset.

Data Type Indicators

It would be singularly unproductive to have to guess which column was set to which data type. So Power BI Desktop comes to your aid by indicating, visually, the corresponding data type for each column. If you look closely to the left of each individual column header, you will see a tiny icon. Each icon specifies the column's data type. The meaning of each icon is given in Table 8-2.

Table 8-2. *Data Type Icons in Power BI Desktop Query Editor*

Data Type Icon	Description
ABC 123	Any data type from among the possible data types
1²3	Whole Number
1.2	Decimal Number
$	Fixed Decimal Number
%	Percentage
A B C	Text
×√	True/False
🕘	Date/Time
📅	Date
🕐	Time
🌐	Date/Time/Timezone
🕐	Duration
📄	Binary

Switching Data Types

Another quick way to alter the data type for a column is to click the data type icon to the left of the column title and select the required data type from the context menu that you can see in Figure 8-4.

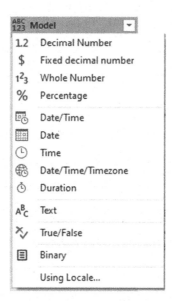

Figure 8-4. *The data type context menu*

Data Type Using Locale

When you are converting data types, you can also choose to use the current locale to specify date, time, and number formats. This means that users opening the Power BI Desktop file in another country will see date, time, and number formats adapted to the local formatting conventions. To do this:

1. Open the Query Editor (unless it is already open).

2. Click the data type icon to the left of the column title.

3. Select Using Locale from the popup menu. The Change Type with Locale dialog will appear.

4. Choose the new data type to apply from the list of available data types.

5. Select the required locale from the list of worldwide locales. The dialog will look like Figure 8-5.

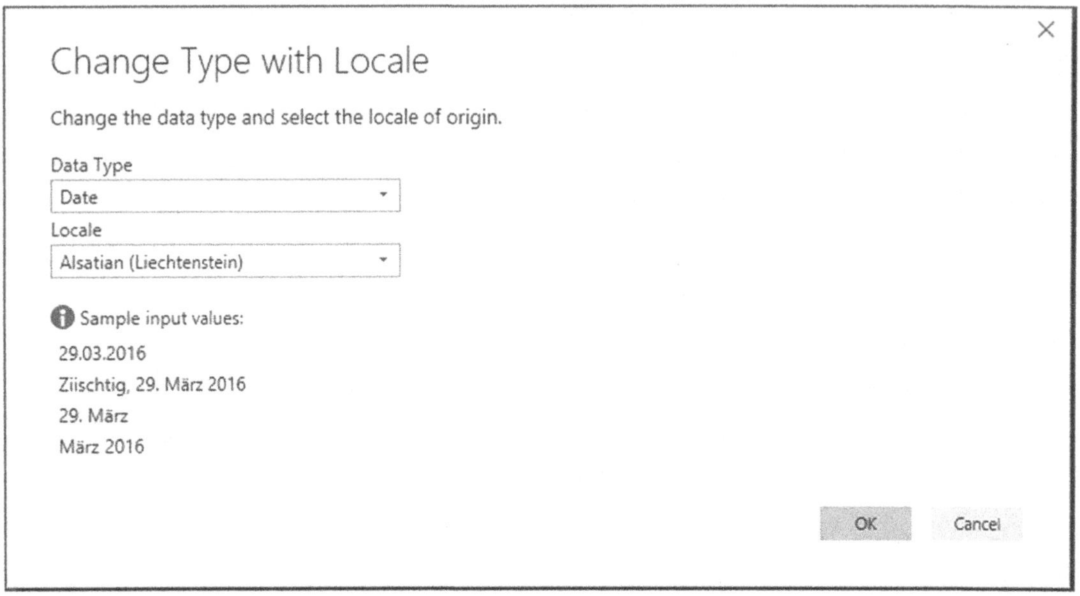

Figure 8-5. *The Change Type with Locale dialog*

6.   Click OK.

The data type will be converted to the selected locale. The Applied Steps list will
contain a step entitled Changed Type with Locale.

Replacing Values

Some data that you load will need certain values to be replaced by others in a kind of
global search-and-replace operation—just as you would in a document. For instance,
perhaps you need to standardize spellings where a make of car (to use the current
sample dataset as an example) has been entered incorrectly. To carry out this particular
data cleansing operation, do the following:

1.   In the Query Editor, click the title of the column that contains
      the data that you want to replace. The column will become
      selected. In this example, I used the Model column from the file
      CH08Sample1.pbix as an example.

2.   In the Home ribbon, click the Replace Values button. The Replace
      Values dialog will appear.

3. In the Value To Find box, enter the text or number that you want to replace. I used Ghost in this example.

4. In the Replace With box, enter the text or number that you want to replace. I used Fantôme in this example, as shown in Figure 8-6.

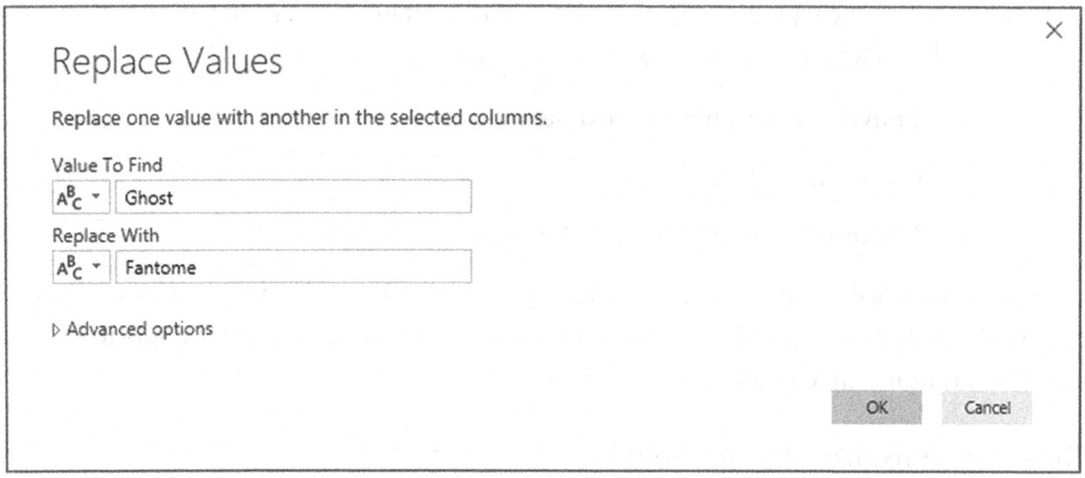

Figure 8-6. *The Replace Values dialog*

5. Click OK. The data is replaced in the entire column. Replaced Values is added to the Applied Steps list.

I only have a few comments about this technique:

- The Replace Values process searches for every occurrence of the text that you are looking for in each record of the selected columns. It does not look for the entire contents of the cell unless you specifically request this by checking the Match Entire Cell Contents check box in the advanced options.

- If you click a cell containing the contents that you want to replace (rather than the column title, as we just did), before starting the process, Power BI Desktop automatically places the cell contents in the Replace Values dialog as the value to find.

- You can only replace text in columns that contain text elements. This does not work with columns that are set as a numeric or date data type. Indeed, you will see a yellow alert triangle in the Replace Values dialog if you enter values that do not match the data type of the selected column(s).

- If you really have to replace parts of a date or figures in a numeric column with other dates or numbers, then you can

  - Convert the column to a text data type

  - Carry out the replace operation

  - Convert the column back to the original data type

The Replace Values dialog also has a few advanced options that you can apply. You can see these if you expand the "Advanced options" item by clicking the triangle to its left. These options are explained in Table 8-3.

Table 8-3. *Advanced Replace Options*

Option	Description
Match Entire Cell Contents	Only replaces the search value if it makes up the entire contents of the column for a row.
Replace Using Special Characters	Replaces the search value with a nonprinting character.
Tab	Replaces the search value with a tab character.
Carriage Return	Replaces the search value with a carriage return character.
Line Feed	Replaces the search value with a line feed character.
Carriage Return and Line Feed	Replaces the search value with a carriage return and line feed.

Note   Replacing words that are subsets of other words are dangerous. When replacing any data, make sure that you don't damage elements other than the one you intend to change.

As a final and purely spurious comment, I must add that I would never suggest rebranding a Rolls Royce, as it would be close to automotive sacrilege.

Transforming Column Contents

Power BI Desktop has a powerful toolbox of automated data transformations that allow you to standardize the contents of a column in several ways. These include

- Setting the capitalization of text columns

- Rounding numeric data or applying math functions

- Extracting date elements such as the year, month, or day (among others) from a date column

Power BI Desktop is very strict about applying transformations to appropriate types of data. This is because transforms are totally dependent on the data type of the selected column. This is yet another confirmation that applying the requisite data type is an operation that should be carried out early in any data transformation process—and certainly *before* transforming the column contents. Remember, you will only be able to select a numeric transformation if the column is a numeric data type, and you will only be able to select a date transformation if the column is a date data type. Equally, the text-based transformations can only be applied to columns that are of the text data type.

Text Transformation

Let's look at a simple transformation operation in action. As an example, I will get Power BI Desktop to convert the Make column into uppercase characters.

1. Still using the file CH08Example1.pbix (and having switched to Query Editor), click anywhere in the column whose contents you wish to transform (Make, in this case).

2. In the Transform ribbon, click the Format button. A popup menu will appear.

3. Select UPPERCASE, as shown in Figure 8-7.

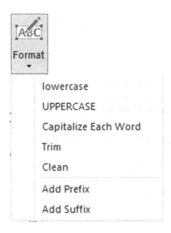

Figure 8-7. *The Format menu*

The contents of the entire column will be converted to uppercase. Uppercased Text will be added to the Applied Steps list.

As you can see from the menu for the Format button, you have five possible options when formatting (or transforming) text. These options are explained in Table 8-4.

Table 8-4. *Text Transformations*

Transformation	Description	Applied Steps Definition
Lowercase	Converts all the text to lowercase.	Lowercased Text
Uppercase	Converts all the text to uppercase.	Uppercased Text
Capitalize Each Word	Converts the first letter of each word to a capital.	Capitalized Each Word
Trim	Removes all spaces before and after the text.	Trimmed Text
Clean	Removes any nonprintable characters.	Cleaned Text
Add Prefix	Adds text at the start of the column contents.	Added Prefix
Add Suffix	Adds text at the end of the column contents.	Added Suffix

Note   I realize that Power BI Desktop Query calls text transformations formatting. Nonetheless, these options are part of the overall data transformation options.

Adding a Prefix or a Suffix

You can also add a prefix or a suffix to all the data in a column. This is as easy as the following:

1. In the Query Editor, click inside the column where you want to add a prefix.

2. In the Transform ribbon, select Format ➤ Add Prefix. The Prefix dialog will be displayed, as you can see in Figure 8-8.

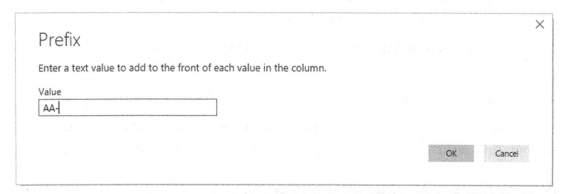

Figure 8-8. *Adding a prefix to a text*

3. Enter the prefix to add in the Value field.

4. Click OK.

The prefix that you designated will be placed at the start of every record in the dataset for the selected field.

Note   If you add a prefix or a suffix to a numeric or date/time column, then the column data type will automatically be converted to text.

Removing Leading and Trailing Spaces

There will inevitably be occasions when you inherit data that has extra spaces before, after, or before *and* after the data itself. This can be insidious, as it can cause

- Data duplication, because a value with a trailing space is *not* considered identical to the same text without the spaces that follow

251

- Sort issues, because a leading space causes an element to appear at the *top* of a sorted list

- Grouping errors, because elements with spaces are not part of the same group as elements without spaces

Fortunately, Power BI Desktop Query has a ruthlessly efficient solution to this problem.

1. Still using the file CH08Example1.pbix (and having switched to Query Editor), click anywhere in the column whose contents you wish to transform (Make, in this case).

2. In the Transform ribbon, click the Format button. A popup menu will appear.

3. Select Trim from the menu.

All superfluous leading and trailing spaces will be removed from the data in the column. This can help when sorting, grouping, and deduplicating records.

Removing Nonprinting Characters

Some source data can contain somewhat insidious elements called nonprinting characters. These can, even if they are nearly always invisible to humans, cause problems when you print reports and dashboards.

If you suspect that your source data contains nonprinting characters, you can remove them simply like this:

1. In the Query Editor, click inside the column (or select the columns) that you know to contain (or that you suspect contain) nonprinting characters.

2. Click Format ➤ Clean.

Power BI Desktop will add Cleaned Text to the list of Applied Steps.

Number Transformations

Just as you can transform the contents of text-based columns, you can also apply transformations to numeric values. As an example, suppose that you want to round up all the figures in a column to the nearest whole number.

1.   In the Query Editor, click anywhere in the column whose contents
     you wish to transform (TotalDiscount, in this case).

2.   In the Transform ribbon, click the Rounding button. A popup
     menu will appear showing all the available options. You can see
     this in Figure 8-9.

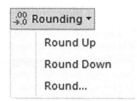

Figure 8-9. *Rounding options*

3.   Select Round Up.

The values in the entire column will be rounded up to the nearest whole number.
Rounded Up will be added to the Applied Steps list.

The other possible numeric transformations that are available are described in
Table 8-5. Because these numeric transformations use several buttons in the Transform
ribbon, I have indicated which button to use to get the desired result.

Table 8-5. *Number Transformations*

Transformation	Description	Applied Steps Definition
Rounding ➤ Round Up	Rounds each number to the specified number of decimal places.	Rounded Up
Rounding ➤ Round Down	Rounds each number down.	Rounded Down
Round…	Rounds each number to the number of decimals that you specify. If you specify a negative number, you round to a given decimal.	Rounded Off
Scientific ➤ Absolute Value	Makes the number absolute (positive).	

(continued)

Table 8-5. (*continued*)

Transformation	Description	Applied Steps Definition
Scientific ➤ Power ➤ Square	Returns the square of the number in each cell.	Calculated Square
Scientific ➤ Power ➤ Cube	Returns the cube of the number in each cell.	Calculated Cube Value
Scientific ➤ Power ➤ Power	Raises each number to the power that you specify.	Calculated Power
Scientific ➤ Square Root	Returns the square root of the number in each cell.	Square Root
Scientific ➤ Exponent	Returns the exponent of the number in each cell.	Calculated Exponent
Scientific ➤ Logarithm ➤ Base 10	Returns the base 10 logarithm of the number in each cell.	Calculated Base 10 Logarithm
Scientific ➤ Logarithm ➤ Natural	Returns the natural logarithm of the number in each cell.	Calculated Natural Logarithm
Scientific ➤ Factorial	Gives the factorial of numbers in the column.	Calculated Factorial
Trigonometry ➤ Sine	Gives the sine of the numbers in the column.	Calculated Sine
Trigonometry ➤ Cosine	Gives the cosine of the numbers in the column.	Calculated Cosine
Trigonometry ➤ Tangent	Gives the tangent of the numbers in the column.	Calculated Tangent
Trigonometry ➤ ArcSine	Gives the arcsine of the numbers in the column.	Calculated ArcSine
Trigonometry ➤ ArcCosine	Gives the arccosine of the numbers in the column.	Calculated ArcCosine
Trigonometry ➤ ArcTangent	Gives the arctangent of the numbers in the column.	Calculated ArcTangent

Note   Power BI Desktop Query will not even let you try to apply numeric transformation to texts or dates. The relevant buttons remain grayed out if you click inside a column of letters or dates.

Calculating Numbers

Power BI Desktop Query can also apply simple arithmetic to the figures in a column. Suppose, for instance, that you want to multiply all the sale prices by 110% as part of your forecasts. This is how you can do just that:

1. Still using the file CH08Example1.pbix (and having switched to Query Editor), click inside any column of numbers. In this example, I used the column SalePrice.

2. Click the Standard button in the Transform ribbon. The menu will appear as you can see in Figure 8-10.

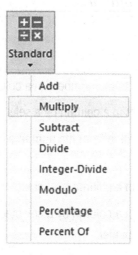

Figure 8-10. Applying a calculation to a column

3. Click Multiply. The Multiply dialog will appear.

4. Enter **1.1** in the Value box. The dialog will look like the one shown in Figure 8-11.

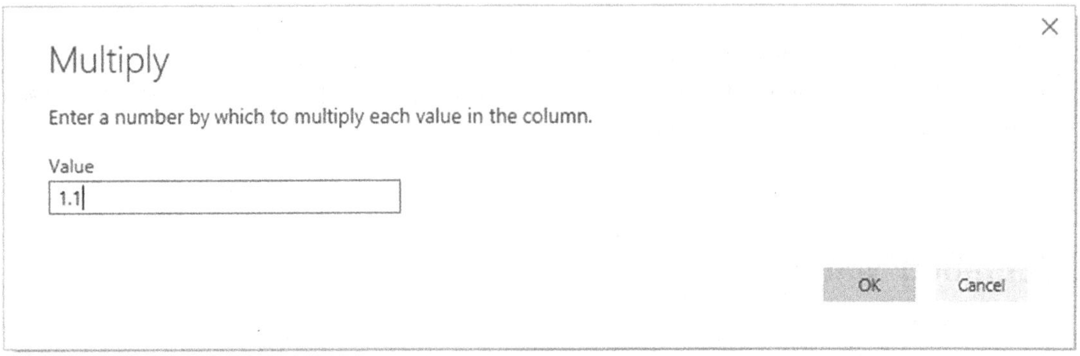

Figure 8-11. *Applying a calculation to a column*

5.   Click OK.

All the numbers in the selected column will be multiplied by 1.1. In other words, they are now 110% of the original value. Table 8-6 describes the possible math operations that you can carry out in Power BI Desktop Query.

Table 8-6. *Applying Basic Calculations*

Transformation	Description	Applied Steps Definition
Add	Adds a selected value to the numbers in a column.	Added to Column
Multiply	Multiplies the numbers in a column by a selected value.	Multiplied Column
Subtract	Subtracts a selected value from the numbers in a column.	Subtracted from Column
Divide	Divides the numbers in a column by a selected value.	Divided Column
Integer-Divide	Divides the numbers in a column by a selected value and removes any remainder.	Integer-Divided Column
Modulo	Divides the numbers in a column by a selected value and leaves only the remainder.	Calculated Modulo
Percentage	Applies the selected percentage to the column.	Calculated Percentage
Percent Of	Expresses the value in the column as a percent of the value that you enter.	Calculated Percent Of

Note   You can also carry out many types of calculations in Power BI Desktop Data View and avoid carrying out calculations in the Query Editor. Indeed, many Power BI Desktop purists seem to prefer that anything resembling a calculation should take place inside the data model rather than at the query stage. As ever, I will let you decide which approach you prefer. Be aware that some heavy transforms can slow the reports down if calculated at runtime, whereas others can only be effective as part of a well-thought-out calculation process.

Finally, it is important to remember that you are altering the data when you carry out this kind of operation. In the real world, you might be safer duplicating a column before profoundly altering the data it contains. This allows you to keep the initial data available, albeit at the cost of increasing both the load time and the size of the Power BI Desktop file.

Date Transformations

Transforming dates follows similar principles to transforming text and numbers. As an example, here is how to isolate the month from a date:

1. Still using the file CH08Example1.pbix (and having switched to Query Editor), click inside the InvoiceDate column.

2. In the Transform ribbon, click the Date button. The menu will appear.

3. Click Year. The submenu will appear.

4. Select Year. The year part of the date will replace all the dates in the InvoiceDate column.

The other possible date transformations that are possible are given in Table 8-7.

Table 8-7. *Date Transformations*

Transformation	Description	Applied Steps Definition
Age	Calculates the date and time difference (in days and hours) between the original date and the current local time.	Calculated Age
Date Only	Converts the data to a date without the time element.	Calculated Date
Year ➤ Year	Extracts the year from the date.	Calculated Year
Year ➤ Start of Year	Returns the first day of the year for the date.	Calculated Start of Year
Year ➤ End of Year	Returns the last day of the year for the date.	Calculated End of Year
Month ➤ Month	Extracts the number of the month from the date.	Calculated Month
Month ➤ Start of Month	Returns the first day of the month for the date.	Calculated Start of Month
Month ➤ End of Month	Returns the last day of the month for the date.	Calculated End of Month
Month ➤ Days in Month	Returns the number of days in the month for the date.	Calculated Days in Month
Month ➤ Name of Month	Returns the name of the month for the date.	Calculated Name of Month
Day ➤ Day	Extracts the day from the date.	Calculated Day
Day ➤ Day of Week	Returns the weekday as a number (Monday is 1, Tuesday is 2, etc.).	Calculated Day of Week
Day ➤ Day of Year	Calculates the number of days since the start of the year for the date.	Calculated Day of Year
Day ➤ Start of Day	Transforms the value to the start of the day for a date and time.	Calculated Start of Day
Day ➤ End of Day	Transforms the value to the end of the day for a date and time.	Calculated End of Day

(*continued*)

Table 8-7. (*continued*)

Transformation	Description	Applied Steps Definition
Day ➤ Name of Day	Returns the weekday as a day of week.	Calculated Name of Day
Quarter ➤ Quarter	Returns the calendar quarter of the year for the date.	Calculated Quarter
Quarter ➤ Start of Quarter	Returns the first date of the calendar quarter of the year for the date.	Calculated Start of Quarter
Quarter ➤ End of Quarter	Returns the last date of the calendar quarter of the year for the date.	Calculated End of Quarter
Week ➤ Week of Year	Calculates the number of weeks since the start of the year for the date.	Calculated Week of Year
Week ➤ Week of Month	Calculates the number of weeks since the start of the month for the date.	Calculated Week of Month
Week ➤ Start of Week	Returns the date for the first day of the week (Sunday) for the date.	Calculated Start of Week
Week ➤ End of Week	Returns the date for the last day of the week (Sunday) for the date.	Calculated End of Week

Time Transformations

You can also transform date/time or time values into their component parts using Power BI Desktop Query. This is extremely similar to how you apply date transformations, but in the interest of completeness, the following explains how to do this:

1. Click inside the InvoiceDate column.

2. In the Transform ribbon, click the Time button. The menu will appear.

3. Click Hour. The hour part of the time will replace all the values in the InvoiceDate column.

Note   Time transformations can only be applied to columns of the date/time or time data types.

The range of time transformations is given in Table 8-8.

Table 8-8. *Time Transformations*

Transformation	Description	Applied Steps Definition
Time Only	Isolates the time part of a date and time.	Extracted Time
Local Time	Converts the date/time to local time from date/time and timezone values.	Extracted Local Time
Parse	Extracts the date and/or date/time elements from a text.	Parsed DateTime
Hour ➤ Hour	Isolates the hour from a date/time or date value.	Extracted Hour
Hour ➤ Start of Hour	Returns the start of the hour from a date/time or time value.	Calculated Start of Hour
Hour ➤ End of Hour	Returns the end of the hour from a date/time or time value.	Calculated End of Hour
Minute	Isolates the minute from a date/time or time value.	Extracted Minute
Second	Isolates the second from a date/time or time value.	Extracted Second
Earliest	Returns the earliest time from a date/time or time value.	Calculated Earliest
Latest	Returns the latest time from a date/time or time value.	Calculated Latest

Note   In the real world, you could well want to leave a source column intact and apply number or date transformations to a copy of the column. To do this, simply apply the same transformation technique, only use the buttons in the Add Column ribbon instead of those in the Transform ribbon.

Duration

If you have values in a column that can be interpreted as a duration (in days, hours, minutes, and seconds), then Power BI Desktop Query can extract the component parts of the duration as a data transformation. For this to work, however, the column *must* be set to the duration data type. This means that the contents of the column have to be interpreted as a duration by Power BI Desktop. Any values that are incompatible with this data type will be set to error values.

If you have duration data, you can extract its component parts like this:

1. Still using the file CH08Example1.pbix (and having switched to Query Editor), click inside the column InvoiceDate.

2. In the Transform ribbon, click the Duration button. The menu will appear.

3. Click Hour. The hour part of the time will replace all the values in the InvoiceDate column.

The range of duration transformations is given in Table 8-9.

Table 8-9. *Duration Transformations*

Transformation	Description	Applied Steps Definition
Days	Isolates the day element from a duration value.	Extracted Days
Hours	Isolates the hour element from a duration value.	Extracted Hours
Minutes	Isolates the minute element from a duration value.	Extracted Minutes
Seconds	Isolates the second element from a duration value.	Extracted Seconds
Total Days	Displays the duration value as the number of days and a fraction representing hours, minutes, and seconds.	Calculated Total Days
Total Hours	Displays the duration value as the number of hours and a fraction representing minutes and seconds.	Calculated Total Hours

(continued)

Table 8-9. (*continued*)

Transformation	Description	Applied Steps Definition
Total Minutes	Displays the duration value as the number of minutes and a fraction representing seconds.	Calculated Total Minutes
Total Seconds	Displays the duration value as the number of seconds and a fraction representing milliseconds.	Calculated Total Seconds
Multiply	Multiplies the duration (and all its component parts) by a value that you enter.	Multiplied Column
Divide	Divides the duration (and all its component parts) by a value that you enter.	Divided Column
Statistics ➤ Sum	Returns the total for all the duration elements in the column.	Calculated Sum
Statistics ➤ Minimum	Returns the minimum value of all the duration elements in the column.	Calculated Minimum
Statistics ➤ Maximum	Returns the maximum value of all the duration elements in the column.	Calculated Maximum
Statistics ➤ Median	Returns the median value for all the duration elements in the column.	Calculated Median
Statistics ➤ Average	Returns the average for all the duration elements in the column.	Calculated Average

Note   If you multiply or divide a duration, Power BI Desktop Query displays a dialog so that you can enter the value to multiply or divide the duration by.

Filling Down Empty Cells

Imagine a data source where the data has come into Power BI Desktop from a matrix-style structure. The result is that some columns only contain a single example of an element and then a series of empty cells until the next element in the list. If this is difficult to imagine, then take a look at the sample file CarMakeAndModelMatrix.xlsx shown in Figure 8-12.

Make	Marque	Sales
Aston Martin	DB4	391000
	DB7	500740
	DB9	915070
	DBS	230000
	Rapide	225000
	Vanquish	746500
	Vantage	320850
	Zagato	178500
Bentley	Arnage	44000
	Azure	239250
	Continental	991250
	Turbo R	347500
Jaguar	XJ12	303500
	XJ6	602000
	XK	1092250
MGB	GT	315000
Rolls Royce	Camargue	810300
	Phantom	178500
	Silver Ghost	649500
	Silver Seraph	288500
	Silver Shadow	308500
	Wraith	178500

Figure 8-12. *A matrix data table in Excel*

All these blank cells are a problem since we need a full data table—or rather, they would be, if Power BI Desktop did not have a really cool way of overcoming this particular difficulty. Do the following to solve this problem:

1. Open a new Power BI Desktop file.

2. In the splash screen, click Get Data.

3. In the Get Data dialog, select Excel. Then click Connect and navigate to `C:\PowerBiDesktopSamples\ CarMakeAndModelMatrix.xlsx`.

4. Click Open, select Sheet 1, and click Transform Data. This will take you directly to the Query Editor.

5. Click inside the column that contains the empty cells; make sure that you click where you want to replace the empty cells with the contents of the first non-empty cell above.

6. In the Transform ribbon, click Fill. The menu will appear.

7. Select Down. The blank cells will be replaced by the value in the first non-empty cell above. Filled Down will be added to the Applied Steps list.

The table will now look like Figure 8-13.

	A^B_C Make	A^B_C Marque	1^2_3 Sales
1	Aston Martin	DB4	391000
2	Aston Martin	DB7	500740
3	Aston Martin	DB9	915070
4	Aston Martin	DBS	230000
5	Aston Martin	Rapide	225000
6	Aston Martin	Vanquish	746500
7	Aston Martin	Vantage	320850
8	Aston Martin	Zagato	178500
9	Bentley	Arnage	44000
10	Bentley	Azure	239250
11	Bentley	Continental	991250
12	Bentley	Turbo R	347500
13	Jaguar	XJ12	303500
14	Jaguar	XJ6	602000
15	Jaguar	XK	1092250

Figure 8-13. *A data table with empty cells replaced by the correct data*

Note   This technique is built to handle a fairly specific problem and only really works if the imported data is grouped by the column containing the missing elements.

Although rare, you can also use this technique to fill empty cells with the value from below. If you need to do this, just select Fill ➤ Up from the Transform ribbon. In either case, you need to be aware that the technique is applied to the entire column.

Extracting Part of a Column's Contents

There could well be times when the contents of a source column contain more data than you actually need. In cases like this, Power BI Desktop can help you by extracting only part of a column. This technique works like this:

1. Load the C:\PowerBiDesktopSamples\CH08Example1.pbix sample file and click Transform Data.

2. Click inside the InvoiceNumber column.

3. In the Transform ribbon, click Extract ➤ Text Before Delimiter. The Text Before Delimiter dialog will be displayed.

4. Enter a hyphen (or a minus sign) in the Delimiter field. The dialog will look like Figure 8-14.

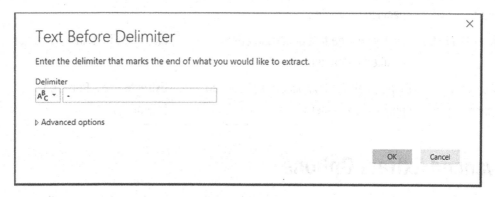

Figure 8-14. *The Text Before Delimiter dialog*

5. Click OK. The contents of the field will be replaced by the characters before the hyphen. A step named Extracted Text Before Delimiter will be added to the Applied Steps list.

The Extract function allows you to choose from a variety of ways in which you can extract a subset of data from a column. The currently available options are explained in Table 8-10.

Table 8-10. *Extract Transformations*

Transformation	Description	Applied Steps Definition
Length	Displays the length in characters of the contents of the field.	Extracted Length
First Characters	Displays a specified number of characters from the left of the field.	Extracted First Characters
Last Characters	Displays a specified number of characters from the right of the field.	Extracted Last Characters
Range	Displays a specified number of characters between a specified start and end position (in characters, from the left of the field).	Extracted Range
Text Before Delimiter	Displays all the text occurring before a specified character.	Extracted Text Before Delimiter
Text After Delimiter	Displays all the text occurring after a specified character.	Extracted Text After Delimiter
Text Between Delimiters	Displays all the text occurring between two specified characters.	Extracted Text Between Delimiters

Advanced Extract Options

Three of the Extract options (Text Before Delimiter, Text After Delimiter, and Text Between Delimiters) let you apply some advanced options that allow you to push the envelope even further when extracting data from a column. These techniques are explained in the following two sections.

Text Before and After Delimiter

If you are extracting part of the contents of a column and you are using a delimiter to isolate the text you want to keep, then you have a couple of additional options available.

You can access these options from the dialog that you saw in Figure 8-14 by clicking Advanced options. The dialog will then look like the one shown in Figure 8-15.

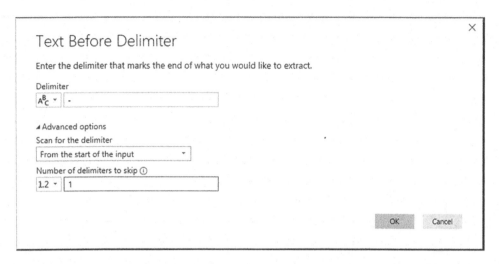

Figure 8-15. *The Advanced options of the Text Before and Text After Delimiter dialogs*

The two options that you now have are

- *Scan for the delimiter*: This option lets you choose between working forward from the start of the contents of the column and working backward from the end of the contents of the column to locate the delimiter you are searching for.

- *Number of delimiters to skip*: Here you can specify that it is the *n*th occurrence of a delimiter that interests you.

Text Between Delimiters

The Advanced options of the Text Between Delimiters dialog essentially lets you apply the same options that you saw previously, only for both the initial delimiter and the final delimiter. In Figure 8-16 you can see this in the Text Between Delimiters dialog.

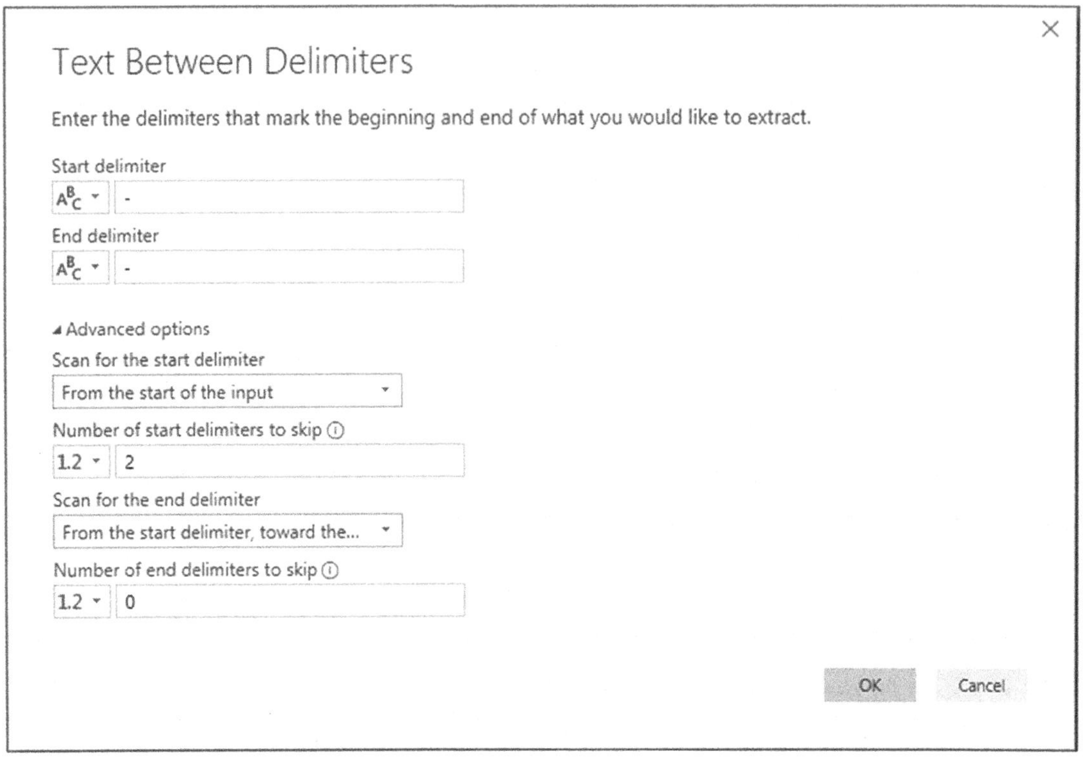

Enter the delimiters that mark the beginning and end of what you would like to extract.

Start delimiter

A^B_C ▾ -

End delimiter

A^B_C ▾ -

⊿ Advanced options
Scan for the start delimiter

From the start of the input   ▾

Number of start delimiters to skip ⓘ

1.2 ▾ 2

Scan for the end delimiter

From the start delimiter, toward the... ▾

Number of end delimiters to skip ⓘ

1.2 ▾ 0

OK   Cancel

Figure 8-16. The Advanced options of the Text Between Delimiters dialog

---

Note   The Extract button can be found in both the Transform and New Column ribbons. If you carry out this operation from the Transform ribbon, then the contents of the existing column will be replaced. If you use the button in the Add Column ribbon, then a new column containing the extracted text will be added at the right of any existing columns.

Duplicating Columns

Sometimes you just need a simple copy of a column, with nothing added and nothing taken away. This is where the Duplicate Column button comes into play.

1. Load the C:\PowerBiDesktopSamples\CH08Example1.pbix
    sample file.

2. Open the Power BI Desktop Query Editor.

3. Click inside (or the title of) the column that you want to duplicate. I will use the Make column in this example.

4. In the Add Column ribbon, click the Duplicate Column button. After a few seconds, a copy of the column is created at the right of the existing table. Duplicated Column will appear in the Applied Steps list.

5. Scroll to the right of the table and rename the existing column; it is currently named Make-Copy.

Note   The duplicate column is named Original Column Name-Copy. I find that it helps to rename copies of columns sooner rather than later in a data mashup process.

Splitting Columns

Sometimes a source column contains data that you really need to break up into smaller pieces across two or more columns. The following are classic cases where this happens:

- A column contains a list of elements, separated by a specific character (known as a *delimiter*).

- A column contains a list of elements, but the elements can be divided at specific places in the column.

- A column contains a concatenated text that needs to be split into its composite elements (a bank account number and a Social Security number are examples of this).

The following short sections explain how to handle such eventualities.

Splitting Column by a Delimiter

Here is another requirement that you may encounter occasionally. The data that has been imported has a column that needs to be further split into multiple columns. Imagine a text file where columns are separated by semicolons, and these subdivisions each contain a column that holds a comma-separated list of elements. Once you have imported the file, you then need to further separate the contents of this column that uses a different delimiter.

Here is what you can do to split the data from one column over several columns:

1. Open the C:\PowerBiDesktopSamples\CH08DataToParse.pbix sample file and switch to the Query Editor.

2. In the Transform ribbon, click Use First Row as Headers.

3. Click inside the ClientList column. You can see that this column contains several data elements, each separated by a semicolon.

4. In the Transform ribbon, click Split Column ➤ By Delimiter. The Split Column by Delimiter dialog appears.

5. Select Semicolon from the list of available options in the "Select or enter delimiter" popup (although the Query Editor could well have detected this already).

6. Click "Each occurrence of the delimiter" as the location to split the text column. The dialog should look like Figure 8-17.

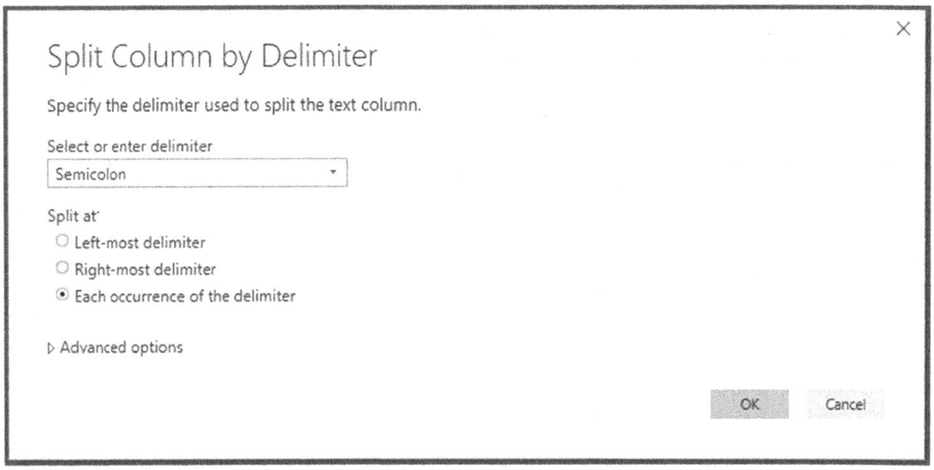

Figure 8-17. *Splitting a column using a delimiter*

7.   Click OK. Split Column by Delimiter will appear in the Applied
      Steps list.

The initial column is replaced and all the new columns are named InvoiceNumber.1,
InvoiceNumber.2, and so forth. As many additional columns as there are delimiters are
created; each is named (*Column.n*) and is sequentially numbered. The result of this
operation looks like Figure 8-18.

	A^BC ClientList.1	A^BC ClientList.2	A^BC ClientList.3	A^BC ClientList.4
1	Aldo Motors	Uttoxeter	Staffs	ST17 99RZ
2	Honest John	London		NSW1 1A
3	Bright Orange	Birmingham	NULL	B1 50AZ
4	Cut'n'Shut	Manchester	NULL	M1 5AZ
5	Wheels'R'Us	London	NULL	SE1 4YY
6	Les Arnaqueurs	Paris	NULL	75010
7	Crippen & Co	Glasgow	NULL	G1 8GH
8	Rocky Riding	New York	New York	NULL
9	Voitures Diplomatiques S.A.	Geneva	NULL	NULL
10	Karz	Stuttgart	NULL	NULL
11	Costa Del Speed	Madrid	NULL	NULL
12	Olde Englande	Shrewsbury	NULL	SY10 9AX
13	Impressive Wheels	Liverpool	NULL	L5 9ZZ
14	Smooth Riders	Telford	NULL	TF6 9RR
15	Luxury Rentals	Gloucester	NULL	GL7 9AS
16	Premium Motor Vehicles	Newcastle upon Tyne	NULL	NE3 3SS
17	Chateau Moi	Lyon	NULL	69001
18	Vive la Vitesse!	Marseille	NULL	13002
19	Carosse Des Papes	Avignon	NULL	84000
20	Three Country Cars	Basle	NULL	NULL

Figure 8-18.   *The results of splitting a column*

This particular process has several options, and their consequences can be fairly
far-reaching as far as the data is concerned. Table 8-11 contains a description of the
available options.

Table 8-11. *Delimiter Split Options*

Option	Description
Colon	Uses the colon (:) as the delimiter.
Comma	Uses the comma (,) as the delimiter.
Equals Sign	Uses the equals sign (=) as the delimiter.
Semi-Colon	Uses the semicolon (;) as the delimiter.
Space	Uses the space ( ) as the delimiter.
Tab	Uses the tab character as the delimiter.
Custom	Lets you enter a custom delimiter.
At the Left-Most Delimiter	Splits the column once only at the first occurrence of the delimiter.
At the Right-Most Delimiter	Splits the column once only at the last occurrence of the delimiter.
At Each Occurrence of the Delimiter	Splits the column into as many columns as there are delimiters.
Split into Columns	This leaves the number of rows as it is in the dataset and creates new columns for each new element resulting from the split operation.
Split into Rows	Creates a new row for each new element resulting from the split operation and duplicates the existing record as many times as there are split elements.

Advanced Options for Delimiter Split

There are a small number of advanced options that are available when splitting text by delimiters. These are displayed when you click the Advanced options element in the Split Column by Delimiter dialog and are explained in Table 8-12.

Table 8-12. *Delimiter Split Options*

Advanced Options ➤ Number of Columns to Split Into	Allows you to set a maximum number of columns into which the data is split in chunks of the given number of characters. Any extra columns are placed in the rightmost column.
Advanced Options ➤ Quote Character	Separators inside a text that is contained in double quotes are not used to split the text into columns. Setting this option to "none" will split elements inside quotes.
Split using special characters	Enables the Insert Special Character button. You can then click this button and select the special character to split data on. The choice is between Tab, Carriage Return, Line-Feed, Carriage Return, and Line-Feed or non-breaking space.

Splitting Columns by Number of Characters

Another variant on this theme is when text in each column is a fixed number of characters and needs to be broken down into constituent parts at specific intervals. Suppose, for instance, that you have a field where each group of (a certain number of) characters has a specific meaning, and you want to break it into multiple columns. Alternatively, suppose you want to extract the leftmost or rightmost n characters and leave the rest. A bank account and a Social Security number are examples of this. This is where splitting a column by the number of characters can come in useful. As the principle is very similar to the process that we just saw, I will not repeat the whole thing again. All you have to do is choose the "By number of characters" menu option at step 5 in the previous exercise. Options for this type of operation are given in Table 8-13.

Table 8-13. *Options When Splitting a Column by Number of Characters*

Option	Description
Number of Characters	Lets you define the number of characters of data before splitting the column.
Once, As Far Left As Possible	Splits the column once only at the given number of characters from the left.
Once, As Far Right As Possible	Splits the column once only at the given number of characters from the right.
Repeatedly	Splits the column as many times as necessary to cut it into segments every defined number of characters.
Advanced Options ➤ Number of Columns to Split Into	Allows you to set a maximum number of columns into which the data is split in chunks of the given number of characters. Any extra columns are placed in the rightmost column.
Split into Columns	This leaves the number of rows as it is in the dataset and crates new columns for each new element resulting from the split operation.
Split into Rows	Creates a new row for each new element resulting from the split operation and duplicates the existing record as many times as there are split elements.

There are a couple of things to note when splitting columns:

- When splitting by a delimiter, Power BI Desktop makes a good attempt at guessing the maximum number of columns into which the source column must be split. If it gets this wrong (and you can see what its guesstimate is if you expand the Advanced options box), you can override the number here.

- If you select a Custom Delimiter, Power BI Desktop displays a new box in the dialog where you can enter a specific delimiter.

- Not every record has to have the same number of delimiters. Power BI Desktop simply leaves the rightmost column(s) blank if there are fewer split elements for a row.

Note   You can only split columns if they are text data. The Split Column button remains grayed out if your intention is to try to split a date or numeric column.

Merging Columns

You may be feeling a certain sense of déjà vu when you read the title of this section. After all, we saw how to merge columns (i.e., how to fuse the data from several columns into a single, wider column) in a previous chapter, did we not?

Yes, we did indeed. However, this is not the only time in this chapter that you will see something that you have tried previously. This is because Power BI Desktop Query repeats several of the options that are in the Transform ribbon in the Add Column ribbon. While these functions all work in much the same way, there is one essential difference. If you select an option from the Transform ribbon, then the column(s) that you selected is *modified*. If you select a similar option from the Add Column ribbon, then the original column(s) will not be altered, but a *new column* is added containing the results of the data transformation.

Merging columns is a case in point. Now, as I went into detail as to how to execute this kind of data transformation in the previous chapter, I will not describe it all over again here. Suffice it to say, if you Ctrl-click the headings of two or more columns and then click Merge Columns in the Add Column ribbon, you will still see the data from the selected columns concatenated into a single column. However, this time the original columns *remain* in the dataset. The new column is named Merged, exactly as was the case for the first of the columns that you selected when merging columns using the Transform ribbon.

The following are other functions that can either overwrite the data in existing columns *or* display the result as a new column:

- *Format*: Trims or changes the capitalization of text

- *Extract*: Takes part of a column and creates another column from this data

- *Parse*: Adds a column containing the source column data as JSON or XML strings

- *Statistics*: Creates a new column of aggregated numeric values

- *Standard*: Creates a new column of calculated numeric values

- *Scientific*: Creates a new column by applying certain kinds of math operations to the values in a column

- *Trigonometry*: Creates a new column by applying certain kinds of trigonometric operations to the values in a column

- *Rounding*: Creates a new column by rounding the values in a column

- *Information*: Creates a new column indicating arithmetical information about the values in a column

- *Date*: Creates a new column by extracting date elements from the values in a date column

- *Time*: Creates a new column by extracting time elements from the values in a time or date/time column

- *Duration*: Creates a new column by calculating the duration between two dates or date/times

When transforming data, the art is to decide whether you want or need to keep the original column before applying one of these functions. Yet, once again, it is not really fundamental if you later decide that you made an incorrect decision, as you can always backtrack. Alternatively, you can always decide to insert new columns as a matter of principle and delete any columns that you really do not need at a later stage in the data transformation process.

Creating Columns from Examples

Creating your own columns can be a little scary if you have not had much experience with Excel or Power Pivot formulas, so the Power BI Desktop development team has tried to make your life easier by adding another way to create custom columns. Instead of referring to columns by the column name (and having to handle square brackets and other peculiar characters), you can build a new column by using the actual data in a row.

The following steps show an example of how to do this:

1. Load the `C:\PowerBiDesktopSamples\CH08Example1.pbix` sample file.

2. Click Transform Data.

3. In the Add Column ribbon, click Column From Examples. A new kind of formula bar will appear above the data. It will look like Figure 8-19. At the same time, a new, empty column will be created at the right of the existing data.

Figure 8-19.   *Creating a column from examples*

4. Double-click inside the new column on the right. A list of data from each field will be displayed, as shown in Figure 8-20.

Figure 8-20.   *Displaying the data from a row when creating a column from examples*

5. Double-click Red to select the data from the Color column.

6. Enter a space, a hyphen, and a space, then type **Camargue** (this is the name of the model for this row).

7. Click OK in the formula bar at the top.

Power BI Desktop will add a new column containing the color, a separator, and the model. Inserted Merged Column will be added as a new step in the Applied Steps list.

Note   In the popup menu for the Column from Examples button, you can choose to take all existing columns as the basis for the example or only any columns that you have previously selected.

As you can see from this short example, creating columns by example lets you use the data from a column rather than the column name. It also removes the need for double quotes and ampersand characters that you had to use when writing the code to create a new column in the previous section.

Tip   If you select Column From Examples ➤ From Selection, then you will only see data from the selected columns when you double-click inside the new column to see samples of data as you did in step 6 of this example.

Adding Conditional Columns

Not all additional columns are a simple extraction or concatenation of existing data. There will be times when you will want to apply some simple conditions that define the contents of a new column. This is where Power BI Desktop's Conditional Column function comes into its own.

Conditional Columns are probably best understood with the aid of a practical example. So let's suppose that you want to add a column that contains a comment on the type of buyer for Brilliant British Cars's products. Here is how you can do this:

1. Load the `C:\PowerBiDesktopSamples\CH08Example1.pbix` sample file.

2. Click Transform Data.

3. In the Add Column ribbon, click Conditional Column. The Add Conditional Column dialog will appear.

4. Enter **BuyerType** in the "New column name" field.

5. Select Make as the column name.

6. Leave Equals as the operator.

7. Enter **Rolls Royce** as the value.

8. Enter **Posh** as the output.

9. Click Add Rule.

10. Select Make as the column name, leave Equals as the operator, enter **Bentley** as the value, and add **Classy** as the output.

11. Enter **Bling** in the Otherwise field. The dialog will look like Figure 8-21.

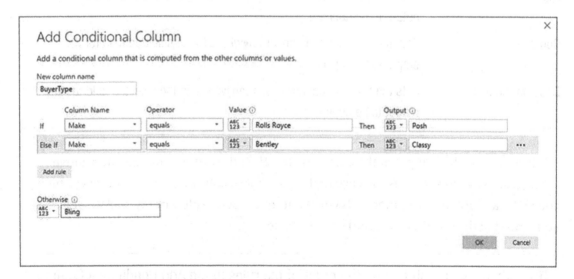

Figure 8-21. *The Add Conditional Column dialog*

12. Click OK. The new column will be added containing either Posh, Classy, or Bling, depending on the make for each record. Added Conditional Columns will appear as the new step in the Applied Steps list.

As you can see from the Add Conditional Column dialog, it has a range of options that you can tweak when defining the logic for the data matching. These options are outlined in Table 8-14.

Table 8-14. *Custom Column Operators*

Operator	Description
Equals	Sets the text that must match the contents of the selected field for the output to be applied.
Does Not Equal	Sets the text that must not match the contents of the selected field for the output to be applied.
Begins With	Sets the text at the left of the selected field for the output to be applied.
Does Not Begin With	Sets the text that must not appear at the left of the selected field for the output to be applied.
Ends With	Sets the text at the right of the selected field for the output to be applied.
Does Not End With	Sets the text that must not appear at the right of the selected field for the output to be applied.
Contains	Sets the text that can appear anywhere in the selected field for the output to be applied.
Does Not Contain	Sets the text that cannot appear anywhere in the selected field for the output to be applied.

It is also worth noting that the comparison value, the output, and the alternative output can be values (as was the case in this example), columns, or parameters (which you will learn about in Chapter 9). If you want to remove a rule, simply click the ellipses at the right of the required rule and select Delete.

Tip   Should you wish to alter the order of the rules in the Add Conditional Column dialog, all you have to do is click the ellipses at the right of the selected rule and select Move Up or Move Down from the popup menu.

Index Columns

An index column is a new column that numbers every record in the table sequentially. This numbering scheme applies to the table, because it is currently sorted and begins at zero. There are many situations where an index column can be useful. The following are some examples:

- Reapply a previous sort order.

- Create a unique reference for every record.

- Prepare a recordset for use as a dimension table in a Power BI Desktop data model. In cases like this, the index column becomes what dimensional modelers call a *surrogate key*.

This list is not intended to be exhaustive in any way; you will almost certainly find other uses as you work with Power BI Desktop. Whatever the need, here is how to add an index column:

1. In the Add Column ribbon, click Index Column. The new, sequentially numbered column is added at the right of the table, and Added Index is added to the Applied Steps list.

2. Scroll to the right of the table and rename the index column; it is currently named Index.

You have a fairly free hand when it comes to deciding how to begin numbering an index column. The choices are as follows:

- Start at 0 and increment by a value of 1 for each row.

- Start at 1 and increment by a value of 1 for each row.

- Start at any number and increase by any number.

As you saw in step 1, the default is for Power BI Desktop Query to begin numbering rows at 0. However, you can choose another option by clicking the small triangle to the right of the Add Index Column button. This displays a menu with the three options outlined.

Selecting the third option, Custom, displays the dialog that you see in Figure 8-22.

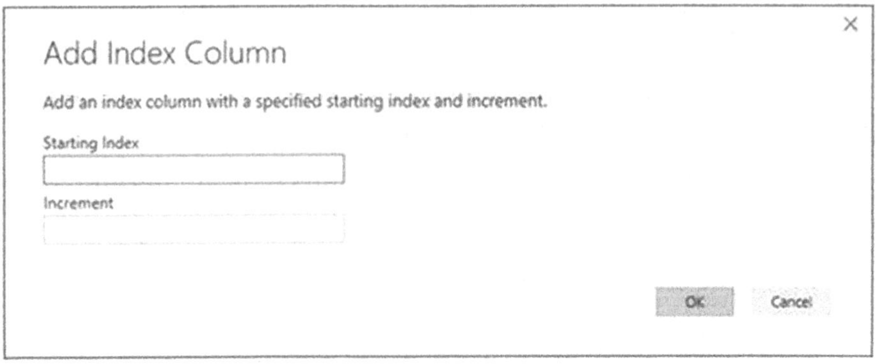

Figure 8-22. *The Add Index Column dialog*

This dialog lets you specify the start number for the first row in the dataset as well as the increment that is added for each record.

Conclusion

In this chapter, you learned some essential techniques that you can use to cleanse and extend datasets. You saw how to round numbers up and down, how to deliver conformed text presentation, and how to remove extraneous spaces and nonprinting characters from columns of data.

You also saw how to replace values inside columns, as well as ways of applying mathematical, statistical, and trigonometric functions to numbers. Other techniques covered extracting date, time, and duration elements from date/time and duration columns.

Finally, you saw a series of techniques that help you to add new columns based on the data in existing columns. These range from simple copies of an entire column or combining columns to extracting parts of a column's data or even deducing different data that is added to a new column using simple logic.

It is now time to see how you can join hitherto separate datasets into single queries and parse complex data types to add them to a dataset. You will even learn how to load multiple identically-structured files in a single query and how to pivot and unpivot and transpose data. All of this will be the subject of the next chapter.

CHAPTER 9

Restructuring Data

In the previous two chapters, you saw how to hone your dataset so that you defined only the rows and columns of data that you really need. Then you learned how to cleanse and complete the data that they contain. In this chapter, you will learn how to build on these foundations to deliver data that is ready to be molded into a structured and usable data model.

The generic term for this kind of data preparation in Power BI Desktop is *restructuring data*. It covers the following:

- *Joining queries*: This involves taking two queries and linking them so that you display the data from both sources as a single dataset. You will learn how to extend a query with multiple columns from a second query as well as how to aggregate the data from a second query and add this to the initial dataset. You will also see how to create complex joins when merging queries.

- *Pivoting and unpivoting data*: If you need to switch data in rows to display as columns—or vice versa—then you can get the Power BI Desktop Query Editor to help you do exactly this. This means that you can guarantee that the data in all the tables that you are using conforms to a standardized tabular structure that is essential for Power BI to function efficiently.

- *Transposing data*: This can be required to switch columns into rows and vice versa.

- *Data quality analysis*: This means using Power BI Query Editor to give you an idea about the quality of the available data.

These techniques can be—and probably will be—used alongside many of the techniques that you saw previously in Chapters 7 and 8. After all, one of the great strengths of Power BI Desktop Query is that it recognizes that data transformation

© Adam Aspin 2020
A. Aspin, *Pro Power BI Desktop*, https://doi.org/10.1007/978-1-4842-5763-0_9

is a complex business and consequently does not impose any strict way of working. Indeed, it lets you experiment freely with a multitude of data transformation options. So remember that you are at liberty to take any approach you want when transforming source data. The only thing that matters is that it gives you the result that you want.

The Power BI Desktop Query Editor View Ribbon

Until now, we have concentrated our attention on the Power BI Desktop Query Editor Home, Transform, and Add Column ribbons. This is for the good and simple reason that these ribbons are where nearly all the action takes place. There is, however, a fourth essential Power BI Desktop Query Editor ribbon—the View ribbon. The buttons that it contains are shown in Figure 9-1, and the options are explained in Table 9-1.

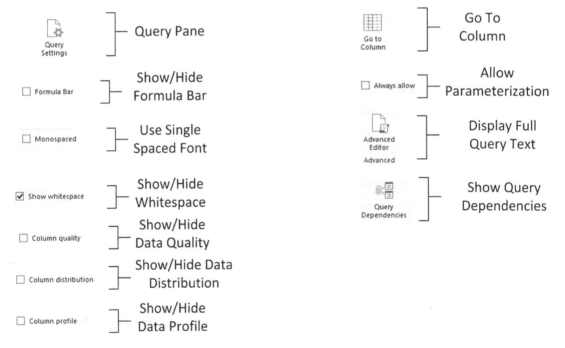

Figure 9-1. *The Power BI Desktop View ribbon*

Table 9-1. *Power BI Desktop View Ribbon Options*

Option	Description
Query Settings	Displays or hides the Query Settings pane at the right of the Power BI Desktop window. This includes the Applied Steps list.
Formula Bar	Shows or hides the formula bar containing the M language code for a transformation step.
Monospaced	Displays previews in a monospaced font.
Show whitespace	Displays whitespace and new line characters.
Column quality	Shows column quality characteristics.
Column distribution	Shows column distribution characteristics.
Column profile	Shows column profile characteristics.
Go to Column	Allows you to select a specific column.
Always allow	Allows parameterization in data source and transformation dialogs.
Advanced Editor	Displays the Advanced Editor dialog containing all the code for the steps in the query.
Query Dependencies	Displays the sequence of query links and dependencies.

Possibly the only option that is not immediately self-explanatory is the Advanced Editor button. It displays the code for all the transformations in the query as a single block of "M" language script. You will learn more about this in Chapter 12.

Tip   Personally, I find that the Query Settings pane and the Formula Bar are too vital to be removed from the Power BI Desktop Query window when transforming data. Consequently, I tend to leave them visible. If you need the screen real estate, however, then you can always hide them for a while.

Merging Data

Until now, we have treated each individual query as if it existed in isolation. The reality, of course, is that you will frequently be required to use the output of one query in conjunction with the output of another to join data from different sources in various ways. Assuming that the results of one query share a common field (or fields) with another query, you can "join" queries into a single "flattened" data table. Power BI Desktop calls this a merge operation, and it enables you, among other things, to

- Look up data elements in another "reference" table to add lookup data. For example, you may want to add a client name where only the client reference exists in your main table.

- Aggregate data from a "detail" table (such as invoice lines) and include the totals in a higher-grained table, such as a table of invoices.

Here, again, the process is not difficult. The only fundamental factor is that the two tables, or queries, that you are merging must have a shared field or fields that enable the two tables to match records coherently. Let's look at a couple of examples.

Adding Data

First, let's try looking up extra data that we will add to a query:

1. In a new, empty Power BI Desktop file, load both the worksheets in the C:\PowerBiDesktopSamples\SalesData.xlsx Excel file.

2. Click the Transform Data button in the Home ribbon.

3. Click the query named Sales in the Queries pane of the Power BI Desktop Query window.

4. Click the Merge Queries button in the Home ribbon. The Merge dialog will appear.

5. In the upper part of the dialog—where an overview of the output from the current query is displayed—scroll to the right and click the ClientName column title. This column is highlighted.

6. In the popup under the upper table, select the Clients query. The output from this query will appear in the lower part of the dialog.

7. In the lower table, select the column title for the column—the join column—that maps to the column that you selected in step 5. This will also be the ClientName column. This column is then selected in the lower table. You may be asked to set privacy levels for the data sources. If this is the case, set them to Public.

8. Select Inner (only matching rows) from the Join Kind popup menu. The dialog will look like Figure 9-2.

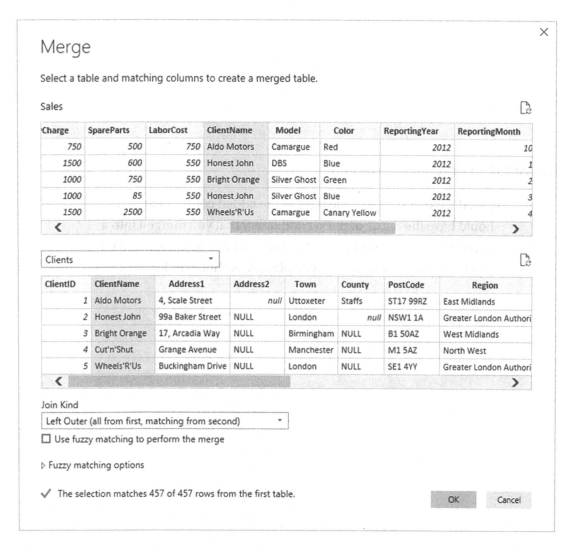

Figure 9-2. The Merge dialog

9. Click OK. A new column is added to the right of the existing data table. It is named Clients—representing the merged table.

10. Scroll to the right of the existing data table. The new column contains the word Table in every cell. This column will look something like Figure 9-3.

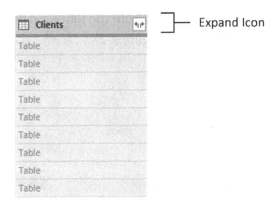

Figure 9-3. *A new, merged column*

11. Click the Expand icon to the right of the added column name (it should have the name of the second query that you merged into a source query). The popup list of all the available fields in this data table (or query, if you prefer) is displayed, as shown in Figure 9-4.

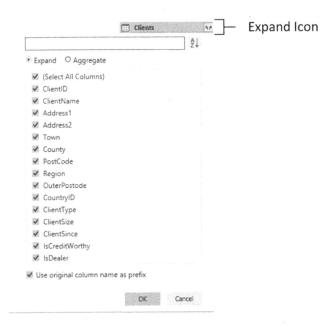

Figure 9-4. *The fields available in a joined query*

12. Ensure that the Expand radio button is selected.

13. Clear the selection of all the columns by unchecking the (Select All Columns) check box.

14. Select the following columns:

    a. ClientName

    b. ClientSize

    c. ClientSince

15. Uncheck Use original column name as prefix.

16. Click OK. The selected columns from the linked table are merged into the main table, and the link to the reference table (New Column) is removed.

17. Rename the columns that have been added, and apply and close the query. The result should look like that in Figure 9-5.

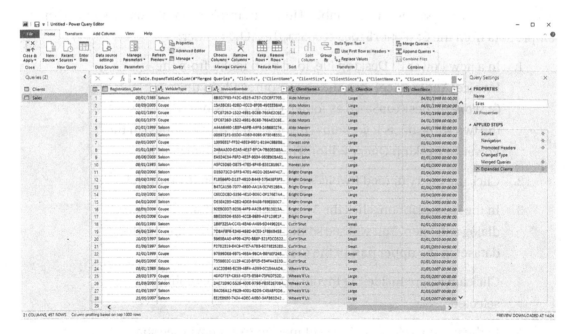

Figure 9-5. *Merged column output*

You now have a single table of data that contains data from two linked data sources. Reprocessing the Sales query will also reprocess the dependent *clients* query and result in the latest version of the data being reloaded into the merged query.

Note   You probably noticed that the Merge dialog indicated how many matching records there were in the two queries. This can be a useful indication that you have selected the correct column(s) to join the two queries.

Aggregating Data During a Merge Operation

If you are not just looking up reference data but need to aggregate data from a separate table and then add the results to the current query, then the process is largely similar. This second approach, however, is designed to suit another completely different requirement. Previously, you saw the case where the current query had many records that mapped to a *single* record in the lookup table. This second approach is for when your current (or main) query has a single record where there are *multiple* linked records in the second query. Consequently, you need to aggregate the data in the second table to bring the data across into the first table. Here is a simple example, using some of the sample data from the C:\PowerBiDesktopSamples\CH09 folder:

1. In a new Power BI Desktop file, load both tables from the InvoicesAndInvoiceLines.xlsx Excel source file in the C:\PowerBiDesktopSamples folder. Click Transform Data to see the two worksheets it contains (Invoices and InvoiceLines) in the Power BI Desktop Query Editor. This will create two queries.

2. Click the query named Invoices in the Queries pane on the left.

3. In the Home ribbon, click the Merge Queries button. The Merge dialog will open. You will see some of the data from the Invoices dataset in the upper part of the dialog.

4. Click anywhere inside the InvoiceID column. This column is selected.

5. In the popup, select the InvoiceLines query. You will see some of the data from the InvoiceLines dataset in the lower part of the dialog.

6. Click anywhere inside the InvoiceID column for the lower table. This column is selected.

7. Select Inner (only matching rows) from the Join Kind popup menu. The dialog will look like Figure 9-6.

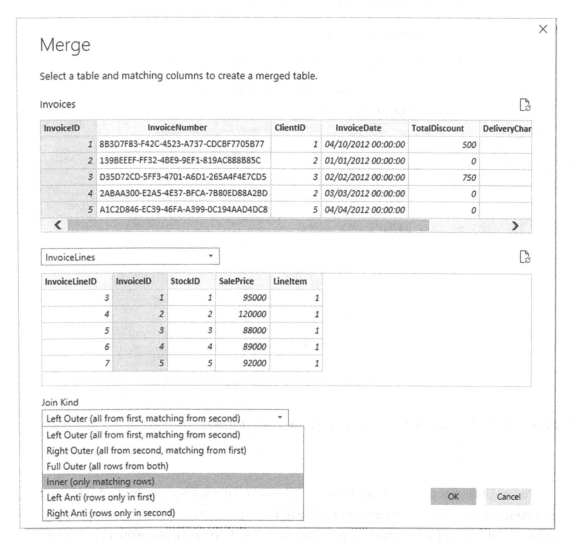

Figure 9-6. *The Merge dialog when aggregating data*

8. Click OK. The Merge dialog will close and a new column named InvoiceLines will be added at the right of the Invoices query.

9. Scroll to the right of the existing data table. You will see the new column (named InvoiceLines) that contains the word *Table* in every cell.

10. Click the Expand icon to the right of the new column title (the two arrows facing left and right). The popup list of all the available fields in the InvoiceLines query is displayed.

11. Select the Aggregate radio button.

12. Select the Sum of SalePrice field and uncheck all the others.

13. Uncheck the "Use original column name as prefix" check box. The dialog will look like Figure 9-7.

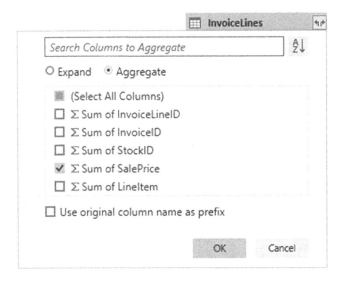

Figure 9-7. *The available fields from a merged dataset*

14. Click OK.

Power BI Desktop will add up the total sale price for each invoice and add this as a new column. Naturally, you can choose the type of aggregation that you wish to apply (before clicking OK), if the sum is not what you want. To do this, place the cursor over the column that you want to aggregate (see step 11 in the preceding exercise) and click the popup menu at the right of the field name. Power BI Desktop will suggest a set of options. The available aggregation options are explained in Table 9-2.

Table 9-2. *Merge Aggregation Options*

Option	Description
Sum	Returns the total value of the field.
Average	Returns the average value of the field.
Median	Returns the median value of the field.
Minimum	Returns the minimum value of the field.
Maximum	Returns the maximum value of the field.
Count (All)	Counts all records in the dataset.
Count (Not Blank)	Counts all records in the dataset that are not empty.

Tip   If you loaded the data instead of editing the query in step 1, simply click the Transform Data button in the Home ribbon to switch to the Query Editor.

The merge process that you have just seen, while not complex in itself, suddenly opens up many new horizons. It means that you can now create multiple separate queries that you can then use together to expand your data in ways that allow you to prepare quite complex datasets.

Here are a couple of comments I need to make about the merge operation:

- Only queries that have been previously created in the Power BI Desktop Query window can be used when merging datasets. So remember to connect to all the datasets that you require before attempting a merge operation.

- Refreshing a query will cause any other queries that are merged into this query to be refreshed also. This way you will always get the most up-to-date data from all the queries in the process.

Types of Join

When merging queries—either to join data or to aggregate values—you are faced with a choice when it comes to how to link the two queries. The choice of join can have a profound effect on the resulting dataset. Consequently, it is important to understand the six join types that are available. These are described in Table 9-3.

Table 9-3. *Join Types*

Join Type	Explanation
Left Outer	Keeps all records in the upper dataset in the Merge dialog (the dataset that was active when you began the merge operation). Any matching rows (those that share common values in the join columns) from the second dataset are kept. All other rows from the second dataset are discarded.
Right Outer	Keeps all records in the lower dataset in the Merge dialog (the dataset that was not active when you began the merge operation). Any matching rows (those that share common values in the join columns) from the upper dataset are kept. All other rows from the upper dataset (the dataset that was active when you began the merge operation) are discarded.
Full Outer	All rows from both queries are retained in the resulting dataset. Any records that do not share common values in the join field(s) contain blanks in certain columns.
Inner	Only joins queries where there is an exact match on the column(s) that are selected for the join. Any rows from either query that do not share common values in the join column(s) are discarded.
Left Anti	Keeps only rows from the upper (first) query.
Right Anti	Keeps only rows from the lower (second) query.

Note   When you use any of the *outer* joins, you are keeping records that do not have any corresponding records in the second query. Consequently, the resulting dataset contains empty values for some of the columns.

When you are expanding the column that is the link to a merged dataset, you have a couple of useful options that are worth knowing about:

- Use original column name as prefix
- Search columns to expand

Use the Original Column Name As the Prefix

You will probably find that some columns from joined queries can have the same names in both source datasets. It follows that you need to identify which column came from which dataset. If you leave the check box selected for the "Use original column name as prefix" merge option (which is the default), any merged columns will include the source query name to help you identify the data more accurately.

If you find that these longer column names only get in the way, you can unselect this check box. This will leave the added columns from the second query with their original names. However, because Power BI Desktop cannot accept duplicate column names, any new columns will have .1, .2, and so forth, added to the column name.

Search Columns to Expand

If you are merging a query with a second query that contains a large number of columns, then it can be laborious to scroll down to locate the columns that you want to include. To narrow your search, you can enter a few characters from the name of the column that you are looking for in the Search columns to aggregate box. The more characters you type, the fewer matching columns are displayed in the Expansion popup dialog.

Joining on Multiple Columns

In the examples so far, you only joined queries on a single column. While this may be possible if you are looking at data that comes from a clearly structured source (such as a relational database), you may need to extend the principle when joining queries from diverse sources. Fortunately, Power BI Desktop allows you to join queries on *multiple* columns when the need arises.

As an example of this, the sample data contains a file that I have prepared as an example of how to join queries on more than one column. This sample file contains data from the sources that you saw in previous chapters. However, they have been modeled as a data warehouse star schema. To complete the model, you need to join a dimension named Geography to a fact table named Sales so that you can add the field GeographySK to the fact table. However, the Sales table and the Geography table share three fields

(Country, Region, and Town) that must correspond for the queries to be joined. The following explains how to perform a join using multiple fields:

1. In a new Power BI Desktop file, click Get Data, select Excel as the source, and in the `C:\PowerBiDesktopSamples\StarSchema.xlsx` Excel file, select the two worksheets (Geography and Sales).

2. Click Transform Data to open the Query Editor. If you are already in the Query Editor, simply click New Source, and select Excel as the source data type and load the two worksheets.

3. Select the Sales query from the list of existing queries from the Queries pane on the left of the Power BI Desktop Query window.

4. In the Home ribbon, click the Merge Queries button. The Merge dialog will appear.

5. In the popup list of queries, select Geography as the second query to join to the first (upper) query.

6. Select Inner (only matching rows) from the Join Kind popup.

7. In the upper list of fields (taken from the Sales table), Ctrl-click the fields CountryName and Region, *in this order*. A small number will appear to the right of each column header, indicating the order that you selected the columns.

8. In the lower list of fields (taken from the Sales table), Ctrl-click the fields CountryName and Region, *in this order*. A small number will appear to the right of each column header, indicating the order that you selected the columns.

9. Verify that you have a reasonable number of matching rows in the information message at the bottom of the dialog. The dialog will look like Figure 9-8.

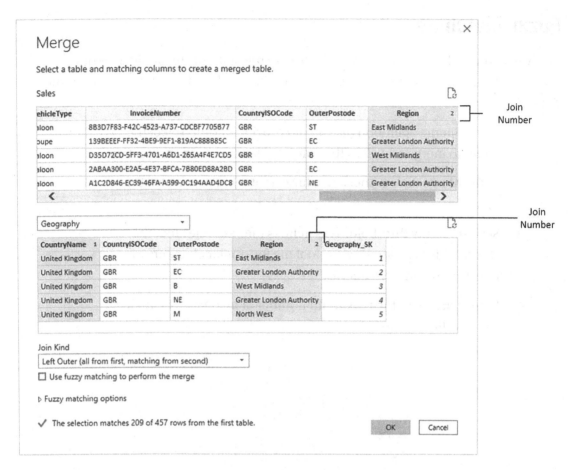

Figure 9-8. *Joining queries using multiple columns*

    10.   Click OK.

You can then continue restructuring your data. In this example, that would be adding the GeographySK field to the Sales query and then removing the Country, Region, and Town fields from the Sales query.

There is no real limit to the number of columns that can be used when joining queries. It will depend entirely on the shape of the source data. However, each column used to define the join must exist in both datasets, and each pair of columns must be of the same (or a similar) data type.

Fuzzy Matching

Fuzzy matching allows you to compare values in the columns to join in a merge operation by using fuzzy matching logic, rather than looking for exact matches in the data.

1. Start a merge operation (as you did previously) and select the two tables to merge as well as the column(s) used to join the queries.

2. In the Merge dialog, check Use fuzzy matching to perform the merge.

3. Set a similarity threshold. This defines the "latitude" that the Query Editor can apply when looking for similar elements to match across the two queries.

4. Enter a figure for the maximum number of matches. The dialog will look like Figure 9-9.

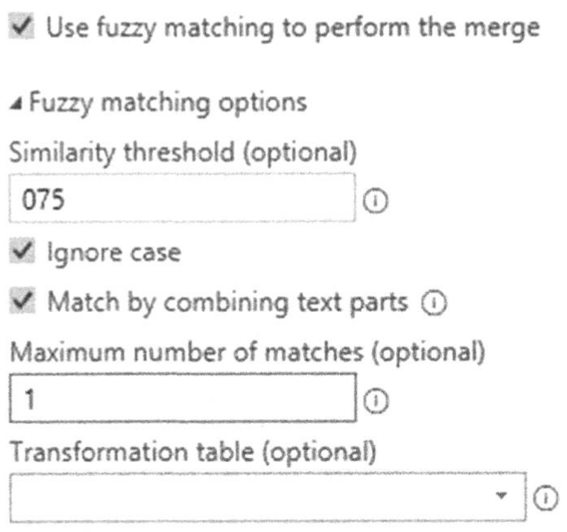

☑ Use fuzzy matching to perform the merge

◢ Fuzzy matching options
Similarity threshold (optional)

| 075 | ⓘ |

☑ Ignore case
☑ Match by combining text parts ⓘ
Maximum number of matches (optional)

| 1 | ⓘ |

Transformation table (optional)

| ▾ | ⓘ |

Figure 9-9. *Fuzzy matching*

Fuzzy Matching Options

There are a few fuzzy matching options that you might want to apply—and that you certainly need to understand when you use this technique. They are explained in Table 9-4.

Table 9-4. *Fuzzy Matching Options*

Option	Explanation
Similarity threshold	Indicates how similar two values need to be in order to match. The minimum value of 0.00 will cause all values to match each other, and the maximum value of 1.00 will only allow exact matches. The default is 0.80.
Ignore case	Ignores uppercase and lowercase characters in the two columns.
Ignore spaces	Ignores whitespace characters in the two columns.
Maximum number of matches	Sets the maximum number of matching rows that will be returned for each input row. The default behavior is to return all matches.
Transformation table	Allows users to specify another query that holds a manually prepared mapping table, so that some values can be auto-mapped as part of the matching.

Fuzzy matching is an extremely powerful technique that can assist you in joining datasets from disparate sources. However, you will probably need to experiment to find the appropriate options to use when merging queries.

Merge As New Query

In the preceding merge process, you merged data into a source table. However, there may be occasions when you prefer to keep the source query (or table, if you prefer) intact and output the result of the merge operation into a new query.

To do this, the trick is to click not the Merge button itself, but the arrow to the right of the Merge button—and selecting Merge Queries as New. You can see this option in Figure 9-10.

Figure 9-10. *Merging tables as a new query*

This will create a new query (named Merge—but you can rename it later) and leave the initial queries intact.

Preparing Datasets for Joins

You could have to carry out a little preparatory work on real-world datasets before joining queries. More specifically, any columns that you join have to be the same basic data type. Put simply, you need to join text-based columns to other text-based columns, number columns to number columns, and date columns to date columns. If the columns are *not* the same data type, you receive a warning message when you try to join the columns in the Merge dialog.

Consequently, it is nearly always a good idea to take a look at the columns that you will use to join queries *before* you start the merge operation itself. Remember that data types do not have to be identical, just similar. So a decimal number type can map to a whole number, for instance.

You might also have to cleanse the data in the columns that are used for joins before attempting to merge queries. This could involve the following:

- Removing trailing or leading spaces in text-based columns

- Isolating part of a column (either in the original column or as a new column) to use in a join

- Verifying that appropriate data types are used in join columns

Correct and Incorrect Joins

Merging queries is the one data restructuring operation that is often easier in theory than in practice, unfortunately. If the source queries were based on tables in a relational or even dimensional database, then joining them could be relatively easy, as a data architect will (hopefully) have designed the database tables to allow for them to be joined. However, if you are joining two completely independent queries, then you could face several major issues:

- The columns do not map.

- The columns map, but the result is a massive table with duplicate records.

Let's take a look at these possible problems.

The Columns Do Not Map

If the columns do not map (i.e., you have joined the data but get no resulting records), then you need to take a close look at the data in the columns that you are using to establish the join. The questions you need to ask are as follows:

- Are the values in the two queries the same data type?

- Do the values really map—or are they different?

- Are you using the correct columns?

- Are you using too many columns and so specifying data that is not in both queries?

The Columns Map, but the Result Is a Massive Table with Duplicate Records

Joining queries depends on isolating *unique* data in both source queries. Sometimes a single column does not contain enough information to establish a unique reference that can uniquely identify a row in the query.

In these cases, you need to use two or more columns to join queries—or else rows will be duplicated in the result. Therefore, once again, you need to look carefully at the data and decide on the minimum number of columns that you can use to join queries correctly.

Examining Joined Data

Joining data tables is not always easy. Neither is deciding if the outcome of a merge operation will produce the result that you expect. So Power BI Desktop Query includes a solution to these kinds of dilemma. It can help you more clearly see what a join has done. More specifically, it can show you for each record in the first query exactly which rows are joined from the second query.

Do the following to see this in action:

1. Carry out steps 1 through 10 in the example you saw earlier ("Joining on Multiple Columns" section).

2. Scroll to the right in the data table. You will see the new column named Geography (as shown in Figure 9-11).

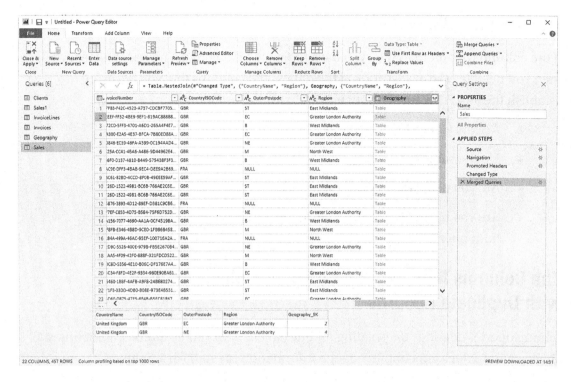

Figure 9-11. *Joined data*

3. Click to the *right* of the word *Table* in the row where you want to
    see the joined data. Note that you must *not* click the word *Table*.
    A second table will appear under the main query's data table
    containing the data from the second query that is joined for this
    particular row. Figure 9-11 shows an example of this.

This technique is as simple as it is useful. There are nonetheless a few comments that
I need to make:

*   You can resize the lower table (and consequently display more or less
    data from the second joined table) by dragging the bottom border of
    the top data table up or down.

*   Clicking to the right of the word *Table* in the NewColumn column will
    enable the Expand and Aggregate buttons in the Transform ribbon.

*   Clicking the word *Table* in the NewColumn column adds a new step
    to the query that replaces the source data with the linked data. You
    can also do this by right-clicking inside the NewColumn column and
    selecting Drill Down.

Note   Drilling down into the merged table in effect limits the query to the row(s) of the subtable. Consequently, you have to delete this step if you want to access all the data in the merged tables.

Appending Data

Not all source data is delivered in its entirety in a single file or as a single database table. You may be given access to two or more tables or files that have to be loaded into a single table in Excel or Power Pivot. In some cases, you might find yourself faced with hundreds of files—all text, CSV, or Excel format—and the requirement to load them all into a single table that you will use as a basis for your analysis. Well, Power BI Desktop can handle these eventualities, too.

Adding the Contents of One Query to Another

In the simplest case, you could have two data sources that are structurally identical (i.e., they have the same columns in the same order), and all that you have to do is add one to another to end up with a query that outputs the amalgamated content of the two sources. This is called *appending data*, and it is easy, provided that the two data sources have *identical* structures; this means

- They have the same number of columns.

- The columns are in the same order.

- The data types are identical for each column.

- The columns have the same names.

As long as all these conditions are met, you can append the output of queries (which Power BI Desktop also calls *Tables* and many people, including me, refer to as datasets) one into another. The queries do not have to have data that comes from identical source types, so you can append the output from a CSV file to data that comes from an Oracle database, for instance. As an example, we will take two text files and use them to create one single output:

1. Create queries to load each of the following text files into Power BI Desktop—without the final load step, which would add them to the data model. Both files are in the `C:\PowerBiDesktopSamples\MultipleIdenticalFiles` folder:

    a. Colours_01.txt

    b. Colours_02.txt

2. Name the queries **Colours_01** and **Colours_02**. You can see the contents of these two queries in Figure 9-12.

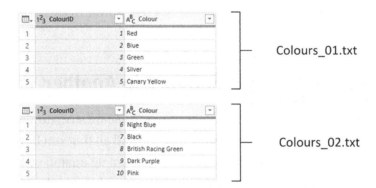

Figure 9-12. *Source data for appending*

3. Open one of the queries (I use Colours_01, but either will do).

4. Click the arrow to the right of the Append Queries button in the Power BI Desktop Query Editor Home ribbon and select Append queries as new. The Append dialog will appear.

5. Ensure that the Two tables radio button is selected.

6. From the Table to Append popup, choose the query Colours_02. The dialog will look like the one in Figure 9-13.

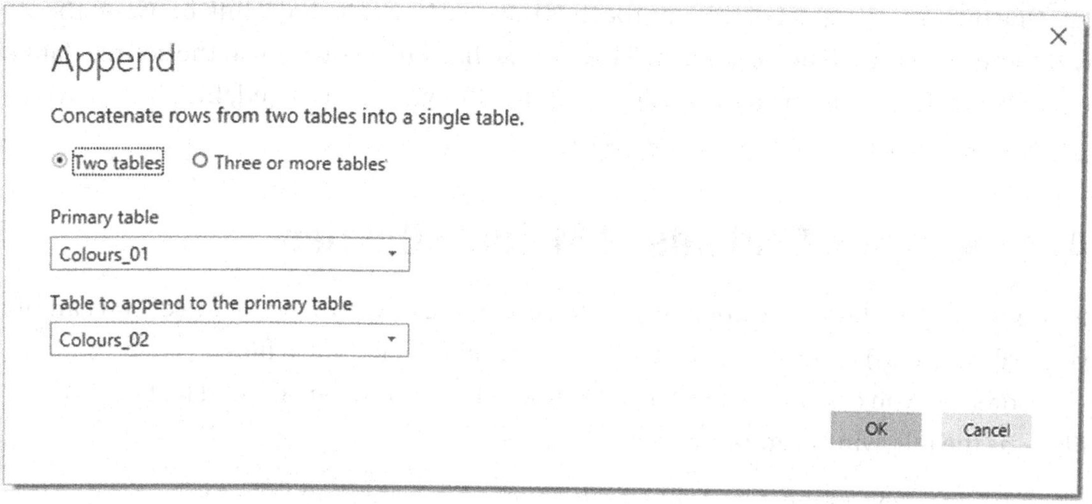

***Figure 9-13.** The Append dialog*

7. Click OK. The data from the two output tables is appended in a new query. You can see an example of the resulting output in Figure 9-14.

	ColourID	Colour
1	1	Red
2	2	Blue
3	3	Green
4	4	Silver
5	5	Canary Yellow
6	6	Night Blue
7	7	Black
8	8	British Racing Green
9	9	Dark Purple
10	10	Pink

***Figure 9-14.** A new query containing appended data*

You can now continue with any modifications that you need to apply. You will notice that the column names are not repeated as part of the data when the tables are appended one to the other.

One interesting aspect of this approach is that you have created a link between the two source tables and the new query. This means that when you refresh the source data, not only are the data in the tables Colours_01 and Colours_02 updated, but the "derived" query that you just created is updated as well.

Appending the Contents of Multiple Queries

Power BI Query Editor does not limit you to appending only two files at once. You can (if you really need to) append a virtually limitless number of identical files.

Moreover, you can append Excel files just as easily as you can append text or CSV files—as the following example shows:

1. In a new, empty Power BI Desktop file, click Transform Data to open the Query Editor.

2. Create queries to load all of the Excel files in the folder `C:\PowerBiDesktopSamples\MultipleIdenticalExcel` (the files are identical, and each one contains a single worksheet named BaseData).

3. Select the query named BaseData in the Queries pane on the left.

4. Click the Append Queries button.

5. Select the Three or more tables radio button in the Append dialog.

6. Ctrl-click the tables "BaseData (2)" and "BaseData (3)" in the Available table(s) list on the left of the dialog.

7. Click the Add button. You can see what the Append dialog now looks like in Figure 9-15.

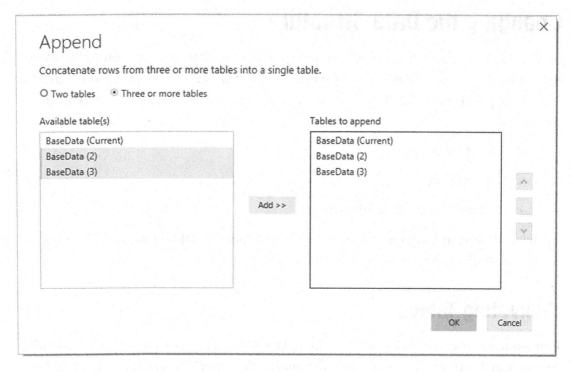

Figure 9-15. *Appending multiple queries*

8. Click OK. The data from the query "BaseData (2)" and "BaseData (3)" will be appended to the current query (BaseData).

It is worth noting that you can

- Remove queries from the list of queries to append on the right by clicking the query (or Ctrl-clicking multiple queries) and subsequently clicking the cross icon on the right of the dialog.

- You can alter the load order of queries by clicking the query to move and then clicking the up and down chevrons on the right of the dialog.

Changing the Data Structure

Sometimes your requirements go beyond the techniques that we have seen so far when discussing data cleansing and transformation. Some data structures need more radical reworking, given the shape of the data that you have acquired. I include in this category the following:

- Unpivoting data

- Pivoting data

- Transforming rows and columns

Each of these techniques is designed to meet a specific, yet frequent, need in data loading, and all are described in the next few pages.

Unpivoting Tables

From time to time, you may need to analyze data that has been delivered in a "pivoted" or "denormalized" format. Essentially, this means that information that really should be in a single column has been broken down and placed across several columns. An example of the first few rows of a pivoted dataset is given in Figure 9-16 and can be found in the `C:\PowerBiDesktopSamples\PivotedDataSet.xlsx` sample file.

	A	B	C	D	E	F	G	H
1	InvoiceDate	Aston Martin	Bentley	Jaguar	MGB	Rolls Royce	Triumph	TVR
2	02/01/2013	75890	25700	88200	4500	62000	8500	
3	09/01/2013	31125						
4	10/01/2013	17500						
5	02/02/2013	75890	25700	63200	8500	62000	17000	37500
6	11/02/2013	22500						
7	02/03/2013	75890	25700	88200	4500	75890	8500	
8	12/03/2013	17500						
9	13/03/2013					31125		
10	14/03/2013	17500						
11	02/04/2013	75890	25700	99500	8500	62000	17000	37500
12	15/04/2013					22500		
13	16/04/2013	17500						
14	02/05/2013	75890	62000	124500	4500	75890	8500	
15	17/05/2013	17500						
16	18/05/2013	17500						
17	19/05/2013	22500						
18	02/06/2013	62000	62000	63200	8500	62000	17000	37500
19	20/06/2013	17500						
20	02/07/2013	62000	25700	88200	4500	62000	17000	
21	21/07/2013					17500		
22	22/07/2013	22500						
23	02/08/2013	62000	62000	38200	8500	62000	17000	37500
24	02/09/2013	62000	62000	124500	4500	75890	17000	
25	23/09/2013	17500						
26	02/10/2013	62000	62000	63200	8500	75890	17000	37500
27	24/10/2013					17500		
28	02/11/2013	125000	25700	87000	4500	75890	17000	37500
29	25/11/2013	31125						
30	26/11/2013	17500						
31	27/11/2013	17500						
32	02/12/2013	125000	25700	137000	4500	62000	17000	

Figure 9-16. *A pivoted dataset*

To analyze this data correctly, we really need the makes of the cars to be switched from being column titles to becoming the contents of a specific column. Fortunately, this is not hard at all:

1. In a new Power BI Desktop file, load the table PivotedCosts from the C:\PowerBiDesktopSamples\PivotedDataSet.xlsx file into Power BI Desktop. Ensure that the first row is set to be the table headers.

2. Switch to the Query Editor (unless it is already open) and select all the columns that you want to unpivot. In this example, this means all columns except the first one (all the makes of cars).

3. In the Transform ribbon, click the Unpivot Columns button (or right-click any of the selected columns and choose Unpivot Columns from the context menu). The table is reorganized and the first few records look as they do in Figure 9-17. Unpivoted Columns is added to the Applied Steps list.

▦▾	▦ InvoiceDate	▾	A^B_C Attribute	▾	1²₃ Value	▾
1	02/01/2013		Aston Martin		75890	
2	02/01/2013		Bentley		25700	
3	02/01/2013		Jaguar		88200	
4	02/01/2013		MGB		4500	
5	02/01/2013		Rolls Royce		62000	
6	02/01/2013		Triumph		8500	
7	09/01/2013		Aston Martin		31125	
8	10/01/2013		Aston Martin		17500	
9	02/02/2013		Aston Martin		75890	
10	02/02/2013		Bentley		25700	
11	02/02/2013		Jaguar		63200	
12	02/02/2013		MGB		8500	
13	02/02/2013		Rolls Royce		62000	
14	02/02/2013		Triumph		17000	
15	02/02/2013		TVR		37500	
16	11/02/2013		Aston Martin		22500	
17	02/03/2013		Aston Martin		75890	
18	02/03/2013		Bentley		25700	
19	02/03/2013		Jaguar		88200	
20	02/03/2013		MGB		4500	
21	02/03/2013		Rolls Royce		75890	
22	02/03/2013		Triumph		8500	

Figure 9-17. *An unpivoted dataset*

4. Rename the columns that Power BI Desktop Query has named Attribute and Value.

The data is now presented in a standard tabular way, and so it can be used to create a data model and then produce reports and dashboards.

Unpivot Options

There are a couple of available options when you unpivot data using the Unpivot Columns button popup in the Transform ribbon:

- *Unpivot Other Columns*: This will add the contents of all the other columns to the unpivoted output.

- *Unpivot Only Selected Columns*: This will only add the contents of any preselected columns to the unpivoted output.

Note   As is the case with so many of the techniques that you apply using the Query Editor, it is really important to select the appropriate column(s) before carrying out pivot and unpivot operations.

Pivoting Tables

On some occasions, you may have to switch data from columns to rows so that you can use it efficiently. This kind of operation is called *pivoting data*. It is—perhaps unsurprisingly—very similar to the unpivot process that you saw in the previous section.

1. Follow steps 1 through 3 of the previous section so that you end up with the table of data that you can see in Figure 9-17.

2. Click inside the column Attribute.

3. In the Transform ribbon, click the Pivot Column button. The Pivot Column dialog will appear.

4. Select Value (the column of figures) as the values column that is aggregated by the pivot transformation.

5. Expand Advanced options and ensure that Sum is selected as the Aggregate Value Function. The Pivot Column dialog will look like Figure 9-18.

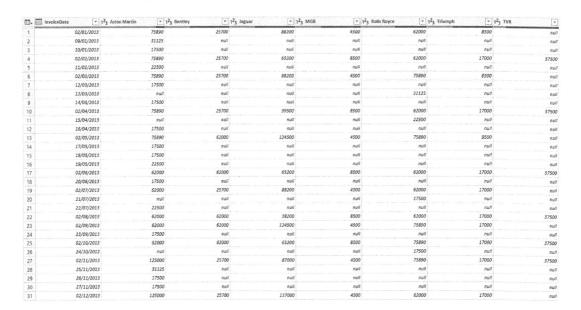

Figure 9-18. *The Pivot Column dialog*

6. Click OK. The table is pivoted and looks like Figure 9-19. Pivoted Column is added to the Applied Steps list.

InvoiceDate	Aston Martin	Bentley	Jaguar	MGB	Rolls Royce	Triumph	TVR
02/01/2013	75890	25700	88200	4500	62000	8500	null
09/01/2013	31125	null	null	null	null	null	null
10/01/2013	17500	null	null	null	null	null	null
02/02/2013	75890	25700	63200	8500	62000	17000	37500
11/02/2013	22500	null	null	null	null	null	null
02/03/2013	75890	25700	88200	4500	75890	8500	null
12/03/2013	17500	null	null	null	null	null	null
13/03/2013	null	null	null	null	31125	null	null
14/03/2013	17500	null	null	null	null	null	null
02/04/2013	75890	25700	99500	8500	62000	17000	37500
15/04/2013	null	null	null	null	22500	null	null
16/04/2013	17500	null	null	null	null	null	null
02/05/2013	75890	62000	124500	4500	75890	8500	null
17/05/2013	17500	null	null	null	null	null	null
18/05/2013	17500	null	null	null	null	null	null
19/05/2013	22500	null	null	null	null	null	null
02/06/2013	62000	62000	63200	8500	62000	17000	37500
20/06/2013	17500	null	null	null	null	null	null
02/07/2013	62000	25700	88200	4500	62000	17000	null
21/07/2013	null	null	null	null	17500	null	null
22/07/2013	22500	null	null	null	null	null	null
02/08/2013	62000	62000	38200	8500	62000	17000	37500
02/09/2013	62000	62000	124500	4500	75890	17000	null
23/09/2013	17500	null	null	null	null	null	null
02/10/2013	62000	62000	63200	8500	75890	17000	37500
24/10/2013	null	null	null	null	17500	null	null
02/11/2013	125000	25700	87000	4500	75890	17000	37500
25/11/2013	31125	null	null	null	null	null	null
26/11/2013	17500	null	null	null	null	null	null
27/11/2013	17500	null	null	null	null	null	null
02/12/2013	125000	25700	137000	4500	62000	17000	null

Figure 9-19. *Pivoted data*

Note   The Advanced options section of the Pivot Column dialog lets you choose the aggregation operation that is applied to the values in the pivoted table.

The Unpivot button contains another menu option that is displayed if you click the small triangle to the right of the Unpivot button. This is the Unpivot Other Columns option that will switch the contents of columns into rows for all the columns that are *not* selected when you run the transformation.

Transposing Rows and Columns

On some occasions, you may have a source table where the columns need to become rows and the rows columns. Fortunately, this is a one-click transformation for Power BI Desktop. Here is how to do it:

1. Edit the `C:\PowerBiDesktopSamples\DataToTranspose.xlsx` Excel file in the Power BI Desktop Query Editor. You will need to select Sheet1. You will see a data table like the one in Figure 9-20.

	ABC 123 Column1	ABC 123 Column2	ABC 123 Column3	ABC 123 Column4	ABC 123 Column5	ABC 123 Column6	
1		1	2	3	4	5	6
2	United Kingdom	France	USA	Germany	Spain	Switzerland	

Figure 9-20. *A dataset needing to be transposed*

2. In the Transform ribbon, click the Transpose button. The data is transposed and appears as two columns, just like the CountryList. txt file that you saw in Chapter 2.

3. Rename the resulting columns.

Data Quality Analysis

Power BI Desktop now includes the ability to help you analyze the quality and composition of your data. It can help you to get a deeper understanding and feel for your source data by providing information on

- Column quality

- Column distribution

- Column profile

313

Column Quality

Power BI Desktop can analyze the following aspects of every column of data in a query:

- Data validity

- Errors

- Empty fields

It then returns the percentages of each of these elements in each column. You can then examine the data in greater detail to track down potential anomalies. Here we will use the file CH08Example1.pbix.

1. In the Query Editor, switch to the View menu.

2. Check the Column quality check box. The column quality analysis will appear under each column header as you can see in Figure 9-21.

InvoiceDate		A^BC Make		A^BC CountryName		A^BC IsDealer		1²3 SalePrice		1²3 CostPrice		1.2 TotalDiscount		1²3 DeliveryCharge	
● Valid	100%	● Valid	100%	● Valid	100%	● Valid	100%	● Valid	100%	● Valid	100%	● Valid	100%	● Valid	100%
● Error	0%	● Error	0%	● Error	0%	● Error	0%	● Error	0%	● Error	0%	● Error	0%	● Error	0%
● Empty	0%	● Empty	0%	● Empty	0%	● Empty	0%	● Empty	0%	● Empty	0%	● Empty	0%	● Empty	0%

Figure 9-21. *Column quality*

Column Distribution

Analyzing the distribution of the data in a column shows unique and distinct values a column contains. This can help you to understand the relevance and usefulness of the data.

1. Check the Column distribution check box. The column distribution analysis will appear under each column header as you can see in Figure 9-22.

Figure 9-22. *Column distribution*

It is worth noting the difference between distinct and unique elements in column distribution:

- *Distinct* elements may occur several times in a column—the total distinct count indicates how many separate elements exist overall.

- *Unique* elements appear only once in a column.

Column Profile

The column profile information indicates the relative percentages of each of the distinct values in a column compared to the total number of elements.

1. Check the Column profile check box. The column profile analysis will appear at the bottom of the screen as shown in Figure 9-23.

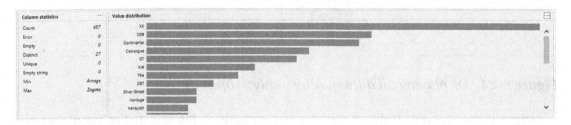

Figure 9-23. Column profile

You may even choose to display all three data quality analysis options at the same time. If you do this, you could end up with a screen like the one shown in Figure 9-24.

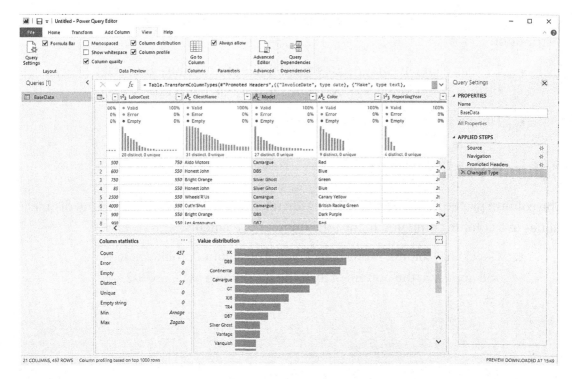

Figure 9-24. *Displaying all data quality analysis options*

Of these options, only Column distribution depends on the selected column. So you need to click each column independently to see the distribution of values for the selected column. Moreover, you can copy—independently—the column statistics and the value distribution for a column by clicking the ellipses at the top right of the column statistics and value distribution windows, respectively, and selecting Copy. This information can then be pasted into, for example, Excel to analyze the metadata for a dataset.

Profiling the Entire Dataset

By default, the built-in data profiling will only look at the first 1000 records in a dataset—presumably to speed up the profiling operation. However, you can force Power BI Desktop to profile the entire dataset.

1. At the bottom left of the Query Editor screen, click Column profiling based on top 1000 rows. The popup that you can see in Figure 9-25 appears.

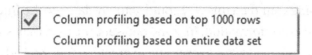

Figure 9-25. *Selecting the extent of the profiling*

2. Select Column profiling based on entire data set. After a short
    delay (that will depend on the size of the dataset), the profiling
    analysis will be updated.

Correcting Anomalies

Power BI's data profiling tools only indicate what the data looks like from a high level.
It does not presume to modify the data—after all, the data might be useful even if it is
flagged as containing errors or anomalies.

However, it can help you to apply some basic data cleansing.

1. Hover over the column quality or column distribution data at the
    top of the screen. A popup containing more detailed information
    appears.

2. Click the ellipses at the bottom right of the popup. The popup that
    you can see in Figure 9-26 appears.

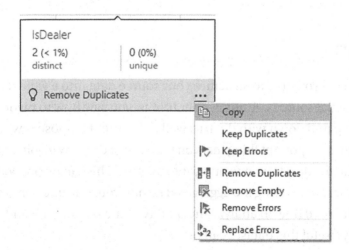

Figure 9-26. *Profiling correction options*

3. Select the option that interests you to correct any anomalies.

Of course, cleansing your data this way could actually damage the integrity of the data—and even remove valuable information. In some datasets, the data that is flagged as being an error could be the data that you want to examine in greater detail. So I advise caution before cleansing data simply to reduce the percentages of errors and empty cells to zero.

Note   Once you select any of the data quality options, they will remain active for future Power BI Desktop sessions until you uncheck the option.

Data Transformation Approaches

I quite understand that you may be bewildered at the sheer number of available transformation options. So it may help, at this point, to remember a few key principles:

- If in doubt, right-click the column that you want to transform. This will list the most common available options in the context menu.

- To alter existing data, use the Transform menu.

- To add a new column, use the New Column menu.

- Remember that you can "unwind" your modifications by deleting steps in the data transformation process.

Conclusion

This chapter showed you how to structure your source data into a valid data table from one or more potential sources. Among other things, you saw how to pivot and unpivot data, to fill rows up and down with data, as well as how to transpose rows and columns.

Possibly the most important thing that you have learned is how to join individual queries so that you can add the data from one query into another. This can involve looking up data from a separate query or carrying the aggregated results from one query into another.

Finally, you learned how to analyze the quality of the source data and understand how immediately useful this dataset can be.

Now it is time to push your data transformation skills to the next level and learn how to set up complex data ingestion and conversion routines. These are the subject of Chapter 10.

CHAPTER 10

Complex Data Loads

Not all data loads are a matter of simply establishing a connection to the source and applying transformations to the source data that is, fortunately, already laid out in neatly structured tables. Sometimes you may want to "push the envelope" when loading data and prepare more complex source data structures for use in your Power BI dashboards. By this, I mean that the source data is not initially in a ready-to-use tabular format and that some restructuring of the data is required to prepare a table for use.

To solve these kinds of challenges, this chapter will explain to you how to

- Add multiple identical files from a source folder

- Select the identical source files to load from a source folder

- Load simple JSON structures from a source file containing JSON data

- Parse a column containing JSON data in a source file

- Parse a column containing XML data in a source file

- Load complex JSON files—and select the elements to use

- Load complex XML files—and select the elements to use

- Convert columns to lists for use in complex load routines

Finally—and purely to complete the overall overview of the Power BI Query Editor and its capabilities—I will mention how to

- Reuse recently used queries

- Modify the list of recently used queries

- Export data from the Power BI Query Editor

© Adam Aspin 2020
A. Aspin, *Pro Power BI Desktop*, https://doi.org/10.1007/978-1-4842-5763-0_10

Adding Multiple Files from a Source Folder

Now let's consider an interesting data ingestion challenge. You have been sent a collection of files, possibly downloaded from an FTP site or received by email, and you have placed them all into a specific directory. However, you do not want to have to carry out the process that you saw in Chapter 2 and load files one by one if there are several hundred files—and then append all these files individually to create a final composite table of data (as you saw in Chapter 9).

Note   Query Editor can only load multiple files if all the files are rigorously identical. This means ensuring that all the columns are in the same order in each file and have the same names.

Here is a much more efficient method to achieve this objective:

1. Create a new Power BI Desktop file.

2. In the Power BI Desktop Home ribbon, click Get Data ➤ File in the Get Data dialog. Then select Folder to the right of the dialog.

3. Click Connect. The Folder dialog is displayed.

4. Click the Browse button and navigate to the folder that contains the files to load. In this example, it is C:\PowerBiDesktopSamples\ MultipleIdenticalFiles. You can also paste in, or enter, the folder path if you prefer. The Folder dialog will look like Figure 10-1.

Figure 10-1. *The Folder dialog*

5.   Click OK. The file list window opens. The contents of the folder
     and all subfolders are listed in tabular format, as shown in
     Figure 10-2.

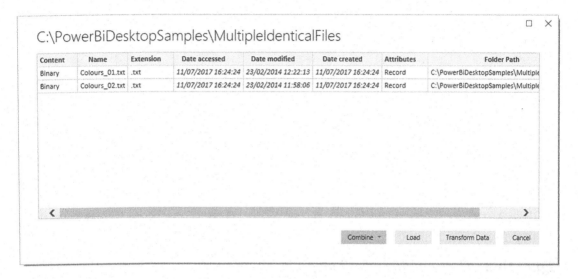

Figure 10-2.   *The folder contents in Power BI Desktop*

6.   Click the popup arrow on the Combine button and select
     Combine & Transform Data. The Combine Files dialog will
     appear, as shown in Figure 10-3. Here you can select which of the
     files in the folder is the *model* for the files to be imported.

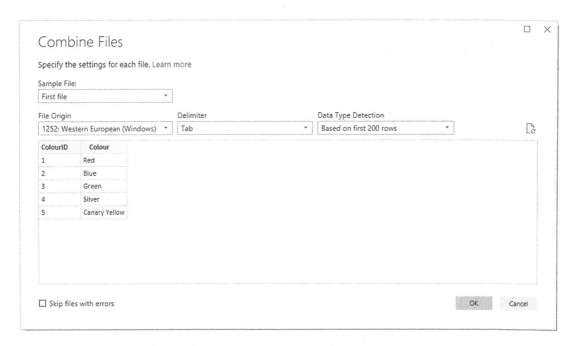

Figure 10-3. *The Combine Files dialog*

7. Click OK. The Power BI Desktop Query Editor will display the imported data. This is shown in Figure 10-4.

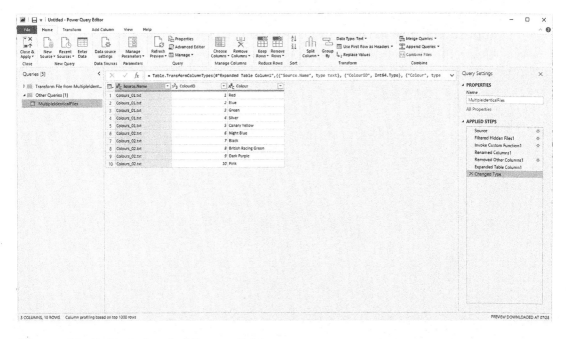

Figure 10-4. *Data loaded from a folder*

8. Click Close & Apply. The data from all the source files will be
    loaded into the Power BI Desktop data model.

Note   The other options in the Combine Files dialog are explained in Chapter 2.

Filtering Source Files in a Folder

There will be times when you want to import only a *subset* of the files from a folder.
Perhaps the files are not identical or maybe you simply do not need some of the available
files in the source directory. Whatever the reason, here is a way to get Power BI Desktop
to do the work of trawling through the directory and *only* loading files that correspond to
a file name specification you have indicated. In other words, the Query Editor allows you
to filter the source file set before loading the actual data. In this example I will show you
how to load multiple Excel files:

1. Carry out the preceding steps 1 through 5 to display the contents
    of the folder containing the files you wish to load. In this scenario
    it is `C:\PowerBiDesktopSamples\MultipleNonIdentical`.

2. Click Transform Data. The Query Editor window will open and
    display the list of files in the directory and many of their attributes.
    You can see an example of this in Figure 10-5.

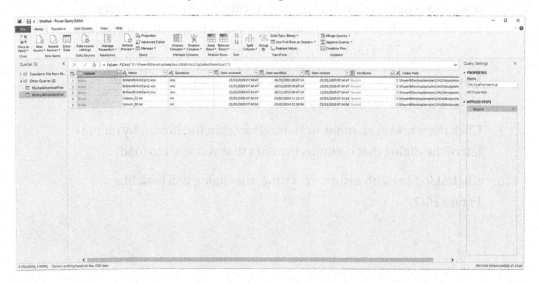

Figure 10-5. *Displaying file information when loading multiple files*

3. As you want to load only Excel files, and avoid files of any other type, click the filter popup menu for the column title Extension and uncheck all elements *except* .xlsx. This is shown in Figure 10-6.

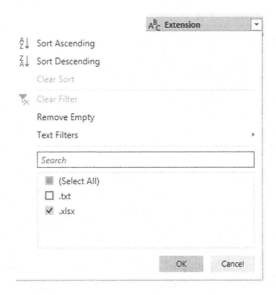

Figure 10-6. *Filtering file types when loading multiple identical files*

4. Click OK. You will now only see the text files in the Query Editor.

5. Click the Expand icon (two downward-facing arrows) to the right of the first column title; this column is called Content and every row in the column contains the word *Binary*. Power BI will display the Combine Files dialog that you saw previously in Chapter 2.

6. Select the file from those available that you want to use as the sample file for the data load.

7. Click the worksheet, table, or named range in the hierarchy on the left of the dialog that contains the data that you wish to load.

8. Click Skip files with errors. This time, the dialog will look like Figure 10-7.

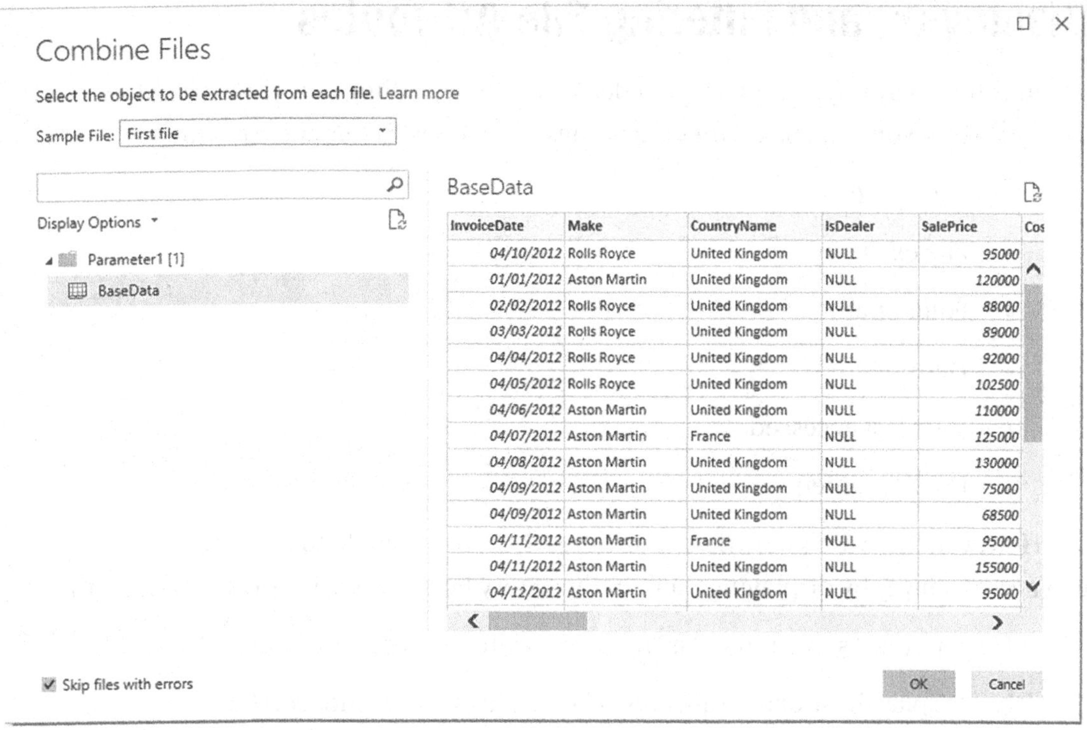

Figure 10-7. *Selecting the source data when loading multiple Excel files*

9. Click OK. Power BI Desktop Query Editor will load all the files and
    display the result.

The contents of all the source files are now loaded into the Power BI Desktop Query
Editor and can be transformed and used like any other dataset. This might involve
removing superfluous header rows (as described in the next but one section). What is
more, if ever you add more files to the source directory, and then click Refresh in the
Home ribbon, *all* the source files that match the filter selection are reloaded, including
any new files added to the specified directory that match the filter criteria.

Note   When loading multiple Excel files, you need to be aware that the data
sources (whether they are worksheets, named ranges, or tables) *must* have the
same name in all the source files or the data will not be loaded.

Displaying and Filtering File Attributes

When you display the contents of a folder in the Query Editor, you see a set of file attributes that you can use to filter data. These cover basic elements such as

- File name

- File extension

- Folder path

- Date created

- Date last accessed

- Date modified

However, there are many more attributes that are available to describe files that you can access simply by displaying them in the Query Editor. Here is how you can do this:

1. Carry out steps 1 and 2 from the previous section.

2. Display the available attributes by clicking the Expand icon (the double-headed arrow) at the right of the Attributes column. The list of available attributes will be displayed, as shown in Figure 10-8.

Figure 10-8. *Selecting the source data when loading multiple Excel files*

3. Select the attributes that you want to display from the list and click OK.

Each attribute will appear as a new column in the Query Editor. You can now filter on the columns to select files based on the expanded list of attributes.

Note   You can also filter on directories, dates, or any of the file information that is displayed. Simply apply the filtering techniques that you learned in Chapter 7.

Removing Header Rows After Multiple File Loads

If the source files contained header rows that were loaded for each source file, here is a practical way to remove them—fast—from the data:

1. If (but only if) each file contains header rows, then scroll down through the resulting table until you find a title element. In this example, it is the word *ColourID* in the ColourID column.

2. Right-click ColourID and select Text Filters ➤ Does Not Equal. All rows containing superfluous column titles are removed.

Note   If your source directory only contains the files that you want to load, then step 2 is unnecessary. Nonetheless, I always add steps like this in case files of the "wrong" type are added later, which would cause any subsequent process runs to fail. Equally, you can set filters on the file name to restrict the files that are loaded.

Loading and Parsing JSON Files

More and more data is now being exchanged in a format called JSON. This stands for JavaScript Object Notation, and it is considered an efficient and lightweight way of transferring potentially large amounts of data. A JSON file is essentially a text file that contains data structured in a specific way.

Now, while Power BI Desktop can connect very easily to JSON data files (they are only a kind of text file, after all), the data they contain are not always instantly comprehensible. So you will now learn how to load the file and then see how this connection can be tweaked to convert it into meaningful information. Transforming the source text into a comprehensible format is often called *parsing* the data.

To connect to a JSON file and parse the data it contains into a usable table:

1. In the Home ribbon, click Get Data ➤ More ➤ File ➤ JSON, then click Connect.

2. Select the file C:\PowerBiDesktopSamples\Colors.json, and click Open. You will see a list of records like the one shown in Figure 10-9.

	List
1	Record
2	Record
3	Record
4	Record
5	Record
6	Record
7	Record
8	Record
9	Record
10	Record

Figure 10-9. *A JSON file after initial import*

3. You will see that the Query Editor has added the List Tools Transform ribbon. This ribbon is explained in detail in the next section. Click the To Table button in this ribbon. The To Table dialog will appear, as shown in Figure 10-10.

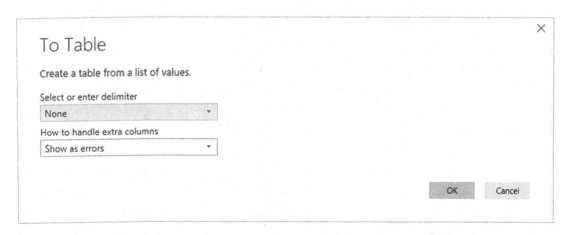

Figure 10-10. *The To Table dialog*

4. Click OK. The list of data will be converted to a table. This means that it now shows the Expand icon at the right of the column title, as you can see in Figure 10-11.

Figure 10-11. *A JSON file converted to a table*

5. Click the Expand icon to the right of the column title, and in the popup dialog, uncheck "Use original column name as prefix."

6. Click OK. The contents of the JSON file now appear as a standard dataset, as you can see in Figure 10-12.

Figure 10-12. *A JSON file transformed into a dataset*

Although not particularly difficult, this process may seem a little counterintuitive. However, it certainly works, and you can use it to process complex JSON files so that you can use the data they contain in Power BI Desktop.

The List Tools Transform Ribbon

Power BI Desktop considers some data to be lists, not tables of data. It handles lists slightly differently and displays a specific ribbon to modify list data. The List Tools Transform ribbon is explained in Figure 10-13 and Table 10-1.

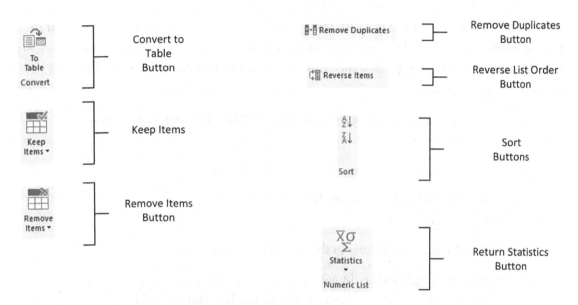

Figure 10-13. *The List Tools Transform ribbon*

Table 10-1. *The List Tools Transform Ribbon Options*

Option	Description
To Table	Converts the list to a table structure.
Keep Items	Allows you to keep a number of items from the top or bottom of the list or a range of items from the list.
Remove Items	Allows you to remove a number of items from the top or bottom of the list or a range of items from the list.
Remove Duplicates	Removes any duplicates from the list.
Reverse Items	Reverses the list order.
Sort	Sorts the list lowest to highest or highest to lowest.
Statistics	Returns calculated statistics about the elements in the list.

Parsing XML Data from a Column

Some data sources, particularly database sources, include XML data actually inside a field. The problem here is that XML data is interpreted as plain text by Power BI Desktop when the data is loaded. If you look at the AvailableColors column in Figure 10-14, you can see that this is not particularly useful.

So once again, Power BI Desktop has a solution to this kind of issue. To demonstrate how to convert this kind of text into usable data, you will find a sample Excel file (C:\PowerBiDesktopSamples\XMLInColumn.xlsx) that contains some XML data as a column. Proceed as follows:

1. In a new, blank Power BI Desktop file, click Edit Queries to switch to the Query Editor.

2. In the Home ribbon, select New Source ➤ Excel.

3. Select the Excel file C:\PowerBiDesktopSamples\ XMLInColumn.xlsx.

4. Select the only worksheet in this file. It is named Sales.

5. Scroll to the right of the dataset and select the last column: AvailableColors. The Navigator dialog looks like Figure 10-14.

Figure 10-14. *A column containing XML*

6. Click OK to connect to the source file.

7. Select the AvailableColors column at the right of the dataset.

8. In the Add Column ribbon, click Parse ➤ XML. A new column will
    be added to the right. It will look like Figure 10-15 and will have
    the title XML.

A^B_C AvailableColors	▼	ABC 123 XML	↑↓
`<root><color1>Red</color1><color2>Blue</color2></root>`		Table	
`<root><color1>Pink</color1><color2>Black</color2></root>`		Table	
`<root><color1>Green</color1><color2>Blue</color2></root>`		Table	
`<root><color1>Red</color1><color2>Blue</color2></root>`		Table	
`<root><color1>Pink</color1><color2>Black</color2></root>`		Table	
`<root><color1>Green</color1><color2>Blue</color2></root>`		Table	
`<root><color1>Red</color1><color2>Blue</color2></root>`		Table	
`<root><color1>Pink</color1><color2>Black</color2></root>`		Table	
`<root><color1>Green</color1><color2>Blue</color2></root>`		Table	
`<root><color1>Red</color1><color2>Blue</color2></root>`		Table	
`<root><color1>Pink</color1><color2>Black</color2></root>`		Table	
`<root><color1>Green</color1><color2>Blue</color2></root>`		Table	

Figure 10-15. *An XML column converted to a table column*

9. Click the Expand icon to the right of the XML column title and uncheck "Use original column name as prefix" in the popup dialog. Ensure that all the columns are selected and click OK. Two new columns (or, indeed, as many new columns as there are XML data elements) will appear at the right of the dataset. The Query Editor will look like Figure 10-16.

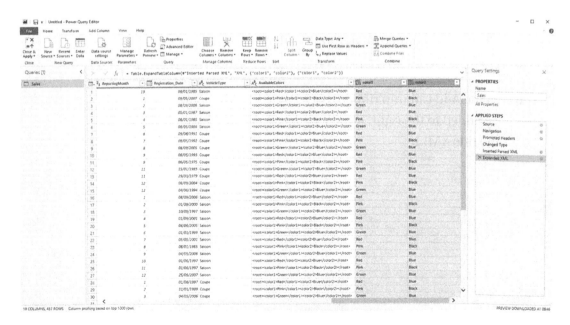

Figure 10-16. *XML data expanded into new columns*

10. Remove the column containing the initial XML data by selecting the column that contains the original XML and clicking Remove Columns in the context menu.

Using this technique, you can now extract the XML data that is in source datasets and use it to extend the original source data.

Parsing JSON Data from a Column

Sometimes you may encounter data containing JSON in a field, too. The technique to extract this data from the field inside the dataset and convert it to columns is virtually identical to the approach that you saw in the previous section for XML data.

Given that the approach is so similar—and is not far removed from what you saw previously when importing JSON files—I will only provide a screenshot for the final result of the process. Here you will be able to see the source JSON as well as the columns of data that were extracted from the JSON and added to the dataset.

1. In a new, blank, Power BI Desktop file load the data from the Excel file `C:\PowerBiDesktopSamples\JSONInColumn.xlsx` and switch to the Query Editor. Select the only worksheet in this file: Sales.

2. Scroll to the right of the dataset and select the last column: AvailableColors.

3. In the Add Column ribbon, click Parse ➤ JSON. A new column will be added to the right and will have the title JSON.

4. Click the Expand icon to the right of the JSON column title and uncheck "Use original column name as prefix" in the popup dialog. Ensure that all the columns are selected and click OK. Two new columns (or, indeed, as many new columns as there are JSON data elements) will appear at the right of the dataset. The Query Editor will look like Figure 10-17.

Figure 10-17. *JSON data expanded into new columns*

5.   Delete the column containing the initial JSON data.

Admittedly, the structure of the JSON data in this example is extremely simple. Real-world JSON data could be much more complex. However, you now have a starting point upon which you can build when parsing JSON data that is stored in a column of a dataset.

Complex JSON Files

JSON files are not always structured as simplistically as the colors.json file that you saw a few pages ago. Indeed, JSON files can contain many sublevels of data, structured into separated *nodes*. Each node may contain multiple data elements grouped together in a logical way. Often you will want to select "sublevels" of data from the source file—or perhaps only select some sublevel elements and not others.

This section shows you how to select the data elements that interest you from a complex JSON structure. Specifically, the sample source data file contains a "root" level which displays core data such as the invoice number, sale date, and sale price (among other elements) and three "sublevels" that contain information on

- The vehicle

- The finance data

- The customer

Note   If you want to get an idea of what a complex JSON file containing several nested nodes looks like, then simply open the file C:\PowerBIDesktopSamples\ CarSalesJSON_Complex.json in a text editor.

In this example you will see how to select elements from one or more (but not all) of the available data in the source file:

1. In the Power BI Desktop ribbon, click Get Data ➤ File and select JSON in the list of file sources on the right of the Get Data dialog.

2. Click Connect and navigate to the folder containing the JSON file that you want to load (C:\PowerBIDesktopSamples\ CarSalesJSON_Complex.json, in this example).

3. Click Open. The Query Editor window will appear and automatically display the Record Tools Convert ribbon. You can see this in Figure 10-18.

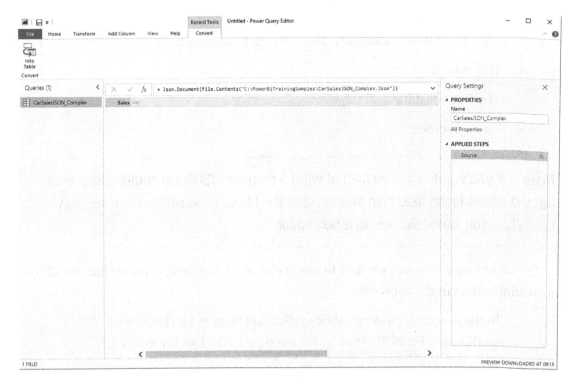

Figure 10-18. *Opening a complex JSON file*

4. Click Into Table from the Record Tools Convert ribbon. The Query
    Editor will look like Figure 10-19.

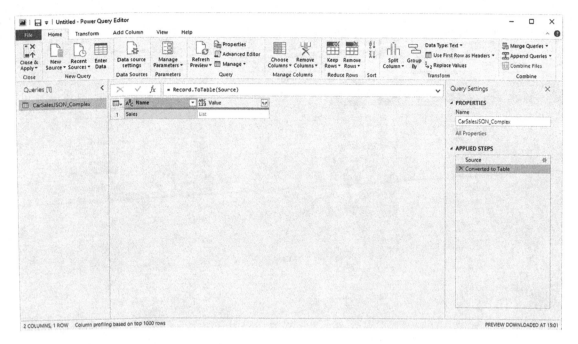

Figure 10-19. *A complex JSON file*

5. Click the Expand icon at the top right of the Value column and
    select Expand to new rows. The Query Editor will look like
    Figure 10-20.

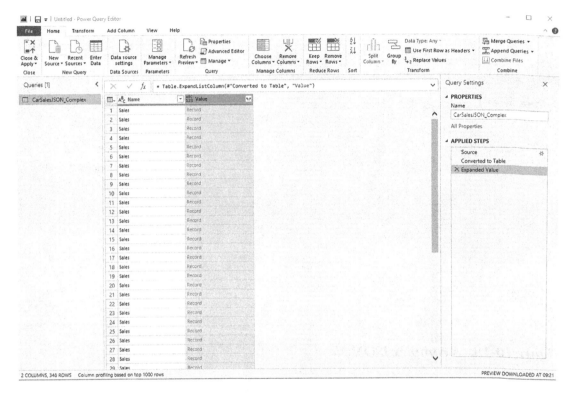

Figure 10-20. *Expanding a JSON file*

6. Click the Expand icon at the top right of the Value column and
    click OK to display all the JSON attributes. The Query Editor
    window will look like Figure 10-21. Each column containing
    the word "record" is, in fact, a JSON node that contains further
    sublevels of data.

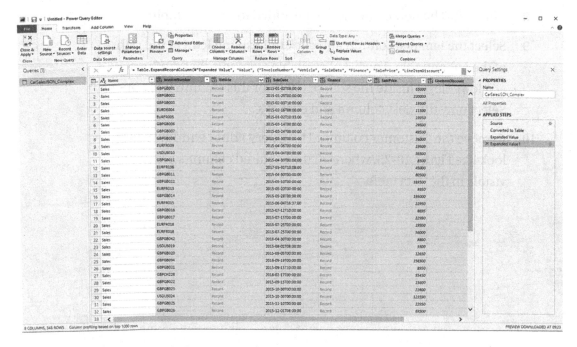

Figure 10-21. *Viewing the structure of a JSON file*

7. Select the Vehicle column and click the Expand icon at the right of the column title. The list of available elements that are "nested" at a lower level inside the source JSON will appear. You can see this in Figure 10-22.

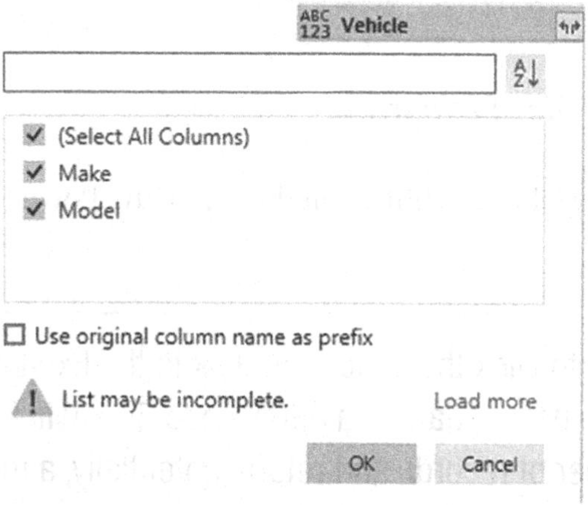

Figure 10-22. *Nested elements in a JSON file*

8. Click OK. The new columns will be added to the data table.

9. Select the Finance column and click the Expand icon at the right of the column title. The list of available elements that are "nested" at a lower level inside the source JSON for this column will appear. Select only the Cost column and click OK.

10. Remove the Customer column. The Query Editor window will look like Figure 10-23, where all the required columns are now visible in the data table.

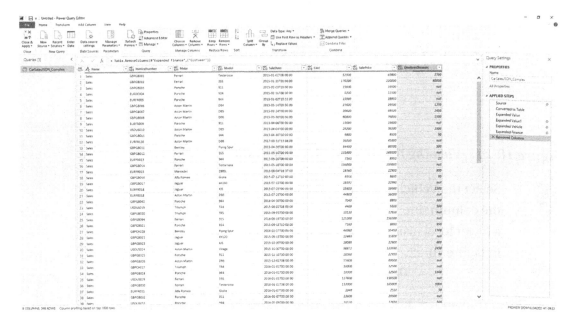

Figure 10-23. *A JSON file after parsing*

11. Click the Apply Changes button at the top of the Power BI Desktop window.

Tip It is a good idea to click the Load more link in the Expand popup menu when you are identifying the nested data in a JSON node. This will force Power Query to scan a larger number of records and return, potentially, a more complete list of nested fields.

This approach allows you to be extremely selective about the data that you load from a JSON file. You can choose to include any column at any level from the source structure. As you saw, you can select—or ignore—entire sublevels of nested data extremely easily.

This section was only a simple introduction to parsing complex JSON files. As this particular data structure can contain multiple sublevels of data, and can mix data and sublevels in each "node" of the JSON file, the source data structure can be extremely complex. Fortunately, the techniques that you just learned can be extended to handle any level of JSON complexity and help you tame the most daunting data structures.

Note   It is important to "flatten" the source data so that all the sublevels (or nodes if you prefer) are removed, and the data that they contain is displayed as a simple column in the query.

Complex XML Files

As is the case with JSON files, XML files can comprise complex nested structures of many sublevels of data, grouped into separate nodes. The good news is that the Power BI Query Editor handles both these data structures in a similar way.

The two approaches are so similar that I will not show all the screens—they are virtually identical to those in the previous section.

1. In the Power BI Desktop ribbon, click Get Data ➤ File and select XML in the list of file sources on the right of the Get Data dialog.

2. Click Connect and navigate to the folder containing the XML file that you want to load (`C:\PowerBIDesktopSamples\ComplexXML.Xml`, in this example).

3. Select the XML node named Sales and click Transform Data. The Query Editor window will appear.

4. Select the Vehicle column and click the Expand icon at the right of the column title. The list of available elements that are "nested" at a lower level inside the source XML will appear.

5. Click OK. The new columns will be added to the data table.

6. Select the Finance column and click the Expand icon at the right of the column title. The list of available elements that are "nested" at a lower level inside the source XML will appear. Select only the Cost column and click OK.

7. Remove the Customer column.

8. Click the Apply Changes button at the top of the Power BI Desktop window.

As was the case with JSON files, this approach allows you to be extremely selective about the data that you load from an XML source file. You can choose to include any column at any level from the source structure. You can select—or ignore—entire sublevels of nested data extremely easily.

Convert a Column to a List

Sometimes you will need to use data in a list format. You will see a practical example of this in Chapter 11 when you learn how to parameterize queries. Fortunately, Power BI Desktop lets you convert a column to a list really easily:

1. Click Get Data ➤ Excel and connect to the Excel file `C:\PowerBiDesktopSamples\BrilliantBritishCars.xlsx`.

2. Select the worksheet BaseData and click Transform Data to open the Query Editor.

3. Select a column to convert to a list by clicking the column header. I will use the column Make in this example.

4. In the Transform ribbon, click Convert to List. The Query Editor will show the resulting list, as you can see in Figure 10-24.

	List
1	Rolls Royce
2	Aston Martin
3	Rolls Royce
4	Rolls Royce
5	Rolls Royce
6	Rolls Royce
7	Aston Martin
8	Aston Martin
9	Aston Martin
10	Aston Martin
11	Aston Martin

Figure 10-24. The list resulting from a conversion-to-list operation

This list can now be used in certain circumstances when carrying out more advanced data transformation processes.

Reusing Data Sources

Over the course of Chapters 2 through 6, you have seen how to access data from a wide variety of sources to build a series of queries across a range of reports. The reality will probably be that you will frequently want to point to the same sources of data over and over again. In anticipation of this, the Power BI development team has found a way to make your life easier.

Power BI Desktop remembers the most recent data sources that you have used and lets you reuse them quickly and easily in any report. Here is how:

1. In the Home ribbon, click the Recent Sources button. The list of the dozen or so most recently used data sources will appear. You can see this in Figure 10-25.

Figure 10-25. *Recently used sources*

2. Click the source that you want to reconnect to, and continue with the data load or connection.

If you cannot see the data source that you want, and you are sure that you have used it recently, then you can scroll to the bottom of this list and click More. Power BI Desktop will display the complete list of recent sources in the Recent Sources dialog that you can see in Figure 10-26.

Figure 10-26. *The Recent Sources dialog*

If you are connecting to any of the database or data warehouse sources that allow DirectQuery or Live Connection, you will see a dialog like the one in Figure 10-27.

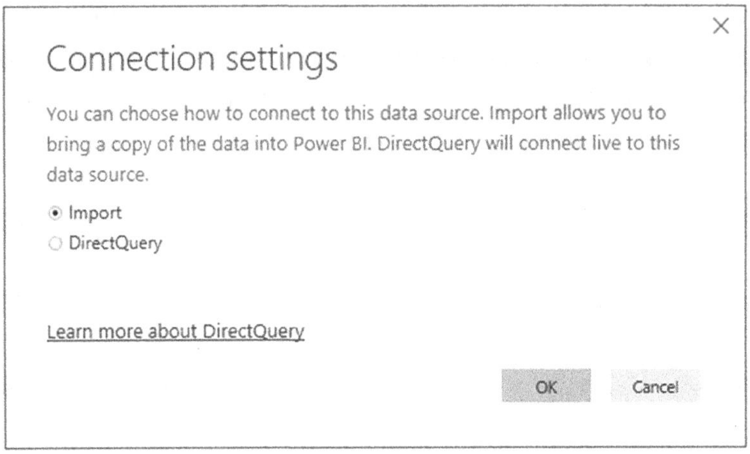

Figure 10-27. *Defining connection settings when reusing an existing connection*

Here you can decide whether to load data or use a direct connection, this time with the chosen data source.

Pinning a Data Source

If you look closely at Figure 10-26, you see that the Excel file CarMakeAndModelMatrix. xlsx (among others) is pinned to the top of the Recent Sources dialog. This allows you to make sure that certain data sources are always kept on hand and ready to reuse.

Do the following to pin a data source that you have recently used to the menu and dialog of recent sources:

1. Click the Recent Sources button in the Power BI Desktop Home ribbon.

2. Scroll down to the bottom of the menu and click More. The Recent Sources dialog will appear.

3. Hover the mouse over a recently used data source. A pin icon will appear at the right of the data source name.

4. Click the pin icon. The data source is pinned to the top of both the Recent Sources menu and the Recent Sources dialog. A small pin icon remains visible at the right of the data source name.

> **Note**   To unpin a data source from the Recent Sources menu and the Recent Sources dialog, all you have to do is click the pin icon for a pinned data source. This unpins it and it reappears in the list of recently used data sources.

If you so wish, you can also apply the following options when deciding which elements you want to make appear in the Recent Sources list:

- Remove from list
- Clear unpinned items from list

Copying Data from Power BI Desktop Query Editor

Power BI Desktop is designed as a data destination. It does not have any data export functionality as such. You can manually copy data from the Power BI Desktop Query Editor, however. More precisely, you can copy any of the following:

- The data in the query
- A column of data
- A single cell

In all cases, the process is the same:

1. Click the element to copy. This can be

   a. The top-left square of the data grid

   b. A column title

   c. A single cell

2. Right-click and select Copy from the context menu.

You can then paste the data from the clipboard into the destination application.

> **Note**   This process is somewhat limited because you cannot select a range of cells. And you must remember that you are only looking at sample data in the Query Editor. You can, however, click Close & Apply and then switch to Table view (as explained in Chapter 13) from where you can copy an entire table.

Conclusion

This chapter pushed your data transformation knowledge with the Power BI Query Editor to a new level, by explaining how to deal with multiple file loads of Excel- and text-based data. You then learned ways of handling data from source files that contain complex, nested source structures—specifically JSON and XML files. You also saw how to parse JSON and XML elements from columns contained in other data sources.

Then, you learned how to reuse data sources and manage frequently used data sources to save time. Finally you learned how to copy sample data resulting from a data transformation process into other applications.

So now the basic tour of data load and transformation with the Power BI Query Editor is over. It is time to move on to more advanced techniques that you can apply to accelerate and enhance, manage, and structure your data transformation processes. These approaches are the subject of the following two chapters.

CHAPTER 11

Organizing, Managing, and Parameterizing Queries

Producing a robust and efficient data query is not just about finding the appropriate load and transform functions and placing them in the correct sequence. It is also about extending, adjusting, and maintaining the process. This can be either to correct an error once the query is being tested or to adapt a query to new requirements. This chapter will introduce you to some of the techniques that you can apply to handle the various stages of the query lifecycle.

Creating an eye-catching dashboard can mean sourcing data from a large range and variety of queries. It may also imply that these queries have to be linked together to create a cascade of data transformations that prepares the core elements of a practical and usable data model collated from multiple sources. It follows that you will therefore need to know how to *manage* the queries that you create to use them efficiently and to keep your queries under control in real-world situations.

However, not all dataflows are rigid and predictable. There will, inevitably, be cases where you also want to shape the data ingestion process depending on aspects of the source data. This can mean parameterizing your queries to allow user interaction or adjusting the dataflow dynamically.

Managing the Transformation Process

Pretty nearly all the transformation steps that we have applied so far have been individual elements that can be applied to just about any data table. However, when you are carrying out even a simple data load and transform process, you are likely to want

© Adam Aspin 2020
A. Aspin, *Pro Power BI Desktop*, https://doi.org/10.1007/978-1-4842-5763-0_11

to step through several transformations in order to shape, cleanse, and filter the data to get the result you want. This is where the Power BI Desktop approach is so malleable, because you can apply most data transformation steps to just about any data table. The art consists of placing them in a sequence that can then be reused any time that the data changes to reprocess the new source data and deliver an up-to-date output.

The key to appreciating and managing this process is to get well acquainted with the Applied Steps list in the Query Settings pane. This list contains the details of every step that you applied, in the order in which you applied it. Each step retains the name that Power BI Desktop gave it when it was created, and each can be altered in the following ways:

- Renamed

- Deleted

- Moved (in certain cases)

The even better news is that, in many cases, steps can be modified. This way you are not stuck with the choices that you made initially, but have the opportunity of tweaking and improving individual steps in a process. This can avoid your having to rebuild an entire sequence of steps in an ETL routine simply by replacing one element in the ETL process.

In order to experiment with the various ways that you can modify queries, you are going to need some initial data. So, to start with, I suggest that you create a query that loads data from the following Excel source file: `C:\PowerBiDesktopSamples\CarSalesDataForQueries.xlsx`. From this source file, select the following tables:

- Clients

- Colors

- Countries

- Invoices

- InvoiceLines

- Stock

Once you have loaded the data, switch to the Query Editor window.

Modifying a Step

How you alter a step will depend on how the original transformation was applied. This becomes second nature after a little practice and will always involve first clicking the step that you wish to modify and then applying a different modification. If you invoke a ribbon option, such as altering the data type, then you change the data type by simply applying another data type directly from the ribbon. If you used an option that displayed a dialog (such as splitting a column, among others), then you can right-click the step in the Applied Steps list and select Edit Settings from the context menu. Alternatively, and if you prefer, you can click the "gear" icon that is displayed to the right of most (but not all) steps to display a dialog where you can adjust the step settings. This dialog will show all the options and settings that you applied initially; in it, you can make any modifications that you consider necessary.

A final possibility that makes it easy to alter the settings for a process is to edit the formula that appears in the formula bar each time you click a step. This, however, involves understanding all the complexities of each piece of the code that underpins the data transformation process. I will provide a short overview of code modification in Chapter 12.

Tip If you can force yourself to organize the process that you are writing with Power BI Desktop, then a little forethought and planning can reap major dividends. For instance, certain tasks, such as setting data types, can be carried out in a single operation. This means that you only have to look in one place for a similar set of data transformations. Not just that, but if you need to alter a data type for a column at a later stage, I suggest that you click the Changed Type step before you make any further alterations. This way, you extend the original step, rather than creating other steps—which can make the process more confusing and needlessly voluminous.

Renaming a Step

Power BI Desktop names steps using the name of the transformation that was applied. This means that if another similar step is applied later, Power BI Desktop uses the same name with a numeric increment. As this is not always comprehensible when reviewing a sequence of transformation steps, you may prefer to give more user-friendly names to individual steps. This is done as follows:

1. Select the query (or source table or worksheet, if you prefer). I will use the Clients query in this example.

2. Right-click the step that you want to rename, Changed Type, for instance.

3. Select Rename from the context menu.

4. Type in the new name. I will use **NewDataTypes**.

5. Press Enter.

The step is renamed and the new name will appear in the Applied Steps list in the Query Settings pane. This way you can ensure that when you come back to a data transformation process days, weeks, or months later, you are able to understand more intuitively the process that you defined, as well as why you shaped the data like you did.

Deleting a Step or a Series of Steps

Deleting a step is all too easy, but doing so can have serious consequences. This is because an ETL process is often an extremely tightly coupled series of events, where each event depends intimately on the preceding one. So deleting a step can make every subsequent step fail. Knowing which events you can delete without drastic consequences will depend on the types of process that you are developing as well as your experience with Power BI Desktop. In any case, this is what you should do if you need to delete a step:

1. Place the pointer over the process step that you want to delete.

2. Click the cross (×) icon that appears.

3. Select Delete. The Delete Step dialog *might* appear, as shown in Figure 11-1.

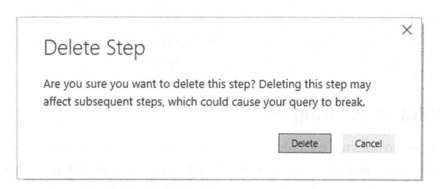

Figure 11-1. *The Delete Step dialog*

    4.   Confirm by clicking the Delete button. The step is deleted.

If—and it is highly possible—deleting this step causes issues for the rest of the process, you will see that the data table is replaced by an error message. This message will vary depending on the type of error that Power BI Desktop has encountered.

When describing this technique, I was careful to state that you *might* see the Delete Step dialog. If you are deleting the final step in a sequence of steps, then you will probably not see it, since there should not be any potentially horrendous consequences; at worst, you will have to re-create the step. If you are deleting a step in the middle of a process, then you might want to think seriously about doing so before you cause a potentially vast number of problems. Consequently, you are asked to confirm the deletion in these cases.

Note   If you realize at this point that you have just destroyed hours of work, then (after drawing a deep breath) click the File menu in the Power BI Desktop window (the downward-facing triangle at the top left) and select Close, then close Power BI Desktop without saving. Don't count on using an undo function as you can in other desktop applications. To lower your blood pressure, you may prefer to save a copy of a file containing an intricate data transformation process *before* deleting any steps. You can also make copies of the entire data transformation process as "M" code—as you will learn in the next chapter.

An alternative technique is to right-click the step that you want to delete and select Delete. You may still have to confirm the deletion.

If you realize that an error in a process step has invalidated all your work up until the end of the process, rather than deleting multiple elements one by one, click Delete Until End from the context menu at step 2 in the preceding exercise.

Modifying an Existing Step

Power BI Desktop does not try and lock you into a rigid sequence of events when you create a series of applied steps to create and transform a dataflow. This really becomes obvious when you discover that you need to alter a step in a process.

Suppose, for instance, that you discover that you have loaded a wrong Excel worksheet when you selected the initial data from Excel. You do not want to repeat the process when you can simply substitute one worksheet name for another.

1. Select the query that you want to modify (Clients in this example).

2. Click the step to modify (in this case it will be Navigation).

3. Click the gear (or cog) icon to the right of the step name. The appropriate dialog will appear. In this case it will be the Navigation dialog that you can see in Figure 11-2.

Figure 11-2. *The Navigation dialog displayed for step modification*

4. Click the table or worksheet that you want to use instead of the current dataset (LatestClients in this example).

5. Click OK.

The Query Editor will replace one source dataset with another. It might also add extra steps to ensure that the data is adapted for use in the query.

As you saw in the previous ten chapters, Power BI Desktop offers a vast range of data ingestion and modification possibilities. So I cannot, here, describe every possible option as far as modifying an Applied Step is concerned. Nonetheless, the principle is simple:

- If the Query Editor can modify a step, the gear icon will be displayed to the right of the step name.

- Clicking the modification (the gear) icon will display the dialog that was used to create the step (or that can be used to modify the step even if the step was created automatically by Power BI Desktop).

Certain steps do not display the modification icon. This is because the step cannot be modified, only removed (at least, using the Query Editor interface). As an example of this, add the following step:

1. Select the query that you want to modify (Clients in this example).

2. Click the last step.

3. Right-click the Address2 column and select Remove.

A new step will appear in the Applied Steps list, named Removed Columns. This step does not have the modification icon. So, for the moment, you can remove it, but *not* modify it—at least, not using the graphical user interface. You can, however, modify the code for a step as you will learn in Chapter 12.

Note   Modifying existing steps is not a "magic bullet." This is because a series of data transformations can be highly dependent on a tailored logic that has been developed for a specific data structure. It follows, for instance, that you can only replace a data source with another one that has a virtually identical structure. However, modifying a step can avoid your having to rewrite an entire dataflow sequence in many cases.

Adding a Step

You can add a step anywhere in the sequence. All you have to do is click the step that *precedes* the new step that you want to insert *before* clicking the icon in any of the ribbons that corresponds to the new step. As is the case when you delete a step, Power BI Desktop will display an alert warning you that this action *could* cause problems with the process from this new step on.

Altering Process Step Sequencing

It is possible—technically—to resequence steps in a process. However, in my experience, this is not always practical, since changing the order of steps in a process can cause as much damage as deleting a step. Nonetheless, you can always try it like this:

1. Right-click the step that you want to resequence.

2. Select Move Up or Move Down from the context menu.

I remain pessimistic that this can work miracles, but it is good to know that it is there.

Tip   Remember that before tweaking the order in which the process is applied, clicking any process step causes the table in the Power BI Desktop window to refresh to show you the state of the data up to and including the selected step. This is a very clear visual guide to the process and how the ETL process is carried out.

An Approach to Sequencing

Given the array of available data transformation options, you may well be wondering how best to approach a new ETL project using Power BI Desktop. I realize that all projects are different, but as a rough and ready guide, I suggest attempting to order your project like this:

1. Load the data into Power BI Desktop.

2. Promote or add comprehensible column headers. For example, you really do not want to be looking at step 47 of a process and wondering what Column29 is, when it could read (for instance) ClientName.

3. Remove any columns that you do not need. The smaller the dataset, the faster the processing. What is more, you will find it easier to concentrate on, and understand, the data if you are only looking at information that you really need. Any columns that have been removed can be returned to the dataset simply by deleting or editing the step that removed them.

4. Alter the data types for every column in the table. Correct data types are fundamental for many transformation steps, and are essential for filtering, so it's best to get them sorted out early on.

5. Filter out any records that you do not need. Once again, the smaller the dataset, the faster the processing. This includes deduplication.

6. Parse any complex JSON or XML elements.

7. Carry out any necessary data cleansing.

8. Carry out any necessary transforms.

9. Carry out any necessary column splits or adding custom columns.

10. Add any derived columns.

11. Add any calculations or logical transformations of data.

12. Handle any error records that the ETL process has thrown up.

Once again, I must stress that this is not a definitive guide. I hope, however, that it will help you to see "the wood for the trees" when you are creating data load and transformation processes using Power BI Desktop.

Error Records

Some data transformation operations will cause errors. This can be a fact of life when mashing up source data. For instance, you could have a few rows in a large dataset where a date column contains a few records that are texts or numbers. If you convert the column to a date data type, then any values that cannot be converted will appear as error values.

Removing Errors

Assuming that you do not need records that Power BI Desktop has flagged as containing an error, you can remove all such records in a single operation:

1. Click inside the column containing errors; or if you want to remove errors from several columns at once, Ctrl-click the titles of the columns that contain the errors.

2. Click Remove Errors in the Home ribbon. Any records with errors flagged in the selected columns are deleted. Removed Errors is added to the Applied Steps list.

You have to be very careful here not to remove valid data. Only you can judge, once you have taken a look at the data, if an error in a column means that the data can be discarded safely. In all other cases, you would be best advised to look at cleansing the data or simply leaving records that contain errors in place. The range and variety of potential errors are as vast as the data itself.

Managing Queries

Once you have used Power BI Desktop for any length of time, you will probably become addicted to creating more and deeper analyses based on wider-ranging data sources. Inevitably, this will mean learning to manage the data sources that feed into your data models efficiently and productively.

Fortunately, Power BI Desktop Query comes replete with a small arsenal of query management tools to help you. These include

- Organizing queries

- Grouping queries

- Duplicating queries

- Referencing queries

- Documenting queries

- Adding a column as a new query

- Enabling data load

- Enabling report refresh

Let's take a look at these functions, one by one.

Organizing Queries

When you have a dozen or more queries that you are using in the Power BI Desktop Query Editor, you may want to exercise some control over how they are organized. To begin with, you can modify the order in which queries appear in the Queries pane on the left of the Power BI Desktop Query Editor window. This lets you override the default order, which is that the most recently added data source appears at the bottom of the list.

Do the following to change the position of a query in the list:

1. Right-click the query that you want to move.

2. Select Move Up (or Move Down) from the context menu.

You have to carry out this operation a number of times to move a query up or down a number of places.

Grouping Queries

You can also create custom groups to better organize the queries that you are using in a Power BI Desktop file. This will not have any effect on how the queries work. Grouping queries is simply an organizational technique, and it will not change in any way the data tables that you see in report mode in Power BI Desktop.

Creating a New Group

The following explains how to create a new group:

1. Right-click the query that you want to add to a new group. I will use the Colors query.

2. Select Move To Group ➤ New Group from the context menu. The New Group dialog will appear.

3. Enter a name for the group and (optionally) a description. I will name the group **ReferenceData**. The dialog will look something like Figure 11-3.

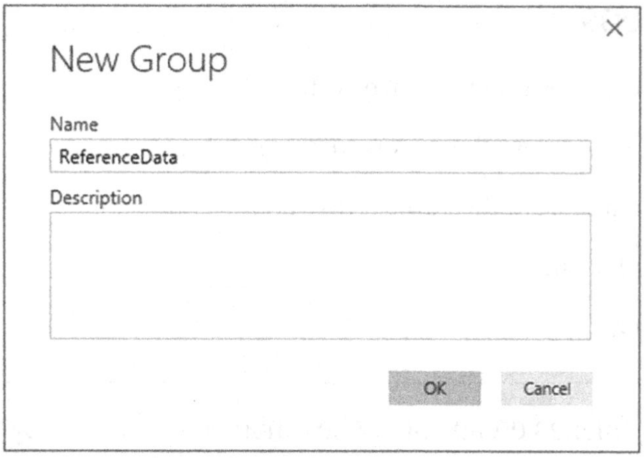

New Group

×

Name

ReferenceData

Description

OK   Cancel

Figure 11-3. *The New Group dialog*

    4.   Click OK.

The new group is created and the selected query will appear in the group. The Queries pane will look something like Figure 11-4.

Figure 11-4. *The Queries pane with a new group added*

Note   By default, all other queries are added to a group named Other Queries.

Renaming Groups

You can rename any groups that you have added.

1. Right-click the query that you want to rename.

2. Select Rename from the context menu.

3. Edit or replace the name.

4. Press Enter.

Note   The Other Queries group cannot be renamed or deleted. By default, all new queries will be added to this group.

Adding a Query to a Group

To move a query from its current group to another group, you can carry out the following steps:

1. Right-click the query that you want to add to another existing group.

2. Select Move To Group ➤ *Destination Group Name* from the context menu.

The selected query is moved to the chosen group.

Duplicating Queries

If you have done a lot of work transforming data, you could well want to keep a copy of the original query before trying out any potentially risky alterations to your work. Fortunately, this is extremely simple.

1. Right-click the query that you want to copy.

2. Select Duplicate from the context menu.

The query is copied and the duplicate appears in the list of queries inside the same group as the source query. It has the same name as the original query, with a number in parentheses appended. You can always rename it in the Query Settings pane or in the Queries pane on the left of the Query Editor window.

Note   You can copy and paste queries if you prefer. The advantage of this technique is that you can choose the destination group for the copied query simply by clicking the folder icon for the required group *before* pasting the copy of the query.

Referencing Queries

If you are building a complex ETL (Extract, Transform, Load) routine, you might conceivably organize your work in stages to better manage the process. To help you with this, the Power BI Desktop Query Editor allows you to *use the output from one query as the source for another query*. This enables you to break down different parts of the process (e.g., structure, filters, then cleansing) into separate queries so that you can concentrate on different aspects of the transformation in different queries.

To use the output of one query as the source data for another, you need to *reference* a query. The following explains how to do it:

1. Right-click the query that you want to use as the source data for a new query.

2. Select Reference from the context menu. A new query is created in the list of queries in the Queries pane.

3. Right-click the new query, select Rename, and give it a meaningful name.

Unless you rename the query, the new query has the same name as the original query, with a number in parentheses appended. If you click the new query, you see exactly the same data in the referenced query as you can see if you click the final step in the source query.

From now on, any modifications that you make in the referenced (source) query produce an effect on the data that is used as the source for the second query.

In practice, I suspect, you will not want to use two copies of the same query to create reports. Indeed, if a query is being used as an "intermediate" query, the data that it contains might not even be fully usable. So you could want to *make the intermediate query unavailable to reports and dashboards* in Power BI Desktop. To do this:

1. Right-click the original (source) query.

2. Deselect Enable Load from the context menu. The check mark to the left of the menu item will disappear.

The source query will no longer appear in Report View and so cannot be used in visuals. It is worth noting that any queries that are "intermediate" queries (i.e., queries that you use to modify data but that do not show in Data View or Report View) are in italics.

You may be wondering why you would want to create "intermediate" queries. Some ideas are

- You want to isolate complex data transformations into more manageable subsets. You may, for instance, want one intermediate query that transforms the data while a subsequent query cleanses the data.

- You could want to apply a common set of initial transformations that then feed into two separate data preparation paths—a detailed view of the data and an aggregated view.

Note   Ensure that any existing reports do not use a query that you subsequently make unavailable in this way, or you will end up with broken visuals in your reports.

Documenting Queries

In a complex ETL process, it is easy to get confused—or simply forget—which query does what. Consequently, I always advise documenting queries by adding a meaningful description.

1. Right-click the query that you want to annotate.

2. Select Properties from the context menu. The Query Properties dialog will appear.

3. Add a description. The result could be like the dialog shown in Figure 11-5.

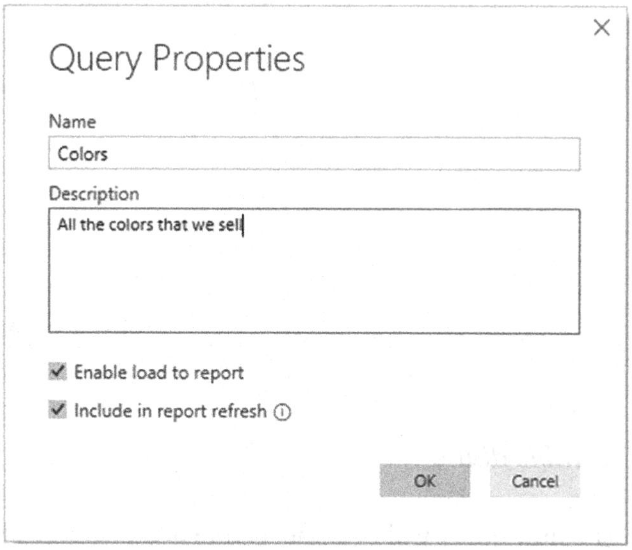

Figure 11-5. Adding a description to a query

4. Click OK.

The description that you added is now visible as a tooltip if you hover the cursor over the query name in the list of queries in the Query Editor.

Adding a Column As a New Query

There are occasions when you might want to extract a column of data and use it as a separate query. It could be that you need the data that it contains as reference data for another query, for example. The following steps explain how you can do this:

1. In the Queries list on the left, select the query containing the column that you want to isolate as a new query.

2. Right-click the title of the column containing the data that you want to isolate.

3. Select Add as New Query from the context menu. A new query is created. It is named after the original query and the source column.

4. In the Transform ribbon, click To Table. The To Table dialog will appear, as you can see in Figure 11-6.

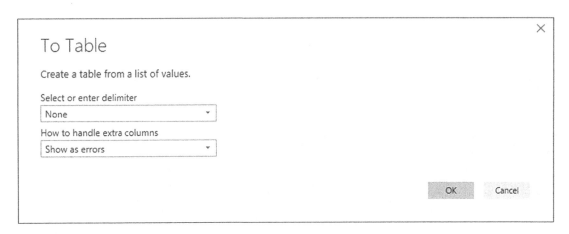

Figure 11-6. *The To Table dialog*

5. Click OK. The new query will become a table of data and will have the name of the column that you selected.

6. Rename the query, if you judge this necessary.

You can now use this query in your data model and as part of a linked set of query processes.

Note   A query created in this way is completely disconnected from the source query from where the data was taken. Put another way, any refresh of the source data will have *no* effect on the new query that you created from a column.

Enabling Data Load

You may have gained the impression that any query that you create will always become part of the Power BI Desktop data model. This is emphatically *not* the case as I mentioned briefly in the section on reference queries. You can create queries that are in effect only "staging" queries that are part of a more complex sequence of transformations or queries that contain only lookup data that is added to another table but not needed in the data model, for instance. In cases like these, you certainly do not want these tables adding clutter to the data model.

To prevent a query being added to the data model, do the following:

1.   In the Queries list on the left, select the query that you want to keep in the Query Editor—but not in the data model.

2.   Right-click the query and uncheck Enable Load.

The query will no longer be loaded into the data model with the other queries.

To reset a query as a candidate for loading into the data model, merely carry out the same operation and ensure that Enable Load is checked. You can see from the check mark in the context menu if the query is due to be loaded or not. As an alternative, you can right-click the query and display the query properties, where you can check (or uncheck) the "Enable load to report" check box.

Note   You can also set this property in the Query Properties dialog that you saw in Figure 11-5.

Enabling Report Refresh

By default, all queries can be refreshed. This lets you gather the very latest data from the source into the Power BI Desktop Query Editor and then into the data model.

There could be times when you do not want to refresh a query. Perhaps the data source is unobtainable, or is slow, or you want to return later for the latest data. Power BI Desktop Query Editor lets you set the refresh option for each query like this:

1.   In the Queries list on the left, right-click the query whose refresh status you want to modify.

2.   Uncheck "Include in report refresh."

Note   Only queries that are enabled for load can have the refresh property modified.

Pending Changes

When you are dealing with data sources and switch from the Query Editor to the Power BI Desktop view, normally, you then want to load the full data from the source into the data model.

The downside to this approach is that a huge set of source data can take a long time to load, or reload, when you move back to creating and modifying visualizations. This is why Power BI Desktop will let you select Close from the Close & Apply button in the Query Editor Home ribbon. Doing this will return you instantly to the Data View, but will not apply any changes that you have made. As a reminder, you will see an alert like the one shown in Figure 11-7 at the top of the Data View.

 There are pending changes in your queries that haven't been applied.   Apply changes

Figure 11-7. *The pending changes alert*

You can continue to work in Data View as long as you like. Click the Apply changes button when you have time to reload the modified source data into the data model. You need to be aware, however, that you will not see all the latest changes to the structure of the tables and fields in the Fields list—as well as the latest data, of course—until you apply the changes.

Parameterizing Queries

Parameters in Power BI Desktop enable you to define and apply specific criteria to certain aspects of queries. At their heart, they are a technique that enables you to

- Store a value that can then be used in multiple queries
- Restrict a selection of potential values to a specific list of options

There are currently three basic ways of creating parameters:

- A single value that you enter
- A selection of a value from a list of possible values that you enter manually
- A selection of a value from a list of possible values that you create using existing queries

It follows that using parameters is a two-step process:

- Create a parameter.

- Apply it to a query.

A parameter is really nothing more than a specialized type of query. As it is a query, you can

- Load it into the data model (although this is rarely required)

- Reference it from another query

- Use it in DAX formulas

The next three short subsections will explain how you can create parameters. I will then show you some of the ways that you can apply parameters in the Query Editor to filter or transform the data.

Creating a Simple Parameter

At its simplest, a parameter is a value that you store so that you can use it later to assist you in your data transformation. Here is how you can store a parameter containing a "True" value ready for use in filtering subsequent datasets:

1. Load the data contained in the Excel file `C:\PowerBiDesktop Samples\CarSalesOverview.xlsx` (using the worksheet that is also called CarSalesOverview) into Power BI Desktop.

2. In the Home ribbon, click Transform Data. The Query Editor will open.

3. In the Query Editor Home ribbon, click the small triangle at the bottom of the Manage Parameters button, then select New Parameter from the available menu options. The Parameters dialog will appear.

4. Enter **DealerParameter** as the parameter name and **Filter dealer types** as the description.

5. Ensure that the Required check box is selected.

6. Choose True/False from the popup list of types.

7. Enter True as the current value from the popup list. The dialog will look like the one in Figure 11-8.

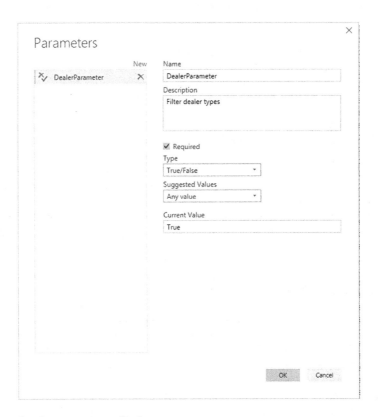

Figure 11-8. *The Parameters dialog*

8. Click OK. The new parameter will appear in the Queries list on the left. You can see this in Figure 11-9.

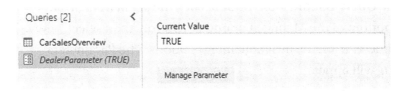

Figure 11-9. *A parameter in the Queries list*

For the moment, all you have done is create a parameter and store a value in it. You will see how to use this parameter in a few pages' time. As you can see, a parameter is stored as a type of query, and the default value is displayed after the query name in parentheses.

Creating a Set of Parameter Values

While a single parameter can always be useful, in reality you are likely to need lists of potential parameters. This will allow you to choose a parameter value from a predefined list in certain circumstances. Here is an example of creating a parameter containing a subset of the available country names used in the sample data:

1. Using the Power BI Desktop file that you created in the previous section (the one based on the Excel file `C:\PowerBiDesktopSamples\CarSalesOverview.xlsx`), open the Query Editor unless the Query Editor is already open.

2. In the Query Editor Home ribbon, click the small triangle at the bottom of the Manage Parameters button, then select New Parameter from the available menu options. The Parameters dialog will be displayed.

3. Enter **CountriesParameter** as the parameter name.

4. Ensure that the Required check box is selected.

5. Choose Text from the popup list of types.

6. In the Suggested Values popup list, select List of Values.

7. Enter the following three values in the grid that has now appeared:

    a. France

    b. Germany

    c. Spain

8. Select France as the Default Value from the popup list.

9. Select France as the Current Value from the popup list. The dialog will look like the one shown in Figure 11-10.

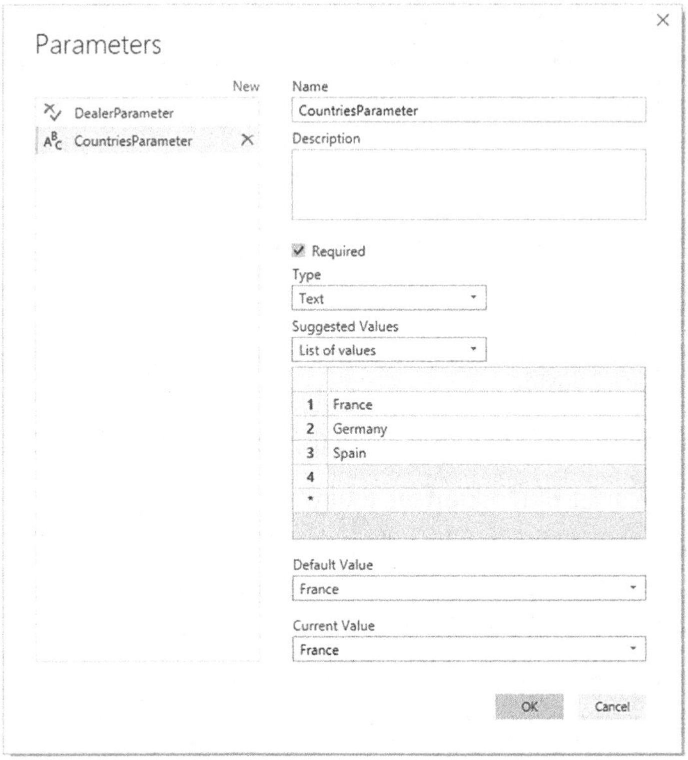

Figure 11-10. *The Parameters dialog*

10. Click OK. The new parameter will appear in the Queries list on
     the left.

Once again, all you have done is create the parameter. You will see how it can be
applied in a couple of pages' time.

Note   As you can see, any current value that you have chosen will appear in the
Queries pane in parentheses to the right of the parameter name. This is to help you
remember which value is current and is possibly being used to filter data.

Creating a Query-Based Parameter

Typing lists of values that you can use to choose a parameter is not only laborious, it is also potentially error-prone. So you can use the data from existing queries to create the series of available elements that you use in a parameter instead of typing lists of values. As an example of this, suppose that you want a parameter that contains all the available makes of car that the company sells:

1. Using the Power BI Desktop file that you created in the previous section (the one based on the Excel file `C:\PowerBiDesktopSamples\CarSalesOverview.xlsx`), open the Query Editor.

2. Select the query CarSalesOverview in the Queries list.

3. Right-click the title of the column named Model, and select Add as New Query. A new query named Model will appear in the Queries list. This query contains the contents of the column you selected.

4. Right-click the Model query and uncheck Enable Load. This prevents the query from appearing in the Power BI Desktop interface as a table.

5. In the newly created query, click Remove Duplicates in the Transform ribbon. The List column will only display unique values.

6. Rename the newly created query **ModelList**.

7. In the Query Editor Home ribbon, click the small triangle at the bottom of the Manage Parameters button, then select New Parameter from the available menu options. The Parameters dialog will be displayed.

8. Enter **ModelsParameter** as the parameter name.

9. Ensure that the Required check box is selected.

10. Choose Text from the popup list of types.

11. In the Suggested Values popup list, select Query.

12. Select ModelList as the query containing a list of values to use from the popup list of available lists.

13. Enter DB9 as the Current Value.

14. Click OK. The new parameter will appear in the Queries list on the left.

You should now be able to see all three parameters that you have created in the Queries pane, as shown in Figure 11-11.

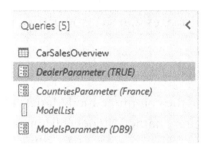

Figure 11-11. *Parameters in the Queries list*

Note   It is normal to prevent a list that is being used to provide a series of values for a parameter from being loaded into the data model (as you did in step 4). This is because this query (or list, if you prefer) is not required in the data model, and you do not want to confuse users by having it appear in the Fields list.

Once your parameters have been created, you can quit the Query Editor by clicking the Close & Apply button. You should see no change in the Power BI Desktop Report View. This is because parameters are used to shape a dataflow process, but *not* as the data in the data model.

Tip   It is also possible to create parameters "on the fly" (that is directly from inside a dialog that uses a parameter) when you want to use them. However, I find it better practice—and more practical—to prepare parameters beforehand. This forces you to think through the reasons for the parameter as well as the potential range of its use. It can also avoid your making errors when trying to do two different things at once.

Modifying a Parameter

Fortunately, parameters are not set in stone once they are created. You can easily modify

- The structure of a parameter

- The selected parameter element (the current value)

Modifying the Structure of a Parameter

Should you need to modify the way that a parameter is constructed, one way is to do the following:

1. In the Query Editor Home ribbon, click Manage Parameters. The Parameters dialog will be displayed as seen in the previous sections.

2. In the left pane of the dialog, click the parameter that you want to modify. The parameter definition will appear on the right.

3. Carry out any required modifications.

4. Click OK.

Alternatively, you can do this:

1. Click the parameter in the Queries pane on the left of the Query Editor.

2. Click the Manage Parameter button. The Parameters dialog will appear.

3. Carry out any required modifications.

4. Click OK.

You can also, if you prefer, right-click a parameter in the Queries pane and select Manage from the popup menu to display the Parameters dialog.

Applying a Parameter When Filtering Records

Now that you have seen how parameters are created, it is time to see them in action. As a first example of applying a parameter, you will see how to use a parameter to filter a query:

1. Open the file `C:\PowerBiDesktopSamples\ParametersExample.pbix`. This file contains the three parameters created previously.

2. Open the Power BI Desktop Query Editor.

3. Click the CarSalesOverview query in the Queries list. A dataset of car sales information will appear.

4. Click the popup menu for the CountryName column.

5. Select Text Filters ▣⊙➤ Equals. The Filter Rows dialog will appear.

6. Leave Equals as the first choice.

7. Click the second popup and select Parameter from the list. You can see this in Figure 11-12.

Figure 11-12. *Selecting a parameter for a filter*

8. Select CountriesParameter for the third popup. The dialog will look like the one shown in Figure 11-13.

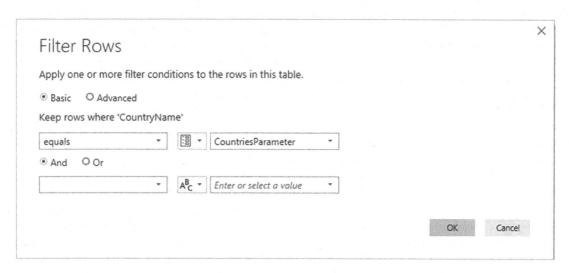

Figure 11-13. *Applying a parameter for a filter*

9. Click OK. The current parameter value (the country that you selected) will be applied, and the dataset will be filtered using the current parameter value.

Note   To remove a parameter from a filter, simply delete the relevant step in the Applied Steps list.

Modifying the Current Value of a Parameter

You could be forgiven for wondering if it is worth setting up a parameter merely to filter a dataset. However, this whole approach becomes more interesting if you modify the current parameter value and then refresh the data to apply the new parameter. Here is an example of this:

1. In the Query Editor Home ribbon, click the small triangle to display the menu for the Manage Parameters button.

2. Select Edit Parameters. The Enter Parameters dialog will appear.

3. From the popup list of values for the CountriesParameter, select one of the available values (and not the value that was previously selected). The dialog should look like the one shown in Figure 11-14.

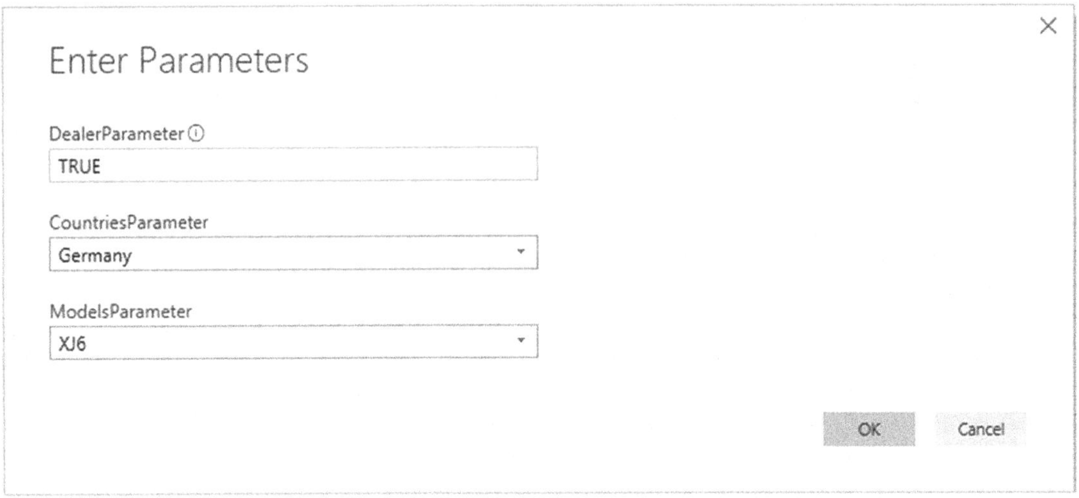

Figure 11-14. *Modifying the current value of a parameter*

4. Click OK.

5. In the Query Editor Home ribbon, click Refresh Preview. The data will be refreshed and the new parameter values applied to the filters that use these parameters.

This approach becomes particularly useful if you have many combinations of filter values to test. In essence, you can apply a series of filters to several columns (or create complex filters) using several parameters and then test the results of different combinations of parameters on a dataset using the Enter Parameters dialog. This technique avoids having to alter multiple filters manually—and repeatedly. As an added bonus, you can restrict the user (or yourself) to specific lists of parameter choices by defining the lists of available parameter options. You can see this for the popup lists that appear when you select the CountriesParameter popup or the ModelsParameter popup.

Applying a Parameter in a Search and Replace

Another use for parameters is to apply them as either the search value or the replacement value in a search and replace operation. You can see this in the following example:

1. Open the Power BI Desktop file C:\PowerBiDesktopSamples\ ParametersExample.pbix.

2. Open the Power BI Desktop Query Editor.

3. Click the CarSalesOverview query in the Queries pane.

4. Click inside the CountryName column.

5. In the Transform ribbon, click Replace Values (or right-click
    and select Replace values). The Replace Values dialog will be
    displayed.

6. Click the popup list to the left under Value To Find, and select
    Parameter.

7. Choose CountriesParameter as the parameter to apply.

8. Enter Luxemburg (for instance) as the replacement value. The
    dialog will look like the one in Figure 11-15.

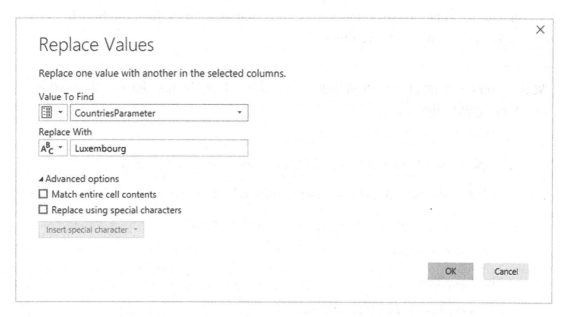

Figure 11-15.   *Using a parameter in search and replace*

9. Click OK. The parameter's current value will be replaced in the
    dataset for the selected column.

Applying a Parameter to a Data Source

In some corporate environments, there are many database servers that are available, and possibly even more databases. You may find it difficult to remember all of these—and so may the users that you are preparing Power BI Desktop reports for.

One solution that can make a corporate environment easier to navigate is to prepare parameters that contain the lists of available servers and databases. These parameters can then be used—and updated—to guide users in their choice of SQL Server, Oracle, or other database data sources.

To see this in action, you will first have to prepare two parameters:

- A list of servers

- A list of databases

You can then see how to use these parameters to connect to data sources. Of course, you will have to replace the example server and database names that I use here in steps 3 and 4 with names from your own environment.

Note   You can only apply parameters if the check box Always allow is checked in the Query Editor View menu.

---

1. Open a new Power BI Desktop file and close the splash screen.

2. Click Transform Data to open the Query Editor.

3. Create a new parameter using the following elements:

   a. *Name*: Servers

   b. *Type*: Text

   c. *Suggested Values*: List of Values

   d. *Values in the list*: ADAM03 and ADAM03\SQLServer2016 (or your database server)

   e. *Default Value*: ADAM03\SQLServer2016 (or your database server)

   f. *Current Value*: ADAM03\SQLServer2016 (or your database server)

4. Create a new parameter using the following elements:

   a. *Name*: Databases

   b. *Type*: Text

   c. *Suggested Values*: List of Values

   d. *Values in the list*: CarSalesData and CarSalesMemoryBased

   e. *Default Value*: CarSalesData

   f. *Current Value*: CarSalesData

5. Click Close & Apply to close the Query Editor.

6. In the Power BI Desktop Report screen, click the SQL Server button.

7. On the Server line, click the popup for the server and choose Parameters. Select the Servers parameter.

8. On the Database line, click the popup for the database and choose Parameters. Select the Databases parameter. The SQL Server dialog will look like the one shown in Figure 11-16.

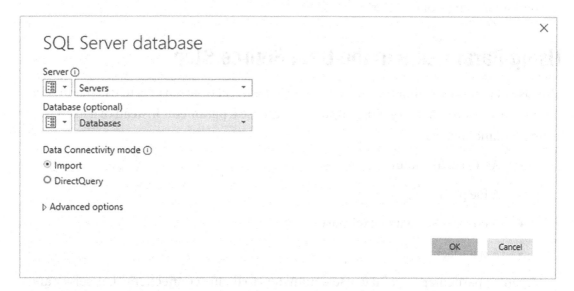

Figure 11-16. *Using a parameter to select the server and database*

9. Choose the data connectivity mode and any advanced options that you want to set.

10. Click OK. The server connection process and dialogs will appear, and you will then see the Navigator dialog displaying the tables and views for the current server and database values in the two parameters.

Note   Preparing parameters for data connection is particularly useful if you then save the file as a template that can be used as the basis for multiple different Power BI Desktop report files. You will learn how to create templates in a few pages.

Other Uses for Parameters

These examples only cover a few of the cases where parameters can be applied in Power BI Desktop. Indeed, the range of circumstances where a parameter can be applied is increasing with each release of the product. So look out for all the dialogs that give you the option of using a parameter!

Using Parameters in the Data Source Step

One use of parameters that can quickly prove to be a real time-saver is to use parameters in the Source step of a query. Put simply, you can use a parameter instead of a fixed element name such as

- An Excel file name

- A file path

- A database or data warehouse server

- A database

It can be particularly useful to use parameters to define connections (i.e., server and database references), as this

- Provides a central reference point for connection information

- Avoids you having to type connection details for similar queries from the same server—and minimizes the risk of introducing typos

- Makes it easier to switch between development, test, and production servers

To illustrate this, and assuming that you have created the parameters "Servers" and "Databases" from the previous section, try the following:

1. Create a connection to a SQL Server database (as described in Chapter 3).

2. Click the Transform Data button in the Home ribbon.

3. In the Query Editor, select the query created by the database connection.

4. Click the first of the Applied Steps on the right. This step should be named "Source."

5. In the formula bar, replace the code that looks something like this:

```
= Sql.Database("ADAMO3\SQL2017", "PrestigeCars")
```

6. With this:

```
= Sql.Database(Servers, Databases)
```

7. Confirm your modifications by clicking the check box in the formula bar—or by pressing Enter. You will almost certainly have to confirm your database credentials.

Note   You need to be aware that hard-coded server and database names must be contained in double quotes, whereas parameters must *not* be enclosed in quotes. Also remember that the M language used in the formula bar is case-sensitive. So you need to enter parameter names *exactly* as they were created.

Applying a Parameter to a SQL Query

If you are using a relational database, such as Oracle or SQL Server, as a data source (and if you are reasonably up to speed with the flavor of SQL that the source database uses), you can query a database using SQL and then apply Power BI Desktop parameters to the source query.

Let's see this in action:

1. Open a new Power BI Desktop file, open the Query Editor, and create the parameter named CountriesParameter that you saw a few pages ago.

2. Click Close & Apply to close the Query Editor.

3. In the Power BI Desktop Report screen, click SQL Server database.

4. Enter the server and database that you are using. (If you are using the examples from the Apress website, then it will be your server and the database CarSalesData.)

5. Click Advanced options and enter the following SQL statement:

```
SELECT  *
FROM    CarSalesData.Data.CarSalesData
WHERE   CountryName = 'Germany'
```

6. Click OK and confirm any dialogs about data access and permissions.

7. Click Edit to connect to the data and open the Query Editor.

8. There should only be one Applied Step for the data connection. Expand the formula bar and tweak the formula so that it looks like this:

```
= Sql.Database("ADAMO3\SQLSERVER2016", "CarSalesData",
[Query="SELECT  *#(lf)FROM    CarSalesData.Data.CarSalesData#(lf)
WHERE   CountryName = '"& CountriesParameter &"'"])
```

9. Click the tick icon in the formula bar to confirm your changes.

    The data will change to display the data for France (the current parameter value) rather than Germany (the initial value in the SQL.)

You can now alter the parameter value and refresh the data. This will place the current parameter inside the SQL WHERE clause and only get the data for the current parameter.

In case this seems a little succinct, let's look at the code used by Power BI Desktop *before* you made the change in step 8. The M language read:

```
= Sql.Database("ADAMO3\SQLSERVER2016", "CarSAlesDAta",
[Query="SELECT *#(lf)FROM    CarSalesData.Data.CarSalesData#(lf)WHERE
CountryName = 'France'#(lf)"])
```

The change was to replace

France

with

"& CountriesParameter &"

What you did was to replace the hard-coded criterion "France" with the parameter reference. Indeed, much as you would in Excel, you added double quotes and ampersands to the formula to allow the code to include an extraneous element.

This was an extremely simple example, but I hope that it opens the door to some fairly advanced use of parameters in database connections.

Note   Updating data once a parameter has changed might require accepting data changes and new permissions.

Query Icons

As you could see previously in Figure 11-16, there are three query icons. These are explained in Table 11-1.

Table 11-1. *Query Icons*

Icon	Query Type	Description
▦	Query	The icon for a standard query.
▯	List	The icon for a list.
▤	Parameter	The icon for a parameter.

Power BI Templates with Parameters

If you have created a Power BI model that contains powerful data transformation routines or simply a set of data connection options—like the ones that you saw in the previous pages—you could want to use any or all of these as the common basis for multiple reports.

The solution to this is extremely simple. You just save a Power BI Desktop file containing all the code, ETL, and other resources that you will need in future reports as a template. You can then open the template and a new Power BI Desktop file will open using all the template's queries, parameters, and code. You then save the new file perfectly normally as a "standard" Power BI Desktop file.

To save a file as a template:

1. Create the model file containing the queries, parameters, and all other elements that make it the basis for future reports.

2. In the Home ribbon, click File ➤ Save As.

3. In the Save As dialog, select Power BI Template File (*.pbit) as the Save As type.

4. Enter a file name and click OK.

You can now open the template file just as you would any other Power BI Desktop file. Power BI Desktop will open a copy of the template, leaving the template itself untouched.

Conclusion

In this chapter you saw how to manage and extend the contents of the queries that you can create using Power BI Desktop. Specifically, you saw how to modify individual steps in a data load and transformation process. This ranged from renaming steps to changing the order of steps in a process—or even altering the specification of what a step actually does.

Then you saw how to manage whole queries. You learned how to rename and group queries as well as how to chain queries so that the output from one query became the source of data for another query.

Finally, you learned how to add parameters to queries and how to interact with queries in a controlled fashion. This lets you make queries—and so the entire ETL process—more flexible and interactive.

CHAPTER 12

The M Language

Data ingestion and modification are not only interface driven in Power BI Desktop. In fact, the entire process is underpinned and powered by a highly specific programming language. Called "M," this language underlies everything that you have learned to do in the last 11 chapters.

Most users—and most of the time—are unlikely to need to use the M language directly at all. This is because the Power Query Editor interface that you have learned so much about thus far in this book is both comprehensive and extremely intuitive. Yet there may be times when you will need to

- Add some additional functionality that is not immediately accessible through the graphical interface

- Add programming logic such as generating sequences of dates or numbers

- Create or manipulate your own lists, records, or tables programmatically

- Create your own built-in functions to extend or enhance those that are built into the M language

- Use the Advanced Editor to modify code

- Add comments to your data ingestion processes

Before introducing you to these concepts, I need to add a few caveats:

- The "M" language that underpins Power BI Desktop queries is not for the faint of heart. The language can seem abstruse at first sight.

- The documentation is extremely technical and not wildly comprehensible for the uninitiated.

© Adam Aspin 2020
A. Aspin, *Pro Power BI Desktop*, https://doi.org/10.1007/978-1-4842-5763-0_12

- The learning curve can be steep, even for experienced programmers.

- The "M" language is very different from VBA (Visual Basic for Applications), which many Excel power users know well.

- Tweaking a step manually can cause havoc to a carefully wrought data load and transform process.

Moreover, the "M" language is so vast that it requires an entire book. Consequently, I have deliberately chosen to provide only the most superficial of introductions here. For greater detail I suggest that you consult the Microsoft documentation. This is currently available at the following URLs:

- https://msdn.microsoft.com/en-us/library/mt779182.aspx

- https://msdn.microsoft.com/en-us/library/mt807488.aspx

In this chapter I am not going to presume that the reader has any in-depth programming knowledge. I will provide a few comparisons with standard programming concepts to assist any readers that have programmed in VBA, C#, or Java. However, rest assured, the intention is to open up new horizons for passionate Power BI Desktop users rather than spiral off into a complex technical universe.

All of this is probably best understood by building on your existing knowledge and explaining how (simply by using the Power Query graphical interface) you have been writing M code already. Then you can extend this knowledge by learning how to tweak existing code, and finally you will see how to write M code unaided.

What Is the M Language?

I should, nonetheless, begin with a few technical stakes in the ground to explain what the Power Query Formula Language (or M as everyone calls the language now) is and what it can—and cannot—do.

M is a *functional* language. It is certainly *not* designed to perform general-purpose programming. Indeed, battle-hardened programmers will search in vain for coding structures and techniques that are core to other languages.

At the risk of offending programming purists, I prefer to introduce M to beginners as being a functional language in three ways:

- It exists to perform a simple function which is to load and transform data.

- It is built on a compendium of over 700 built-in functions, each of which is designed to carry out a specific piece of data load and/or transformation logic.

- It exists as a series of one or more functions, each of which computes a set of input values to a single output value.

To complete the whirlwind introduction, you also need to know that

- M is case-sensitive, so you need to be very careful when typing in function keywords and variable names.

- M is strongly typed, which means that you must respect the core types of data elements used and convert them to the appropriate type where necessary. M will not do this for you automatically.

- M is built on a set of keywords, operators, and punctuators.

I don't want to get too technical at this juncture. Nonetheless I hope that a high-level overview will prepare you for some of the approaches that you will learn later in this chapter.

M and the Power Query Editor

The good news about M is that you can already write it. By this I mean that every example that you followed in the previous 11 chapters wrote one or more lines of M code for you. Indeed, each step in a data load and transformation process that you generated when using the Power Query Editor created M code for you—automatically.

This means several (very positive) things:

- You do not necessarily have to begin writing M code from a blank slate. Often you can use the Query Editor interface to carry out most of the work—and then tweak the automatically generated code to add the final custom elements that you require.

- You do not have to learn over 700 functions to deliver M code as the Query Editor can find and write many of the appropriate instructions for you.

- The Query Editor interface is tightly linked to the way that M code is written. So understanding how to use the interface helps you in understanding what M code is and how it works.

Modifying the Code for a Step

If you feel that you want to delve into the inner reaches of Power BI Desktop, you can modify steps in a query by editing the code that is created automatically every time that you add or modify a query step.

To get a quick idea of what can be done:

1. Open the Query Editor and load the Excel file
   `C:\PowerBiDesktopSamples\BrilliantBritishCars.xlsx`
   (there is only one source table named BaseData).

2. Select the column IsDealer and remove it.

3. Click the Remove Columns step in the BaseData query.

4. In the View menu, ensure that the formula bar check box is checked. You will see the "M" code in the formula bar. It will look like that shown in Figure 12-1.

```
×  ✓  fx    = Table.RemoveColumns(#"Changed Type",{"IsDealer"})
```

Figure 12-1. *"M" code for an applied step*

5. In the formula bar, edit the M code to replace IsDealer with **ReportingYear**.

6. Press Enter or click the tick icon (check mark) in the formula bar to confirm your changes.

The step and subsequent data will be updated to reflect your changes.

The modification that you carried out in step 5 effectively means that you are adding back the IsDealer column and removing the ReportingYear column instead. You could have done this using the interface (by clicking the gear cog icon in the Applied Steps list for this step), but the whole point is to understand that both options are available and that the Power Query interface is only generating and modifying M code. So you can modify this code directly, if you prefer.

If you are an Excel power user (as many Power BI aficionados are), then you can be forgiven for thinking that this is similar to Excel Macro development. Indeed, it is in some respects:

- The core code can be recorded (VBA for Excel, M for Power BI).

- The resulting code can then be modified.

This is, of course, a very simplistic comparison. The two approaches may be similar, but the two languages are vastly different. Yet if this helps as a metaphor to encourage you to move to M development, then so be it.

There are inevitably a series of caveats when modifying the M code for a query step in the formula bar. These include (but are far from restricted to) the following:

- Any error will not only cause the step to fail, it will cause the whole data load and transformation process to fail from the current step onward.

- You need to remember that M is case-sensitive, and even the slightest error at this level can cause the entire process to fail.

- The use of quotes to define literal elements (such as column names) must be respected.

- M makes lavish use of both parentheses and braces. It can take some practice and understanding of the underlying logic to appreciate their use fully in various contexts.

Fortunately, M will provide fairly clear error messages if (or when) errors creep in. If you enter an erroneous field name, for instance, you could see a message like the one in Figure 12-2.

 Expression.Error: The column 'Reporting Year' of the table wasn't found.
Details:
    Reporting Year

Figure 12-2. *An "M" error message*

I do not want you to feel that modifying M code is difficult or dangerous, however. So, to extend the preceding example, this is what the M code would look like if you extended it to remove two columns, and not just one:

```
= Table.RemoveColumns(#"Changed Type",{"ReportingYear", "IsDealer"})
```

> **Note** More generally, it is often best to look at the code for existing steps—or create "dummy" code using a sample dataset in parallel—to get an idea of what the M code for a particular function looks like. This will then indicate how best to modify the code.

M Expressions

To give you a clearer understanding of what each M "step" contains, Figure 12-3 shows the core structure of a step. However, only the Power Query interface calls this a step. M actually calls this an *expression*. So that is the term I will use from now on.

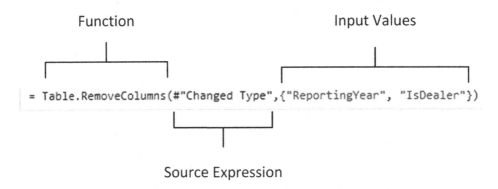

Figure 12-3. *An M expression*

There are several fundamental points that you need to be aware of here:

- Each M *expression* is made up of *functions*. These can be any of the built-in functions (such as the Table.RemoveColumns function used here)—or functions that you have defined (which is explained a little later in this chapter). They can also be calculations or simple logic.

- As you learned in the course of this book so far, data mashup is essentially a series of individual actions (or *steps* as the Power Query interface calls them). These actions are linked in a "chain" where each expression is built on—and refers to—a preceding expression. In Figure 12-3 this specific expression refers to the output of the #"Changed Type" expression which preceded it.

- M expressions can become extremely complex and include multiple functions—rather like complex Excel formulas. As functions can be nested, this can lead to quite complex expressions.

Writing M by Adding Custom Columns

Another way to write certain types of M code is to add custom columns. Although these are known as *custom columns* in Power BI Desktop, they are also known more generically as *derived columns* or *calculated columns*. Although they can do many things, their essential role is to

- Concatenate (or join, if you prefer) existing columns

- Add calculations to the data table

- Extract a specific part of a column

- Add flags to the table based on existing data

The best way to understand these columns is probably to see them in action. You can then extend these principles in your own processes. This can, however, be an excellent starting point to learn basic M coding—albeit limited to a narrowly focused area of data wrangling in M.

Initially, let's perform a column join and create a column named Vehicle, which concatenates the Make and Model columns with a space in between.

1. Open a blank Power BI Desktop file.

2. Connect to the C:\PowerBiDesktopSamples\ BrilliantBritishCars.xlsx data source.

3. Click Transform to open the Power Query Editor.

4. In the Add Column ribbon, click Custom Column. The Add Custom Column dialog is displayed.

5. Click the Make column in the column list on the right, then click the Insert button; `=[Make]` will appear in the Custom column formula box at the left of the dialog.

6. Enter & " " & in the Custom column formula box after `=[Make]`.

7. Click the Model column in the column list on the right, and then click the Insert button.

8. Click inside the New column name box and enter a name for the column. I call it CarType. The dialog will look like Figure 12-4.

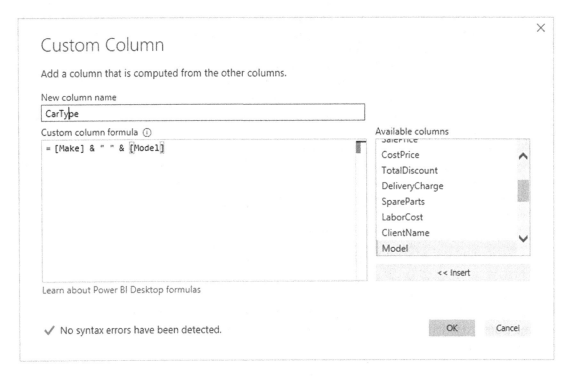

Figure 12-4. *The Custom Column dialog*

9. Click OK. The new column is added to the right of the data table; it contains the results of the formula. Inserted Column appears in the Applied Steps list. The formula bar contains the following formula:

```
= Table.AddColumn(#"Changed Type", "CarType", each [Make]
& " " & [Model])
```

You can always double-click a column to insert it into the Custom column formula box if you prefer. To remove a column, simply delete the column name (including the square brackets) in the Custom column formula box.

Tip   You must always enclose a column name in square brackets.

You can see that this line of M code follows the principles that you have already seen. It uses an M formula (Table.AddColumn) that refers to a previous expression (#"Changed Type") and then applies the code that carries out the expression requirements—in this case adding a new column that contains basic M code.

Note   The *each* keyword is an M convention to indicate that every record in the column will have the formula applied.

The Advanced Editor

The formula bar is only the initial step to coding in M. Nearly always you will write M code in the Power Query Advanced Editor. There are several fundamental reasons for this:

- The Advanced Editor shows all the expressions that make up an M query.

- It makes understanding the sequencing of events (or steps or expressions if you prefer) much easier.

- The Advanced Editor has built-in IntelliSense. This means that you can see M functions listed as you type.

- It has a syntax checker that helps isolate and identify syntax errors.

- It color-codes the M code to make it more readable and comprehensible.

Expressions in the Advanced Editor

The M expressions that you can see individually in the formula bar do not exist in a vacuum. Quite the contrary, they are always part of a coherent sequence of data load, cleansing, and transformation events. This is probably best appreciated if you now take a look at the whole block of M code that was created when you loaded a table from an Excel file previously.

To see the M code, you need to open the Advanced Editor:

1. In the Home ribbon, click the Advanced Editor button. The Advanced Editor window will open, as shown in Figure 12-5. You can also see the Applied Steps list from the Power Query Editor to help you understand how each step is, in fact, an M expression.

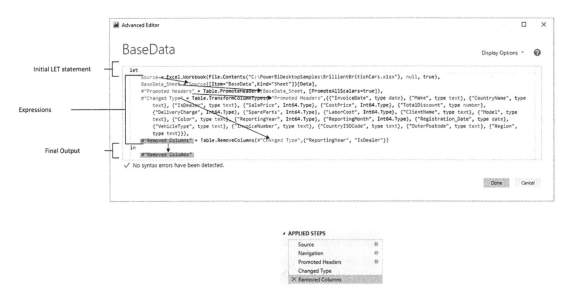

Figure 12-5. *Syntax checking in the Advanced Editor*

This dialog contains the entire structure of the connection and transformation process that you created. It contains the following core elements:

- A sequence of expressions (which are steps)

- A *let* expression that acts as an outer container for sequence of data transformation expressions

- An *in* expression that returns the output of the entire query

If you look at Figure 12-5, you can see several important things about the sequence of expressions that are inside the Let...In block:

- Each expression is named—and you can see its name in the Applied Steps list.

- Each expression refers to another expression (nearly always the previous expression) except for the first one.

- All but the final expression are terminated by a comma.

- An expression can run over several lines of code. It is the final comma that ends the expression in all but the last expression.

- The final expression becomes the output of the query.

Although this is a fairly simple M query, it contains all the essential elements that show how M works. Nearly every M query that you build will reflect these core principles:

- Have a Let...In block

- Contain one or more expressions that contain functions

The Let Statement

The *let* statement is a core element of the M language. It exists to allow a set of values to be evaluated individually where each is assigned to a variable name. These variables form a structured sequence of evaluation processes that are then used in the output expression that follows the *in* statement. You can consider it to be a "unit of processing" in many respects. Let statements can be nested to add greater flexibility.

In most let statements, the sequence of variables will be ordered from top to bottom (as you can see in Figure 12-6) where each named expression refers to, and builds on, the previous one. This is the way that the Query Editor presents named expressions as steps and is generally the easiest way to write M scripts that are easy to understand. However it is not, technically, necessary to order the expressions like this as the expressions can be in any order.

Modifying M in the Advanced Editor

As with all things Power BI related, the Advanced Editor is best appreciated through an example. You saw in Chapter 3 how to create and modify connections to data sources. You can also modify connections directly in the "M" language. This assumes that you know and understand the database that you are working with.

1. Add a new query that connects to a SQL Server database. I am using a SQL instance and database on my PC.

2. Select this query in the Queries list on the left.

3. In the Home ribbon, click the Advanced Editor button. The Advanced Editor dialog will appear, as shown in Figure 12-6.

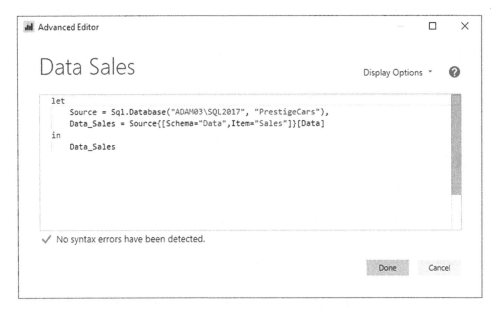

Figure 12-6. The Advanced Editor dialog to alter a database connection

4. Alter any of the following elements:

   a. The server name in the Source line (currently "ADAM03\SQL2017").

   b. The database name in the second line (currently Name="PrestigeCars").

     c. The schema name in the third line (currently Schema="Data").

     d. The table name in the third line (currently Item="Sales").

5. Click Done to confirm any changes and close the Advanced Editor.

This approach really is working without a safety net, and I am showing you more to raise awareness than anything else. However, it does open the door to some far-reaching possibilities if you wish to continue learning all about the "M" language.

Note   You can, of course, click Cancel to ignore any changes that you have made to the M code in the Advanced Editor. The Query Editor will ask you to confirm that you really want to discard your modifications.

Syntax Checking

If you intend to write and modify M code, you are likely to be using the Advanced Editor—a lot. Consequently, it is certainly worth familiarizing yourself with the help that it can provide. Specifically, its syntax checking can be extremely useful and is entirely automatic.

Suppose that you have (heaven forbid!) made an error in your code. The Advanced Editor could look something like the one in Figure 12-7.

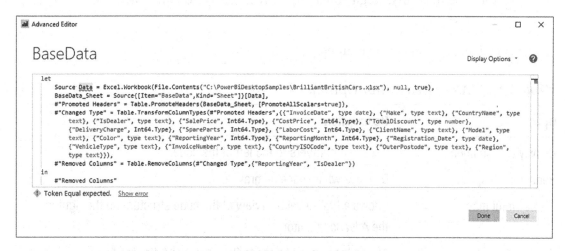

Figure 12-7. *Syntax checking in the Advanced Editor*

As you can see, in this case the Advanced Editor no longer displays a check box under the code and the reassuring message "No syntax errors have been detected." Instead you see an error message, and any errors are underlined in red. Clicking the Show error link will highlight the source of the error by displaying it on a gray background.

Advanced Editor Options

The Advanced Editor also has a few optional settings that you can configure.

1. In the top right of the Advanced Editor dialog, click the popup triangle to the right of Display Options. You can see this in Figure 12-8.

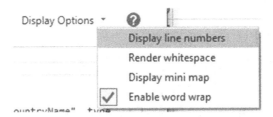

Figure 12-8. *Advanced Editor options*

2. Select Enable word wrap. Any individual M expressions that are too long to fit on a single line in the Advanced Editor will flow onto the next line.

The available options are explained in Table 12-1.

Table 12-1. *Advanced Editor Options*

Option	Description
Display line numbers	Adds line numbers to the left of the code.
Render whitespace	Displays whitespace as gray dots.
Display mini map	Shows a high-level overview of the code structure on the right of the Advanced Editor.
Enable word wrap	Allows long lines of code to flow onto the following line.

Basic M Functions

The M language is vast—far too vast for anything other than a cursory overview in a single chapter. Nonetheless, to give some structure to the overview, it is worth knowing that there are a few key categories of M functions that you might find useful when beginning to use M.

The following list is not exhaustive by any means, but can, hopefully, serve as a starting point for your journey into M functions. The elementary categories are

- Text functions
- Date functions
- Time functions
- DateTime functions
- Logical functions
- Number functions

I am focusing on these categories as they are probably the most easily comprehensible in both their application and their use. Once you have seen some of these functions, we can move on to other functions from the range of those available.

Most of the more elementary M functions can be applied in ways that will probably remind you of their Excel counterparts. For instance, if you want to extend the formula that you used to concatenate the Make and Model columns so that you are only extracting the leftmost three characters from the Make, you can use code like this:

```
= Table.AddColumn(#"Changed Type", "CarType", each Text.Start([Make], 3) &
" " & [Model])
```

The result is shown in Figure 12-9.

ABC 123 CarType
Rol Camargue
Ast DBS
Rol Silver Ghost
Rol Silver Ghost
Rol Camargue
Rol Camargue
Ast DBS
Ast DB7
Ast DB9

Figure 12-9. *Applying a first text function*

As you can see, wrapping the Make column inside this particular text function has added an extra layer of data transformation to the expression.

Text Functions

Rather than take you step by step through every possible example of text functions, I prefer to show you some of the more useful text functions (at least, in my experience). These code snippets are given in Table 12-2, where you will doubtless recognize many of the functions that you have been accessing up until now through the Power Query user interface.

Table 12-2. *Text Function Examples*

Output	Code Snippet	Description
Left	Text.Start([Make],3)	Returns the first three characters from the Make column.
Right	Text.End([Make],3)	Returns the last three characters from the Make column.
Up to a specific character	Text.Start([Make], Text.PositionOf([Make]," "))	Returns the leftmost characters up to the first space.

(continued)

Table 12-2. (*continued*)

Output	Code Snippet	Description
Up to a delimiter	Text.BeforeDelimiter([InvoiceNumber], "-" ,"2")	Returns the text before the third hyphen.
Text length	Text.Length([Make])	Finds the length of a text.
Extract a substring	Text.Range([Make], 2, 3)	Extracts a specific number of characters from a text—starting at a specified position.
Remove a subtext	Text.RemoveRange([Make], 2, 3)	Removes a specific number of characters from a text—starting at a specified position.
Replace a text	Text.Replace([Make], "o", "a")	Replaces all the o characters with an a in the text or column.
Trim spaces	Text.Trim([Make])	Removes leading and trailing spaces in the text or column.
Convert to uppercase	Text.Upper([Make])	Converts the text or column to uppercase.
Convert to lowercase	Text.Lower([Make])	Converts the text or column to lowercase.
Add initial capitals	Text.Proper([Make])	Adds initial capitals to each word of the text or column.

Note   You have probably noticed if you looked closely at these functions that any numeric parameters are zero based. So, to define the third hyphen when splitting text in a column, you would use *2*, not *3*.

There are, inevitably, many more text functions available in M. However the aim is not to drown the reader in technicalities, but to make you aware of both the way that M works and what is possible.

Once you also learn the DAX language to create calculations in Power BI, you may well wonder why you carry out operations like this in Power BI Desktop Query when you can do virtually the same thing in the data model. Well, it is true that there is some overlap; so you have the choice of which to use. You can perform certain operations at multiple stages in the data preparation and analysis process. It all depends on how you are using the data and with what tool you are carrying out the analyses.

Table 12-2 is only a subset of the available text functions in M. If you want to see the complete list, it is on the Microsoft website at `https://docs.microsoft.com/en-us/powerquery-m/text-functions`.

Number Functions

To extend your knowledge, Table 12-3 shows a few of the available number functions in M. Here I have concentrated on showing you some of the numeric type conversions as well as the core calculation functions.

Table 12-3. *Number Function Examples*

Output	Code Snippet	Description
Returns an 8-bit integer	`Int8.From("25")`	Converts the text or number to an 8-bit integer.
Returns a 16-bit integer	`Int16.From("2500")`	Converts the text or number to a 16-bit integer.
Returns a 32-bit integer	`Int32.From("250,000")`	Converts the text or number to a 32-bit integer.
Returns a 64-bit integer	`Int64.From("2500000000")`	Converts the text or number to a 64-bit integer.
Returns a decimal number	`Decimal.From("2500")`	Converts the text or number to a decimal.
Returns a Double number value from the given value	`Double.From("2500")`	Converts the text or number to a floating point number.

(continued)

Table 12-3. (*continued*)

Output	Code Snippet	Description
Takes a text as the source and converts to a numeric value	`Number.FromText("2500")`	Converts the text to a number.
Rounds a number	`Number.Round(5000, 0)`	Rounds the number up or down to the number of decimals (or tens, hundreds, etc., for negative parameters).
Rounds a number up	`Number.RoundUp(5020, -2)`	Rounds the number up to the number of decimals (or tens, hundreds, etc., for negative parameters).
Rounds a number down	`Number.RoundDown(100.01235, 2)`	Rounds the number down to the number of decimals (or tens, hundreds, etc., for negative parameters).
Removes the sign	`Number.Abs(-50)`	Returns the absolute value of the number.
Raises to a power	`Number.Power(10, 4)`	Returns the value of the first parameter to the power of the second.
Modulo	`Number.Mod(5, 2)`	Returns the remainder resulting from the integer division of number by divisor.
Indicates the sign of a number	`Number.Sign(-1)`	Returns 1 if the number is a positive number, -1 if it is a negative number, and 0 if it is zero.
Gives the square root	`Number.Sqrt(4)`	Returns the square root of the number.

Note   If you are an Excel user, you can probably see a distinct similarity with how you build formulas in Excel and Power Pivot, except that here (as in Power Pivot) you use column names rather than cell references.

Table 12-3 is only a minor subset of the vast range of number functions that are available in M. If you want to see the complete list, it is on the Microsoft website at https://docs.microsoft.com/en-us/powerquery-m/number-functions.

Date Functions

M has many date functions. Table 12-4 contains a potentially useful sample of the available functions.

Table 12-4. *Date Function Examples*

Output	Code Snippet	Description
Day	`Date.Day(Date.FromText("25/07/2020"))`	Returns the number of the day of the week from a date.
Month	`Date.Month(Date.FromText("25/07/2020"))`	Returns the number of the month from a date.
Year	`Date.Year(Date.FromText("25/07/2020"))`	Returns the year from a date.
Day of week	`Date.DayOfWeek(Date.FromText("25/07/2020"))`	Returns the day of the week from a date.
Name of weekday	`Date.DayOfWeekName(Date.FromText("25/07/2020"))`	Returns the weekday name from a date.
First day of month	`Date.StartOfMonth(Date.FromText("25/07/2020"))`	Returns the first day of the month from a date.
Last day of month	`Date.EndOfMonth(Date.FromText("25/07/2020"))`	Returns the last day of the month from a date.

(continued)

Table 12-4. (*continued*)

Output	Code Snippet	Description
First day of year	Date.StartOfYear(Date.FromText("25/07/2020"))	Returns the first day of the year from a date.
Last day of year	Date.EndOfYear(Date.FromText("25/07/2020"))	Returns the last day of the year from a date.
Day of year	Date.DayOfYear(Date.FromText("25/07/2020"))	Returns the day of the year from a date.
Week of year	Date.WeekOfYear(Date.FromText("25/07/2020"))	Returns the week of the year from a date.
Quarter	Date.QuarterOfYear(Date.FromText("25/07/2020"))	Returns the number of the quarter from a date.
First day of quarter	Date.StartOfQuarter(Date.FromText("25/07/2020"))	Returns the first day of the quarter from a date.
Last day of quarter	Date.EndOfQuarter(Date.FromText("25/07/2020"))	Returns the last day of the quarter from a date.

Table 12-4 is only a subset of the available date functions in M. If you want to see the complete list, it is on the Microsoft website at `https://docs.microsoft.com/en-us/powerquery-m/date-functions`.

Time Functions

M also has many time functions. Table 12-5 contains a potentially useful sample of the available functions.

Table 12-5. *Time Function Examples*

Output	Code Snippet	Description
Hour	`Time.Hour(#time(14, 30, 00))`	Returns the hour from a time.
Minute	`Time.Minute(#time(14, 30, 00))`	Returns the minute from a time.
Second	`Time.Second(#time(14, 30, 00))`	Returns the second from a time.
Time from fraction	`Time.From(0.5)`	Returns the time from a fraction of the day.

Table 12-5 is only a subset of the available time functions in M. If you want to see the complete list, it is on the Microsoft website at `https://docs.microsoft.com/en-us/powerquery-m/time-functions`.

Equally, as they are so similar to the date and time functions, I have not shown here the datetime functions and the datetimezone functions. These are also available on the Microsoft website.

Duration Functions

M can also extract durations—in days, hours, minutes, and seconds. Table 12-6 shows some of the basic duration functions.

Table 12-6. *Duration Function Examples*

Output	Code Snippet	Description
Days	`Duration.Days(#duration(10, 15, 55, 20))`	Duration in days.
Hours	`Duration.Hours(#duration(10, 15, 55, 20))`	Duration in hours.
Minutes	`Duration.Minutes(#duration(10, 15, 55, 20))`	Duration in minutes.
Seconds	`Duration.Seconds(#duration(10, 15, 55, 20))`	Duration in seconds.

Table 12-6 is nearly all the available duration functions in M. If you want to see the remaining few functions, they are on the Microsoft website at `https://docs.microsoft.com/en-us/powerquery-m/duration-functions`.

M Concepts

The time has now come to "remove the stabilizers" from the bicycle and learn how to cycle unaided. This means, firstly, becoming acquainted with several M structural concepts.

This means moving on from the "starter" functions that you can use to modify the contents of the data to creating and modifying data structures themselves. M is essentially focused on loading and presenting tabular data structures, so tables of data are an essential data structure. However, there are other data structures that it can manipulate—and that you have seen in passing in previous chapters. In this chapter, then, we will look at the three core data structures. Collectively, these are classified as *structured* values—as opposed to the *primitive* values such as text, number, or date and time. Some of these are

- Lists
- Records
- Tables

However, before delving into these structured data elements, you need to understand two fundamental aspects of the M language. These are

- Data types
- M values (also referred to as variables or identifiers)

So, without further ado, let's start your journey into M.

M Data Types

If you are creating your own lists, records, and tables, then it will help to know the basics about data types in M.

When beginning to use M, you need to remember that primitive data values must always be one of the following types:

- Number
- Text
- Date
- Time
- DateTime

- DateTimeZone

- Duration

- Logical (Boolean if you prefer)

- Binary

- Null

There are other types such as function, any, or anynonnull, but we will not be covering them in this chapter.

All data types expect to be entered in a specific way. Indeed, you must enter data in the way shown in Table 12-7 to avoid errors in your M code.

Table 12-7. *Data Type Entry*

Data Type	Code Snippet	Comments
Number	100 0.12345 2.4125E8	Do not use formatting such as thousands separators or monetary symbols.
Text	"Calidra Power BI Training"	Always enclose in double quotes. Use two double quotes to enter the actual quotes text.
Date	#date(2020,12,25)	Dates must be year, month, and day in the #date() function.
Time	#time(15,55,20)	Times must be hour, minute, and second in the #time() function.
DateTime	#datetime(2020,12, 25,15,55,20)	Datetimes must be year, month, day, hour, minute, and second in the #datetime() function.
DateTimeZone	#datetimezone(2020,12, 25,15,55,20,-5,-30)	Datetimezones must be year, month, day, hour, minute, second, day offset, and hour offset in the #datetimezone() function.
Duration	#duration(0,1,0,0)	Days, hours, minutes, and seconds comma-separated inside the #duration() function.
Logical	true	true or false in lowercase

M Values

Before diving deeper into actual coding, you really need to know a few fundamentals concerning M values:

- Values are the output of expressions.

- Values are also variables.

- The names of values are case-sensitive.

- If the value name contains spaces or restricted characters, they must be wrapped in #"" (pound sign followed by double quotes).

This fourth bullet point clearly begs the question "what is a restricted character?" The simple answer—that avoids memorizing lists of glyphs—is "anything not alphanumeric."

Note   The Power Query Editor interface makes the steps (which are the values returned by an expression) more readable by adding spaces wherever possible. Consequently, these values always appear in the M code as #"Step Name".

Defining Your Own Variables in M

As the values returned by any expression are also variables, it follows that defining your own variables in M is breathtakingly simple. All you have to do is to enter a variable name (with the pound sign and in quotes if it contains spaces or restricted characters), an equals sign, and the variable definition.

As a really simple example, take a look at Figure 12-10. This M script defines the three parameters required for the List.Numbers() function that you will see in Table 12-8 and then uses the variables inside the function.

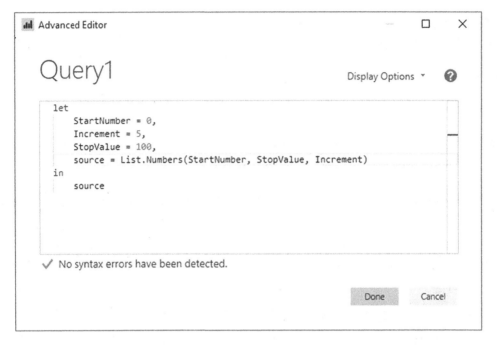

Figure 12-10. *User variables in M*

There are only a few things to remember when defining your own variables:

- They respect the same naming convention as output values in M.

- A variable can be referenced inside the subexpression where it is defined and any expressions that contain the subexpression.

- A variable can be a simple value or a calculation that returns a value.

Writing M Queries

Before actually writing M, you need to know how and where to write your code. Suppose that you need an environment to practice the examples in the remainder of this chapter:

1. Open a new, blank Power BI Desktop file.

2. In the Home ribbon, click New Source ➤ Blank Query. The Power Query Editor will open.

3. Click Advanced Editor. An Advanced Editor dialog will open containing only an outer let expression, as shown in Figure 12-11.

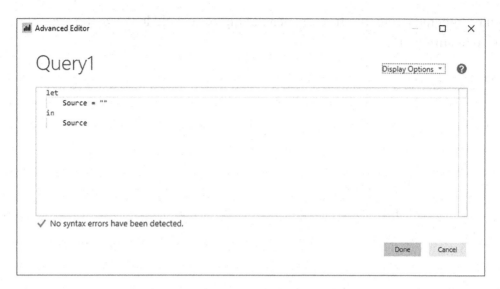

Figure 12-11. *Preparing the Advanced Editor to write M code*

Note Technically, a let clause is not required in M. You can simply enter an expression. However, I prefer to write M "by the book"—at least to begin with.

Lists

You met M lists in Chapter 11 when creating popup lists for query-based parameters (showing, once again, that everything in the Query Editor is based on M). Lists are nothing more than a series of values.

Lists have specific uses in M and can be used directly in a data model. However, they are more generally used as intermediate steps in more complex data transformation processes. If you have a programming background, you might find it helpful to consider lists as being something akin to arrays.

Creating Lists Manually

A list is simply a comma-separated set of values enclosed in braces—such as

```
{1,2,3}
```

Once integrated into the structure of an M query, it could look like the example shown in Figure 12-12.

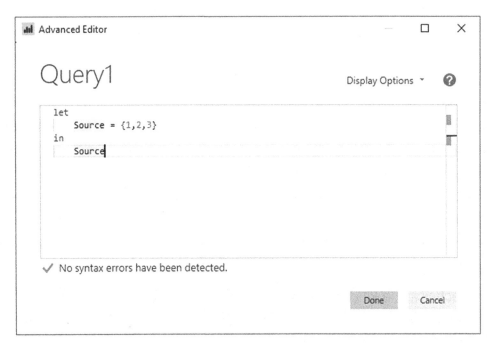

Figure 12-12. *A list in the Advanced Editor*

Once created—either as an intermediate step in a query or as the final output of the query—the list can be used by anything that requires a list as its input. Indeed, if you click the Done button for the preceding example, the Power Query Editor will display this piece of M code as a functioning list—exactly like the one that you created in Chapter 11. So you can now create custom lists for parameters (for instance) quickly and easily.

There is some technical information that you need to know about lists:

- Lists are unlimited in size.

- Lists can contain data of the same type (i.e., all elements are numeric values, dates, or texts, for instance)—or the data can be of different types.

- Lists can be empty—that is, composed of a pair of empty braces.

- Lists can be entered horizontally or vertically. That is, the list shown earlier could have been typed in as

```
Source = {
            1,
            2,
            3
        }
```

Generating lists is really easy; knowing when to use lists is the hard part.

Generating Sequences Using Lists

Lists have many uses in M, but there is one area where they shine, and that is generating sequences of numbers, dates, or texts. Rather than laboriously explain each approach individually, I have collated a set of examples of M code snippets for list generation in Table 12-8.

Table 12-8. *List Generation*

Code Snippet	Description
`{1..100}`	An uninterrupted sequence of numbers from 1 to 100, inclusive.
`{1..100, 201..400}`	An uninterrupted sequence of numbers from 1 to 100, then from 201 to 400.
`List.Numbers(0, 100, 5)`	Starting at zero increments by 5 until 100 is reached.
`{"A".."Z"}`	The uppercase letters A through Z.
`List.Dates(#date(2020, 1, 1), 366, #duration(1, 0, 0, 0))`	Each individual day for the year 2020—starting on January 1, 2020, 366 days (expressed as a duration in days) are added.
`List.Times(#time(1, 0, 0), 24, #duration(0, 1, 0, 0))`	Each hour in the day starting with 1 AM.

Accessing Values from a List

If you move to more advanced M coding, you may well want to refer to a value from a list in your M script. At its simplest, this is done using *positional references*. Here is a short piece of M code that does just this:

```
let
    Start = {"George","Bill","George W.", "Barack", "Donald"},
    source = Start{3}
in
    source
```

The output of this code snippet is the fourth element in the list—making the point that lists in M are *zero based*. That is, the first element in a list is the element 0.

List Functions

There are many dozens of list functions available in M. Far too many to go through in detail here. So, to give you an idea of some of the possible ways that you can manipulate lists, take a look at Table 12-9. All of them use the very simple list that you saw previously.

Table 12-9. *List Functions*

Output	Code Snippet	Description
First value	`List.First(MyList)`	Returns the first element in a list.
Last value	`List.Last(MyList)`	Returns the last element in a list.
Sort list values	`List.Sort(MyList)`	Sorts the values in a list.
Extract range	`List.Range(MyList, 4)`	Extracts a range of values from a list.
Return value(s)	`List.Select(MyList , each _ ="Adam")`	Returns the elements from a list that match a criterion.
Generate a list	`List.Generate()`	Creates a list of sequential values.
Aggregate values	`List.Sum(MyList)`	Aggregate the numeric values in a list.
Replace values	`List.ReplaceMatchingItems (MyList, {"Joe", "Fred"})`	Replaces a range of values in a list.
Convert to list	`Table.Column(MyList)`	Returns a column from a table as a list.

Table 12-9 is only a small subset of the available list functions in M. If you want to see the full range of functions, it is on the Microsoft website at `https://docs.microsoft.com/en-us/powerquery-m/list-functions`.

Records

If lists can be considered as columns of data that you can use in your M code, *records* are rows of data. You might well find yourself needing to define records when creating more complex data transformation routines in M.

At its simplest, here is a sample record created in M:

```
let
    Source = [Surname = "Aspin", FirstName = "Adam"]
in
    Source
```

If you need to access the data in a record, you append the record variable name with the field name in square brackets, like this:

```
let
    Source = [Surname = "Aspin", FirstName = "Adam"],
    Output = Source[Surname]
in
    Output
```

There are a few record functions that you may find useful. These are outlined in Table 12-10.

Table 12-10. *Record Functions*

Output	Code Snippet	Description
Add field	`Record.AddField()`	Adds a field to a record.
Remove field	`Record.RemoveFields()`	Removes a field from a record.
Rename fields	`Record.RenameFields()`	Renames a field in a record.
Output field	`Record.Field()`	Returns the value of the specified field in the record.
Count	`Record.FieldCount()`	Returns the number of fields in a record.

Table 12-10 is only a subset of the available record functions in M. If you want to see the complete list, it is on the Microsoft website at `https://docs.microsoft.com/en-us/powerquery-m/record-functions`.

Tables

The final structured data type that you could well employ in M code is the *table* type. As you might expect in a language that exists to load, cleanse, and shape tabular data, the table data type is fundamental to M.

If you decide to create your own tables manually in M, then you will need to include, at a minimum, the following structural elements:

- The #table() function

- A set of column/field headers where each field name is enclosed in double quotes, and the set of field names is wrapped in braces

- Individual rows of data, each enclosed in braces and comma-separated, where the collection of rows is also wrapped in braces

A very simple example of a hand-coded table could look like this:

```
#table(
        {"Surname", "FirstName"},
        {
            {"Johnson","Vladimir"},
            {"Putin","Emmanuel"},
            {"Macron","Angela"},
            {"Merkel","Boris"}
        }
    )
```

However, the weakness with this approach is that there are no type definitions for the fields. Consequently, a much more robust approach would be to extend the table like this:

```
#table(
        type table
                    [
```

```
            #"Surname" = text,
            #"FirstName" = text
        ],
    {
        {"Johnson","Vladimir"},
        {"Putin","Emmanuel"},
        {"Macron","Angela"},
        {"Merkel","Boris"}
    }
)
```

Note   The data type keywords that you specify to define the required data type were outlined earlier in this chapter.

There are many table functions available in M. I have outlined a few of the more useful ones in Table 12-11.

Table 12-11.   *Table Functions*

Output	Code Snippet	Description
Merge tables	Table.Combine()	Merges tables of similar or different structures.
Number of records	Table.RowCount()	Returns the number of records in a table.
First	Table.First()	Returns the first record in a table.
Last	Table.Last()	Returns the last record in a table.
Find rows	Table.FindText()	Returns the rows in the table that contain the required text.
Insert rows	Table.InsertRows()	Inserts rows in a table.
Output rows	Table.Range()	Outputs selected rows.
Delete rows	Table.DeleteRows()	Deletes rows in a table.
Select columns	Table.SelectColumns()	Outputs selected columns.

Table 12-11 is, as you can probably imagine, only a tiny subset of the available table functions in M. If you want to see the complete list, it is on the Microsoft website at `https://docs.microsoft.com/en-us/powerquery-m/table-functions`.

Other Function Areas

As I mentioned previously, M is a vast subject that could fill an entire (and very large) book. We have taken a rapid overview of some of the core concepts and functions, but there is much that remains to be learned if you wish to master M. If you are really interested in learning more, then I suggest that you search the Microsoft documentation for the elements outlined in Table 12-12 to further your knowledge.

Table 12-12. *Other Function Areas*

Function Area	Description
Accessing data functions	Access data and return table values.
Binary functions	Access binary data.
Combiner functions	Used by other library functions that merge values to apply row-by-row logic.
DateTime functions	Functions applied to datetime data.
DateTimeZone functions	Functions applied to datetime data with timezone information.
Expression functions	M code that was used for expressions.
Line functions	Convert data to lists of values.
Replacer	Used by other functions in the library to replace a given value in a structure.
Splitter	Splits values into sub-elements.
Type	Returns M types.
Uri	Handles URLs and URIs.
Value	Handles M values.

Custom Functions in M

M also allows you to write custom functions that can carry out highly specific tasks repeatedly.

As an example of a very simple custom function, try adding the following code snippet to a new, blank query:

```
let DiscountAnalysis =
                (Discount as number) =>
                            if Discount < 10 then
                            "Poor" else "Excellent" in
                            DiscountAnalysis
```

When you close the Advanced Editor, you will see that this query has been recognized as being an M function and appears as such in the list of queries. You can see this in Figure 12-13 (where I have renamed it to "DiscountAnalysis").

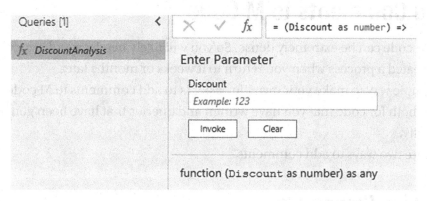

Figure 12-13. *User-defined functions in M*

You can now invoke the function at any time interactively by entering a value as the discount and clicking the Invoke button. You can also use this function inside other M functions. Indeed, this is probably why you created a custom function in the first place.

If you want to see a more advanced function, take a look at the following code snippet, which pads out a date to add leading zeroes to the day and month if these are required:

```
let
      FormatDate = (InDate as date) =>
let
      Source = Text.PadStart(Text.From(Date.Month(InDate)),2,"0") & "/"
      & Text.PadStart(Text.From(Date.Day(InDate)),2,"0") & "/" &Text.
      From(Date.Year(InDate))
in
      Source
in
      FormatDate
```

Adding Comments to M Code

Complex M code can be extremely dense. So you will likely need ways of remembering why you created a process when you return to it weeks or months later.

One simple way to make your own life easier is to add comments to M code. You can do this both for code that you have written and queries that have been generated automatically.

There are two ways to add comments.

Single-Line Comments

To comment a single line (which you can do either at the start of the line or partway through the line), simply add two forward slashes—like this:

```
//This is a comment
```

Everything from the two slashes until the end of the line will be considered to be a comment and will not be evaluated by M.

Multiline Comments

Multiline comments can cover several lines—or even part of a line. They cover all the text that is enclosed in /∗ ... ∗/.

```
/* This is a comment
Over
Several lines */
```

Everything inside the /∗ ... ∗/ will be considered to be a comment and will not be evaluated by M.

Conclusion

This chapter closes the section on loading and transforming source data. In this chapter you learned the basics of the M language that underpins everything that you learned in this book up until now.

You began by seeing how you can use the Power Query Editor interface to assist you in writing short snippets of M code. Then you moved on to discovering the fundamental M concepts such as expressions, variables, and values. Finally, you learned about data types in M and the more complex data types such as lists and tables that underlie complex data transformations. This involved learning to use the Advanced Editor to write and debug your code.

In this chapter and the 11 previous chapters, you have seen essentially a three-stage process: first, you find the data, then you load it into Power BI Desktop Query, and from there, you cleanse and modify it. The techniques that you can use are simple but powerful and can range from changing a data type to merging multiple data tables. Now that your data is prepared and ready for use, you can add it to the Power BI Desktop data model and start creating your Power BI Desktop dashboards. You will now move on to structuring an entire data model using the output from queries. This is the subject of the next chapter.

CHAPTER 13

Creating a Data Model

You need only one thing to create stunning visualizations and that is good data. Specifically, you need clean and accurate data loaded into the Power BI Desktop data model. There you can hone tens of millions of rows from multiple data sources into a coherent and powerful framework on which you can build your analyses and dashboards.

Finding, transforming, and loading the source data using queries (as you learned in Chapters 1 through 12) are fundamental to preparing your data for the data model. However, the process does not stop there. Once you have made accessible the data that you need, you still have a few more tasks to carry out. To complete the process, you need to assemble these queries into a coherent structure that is clear and comprehensible to anyone who uses it.

To guarantee that you are at ease when creating a data model in Power BI Desktop for later analysis in your dashboards, this chapter introduces you to some of the techniques that you need to apply to model your data. You will discover how to take the data tables that you loaded and convert them into a structured dataset in the Power BI Desktop data model. This framework includes applying the appropriate data types, categorizations, and formats that enable you to deliver information, insight, and analysis from the data in the model. This learning curve covers a process that includes

- Defining the appropriate semantic layer—that is, ensuring that all the tables and fields have clearly comprehensible names

- Ensuring that all the data types are correct

- Formatting data

- Setting the default aggregation that Power BI will use in dashboards for each field

- Joining the tables in a data model

© Adam Aspin 2020
A. Aspin, *Pro Power BI Desktop*, https://doi.org/10.1007/978-1-4842-5763-0_13

The fifth point in this list is probably the most fundamental aspect of data modeling. Indeed, this will take up nearly half the current chapter. To report on data accurately and precisely, you must allow Power BI Desktop to understand how the data in one table is linked to the data contained in another table. Chaining one table to another will let you use the data to deliver accurate and cogent results.

Once again, all the sample files used in this chapter are available on the Apress website. Once downloaded, they should be in the `C:\PowerBiDesktopSamples` folder.

The Power BI Desktop Data View

To start using Power BI Desktop to prepare all the tables and fields, it is generally easiest to work in Data View. This means

1. Run Power BI Desktop and load any queries that you need to access your data. To follow the examples in this chapter, open the `C:\PowerBiDesktopSamples\CarSalesDataFromDataModel.pbix` file.

2. If you are using your own data, make sure that you have closed the Power BI Desktop Query window, applying any changes that you have made, and reverted to the Power BI Desktop environment.

3. Click the Data View icon on the left. You will switch to the Data View, where you can see all the available tables in the Fields list on the right. One of the tables will be selected and its data will be visible in the Data pane, as shown in Figure 13-1. Visuals and Filter panes are no longer visible, and two new menus—Table tools and Column tools (if a column is selected)—have appeared.

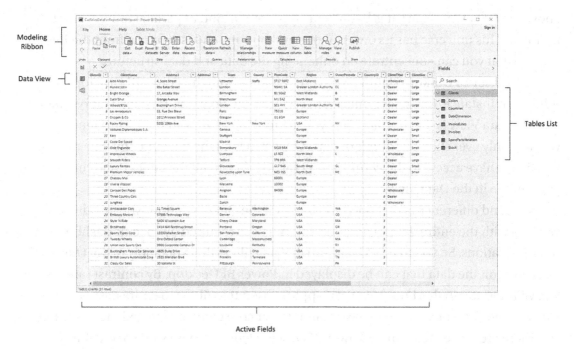

Figure 13-1. *Data View*

Note   Modeling data is only possible once data has been loaded into the Power BI Desktop data model. By this I mean that editing data in the Query Editor and returning to the Power BI Desktop window without applying your changes will hinder your data modeling—or at the very least will prevent you from returning accurate results.

Data View or Query?

You could well be thinking that Data View does not look like very much at all yet. If anything, it looks like an extension of the Power BI Desktop Query window. However, be reassured, you will soon see what you can do in Data View and exactly how powerful a tool Power BI Desktop really is when it comes to data modeling. For the moment, it is essential to remember that you have (so to speak) opened a door into the engine room of Power BI Desktop. Although this new world is part of Power BI Desktop (and you can return to Power BI visualizations instantaneously just by clicking the Report View icon above the Data View icon), it is best if you consider it a kind of parallel universe for the moment. This universe has its own ribbons and buttons and is separate from the Report View so that you can concentrate on enhancing the data and data structure.

The Power BI Desktop Data View is also different from the Power BI Desktop Query Editor. For instance, one major difference between the Power BI Desktop Query window and the Data View is that in Data View you are looking at *all* your data. The Query window only ever shows a *sample* of data. Once you load the data into the data model, you finally have access to the *entire* dataset (all the data in all the tables), and this is what you can see in the Data View.

A second difference is that once you have left the Query window, you are always working with the entire dataset and only filtering it as required by specific dashboards or visualizations. So you need to be aware that any filters that you apply in the Query window limit the data that can be displayed in Power BI Desktop. By contrast (and as you will see later in this book), you can apply subsequent filters to entire dashboards or specific visualizations once you have defined your core data and created the data model.

There are some areas where Power BI Desktop Query can do some of the things that can also be done in the Data View or Relationships View. For instance, you can create calculated fields in both (you will see how to do this in Data View in the following chapter). My advice is to try to remember that Power BI Desktop Query is for finding, filtering, and mashing up data, whereas Data View is for refining and calculating the data layer and metrics in your data model. However, each user can take the approach that they prefer and carry out any necessary calculations in either the Query Editor or the Data View. After all, it is the result that counts.

Note   *Always* make sure that you have clicked Close & Apply when using the Query Editor *before* modeling the data. This guarantees that you are working on the most up-to-date version of the data transformations that you have made, as well as the most recent data. If you have not clicked Close & Apply, you will see an alert at the top of the Power BI Desktop window.

The Data View is essentially used to prepare data for the final modeling step. This covers

- Manipulating tables
- Adding "sort by" fields that ensure the correct sort order in dashboard elements

- Renaming tables and columns

- Defining data types

- Setting data categories

- Formatting data

- Creating groups based on field values

- Setting Sort by column (to sort columns using the contents of another column)

- Setting tables as date tables to apply time intelligence

Once these core elements are defined, you can proceed to the modeling step where you join the tables in a coherent data model.

The Power BI Desktop Data View Ribbons

So what, exactly, are you looking at when you look at Power BI Desktop data? Essentially, you can see three ribbons, which are all devoted to preparing the fundamental aspects of the data model:

- The Home ribbon

- The Table tools ribbon

- The Column tools ribbon (when a column is selected)

These latter two ribbons will be explained in detail later in this chapter. The Home ribbon will be explained in detail in the following chapter.

Managing Power BI Desktop Data

Assuming that all has gone well, you now have a series of tables from various sources successfully added to your Power BI Desktop data model. If you have opened the file `C:\PowerBiDesktopSamples\CarSalesDataFromDataModel.pbix`, you can see a set of data tables in the Fields list at the right of the Power BI Desktop window. Clicking a table will display the data from that table in the central area of the Data View window. It will soon be time to see what you can do with this data, but first, to complete the roundup of the overall data management, you need to know how to do the following:

- Rename tables

- Delete tables

- Move tables

- Move around a table

- Rename a field

- Delete fields

- Set field width

Note   When loading and editing source data, I generally use the term dataset to describe the source data. Now that the data is finally loaded, I will use the term (data) table to describe the data entities that Power BI Desktop uses when shaping and extending the data model. This is because a table is, virtually always, the output resulting from all transformations produced by a query. Equally, I prefer to refer to the columns of data that are shown in the Fields list as fields—even if Power BI Desktop does refer to them frequently as columns.

Manipulating Tables

Let's begin by seeing how you can tweak the tables that you have successfully imported and transformed.

Renaming Tables

Suppose that you wish to rename a table that you previously imported using Power BI Desktop Query. These are the steps to follow:

- Click the table name in the Fields list at the right of the Power BI Desktop window.

- Select the Table tools ribbon.

- Enter the new name or modify the existing name in the Name field.

- Press Enter.

This also renames the query on which the table is based. In essence, Power BI will let you rename datasets either as queries in the Power BI Desktop Query window or in the Data window. Because the query *is* the table, renaming one renames the other.

Note   You can also right-click the table name in the Fields list at the right of the Power BI Desktop window and select Rename, then enter the new name or modify the existing name.

Deleting a Table

Deleting a table is virtually identical to the process of renaming one—you just right-click the table name tab and select Delete instead of Rename. As this is a potentially far-reaching operation, Power BI Desktop will demand confirmation.

Note   When you delete a table, you are removing it from Power BI Desktop completely. This means that it is *also* removed from the set of queries that you may have used to transform the data. So you need to be careful when deleting tables, because you could lose all your carefully wrought transformation steps as well.

Selecting a Field from the List of Available Field Names

If you want to leap straight to a field of data (and presuming you know which field contains the data that interests you), all you have to do is

1. In the Fields list, click the expand triangle to the left of the table containing the field that you want to jump to. A list of the fields in the table appears, as shown in Figure 13-2.

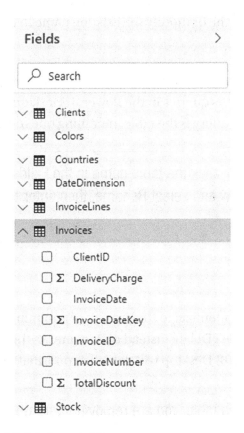

Figure 13-2. *The list of fields in a table*

2. Click the name of the field that contains the data that you want to study. The field will be selected in the table.

Manipulating Fields

Now let's see how to perform similar actions—but this time inside a table—to the fields containing data that make up the table.

Renaming a Field

Renaming a field is pretty straightforward. All you have to do is

1. In the Fields list, right-click the title of the field that you wish to rename (or click the ellipses to the right of the field name). In this example, it is the field ClientType in the Data Clients table. The field will be selected and the context menu will appear. This is shown in Figure 13-3.

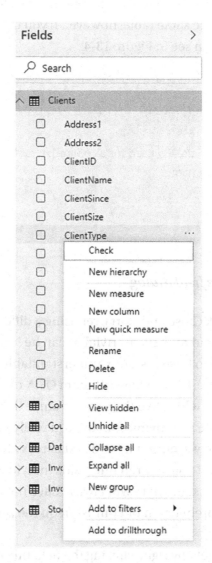

Figure 13-3. *The Power BI Desktop context menu*

2.   Select Rename from the context menu. The current field name will
     be highlighted.

3.   Type in the new name for the field (**TypeOfClient**) and press
     Enter.

And that is it. Your field has been renamed; it is also selected. You cannot use the
name of an existing field in the same table, however. If you try, Power BI Desktop will
display the dialog that you can see in Figure 13-4.

Figure 13-4. *The Rename field dialog*

If this happens, just click Close and start over using a different new field name.

Although renaming a field may seem trivial, it can be important. Consider other
users first; they need fields to have instantly understandable names that mean
something to them. Then there is the PowerBI.com Q&A natural language feature.
This only works well if your fields have the sort of names that are used in the queries—
or ones that are recognizable synonyms. Finally, you really need to give your fields
the names that you are happy seeing standardized across all the dashboards that are
based on this dataset (even if you can rename fields individually in visualisations).
The upside to this is that the same data will always have the same name, thus
removing potential incomprehension or confusion on the part of the audience—and
yourself.

You can also rename a field by right-clicking the field title that interests you and
selecting Rename from the context menu or by clicking inside the column and then
selecting the Column tools ribbon, where you can alter the contents of the Name field.

Tip   Power BI Desktop is very forgiving when it comes to renaming fields (or, indeed, tables and calculations too). You can rename *most* elements in the Query window, the Data View, the Report View, or the Relationships View (depending where they were added), and the changes will ripple through the entire Power BI Desktop data model. Better still, renaming fields, calculations, and tables generally does not cause Power BI Desktop any difficulties if these elements have already been applied to dashboards, as these are also updated to reflect the change of name. Just be aware that if you customize a lot of names and don't document the fields for reference, you will find that reverse engineering a report can be quite a task. In practice, it can save you a lot of effort if you always keep a reference of alias fields back to source in the query.

Deleting Fields

Deleting a field is equally easy. You will probably find yourself doing this when you bring in a field that you did not mean to import or when you find that you no longer need a field. So, to delete a field, you need to do the following:

1. Right-click the title of the field that you wish to delete. Alternatively, right-click the field name in the Fields list. The field will be selected and the context menu will appear.

2. Select Delete Fields from the context menu. Unless the field is empty, the confirmation dialog will appear as shown in Figure 13-5.

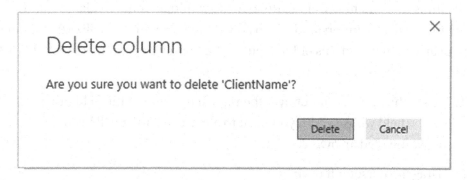

Figure 13-5.   *Deleting a field*

3. Click OK. The field will be deleted from the table.

Deleting unused fields is good practice because you will

- Reduce the memory required for the dataset

- Speed up data refresh operations

- Reduce the size of the Power BI Desktop file

Note   Deleting a field really is permanent. You cannot use the undo function to recover it. Indeed, refreshing the data will not add the field back into the table either. If you have deleted a field by accident, you can choose to close the Power BI Desktop file without saving and reopen it, thus reverting to the previous version. Otherwise, you can return to the source query and add the field name back into the query, as deleting a field in Power BI Desktop has added a Remove Field step to the sequence of steps underlying the relevant query.

Moving Fields

Once in the data model, you *cannot* move fields around. So if you want to change the field order for any reason, you have to switch to the Power BI Desktop Query Editor and move the field there. Once you save and apply your changes, the modified field order is visible in the data model. However, fields will always appear in alphabetical order in the Fields list in Report View.

Setting Field Widths

One final thing that you may want to do to make your data more readable—and consequently easier to understand—is to adjust the field width. I realize that as an Excel or Word user, you may find this old hat, but in the interests of completeness, this is how you do it:

1. Place the mouse pointer over the right-hand limit of the field title in the field whose width you want to alter. The cursor will become a two-headed arrow.

2. Drag the cursor left or right.

Note   You cannot select several adjacent fields before widening (or narrowing) one of them to set them all to the width of the field that you are adjusting. You can double-click the right-hand limit of the field title in the field whose width you want to alter so that Power BI Desktop can set the width to that of the longest element in the field.

Adjusting the field width is purely to help you read the data and will have *no effect* on the width of the columns in any visuals.

Preparing Data

Now that your tables and columns are prepared (which can be referred to as "preparing the semantic layer"), you can start defining essential aspects of each field. This covers

- Data type attribution

- Formatting data

- Categorizing data

- Setting default summarizations

- Preparing groups of data

Virtually all of these operations are carried out using the Column tools ribbon. You can see this ribbon in Figure 13-6. The contents of the ribbon are explained in Table 13-1.

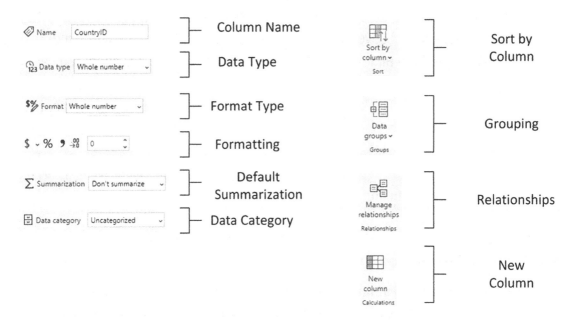

Figure 13-6.   *The Column tools ribbon*

Table 13-1.   *The Column Tools Ribbon*

Button	Description
Name	Allows you to modify the column name.
Data type	Sets the data type for the column.
Format type	Sets the overall format type.
Format	Specifies the precise formatting.
Default summarization	Sets the default summarization from the available options.
Data category	Applies a data category.
Sort by column	Applies a sort by column (sorts using the data in a different column).
Data groups	Allows you to group data.
Relationships	Displays the Manage relationships dialog.
New column	Adds a new column using DAX.

You are also likely to use the Table tools ribbon for some operations. The contents of this ribbon are explained in Table 13-2. You can see this ribbon in Figure 13-7.

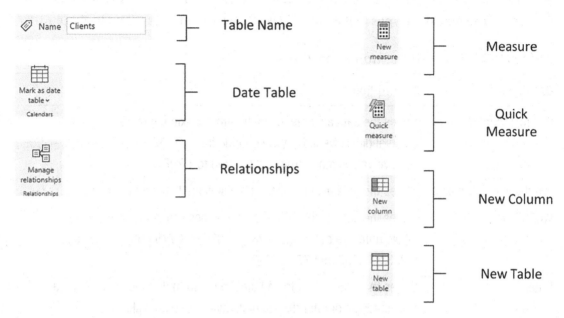

Figure 13-7.   *The Table tools ribbon*

Table 13-2.   *The Table Tools Ribbon*

Button	Description
Table name	Allows you to modify the table name.
Date table	Sets the selected table as a date table.
Relationships	Displays the Manage relationships dialog.
Measure	Adds a new measure using DAX.
Quick measure	Lets you create a measure using examples.
New column	Adds a new column using DAX.
New table	Adds a new table using DAX.

Power BI Desktop Data Types

When you are importing data from an external source, Power BI Desktop tries to convert it to one of the nine data types that it uses. These data types are described in Table 13-3.

Table 13-3. *Power BI Desktop Data Types*

Data Type	Description
Decimal Number	Stores the data as a real number with a maximum of 15 significant decimal digits. Negative values range from −1.79E +308 to −2.23E −308. Positive values range from 2.23E −308 to 1.79E + 308.
Fixed Decimal Number	Stores the data as a number with a specified number of decimals.
Whole Number	Stores the data as integers that can be positive or negative but are whole numbers between 9,223,372,036,854,775,808 (−2^63) and 9,223,372,036,854,775,807 (2^63−1).
Date/Time	Stores the data as a date and time in the format of the host computer. Only dates on or after the 1st of January 1900 are valid.
Date	Stores the data as a date in the format of the host computer.
Time	Stores the data as a time element in the format of the host computer.
Text	Stores the data as a Unicode string of 536,870,912 bytes at most.
True/False	Stores the data as Boolean—true or false.
Binary	Stores the data as binary (machine-readable) data.

You can set the data type of a column like this:

1. In Data View, select (or click inside) the column whose data type you wish to change.

2. Activate the Column tools ribbon.

3. Select a data type from the Data type popup list.

As was the case when setting data types in the Query Editor, you will not be allowed to apply an inappropriate data type.

Formatting Power BI Desktop Data

Power BI Desktop allows you to apply formatting to the data in the tables that it contains. When you format the data in the Power BI Desktop data model, you are defining the format that will be used in *all visualizations in all the dashboards* that you create using this metric. So it is probably worth learning to format data for the following reasons:

- You will save time and multiple repetitive operations when creating reports and presentations by defining a format once and for all in Data View. The data will then appear using the format that you applied in multiple visualizations in this Power BI Desktop file.

- It can help you understand your data more intuitively if you can see the figures in a format that has intrinsic meaning.

This explains how to format a field (of figures in this example):

1. Assuming that you are working in the Power BI Desktop Data View, click the table name in the Fields list that contains the metric you wish to format.

2. Click inside the field that you want to format (SalePrice from the InvoiceLines table in the CarSalesDataFromDataModel.pbix sample file).

3. In the Column tools ribbon, click the Thousands Separator icon (the comma in the Formatting section). All the figures in the field will be formatted with a thousands separator and two decimals.

The various formatting options available are described in Table 13-4.

Table 13-4. *Currency Format Options*

Format Option	Icon	Description	Example
General		Leaves the data unformatted.	100000.01
Currency	$ ˅	Adds a thousands separator and two decimals as well as the current monetary symbol.	$100,000.01
Date/Time		Formats a date and/or time value in one of a selection of date and time formats.	
Decimal Number		Adds a thousands separator and two decimals.	100,000.01
Whole Number		Adds a thousands separator and truncates any decimals.	100,000
Percentage	%	Multiplies by 100, adds two decimals, and prefixes with the percentage symbol.	28.78%
Thousands Separator	,	Adds a thousands separator.	
Scientific		Displays the numbers in scientific format.	1.00E+05
Text		Formats the field contents as text.	
Binary		Leaves the field contents as a binary representation of the data.	
True/False		Formats the field contents as true/false.	
Decimal Point	-⁰⁰ [1 ˅]	Increases or reduces the number of decimals.	

If you wish to return to "plain vanilla" data, then you can do this by selecting the General format. Remember that you are not in Excel, and you cannot format only a range of figures—it is the whole field or nothing. Also, there is no way to format nonadjacent fields by Ctrl-clicking to perform a noncontiguous selection. And, you cannot select multiple adjacent fields and format them in a single operation.

By now, you have probably realized that Power BI Desktop operates on a "Format once/apply everywhere" principle. However, this does not mean that you have to prepare the data exhaustively before creating dashboards and reports. You can flip between the data model and the Report View at any time to select another format, secure in the knowledge that the format that you just applied is used throughout all of your dashboards wherever the relevant metric is used.

Note   Numeric formats are not available for selection if the data in a field is of text or date/time data type. Similarly, date and time formats are only available if the field contains data that can be interpreted as dates or times. Only Boolean (true/false) data types can be formatted as true/false. Finally, only fields containing binary data can be formatted as binary.

Currency Formats

Power BI Desktop will propose a wide range of currency formats. To choose the currency that you want:

1. Click the popup (the downward-facing triangle) to the right of the currency format icon. This will display a list of available formats.

2. Select the currency symbol that you want, or scroll through the list to view all the available currency formats, as shown in Figure 13-8, then click OK.

Figure 13-8. *The currency format popup list*

Note   The thousands separator that is applied, as well as the decimal separator, depends on the settings of the PC on which the formatting is applied.

Preparing Data for Dashboards

Corralling data into a structure that can power your dashboards necessitates a good few tweaks above and beyond specifying data types and formats for final presentation. As part of the groundwork for your dashboards, you could also have to

- Categorize data

- Apply a default summarization

- Define Sort by fields

- Hide fields

These ideas probably seem somewhat abstruse at first sight, so let's see them in action to make it clear why you need to add these touches to your data model.

Categorizing Data

Power BI dashboards are not just made up of facts and figures. They can also contain geographical data or hyperlinks to websites or documents. While we humans can recognize a URL pretty easily and we can guess that a field with postcodes contains, well, postcodes, such intuitions may not be quite as self-evident for a computer.

So, if you want Power BI to be able to add maps or hyperlinks (for instance), you will make life easier for both you and the application if you categorize any fields that contain the types of data that are used for maps and links.

For instance, suppose that you want to prepare the Countries table as a potential data source for a dashboard map (and assuming that you have loaded the CarSalesDataFromDataModel.pbix sample file):

1. In the Data View, select the Countries table in the Fields list. The data in the Countries table will appear in the center of the Power BI Desktop window.

2. Click inside the CountryName field. The field will be highlighted.

3. In the Column tools ribbon, click the popup to the right of the Data category button. You can see this context menu in Figure 13-9.

Figure 13-9. *The Data category options*

4.   Select Country/Region from the menu.

The ribbon will show Data Category: Country/Region. This means that Power BI Desktop now knows how to use the contents of this field as a country when generating maps in dashboards.

The Data category options that are available are described in Table 13-5.

Table 13-5. *Data Category Options*

Data Category Option	Description
Uncategorized	Applies to data that is not used for hyperlinks or creating maps.
Address	Specifies an address for mapping.
Place	Specifies a location or place for mapping.
City	Specifies a city for mapping.
County	Specifies a county for mapping.
State or Province	Specifies a state or province for mapping.
Postal Code .	Specifies a postal (ZIP) code for mapping.
Country	Specifies a country or region for mapping.
Continent	Specifies a continent for mapping.
Latitude	Specifies a latitude for mapping.
Longitude	Specifies a longitude for mapping.
Web URL	Indicates a URL for a hyperlink.
Image URL	Indicates a URL for the source of an image in a dashboard.
Barcode	Specifies that the field contains a barcode.

Note   Not specifying a data category does not mean that Power BI Desktop cannot create maps in dashboards or recognize URLs. However, the results cannot be guaranteed of a reasonable chance of success unless you have indicated to the application that a field contains a certain type of data.

Applying a Default Summarization

When you are creating dashboards, you are often aggregating numeric data. Most times, this means adding up the figures to return the field total. However, there could be fields of data where you want another aggregation applied. Do the following to set your own default aggregation (assuming that you have loaded the CarSalesDataFromDataModel. pbix sample file):

1. In the Data View, select the Colors table in the Fields list. The Colors data will appear in the center of the Power BI Desktop window.

2. Click inside the Color field. The field will be highlighted.

3. In the Column tools ribbon, click the popup to the right of the Summarization button. The Summarization popup menu appears, as shown in Figure 13-10.

Figure 13-10. *The Default Summarization popup menu*

4. Select Count from the context menu.

The ribbon will show Default Summarization: Count.

The Default Summarization options that are available are described in Table 13-6.

Table 13-6. *Default Summarization Options*

Default Summarization Option	Description
Don't summarize	The data in this field is not summarized.
Sum	The data in this field is added (summed).
Average	The average value for the data in this field is returned.
Minimum	The minimum value for the data in this field is returned.
Maximum	The maximum value for the data in this field is returned.
Count	The number of elements in this field is returned.
Count (Distinct)	The number of individual (distinct) elements in this field is returned.

Obviously, you can only apply mathematical aggregations to numeric values. However, you can apply counts to any type of data.

Note   Specifying a default aggregation does not prevent you from overriding the default in dashboards. It merely sets a default that is applied as a standard when aggregating data from a field. In the real world, this can be really useful because it reduces the time you spend building dashboards.

Defining Sort By Fields

Sometimes you will want to sort data in a dashboard visualization based not on the contents of the selected field, but on the contents of another field. As an example, imagine that you have a table of data that contains the month for a sale. If you sort by month, you probably do not want to see the months in alphabetical order, starting with April. In cases such as this, you can tell Power BI Desktop that you want to sort the month *name* element by the month *number* that is contained in another field.

1. Load the C:\PowerBiDesktopSamples\CarSalesDataFromDataModel. pbix sample file (unless you have already loaded it, of course).

2. In the Data View, select the DateDimension table in the Fields list. The date data will appear in the center of the Power BI Desktop window.

3. Click inside the MonthFull field. The field will be highlighted.

4. In the Column tools ribbon, click the Sort by column button and select MonthNum from the list of available fields.

Now if you sort by MonthFull in a visualization, you see the months in the order that you probably expect—from January to December. Had you *not* applied a Sort by column, then calendar months would have been sorted in alphabetical order, which is from April to September! Once again, this choice applies to *any* visualization that you create in a Power BI Desktop dashboard that is based on this data model. So remember to add numeric sort fields alongside textual fields, such as dates and so forth, at the source.

To remove the Sort by column, leave the field selected and simply click the Sort by column button again and select the original field name from the list of available fields.

Tip   If you want to see which field has been set as a Sort By field, simply click inside the field to be sorted and then click the Sort By field button. The popup list of fields shows a tick to the left of the field that is being used to sort the selected field.

The sample file for this chapter (CarSalesDataFromDataModel.pbix) already contains fields that you can use as Sort By fields. In the real world, your source data might not always be this instantly usable. So remember that you can always switch to the Power BI Desktop Query Editor and enhance source tables with extra fields that you can then use to sort data in Data View.

Hiding Tables and Fields from the User

A data model can conceivably contain many more fields than those that you need to create reports and dashboards. These could include (among others)

-   Sort by column

-   Fields that already appear in hierarchies (as you will see in a couple of pages' time)

-   Fields that contain intermediate calculations (these are explained in the next chapter)

-   Fields that contain data that you have loaded "just in case" but don't need yet

It follows that, in the interests of clarity, you may want to hide fields (or even entire tables) that are not strictly relevant to your analysis. This not only reduces clutter, it can avoid confusion when new users start to work with a data model that you have created. It also guarantees that only essential data will be available.

Hiding Fields and Tables

As a first step, you need to flag fields (or fields, if you prefer) and tables as hidden. Here is how:

1. Click the field or table that you want to hide.

2. Select Hide in Report View from the popup menu.

Hidden fields and tables will still appear in the Fields list for the moment, but will be grayed out. Hidden fields and the fields in hidden tables can, nonetheless, still be used in visualizations.

To redisplay a hidden field or table, simply right-click the requisite field or table and uncheck the Hide in Report View option in the popup menu.

Removing Hidden Fields and Tables from View

If your objective is to "declutter" the Fields list, you can then remove hidden fields and tables from view completely, as follows:

1. Click any table or field in the Fields list and uncheck the View Hidden option in the popup menu.

All the hidden fields and tables will disappear from the Fields list. To redisplay all the hidden fields and tables, simply check the Unhide all option in the popup menu.

Sorting Data in Power BI Desktop Tables

A Power BI Desktop table could contain millions of rows, so the last thing that you want to have to do is to scroll down through a random dataset. Fortunately, ordering data in a table is simple:

1. Activate the table that contains the field to sort.

2. In the table (not in the Fields list) right-click inside the field you want
    to order the data by. I will choose the Make field in the Stock table.

3. Click the Sort Ascending option in the context menu to sort this
    field in ascending (alphabetical) order.

The table is sorted using the selected field as the sort key, and even a large dataset
appears correctly ordered in a very short time. If you want to sort a table in descending
order (reverse alphabetical or largest to smallest order), click the Sort Descending option
in the context menu.

At this juncture, you need to remember that the data model is not really designed for
interactive data analysis. That is what dashboards are for. Consequently, you should not
expect to use the data tables in Power BI Desktop as if they were vast Excel spreadsheets.

Tip   If you need a visual indication that a field is sorted, look at the right of the
field name. You will see a small arrow that faces upward to indicate a descending
sort or downward to indicate an ascending sort.

If you want to remove the sort operation that you applied and return to the initial
dataset as it was imported, all you have to do is click the Clear Sort icon in the context
menu for the field.

Note   You cannot perform complex sort operations; that is, you cannot sort first
on one field, then carry out a secondary sort in another field (if there are identical
elements in the first field). You also cannot perform multiple sort operations sorting
on the least important field and then progressing up to the most important field
to sort on to get the effect of a complex sort. This is because Power BI Desktop
always sorts the data based on the dataset as it was initially loaded. Remember
that you can add index fields (as you saw in Chapter 8) in Power BI Desktop Query
and then sort on these if you want to reapply an initial sort order.

Creating and Modifying Groups

There could be times when you have multiple individual items in a list and you wish to gather separate sets of values into groups. This could be to get a higher-level view of separate subdomains or simply to isolate certain values from a recordset. It can be particularly useful when you want to

- Visualize a disparate set of values as a single element

- Group a "long tail" of values into a single category

Tip   If you like, you can consider that groups are to "horizontal" organization what hierarchies are to "vertical" selection.

Creating a Group

Suppose that you will frequently be using a set of colors as the basis for tables and charts in your dashboards. Here is how to create a group containing a subset of the available colors:

1. Click the Data icon on the top left of the Power BI Desktop window.

2. Select the Colors table.

3. Click inside the Color field.

4. In the Column tools ribbon, click the New Group icon. The Groups dialog will appear.

5. In the Name field, enter a name for the group. I will use PowerColors in this example.

6. In the list of ungrouped values on the left, Ctrl-click the following five elements:

   a. Black

   b. Blue

   c. British Racing Green

   d. Dark Purple

   e. Green

7. Click Group.

8. Rename the color group (which is currently highlighted).

9. Press Enter. The dialog will look like the one shown in Figure 13-11.

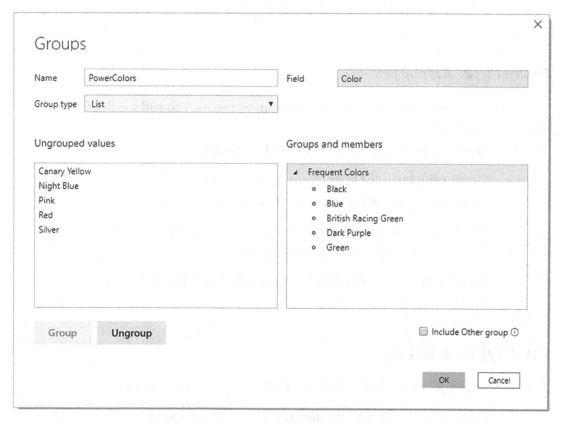

Figure 13-11. *The Groups dialog*

10. Click OK. A new field will be created containing the group definitions, as you can see in Figure 13-12. The name of the group becomes the new field name.

ColorID	Color	PowerColors
1	Red	Red
2	Blue	Frequent Colors
3	Green	Frequent Colors
4	Silver	Silver
5	Canary Yellow	Canary Yellow
6	Night Blue	Night Blue
7	Black	Frequent Colors
8	British Racing Green	Frequent Colors
9	Dark Purple	Frequent Colors
10	Pink	Pink

Figure 13-12. *A group field*

You can now use this field in visuals to group elements. You will see this in greater detail in Chapter 16.

There are a couple of final points to note when creating groups:

- Clicking the Include Other group check box will take all remaining items in the original field and use them to create an "Other" group.

- You can create multiple groups. Simple carry out steps 6 and 7 as many times as you want separate groups.

- No value from the original field can appear more than once in a group.

Modifying a Group

Any existing group can be altered easily, simply by doing the following:

1. Click inside the field containing the group that you want to modify.

2. In the Column tools ribbon, click the Edit Groups icon. The Groups dialog will appear.

3. Remove any items from the group by clicking the value in the Groups and Members list on the right. Then click Ungroup.

4. Add any new values by selecting the item on the left and, once
   you have selected the appropriate group on the right, clicking the
   Group button.

5. Click OK. The modified group will be applied to the selected field.

Deleting a Group

As a group is, to all intents and purposes, a field, you delete a group exactly as you would
delete a field:

1. In the Fields list, expand the table containing the new field. You
   will see that group fields have a small icon with two empty squares
   to the left of the field name.

2. Right-click the group field and select Delete.

3. Confirm the deletion.

Note You can "mix and match" groups in a table. You can, for instance, allocate all
the separate values in a table to different groups, or you can create multiple groups
to handle certain values and nonetheless leave other values outside a group.

Marking a Table as a Date Table

Power BI Desktop now needs to know that the table you have imported is, in fact, a date
table that it can use to add time intelligence. This is easier to do than to talk about:

1. Switch to the Data View.

2. Click the DateDimension table.

3. In the Table tools ribbon, click the Mark as date table button. The
   Mark as date table dialog will appear.

4. Select the column that contains the contiguous list of dates. In the
   example used in this book, it is the DateKey column. The dialog
   should look like the one shown in Figure 13-13.

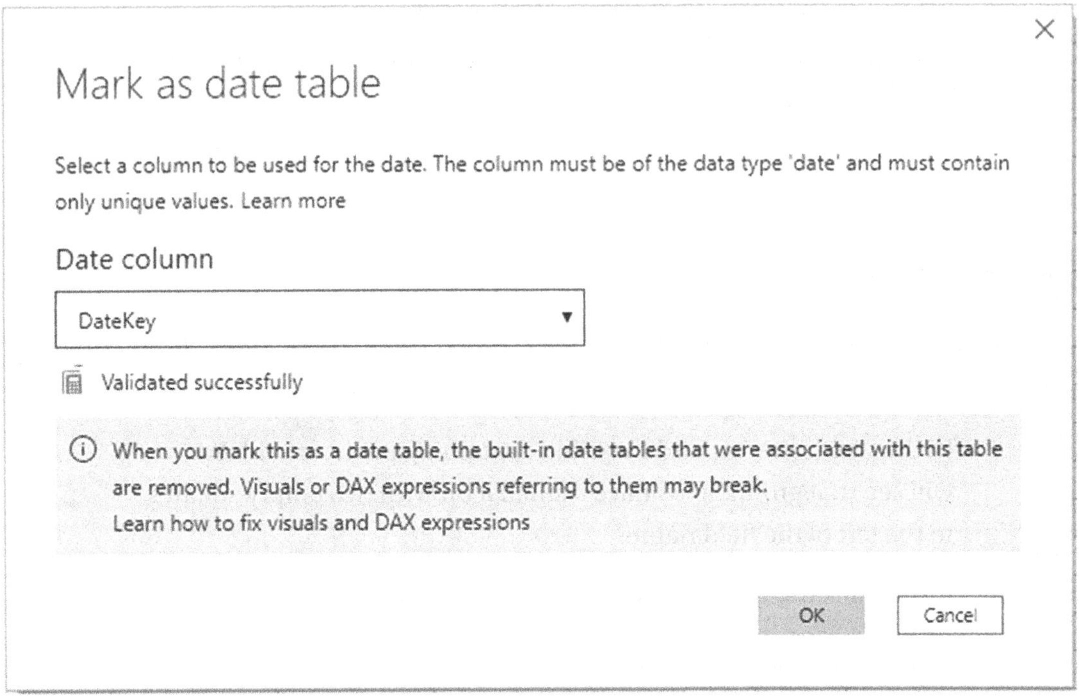

Figure 13-13. *The Mark as date table dialog*

5.   Click OK.

Now Power BI Desktop knows that this table is slightly special and that it contains only a list of dates that can be used to add time intelligence to your analyses. The final thing to do is define a relationship between the DateKey column in the date table and a date field in the table that contains the data you want to analyze over time. In the sample data that we are using, this will be the InvoiceDate field in the SalesDate table. This way the dataset knows that you may be looking at sales by invoice date, but that the DateTable will provide the list of days, months, quarters, and years used to display metrics over time.

Note   Creating date dimensions can be done in Excel, DAX, or M. However, the techniques required are beyond the scope of this book.

Designing a Power BI Desktop Data Model

Congratulations! You are well on the way to developing a high-performance data model for self-service business intelligence (BI). You have imported data from one or even from several sources into the Power BI Desktop data model. You have taken a good look at your data using the Power BI Desktop data model window, and you can carry out essential operations to rename tables and fields. The final step to ensure that your dataset is ready for initial use as a self-service BI data repository is to create and manage relationships between tables. This is a fundamental part of designing a coherent and usable dataset in Power BI Desktop.

Before leaping into the technicalities of table relationships, we first need to answer a couple of simple questions:

- What are relationships between tables?

- Why do we need them?

Table relationships are links between tables of data that allow fields in one table to be used meaningfully in another table. If you have opened the Power BI Desktop example file CarSalesDataFromDataModel.pbix, then you can see that there is a Stock table of stock data that contains a ColorID field, but not the actual color itself. As a complement to this, there is a reference table of colors, named Colors. It follows that, if we want to say what color a car was when it was bought, we need to be able to link the tables so that the Stock table can "look up" the actual color of the car that was bought. This requires some commonality between the two tables and, fortunately, both contain a field named ColorID. So if we are able to join the two tables using this field, we can see which color is represented by the color ID for each car in stock.

You can see another example of linking tables if you take a look at the Invoices and InvoiceLines tables. These two tables have been designed using a technique called relational modeling. Essentially this means that two tables have been created to avoid pointless data duplication. So any data that is used to describe an invoice (such as the invoice date or invoice number) is stored in the Invoices table, whereas all the details concerning the vehicles sold are held in a separate table named InvoiceLines. The two tables then share a field that allows them to be joined so that users can see the data from the two tables together if they need to. This means that any elements that would otherwise be repeated are stored in a "header" table such as the Invoices table, and nonrepeating data is stored in a detail table (the InvoiceLines table in this example).

It is possible to store the data from these two tables as one table. However, this would mean repeating elements such as the invoice date or invoice number each time that an invoice contained more than one item. This would entail repeated data elements and vastly increased file sizes.

Clearly, these examples are extremely simple. However, they are not unduly contrived. They represent the way many relational databases store data. So there is every chance that you will see potential links or relationships like this in the real-world data that you import from corporate databases. In any case, if you want to use data from multiple sources in your data analysis, you will have to find a way to link the tables using a common field, like the ColorID field that I just mentioned. The reality may be messier (the fields may not have the same name in the two tables, for instance), but the principle always applies.

Tip   If you have the necessary permissions as well as the SQL knowledge, then you can join tables directly in the source database using a query. This way you can create fewer "flattened" tables in Power BI Desktop from the start and avoid having to create a spider's web of new table relationships in Power BI Desktop.

Data Modeling in the Power BI Desktop Environment

Before leaping into the detail of what you can do to create and enhance a data model, I think that it is best if you first familiarize yourself with the Modeling ribbon which is the starting point for data modeling.

The Modeling Ribbon

The Modeling ribbon is used to categorize and organize data and tables as well as to add calculated fields and additional metrics and categorize and format data. The buttons that it contains are shown in Figure 13-14 and explained in Table 13-7.

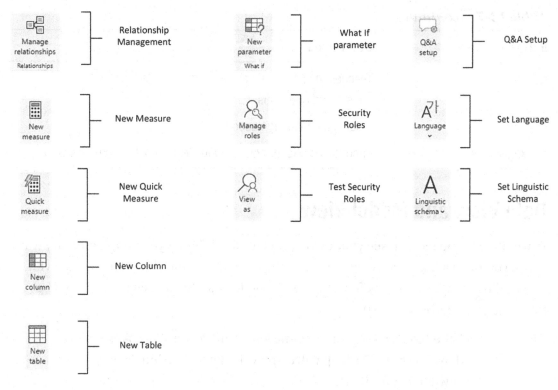

Figure 13-14. *Buttons in the Column tools ribbon*

Table 13-7. *The Column Tools Ribbon Buttons*

Button	Description
Manage relationships	Lets you join tables as well as delete these joins (called *relationships*) and modify them.
New measure	Used to add a new value or calculation to a table.
New quick measure	Used to add a new value or calculation to a table with help from Power BI Desktop.
New field	Adds a new calculated field to a table.
New table	Adds a new table.
What-if parameter	Lets you add a new interactive "what-if" parameter.
Manage roles	Allows you to restrict data access for given users.
View as roles	Lets you see the data available for a given role or roles.

(continued)

Table 13-7. (*continued*)

Button	Description
Q&A setup	Teaches the Power BI natural language interface to better understand questions.
Set language	Selects the language used by Q&A.
Set linguistic schema	Imports, exports, or edits a linguistic schema used by Q&A.

Data View and Model View

Power BI Desktop lets you see your data model in two different yet complementary ways. When you need a high-level overview of all the data tables, you should use Model view, as this allows you to step back from the detail and look at the dataset as a whole. The following explains how to do this:

1. Click the Model view button on the left of the Power BI Desktop window. Power BI Desktop will display the tables in Model view, as shown in Figure 13-15.

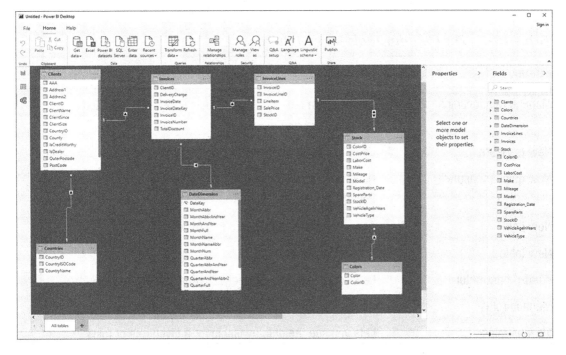

Figure 13-15. *Model view*

As you can see from Figure 13-15, you are now looking at most or all of your tables, and although you can see the table and field names, you cannot see the data. Not only that, but you can also see that some tables are already joined—though not all of them. This is because Power BI Desktop always attempts to guess any possible relationships between tables and creates relationships automatically, if it can, to save you time and effort.

This is exactly what we need, because now it is time to think in terms of overall structures rather than the nitty-gritty. You can use this view to move and resize the tables. Moving a table is as easy as dragging the table's title bar. Resizing a table means placing the pointer over a table edge or corner and dragging the mouse.

Tip   Although repositioning tables can be considered pure aesthetics, I find that doing so is really useful. A well-laid-out dataset design helps you understand the relationships between the tables and the inherent structure of the data.

Model View Display Options

The whole point of Model view is to let you get a good look at the entire dataset and, if necessary, modify the layout in order to see the relationships between tables more clearly.

Creating Relationships

Creating relationships is easy once you know which fields are common between tables. Since we already agreed that we need to join the Colors table to the Stock table, let's look at how to do this using the file C:\PowerBiDesktopSamples\ CarSalesDataForLinkingTables.pbix. This file contains the data tables that you saw up until now in this chapter, but without any of the relationships between the tables.

1. Open the Power BI Desktop file CarSalesDataForLinkingTables. pbix in the folder C:\PowerBiDesktopSamples.

2. Drag the ColorID field from the Stock table over the ColorID field in the Colors table, as shown in Figure 13-16.

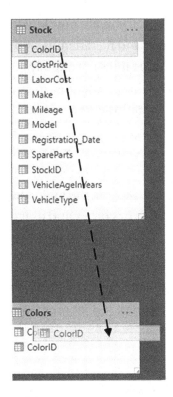

Figure 13-16. *A table relationship*

This is all that you have to do. The two tables are now joined and the data from both tables can be used meaningfully in reports and dashboards.

Note   Currently, in the Power BI Desktop data model, you can only join tables on a single field. You may need to take this into account when preparing queries in the Power BI Desktop Query Editor for later use in the data model.

Creating Relationships Manually

You do not have to drag and drop field names to create relationships. If you prefer, you can specify the tables and fields that will be used to create a relationship between tables. What is more, you do not have to be in Model view to do this. So, just to make a point and to show you how flexible Power BI Desktop can be, in this example, you will join the Invoices and InvoiceLines tables on their common InvoiceID field:

1. Select a table that you want to make appear in a relationship. I will use the Invoices table for this example.

2. Click the Manage relationships button in the Modeling ribbon (or in the Table tools ribbon if you are in Data View). The Manage relationships dialog will appear.

3. Click New. The Create relationship dialog will appear.

4. In the upper part of the dialog, select the Invoices table from the popup list of tables.

5. In the lower part of the dialog, select the InvoiceLines table as the related lookup table. The InvoiceID field should appear automatically as the field to join on (it will be selected in both tables). If Power BI Desktop has guessed the field, it will appear selected. If it does not, or if it has guessed incorrectly, you can always select the correct field for both tables. The Create relationship dialog should look like Figure 13-17.

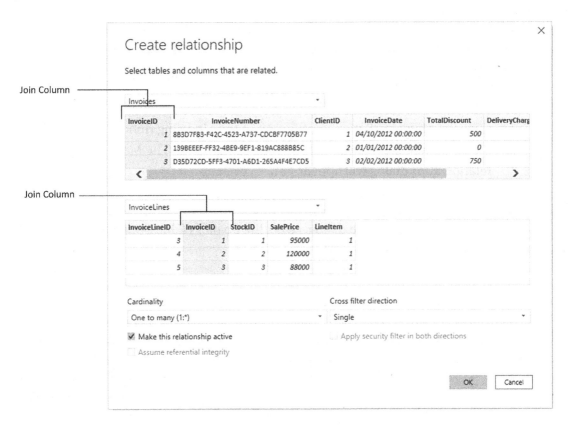

Figure 13-17. *The Create relationship dialog*

6. Click OK. The Create relationship dialog will close and return you
    to the Manage relationships dialog. It should look like Figure 13-18
    at the moment. You can see that it indicates which field in which
    table is used to join to which other field in which other table.

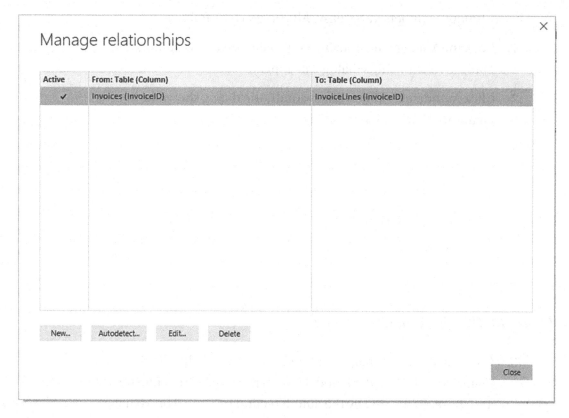

Figure 13-18. *The Manage relationships dialog*

7. Click Close. The Manage relationships dialog will close and the relationship will be created.

Creating Relationships Automatically

Whatever the data source, you can have Power BI Desktop detect the relationships automatically. This approach has a couple of advantages:

- You avoid a lot of manual work.

- You reduce the risk of error (i.e., creating relationships between tables on the wrong fields, or even creating relationships between tables that are not related).

This technique is unbelievably easy. All you do is the following:

1. Click the Manage relationships button in the Home ribbon. The Manage relationships dialog will appear.

2. Click Autodetect. After a few seconds, the dialog shown in Figure 13-19 will appear.

Figure 13-19. *The Autodetect dialog*

3. Click Close. The Manage relationships dialog will list all the relationships in the data model—both preexisting relationships and those discovered by the autodetection process. The Manage relationships dialog will now look like the one in Figure 13-20.

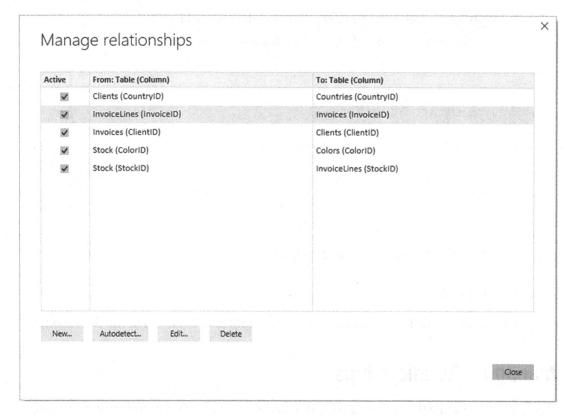

Figure 13-20. *The Manage relationships dialog after automatically detecting relationships*

4. Click Close to return to the Relationships View.

You will see that the tables you just imported already have the relationships generated in Power BI Desktop.

Deleting Relationships

In addition to creating relationships, you will inevitably want to remove them at some point. This is both visual and intuitive.

1. Click the Design View button in the Home ribbon. Power BI Desktop will display the tables in Model view.

2. Select the relationship that you want to delete. The arrow joining the two tables will become a double link, and the two tables will be highlighted.

3. Right-click and choose Delete (or press the Delete key). The Confirmation dialog will appear, as shown in Figure 13-21.

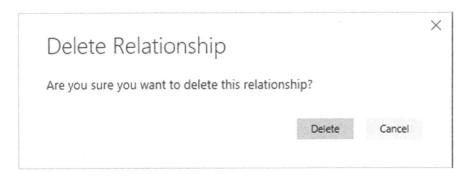

Figure 13-21. The Delete Relationship dialog

4. Click Delete.

The relationship will be deleted. However, the tables will remain in the data model.

Managing Relationships

If you wish to change the field in a table that serves as the basis for a relationship, then you have another option. You can use the Manage relationships dialog. This approach may also be useful if you want to create or delete several relationships at once. If you want to use this dialog

1. In the Design tab, of the Home ribbon, click Manage relationships. The Manage relationships dialog appears, as was shown previously in Figure 13-18.

2. Click the relationship you wish to modify.

3. Click Edit (or double-click the relationship). The Edit relationship dialog appears (it is virtually identical to the Create relationship dialog shown in Figure 13-17).

4. Continue modifying the relationship as described previously.

As you can see from this dialog, you also have the option of creating or deleting relationships. Since the processes here are identical to those I have already described, I will not repeat them.

The techniques used to create and manage relationships are not, in themselves, very difficult to apply. It is nonetheless *absolutely fundamental* to establish the correct relationships between the tables in the dataset. Put simply, if you try to use data from unconnected tables in a single Power BI Desktop dashboard, not only will you get an alert warning you that relationships need to be created, you will also get visibly inaccurate results. Basically, all of your analyses will be false. So it is well worth it to spend a few minutes upfront designing a clean, accurate, and logically coherent dataset.

Tip   Double-clicking a relationship in the Model view will also display the Edit relationship dialog.

Deactivating Relationships

If you no longer need a relationship between tables but do not want to delete it, you also have the option of deactivating the relationship. This means that the relationship no longer functions, but that you can reactivate it quickly and easily.

Deactivating—or reactivating—a relationship is as simple as selecting or unselecting the box in the Active field of the Manage relationships dialog (shown earlier in Figure 13-18).

Advanced Relationship Options

The Edit relationship dialog contains a few advanced options that you could find useful on occasion. These include a couple of fundamental options that you have to take into consideration when defining the structure of a data model:

- Cardinality

- Cross-filter direction

These are the subject of the next two subsections.

Cardinality

Cardinality defines how many fields in one table relate to the matching field in the linked table. You can see the available choices in the cardinality popup in Figure 13-22.

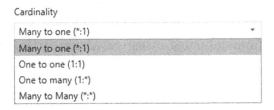

Figure 13-22. *Cardinality in table relationships*

These various options are described in Table 13-8.

Table 13-8. *Power BI Desktop Relationship Types*

Relationship Option	Description
Many to one	Specifies that there are many records in one table for a single record that maps in the table that is joined.
One to one	Specifies that there is a single record in one table for a single record that maps in the table that is joined.
One to many	Specifies that there is a single record in one table for many records that map in the table that is joined.
Many to many	Specifies that many records in one table may be joined to multiple records in another table.

Power BI Desktop will nearly always detect the correct cardinality for a relationship. However, if you want to override the choice made by the software because you suspect that another type of cardinality will be required in the future, for instance, then you simply select the cardinality that you want from the popup list.

Cardinality Issues

Data is not always perfect, unfortunately. So there will be times when you will select the cardinality that you want to use to join two tables and will get strange results when you create your dashboards.

It is impossible to cover all the multiple reasons that can provoke this error. So, if you see this message, here are a few pointers to try and help you sort out this issue, should you encounter it:

- For a one-to-many cardinality, ensure that the values for the field on the "one" side of the relationship exist for *all* the corresponding values on the "many" side.

- For a one-to-one cardinality, check that there are *no duplicate values* for the fields on either side of the table relationship.

- For a one-to-one cardinality, make sure that there are no empty or null values for the fields on either side of the table relationship.

- For a one-to-many cardinality, ensure that the values for the field on the "one" side of the relationship do not contain empty or null values.

Managing Relationships Between Tables

Managing relationships in Power BI Desktop is often the key to creating an efficient data model. It is, however, outside the scope of this book to provide a complete course in data modeling. Nonetheless, here are a few tips to bear in mind when creating your initial data models:

- It can help to think in terms of *main* tables and *lookup* tables. In the data model that you have looked at in this chapter, you can consider certain tables as lookup tables for the main data, such as the Colors, Countries, and Clients tables.

- Lookup tables generally contain a series of values that are not repeated in the table (a list of countries, for instance). These values are called the "one" side of a relationship and are linked to another table where they are referred to on many occasions. Hence the table that contains the multiple references is called the "many" side of the relationship. This is also called the *cardinality* of a relationship by database and data warehouse designers.

- If you take a look at Figure 13-15 (the Power BI Desktop Model view), you can see that the different types of relationship are indicated in the join between related tables. A small 1 at the end of a relationship indicates the "one" side of a relationship, and an asterisk indicates the "many" side of the relationship.

- If your source data contains many lookup tables that cascade down through a series of relationships (a classic case is the Category ➤ Subcategory ➤ Product hierarchy that you find in many retail environments), to avoid overcomplicating the data model, you may prefer to merge multiple tables into a single table using Power BI Desktop Query *before* developing the data model in Power BI Desktop itself.

- Sometimes—and this can be the case when importing data from relational databases—you need to join tables on more than one field. This is not possible in Power BI Desktop. However, you can often find workarounds to this, again using Power BI Desktop Query before modeling the data. In cases like this, you can merge tables by creating joins using multiple fields (as you saw in Chapter 8), for instance.

- Data imported from data warehouses can have a built-in structure of facts (main tables containing metrics) and dimensions (containing lookup elements). However, you may want to "flatten" complex hierarchies of dimensions and create single-level tables of lookup elements here, too, using Power BI Desktop Query.

- Sometimes you may want to use the same table twice in different contexts. For instance, a date table may be useful to join to a sale date and a purchase date. In cases like this, you can reimport the date table a second time (and give it another name) and then create two separate joins from a lookup table to the two different lookup tables. This allows you to filter and aggregate data by separate date criteria. A lookup table like this is often called a *role-playing dimension*.

- It is possible to create multiple relations between one table and another and to specify that only one of them is active. You can then force a calculation to apply a nonactive relationship using the USERELATIONSHIP() function in DAX. However, we are already starting to reach more complex levels of data modeling, so I will only mention the possibility here.

Cross-Filter Direction

You can see the two cross-filtering options in Figure 13-23. These allow you to specify whether filters will apply to all tables in a joined set of tables or only in the table where an aggregation is being carried out.

Figure 13-23. *Cross-filter direction in table relationships*

The two options are described in Table 13-9.

Table 13-9. *Cross-Filter Direction Options*

Cross-Filter Direction Option	Description
Single	Filters on the linked table will apply to the table where the data aggregations take place, but not the reverse.
Both	For filtering purposes, both tables are considered as if they are a single, larger, table. All data in all tables will be filtered.

Other Relationship Options

The fundamental remaining options for relationships are

- Make this relationship active
- Assume referential integrity

Make This Relationship Active

In some data models, there can be multiple relationships (on different fields) between tables. However, only one of these relationships can be active at any one time. Clicking the "Make this relationship" active check box tells Power BI Desktop that the selected relationship is the active one. Other relationships can, however, be used in DAX code.

Assume Referential Integrity

This option is only available when using DirectQuery (which you learned to use in Chapter 4). By definition, this option applies only to a relational database. Enabling this lets Power BI Desktop send more efficient queries to the underlying data source. This means that data is updated faster. For this to work, there are a couple of basic requirements:

- Data in the "from" field in the relationship can never be null or blank.

- For each data element in the "from" field, there is a corresponding value in the "to" field.

- The "from" field is on the "many" side in a one-to-many relationship, or the relationship is a one-to-one type of join.

Note   You need to be aware that setting the "Assume referential integrity" option when the underlying data does not fulfill the preceding requirements will not prevent the option from being applied, or even data being returned. However, the results might be erroneous.

Reimporting Related Tables

There is one fairly important point to make to conclude this chapter. This is that if you delete a set of related tables and subsequently reimport them without importing the relationships, then Power BI Desktop will *not* remember the relationships that existed previously. Consequently, you will have to re-create any relationships manually. The same is true if you delete and reimport any table that you linked to an existing table in Power BI Desktop—once a relationship has been removed through the process of deleting a table, you will have to re-create it.

Table and Field Properties

Power BI data models can rapidly become extremely complex. Consequently, it can be useful (not to say fundamental) to document them thoroughly. The Properties pane of the Model view allows you to do just this:

1.   Switch to Model view.

2.   Click the table you wish to document.

3.   In the Properties pane, click inside the Description field and enter a description. The Properties pane will look something like the one shown in Figure 13-24.

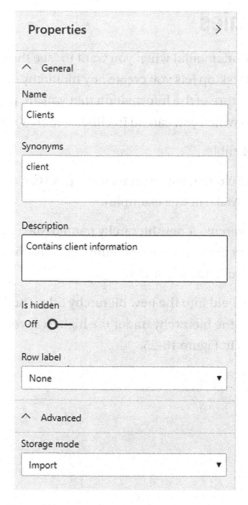

Figure 13-24.   *The Properties pane*

Clicking a field name allows you to document the selected field in the same way. The Properties pane also lets you set the following attributes of the selected field:

- The data type

- The numeric formatting

- The field visibility (this applies to tables as well)

- The data categorization

- The default summarization

- The Sort by column (if one is needed)

Adding Hierarchies

Organizing data can be fundamental when you want to "see the wood for the trees." Consequently Power BI Desktop lets you create any hierarchy on the fly so that you can better appreciate the structure of the information that you are presenting.

To create a hierarchy (which you can do in either Report View or Data View):

1. Select the Stock table.

2. Right-click the field that will become the top-level element in the new hierarchy (Make in this example).

3. Select New Hierarchy. A new hierarchy named Make Hierarchy will appear in the Stock table, containing the Make field as the top-level element in the hierarchy.

4. Drag the Model field into the new hierarchy title. The Model field will be added to the hierarchy under the highest-level element. You can see this in Figure 13-25.

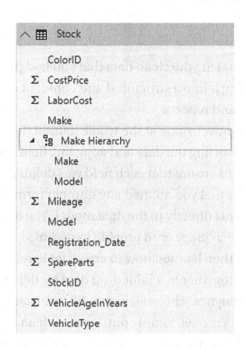

Figure 13-25. *An added hierarchy*

This is all that you have to do! You can now drag the hierarchy into the report canvas to create a table that is based on the multiple elements that make up the hierarchy. The data can be used anywhere—and in any visual—where the multiple fields that make up the hierarchy would be used. They are particularly useful as the basis for matrices and drill-down charts, which you will discover in Chapters 15 and 16.

You can, of course, rename or delete the hierarchy or any level in a hierarchy just as you would any standard data field.

Tip   Adding a field to a hierarchy means that the field now exists twice in the table—once as a "stand-alone" field and once inside a hierarchy. In most cases it is best to hide the original version of the field so that users (and you) don't see the field twice in the data model.

Conclusion

This chapter was all about taking the clean data that you had prepared using Power BI Desktop Query and molding it into a structured and coherent data model that will be the basis for your dashboards and reports.

To begin with, you saw how to look at the whole dataset that was now available in the data model. This included sorting the data and adjusting field widths.

Then you learned how to ensure that each field was defined as having the appropriate data type. After that you applied any number formats that would be required in future dashboard elements directly to the data model. You also saw how to prepare certain types of field for use in maps or to provide hyperlinks.

Most importantly, you then learned how to create table relationships that pull all the disparate data sources together in a joined-up data model that has now become the basis for some in-depth analytics. This will, in most circumstances, be the singular most important aspect of the data model. Simply put, a good, clean, and well-structured data model will allow you to get the most out of your data visualization—which is the subject of the remaining chapters in this book.

CHAPTER 14

Table Visuals

You are now entering the final straight on your race to deliver clear, powerful, and visually compelling analytics. The time has come to transform data into attention-grabbing dashboards that capture the imagination of your audience. In this chapter, you will start learning how to use Power BI Desktop to

- Delve deeply into data and produce valuable information from the mass of facts and figures available

- Create interactive views of your insights, where you can test your analyses quickly and easily

- Enhance the presentation of your results to grab your audience's attention

This chapter and the next one take you through the process of creating text-based visualizations (or visuals if you want to call them that) in Power BI Desktop. In these two chapters, you will learn how to create and enhance

- Tables

- Matrices

- Cards

- Multirow cards

What these types of visuals all have in common is that they are designed to use *text* to convey information rather than using the more graphical display types, which you will discover in Chapters 16 through 20. Text-based visuals are essential when it comes to

- Presenting lists of detailed information

- Displaying cross sections of key data

- Focusing the audience's attention on a single essential figure

© Adam Aspin 2020
A. Aspin, *Pro Power BI Desktop*, https://doi.org/10.1007/978-1-4842-5763-0_14

- Delivering a clear overview of a few key metrics

- Drilling down into hierarchies of data

As you are on the first step of the learning curve, this chapter will focus solely on all that you can do with *tables* of data in Power BI Desktop. This will allow you to familiarize yourself with the core techniques that you can then apply to other text-based visuals—as well as many, if not all, of the vast range of graphical and geographical visualizations that Power BI Desktop lets you use to deliver your analyses.

The techniques that you will learn in this chapter use a Power BI Desktop file called `C:\PowerBiDesktopSamples\CarSalesDataForReports.pbix`. It is available on the Apress website as part of the downloadable material that accompanies this book.

Power BI Desktop Report View

So far in this book, you have used two of the three core interface modes of Power BI Desktop: Data View and Relationships View. Now that you are moving on to create reports and dashboards, you will use the final part of the trilogy: Report View.

You always use Report View to build your dashboards (or reports, if you prefer). It is here that you add and configure visuals that use the data that you have already loaded, cleansed, structured, and enhanced in the data model. This activity is carried out in the report canvas of Power BI Desktop.

Switching to Report View

Although Report View is the default mode when you open Power BI Desktop, you need to switch back to it if you have spent any time working on the underlying data model. The following explains how to activate Report View:

Click the Report View icon at the top left of the Power BI Desktop screen.

You can see the Report View icon in Figure 14-1.

The Power BI Desktop Window

Before we go any further, I would like to explain the Power BI Desktop window, since it is something that you will use a lot in this book from this point onward. The Power BI Desktop window contains the elements that are outlined in Figure 14-1.

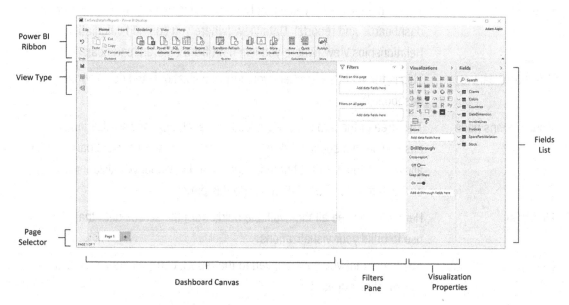

Figure 14-1. *The Power BI Desktop*

As you can see, the Power BI Desktop screen is simple and uncluttered. The various elements that it contains are explained in Table 14-1.

Table 14-1. *Power BI Desktop Options*

Option	Description
Power BI ribbon	This contains the principal options that are available to you when developing dashboards with Power BI Desktop.
View type	These three icons let you flip between Dashboard View (where you create dashboards and reports), Data View (where you can add calculations), and Relationships View (where you join data from different sources).
Dashboard canvas	This is the main area, where you add visualizations and design your dashboards.
Visualizations pane	This area of the application is specific to each type of visualization and lets you set the specific attributes of each element on a dashboard. It also allows you to filter dashboards, pages, and individual visualizations. You can also format visualizations using this pane.
Fields list	Here you can see all the available fields from the source data that you can use to build your visualizations.
Filter pane	Any filters that you have applied to the report, current page, or selected visualization appear here.
Visualization palette	This area contains all the currently available types of visualization that you can add to a dashboard.
Page selector	These are tabs that let you switch from page to page in a report.
Other panes	There are several other panes that are available in Power BI Desktop. However, they remain hidden until you choose to display them. You will learn how to use these panes in future chapters.

Power BI Desktop—like most Microsoft applications—has several available ribbons. These are explained as the need arises in the course of this book.

View Types

There are three principal views over your data in Power BI Desktop. These are outlined in Table 14-2.

Table 14-2. *View Types*

Option	Icon	Description
Report View		This is where you create reports (dashboards) in Power BI Desktop. It will be the focus of the remaining chapters in this book.
Data View		This view allows you to look at the data that you have loaded.
Model View		This view (as you saw in Chapter 13) lets you join tables to create a coherent data model.

We will be working exclusively in Report View in this chapter and in all the chapters devoted to creating dashboards and reports.

Working with Tables

Tables are probably the simplest and most elementary way of displaying data. However, this simplicity should not detract from their usefulness. Indeed, for Power BI Desktop, the humble table is often the default visualization. Moreover, and as you will see in this chapter, the table is the default presentation style for non-geographical data.

I realize, of course, that it may seem contradictory to spend time on a subject that is generally described as intuitive. In answer to this, I can only say that, while getting up and running is easy, attaining an in-depth understanding of all of the potential of this powerful tool does require some explanation. Consequently, the approach that I am taking is to go through all the possibilities of each item as thoroughly as possible. So feel free to jump ahead (and back) if you don't need all the detail just yet—or if you want to skim over the intricacies in order to get a high-level overview of the subject.

Creating a Basic Table

The following example introduces you to tables in Power BI Desktop by creating an initial table that will display the list of clients and their total sales:

1. Open the C:\PowerBiDesktopSamples\CarSalesDataForReports. pbix file from the downloadable samples.

2. In the Fields list, expand the Clients table.

3. Drag the ClientName field into the dashboard canvas. A table displaying all the clients of Brilliant British Cars will appear.

4. Leave this new table selected and, in the Fields list, expand the InvoiceLines table.

5. Click the check box to the left of the SalePrice field. This will add the cumulative sales per client to the table. It should look like Figure 14-2.

ClientName	SalePrice
	£141,250
Aldo Motors	£2,876,250
Ambassador Cars	£1,686,930
Bright Orange	£2,880,500
British Luxury Automobile Corp	£302,690
BritWheels	£2,068,750
Buckingham Palace Car Services	£402,000
Carosse Des Papes	£404,040
Chateau Moi	£311,790
Classy Car Sales	£200,250
Costa Del Speed	£207,750
Crippen & Co	£390,750
Cut'n'Shut	£2,825,500
Embassy Motors	£1,254,550
Total	£31,839,190

Figure 14-2. *A basic table of sales per client*

This is a very tiny table. In the real world, you could be looking at tables that contain thousands, or tens of thousands (or even millions), of records. Power BI Desktop accelerates the display of large datasets by only loading the data that is required as you scroll down through a list and starts with the initial few records in the data. So you might see the scroll bar advance somewhat slowly as you progress downward through a large table.

If a table contains fields that you have used in a visual, then the table name appears in yellow in the Fields list when you select the visualization. You can always see which fields have been selected for a table by expanding the table in the Fields list. The fields used are instantly displayed in both the Fields list (as selected fields) and the field well of the Visualizations pane. To get you used to this idea, see Figure 14-3, which shows both these elements for the table that you just created.

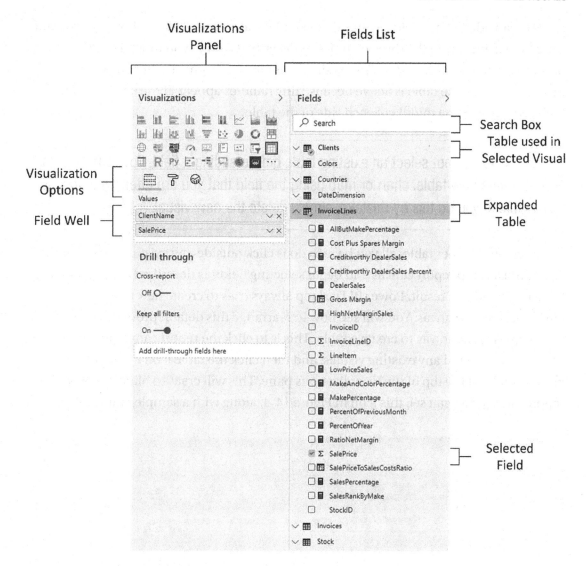

Figure 14-3. *The fields used in a visual*

As befits such a polished product, Power BI Desktop does not limit you to just one way of adding fields to a table. The following are ways in which you can add fields to a table:

- By dragging the field name into the field well in the Visualizations pane

- By selecting a field (which means checking the check box to the left of the field) in the Fields list—assuming that the table is already selected

- By dragging a field into an existing visualization

489

You can add further fields to an existing table at any time. The key thing to remember (if you are using any of the three techniques described) is that you must *select the table that you want to modify first*. This is as simple as clicking inside it. After you click, you instantly see that the table is active because tiny handles appear at the corners of the table as well as in the middle of each side of the table.

Note   If you do not select an existing table before adding a field, Power BI Desktop will create a new table, chart or map using the field that you are attempting to add to a table. If you do this by mistake, simply delete the new visual.

To create another table, all you have to do is click outside any existing visuals in the Power BI Desktop report canvas and begin selecting fields as described earlier. A new table is created as a result. Power BI Desktop always tries to create new tables in an empty part of the canvas. You will see how to rearrange this default presentation shortly.

There is another way to create a table. This is to click the report canvas to ensure that you have deselected any existing visuals, and then click the table icon in the palette of visualizations at the top of the Visualizations pane. This will create a blank table on the report canvas. You can see this icon in Figure 14-4, along with a sample empty table.

Figure 14-4. The table icon

Selecting a Table

Even if it may seem self-evident, I prefer to point your attention at a couple of intricacies of table selection that can flummox newcomers to Power BI Desktop:

- When selecting a table, *avoid* clicking any of the data in the table, as this will highlight the row and gray out other data. Apart from the effect on visibility, this will also apply cross-filtering—which you probably do not want to apply unintentionally (and which you will learn about in Chapter 22).

- Always select a table by clicking outside any data—or better still, by clicking the top bar of the table. You can also click the table border to select it safely.

Note   If you have highlighted a row in a table by accident (and consequently grayed out the remaining rows), just click a second time on the selected row to reset the table.

Deleting a Table

Suppose that you no longer need a table in a Power BI Desktop report. Well, deleting it is simple:

1. Select the table. You can do this by clicking anywhere inside the table. The table borders will appear, even if you move the mouse pointer away from the table.

2. Press the Delete key.

Another way to select a table is to click the options button (the ellipses) that appears at the top right of any visual once it is selected. The options menu for the visual (the table in this example) will appear. Clicking the Remove option will delete the table. You can see the context menu in Figure 14-5.

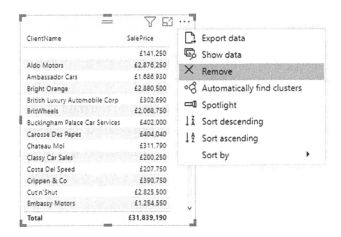

Figure 14-5. *The table visualization options menu*

Deleting a table is so easy that you can do it by mistake, so remember that you can restore an accidentally deleted table by pressing Ctrl+Z or using the Undo arrow at the top left of the Power BI window ribbon.

Copying a Table

You need to copy tables on many occasions. There could be several reasons for this:

- You are creating a new visual on the Power BI Desktop report and need the table as a basis for the new element, such as a chart.

- You are copying visuals between reports.

- You want to keep an example of a table and try some fancy tricks on the copy, but you want to keep the old version as a failsafe option.

In any case, all you have to do (as you might expect) is

1. Select the table (as described previously)

2. In the Home ribbon, select Copy (or press Ctrl+C)

To paste a copy, click outside any visual in a current or new Power BI Desktop report, and select Paste from the Home ribbon (or press Ctrl+V).

Changing the Table Size and Position

A table can be resized and moved (just like any other visual in a Power BI Desktop report) using the techniques that you saw, briefly, in Chapter 1. Although you have already seen these possibilities, I will explain them here in full for the sake of completeness.

Resizing a Table

Resizing a table is mercifully easy. All you have to do is to click any of the table handles and drag the mouse. Lateral handles will alter the table width; top and bottom handles will change the table's height; corner handles modify both height and width by changing the size of the two sides that touch on the selected corner.

Moving a Table

Moving a table is as easy as placing the pointer over the table so that the edges appear and dragging the table to its new position.

You may prefer to use the keyboard when fine-tuning the position of a visual on the dashboard. The keyboard options for doing this are shown in Table 14-3.

Table 14-3. Keyboard Shortcuts for Moving Visuals

Option	Description
Nudge left	Left cursor key
Nudge right	Right cursor key
Nudge up	Up cursor key
Nudge down	Down cursor key

Changing Column Order

If you have built a Power BI Desktop table, you are eventually going to want to modify the order in which the columns appear from left to right. The following explains how to do this:

1. Activate the Fields list (unless it is already displayed).

2. In the Visualizations pane, ensure that the Fields options are displayed (by clicking the small bar chart icon under the collection of available visuals).

3. Click the name of the field that you wish to move.

4. Drag the field vertically to its new position. This can be between existing fields, at the top or at the bottom of the Fields list. A thick yellow line indicates where the field will be positioned.

Figure 14-6 shows how to drag a field from one position to another.

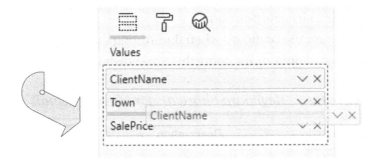

Figure 14-6. *Changing column order by moving fields*

Note   You cannot change the position of a column in a table by dragging it sideways inside the table itself.

Renaming Fields

You also have the ability to rename fields in visuals without having to rename the underlying column in the data table. While this can cause a certain disconnect between the data and its display, it is a technique that can be extremely useful in certain circumstances. To do this:

1. Select the visual containing the data element that you want to rename (I will use the table that you just created in this example).

2. Right-click the field to rename in the field well of the Visualizations pane.

3. Select Rename from the popup menu.

4. Edit the field name—or delete the current name and enter a new name.

5. Press Enter.

The field is now renamed. The new name will appear only in the selected visual, and the data element will keep its original name.

Note   Renaming a field in the field well will also rename the field. However, this will apply the new name to every visual in the report.

Removing Columns from a Table

Another everyday task in Power BI Desktop is removing columns from a table when necessary. As is the case when rearranging the order of columns, this is not done directly in the table but is carried out using the Fields list. There are, in fact, several ways of removing columns from a table, so I will begin with the way that I think is the fastest and then describe the others:

1. Display the Fields list—unless it is already displayed.

2. Uncheck the field name in the Fields list.

Assuming that a visual is selected, the following are other ways to remove a field:

- In the Visualizations pane, click the cross icon at the right of the field name in the field well.

- In the Visualizations pane, click the small triangle at the right of the name in the field well (remember that these are the fields used in the visualization). When the popup menu appears, select Remove Field.

Note   Do *not* click the popup menu icon (the ellipses at the right of the field name) and select Delete in the *Fields list* to remove a field from the table. Doing this deletes the field from the data model.

Table Granularity

A Power BI Desktop table will automatically aggregate data to the lowest available level of grain. Put simply, this means that it is important to select data at the lowest useful level of detail but not to add pointlessly detailed elements.

This is probably easier to understand if I use an example. Suppose you start with a high level of aggregation—the country, for instance. If you create a table with CountryName and SalePrice columns, it will give you the total sales by country. If you use the sample data given in the examples for this book (the CarSalesDataForReports. pbix file), this table only contains half a dozen or so lines.

Then add the ClientName column after the CountryName column. When you do this, you obtain a more finely grained set of results, with the aggregate sales for *each client in each country*. If you (finally) add the InvoiceNumber, you get a very detailed level of data. Indeed, adding such a fine level of grain to your table could produce an extremely large number of records—as indicated by the appearance of a vertical scroll bar in this table. These progressive levels of granularity are shown in Figure 14-7.

CountryName	SalePrice
	£141,250
France	£2,524,510
Germany	£145,750
Spain	£207,750
Switzerland	£1,440,970
United Kingdom	£15,725,000
USA	£11,653,960
Total	£31,839,190

CountryName	ClientName	SalePrice
		£141,250
France	Carosse Des Papes	£404,040
France	Chateau Mol	£311,790
France	Les Arnaqueurs	£1,366,250
France	Vive la Vitesse!	£442,430
Germany	Karz	£145,750
Spain	Costa Del Speed	£207,750
Switzerland	Jungfrau	£501,870
Switzerland	Three Country Cars	£233,600
Switzerland	Voitures Diplomatiques S.A.	£705,500
United Kingdom	Aldo Motors	£2,876,250
United Kingdom	Bright Orange	£2,880,500
United Kingdom	Crippen & Co	£390,750
United Kingdom	Cut'n'Shut	£2,825,500
United Kingdom	Honest John	£2,706,750
United Kingdom	Impressive Wheels	£182,750
United Kingdom	Luxury Rentals	£214,750
United Kingdom	Olde Englande	£297,500
United Kingdom	Premium Motor Vehicles	£85,250
Total		£31,839,190

CountryName	ClientName	InvoiceNumber	SalePrice
		0BDA8D88-B2F8-4DD5-815C-1184E7159C0D	£25,250
		67A4561B-68D0-4865-910F-3F531F3157F5	£44,000
		B2F2E58C-12C8-41E6-948E-3546F1CE50FD	£25,250
		C2FC2EB7-EE58-4741-8688-2AACFC735094	£46,750
France	Carosse Des Papes	3E85A0EF-EFDA-424E-B721-A9A797A0F46C	£72,000
France	Carosse Des Papes	45275E14-7807-4788-BD7D-1E505F8AB515	£77,250
France	Carosse Des Papes	45D5D28D-9EE7-49CF-93C5-FDA9E73E684D	£77,250
France	Carosse Des Papes	4D4E5593-7DAA-4FFF-A493-2FF65C4625A1	£37,690
France	Carosse Des Papes	6FBA08C3-1BA1-41F6-96DD-1D9F1C60C79C	£25,500
France	Carosse Des Papes	78273430-FD2E-4E06-847C-6E3B1165FDD7	£22,750
France	Carosse Des Papes	B2B8A324-C314-413B-AA67-C16DB117869C	£45,800
France	Carosse Des Papes	C41A9EFE-E0A8-4C13-8AAD-ADD268CA40A4	£45,800
France	Chateau Mol	311AA133-E929-47E6-9EB9-C39987FD01A5	£74,500
France	Chateau Mol	52D515E5-3BAA-42E1-9D28-C39E9A795A5B	£28,000
France	Chateau Mol	AFFFAD41-2D1D-4732-98E5-3BD0DC828F10	£77,250
France	Chateau Mol	E027A469-FDDE-4D3E-88A8-238F18645E21	£45,800
France	Chateau Mol	E34523F3-A2DC-40B9-BE7F-60E368328508	£48,550
France	Chateau Mol	E3EBBF63-ABF3-4A0D-87A1-8105FAFA96D2	£37,690
France	Les Arnaqueurs	064F3E61-A9DC-470B-A3A6-9859C31D321B	£42,250
France	Les Arnaqueurs	0A07E861-9E26-4EB9-95C9-48B7CCFD8462	£46,750
France	Les Arnaqueurs	0BD18246-A958-4817-A7F2-537F17A9C443	£44,000
France	Les Arnaqueurs	23841002-BE8F-4080-8516-DCE689B37C50	£44,000
France	Les Arnaqueurs	3E106580-BF01-4CD8-A19C-4857E2ABEBE0	£39,500
France	Les Arnaqueurs	4799184A-499A-46AC-95EF-100716A2A270	£130,000
France	Les Arnaqueurs	5273FF25-EFC7-4A58-9CEA-9CFFE28D047C	£42,250
France	Les Arnaqueurs	605A276C-B403-4A6A-AC95-55093368A316	£110,000
France	Les Arnaqueurs	79203209-7C00-4161-918E-98CC9BC0D6E1	£181,250
France	Les Arnaqueurs	7A48D828-795B-49DE-AD0E-8CA679EF3642	£127,750
France	Les Arnaqueurs	7D49EF49-27F5-4459-AE33-28710E0E7A76	£44,000
France	Les Arnaqueurs	9C4F7810-8B87-4D91-B73F-817354FCE5F5	£110,000
France	Les Arnaqueurs	9E31A8B0-8DE3-4D1E-88F8-8A47B7470009	£29,750
France	Les Arnaqueurs	ADFFAC9E-DFF3-4BAB-9EC4-DEE9A2B69350	£125,000
Total			£31,839,190

Figure 14-7. *Progressive table granularity*

Power BI Desktop always attempts to display the data using the information available to it in the underlying data model.

Types of Data

Not all data is created equal (or at least identical), and the data model that underlies Power BI Desktop will provide you with different types of data. The two core data types are

- Descriptive (non-numeric) attributes

- Values (or numeric measures)

Power BI Desktop indicates the precise data type by using a descriptive icon beside many of the fields, which you can see when you expand a data table in the Fields list. These data types are described in Table 14-4.

Table 14-4. *Data Types*

Data Type	Icon	Description
Attribute	None	A descriptive element and is non-numeric. It can be counted but not summed or averaged.
Aggregates	Σ	A numeric field whose aggregation type can be changed.
Calculated column		The result of a formula applied to create a new, calculated column.
Calculation		A numeric field whose aggregation type cannot be changed as it is the result of a specific calculation.
Geography		This field can potentially be used in a map to provide geographical references.
Binary data		This field contains data, such as images.

Numeric fields are not the only ones that can be added as aggregates. If you add an attribute field to a table and then display the popup menu for this field by clicking the small triangle to the right of the field name in the Visualizations pane, you can select Count. You will display the *number* of elements for this attribute in the column of the table instead of the text of the element. Figure 14-8 shows you a sample popup field menu for a text field.

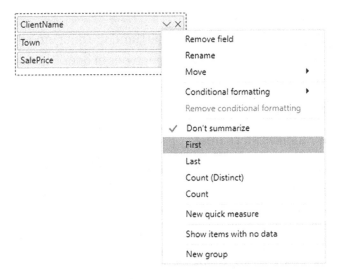

Figure 14-8. *The popup menu for a text field*

Searching for Fields

If you are building a dashboard using a new and as-yet unknown dataset, you could, potentially, waste a lot of time trawling through the available tables looking for the field that you require.

Power BI Desktop makes finding data easier using the Search field. You can see this at the top of the Fields list. Simply typing in part of a field name will instantly filter the Fields list to show only fields containing the text that you just entered. You can see an example of this in Figure 14-9.

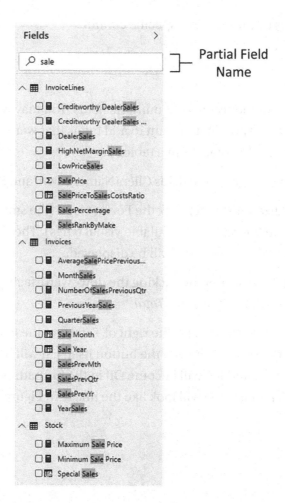

Figure 14-9. Searching for a field

To reset the Fields list so that it displays all the available tables and fields, simply delete the search text.

Enhancing Tables

So you have a basic table set up and it has the columns you want in the correct order. Quite naturally, the next step is to want to spice up the presentation of the table a little. So let's see what Power BI Desktop has to offer here. Specifically, we will look at

- Adding and removing totals

- Adjusting text sizes in tables

- Changing column widths

- Sorting rows by the data in a specific column

Row Totals

Row totals are added automatically to all numeric fields. You may wish to remove the totals, however. Conversely, you could want to add totals that were removed previously. In any case, to remove all the totals from a table:

1. Create a table based on the fields ClientName, Town, and SalePrice.

2. In the Visualizations pane, click the Format icon (the small paint roller beneath the palette of available visual types). The formatting options for the selected table will be displayed.

3. Expand the Total section by clicking the downward-facing chevron to the left of the word *Total*.

4. Drag the full circle button (to the right of Totals) to the left (or click to the left of the button or even the button itself). It will become an empty circle, and On will become Off in the formatting options. The Visualizations pane will look like the image in Figure 14-10.

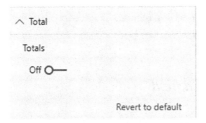

Figure 14-10. *Formatting options for tables in the Visualizations pane*

To add totals where there are none, follow the process described (with the table selected), and at step 4, drag the Off button to the right for Totals to set the totals to On. You can see the table you created previously—without totals—in Figure 14-11.

ClientName	Town	SalePrice
		£141,250
Carosse Des Papes	Avignon	£404,040
Three Country Cars	Basle	£233,600
Ambassador Cars	Bellevue	£1,686,930
Bright Orange	Birmingham	£2,880,500
Tweedy Wheels	Cambridge	£641,000
Style 'N Ride	Chevy Chase	£1,714,550
Embassy Motors	Denver	£1,254,550
British Luxury Automobile Corp	Franklin	£302,690
Voitures Diplomatiques S.A.	Geneva	£705,500
Crippen & Co	Glasgow	£390,750
Luxury Rentals	Gloucester	£214,750
Impressive Wheels	Liverpool	£182,750
Honest John	London	£2,706,750
Wheels'R'Us	London	£3,132,750
Union Jack Sports Cars	Louisville	£358,690
Chateau Moi	Lyon	£311,790
Costa Del Speed	Madrid	£207,750
Cut'n'Shut	Manchester	£2,825,500
Vive la Vitesse!	Marseille	£442,430
Buckingham Palace Car Services	Mason	£402,000
Rocky Riding	New York	£1,027,500
Premium Motor Vehicles	Newcastle upon Tyne	£85,250
Les Arnaqueurs	Paris	£1,366,250
Classy Car Sales	Pittsburgh	£200,250
BritWheels	Portland	£2,068,750
Sporty Types Corp	San Francisco	£1,997,050
Olde Englande	Shrewsbury	£297,500
Karz	Stuttgart	£145,750
Smooth Riders	Telford	£132,250
Aldo Motors	Uttoxeter	£2,876,250
Jungfrau	Zurich	£501,870

Figure 14-11. *The initial table without totals*

Note   You can only add or remove totals if a table displays multiple records. If a table is displaying the highest level of aggregation for a value, then no totals can be displayed, as you are looking at the grand total already. In this case, the Totals button is grayed out.

Formatting Numbers in Reports

You cannot (as things stand) format numbers directly in tables in a Power BI Desktop report. This is because all number formatting is centralized in the data model. So if you want to apply a different numeric format from the one that appears when you add a value to a table, you will have to switch to Data View and apply the formatting there. If you need to remind yourself exactly how this is done, then just flip back to Chapter 13 for a quick refresher course on how to format numbers in Power BI Desktop.

Font Sizes in Tables

You may prefer to alter the default font size that Power BI Desktop applies when a table is first created. This is easy to do:

1. Select the table.

2. In the Visualizations pane, click the Format icon.

3. Expand the Values section by clicking the downward-facing chevron to the left of the word Values.

4. Click the up or down arrows to the right of the current text size. The new text size in points will be displayed in the Text Size box, and the actual size of the text in the table will increase.

Here are a few points regarding font sizes in tables:

- You can enter a font size in the Text Size box to specify an exact size, if you prefer.

- Altering the font size will *not* cause the table to grow or shrink, as Power BI Desktop will continue to display the same number of characters per column as were visible using the previous font size. So you may end up having to alter the column widths by setting Auto-size to On (this is described in an upcoming section) or adjusting the table size (as described previously) to make your table look exactly the way you want it.

- This formatting option only affects the size of the *records* in the table, not the column headings. To change the size of the header font, expand the Column Headers section of the Formatting pane and use exactly the same techniques to set the font size. This time it will be the header font that is altered.

Changing Column Widths

Power BI Desktop will automatically set the width of a column so that all the data is visible when you create an initial table.

However—and as you would expect—you can also manually adjust the size of individual columns in a table. You do this more or less as you would in Excel:

1. In the column header row, place the mouse pointer over the rightmost edge of the column.

2. Drag left or right to adjust the column width.

Note   As you would probably expect from a product that aims at Excel users, you can double-click the column separator at the right of a column's header to have Power BI Desktop adjust the width of the column automatically to fit the widest currently visible data element.

Inhibiting Automatic Adjustment of Column Width and Enabling Word Wrap

If you want to, you can prevent Power BI Desktop from resetting column widths automatically, and you can also activate word wrap to make sure that text in a column is not truncated, but flows onto the following line. Here is how:

1. Select the table. In this example, I use the table that you saw in Figure 14-11.

2. In the Visualizations pane, click the Format icon (the small paint roller beneath the palette of available visual types). The formatting options for the selected table will be displayed.

3. Expand the Column Headers section by clicking the downward-facing chevron to the left of the word Column Headers.

4. Click the "Auto-size column width" button. It will become an empty circle, and On will become Off in the formatting options.

5. Set Word wrap to On. The Visualizations pane will look like Figure 14-12.

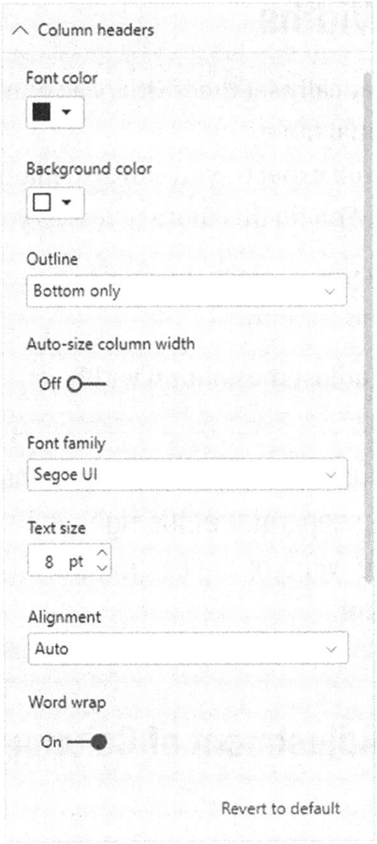

Figure 14-12. *Inhibiting automatic column resizing for tables*

You can now alter the size of the font used in the table without causing column widths to grow or shrink. Inversely, resetting the Auto-size option to On causes the column width to be readjusted automatically to display the widest element in the column.

Note   If you are formatting a table and you start to get a little confused as to which options are active and how best to start over, you can always click "Revert to default" to reapply the standard "factory settings" for tables—or for any visual.

Sorting by Column

Any column can be used as the sort criterion for a table, whatever the column data type. To sort the table, merely click the column header. The rows in the table are sorted according to the elements in the selected column. The sort order is A to Z (or lowest to highest for numeric values) the first time that you sort a column.

Once a table has been sorted, you cannot unsort it. You can use another column to resort the data, however. Alternatively, you can click the column title again to sort in the opposing order—Z to A (or highest to lowest for numeric values).

For an example of sorting a column, look at Figure 14-13 (I will use the table you created for Figure 14-11). You can see that the data is sorted by SalePrice from highest to lowest. Moreover, you can see a small down-facing triangle below the title of the SalePrice column. This indicates that the column is sorted from the highest to the lowest value.

ClientName	Town	SalePrice
Wheels'R'Us	London	£3,132,750
Bright Orange	Birmingham	£2,880,500
Aldo Motors	Uttoxeter	£2,876,250
Cut'n'Shut	Manchester	£2,825,500
Honest John	London	£2,706,750
BritWheels	Portland	£2,068,750
Sporty Types Corp	San Francisco	£1,997,050
Style 'N Ride	Chevy Chase	£1,714,550
Ambassador Cars	Bellevue	£1,686,930
Les Arnaqueurs	Paris	£1,366,250
Embassy Motors	Denver	£1,254,550
Rocky Riding	New York	£1,027,500
Voitures Diplomatiques S.A.	Geneva	£705,500
Tweedy Wheels	Cambridge	£641,000
Jungfrau	Zurich	£501,870
Vive la Vitesse!	Marseille	£442,430
Total		£31,839,190

Sort Indicator — (points to the down-facing triangle below the SalePrice title)

Figure 14-13. *Sorting a table by a numeric column*

Sometimes you are sorting a column on one field (as was the case in all the examples so far), but the actual sort uses another column as the basis for the sort operation. For example, you could sort by month name but see the result by the month number (so that you are not sorting months alphabetically, but numerically). You saw how this is configured in Chapter 13.

Formatting Tables

As befits such a polished product, Power BI Desktop can enhance the presentation of even a humble table so that it stands out from the crowd and delivers that attention-grabbing effect that your audience expects. The currently available formatting options include

- Adding automatic table styles

- Formatting titles

- Modifying the table background

- Adding and removing table borders

- Formatting rows—including alternating rows

- Adding and removing a table grid

- Formatting column headers

- Column formatting

- Formatting totals

- Conditional formatting—including color scales, font colors, data bars, and "KPI-style" icons

I confidently expect that these options will continue to be developed as Power BI Desktop matures. Consequently, you could see further presentation enhancements by the time that you read this book. However, for the moment, let's take a look at the currently available options.

Note   There are no specific options for formatting the figures in tables. You format the data by clicking the data icon on the left of the Power BI Desktop window, select the column to format, and, in the Modeling ribbon, select a number format. This format will then apply to the selected field in the same way in every visual where it is used.

Table Style

Power BI Desktop allows you to choose from nine different ways of instantly formatting a table in a few clicks. This includes the option of removing all table formatting. To format an entire table:

1. Click inside the table to format.

2. In the Visualizations pane, click the Format icon.

3. Expand the Table Style section. Select a table style from the available options.

You can see the range of available table styles in Table 14-5.

Table 14-5. *The Available Table Styles*

Matrix Style	Description
Default	Adds a gray background to alternating rows.
None	Removes all formatting.
Minimal	Adds a light spacing between records.
Bold header	Adds a dark background to the title row.
Alternating rows	Adds a gray background to alternating rows and a dark background to the title and totals rows.
Contrast alternating rows	Alternates the row background between light and darker gray. Adds a dark background to the title and totals rows.
Flashy rows	Alternates the row background between light and darker green.
Bold header flashy rows	Alternates the row background between light and darker green. Adds a dark background to the title and totals rows.
Sparse	Adds a dark background to the title and totals rows and removes the light line separating rows.
Condensed	Adds a dark background to the title and totals rows and adds vertical and horizontal lines between rows and columns.

The table styles that you can add are really nothing more than preset values. If you want to be precise in the definition of how the records in a table appear, you can apply the various options that are explained in the next few sections.

Note   To remove a table style and revert to a "plain vanilla" presentation, simply select None from the popup list of available table styles.

Adding and Formatting Titles

Like most visualizations in Power BI Desktop, tables can have titles. Once you have added a title, you can set its

- Font color

- Background color

- Text alignment

As simple as this is, I prefer to explain all the options for the sake of completeness.

1. Select the table. In this example, I use the table that you saw in Figure 14-11 based on Town, ClientName, and SalePrice.

2. In the Visualizations pane, click the Format icon (the small paint roller beneath the palette of available visualization types). The formatting options for the selected table will be displayed.

3. Expand the Title section by clicking the downward-facing chevron to the left of the word Title.

4. Click to the right of the empty circle to the right of the word Off. This will activate a title for the selected table.

5. In the empty box to the right of Title text, enter a title for the table. I suggest **Sales by Town**.

6. Click the popup menu triangle to the right of Font color and select a color from the palette of available hues.

7. Click the popup menu triangle to the right of Background color and select a color from the palette of available tones.

8. Click the middle icon to the right of Alignment. This will center the text relative to the width of the table.

9. Use the arrows to increase the size of the title font.

The formatting options and the table will look like they do in Figure 14-14.

Sales by Town		
ClientName	Town	SalePrice
Wheels'R'Us	London	£3,132,750
Bright Orange	Birmingham	£2,880,500
Aldo Motors	Uttoxeter	£2,876,250
Cut'n'Shut	Manchester	£2,825,500
Honest John	London	£2,706,750
BritWheels	Portland	£2,068,750
Sporty Types Corp	San Francisco	£1,997,050
Style 'N Ride	Chevy Chase	£1,714,550
Ambassador Cars	Bellevue	£1,686,930
Les Arnaqueurs	Paris	£1,366,250
Embassy Motors	Denver	£1,254,550
Rocky Riding	New York	£1,027,500
Voitures Diplomatiques S.A.	Geneva	£705,500
Tweedy Wheels	Cambridge	£641,000
Jungfrau	Zurich	£501,870
Vive la Vitesse!	Marseille	£442,430
Carosse Des Papes	Avignon	£404,040
Buckingham Palace Car Services	Mason	£402,000
Crippen & Co	Glasgow	£390,750
Union Jack Sports Cars	Louisville	£358,690
Chateau Moi	Lyon	£311,790
British Luxury Automobile Corp	Franklin	£302,690
Olde Englande	Shrewsbury	£297,500
Three Country Cars	Basle	£233,600
Luxury Rentals	Gloucester	£214,750
Costa Del Speed	Madrid	£207,750
Classy Car Sales	Pittsburgh	£200,250
Impressive Wheels	Liverpool	£182,750
Karz	Stuttgart	£145,750
		£141,250
Smooth Riders	Telford	£132,250
Premium Motor Vehicles	Newcastle upon Tyne	£85,250

Figure 14-14. *Options for titles in tables*

Note   You can, if you prefer, enter the desired font size in the Text Size field.

Modifying the Table Background

The table title is not the only aspect of a table that you can modify for visual effect. You can also change a couple of elements of the table itself to add pizzazz to your dashboards. The following are the two things that you can modify:

- The background color

- The table transparency

The following example illustrates both of these possibilities:

1. Select the table. In this example, I use the table that you saw in Figure 14-14.

2. In the Visualizations pane, click the Format icon (the small paint roller beneath the palette of available visual types). The formatting options for the selected table will be displayed.

3. Set the Style to None.

4. Expand the Background section by clicking the downward-facing chevron to the left of the word Background.

5. Ensure that the switch to the right of the word Background is set to On (if it is not, then click to the right of the empty circle to change this).

6. Click the popup menu triangle to the right of Color and select a color from the palette of available colors.

7. Click the Transparency slider switch and slide it to the left to intensify the background color by reducing the percentage of transparency. The formatting options and the table will look like Figure 14-15.

Sales by Town		
ClientName	Town	SalePrice
Wheels'R'Us	London	£3,132,750
Bright Orange	Birmingham	£2,880,500
Aldo Motors	Uttoxeter	£2,876,250
Cut'n'Shut	Manchester	£2,825,500
Honest John	London	£2,706,750
BritWheels	Portland	£2,068,750
Sporty Types Corp	San Francisco	£1,997,050
Style 'N Ride	Chevy Chase	£1,714,550
Ambassador Cars	Bellevue	£1,686,930
Les Arnaqueurs	Paris	£1,366,250
Embassy Motors	Denver	£1,254,550
Rocky Riding	New York	£1,027,500
Voitures Diplomatiques S.A.	Geneva	£705,500
Tweedy Wheels	Cambridge	£641,000
Jungfrau	Zurich	£501,870
Vive la Vitesse!	Marseille	£442,430
Carosse Des Papes	Avignon	£404,040
Buckingham Palace Car Services	Mason	£402,000
Crippen & Co	Glasgow	£390,750
Union Jack Sports Cars	Louisville	£358,690
Chateau Moi	Lyon	£311,790
British Luxury Automobile Corp	Franklin	£302,690
Olde Englande	Shrewsbury	£297,500
Three Country Cars	Basle	£233,600
Luxury Rentals	Gloucester	£214,750
Costa Del Speed	Madrid	£207,750
Classy Car Sales	Pittsburgh	£200,250
Impressive Wheels	Liverpool	£182,750
Karz	Stuttgart	£145,750
		£141,250
Smooth Riders	Telford	£132,250
Premium Motor Vehicles	Newcastle upon Tyne	£85,250

Figure 14-15. *Setting the background color for a table*

Note   You can see that, using this technique, you have only formatted the background of the table visual, not the rows and columns that make up the table itself. You will learn how to format the rows and columns in a couple of pages' time.

Table Borders

To add another flourish, you can add an outside border to any table. The following explains how to do this:

1. Select the table. In this example, I use the table that you saw in Figure 14-15.

2. In the Visualizations pane, click the Format icon. The formatting options for the selected table will be displayed.

3. Slide the Border button to the right. This will apply a border to the table.

4. Expand the Border section.

5. Select a border color from those available in the popup palette.

6. Drag the Radius button to the right to define the rounding of the corners of the border.

Row Formatting

In an earlier section, you saw how to change the font size for the rows in a table. This is only one of the available formatting options that you can apply to the rows in a table. Here are some of the other possibilities:

1. Select the table that you want to enhance. In this example, I use the table that you saw in Figure 14-10.

2. In the Visualizations pane, click the Format icon.

3. Expand the Values section.

4. Select a background color as well as an alternate background color.

5. Select a font color as well as an alternate font color.

6. Select Outline from the available outline styles.

7. Adjust the width of the left two columns. The table should look something like the one shown in Figure 14-16.

Figure 14-16. *Formatting alternate rows in a table*

There are currently seven outline styles available, plus the option of removing all outline styles. These are explained in Table 14-6.

Table 14-6. *The Available Outline Styles*

Outline Style	Description
None	Removes borders from the title.
Bottom only	Adds a bottom border to the title.
Top only	Adds a top border to the title.
Left only	Adds a left border to the title.
Right only	Adds a right border to the title.
Top + bottom	Adds both top and bottom borders to the title.
Left + right	Adds both left and right borders to the title.
Frame	Adds a frame around the title.

I have a couple of minor explanations to add at this juncture:

- Selecting an outline style will add a border to the entire table *inside* the visual, as opposed to the table border that you added previously that applies to the outer edge of the entire visual.

- Enabling word wrap will enable text to flow to the next line in all columns. This will increase the height of any affected rows.

- Enabling the URL Icon option in the Values section will convert a URL text to an icon.

Table Grid

You can extend the presentation of a table with much greater precision if you use the Table Grid section of the formatting options in the Visualizations pane.

Let's see how this works, taking the table from Figure 14-16:

1. Select the table to format, and in the Visualizations pane, click the Format icon.

2. Expand the Grid section.

3. Display the vertical grid by switching Vert Grid to On.

4. Select a color from the palette of available colors for the vertical grid.

5. Enter **3** in the field for Vert Grid thickness.

6. Select a color from the palette of available colors for the horizontal grid (this should be on by default; if not, simply slide the button for Horiz Grid to the right).

7. Slide the Horiz Grid button to the right to set a different thickness for the horizontal grid.

8. Enter **5** in the field for Row padding.

9. Select a color from the palette of available colors for the outline color.

10. Enter **5** in the field for Outline weight.

11. Enter **10** in the field for Text Size.

12. Adjust the column widths to display all the text and numbers in the columns.

You can see the results of these changes in Figure 14-17. I am in no way pretending that there is any profound aesthetic value to these enhancements—but you can, at least, see how Power BI Desktop can be used to format your data.

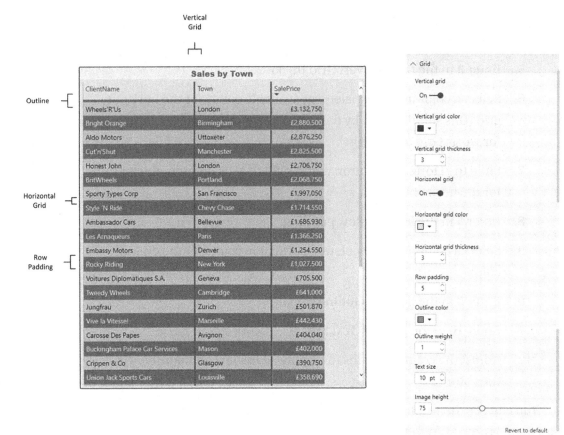

Figure 14-17. *Table grid settings*

Note   Depending on the resolution of your monitor, you might have to scroll down inside the Grid section of the Formatting pane. You do this using the gray vertical bar at the right of the Grid section.

Column Headers

Power BI Desktop also allows you to modify the formatting of column headers. You could carry out the following tweaks to see this in action:

1. Re-create the initial table from Figure 14-14, with the default table style.

2. Expand the Column Headers section.

3. Set a font and background color using the appropriate palettes for each.

4. Click the up arrow to increase the font size for the title.

5. Select Center as the Alignment.

6. In the Outline popup, select Top + Bottom. These styles are the same as those that you previously applied to row values and are described in Table 14-6. You can see the resulting format in Figure 14-18.

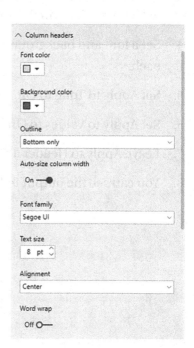

Figure 14-18. *Formatting column headers*

Note   If you choose to enter a text size in the Text Size field, be aware that there are limits that you cannot exceed. For instance, if you enter a figure less than 8, Power BI Desktop will refuse to apply the requested font size and will add a red outline to the Text Size field. You will then have to enter a valid number.

Field Formatting

Each individual column can be formatted separately. Power BI Desktop calls this field formatting. You need to be aware that, in practice, overuse of this technique can easily lead to total illegibility. Nonetheless, it is worth learning how to format an individual column.

1. Re-create the table from Figure 14-11, and with the default style.

2. Expand the Field Formatting section.

3. Select the column header for the column that you wish to format from the popup list at the top of the Column Formatting section. I will choose Town in this example.

4. Set a font and background color using the appropriate palettes for each.

5. Set Apply to Total to On.

6. Set Apply to Values to On.

7. Leave Apply to Header as Off.

8. You can see the output in Figure 14-19.

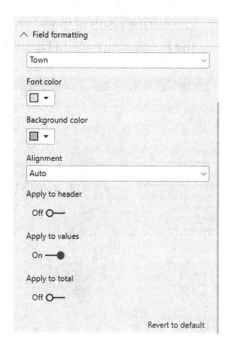

ClientName	Town	SalePrice
		£141,250
Carosse Des Papes	Avignon	£404,040
Three Country Cars	Basle	£233,600
Ambassador Cars	Bellevue	£1,686,930
Bright Orange	Birmingham	£2,880,500
Tweedy Wheels	Cambridge	£641,000
Style 'N Ride	Chevy Chase	£1,714,550
Embassy Motors	Denver	£1,254,550
British Luxury Automobile Corp	Franklin	£302,690
Voitures Diplomatiques S.A.	Geneva	£705,500
Crippen & Co	Glasgow	£390,750
Luxury Rentals	Gloucester	£214,750
Impressive Wheels	Liverpool	£182,750
Honest John	London	£2,706,750
Wheels'R'Us	London	£3,132,750
Union Jack Sports Cars	Louisville	£358,690
Chateau Moi	Lyon	£311,790
Costa Del Speed	Madrid	£207,750
Cut'n'Shut	Manchester	£2,825,500
Vive la Vitesse!	Marseille	£442,430
Buckingham Palace Car Services	Mason	£402,000
Rocky Riding	New York	£1,027,500
Premium Motor Vehicles	Newcastle upon Tyne	£85,250
Les Arnaqueurs	Paris	£1,366,250
Classy Car Sales	Pittsburgh	£200,250
BritWheels	Portland	£2,068,750
Sporty Types Corp	San Francisco	£1,997,050
Olde Englande	Shrewsbury	£297,500
Karz	Stuttgart	£145,750
Smooth Riders	Telford	£132,250
Aldo Motors	Worcester	£2,876,250

Figure 14-19. *Adding column formatting*

Formatting Totals

Power BI Desktop lets you do more to totals in tables than just switch them on and off. You can format the total to enhance the visibility (or, inversely, try and divert attention from poor figures), like this:

1. Re-create the table that you can see in Figure 14-19.

2. In the Visualizations pane (and, of course, leaving the table selected), activate the Format panel and expand the Total section.

3. Ensure that the Totals option is set to On.

4. Choose a font color from those in the palette.

5. Choose a background color from those in the palette.

6. Enter an appropriate total label.

7. Set the outline to None.

8. Enter a figure or adjust the slider to obtain a larger font size. You can see the result of these actions as well as the Total section of the Formatting pane in Figure 14-20.

Figure 14-20. *Formatting totals*

Conditional Formatting

Tables of data may convey vast amounts of information, but they rarely enable instant understanding of the meaning of the figures. This is where conditional formatting can be applied to convert data into instantly useful information. Indeed, you may already be used to applying these kinds of enhancements to Excel spreadsheets.

In Power BI Desktop, there are four types of conditional formatting that you can apply to add meaning to your figures:

- *Background color*: Adds shades of color to the entire background of a table cell. The intensity of the shading reflects a selected value in the data.

- *Text color*: Alters the color of the text as a function of a selected value.

- *Data bars*: Add a background bar to a table cell. Here the size of the bar represents the value in the cell.

- *Icons*: Add an icon (a KPI indicator) to draw attention to the value of a cell relative to another value.

Note   Conditional formatting can only be used when based on the values in fields containing numeric values, not text elements. However, the field (or column if you prefer) that displays the conditional formatting need not necessarily be the field whose data is used to define the conditional formatting.

Background Color

Color scales are a background color that you apply to each cell in a column. The actual color will vary according to the value of each row. As an example of how color scales work, try the following:

1. Re-create the table from Figure 14-11. Make sure that you leave the table selected.

2. Click the Format icon in the Visualizations pane and expand the Conditional Formatting section.

3. Select the name of the column to format from the popup list of the columns in the table (in this example this is the SalePrice column).

4. Set the Background color button to On.

5. Click the Advanced Controls link. The Background color dialog will be displayed.

6. Select Color scale from the "Format by" popup.

7. Choose a Summarization from the Summarization popup. In this example I suggest selecting Sum.

8. Choose the SalePrice field in the "Based on field" popup. You will see that this is represented in the dialog as "Sum of SalesPrice."

9.   In the "Format blank values" popup, select As Zero.

10. Set the color for the minimum to a light color from the popup palette.

11. Click the Diverging check box.

12. Set the color for the center to a medium color from the popup palette.

13. In the popup for Center, select Number.

14. Enter **25000** in the number field that is now enabled.

15. Set the color for the maximum to a dark color from the popup palette. The Color scales dialog will look like the one shown in Figure 14-21.

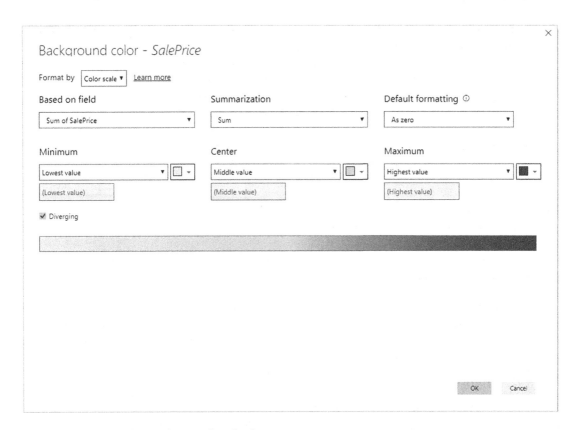

Figure 14-21. *The Color scales dialog*

16. Click OK. The table will look like the one in Figure 14-22.

Town	ClientName	SalePrice
		£141,250
Avignon	Carosse Des Papes	£404,040
Basle	Three Country Cars	£233,600
Bellevue	Ambassador Cars	£1,686,930
Birmingham	Bright Orange	£2,080,500
Cambridge	Tweedy Wheels	£641,000
Chevy Chase	Style 'N Ride	£1,714,550
Denver	Embassy Motors	£1,254,550
Franklin	British Luxury Automobile Corp	£302,690
Geneva	Voitures Diplomatiques S.A.	£705,500
Glasgow	Crippen & Co	£390,750
Gloucester	Luxury Rentals	£214,750
Liverpool	Impressive Wheels	£182,750
London	Honest John	£2,706,750
London	Wheels'R'Us	£3,152,700
Louisville	Union Jack Sports Cars	£358,690
Lyon	Chateau Moi	£311,790
Madrid	Costa Del Speed	£207,750
Manchester	Cut'n'Shut	£4,025,500
Marseille	Vive la Vitesse!	£442,430
Mason	Buckingham Palace Car Services	£402,000
New York	Rocky Riding	£1,027,500
Newcastle upon Tyne	Premium Motor Vehicles	£85,250

Figure 14-22. *A table with color scales applied*

There are a few points that are worth noting when defining conditional formatting:

- You can choose any field as the basis for the background color shading—it does not have to be the field that actually displays the shading in the table.

- As you saw in step 15, you can either let Power BI Desktop detect the minimum, maximum, and median values when setting a background color or you can define specific values.

- If you do not check the Diverging check box, you only define a range of two colors.

- You can define a background color in three ways:

  - Color scale (which we did here)

  - Rules (which we will look at in the next section when defining a text color)

  - Field value (which I will explain in the next section)

- As you saw in step 8, you can select a field to use as the basis for the conditional formatting from the entire data model.

- The standard summarizations that you probably expect (Sum, Average, Count, etc.) are available when defining conditional formatting.

Text Color

Another conditional formatting option is to set the color of the text for the text of each value using conditional formatting. This is very similar to applying conditional formatting to the cell background. Indeed, in this example I will extend the previous example to apply conditional formatting to the text of the table that you just created. Only this time, we will apply rules-based formatting to the Town column.

1. Select the table that you created in the previous section.

2. In the Visualizations pane, click the Format icon.

3. Expand the Conditional Formatting section.

4. Select the Make column from the popup of columns to format.

5. Set Font color scales to On.

6. Click Advanced Controls for Font color. The Font color dialog will appear.

7. Select Rules from the Format by popup.

8. Select Make for the Based on field.

9. Leave the Summarization as Count.

10. Select a color for the minimum from the palette.

11. Set the If value to the following: Is greater than or equal to 0 (number) and Is less than 10 (number).

12. Select a color for this rule from the palette.

13. Click the + New rule button. A new rule row will appear below the rule that you just created.

14. Set the If value for this rule to the following: Is greater than or equal to 11 (number) and Is less than 100 (number).

15. Select a color for this rule from the palette. The dialog will look like the one shown in Figure 14-23.

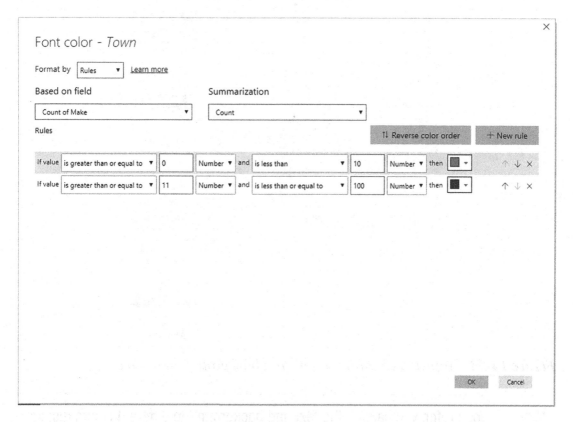

Figure 14-23. *The Background color scales dialog*

16. Click OK. The table will look like it does in Figure 14-24.

Town	ClientName	SalePrice
		£141,250
Avignon	Carosse Des Papes	£404,040
Basle	Three Country Cars	£233,600
Bellevue	Ambassador Cars	£1,686,930
Birmingham	Bright Orange	£2,880,500
Cambridge	Tweedy Wheels	£641,000
Chevy Chase	Style 'N Ride	£1,714,550
Denver	Embassy Motors	£1,254,550
Franklin	British Luxury Automobile Corp	£302,690
Geneva	Voitures Diplomatiques S.A.	£705,500
Glasgow	Crippen & Co	£390,750
Gloucester	Luxury Rentals	£214,750
Liverpool	Impressive Wheels	£182,750
London	Honest John	£2,706,750
London	Wheels'R'Us	£3,132,750
Louisville	Union Jack Sports Cars	£358,690
Lyon	Chateau Moi	£311,790
Madrid	Costa Del Speed	£207,750
Manchester	Cut'n'Shut	£2,825,500
Marseille	Vive la Vitesse!	£442,430
Mason	Buckingham Palace Car Services	£402,000
New York	Rocky Riding	£1,027,500
Newcastle upon Tyne	Premium Motor Vehicles	£85,250
Paris	Les Arnaqueurs	£1,366,250
Pittsburgh	Classy Car Sales	£200,250
Portland	BritWheels	£2,068,750
San Francisco	Sporty Types Corp	£1,997,050
Shrewsbury	Olde Englande	£297,500
Stuttgart	Karz	£145,750
Telford	Smooth Riders	£132,250
Uttoxeter	Aldo Motors	£2,876,250
Zurich	Jungfrau	£501,870
Total		£31,839,190

Figure 14-24. Applying conditional text and background to a table

Note   If you prefer, you can set the text and background to different colors (using identical or different sets of rules) to obtain a completely different effect from the application of conditional text.

There are a few points you may find interesting when setting the conditional formatting for a text:

- If you choose a non-numeric field as the basis for the background color shading, you can only use Count or Count distinct as the summarization.

- You can add multiple rules when defining rules-based conditional formatting.

- Rules can be deleted by clicking the cross icon at the right of each rule.

- Rules-based conditional formatting can be applied equally well to the cell background.

- If you want to alter the order in which the rules are applied, simply click the up and down arrows to the right of each rule.

- Clicking the Reverse color order button keeps the rules, but reverses the colors that are applied.

- When applying rules-based conditional formatting, be careful that you set the threshold values accurately so that you do not exclude any values.

Data Bars

Data bars are a presentation technique that represents the figure as a colored bar behind the actual value in a table cell. You can add data bars using the following steps:

1. Create a table based on Make and CostPrice.

2. Click the Format icon in the Visualizations pane and expand the Conditional Formatting section.

3. Select the name of the column to format from the popup list of the columns in the table (in this example it will be the SalePrice column).

4. Set the Data bars button to On. Power BI Desktop applies data bars to the SalePrice column.

5. Click the Advanced Controls link. The Data bars dialog will be displayed.

6. In the Minimum popup, select Number.

7. Enter **250000** as the value in the number field that is now enabled.

8. Choose colors for the positive bar and negative bar and the Axis. The dialog should look like the one in Figure 14-25.

Figure 14-25. *The Data bars dialog*

9. Click OK. The table will look like the one in Figure 14-26.

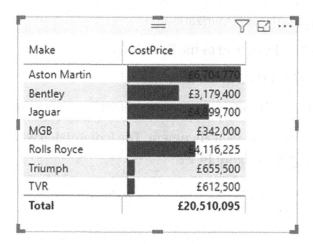

Make	CostPrice
Aston Martin	£6,704,770
Bentley	£3,179,400
Jaguar	£4,899,700
MGB	£342,000
Rolls Royce	£4,116,225
Triumph	£655,500
TVR	£612,500
Total	**£20,510,095**

Figure 14-26. *Data bars applied to a table*

There are a few points you may find of note when applying data bars:

- You can choose to apply the bars only (and not the actual figures).

- Data bars can only be applied to a column containing numeric values.

You can choose to add data bars and color scales to the same column at the same time. However, this may detract from the visual rather than enabling the reader to understand the meaning of the data.

Icons

A fairly recent addition to the panoply of available data visualization techniques in Power BI Desktop is the ability to display key performance indicators (KPIs) as icons. You can add these to any existing column in a table like this:

1. Select the table that you created in the previous section.

2. Click the Format icon in the Visualizations pane and expand the Conditional Formatting section.

3. Select the name of the column to format from the popup list of the columns in the table (in this example it will be the Make column).

4. Set the Icons button to On. The Icons dialog appears.

5. Select Sum as the summarization.

6. Select the SalePrice field as the Based on field.

7. Choose Right of Data as the Icon layout.

8. Select one of the available icon style sets from the Style popup.

9. Select Middle as the Icon alignment. The Icons dialog will look like that shown in Figure 14-27.

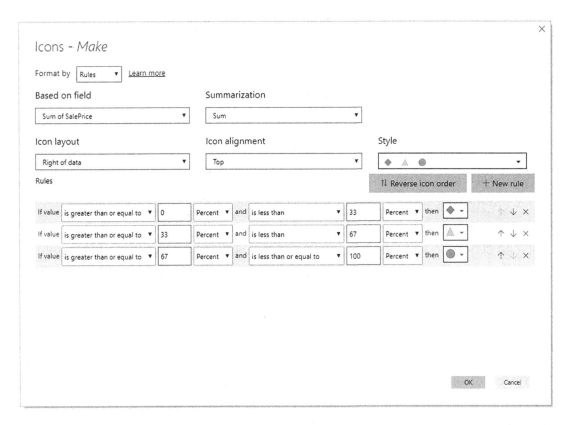

Figure 14-27. *The Icons dialog*

10. Click OK. The table will look like that shown in Figure 14-28.

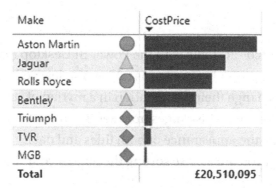

Figure 14-28. *Icons applied to a table*

Icons are a great addition to the available data display techniques in Power BI Desktop. There are, nonetheless, a few things that you need to know:

- The number of rules that appear in the dialog will automatically map to the number of icons in the style that you selected.

- If you delete or add a rule, the Style switches to Custom. You can now select the type of icon that you wish for each rule.

- You can, if you wish, select a specific icon for each rule that is applied.

Exporting Data from a Visualization

Finally, it is worth noting that you can export the data that underlies a visualization. This applies to any visual, from tables to charts. All you have to do is

1. Click the menu for the visual—the ellipses at the top right of the chart, table, or map. Then select Export Data from the popup menu.

2. Select a destination directory and file name.

3. Click OK and the relevant data will be exported. The only current export format is a CSV file.

Note   Any existing filters are applied when the data is exported. This means that, potentially, only a subset of the data will be exported to the CSV file.

Conclusion

I hope that you are now comfortable with the Power BI Desktop report interface and are relaxed about using it to present your data as tables. You learned not just how to create tables but also how to change their presentation in a myriad of subtle (and not so subtle) ways to enhance their impact. This ranges from setting font attributes to conditional formatting via adjusting the appearance of both titles and data.

Equally, I hope that you are at ease sorting the data in your tables using the available techniques.

This chapter was just a taster of the many ways in which Power BI Desktop can help you analyze and display the information that you want your audience to appreciate. So, as tables are the basis for just about every other form of visual, it is well worth mastering the techniques and tricks of table creation. This way, you are well on the way to a fluent mastery of Power BI Desktop, which lays the foundations for some truly impressive presentations.

Now that you have mastered the basics, it is time to move on to the next level of dashboard creation where you will discover how to create and enhance matrices and cards. These are explained in the next chapter.

CHAPTER 15

Matrix and Card Visuals

This chapter takes you through the process of creating further text-based visualizations in Power BI Desktop. You will learn how to further develop the skills that you acquired in the previous chapter to create and enhance

- Matrices

- Cards

- Multirow cards

The techniques that you will learn in this chapter use a Power BI Desktop file that results from the application of much of what you saw in the last four chapters. This file is called `C:\PowerBiDesktopSamples\CarSalesDataForReports.pbix`. It is available on the Apress website as part of the downloadable material that accompanies this book.

Creating a Matrix

In the previous chapter, you saw how tables can be used to display the information as full columns of lists. Lists do not, however, always give an intuitive feeling for how data should be grouped at various levels. Presenting information in a neat hierarchy with multiple grouped levels is the task of a matrix visual.

Creating a Row Matrix

When creating a matrix, I find that it helps to think in terms of a hierarchy of information and to visualize this information flowing from left to right. For instance, suppose that we want to create a matrix with the country name as the highest level in the hierarchy (and consequently the leftmost item). Then we want the make of car to be the second level,

© Adam Aspin 2020
A. Aspin, *Pro Power BI Desktop*, https://doi.org/10.1007/978-1-4842-5763-0_15

and the next element in from the left. Finally, we want the color of car sold, followed by all the numeric fields that interest us. You can see this progression illustrated in Figure 15-1.

Country Name   Make   Colour

Figure 15-1. *An information hierarchy*

When creating a matrix, it is important to have the Visualizations pane reflect the hierarchy. Put another way, you must ensure that the order of the fields that you select for the matrix and that you place in the field well follows the display hierarchy that you want. Consequently, to create a matrix like the one just described, you need to do the following:

1. Use the `C:\PowerBiDesktopSamples\CarSalesDataForReports.pbix` file as your source of data.

2. Click the Matrix icon in the Visualizations pane. This is shown in Figure 15-2. An empty matrix will appear on the report canvas.

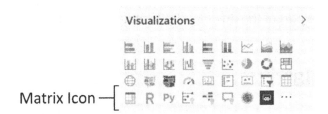

Figure 15-2. *A matrix table*

3. Drag the fields CountryName (from the Countries table), Make (from the Stock table), and Color (from the Colors table) in this order to the Rows well in the Visualizations pane. Then add the fields SalePrice and Cost Plus Spares Margin (from the InvoiceLines table) and Mileage (from the Stock table). The matrix should look something like Figure 15-3.

CountryName	SalePrice	Cost Plus Spares Margin	Mileage
	£141,250	£37,280	222,750
France	£2,524,510	£1,021,980	2,037,750
Germany	£145,750	-£15,850	284,720
Spain	£207,750	£24,630	415,220
Switzerland	£1,440,970	£709,505	1,530,165
United Kingdom	£15,725,000	£5,303,870	11,571,260
USA	£11,653,960	£3,748,850	9,175,385
Total	**£31,839,190**	**£10,830,265**	**25,237,250**

Figure 15-3. *A matrix showing the top level of data*

4. Click the "Expand all down one level in the hierarchy" icon at the top of the matrix. This is the third icon from the left that looks like a small pitchfork (you can see this icon in Figure 15-11 if you want to jump ahead slightly). The matrix should look something like Figure 15-4 (note that it is perfectly normal that there is no country name for the first set of rows).

CountryName	SalePrice	Cost Plus Spares Margin	Mileage
	£141,250	£37,280	222,750
Bentley	£46,750	£13,480	65,250
Triumph	£50,500	£22,700	105,000
TVR	£44,000	£1,100	52,500
France	£2,524,510	£1,021,980	2,037,750
Aston Martin	£1,487,210	£689,670	1,086,500
Bentley	£394,250	£103,210	315,000
Jaguar	£212,000	£51,300	238,750
Rolls Royce	£373,300	£180,100	292,500
Triumph	£28,000	£5,850	52,500
TVR	£29,750	-£8,150	52,500
Germany	£145,750	-£15,850	284,720
Jaguar	£74,750	-£11,050	179,720
TVR	£71,000	-£4,800	105,000
Spain	£207,750	£24,630	415,220
Bentley	£46,750	£13,480	65,250
Jaguar	£69,250	-£6,550	179,720
Triumph	£47,750	£16,600	117,750
TVR	£44,000	£1,100	52,500
Switzerland	£1,440,970	£709,505	1,530,165
Aston Martin	£543,170	£242,675	814,000
Bentley	£222,750	£161,830	71,195
Jaguar	£450,250	£196,910	418,470
Rolls Royce	£192,300	£118,490	174,000
TVR	£32,500	-£10,400	52,500
Total	£31,839,190	£10,830,265	25,237,250

Figure 15-4. *A two-level matrix*

5. Click the "Expand all down one level in the hierarchy" icon again.
    The matrix should look something like Figure 15-5.

Top Level
(Country)

Second Level
(Make)

Third Level
(Color)

CountryName	SalePrice	Cost Plus Spares Margin	Mileage
France	£2,524,510	£1,021,980	2,037,750
Aston Martin	£1,487,210	£689,670	1,086,500
Blue	£141,250	£99,750	66,000
British Racing ...	£181,250	£50,650	8,000
Canary Yellow	£284,440	£99,295	193,000
Green	£108,990	£30,325	246,000
Night Blue	£165,600	£19,850	156,500
Red	£450,300	£309,460	261,000
Silver	£155,380	£80,340	156,000
Bentley	£394,250	£103,210	315,000
Blue	£44,000	£11,350	52,500
British Racing ...	£39,500	-£25,070	52,500
Canary Yellow	£110,000	£46,050	52,500
Dark Purple	£44,000	-£25,570	52,500
Red	£110,000	£82,350	52,500
Silver	£46,750	£14,100	52,500
Jaguar	£212,000	£51,300	238,750
Black	£84,500	£33,100	81,250
Canary Yellow	£88,000	£5,650	105,000
Night Blue	£39,500	£12,550	52,500
Rolls Royce	£373,300	£180,100	292,500
Black	£48,250	-£3,540	66,000
Blue	£72,000	£48,605	52,000
Canary Yellow	£207,250	£107,630	113,500
Night Blue	£45,800	£27,405	61,000
Triumph	£28,000	£5,850	52,500
Silver	£28,000	£5,850	52,500
TVR	£29,750	-£8,150	52,500
Silver	£29,750	-£8,150	52,500
Germany	£145,750	-£15,850	284,720
Jaguar	£74,750	-£11,050	179,720
Green	£42,250	-£650	52,500
Red	£32,500	-£10,400	127,220
TVR	£71,000	-£4,800	105,000
Blue	£41,250	£3,350	52,500
Silver	£29,750	-£8,150	52,500
Total	£31,839,190	£10,830,265	25,237,250

Figure 15-5. *A three-level matrix*

As you can see, a matrix display not only makes data easier to digest, but it automatically groups records by each element in the hierarchy and adds totals for each level as well. What is more, each level in the hierarchy is sorted in ascending order. You can expand all the levels that are available in the data that you added to the matrix definition. This final level will display all available detail at that level.

You can also add fields directly to a table by dragging them into the table. When you do this, Power BI Desktop always adds a text field to the *right* of existing fields. In a matrix, this means that any aggregate/numeric field is added to the right of existing aggregate fields (and appears in the Values box), whereas any text or date/time fields are added to the right of any existing hierarchy fields (and appear in the Rows box). However, it is always a simple matter to reorganize them by dragging the required fields up and down in the Rows and Values boxes to define the correct hierarchy and the overall type of display that you want to achieve. You can see how the Visualizations pane reflects the matrix hierarchy in Figure 15-6.

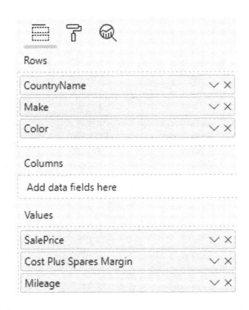

Figure 15-6. *The Visualizations pane showing the matrix hierarchy*

When creating matrices, my personal preference is to drag the fields that constitute the hierarchy of non-numeric values into the Rows well, which means I am placing them accurately above, below, or between any existing elements. This ensures that your matrix looks right the first time, which can help you avoid some very disconcerting double takes! Also as Power BI Desktop will add additional fields to the Columns well by default, it helps to be precise when building a matrix. This means carefully placing the fields for the row headers in the Rows well.

Adding or Removing Subtotals in a Matrix

By default, a new matrix will include the subtotals for every level of the data. Should you prefer to remove the subtotals from a matrix:

1.   Select the matrix visual that you used in the previous section.

2.   In the Visualizations pane, click the Format icon.

3.   Expand the Subtotals section.

4.   Click the Row Subtotals button to turn the row subtotals off. This will remove all the totals from the matrix, as you can see in Figure 15-7.

CountryName	SalePrice	Cost Plus Spares Margin	Mileage
Bentley			
Canary Yellow	£46,750	£13,480	65,250
Triumph			
British Racing ...	£25,250	£11,350	52,500
Canary Yellow	£25,250	£11,350	52,500
TVR			
Blue	£44,000	£1,100	52,500
France			
Aston Martin			
Blue	£141,250	£99,750	66,000
British Racing ...	£181,250	£50,650	8,000
Canary Yellow	£284,440	£99,295	193,000
Green	£108,990	£30,325	246,000
Night Blue	£165,600	£19,850	156,500
Red	£450,300	£309,460	261,000
Silver	£155,380	£80,340	156,000
Bentley			
Blue	£44,000	£11,350	52,500
British Racing ...	£39,500	-£25,070	52,500
Canary Yellow	£110,000	£46,050	52,500
Dark Purple	£44,000	-£25,570	52,500
Red	£110,000	£82,350	52,500
Silver	£46,750	£14,100	52,500

Figure 15-7. A matrix without subtotals

Column Matrix

Power BI Desktop does not limit you to adding row-level hierarchies; you can also create column-level hierarchies, or mix the two. Suppose that we want to get a clear idea of sales and gross margin by country, make, and vehicle type and how they impact one another. To achieve this, I suggest extending the matrix that you created previously by adding a VehicleType level as a column hierarchy.

Here is how you can do this:

1. Click inside the matrix that you created previously to select it. The Visualizations pane will display the fields that are used for this table in the Rows and Values boxes.

2. Drag the VehicleType field from the Stock table down into the Columns well in the Visualizations pane. This will add a hierarchy to the columns in the table. The table will look like Figure 15-8.

VehicleType	Convertible				Coupe				Saloon				Total		
CountryName	SalePrice	Cost Plus Spares Margin	Mileage	SalePrice	Cost Plus Spares Margin	Mileage	SalePrice	Cost Plus Spares Margin	Mileage	SalePrice	Cost Plus Spares Margin	Mileage	SalePrice	Cost Plus Spares Margin	Mileage
Bentley															
Canary Yellow	£46,750	£13,480	65,250										£46,750	£13,480	65,250
Triumph															
British Racing ...				£25,250	£11,350	52,500							£25,250	£11,350	52,500
Canary Yellow				£25,250	£11,350	52,500							£25,250	£11,350	52,500
TVR															
Blue				£44,000	£1,100	52,500							£44,000	£1,100	52,500
France															
Aston Martin															
Blue				£141,250	£99,750	66,000							£141,250	£99,750	66,000
British Racing ...				£181,250	£50,650	8,000							£181,250	£50,650	8,000
Canary Yellow	£37,690	£19,295	52,000	£246,750	£80,000	141,000							£284,440	£99,295	193,000
Green				£108,990	£30,325	246,000							£108,990	£30,325	246,000
Night Blue				£165,600	£19,850	156,500							£165,600	£19,850	156,500
Red	£151,750	£82,710	104,000	£298,550	£226,750	157,000							£450,300	£309,460	261,000
Silver	£78,130	£26,340	104,000	£77,250	£54,000	52,000							£155,380	£80,340	156,000
Bentley															
Blue							£44,000	£11,350	52,500	£44,000	£11,350	52,500			
British Racing ...							£39,500	-£25,070	52,500	£39,500	-£25,070	52,500			
Canary Yellow							£110,000	£46,050	52,500	£110,000	£46,050	52,500			
Dark Purple				£44,000	-£25,570	52,500				£44,000	-£25,570	52,500			
Red							£110,000	£82,350	52,500	£110,000	£82,350	52,500			
Silver							£46,750	£14,100	52,500	£46,750	£14,100	52,500			
Jaguar															
Black				£42,250	£22,800	28,750	£42,250	£10,300	52,500	£84,500	£33,100	81,250			
Canary Yellow				£44,000	£4,550	52,500	£44,000	£1,100	52,500	£88,000	£5,650	105,000			
Night Blue							£39,500	£12,550	52,500	£39,500	£12,550	52,500			
Rolls Royce															
Black							£48,250	-£3,540	66,000	£48,250	-£3,540	66,000			
Blue							£72,000	£48,605	52,000	£72,000	£48,605	52,000			
Canary Yellow				£77,250	£40,230	61,000	£130,000	£67,400	52,500	£207,250	£107,630	113,500			
Night Blue							£45,800	£27,405	61,000	£45,800	£27,405	61,000			
Triumph															
Silver				£28,000	£5,850	52,500				£28,000	£5,850	52,500			
TVR															

Figure 15-8. *A row and column matrix table*

The Visualizations pane now looks like the snippet shown in Figure 15-9.

Figure 15-9. *The Visualizations pane for a row and column matrix table*

As you can see, you now have the sales and gross margin by country name, color, make, and vehicle type, but it is in a cross-matrix, where the data is broken down by both rows and columns.

To conclude the section on creating matrices, there are a few things that you might like to note:

- If you add totals, then *every level* of the hierarchy has totals.

- Adding non-numeric data to the values field well makes Power BI Desktop display the Count aggregation.

- Matrices can get very wide, especially if you have a multilevel hierarchy. Power BI Desktop matrices reflect this in the way in which horizontal scrolling works. A matrix table freezes the non-aggregated data columns on the left and allows you to scroll to the right to display aggregated (numeric) data.

- Moving the fields in the Columns and Rows wells of the Visualizations pane (using drag and drop, as described previously) reorders the aggregated data columns in the table.

Expanding and Drilling Down and Up

When creating the original matrix, you saw how to expand the matrix to include sublevels. However, Power BI Desktop offers a wide range of possibilities when it comes to navigating through layers of data in a matrix. These cover

- Displaying one or all sublevels of data in a hierarchy

- Displaying only a deeper level of data

- Drilling down to display only lower levels of a specific item

- Drilling up to show the only previous level of a hierarchy

Navigating between levels of data is done using a combination of four interface elements:

- The Data/Drill ribbon

- The icons at the top of every matrix

- The context menu for a data element

- The +/- icons for each individual item in a level

It will probably help to get an overview of all three before learning to move through levels of data.

The Data/Drill Ribbon

One important tool when drilling through hierarchical data is the Data/Drill ribbon. The buttons that this ribbon contains are shown in Figure 15-10 and explained in Table 15-1.

Figure 15-10. *The Data/Drill ribbon*

Table 15-1. *The Available Matrix Styles*

Button	Description
Apply drilling to	Drills down or up either for all visuals on the page or just the selected visual.
See data	Shows the data, unformatted, in a separate pane.
Switch to next level	Displays the data segmented by the data at the next level in the hierarchy.
Expand all down one level in the hierarchy	Shows all data items with the next level of data.
Drill up	Returns to the previous data level (expanded or drilled down).
Drill down	Shows the selected data item and any sublevel of data only for this item.
Visual table	Displays the data for the records making up an aggregate row.
Group	Creates a group to highlight the selected values in a visual.
Drillthrough	Drills through to another page containing detailed information.

The Matrix Navigation Icons

Any matrix has a series of icons above the data. You can see these in Figure 15-11. I suggest that you familiarize yourself with these as they are fundamental when drilling through hierarchies of information. This applies not only to matrices but to certain types of chart, too.

Figure 15-11. *The drill and expand icons for a matrix*

The Context Menu for Matrix Items

The final approach that you might need when navigating through hierarchies of data in matrices is the popup menu that appears when you right-click any record in a matrix. You can see this in Figure 15-12.

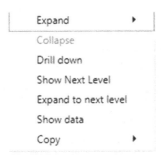

Figure 15-12. *The context menu for matrix items*

The +/- Icons for Each Individual Item in a Level

You do not have to expand every element at a specific level in a matrix if you do not want to. You can (now) choose to expand or collapse each level individually.

Enabling expansion of individual levels of a matrix can be done like this:

1. Create a matrix using the Make and Model fields for the Rows and SalePrice for the Values.

2. With the matrix selected, click the Formatting icon in the Visualizations pane.

3. Expand Row Headers.

4. Set the +/- icons to On. The matrix will look like the one shown in
   Figure 15-13.

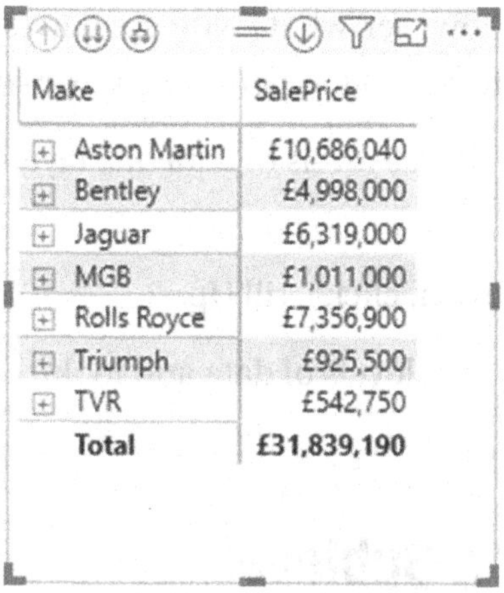

Figure 15-13. *A matrix with the +/- (expand and collapse) icons displayed*

5. Click the plus icon for Bentley. The entire section for the selected
   item will be expanded—but nothing else. The matrix will look like
   the one shown in Figure 15-14.

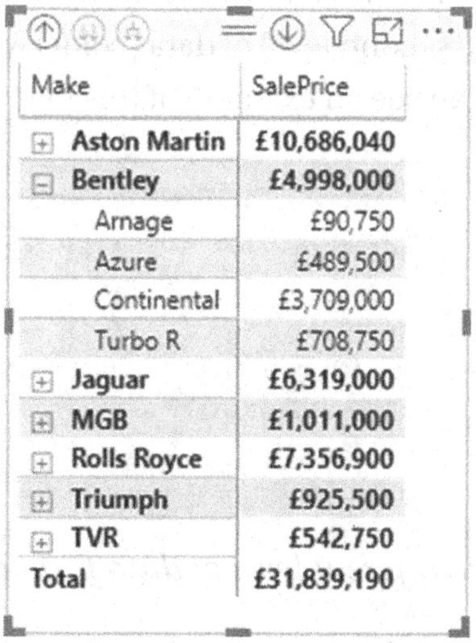

Figure 15-14. *A matrix with a specific element for one level expanded*

- As you have doubtless guessed, clicking the minus icon for an
  expanded item will collapse that specific level.

Displaying Data at the Previous Level

A few pages back you saw how to expand all the sublevels when creating a matrix, so I do not need to repeat this here. However, what if you are currently showing, say, three levels of a data hierarchy and want to return to displaying only two levels?

1. Take the matrix with three levels of data displayed that you can see in Figure 15-5.

2. In the Data/Drill ribbon, click Drill Up.

The matrix will show only two levels of data and look, once again, like the image in Figure 15-4.

Displaying Data for a Sublevel

A matrix does not oblige you to display all levels of data at once. You can, if you prefer, display only the data for a lower level of the matrix hierarchy, as follows:

1. Create the matrix that you began with in Figure 15-3, showing only the top-level data.

2. Click the "Go to the next level in the hierarchy" icon at the top of the matrix. Only the second level of data (color) will be displayed in the matrix. You can see an example of this in Figure 15-15.

Make	SalePrice	Cost Plus Spares Margin	Mileage
Aston Martin	£10,686,040	£3,891,790	6,120,170
Bentley	£4,998,000	£1,655,880	3,494,370
Jaguar	£6,319,000	£1,248,540	7,432,890
MGB	£1,011,000	£657,750	1,966,500
Rolls Royce	£7,356,900	£3,191,280	3,507,570
Triumph	£925,500	£260,775	1,928,250
TVR	£542,750	-£75,750	787,500

Figure 15-15. *Displaying a different level of data from a matrix*

As you can see, the totals are identical. Only the data segmentation has changed.

To return to the previous level in the data hierarchy, simply click the Drill Up button in the Data/Drill ribbon—or the Drill Up icon at the top left of the matrix.

Drilling Down at Row Level

Another completely different option when navigating hierarchies of data is to drill up and down into a specific element of a hierarchy. The key difference between expanding and drilling are as follows:

- Expanding a hierarchy will display the next level of data for *all* top-level elements.

- Drilling down will only display the next sublevel for the *selected* data element.

To see this in practice, try the following:

1. Right-click any top-level data element in a matrix (I will take France in the matrix that you can see in Figure 15-5).

2. Select Drill down from the context menu. The matrix will now look like the one in Figure 15-16.

CountryName	SalePrice	Cost Plus Spares Margin	Mileage
France			
Aston Martin	£1,487,210	£689,670	1,086,500
Bentley	£394,250	£103,210	315,000
Jaguar	£212,000	£51,300	238,750
Rolls Royce	£373,300	£180,100	292,500
Triumph	£28,000	£5,850	52,500
TVR	£29,750	-£8,150	52,500

Figure 15-16. *Drilling down in a matrix*

3. You can continue to drill down into further levels of data simply by right-clicking any data element at the second level and selecting Drill down from the context menu (Bentley, for instance, in this example). The matrix will now look like the one in Figure 15-17.

CountryName	SalePrice	Cost Plus Spares Margin	Mileage
France			
Bentley			
Blue	£44,000	£11,350	52,500
British Racing ...	£39,500	-£25,070	52,500
Canary Yellow	£110,000	£46,050	52,500
Dark Purple	£44,000	-£25,570	52,500
Red	£110,000	£82,350	52,500
Silver	£46,750	£14,100	52,500

Figure 15-17. *Drilling down further in a matrix*

To return to a previous level, all you have to do is click the Drill Up button in the Data/Drill ribbon—or the Drill Up icon at the top left of the matrix. Alternatively, you can right-click a data item and select Drill Up from the context menu.

Drill Down Using Click-Through

If you find it a little wearing to right-click and select the Drill down option, then you have an alternative solution. You can switch a matrix to drill down with a simple click on a data item. Here is how you can do this:

1. At the top right of a matrix, click the "Click to turn on drill down" icon. This will become a light arrow on a dark background.

2. Click any data element (a country, for instance). You will drill down to the next level.

You can turn off this option at any time by reclicking the "Click to turn on drill down" icon. It will return to being a light arrow on a clear background, indicating that this form of drill down is deactivated.

Drilling Down at Column Level

The same drill-down and drill-up logic applies to columns as to rows. Take the column matrix that you created previously (and that you can see in Figure 15-8):

1. Add the Model (from the Stock table) to the data for the matrix to the Columns well, under the VehicleType field. A popup appears at the top left of the matrix containing the choice between rows and columns. You can see this in Figure 15-18.

Figure 15-18. *The drill-down option in complex matrices*

2. Click the popup and select Columns.

3. Click the "Go to the next level in the hierarchy" icon. You will see something like Figure 15-19, where the vehicle type has been replaced by model as the column header.

Model	Arnage				Azure				Camargue				Cerbera				Continental	
CountryName	SalePrice	Cost Plus Spares Margin	Mileage	SalePrice	Cost Plus Spares Margin	Mileage	SalePrice	Cost Plus Spares Margin	Mileage	SalePrice	Cost Plus Spares Margin	Mileage	SalePrice	Cost Plus Spares Margin	Mileage	SalePrice	Cost Plus S
																	£46,750	
France				£44,000		£11,350	52,500	£243,300		£112,700	240,000	£29,750		-£8,150	52,500	£193,500	
Germany												£29,750		-£8,150	52,500		
Spain																	
Switzerland				£110,000		£82,350	18,695	£192,300		£118,490	174,000	£32,500		-£10,400	52,500	£112,750	
United Kingdom	£90,750	£29,210	105,000	£222,750		£72,020	411,940	£1,209,750		£419,370	340,000	£32,500		-£10,400	52,500	£1,675,250	
USA				£112,750		£80,100	18,695	£2,471,550		£1,048,010	1,169,190					£1,680,750	

Figure 15-19. *Drilling down in a multilevel column hierarchy*

As you can see, a hierarchy can be applied equally to columns and rows. This boils down to

- Adding the field to the correct well in the Visualizations pane (Rows or Columns)

- Selecting the appropriate drill-down mode from the popup at the top of the matrix (Columns or Rows)

Visualize Source Data

If a formatted table or matrix becomes, paradoxically, too large or complex, you can opt to look at the underlying data without any formatting applied. This often lets you see more information than you can in a carefully formatted visualization.

1. Select the table or matrix whose data you want to display without formatting.

2. In the Data/Drill ribbon, click the See Data button. The unformatted version of the data for the selected table or matrix will be displayed in a second window. You can see this in Figure 15-20.

Figure 15-20. *Visualizing source data*

3. Click the Back to report button above the formatted table (or click again the See Data button in the Data/Drill ribbon) to return to the normal Power BI Desktop Report View.

Note   You cannot currently resize the two windows when viewing unformatted data. You can, however, scroll up and down in either window. If you prefer to see the data to the right of the visual (rather than underneath it), then click the Switch Layout icon at the top right of the window.

Viewing Records

When dealing with aggregated data, you can sometimes lose sight of valuable details. You might miss a large outlier that is skewing an average value, for instance. Or, perhaps, an excessive value for a single record is making a total higher than is normal—or healthy.

To help you follow your intuitions and weight aggregated values against detailed numbers, Power BI Desktop lets you view the underlying records "behind" a total at any time in a matrix. Here's an example:

1. Create a matrix based on the following fields (all of them are from the Stock table):

    a. Make (Rows)

    b. Model (Rows)

    c. LaborCost

    d. CostPrice

2. In the Data/Drill menu, click Expand all down one level in the hierarchy to see the complete hierarchy of makes and models.

3. Right-click the figure for the labor cost for Aston Martin Vanquish and select See records from the context menu. You will see all the detail records that make up this total figure. This is shown in Figure 15-21.

Make	Model	LaborCost	CostPrice	VehicleType	Vehicle	Excessive Parts Cost	PriceCheck	Mileage Range	Vehicle Age Category	Vehicle Age Category Sort	Special Sales	High Mileage
Aston Martin	Vanquish	£325	£62,000	Coupe	Aston Martin Vanquish		Price OK	High	11-20	4	Special	Yes
Aston Martin	Vanquish	£325	£67,000	Coupe	Aston Martin Vanquish		Price OK	High	11-20	4	Special	Yes
Aston Martin	Vanquish	£654	£62,000	Coupe	Aston Martin Vanquish		Price OK	Medium	11-20	4	Normal	No
Aston Martin	Vanquish	£654	£67,000	Coupe	Aston Martin Vanquish		Price OK	Medium	11-20	4	Normal	No
Aston Martin	Vanquish	£750	£125,000	Coupe	Aston Martin Vanquish		Price too high	High	>30	7	Normal	Yes
Aston Martin	Vanquish	£750	£130,000	Coupe	Aston Martin Vanquish		Price too high	High	>30	7	Normal	Yes
Aston Martin	Vanquish	£752	£125,000	Coupe	Aston Martin Vanquish		Price too high	Medium	11-20	4	Special	No
Aston Martin	Vanquish	£752	£130,000	Coupe	Aston Martin Vanquish		Price too high	Medium	11-20	4	Special	No
Aston Martin	Vanquish	£984	£62,000	Coupe	Aston Martin Vanquish		Price OK	Medium	11-20	4	Normal	No
Aston Martin	Vanquish	£984	£67,000	Coupe	Aston Martin Vanquish		Price OK	Medium	11-20	4	Normal	No

Figure 15-21. *Displaying data records from a matrix*

4. Click the Back to report button above the records that are now displayed to return to the normal Power BI Desktop Report View.

Note   Alternatively, you can right-click any value in a matrix and select See records to drill through to the detailed records that give the selected aggregate figure.

Including and Excluding Matrix Elements

Some matrices can swamp you in data. So you might need to focus on a few selected elements. This is really simple in Power BI Desktop:

1. Re-create the matrix from the previous section (Make, Model, LaborCost, and CostPrice).

2. Click Expand all down one level in the hierarchy to see the complete hierarchy of makes and models.

3. Ctrl-click any element (make, model, or a value) for

   a. Aston Martin DB4

   b. Bentley Arnage

   c. Jaguar XJ12

4. Right-click one of the selected elements and select Include from the popup menu. All other elements will be removed from the matrix. The result is shown in Figure 15-22.

Make	LaborCost	CostPrice
Aston Martin	£5,424	£673,340
DB4	£5,424	£673,340
Bentley	£2,500	£56,400
Arnage	£2,500	£56,400
Jaguar	£4,890	£270,000
XJ12	£4,890	£270,000
Total	£12,814	£999,740

Figure 15-22. *Including selected elements from a matrix*

Note   As an alternative to including certain elements, you can select all the elements that you wish to *exclude*, and choose Exclude from the popup menu.

For the moment, the only way to return to a complete matrix containing all the rows of data seems to be to press Ctrl+Z and undo this operation.

Displaying Multiple Values As Rows

A feature that is really useful in Power BI Desktop fairly recently is the possibility of creating complex matrices where the columns of data can now be displayed as rows. That is, instead of seeing possibly multiple data values side by side for a complex column hierarchy, you can see all the numeric data displayed as rows.

This is possibly best appreciated with the help of an example:

1. Create a matrix using the following elements:

    a. *Rows*: CountryName from the Countries table and Make from the Stock table (in this order).

    b. *Column*: VehicleType (from the Stock table).

    c. *Values*: Mileage and LaborCost (in this order). Both are from the Stock table.

2. Expand all down one level. The matrix will look like the one shown in Figure 15-23.

VehicleType CountryName	Convertible Mileage	LaborCost	Coupe Mileage	LaborCost	Saloon Mileage	LaborCost	Total Mileage	LaborCost
	65,250	£486	157,500	£975			222,750	£1,461
Bentley	65,250	£486					65,250	£486
Triumph			105,000	£650			105,000	£650
TVR			52,500	£325			52,500	£325
France	260,000	£5,650	1,126,250	£19,767	651,500	£11,054	2,037,750	£36,471
Aston Martin	260,000	£5,650	826,500	£16,020			1,086,500	£21,670
Bentley			52,500	£486	262,500	£4,223	315,000	£4,709
Jaguar			81,250	£1,236	157,500	£1,561	238,750	£2,797
Rolls Royce			61,000	£1,250	231,500	£5,270	292,500	£6,520
Triumph			52,500	£450			52,500	£450
TVR			52,500	£325			52,500	£325
Germany			232,220	£1,136	52,500	£325	284,720	£1,461
Jaguar			127,220	£486	52,500	£325	179,720	£811
TVR			105,000	£650			105,000	£650
Spain	65,250	£486	297,470	£1,461	52,500	£325	415,220	£2,272
Bentley	65,250	£486					65,250	£486
Jaguar			127,220	£486	52,500	£325	179,720	£811
Triumph			117,750	£650			117,750	£650
TVR			52,500	£325			52,500	£325
Switzerland	290,500	£5,325	816,720	£13,512	422,945	£8,370	1,530,165	£27,207
Aston Martin	238,000	£5,000	576,000	£10,950			814,000	£15,950
Bentley					71,195	£2,237	71,195	£2,237
Jaguar	52,500	£325	127,220	£987	238,750	£3,933	418,470	£5,245
Rolls Royce			61,000	£1,250	113,000	£2,200	174,000	£3,450
TVR			52,500	£325			52,500	£325
United Kingdom	668,250	£6,394	5,956,420	£61,453	4,946,590	£62,105	11,571,260	£129,952
Aston Martin			2,109,780	£26,268			2,109,780	£26,268
Bentley	353,250	£4,444	234,700	£5,934	1,113,990	£20,865	1,701,940	£31,243
Jaguar			1,343,190	£15,476	1,960,720	£18,930	3,303,910	£34,406
MGB	315,000	£1,950	996,000	£5,850			1,311,000	£7,800
Rolls Royce					1,871,880	£22,310	1,871,880	£22,310
Triumph			1,115,250	£6,950			1,115,250	£6,950
Total	2,109,500	£28,624	13,306,950	£152,160	9,820,800	£131,175	25,237,250	£311,959

Figure 15-23. *A standard matrix with values as columns*

3. In the Visualizations pane, click the Format icon and expand the Values section.

4. Set Show on rows to On. The matrix will now look like the one shown in Figure 15-24, where the multiple columns of data have become rows of data.

CountryName	Convertible	Coupe	Saloon	Total
Mileage	65,250	157,500		222,750
LaborCost	£486	£975		£1,461
Bentley				
Mileage	65,250			65,250
LaborCost	£486			£486
Triumph				
Mileage		105,000		105,000
LaborCost		£650		£650
TVR				
Mileage		52,500		52,500
LaborCost		£325		£325
France				
Mileage	260,000	1,126,250	651,500	2,037,750
LaborCost	£5,650	£19,767	£11,054	£36,471
Aston Martin				
Mileage	260,000	826,500		1,086,500
LaborCost	£5,650	£16,020		£21,670
Bentley				
Mileage		52,500	262,500	315,000
LaborCost		£486	£4,223	£4,709
Jaguar				
Mileage		81,250	157,500	238,750
LaborCost		£1,236	£1,561	£2,797
Rolls Royce				
Mileage		61,000	231,500	292,500
LaborCost		£1,250	£5,270	£6,520
Triumph				
Mileage	2,109,500	13,306,950	9,820,800	25,237,250
LaborCost	£28,624	£152,160	£131,175	£311,959

Figure 15-24. *A matrix with values as rows*

Simply switching Show on rows to Off will revert the matrix to its initial format.

Formatting a Matrix

Fortunately, the techniques that you apply to format a matrix are largely identical to those you applied to tables. So I will not cover, again, the principles that you saw in the previous chapter to change the presentation of

- Matrix style (this is the table style, but applied to a matrix)
- Grid
- Column headers
- Row headers

- Values

- Totals

- Title

- Background

- Conditional formatting

There are, nonetheless, a few extra formatting tweaks that you can add to matrices. These are

- Stepped layout

- Subtotals

I will explain these in the following sections.

Stepped Layout

In Figure 15-5 you can see the multiple levels of a matrix. These are shown using levels of indentation. However, you may prefer to display each level in a separate column. Here is how you can do this:

1. Select (or re-create) the matrix using CountryName, Make, and Color as the Row data and Mileage and LaborCost as the values.

2. Click Expand all down one level in the hierarchy twice to display all the levels of data.

3. In the Visualizations pane, click the Format icon.

4. Expand the Row Headers section.

5. Set Stepped Layout to Off.

6. Adjust the width of the matrix if necessary. The matrix will look like the one in Figure 15-25.

CountryName	Make	Color	Mileage	LaborCost
	Bentley	Canary Yellow	65,250	£486
		Total	**65,250**	**£486**
	Triumph	British Racing Green	52,500	£325
		Canary Yellow	52,500	£325
		Total	**105,000**	**£650**
	TVR	Blue	52,500	£325
		Total	**52,500**	**£325**
	Total		**222,750**	**£1,461**
France	Aston Martin	Blue	66,000	£2,500
		British Racing Green	8,000	£570
		Canary Yellow	193,000	£4,500
		Green	246,000	£3,450
		Night Blue	156,500	£2,650
		Red	261,000	£4,850
		Silver	156,000	£3,150
		Total	**1,086,500**	**£21,670**
	Bentley	Blue	52,500	£750
		British Racing Green	52,500	£486
		Canary Yellow	52,500	£1,250
		Dark Purple	52,500	£486
		Red	52,500	£750
		Silver	52,500	£987
		Total	**315,000**	**£4,709**
	Jaguar	Black	81,250	£1,236
		Canary Yellow	105,000	£811
		Night Blue	52,500	£750
		Total	**238,750**	**£2,797**
	Rolls Royce	Black	66,000	£2,500
		Blue	52,000	£950
		Canary Yellow	113,500	£1,820
		Night Blue	61,000	£1,250
		Total	**292,500**	**£6,520**
	Triumph	Silver	52,500	£450
		Total	**52,500**	**£450**

Figure 15-25. *A matrix without stepped layout*

Subtotals

Whereas a table only has a grand total (assuming that you want to display it), a matrix can have subtotals for each level of data displayed. Although formatting subtotals is similar to formatting the total in a table, I prefer, for the sake of completeness, to describe the possibilities here:

1. Select the matrix visual that you used in the previous section.

2. In the Visualizations pane, click the Format icon.

3. Expand the Subtotals section.

4. Choose a different font color from the Font color palette.

5. Select a different font from the Font family popup list.

6. Enter a number in the Text size field (or adjust using the arrows) to set a larger font size.

7. Set Apply to labels to On—this will ensure that the subtotal labels as well as numbers are formatted. The matrix should look like the one in Figure 15-26.

CountryName	Make	Color	Mileage	LaborCost
	Bentley	Canary Yellow	65,250	£486
		Total	65,250	£486
	Triumph	British Racing Green	52,500	£325
		Canary Yellow	52,500	£325
		Total	105,000	£650
	TVR	Blue	52,500	£325
		Total	52,500	£325
	Total		222,750	£1,461
France	Aston Martin	Blue	66,000	£2,500
		British Racing Green	8,000	£570
		Canary Yellow	193,000	£4,500
		Green	246,000	£3,450
		Night Blue	156,500	£2,650
		Red	261,000	£4,850
		Silver	156,000	£3,150
		Total	1,086,500	£21,670
	Bentley	Blue	52,500	£750
		British Racing Green	52,500	£486
		Canary Yellow	52,500	£1,250
		Dark Purple	52,500	£486
		Red	52,500	£750
		Silver	52,500	£987
		Total	315,000	£4,709
	Jaguar	Black	81,250	£1,236
		Canary Yellow	105,000	£811
		Night Blue	52,500	£750
		Total	238,750	£2,797
	Rolls Royce	Black	66,000	£2,500
		Blue	52,000	£950
		Canary Yellow	113,500	£1,820
		Night Blue	61,000	£1,250
		Total	292,500	£6,520
	Triumph	Silver	52,500	£450

Figure 15-26. Formatting subtotals in a matrix

Note   As the grand total is essentially formatted in the same way as the Total for a table, I will not re-explain how to do this here. If you need to refresh your memory, then just flip back to the previous chapter.

Placing Subtotals

You can also decide whether the subtotals are placed above a group of elements, alongside the element header, or under a group, on a separate row. Simply do the following to place subtotals:

1. Re-create the matrix that you used in Figure 15-21 (following only steps 1 and 2).

2. In the Visualizations pane, click the Format icon and expand the Subtotals section.

3. In the popup for Row Subtotal Position, select Top. The matrix should now look like the one in Figure 15-27.

CountryName	Make	Color	Mileage	LaborCost
Total			25,237,250	£311,959
	Total		222,750	£1,461
	Bentley	Total	65,250	£486
		Canary Yellow	65,250	£486
	Triumph	Total	105,000	£650
		British Racing Green	52,500	£325
		Canary Yellow	52,500	£325
	TVR	Total	52,500	£325
		Blue	52,500	£325
France	Total		2,037,750	£36,471
	Aston Martin	Total	1,086,500	£21,670
		Blue	66,000	£2,500
		British Racing Green	8,000	£570
		Canary Yellow	193,000	£4,500
		Green	246,000	£3,450
		Night Blue	156,500	£2,650
		Red	261,000	£4,850
		Silver	156,000	£3,150
	Bentley	Total	315,000	£4,709
		Blue	52,500	£750
		British Racing Green	52,500	£486
		Canary Yellow	52,500	£1,250
		Dark Purple	52,500	£486
		Red	52,500	£750
		Silver	52,500	£987
	Jaguar	Total	238,750	£2,797
		Black	81,250	£1,236
		Canary Yellow	105,000	£811
		Night Blue	52,500	£750
	Rolls Royce	Total	292,500	£6,520
		Black	66,000	£2,500
		Blue	52,000	£950
		Canary Yellow	113,500	£1,820

Figure 15-27. *Placing subtotals below groups*

Custom Subtotal Settings per Level of Matrix

Power BI Desktop now lets you define whether subtotals are displayed for each level of the matrix hierarchy for both rows and columns. To see this in action:

1. Re-create the matrix that you used in Figure 15-23 (following only steps 1 and 2).

2. Click Expand all down one level in the hierarchy (either the icon in the matrix or in the Data/Drill menu).

3. In the Visualizations pane, click the Format icon and expand the Subtotals section.

4. Set Per row level to On. This will add the list of all the row data elements to the Visualizations pane.

5. Set Per column level to On. This will add the list of all the column data elements to the Visualizations pane.

6. Set the button to Off for both Make and VehicleType. As you can see in Figure 15-28, the subtotals have been removed for these elements.

VehicleType	Convertible		Coupe		Saloon	
CountryName	Mileage	LaborCost	Mileage	LaborCost	Mileage	LaborCost
Bentley	65,250	£486				
Triumph			105,000	£650		
TVR			52,500	£325		
France						
Aston Martin	260,000	£5,650	826,500	£16,020		
Bentley			52,500	£486	262,500	£4,223
Jaguar			81,250	£1,236	157,500	£1,561
Rolls Royce			61,000	£1,250	231,500	£5,270
Triumph			52,500	£450		
TVR			52,500	£325		
Germany						
Jaguar			127,220	£486	52,500	£325
TVR			105,000	£650		
Spain						
Bentley	65,250	£486				
Jaguar			127,220	£486	52,500	£325
Triumph			117,750	£650		
TVR			52,500	£325		
Switzerland						
Aston Martin	238,000	£5,000	576,000	£10,950		
Bentley					71,195	£2,237
Jaguar	52,500	£325	127,220	£987	238,750	£3,933
Rolls Royce			61,000	£1,250	113,000	£2,200
TVR			52,500	£325		
United Kingdom						
Aston Martin			2,109,780	£26,268		
Bentley	353,250	£4,444	234,700	£5,934	1,113,990	£20,865
Jaguar			1,343,190	£15,476	1,960,720	£18,930
MGB	315,000	£1,950	996,000	£5,850		
Total	2,109,500	£28,624	13,306,950	£152,160	9,820,800	£131,175

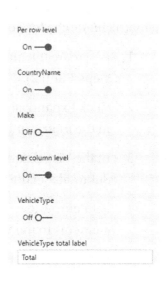

Figure 15-28. *Selective subtotals*

Sorting Data in Matrices

When you sort data in a matrix table, the sort order will respect the matrix hierarchy. This means that if you sort on the second element in a hierarchy (Make, in the example table we just created), then the primary element in the hierarchy (CountryName, the leftmost column) will switch back to the initial (alphabetical) sort order, as will any lower levels in the hierarchy of row elements.

If you sort by any value in a matrix, then the total for the highest level of the hierarchy is used to reorder the whole table. You can see this in Figure 15-29, where the matrix from Figure 15-25 has been sorted on the total labor cost in descending order. This has made the country with the greatest labor cost move to the top of the table. As well, if you have a column matrix (as in this example), then you will end up sorting on the grand total of the columns (the two rightmost columns in this example) to make the matrix sort by numeric values, albeit in ascending order.

CountryName	Make	Color	Mileage	LaborCost
United Kingdom	Jaguar	Canary Yellow	757,220	£6,506
		Red	315,000	£5,185
		Silver	430,000	£4,500
		Dark Purple	340,500	£4,448
		British Racing Green	269,250	£4,211
		Green	337,220	£3,797
		Blue	463,250	£2,786
		Black	211,750	£2,237
		Night Blue	179,720	£736
		Total	**3,303,910**	**£34,406**
	Bentley	Canary Yellow	347,450	£8,184
		Red	445,940	£6,460
		Night Blue	267,500	£5,446
		Blue	138,050	£4,500
		Dark Purple	235,500	£2,708
		Green	57,500	£1,500
		British Racing Green	105,000	£1,473
		Black	105,000	£972
		Total	**1,701,940**	**£31,243**
	Aston Martin	Blue	289,900	£4,467
		Black	288,000	£3,807
		Silver	289,720	£3,558
		Canary Yellow	195,000	£3,349
		Dark Purple	255,000	£3,074
		Red	341,940	£2,718
		Green	105,000	£1,968
		Night Blue	284,720	£1,794
		British Racing Green	60,500	£1,533
		Total	**2,109,780**	**£26,268**
	Rolls Royce	Red	420,000	£4,923
		British Racing Green	267,500	£3,908
		Black	335,690	£3,615
		Silver	288,000	£3,178
		Green	210,000	£3,074

Figure 15-29. Sorting a matrix on values

Note   As was the case with tables, there are no specific options for formatting the figures in matrices. You format the data by clicking the Data View icon on the left of the Power BI Desktop window, select the column to format, and, in the Modeling ribbon, select a number format.

Cards

On some occasions, you will want to display a single figure more prominently than others. Perhaps you need to attract the viewer's attention to your new sales record, or you would like the boss to appreciate the customer satisfaction ratings that you have achieved.

Whatever the motivation, cards are the solution. Power BI Desktop cards are a simple and powerful way to isolate and emphasize a single figure. Suppose that you want to display all vehicle sales to date in a dashboard, for instance; the following explains how you can do it:

1. Using the C:\PowerBiDesktopSamples\CarSalesDataForReports.
   pbix file as your source of data, click outside any existing
   visualizations.

2. In the gallery of available visuals, click the Card icon. You can
   see this icon in Figure 15-30. An empty card will appear on the
   dashboard canvas.

Figure 15-30. *The Card icon in the gallery of available visuals*

3. Expand the InvoiceLines table fields in the Fields list and select
   the SalePrice field. The total for all sales will appear in the card.

4. Resize the card so that the figure fits inside the card borders
   without any wasted space. The final card will look like Figure 15-31.

£32M

SalePrice

Figure 15-31. *A card visual*

Formatting Cards

As you just saw, cards are an extremely effective way of focusing your audience's attention on key data. Yet there is a lot more that you can do to extend this emphasis, including the following:

- Change the units, number of decimals, color, and text size of the data that is displayed.

- Remove the label that is displayed automatically, as well as alter its text size.

- Add a title that you can format independently.

- Change the background color of the card.

- Modify the border style.

Let's see how to tweak the card that you just created:

1. Select the card. In this example, I use the card that you saw in Figure 15-31.

2. In the Visualizations pane, click the Format icon (the small paint roller beneath the palette of available visualization types). The formatting options for the selected card will be displayed.

3. Expand the Background section by clicking the downward-facing chevron to the left of the word Background.

4. Make sure that the switch to the right of the word Background is set to On (if it is not, then click to the right of the empty circle to change this).

5. Click the popup menu triangle to the right of Color and select a color from the palette of available colors.

6. Click the Transparency slider switch and slide it to the left to intensify the background color by reducing the percentage of transparency.

7. Expand the Category label section by clicking the downward-facing chevron to the left of the words Category label.

8. Adjust the text size either by clicking the up and/or down chevrons or entering the required text size. You can change the color and font as well if you want to.

9. Expand the Title section by clicking the downward-facing chevron to the left of the word Title.

10. Set the title to On by clicking immediately to the right of the On/Off button to the right of Title.

11. Enter **To Date** as the Title text.

12. Click the popup menu triangle to the right of Font color and select a color for the font from the palette of available colors.

13. Click the popup menu triangle to the right of Background color and select a background color from the palette of available colors.

14. Click the middle icon of the Alignment icons to center the card title.

15. Choose a different font and font size if you want to.

16. Expand the Data labels section by clicking the downward-facing chevron to the left.

17. Click the popup menu triangle to the right of Color and select a data label color from the palette of available colors.

18. Adjust the text size—or enter the required text size.

19. Select a display unit for the figure in the card by clicking the popup list of Display units.

20. Select the number of decimals to be used for the card data by clicking the up and down triangles to the right of the Precision box. You can also enter the number of decimals directly, if you prefer.

21. Expand the Border section and switch the border on. Change the border color if you want to.

22. Adjust the Radius slider to set the rounded corners of the card. The card (along with the formatting palette) will now look something like the elements that you can see in Figure 15-32.

Figure 15-32. *A formatted card*

The available display units for formatting the value in a card are described in Table 15-2.

Table 15-2. *Display Units*

Display Unit	Description
Auto	Chooses an appropriate display unit from those available depending on the size of the figure.
None	Displays the actual figure.
Thousands	Displays the figure in thousands followed by a K.
Millions	Displays the figure in millions followed by an M.
Billions	Displays the figure in billions followed by a bn.
Trillions	Displays the figure in trillions followed by a T.

Multirow Cards

Tabular data can also be displayed in an extremely innovative way using the Power BI Desktop card style of output. As is the case with matrices, you begin by choosing the fields that you want to display as a basic table and then you convert this to another type of visual. Here is an example of how this can be done:

1. Using the C:\PowerBiDesktopSamples\CarSalesDataForReports. pbix file as your source of data, click outside any existing visuals.

2. In the Visualizations pane, click the Card icon. You can see this in Figure 15-33. An empty multirow card will appear on the dashboard canvas.

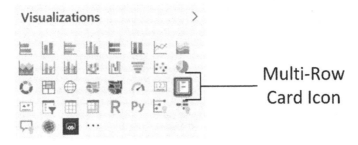

Figure 15-33. *The multirow card icon in the Visualizations pane*

3. Add the following fields, in this order:

    a. CountryName (from the Countries table)

    b. CostPrice (from the Stock table)

    c. LaborCost (from the Stock table)

    d. SpareParts (from the Stock table)

4. Resize the multirow card to display all the countries, with all of the figures on a single row per country. The visual will look something like the one in Figure 15-34. Don't worry about the (Blank) costs; these correspond to vehicles in stock that are not yet sold and so do not have a client country yet.

(Blank)

| £100,200 | £1,461 | £3,770 |
| CostPrice | LaborCost | SpareParts |

France

| £1,460,100 | £36,471 | £42,430 |
| CostPrice | LaborCost | SpareParts |

Germany

| £160,000 | £1,461 | £1,600 |
| CostPrice | LaborCost | SpareParts |

Spain

| £178,700 | £2,272 | £4,420 |
| CostPrice | LaborCost | SpareParts |

Switzerland

| £701,150 | £27,207 | £30,315 |
| CostPrice | LaborCost | SpareParts |

United Kingdom

| £10,193,880 | £129,952 | £227,250 |
| CostPrice | LaborCost | SpareParts |

USA

| £7,716,065 | £113,135 | £189,045 |
| CostPrice | LaborCost | SpareParts |

Figure 15-34. *A card visualization*

Card-type tables will display the selected fields in the order in which they appear in the field well in the Visualizations pane, and it is here that they can be reordered, as with any table. This makes each card into a data record. The fields will flow left to right and then onto the following line in each card. What is interesting here is that adjusting the size of the table can change the appearance of the table quite radically. A very narrow table will list the fields vertically, one above the other. If you can fit all the fields into a single row, then you will get a highly original multiple-record display.

Formatting Multirow Cards

There are a few visual aspects of multirow cards that you can tweak for added effect. These include adding a title and changing the background color. Let's try both of these:

1. Select the multirow card visualization. In this example, I use the card that you saw in Figure 15-34.

2. In the Visualizations pane, click the Format icon (the small paint roller beneath the palette of available visual types). The formatting options for the selected multirow card are displayed.

3. Expand the Background section by clicking the downward-facing chevron to the left of the word Background.

4. Make sure that the switch to the right of the word Background is set to On (if it is not, then click to the right of the empty circle to change this).

5. Click the popup menu triangle to the right of Color and select a color from the palette of available tones.

6. Click the Transparency slider switch and slide it to the left to intensify the background color by reducing the percentage of transparency.

7. Expand the Title section by clicking the downward-facing chevron to the left of the word Title.

8. Set the title to On by clicking immediately to the right of the On/ Off button to the right of Title.

9. Enter **Key Figures By Country** as the Title text.

10. Click the popup menu triangle to the right of Font color and select a color for the font from the palette of available colors.

11. Click the popup menu triangle to the right of Background color and select a background color from the palette of available colors.

12. Set a larger font for the title.

13. Click the icon in the center for the Alignment. This will center the title.

14. Click the popup menu triangle to the right of Card and select Bottom only as the outline style.

15. Click inside the Outline weight field and enter **4**.

16. Select a different bar color from the palette of available bar colors.

17. Set the Bar thickness to 10 to increase the width of the bar.

18. Set the Padding button to 10 to reduce the padding between individual elements in the card.

19. Choose a background color from the palette of colors available for the Background.

20. Expand the Data labels section and increase the size of the font. Change the font and font size if you wish.

21. Expand the Card Title section and increase the text size.

22. Choose a text color from the palette of available colors.

23. Expand the Category labels section and select a text color, font, and font size. The multirow card visual will now look like the one in Figure 15-35. You might have to tweak its size to get the correct effect.

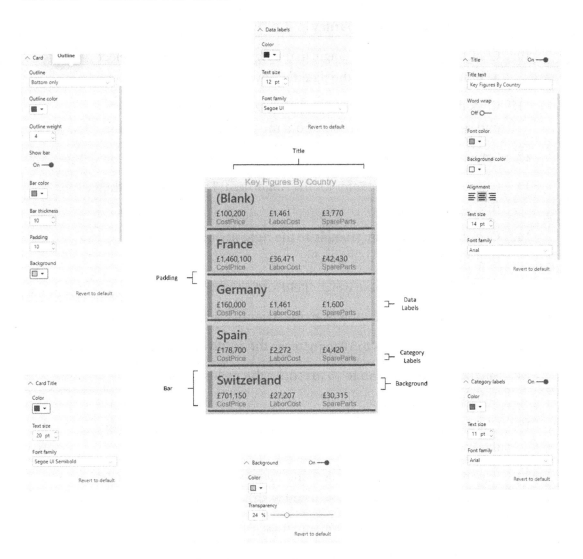

Figure 15-35. *A formatted multirow card*

Note   You can also fix the aspect ratio of a multirow card visual just as you did for the initial table at the start of this chapter. Equally, you can add a border as you saw previously for a card visual.

Sorting Multirow Cards

Like tables and matrices, multirow cards can be sorted. However, there is a specific way to apply a sort order to this kind of visual:

1. Click the ellipses at the top right of the multirow card visual.

2. Select Sort by.

3. Select the column name to sort by from the list of columns in the popup menu.

The elements in the multirow card will now be ordered according to the values in the chosen column. You can see an example of the popup menu in Figure 15-36. This example uses the multirow card that you created previously.

Figure 15-36. *Sorting a multirow card*

Note   Sorting on the category in a multirow card (the country in this example) will initially sort in reverse alphabetical order (as a multirow card is initially ordered in alphabetical order). Reselecting a sort on the category will reset the sort order to alphabetical. Sorting on a value will always order from highest to lowest—and reclicking the value in the popup menu will remove the sort order and revert to the initial order.

Switching Between Table Types

One of the fabulous things about Power BI Desktop is that it is designed from the ground up to let you test ideas and experiment with ways of displaying your data quickly and easily. So, quite naturally, you can switch table types easily to see which style of presentation is best suited to your ideas and the message that you want to convey. To switch table types, all you have to do is select the current text-based visualization (table, multirow card, or matrix) and select one of these options from the gallery of available visuals:

- Table

- Matrix

- Multirow card

What is even more reassuring is that Power BI Desktop remembers the attributes of the previous table type you used. So, for instance, if you set up a matrix with a carefully crafted hierarchy and then switch to a card-type table, Power BI Desktop remembers how you set up the matrix should you want to switch back to it.

To see an example of how this works in practice, take a look at Figure 15-37. This shows the same initial visual that has been copied and then switched between the text-based core types of visual. I have added the Color field to the matrix and expanded the next level to make the difference between the table and matrix clearer.

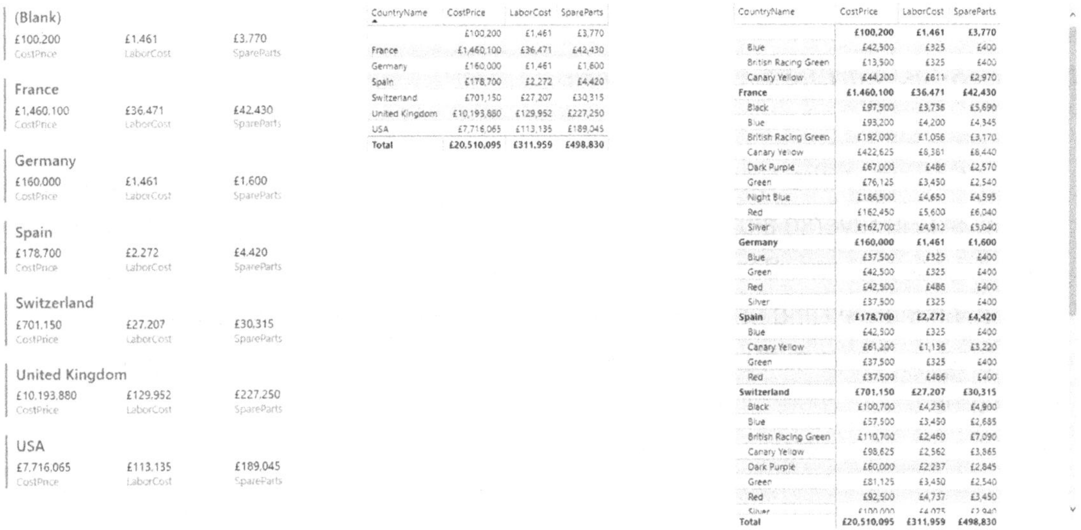

Figure 15-37. *Switching visuals using the same data and formatting*

The following are the main things to note here:

- The visual remains the same size when you switch types. Consequently, you will probably have to resize it.

- All formatting that can be retained is retained. This can be seen in the titles and background of all three visuals in Figure 15-37.

Conclusion

This chapter extended the knowledge that you acquired in the previous chapter to show you how to create matrices. You then learned how to drill down into any matrix to display a hierarchy of information—or only a sublevel in the data hierarchy.

You then learned how to create card visuals and Power BI Desktop's unique and effective multirow cards.

Now that you have mastered the basics of creating visuals, it is time to move on to the next level of dashboard creation. In the next two chapters, you will discover how to create and enhance charts. This will allow you to give freer rein to your imagination and help you let your data speak for itself.

CHAPTER 16

Charts in Power BI Desktop

It is one thing to have a game-changing insight that can fundamentally alter the way your business works. It is quite another to be able to convince your colleagues of your vision. So what better way to show them—intuitively and instantaneously—that you are right than with a chart that irrefutably makes your point?

Power BI Desktop is predicated on the concept that a picture is worth many thousands of words. Its charting tools let you create clear and convincing visuals that tell your audience far more than a profusion of figures ever could. This chapter, therefore, will show you how simple it can be not just to make your data explain your analysis but to make it seem to leap off the screen. You will see over the next few pages how a powerful chart can persuade your peers and bosses that your ideas and insights are the ones to follow.

A little more prosaically, Power BI Desktop lets you make a suitable dataset into

- Pie charts
- Bar charts
- Column charts
- Line charts
- Area charts
- Scatter charts
- Bubble charts
- Funnel charts
- Waterfall charts
- Donut charts
- Ribbon charts

577

© Adam Aspin 2020
A. Aspin, *Pro Power BI Desktop*, https://doi.org/10.1007/978-1-4842-5763-0_16

In this chapter, we get up and running by looking at all these types of charts and then extend some of them to create stacked bar, stacked column, and stacked area charts, 100% stacked bar and stacked column charts, as well as dual-axis charts. Once you have decided upon the most appropriate chart type, you can then enhance your visualization with a title, data labels, and legends, where they are appropriate. In the next chapter, you will learn how to format all of these elements to give your charts the wow factor that they deserve.

A First Chart

It is generally easier to appreciate the simplicity and power of Power BI Desktop by doing rather than talking. So I suggest leaping straight into creating a first chart. In this section, we will look only at "starter" charts that all share a common thread—they are based on a single column of data values and a single column of descriptive elements. The data will include

- A list of clients

- Car sales for a given year

So, let's get charting! In this chapter, you will use the `C:\PowerBiDesktopSamples\CarSalesDataForReports.pbix` Power BI Desktop file that is available on the Apress website for download.

Creating a First Chart

Any Power BI Desktop chart begins as a dataset. So, let me introduce you to the world of charts by showing you how to make a bar chart in a few clicks; the following explains how to begin:

1. Open the file `C:\PowerBiDesktopSamples\CarSalesDataForReports.pbix` from the downloadable samples.

2. Click the Stacked Bar Chart icon at the top left of the Visualizations pane. This icon is illustrated in Figure 16-1. An empty bar chart visual will appear on the dashboard canvas.

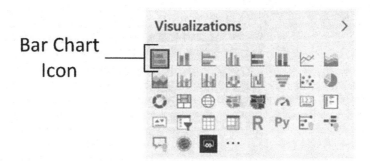

Figure 16-1. *The Bar Chart icon in the Visualizations pane*

3. Leave the empty bar chart visual selected and expand the Clients table in the Fields list.

4. Select the box to the left of the ClientName field.

5. Leaving this new bar chart visual selected, expand the InvoiceLines table in the Fields list.

6. Click the check box to the left of the SalePrice field. This will add the cumulative sales per client to the chart.

7. Resize the chart (I suggest widening it and increasing the height) until the axis labels are clearly visible, as shown in Figure 16-2.

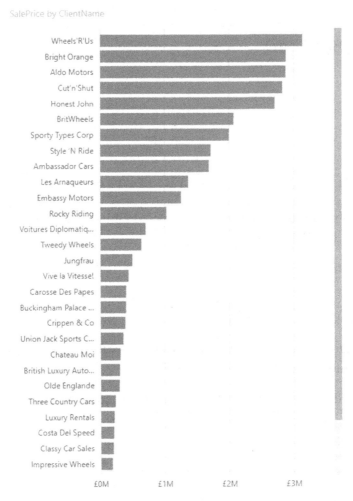

Figure 16-2. *A bar chart after resizing*

And that is all that there is to creating a simple starter chart. This process might only take a few seconds, and once it is complete, it is ready to be shown to your audience or be remodeled to suit your requirements.

Nonetheless, a few comments are necessary to clarify the basics of chart creation in Power BI Desktop:

- When creating the chart, you can use any of the techniques described in Chapters 14 and 15 to add fields to visuals. You can drag fields into the field well of the Visualizations pane or into the visual directly if you prefer.

- When using only a single dataset, you can choose either clustered or stacked as the chart type for a bar or column chart; the result is the same in either case. As you will see as we progress, this will not be the case when the chart is based on multiple data fields.

- Power BI Desktop will add a title at the top left of the chart explaining what data the chart is based on. You can see an example of this in Figure 16-2.

- Creating a chart is very much a first step. You can do so much more to enhance a chart and accentuate the insights that it can bring. All of this follows further on in this chapter and in the next one.

Converting a Table into a Chart

Another way to create a chart is to create a table first (by dragging the data fields into the Power BI desktop canvas without first clicking a chart icon, for instance). Then select the table and click a chart icon in the Visualizations pane to convert the table into a chart.

However, if you create a table first, then transform a table into a chart (by selecting a table and clicking the Stacked Bar Chart icon), the field well of the Visualizations pane changes to reflect the options available when creating or modifying a chart. If you select the chart that you just created, you will see that the ClientName field has been placed in the Axis box, and the SalePrice field has been placed in the Value box. Neither of these boxes exists if the visual is a table. This can be seen in Figure 16-3.

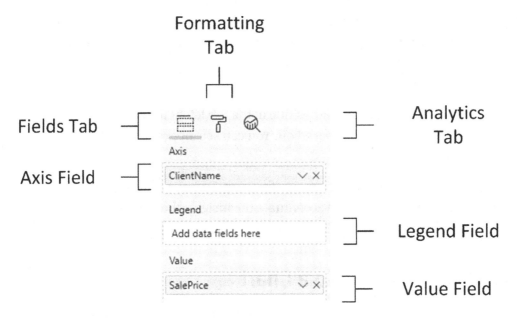

Figure 16-3. *The Fields list for a bar chart*

Deleting a Chart

Deleting a chart is as simple as deleting a table, a matrix, or a card. All that you have to do is

1. Click inside the chart.

2. Press the Delete key.

If you remove all the fields from the Layout section of the field well of the Visualizations pane (with the chart selected), then you will also delete the chart.

Basic Chart Modification

So you have an initial chart. Suppose, however, that you want to change the fields on which the chart is based. Well, all you have to do to change both the axis elements (the client names and the values represented) is

1. Click the bar chart that you created previously. Avoid clicking any of the bars in the chart for the moment.

2. In the field well of the Visualizations pane, click the small cross at the right of SalePrice in the Values well (or click the popup menu for SalePrice, and select Remove Field). The bars will disappear from the chart.

3. Drag the field LaborCost from the Stock table in the Fields list into the Values well.

4. In the field well of the Visualizations pane, click the popup menu for ClientName in the Axis box, and select Remove Field. The client names will disappear from the chart and a single bar will appear.

5. In the Fields list, expand the Colors table and drag the Color field from the Colors table into the Axis box. The list of colors will replace the list of clients on the axis, and a series of bars will replace the single bar. Look at Figure 16-4 to see the difference.

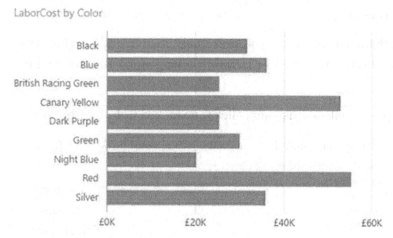

Figure 16-4. A simple bar chart with the corresponding Layout section

That is it. You have changed the chart completely without rebuilding it. Power BI Desktop has updated the data in the chart and the chart title to reflect your changes.

Basic Chart Types

When dealing with a single set of values, you will probably be using the following six core chart types to represent data:

- Bar chart
- Column chart

- Line chart

- Pie chart

- Donut chart

- Funnel chart

Let's see how we can try out these types of chart using the current dataset—the colors and labor cost that you applied previously.

Column Charts

A column chart is, to all intents and purposes, a bar chart where the bars are vertical rather than horizontal. So, do the following to switch your bar chart to a column chart:

1. Click the bar chart that you previously created and modified (the one shown in Figure 16-4). Avoid clicking any of the bars in the chart.

2. In the Visualizations pane, click the Stacked Column Chart icon.

3. Resize the chart as required. Your chart should look like Figure 16-5.

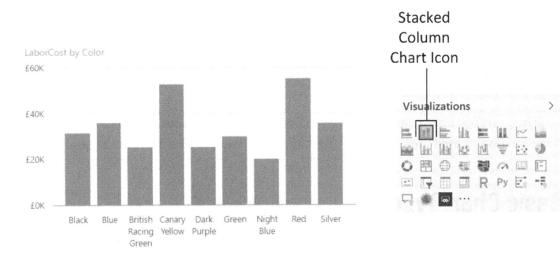

Figure 16-5. *An elementary column chart*

Line Charts

A line chart displays the data as a set of points joined by a line. Do the following to switch your column chart to a line chart:

1. Click the column chart that you created previously. Avoid clicking any of the columns in the chart for the moment.

2. In the Visualizations pane, click the Line Chart icon. Your chart should look like Figure 16-6.

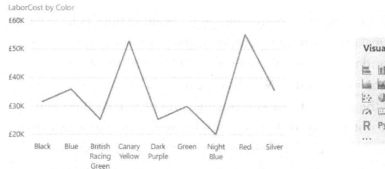
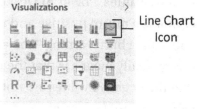

Figure 16-6. *A simple line chart*

Pie Charts

Pie charts can be superb at displaying a limited set of data for a single series, like we have in this example. To switch the visual to a pie chart:

1. Click the line chart that you created previously. Avoid clicking any of the lines in the chart for the moment.

2. In the Visualizations pane, click the Pie Chart icon. The line chart will become a pie chart.

3. Resize the pie chart, if necessary, to display the text for all the colors correctly. Your chart should look like Figure 16-7. You will notice that the Layout section has changed slightly for a pie chart, and the Axis box has been replaced by a Legend box.

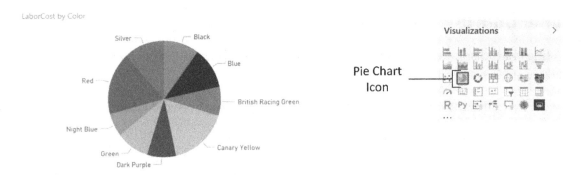

Figure 16-7. *A basic pie chart*

A pie chart is distorted if it includes negative values at the same time as it contains positive values. Power BI Desktop will not display the negative values. If your dataset contains a mix of positive and negative data, then Power BI Desktop displays an alert above the chart warning "Too many values. Not showing all data." What this nearly always really means is that the pie chart contains positive *and* negative values and that the negative values are not displayed. This also applies to donut charts. Negative values can make funnel charts appear a little peculiar, too. If you want to see this for yourself, try creating a table of makes and gross margin. You will see that the table contains seven rows, but the corresponding pie or donut chart only displays six sections. This is because the make with a negative gross margin (TVR) does not appear in the pie chart.

In practice, you may prefer not to use pie or donut charts when your data contains negative values, or you may want to separate out the positive and negative values into two datasets and display two charts, using filters (this is explained in Chapter 20).

Note   Juggling chart size and font size to fit in all the elements and axis and/or legend labels can be tricky. One useful trick is to prepare "abbreviated" data fields in the source data, as has been done in the case of the QuarterAbbr field in the Date table that contains Q1, Q2, and so on, rather than Quarter 1, Quarter 2, and so on, to save space in the chart.

Essential Chart Adjustments

I hope you will agree that creating a chart in Power BI Desktop is extremely simple. Yet the process of producing a telling visualization does not stop when you take a dataset and display it as a chart. At the very least, you want to make the following tweaks to your new chart:

- Resize the chart

- Reposition the chart

- Sort the elements in the chart

- Alter the size of the fonts in the chart

None of these tasks is at all difficult. Indeed, it can take only a few seconds to transform your initial chart into a compelling visual argument—when you know the techniques to apply.

Resizing Charts

A chart is like any other visual on the Power BI Desktop dashboard canvas and can be resized to suit your requirements. The following explains how to resize a chart:

1. Click inside the chart (but not on any of the bars, columns, lines, or pie segments).

2. Place the mouse pointer over any of the eight handles that appear at the corners and in the middle of the edges of the chart that you wish to adjust. The pointer becomes a two-headed arrow.

3. Drag the mouse pointer to resize the chart.

Note   Remember that the lateral handles let you resize the chart only horizontally or vertically and that the corner handles allow you to resize both horizontally and vertically.

Resizing a chart can have a dramatic effect on the text that appears on an axis. Power BI Desktop always tries to keep the space available for the text on an axis proportionate to the size of the whole chart.

For column, line, and bar charts, this can mean that the text can be truncated, with an ellipsis (three dots) indicating that not all the text is visible. With column and line charts, the text may even be angled at 45 degrees or possibly swiveled to appear vertically.

If you reduce the height (for a bar chart) or the width (for a column or a line chart) below a certain threshold, Power BI Desktop will stop trying to show all the elements on the non-numeric axis. Instead, it only shows a few elements and adds a scroll bar to allow you to scroll through the remaining data. What is more, if axis labels cannot be displayed in their entirety, they will be truncated (and ellipses added). You can see an example of these outcomes for a bar chart in Figure 16-8.

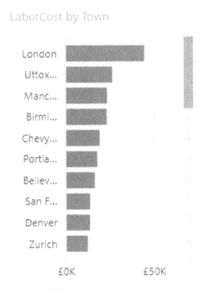

Figure 16-8. *A chart with a scroll bar visible*

All that this means is you might have to tweak the size and height-to-width ratio of your chart until you get the best result. If you are in a hurry to get this right, I advise using the handle in the bottom-right corner to resize a chart, as dragging this up, down, left, and right will quickly show you the available display options.

Repositioning Charts

You can move a chart anywhere inside the Power BI Desktop report, as follows:

1. Place the mouse pointer over the border of the chart.

2. Drag the mouse pointer.

Sorting Chart Elements

Sometimes you can really make a point about data by changing the order in which you have it appear in a chart. Up until this point, you have probably noticed that when you create a chart, the elements on the axis (and this is true for a bar chart, column chart, line chart, or pie chart) are in alphabetical order by default. If you want to confirm this, then just look at Figures 16-5 to 16-8.

Suppose now, for instance, you want to show the way that the gross margin is affected by the color of the vehicle. In this case, you want to sort the data in a chart from highest to lowest so that you can see the way in which the figures fall, or rise, in a clear order. The following steps explain how to do this:

1. Select the bar chart type for Color and LaborCost, as described earlier (and shown in Figure 16-4).

2. Place the mouse pointer over the chart. You will see that the chart border and options button (the ellipses at the top right) appear.

3. Click the ellipses to display the chart menu and then click the chevron to the right of Sort by and select the appropriate field to order the data (LaborCost in this example).

4. Click Sort descending. This is shown in Figure 16-9, where the columns are sorted in reverse alphabetical order.

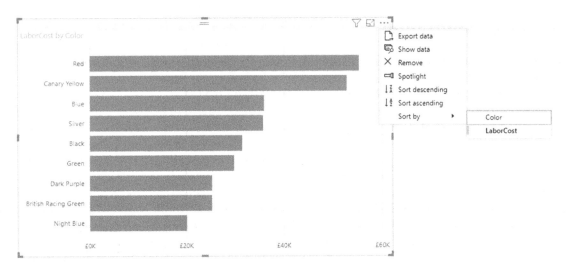

Figure 16-9. *Using the popup menu in a chart to sort data*

As you can see, the initial sort is in descending order when you sort by a numeric value. Let's suppose now that you want to see the sales by color in *ascending* order. All you have to do is repeat the operation that you just carried out and the chart will be resorted. Only this time, it is sorted in ascending order. Equally, the *first* time that you sort on a *text* element, the chart is sorted in *ascending* order, and the *second* time it is sorted in *descending* order.

I should add just a short remark about sorting pie charts. When you sort a pie chart by a numeric field, the pie chart is sorted clockwise, starting at the top of the chart. So if you are sorting colors by LaborCost in descending order, the top selling color is at the top of the pie chart (at 12 o'clock), with the second bestselling color to its immediate right (e.g., 2 o'clock), and so on. An example of this is shown in Figure 16-10.

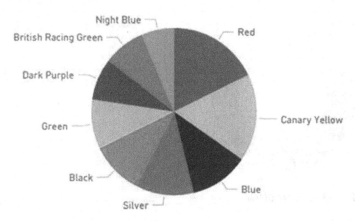

Figure 16-10.   Sorting data in a pie chart

Donut Charts

Donut charts are essentially a variation of a pie chart. However, they can make a welcome presentational change from their overexposed older sibling. Fortunately, they are equally easy to create. In this example, you are going to see how to visualize the parts cost incurred for each make of vehicle purchased. To vary the approach, in this example you will first create a table and then convert it to a donut chart:

1. Continue using (or open) the file C:\PowerBiDesktopSamples\ CarSalesDataForReports.pbix.

2. Ensure that no current visual is selected.

3. Expand the Stock table in the Fields list.

4. Select the box to the left of the Make field. A table containing the list of makes purchased will appear in the dashboard canvas.

5. Leave this new table selected and click the check box to the left of the SpareParts field. This will add the cumulative cost of spare parts per make to the table.

6. Click the Donut Chart icon in the Visualizations pane. This will convert the table to a donut chart.

7. Resize the chart if necessary to show the names of the makes clearly, as shown in Figure 16-11.

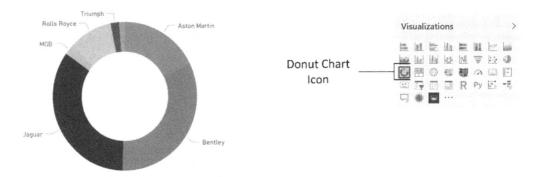

Figure 16-11. *A donut chart*

Funnel Charts

Funnel charts are excellent when it comes to comparing the relative values of a single series of figures. As you are now well versed in the art of creating charts with Power BI Desktop, designing a funnel chart that displays parts cost per color should not be a problem for you.

1. Carry on using the file C:\PowerBiDesktopSamples\
    CarSalesDataForReports.pbix.

2. Expand the Colors table in the Fields list.

3. Drag the Color field into an empty part of the dashboard canvas.
    A table containing the list of vehicle colors will appear.

4. Leave this new table selected and click the check box to the left of
    the SpareParts field in the Stock table. This will add the cumulative
    cost of parts per make to the table.

5. Click the Funnel Chart icon in the Visualizations pane. This will
    convert the table to a funnel chart. The funnel chart will display
    the color with the highest value for the cost of spare parts at the
    top of the visual.

6. Resize the chart if necessary to show the names of the colors
    clearly as well as make the relative weights for all the colors more
    clearly comprehensible, as shown in Figure 16-12.

Figure 16-12. *A funnel chart*

Multiple Data Values in Charts

So far in this chapter, we have seen simple charts that display a single value. Life is, unfortunately, rarely that simple, and so it is time to move on to slightly more complex, but possibly more realistic, scenarios where you need to compare and contrast multiple data elements.

For this set of examples, I will presume that we need to take an in-depth look at the following indirect cost elements of our car sales to date:

- Parts

- Labor

Consequently, to begin with a fairly simple comparison of these indirect costs, let's start with a clustered column chart:

1. Open (or continue to use) the file `C:\PowerBiDesktopSamples\` `CarSalesDataForReports.pbix` from the downloadable samples.

2. Starting with a clean Power BI Desktop report, create a table that displays the following fields:

   a. ClientName (from the Clients table)

   b. SpareParts (from the Stock table)

   c. LaborCost (from the Stock table)

3. Leaving the table selected, click the Clustered Column icon in the Visualizations pane.

4. Resize the chart to make it clear and comprehensible, as shown in Figure 16-13. (I have included the fields from the Visualizations pane so that you can see this, too.)

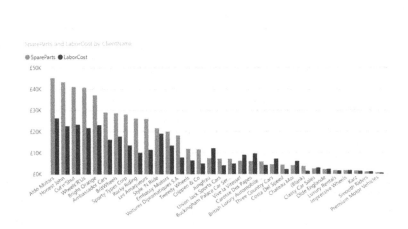

Figure 16-13. *Multiple data values in charts—a clustered column chart with the Layout section shown*

You will notice that a chart with multiple datasets has a legend by default and that the automatic chart title now says SpareParts and LaborCost by ClientName. Also you will note that the chart is automatically sorted with the highest values (for the first data series added) on the left.

The same dataset can be used as a basis for other charts that can effectively display multiple data values:

- Stacked charts

- Clustered column and stacked column

- Line charts

- Area charts

- Stacked area charts

Since column charts are essentially bar charts pivoted 90 degrees, I will not show examples. However, in Figures 16-14, 16-15, 16-16, and 16-17, you will see examples of a stacked column chart, a line chart, an area chart, and a stacked area chart, respectively—all created from the same data. You also see that when creating these types of visualization, the Layout section of the field well of the Visualizations pane remains the same for all of these charts.

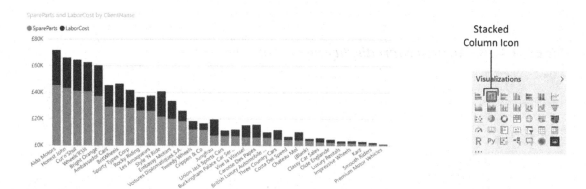

Figure 16-14. *A simple stacked column chart*

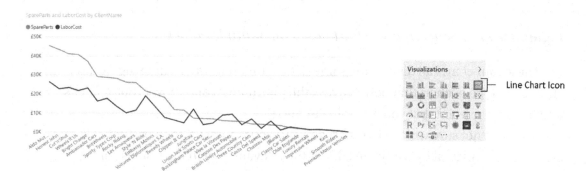

Figure 16-15. *A line chart that displays multiple values*

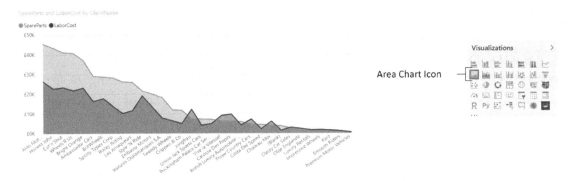

Figure 16-16. *An area chart displaying multiple values*

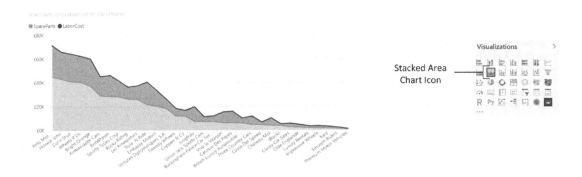

Figure 16-17. *A stacked area chart based on multiple values*

These four charts all display the same data in different ways. Knowing this, you can choose the type of chart that best conveys the information and draws your reader's attention to the point that you are trying to make.

If you are not sure which chart best conveys your message, then try them all, one after another. All it takes is a single click of the relevant icon in the visuals gallery to convert a chart to another chart type. Indeed, sometimes the differences can be extremely subtle. For instance, the essential difference between the area chart and the stacked area chart is the X (vertical) axis. In the case of Figure 16-17, this is a cumulative value. Figure 16-16, in contrast, shows two values directly compared one to the other with the higher value placed behind the lower value.

Note   Any of these chart types can be used to display a single data series if you want to. It all depends on the effect and the clarity of the insights that you are projecting using the chart.

100% Stacked Column and Bar Charts

One way to compare data from multiple datasets is to present each individual data series as a percentage of the total. Power BI Desktop includes two chart types that can do this "out of the box." They are the 100% stacked column and 100% stacked bar charts.

Since you now know how to create charts that use multiple series of data, I will not explain how to produce these two chart types in detail; all you have to do is select the correct chart icon from the Visualizations pane. So instead, I suggest that you look at Figures 16-18 and 16-19, which show an example of each of these charts using the same data that you used to create the clustered column chart shown in Figure 16-14.

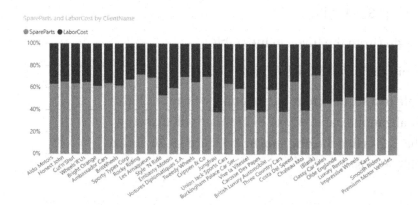

100 %
Stacked
Column
Chart Icon

Figure 16-18. *A 100% stacked column chart*

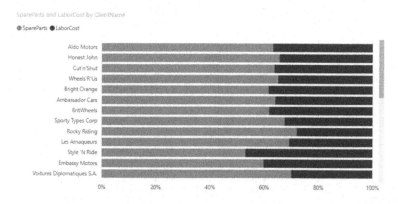

100 %
Stacked Bar
Chart Icon

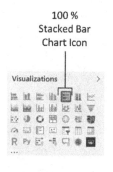

Figure 16-19. *A 100% stacked bar chart*

Scatter Charts

A scatter chart is a plot of data values against two numeric axes, and so by definition, you need two sets of numeric data to create a scatter chart. To appreciate the use of these charts, let's imagine that you want to see the sales and margin for all the makes and models of car you sold overall. Hopefully, this allows you to see where you really made money selling cars. The following explains how to do it:

1. Using the file `C:\PowerBiDesktopSamples\CarSalesDataForReports.pbix`, delete any existing visualizations.

2. Create a table with the following fields in this order:

    a. Vehicle (from the Stock table)

    b. RatioNetMargin (from the InvoiceLines table)

    c. SalePrice (from the InvoiceLines table)

3. Convert the table to a scatter chart by clicking the Scatter Chart icon in the Visualizations pane. Power BI Desktop will display a scatter chart that looks like the one shown in Figure 16-20. Resize the chart to suit your taste.

Figure 16-20. *A scatter chart*

If you look at the Fields area of the Visualizations pane (which is also shown in Figure 16-20), you will see that Power BI Desktop has used the fields that you selected like this:

- *Vehicle*: Placed in the Details box.

- *RatioNetMargin*: Placed in the X Axis box. This is the vertical axis.

- *SalePrice*: Placed in the Y Axis box. This is the horizontal axis.

If you hover the mouse pointer over one of the points in the scatter chart, you see the data for the specific car model.

Note   By definition, a scatter chart requires numeric values for both the X and Y axes. So if you add a non-numeric value to either the X Value or Y Value boxes, then Power BI Desktop converts the data to a count aggregation.

We made this chart by adding all the required fields to the initial table first. We also made sure that we added them in the right order so the scatter chart would display correctly the first time. In the real world of interactive data visualization, things may not be quite this coherent, so it is good to know that Power BI Desktop is very forgiving. And, it lets you build a scatter chart (just like any other chart) step by step if you prefer. In practice, this means that you can start with a table containing just two of the three fields that are required at a minimum for a scatter chart, convert the table to a scatter chart, and then add the remaining data field. Power BI Desktop always attributes numeric or time fields to the X and Y axes (in the order in which they appear in the Fields box) and places the first descriptive field into the Details box.

Once a scatter chart has been created, you can swap the fields around and replace existing fields with other fields from the tables in the data to your heart's content.

Bubble Charts

A variant of the scatter chart is the bubble chart. This is one of my favorite chart types, though of course you cannot overuse it without losing some of its power. Essentially, a bubble chart is a scatter chart with a third piece of data included. So whereas a scatter chart shows you two pieces of data (one on the X axis, one on the Y axis), a bubble chart lets you add a third piece of information, which becomes the *size* of the point. Consequently, each point becomes a bubble.

The best way to appreciate a bubble chart is to create one. So here we assume that you want to look at the following for all makes of car sold in a single chart:

- The total sales

- The net margin ratio

- The gross margin

This explains how a bubble chart can do this for you:

1. Using the file `C:\PowerBiDesktopSamples\`
   `CarSalesDataForReports.pbix`, delete any existing visualizations.

2. Create a table with the following fields from the SalesData table, in this order:

   a. Make (from the Stock table)

   b. SalePrice (from the InvoiceLines table)

   c. RatioNetMargin (from the InvoiceLines table)

   d. Gross Margin (from the InvoiceLines table)

3. Convert the table to a scatter chart by clicking the Scatter Chart icon. Yes, a bubble chart is a scatter chart, with a fresh tweak added.

4. Drag the ClientSize field from the Clients table into the Legend well of the Visualizations pane. Power BI Desktop will display a bubble chart that looks like that shown in Figure 16-21.

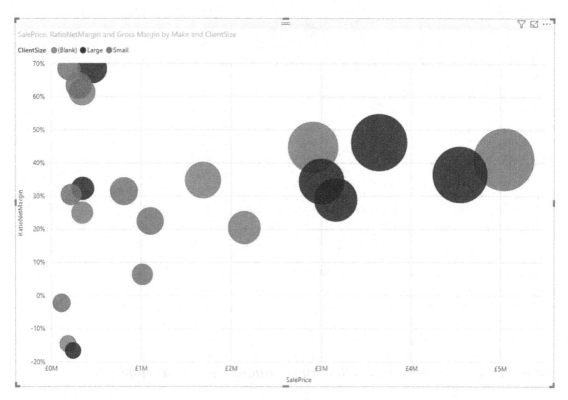

Figure 16-21. *An initial bubble chart*

5.   Resize the chart if you need to.

If you look at the field well in the Visualizations pane (shown in Figure 16-22), you will see that Power BI Desktop has used the fields that you selected like this.

Figure 16-22. *The field well of the Visualizations pane for a bubble chart*

- *Make*: Placed in the Details box. This defines the core bubbles.

- *ClientSize*: Added to the Legend box. This creates bubbles for each combination of the detail element (make) and legend item (client size).

- *SalePrice*: Placed in the X Axis box. This is the vertical axis.

- *RatioNetMargin*: Placed in the Y Axis box. This is the horizontal axis. Each bubble is placed at the intersection of the values on the vertical and horizontal axes.

- *Gross Margin*: Placed in the Size box. This defines the size of the points, which have consequently become bubbles of different sizes.

Hover the mouse pointer over one of the points in the bubble chart. You will see all the data that you placed in the Fields list Layout section for each make, including the Gross Margin.

Waterfall Charts

What I want to look at now is one of the more original chart types that Power BI Desktop offers—the waterfall chart. This chart type is excellent at displaying the component parts of a final figure; in this example, it is used to show how the various makes sold make up the total sales figure:

1. Open the file `C:\PowerBiDesktopSamples\CarSalesDataForReports.pbix` and delete any existing visualizations.

2. Click the Waterfall Chart icon. You can see this in Figure 16-23. An empty waterfall chart will appear on the dashboard canvas.

3. Expand the Stock table and check the following fields:

   a. Make

   b. CostPrice

4. Resize the chart to suit your aesthetic requirements. It should look something like Figure 16-23.

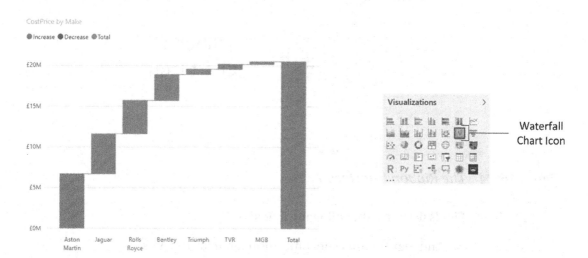

Figure 16-23. *A waterfall chart*

Waterfall charts can be extremely useful when you are analyzing the constituent elements of a whole. For instance, you could try using one to break down all the cost elements. It is worth noting that if you have any negative values in the chart, these will appear in a different color from positive values and will, inevitably, reduce the value of the total bar on the right.

Ribbon Charts

One addition to the range of chart options that Power BI Desktop has on offer is the ribbon chart. Ribbon charts virtually always use a time element as the X axis and are designed to show evolution over time. More specifically, they always place the highest value as the upper ribbon of the chart.

This is probably best understood with the help of an example. So I suggest that you try out the following:

1. Click the Ribbon Chart icon in the Visualizations pane (this is shown in Figure 16-24).

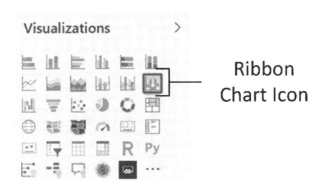

Figure 16-24. The Ribbon Chart icon

2. In the Fields list, click the following fields:

    a. MonthAndYear (in the DateDimension table) as the Axis

    b. SalePrice (in the InvoiceLines table) as the Legend

    c. Make (in the Stock table) as the Value

3. Resize the chart until it looks like the one shown in Figure 16-25.

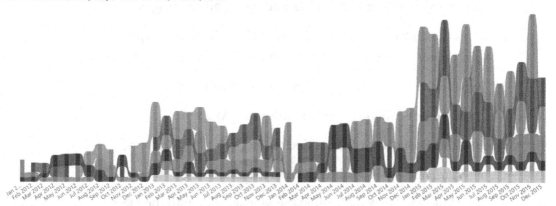

Figure 16-25. *A ribbon chart*

As you can see, the ribbon chart shows the ebb and flow of sales of different makes of vehicle over time. Indeed—and at the risk of anticipating the contents of Chapter 17—I suggest that you click one of the makes in the chart legend. This will highlight the make and show its evolution over time.

Dual-Axis Charts

To conclude our tour of chart types, let's take a look at a couple of charts that combine two of the basic chart types that you have seen previously in this chapter:

- Line and clustered column chart

- Line and stacked column chart

Let's discuss each of these in turn.

Line and Clustered Column Chart

Suppose that the CEO of Brilliant British Cars has decided to embark on an analysis of vehicle purchases. He wants to isolate any interesting correlations that could influence purchases in order to maximize profits. So, determined to satisfy his request (or possibly to humor him), you have in turn decided to take a look at indirect costs and mileage to see if there are any correlations.

1. Open the file `C:\PowerBiDesktopSamples\` `CarSalesDataForReports.pbix` and delete any existing visual.

2. Click the Line and Clustered Column Chart icon. An empty line and clustered column chart will appear on the dashboard canvas.

3. Expand the Stock table and check the following fields:

   a. Make (this will be added to the Shared Axis box)

   b. LaborCost (this will be added to the Column Values box)

   c. SpareParts (this will be added to the Column Values box)

4. Also from the Stock table, drag the Mileage field into the Line Values box in the field well of the Visualizations pane.

5. Resize the chart to suit your aesthetic requirements. It should look something like Figure 16-26.

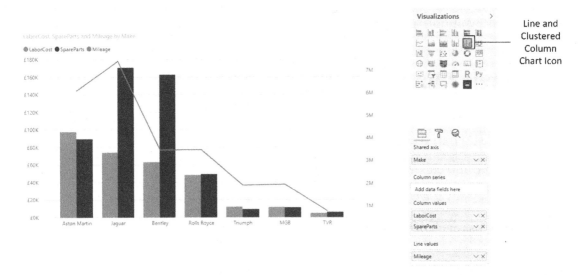

Figure 16-26. *A line and clustered column chart*

As you can see, this chart combines a clustered column chart that displays the labor and parts costs using the left axis with a line chart that displays the mileage using the right axis. Both of these charts share the X (or horizontal) axis.

Moreover, this kind of analysis makes it immediately clear that there is one make where low mileage does not necessarily mean lower repair costs. So the boss should be happy that you have isolated this unexpected correlation.

Line and Stacked Column Chart

One of the key advantages of dual-axis charts is that the two X axes can have vastly different scales. So, for instance, when you want to see how the parts and labor cost relate to the purchase cost (which is orders of magnitude higher than the other two costs), a line and stacked column chart can be really useful to get a clearer view of the data.

1. Open the file `C:\PowerBiDesktopSamples\` `CarSalesDataForReports.pbix` and delete any existing visualizations.

2. Expand the Stock table and check the following fields to display a table on the dashboard canvas:

    a. Make

    b. LaborCost

    c. SpareParts

3. Click the Line and Stacked Column Chart icon. The table will be converted to a line and stacked column chart.

4. Also from the Stock table, drag the CostPrice field into the field well of the Visualizations pane. Place it in the Line Values box.

5. Resize the chart to suit your aesthetic requirements. It should look something like Figure 16-27.

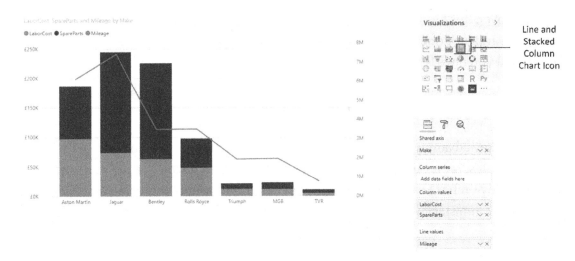

Figure 16-27. *A line and stacked column chart*

This way you can compare values where the use of a single chart type would lead to one value (the cost price in this example) dwarfing the other values to the point of making them unreadable.

Data Details

To conclude our tour of chart types, I just want to make a few comments:

- You can always see exactly what the figures behind a bar, column, line, point, or pie segment are just by hovering the mouse pointer over the bar (or column, or line, or pie segment). This works whether the chart is its normal size or has been popped out to cover the Power BI Desktop report area.

- However much work you have done to a chart, you can always switch it back to a table if you want. Simply select the chart, and select the required table type from the Table button in the Design ribbon. If you do this, you see that the table attempts to mimic the design tweaks that you applied to the chart, keeping the font sizes the same as in the chart and the size of the table identical to that of the chart. Should you subsequently switch back to the chart, then you should find virtually all of the design choices that you applied are still present—unless, of course, you made any changes to the table before switching back to the chart visualization.

- You can always juxtapose the raw data that powers a chart under the chart itself, as you could with text-based visuals. Simply click the ellipses at the top right of a chart and select Show Data to display the source data. You can see an example of this in Figure 16-28 (where you can also see how a data point is displayed in line, area, and stacked area charts).

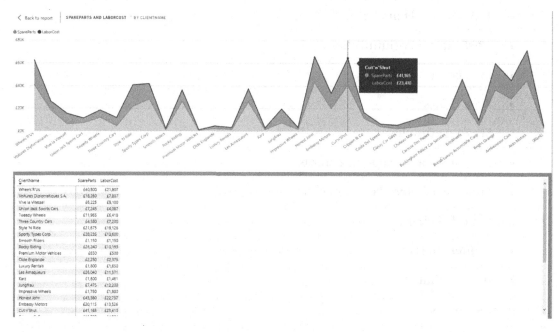

Figure 16-28. *Displaying pop-out data for a chart*

To switch back to the dashboard canvas, click Back to report at the top left of the chart.

Drilling into and Expanding Chart Data Hierarchies

An extremely useful aspect of Power BI Desktop charts is that you can use them as an interactive presentation tool. One of the more effective ways to both discover what your data reveals and deliver the message to your public is to drill into, or expand, layers of data. All the standard Power BI chart types let you do just this.

Drill down works with all the standard chart types. This means that you can drill into

- Stacked bar charts
- Stacked column charts
- Clustered bar charts
- Clustered column charts
- 100% stacked bar charts
- 100% stacked column charts
- Line charts
- Area charts
- Stacked area charts
- Line and stacked column charts
- Line and clustered column charts
- Waterfall charts
- Scatter charts
- Bubble charts
- Pie charts
- Funnel charts
- Donut charts
- Tree map charts

The key point to remember when you are creating drill-down charts is that you *must* place the fields that you wish to drill into in the Axis area (the Shared Axis area for double-axis charts) of the field well, *not* in the Legend area (and not in the Details area for a pie chart).

Drill Down

Fortunately, you use the same techniques that you saw in the previous chapter when navigating data hierarchies to drill down into charts. So extending this approach from tables and matrices to charts is really easy. Here, then, is a simple example of how you can analyze the hierarchy of makes, models, and colors of vehicles sold in a drill-down chart:

1. Click the Clustered Column Chart icon in the Visualizations pane. An empty chart visual will be created on the dashboard canvas.

2. Drag the following fields into the Axis area of the field well in this order:

   a. Make (from the Stock table)

   b. Model (from the Stock table)

   c. Color (from the Colors table)

3. Drag the SalePrice (from the InvoiceLines table) and the Mileage (from the Stock table) fields into the chart. The chart will look like the one in Figure 16-29. As you can see, it only displays the top-level element from the Axis field well—the make of vehicle.

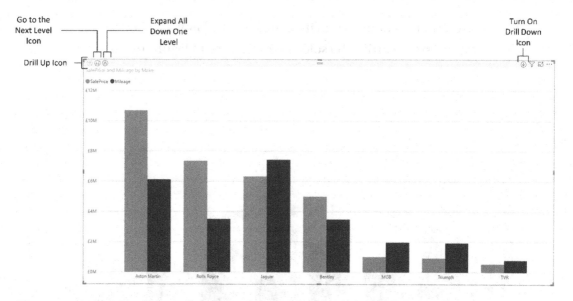

Figure 16-29. *A column chart displaying the top level of data in a hierarchy*

4. Click the Turn on Drill Down icon at the top right of the chart. This icon will become a white arrow on a dark background.

5. Click either of the columns for Aston Martin. The chart will now display the models of Aston Martin sold, as you can see in Figure 16-30.

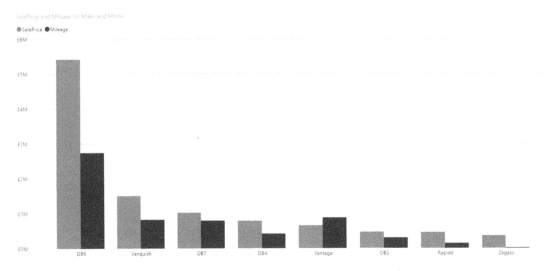

Figure 16-30. *A column chart displaying the second level of data in a hierarchy*

6.   Click one of the columns for DB9. The chart will now display the colors of Aston Martin DB9 sold, as you can see in Figure 16-31.

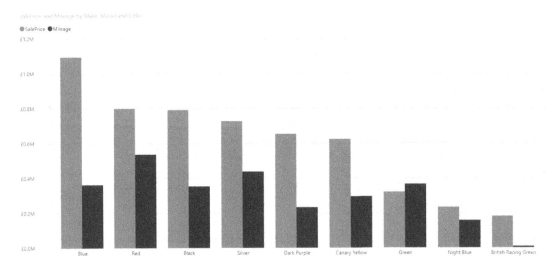

Figure 16-31. *A column chart displaying the lowest level of data in a hierarchy*

Once you have drilled down to a lower level in a chart, you can always return to the previous level (and from there continue drilling up until you reach the top level) by clicking the Drill Up icon at the top left of the chart.

Expand All Down One Level in the Hierarchy

The Expand all down one level in the hierarchy icon produces a different result to drilling down by clicking a bar in the chart. If you click the Expand all down one level in the hierarchy icon, you see *all* the elements at the next level down, not just the elements in the hierarchy that are a subgroup. To see this, try out the following steps:

1. Re-create the chart from the previous section (follow steps 1 through 3) until you can once again see the chart from Figure 16-29.

2. Click the Expand all down one level in the hierarchy icon.

3. Resize the chart to enhance its visibility. You will see a chart that looks like the one shown in Figure 16-32.

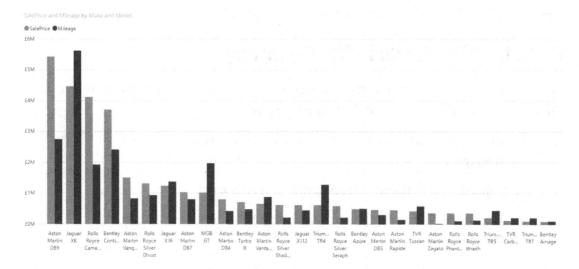

Figure 16-32. *Expanding a chart down one level*

4. Click the Expand all down one level in the hierarchy icon a second time.

5. Resize the chart if necessary. This time the chart looks like the one shown in Figure 16-33.

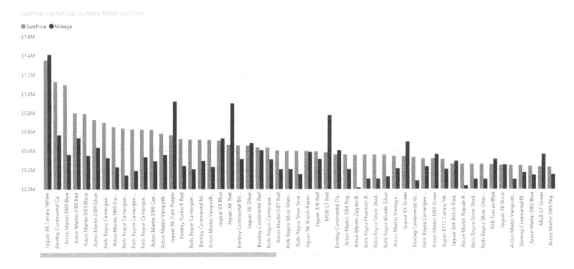

Figure 16-33. *Expanding a chart down one more level*

Go to the Next Level in the Hierarchy

The final hierarchy navigation technique that you can apply is to Go to the next level in the hierarchy. To test this, try out the following steps:

1. Re-create the chart from the last but one section (follow steps 1 through 3).

2. Click the Go to the next level in the hierarchy icon.

3. Resize the chart to enhance its visibility. You should see a chart like the one shown in Figure 16-34.

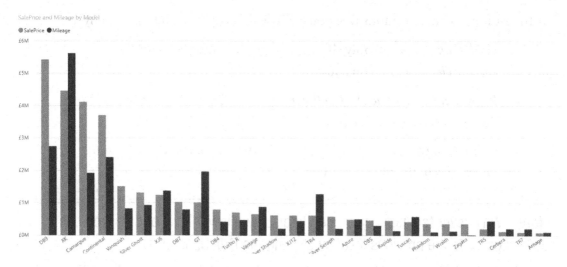

Figure 16-34. *Going to the next level in a chart*

4.   Click the Go to the next level in the hierarchy icon one more time. You will see a chart that looks like the one shown in Figure 16-35.

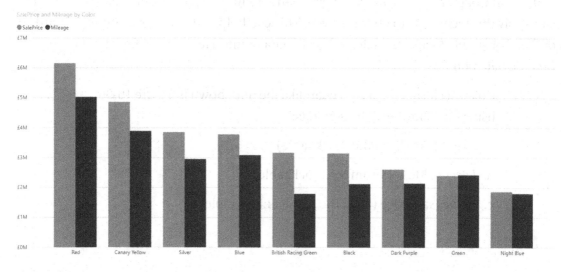

Figure 16-35. *Going to a deeper level in a chart*

To resume, the three options that you can use to navigate a chart hierarchy are

- *Drill down*: This will only show the data at the next level for the *specific element* that you clicked.

- *Expand all down one level in the hierarchy*: This will show the data at the next level for *all* elements.

- *Go to the next level in the hierarchy*: This will display data *only for the lower level* in the data hierarchy.

Note   Whichever technique you used to display a lower level of data, you can always go up to the previous level by clicking the Drill Up icon.

Including and Excluding Data Points

You saw in Chapter 15 that you can include and exclude records from a matrix. Well, you can apply this technique to charts as well. This can help you to remove clutter, discard outliers, or simply focus on a selected set of data points. Here's an example of how to exclude data points:

1. Create a clustered column chart like the one shown in Figure 16-36 using the following data elements:

    a. *Axis*: Make (from the Stock table)

    b. *Legend*: Model (from the Stock table)

    c. *Value*: SalePrice (from the InvoiceLines table)

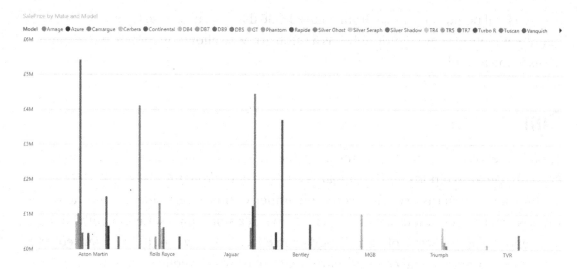

Figure 16-36. *A column chart before excluding data points*

2. Ctrl-click to select the four tallest columns.

3. Right-click any of the selected columns and choose Include
    from the popup menu. The chart will look like the one shown in
    Figure 16-37.

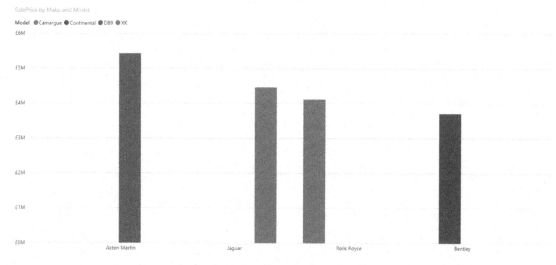

Figure 16-37. *A column chart after excluding data points*

The remaining data is exactly the same as before, but removing the very tall columns
allows you to see more clearly any differences among the remaining data elements.

As a final point, you can see from Figure 16-36 that a chart whose legend contains too many elements to view comfortably has a scroll arrow to allow you to view the remaining items in the legend.

Conclusion

This chapter took you on a tour of the available chart types that you can use in your Power BI Desktop reports and dashboards. These extend from the classic pie, line, column, and bar charts to the less common funnel, donut, area, scatter, bubble, and waterfall charts. You saw that there are charts to suit a single data series and others that can handle multiple series of data. To add extra effect, you saw how to create mixed chart types, create 100% bar and column charts, and tweak axis elements.

However, these charts can be presented at a higher level if you decide to add some compelling formatting. This is what you will learn to do in the next chapter.

CHAPTER 17

Formatting Charts in Power BI Desktop

Now that you have mastered basic charts, it is time to move on to the next step and learn how to tweak your charts to the greatest effect. This chapter is devoted to the various techniques available in Power BI Desktop to give your charts real clarity and power. Some of these enhancements apply to all chart types, whereas others are specific to a single type of chart—or even one or two chart types.

Sometimes you change the configuration of a chart—and consequently enhance it—by altering the mapping of the data to the chart elements. However, on most occasions, you enhance a chart by modifying the various formatting options that are displayed when you select a chart and then clicking the paint roller icon (the Format icon) in the Visualizations pane. I refer to this as the "format section" for ease of reference from now on.

As well as looking at formatting charts in this chapter, we will also look at a really interesting aspect of Power BI Desktop. This will involve a tour of the built-in analytics functions that are available. These can help you to isolate and highlight key trends and information in the charts that you create.

In this chapter you will use the `C:\PowerBiDesktopSamples\` `CarSalesDataForReports.pbix` Power BI Desktop file (that is available on the Apress website for download) as the basis for any charts that you will create.

Multiple Chart Formatting

It is worth noting from the outset that you can apply identical modifications to a set of charts on the same dashboard page by Ctrl-clicking to select multiple charts before you make any formatting changes.

However, simultaneous modification of several charts only works if *all* the selected charts are the same type.

© Adam Aspin 2020
A. Aspin, *Pro Power BI Desktop*, https://doi.org/10.1007/978-1-4842-5763-0_17

Chart Legends

If you have a chart with more than one field that provides the values on which the chart is based (or if you are creating a pie or donut chart), then you see a legend appear automatically.

You can format a legend by modifying any of the following options:

- Legend display
- Position
- Legend title

Let's look at each of these in turn.

Note   A legend can only be displayed if there is more than one field added to the Values well (except in the case of pie and donut charts).

Legend Display

Power BI Desktop may automatically display legends in some cases, but you have the final decision as to whether a legend is required. To turn a legend off, do the following:

1. Select the chart whose legend you want to hide.

2. In the Visualizations pane, click the Format icon to display the format section.

3. Drag the Legend button to the left (or click to its left) so that it changes from a full circle to an empty circle.

The legend will disappear from the selected chart.

Legend Position

The default for the legend is for it to be placed at the top left of the chart. However, you can choose where to place the legend inside the chart area. Follow these steps:

1. Select the chart whose legend you want to modify.

2. In the Visualizations pane, click the Format icon.

3. Expand the Legend section.

4. Select one of the available legend positions from the Position popup.

The available options are given in Table 17-1.

Table 17-1. *Legend Position Options*

Legend Option	Description
Top	The legend is displayed above the chart on the left.
Bottom	The legend is displayed below the chart on the left.
Left	The legend is displayed at the left of the chart at the top.
Right	The legend is displayed at the right of the chart at the top.
Top center	The legend is displayed above the chart on the left in the center.
Bottom center	The legend is displayed below the chart on the left in the center.
Left center	The legend is displayed at the left of the chart in the middle.
Right center	The legend is displayed at the right of the chart in the middle.

If one of the legend options is grayed out, it is the option that is currently active.

Legends can require a little juggling until they display their contents in a readable way. This is because the text of the legend is often truncated when it is initially displayed. If this is the case, the only real option is to modify the chart size or the legend font size.

Note   You cannot add a legend to an area, column, bar, or line chart that only has a *single* data series.

Legend Title

You can add a title to a legend if you want:

1. Create a clustered column chart using the following fields (I am assuming that you are, by now, familiar enough with the source data tables to locate these fields using the file CarSalesDataForReports.pbix):

   a. Make

   b. SalePrice

   c. Mileage

2. In the Visualizations pane, click the Format icon.

3. Expand the Legend section.

4. Ensure the Legend button is set to On.

5. Select a position from the popup list of available options.

6. Ensure the Title button is set to On.

7. Enter the legend title in the Legend Name box. I suggest adding **Sales Analysis:**.

8. Select a color for the text in the legend from the color palette.

9. Select a font family and text size.

An example of a legend with a title is shown in Figure 17-1.

Figure 17-1. A legend with a title

Chart Title

Each chart is created with a title explaining what the chart is displaying, that is, the fields on which it is based. The available options are fairly simple:

- Hide or display the title

- Modify the default text of the title

- Change the font color

- Change the background color for the title

- Alter the alignment

Let's see how to apply all of these options to the title of the chart that you created earlier:

1. Select the chart containing the title that you want to modify.

2. In the Visualizations pane, click the Format icon.

3. Expand the Title section.

4. Ensure the Title button is in the On position. Alternatively, switch to the Off position to hide the title.

5. Modify the title text in the Title text box. In this example, I set it to **Profitability**.

6. Set Word wrap to On if the title needs to flow over more than one line.

7. Click the popup menu triangle to the right of Font color and select a color from the palette of available colors.

8. Click the popup menu triangle to the right of Background color and select a color from the palette of available hues.

9. Click the middle icon to the right of Alignment. This will center the text relative to the width of the table.

10. Adjust the Text size to set a larger font size. You can see the result of these kinds of adjustments in Figure 17-2.

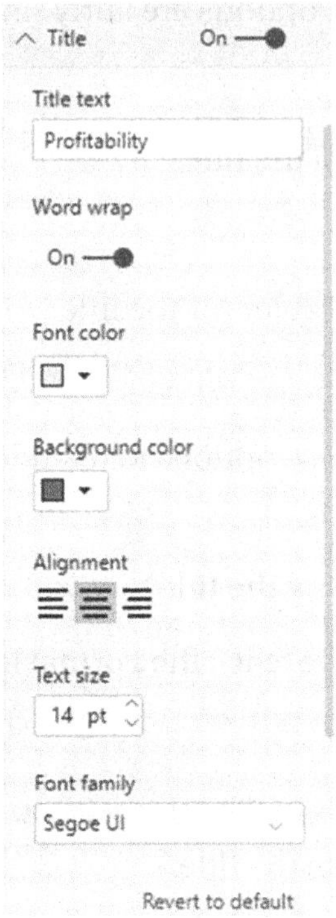

Figure 17-2. *Chart title adjustments*

You can always add further annotations to a chart using free-form text boxes. This technique is described in Chapter 23.

Chart Data Labels

As you have seen already, you can display the exact data behind a column, bar, or point in a line chart simply by hovering the mouse pointer over the data that interests you. Yet there could be times when you want to display the values behind the chart permanently on the visualization. This is where data labels come into play.

To add data labels to a chart (in this example, I continue using the chart that you created at the start of this chapter), all you have to do is this:

1.   Select the chart to which you wish to add data labels.

2.   In the Visualizations pane, click the Format icon.

3.   Expand the Data labels section.

4.   Set the Data labels button to On.

5.   Select a display unit for the figure in the card by clicking the popup list of display units. I will apply thousands as the unit in this example.

6.   Select a number of decimals to be used for the card data by clicking the up and down triangles to the right of the Precision box. You can also enter the number of decimals directly if you prefer.

7.   Select a color for the data labels from the popup palette of colors.

8.   Choose an alignment style (vertical or horizontal) from the Orientation popup list.

9.   Set the Overflow text to On if you are happy for the text to overflow. This means that a text element that does not fit inside a bar will nonetheless be displayed—even if it is truncated.

10.   Select a position for the label relative to the data (this only applies to bar and column charts).

11.   Tweak the text size and font if you wish.

12.   Set the data labels' background color to on—and select a background color from the color palette—if you want the data labels to appear against a specific colored background.

13.   Using the slider, adjust the transparency of the data label background. You can see a sample of the output from this in Figure 17-3.

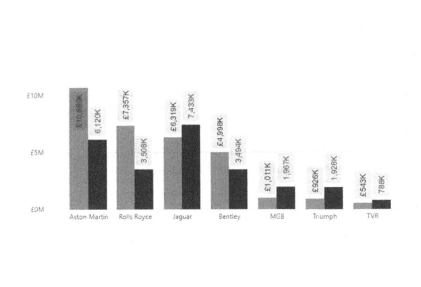

Figure 17-3. *Data labels in a column chart*

Note   When applying data labels to column, bar, and line charts, you notice that sometimes Power BI Desktop cannot physically place all the data labels exactly where the option that you have selected implies that they should appear. This is because sometimes there is simply not enough space inside a bar or column to fit the figures. In these cases, Power BI Desktop places the data outside the bar or column. On other occasions, the data cannot fit outside a line, column, or bar without being placed above the upper end of the axis. Here again, Power BI Desktop tweaks the presentation to get as close as possible to the effect that you asked for. This can mean that data labels are not displayed at all.

The various options for positioning the data labels are given in Table 17-2.

Table 17-2. *Data Label Position Options*

Data Label Position	Description
Auto	Power BI Desktop places the data label for the best effect.
Inside end	The data label is placed inside the bar at the right or inside the column at the top.
Outside end	The data label is placed outside the bar at the right or outside the column at the top.
Inside center	The data label is placed inside the center of the bar or column.
Inside base	The data label is placed inside the bar at the left or inside the column at the bottom.

There are a few final points to note on the subject of data labels:

- Scatter charts and balloon charts do not display data labels.

- You can, if you prefer, show and tweak data labels for one or all of the data series in a chart. Simply click the Customize series button to set it to On and then select the data element to format from the popup list. You can then format this selected series in the same way that you formatted the data labels for the entire chart.

Chart Background

If you need to alter the aesthetics of a chart, or should the need arise to make one chart stand out from the others in a dashboard, you can also modify the background color of the entire chart. So, continuing with the chart that you created previously, this is what you can do:

1. Select the chart whose background you wish to modify.

2. In the Visualizations pane, click the Format icon.

3. Expand the Background section.

4. Ensure that the Background On/Off switch is set to On (a full circle on the right).

5. Click the popup menu triangle to the right of Background color and select a color from the palette of available colors.

6. Move the Transparency slider to the left or right to increase or decrease the transparency (and consequently the intensity) of the background color.

Data Colors

All charts allow you to specify the color of each and every data series. Of course, the amount of effort involved will depend on the number of data series that you want to alter. The way to do it is as follows:

1. Select the chart for which you wish to modify the data colors.

2. In the Visualizations pane, click the Format icon.

3. Expand the Data colors section. The list of chart data series (or data elements for certain chart types) will be displayed.

4. Select a color for each data element or series from the popup palette of available colors.

Figure 17-4 shows modified data colors for the chart that you are currently working on.

Figure 17-4. *Specifying data colors*

Note   If a chart only contains a single data series (this is always the case for pie and donut charts and can be the case for column, line, bar, and area charts), you have the option to set a color for *each data point* of a data series.

Plot Area

For all except pie, donut, and funnel charts, you can set an image as the background for the plot area of the selected chart. Here is an example of how to do this:

1. Select the chart whose plot area you want to alter (I am still using the chart that you first saw at the beginning of this chapter).

2. In the Visualizations pane, click the Format icon.

3. Expand the Plot area section.

4. Click Add image. The standard Windows Open dialog will appear.

5. Navigate to the image file that you want to add. I will use `C:\PowerBiDesktopSamples\Images\GreenShade.png`.

6. Click Open.

7. In the Image Fit popup, select Fit. The image will expand to fill all the plot area. You can see an example of an image applied to a chart in Figure 17-5.

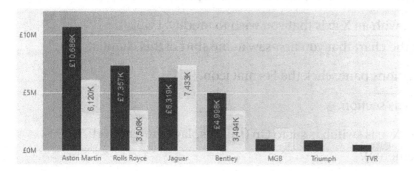

Figure 17-5. *Adding an image to a chart's plot area*

Note   To remove the image that you added, click the small cross to the right of the image file name in the Plot area section of the Format area of the Visualizations pane.

Axis Modification

Most charts—except pie, donut, and funnel charts—allow you to tweak the axis attributes. This means modifying

- The X (horizontal) axis
- The Y (vertical) axis

We will take a quick look at these two separately.

Modifying the X Axis

There are several aspects of the X axis that you can alter:

- The axis display
- The axis title and presentation
- The font attributes of the axis labels
- The category width

A simple example explains how to adjust all of these aspects of the X axis:

1. Select the chart with an X axis that you wish to modify. I will continue with the chart that you first saw at the start of this chapter.

2. In the Visualizations pane, click the Format icon.

3. Expand the X axis section.

4. Ensure that the X axis switch is set to On (this displays the axis and descriptive elements).

5. Select a font, font size, and color for the axis labels.

6. Set the Title to On (this adds the axis title). Enter **Make of Vehicle** as the Axis title.

7. Scroll down inside the Visualizations pane (if necessary) and select a font, font size, and color for the axis title.

8. Set a larger Minimum category width (this is the width of each bar in the chart).

9. Set a larger Inner padding (this is the space between groups of bars).

10. Set a Maximum size (this defines the maximum height of the
     axis elements relative to the height of the plot area). You can see
     the Format area of the Visualizations pane for these attributes in
     Figure 17-6. The final, formatted, chart is shown in Figure 17-8.

Figure 17-6. *Formatting the X axis*

Modifying the Y Axis

If your chart has a Y axis (or in the case of a dual-axis chart, two Y axes), then you can modify the following elements:

- The axis position

- The axis scale type

- The lower axis value

- The upper axis value

- The title display

- The display units

- The numeric precision

- The gridlines and gridline style

Once again, it is probably easiest to see how these various formatting options can be applied using a single example. I continue using the chart that we first saw at the start of this chapter.

1. Select the chart to which you wish to alter the axis attributes. I will continue using the chart that we have been modifying in this chapter.

2. In the Visualizations pane, click the Format icon.

3. Expand the Y axis section.

4. From the Position popup, select Right.

5. Ensure that the Scale type is set to Linear—or set to Log if you need a logarithmic scale.

6. Enter a Start value to set the starting figure for the axis. This can be negative and must be a full, unformatted figure including thousands or millions. In this example I will leave this at Auto.

7. Enter an End value to set the upper figure for the axis. This, too, must be a full, unformatted figure including thousands or millions. In this example I will set it to **15000000**.

8. Set the font, font size, and color for the Y axis elements.

9. Set (or leave) the Display units to Auto.

10. Switch Title to On to display the Y axis title.

11. Set the Style to Show both. This way the axis title will display both numbers and units. You can select either if you prefer.

12. Enter the number of decimals to be displayed on the axis in the Value decimal places field.

13. Enter a title in the Axis title field. I am adding **Massive Profit**.

14. Set the axis title font, font size, and color.

15. Set the Gridlines to On.

16. Choose a color for the gridlines.

17. Select a stroke width and line style. You can see the Format area of the Visualizations pane for the Y axis section in Figure 17-7. The final chart is shown in Figure 17-8.

Figure 17-7. *Formatting the Y axis*

If you are modifying a chart that only has a single axis, you can move the axis from the left side of the chart to the right by selecting Right from the Position popup menu. In the case of a chart with two axes, you can swap the axes around using this setting.

If your chart contains *two* Y axes (one on the left and one on the right), then you can repeat these settings for the other axis. You may have to scroll down in the Visualizations pane to see the settings for the second axis.

Note   Remember that you can define a specific value as a measure in the data model. This can be extremely useful if you need to set reusable maximum and minimum values for the Y axis in charts.

Chart Borders

You can add a border to a chart just like you did to tables in the previous chapter. Simply click the Format icon and set the Border button to On. You can always choose a border color by expanding the Border section and selecting a color from the popup menu of available colors.

General Attributes

As was the case for the text-based visuals that you saw in the previous chapter, you can specify the exact position of a chart on the dashboard canvas in the General section of the Format area of the Visualizations pane.

Chart Aspect Ratio

As a final comment on chart formatting, it is worth remembering that you can lock the aspect ratio of a chart. This ensures that when you resize a chart, the width and height maintain their original proportions relative to each other.

To set the aspect ratio:

1. Click the chart to select it.

2. In the Visualizations pane, click the Format icon.

3. In the Lock Aspect section, click Off to turn the lock on, or alternatively click to the right of the empty circle indicating that the lock is off so that it slides to the right and becomes a filled circle.

Now, when you resize a table using the corner handles, it will keep its height-to-width ratio.

Finally, in Figure 17-8 you can see the chart with all your modifications applied. Before rolling your eyes at my (lack of) taste, please note that I am not suggesting that you should present charts in this way (indeed, you should probably take this as an example of what *not* to do). I am merely showing the result of applying many of the available chart formatting options.

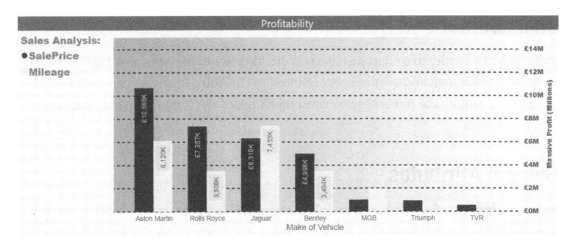

Figure 17-8. *A fully formatted chart*

Specific Chart Formatting

Although most charts share many of the common formatting options that you have seen so far in this chapter, others present different formatting possibilities. This means that while bar, stacked bar, column, and stacked column charts can all be formatted using the techniques that you have recently learned, other chart types require discovering a few new tweaks.

Line, Area, and Stacked Area Charts

One group of charts that all share a new formatting option are line charts, area charts, and stacked area charts. More specifically, they all allow you to adjust the line and point aspects of the chart. Here is an example to show you this in action:

1. Create a new line chart using the following fields (using the file CarSalesDataForReports.pbix):

    a. Color (from the Colors table)

    b. SpareParts (from the Stock table)

    c. LaborCost (from the Stock table)

2. In the Visualizations pane, click the Format icon.

3. Expand the Shapes section.

4. Set the Stroke width to 5.

5.   Set Show marker to On.

6.   Select a marker shape from the Marker shape popup list.

7.   Increase the marker size and change its color.

8.   Set the Line style to Dashed.

9.   Set Customize series to On.

10.   Select SpareParts as the data series to modify from the popup list.

11.   Set the Stroke width to 1 and the Line style to Dotted.

12.   Set Show marker to On.

13.   Select a different marker shape from the Marker shape popup list.

14.   Decrease the marker size and change its color.

15.   Set Stepped to On. You should see a chart like the one in Figure 17-9.

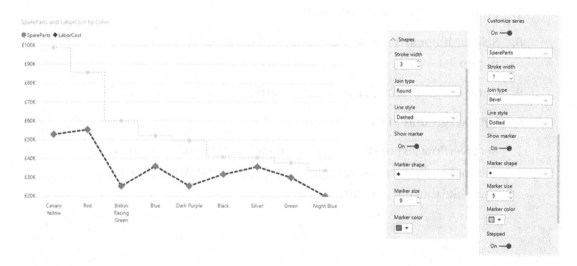

Figure 17-9. *Shape options in a line chart*

Note   If you are not displaying the marker, you can select a join type (the intersection where each line alters direction) from the Join type popup in the Shapes section.

Pie and Donut Charts

Pie and donut charts also have specific formatting possibilities. These consist of the ways that you can alter the detail labels for a pie or donut chart. Try out the following:

1. Create a new pie chart using the following fields (using the file CarSalesDataForReports.pbix):

   a. Color (from the Colors table)

   b. SpareParts (from the Stock table)

2. In the Visualizations pane, click the Format icon.

3. Set the Legend to On and place it at the left in the center.

4. Expand the Detail labels section.

5. Select Data value from the Label style popup list.

6. Choose a color from the color palette.

7. Enter, or select, a larger text size.

8. Select Millions as the display units from the Display units popup list.

9. Enter **4** as the Value decimal places setting.

10. Set Background to On.

11. Set Overflow text to On (this allows data labels to appear even if this makes them cross pie chart segment borders). You will have a chart like the one in Figure 17-10.

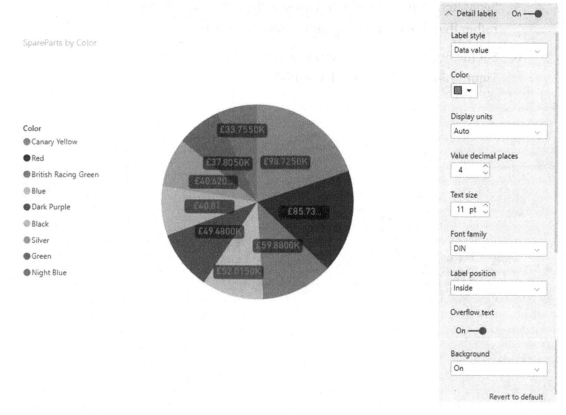

Figure 17-10. *Shape options in a pie chart*

Ribbon Charts

Ribbon charts contain all the standard formatting options that you have seen applied to stacked column charts, so I will not reiterate all these possibilities here. There is, however, one formatting option that is specific to this chart type. This is the ribbon formatting.

To see this in action:

1. Re-create the ribbon chart that you made in Chapter 16.

2. Click the Format icon in the Visualizations pane.

3. Expand the Ribbons section.

4. Set the Spacing to 10. This sets each ribbon apart from the others.

5. Set Match series color to Off. This sets the ribbon color to gray, rather than the color of the bar for each data point.

6. Set the Border to On. The result (which you can compare to Figure 16-25) is shown in Figure 17-11.

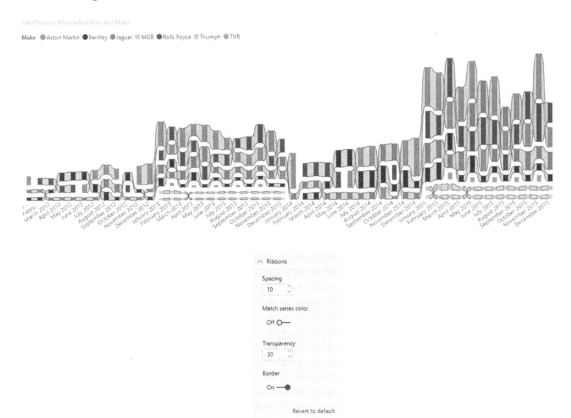

Figure 17-11. *A ribbon chart*

Funnel Charts

Funnel charts allow you to display (or not) and format one element that is specific to this kind of chart—the conversion rate. These are the percentage figures that appear above and below the funnel. This short walk-through explains how you can do this:

1. Using the file CarSalesDataForReports.pbix, create a new pie chart using the following fields:

    a. Color (from the Colors table)

    b. SpareParts (from the Stock table)

2. Sort by SpareParts.

3. Expand the Conversion Rate section of the Format area of the Visualizations pane.

4. Choose a color from the color palette.

5. Enter, or select, a larger text size. You will have a chart like the one in Figure 17-12.

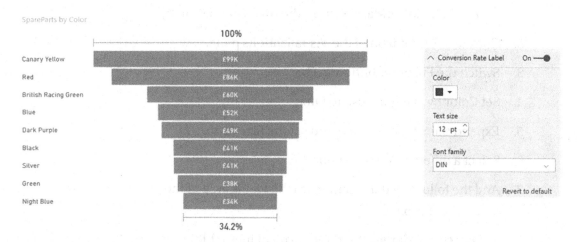

Figure 17-12. *Adjusting the conversion rate in a funnel chart*

Note   To prevent the conversion rate from being displayed, all you have to do is click the Conversion Rate Label button.

Scatter and Bubble Charts

The final set of charts that allow you to apply some particular formatting are scatter and bubble charts. When you are creating these chart types, you can alter the following:

- Fill point

- Category labels

- Color by category

- Color border

- Bubbles

To see these effects, we will create a new chart and then try out some of the available options. We will start with a scatter chart that we will then extend to make into a bubble chart:

1. Create a scatter chart using the following data elements:

   a. *Details*: Make (from the Stock table)

   b. *X axis*: SalePrice (from the InvoiceLines table)

   c. *Y axis*: RatioNetMargin (from the InvoiceLines table)

2. Click the Format icon of the Visualizations pane.

3. Switch the Fill point button to On.

4. Set Color by category also to On.

5. Expand the Shapes section and set the Size to 20.

6. Select a different Marker shape.

7. Add the following data element to the Fields area of the Visualizations pane:

   a. *Size*: Gross Margin (from the InvoiceLines table)

8. Set Color border to On.

9. Expand the Data colors section. The chart will now look like the one in Figure 17-13.

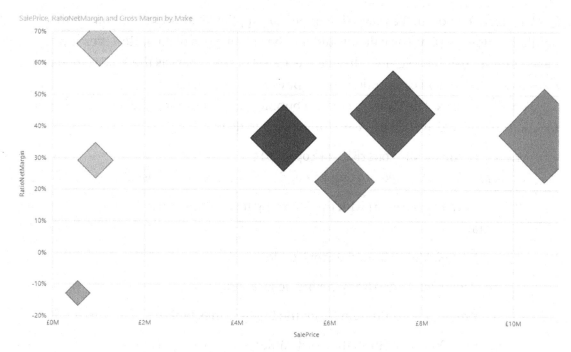

Figure 17-13. *Formatting a bubble chart*

There are a couple of points that need to be made at this juncture:

- Adding a field to express the color saturation will deactivate the Color by category formatting option and will prevent you from attributing specific data colors.

- For a bubble chart, you can specify the actual values used to define the color divergence in the bubbles in the Data colors section (assuming that a value for color saturation has been added).

Bubble Chart Play Axis

So far in this chapter, you have seen various ways of presenting data as charts and how to select and compare the data using a variety of chart types. A final trick with Power BI Desktop (one that can be extremely effective at riveting your audience) is to apply a play axis to the visualization. This animates the chart and, ideally, is suited to showing how data evolves over time. Unfortunately, it is harder to get the "wow" effect using these printed pages, so this really is a technique that you have to try yourself.

You need to know that a play axis can only be applied to scatter or bubble charts. Similarly, adding a play axis will not suit or enhance all types of data. However, if you have a time-dependent element that can be added to your chart as the Y axis (such as sales to date), then you can produce some powerful and revelatory effects.

The following explains how to create a bubble chart that shows the net margin ratio for colors of car sold against the sales for the year to date:

1. Open the file `C:\PowerBiDesktopSamples\` `CarSalesDataForReports.pbix` and delete any existing visuals.

2. Create a bubble chart with the following fields using the following data:

   a. *Legend*: Make (from the Stock table)

   b. *X axis*: YearSales (from the Invoices table)

   c. *Y axis*: RatioNetMargin (from the InvoiceLines table)

   d. *Size*: CostPrice (from the Stock table)

   e. *Play axis*: MonthAndYearAbbr (from the DateDimension table)

3. Adjust the presentation (size, legend placement, data labels, etc.) to obtain the best effect.

Click the Play icon to the left of the play axis. You will see the bubbles reveal how sales progress throughout the year. At one point on the timeline, the visual will look like that shown in Figure 17-14.

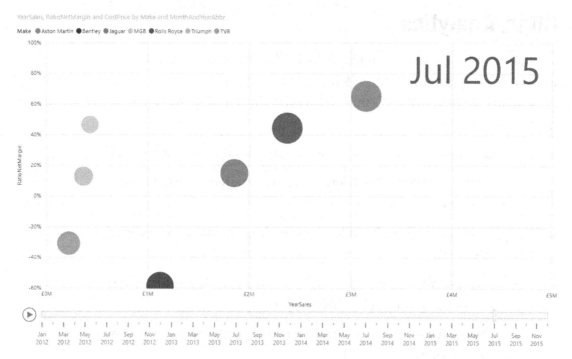

Figure 17-14. *The play axis on a bubble chart*

There are a few points worth noting about the play axis while we are discussing it:

- You can pause the automated display by clicking the Pause icon, which the Play icon has become, while the animation is progressing. You can stop and start as often as you like.

- You can click any month (or any element) in the play axis to display the data just for that element, without playing the data before that point. This essentially means that you can use the play axis as a filter for your data.

- A play axis need not be time based. However, it can be harder to see any coherence or progression in the data if time is not used as a basis for a play axis.

- Using cumulative data (such as the YearSales figure in this example, which is the cumulative year-to-date sales) is particularly effective with a time-based play axis as it lets you appreciate the growth of sales for each data item over time.

- You can use a play axis as another interactive filter for your data, but doing this makes you miss out on a fabulous animation technique!

Chart Analytics

Yet another way to add extra emphasis to the data in a chart is to add analytical enhancements. These are added elements that draw the reader's attention to a value that is calculated automatically. All these items are added as lines to a chart independently of the existing data. They include

- *Constants*: You may wish to add a specific value as an item in a chart.

- *Minimum values*: This allows you to draw attention to a lower threshold.

- *Maximum values*: This allows you to draw attention to an upper threshold.

- *Averages*: You can have Power BI Desktop calculate the average of a set of values and display this as a line.

- *Median values*: Power BI Desktop can also calculate and display a median value.

- *Percentiles*: You can specify a percentile to be displayed.

To see this a little closer, suppose that you want to add the following lines to a chart containing the selling price and mileage of all cars by make:

- The average mileage

- The maximum selling price

Here is how you can do this:

1. Click the Clustered Column Chart icon in the Visualizations pane. An empty chart visual will be created on the dashboard canvas.

2. Drag the following fields into the Axis area of the field well in this order:

   a. Make (from the Stock table)

   b. Model (from the Stock table)

   c. Color (from the Colors table)

3. Drag the following fields into the Value area of the field well:

   a. SalePrice (from the InvoiceLines table)

   b. Mileage (from the Stock table)

4. Click the Analytics icon (to the right of the Format icon in the Visualizations pane).

5. Expand the Average line section.

6. Click Add.

7. Select Mileage from the Measure popup list.

8. Choose a color from the palette of available colors.

9. Set the Line style as Dotted.

10. Click the Data label button to activate the data label.

11. Set the Text to Name and value.

12. Set the Horizontal position to Right.

13. Set the Vertical position to Under.

14. Double-click inside the field containing the text "Average line 1" and enter **Average Mileage**.

15. Close the Average line section.

16. Expand the Max line section.

17. Click Add.

18. Select SalePrice from the Measure popup list.

19. Set the Line style to Solid. The chart should look like the one shown in Figure 17-15.

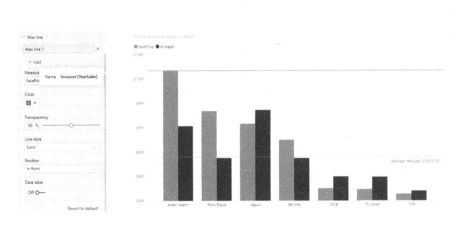

Figure 17-15. *Adding chart analytics*

It is worth noting that you can add several lines for an analytical element. That is, you can add as many averages, for instance, as there are data elements in the chart. To do this, simply click Add once more in the section where you wish to add another line and then define the settings to achieve the result that you want. This is, nonetheless, a technique that can detract from the visibility of a chart as easily as it can add to the data story that you are telling. So it is probably best used sparingly.

If you are adding a percentile line, then you have one extra element that you will probably need to alter. This is the actual percentile value of the maximum value of a data element, which you can alter using the Percentile slider.

Removing an analytical line is as simple as this:

1. Click the Analytics icon.

2. Expand the section corresponding to the line that you wish to remove.

3. Click the cross to the right of the line that you wish to remove.

Note   You cannot actually select an analytical line in a chart.

Scatter Chart Symmetry Shading and Ratio Line

Two features of Power BI Desktop can help you "see the wood for the trees" in scatter charts:

- Symmetry shading

- Ratio lines

They are equally simple to apply, but can really help you to see beyond a mass of data points and isolate valuable trends and salient items of data.

Symmetry Shading

This feature allows you to see which points have a higher value on the X axis compared to the Y axis (and vice versa). Like so much of Power BI Desktop, it is best understood using a practical example:

1. Create a scatter chart using the following elements:

    a. *Details*: Make (from the Stock table)

    b. *X axis*: SalePrice (from the InvoiceLines table)

    c. *Y axis*: Mileage (from the Stock table)

2. Increase the size of the shapes and fill them (as described previously).

3. With the scatter chart selected, click the Analytics icon (the magnifying glass) in the Visualizations pane.

4. Expand the Symmetry shading section.

5. Click Add.

6. Select a color for the upper shading from the palette of available colors.

7. Select a color for the lower shading from the palette of available colors.

8. Adjust the Transparency slider to set the transparency to 15%. The chart will look like the one shown in Figure 17-16.

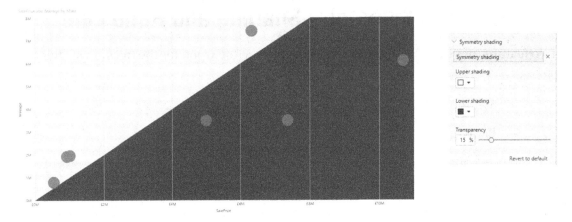

Figure 17-16. *Adding symmetry shading to a scatter chart*

You can remove symmetry shading by clicking the small cross at the right of the Symmetry shading box in the Symmetry shading section.

Note   Symmetry shading will only really be of use if the values on the X and Y axes are comparable in extent.

Ratio Line

One final instant analysis function is the ratio line. This shows you how to apply it:

1. Follow steps 1 and 2 of the previous section to create a scatter chart.

2. Expand the Ratio line section.

3. Click Add.

4. Select a color for the ratio line from the palette of available colors.

5. Select a line style—Dashed, Dotted, or Solid.

6. Select a line type from the popup list of line styles. The chart will look like the one shown in Figure 17-17.

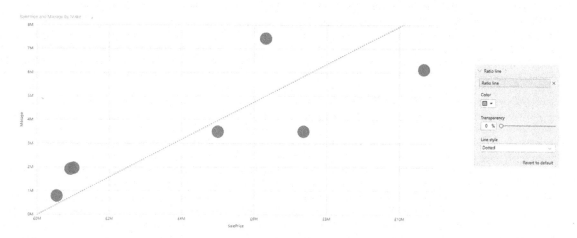

Figure 17-17. *Adding a ratio line to a scatter chart*

As was the case for symmetry shading, you can remove a ratio line by clicking the small cross at the right of the Ratio line box in the Ratio line section.

Conclusion

In this chapter you learned how to enhance Power BI Desktop chart types by formatting them for added effect. This included modifying the colors of data series and data points as well as adding or removing titles. You also saw how to add legends and data labels to certain types of charts.

You then saw how to enhance charts with automatic analytics. These included averages and selected maximum values as well as ratio lines.

As well, you saw how certain types of charts (bubble charts specifically) can even be animated so that you can add time as a descriptive factor to help your audience understand how data evolves.

You are now well on the way to becoming a Power BI Desktop dashboard maestro. All you need to look at now are a few remaining visualization types and you will have attained a complete mastery of high-impact presentations. So now, on to the next three chapters to finish your apprenticeship.

CHAPTER 18

Other Types of Visuals

While text-based visuals and charts can often make your point, there are times when you need to deliver your insights in ways that go beyond the more traditional data displays. This is where Power BI Desktop really comes to your aid. With the right data—and only a few clicks—you can revitalize your dashboards.

- Tree maps

- Gauges

- KPIs

- R visuals

- Python visuals

- Decomposition tree

- Key influencers

Most of these visualization types are as simple to create as the text-based visuals and charts that you saw in the preceding four chapters. Yet their very ease of use should not distract you from the clarity and power that they can bring to your reports and presentations.

This chapter will use the file `C:\PowerBiDesktopSamples\CarSalesDataForReports.pbix` as the basis for the visuals that you will create.

Tree Maps

One type of visual that can really help your audience to see the way that individual values relate to a total is the tree map. While this is not a map in any geographical sense, it can certainly assist users in finding their way around a set of figures.

© Adam Aspin 2020
A. Aspin, *Pro Power BI Desktop*, https://doi.org/10.1007/978-1-4842-5763-0_18

As, yet again, seeing is believing in the world of visuals, let's take a look at a tree map showing how the labor costs stack up for each make and model of car purchased:

1. Open the C:\PowerBiDesktopSamples\CarSalesDataForReports.
   pbix file, or click an empty part of the dashboard canvas.

2. Click the Tree Map icon in the Visualizations pane. A blank tree
   map will appear.

3. Expand the Stock table and drag the Make field into the Group box
   in the field well.

4. Drag the Model field into the Details box in the field well.

5. Drag the LaborCost field into the Values box in the field well. The
   tree map should look like the one in Figure 18-1.

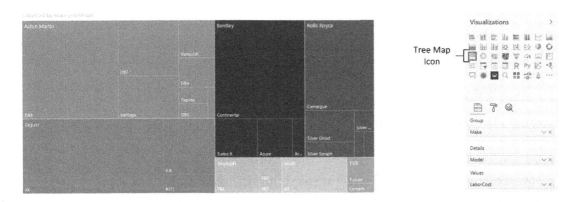

Figure 18-1. *A tree map showing labor cost for each make of car*

As you can see in Figure 18-1, the tree map has grouped each model of car by make and then displayed the labor cost as the relative size of each box in the tree map. This way, your viewers can get a rough idea of

- How the labor cost for each model compares to the total labor cost
  for the make

- How the labor cost for each make compares to the total labor cost

As you are probably expecting by now, you can hover the mouse over any box in the tree map and see a popup tooltip of the exact data.

Power BI Desktop will decide how best to organize the tree map. However, the final appearance will depend on how wide and how tall the visual is. So don't hesitate to resize this particular kind of visualization and see how it changes as you adjust the relative height and width.

There could be cases when a tree map cannot display all the available data, possibly because there are too many data points, or the range of values is too wide to be shown properly, or (as the case with the pie charts) because there are negative values in the data. In these circumstances, the tree map shows a warning information symbol in the top left of the visual. If you hover the mouse pointer over this icon, you will see a message like the one shown in Figure 18-2.

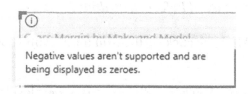

Figure 18-2. *The tree map data alert*

If you see this warning, then you could be advised to apply filters to the data (as described in Chapter 21) to filter out the data that is causing the problem.

Drill Down and Tree Maps

The same drill-down and expand lower-level logic that you have already seen for matrices, charts, and maps also applies to tree maps. As you are used to the concept by now, I will only show a short example of drill down using a tree map:

1. Select the tree map that you just created.

2. Drag the Color field from the Colors table to the group well of the Visualizations pane. Place this *under* the Make field. The field well and the tree map will look like those shown in Figure 18-3. You can see that the relative labor cost by model is no longer visible.

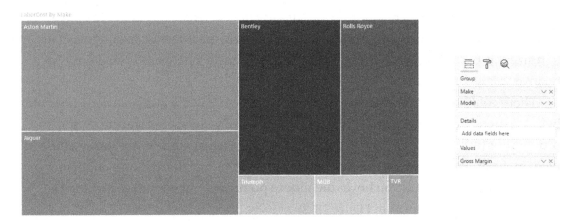

Figure 18-3. *A tree map visual before drill-down*

3. Activate Drill Mode by clicking the drill mode icon at the top right of the visual.

4. Click Aston Martin. You will drill down to the next level (color) for this make, and the visual will look like the one shown in Figure 18-4.

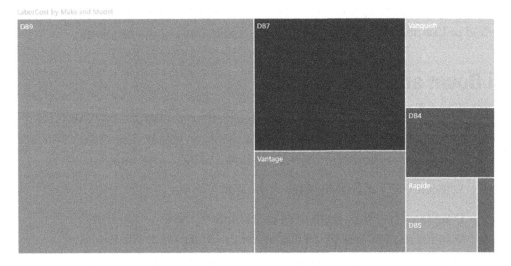

Figure 18-4. *Drilling down into a tree map visual*

Formatting Tree Maps

Tree maps can be formatted just like any other visual. The following are the available options in the Format icon in the Visualizations pane:

- Legend

- Data colors

- Data labels

- Category labels

- Title

- Background

- Lock aspect

- Border

Since applying all of these options was explained (for other types of visual) in previous chapters, I will not explain them in detail again, but I will provide a few comments about the available options.

Legend

In my opinion, a legend is superfluous as it duplicates the information about the grouping data that is already displayed in the tree map. You may find a legend necessary if you choose not to display the category labels, however.

Data Colors

This palette lets you choose a specific color for each grouping element.

Data Labels

You can display (or hide) the actual figures that are behind each segment of a tree map if you wish. This entails switching the Data labels button to On or Off. If you expand the Data labels section of the Formatting pane, you can also modify the color, units, number of decimals, and text size and font of the data labels.

Category Labels

This option lets you decide whether or not to display the grouping elements and the detail element information inside the tree map. If your tree map contains dozens (or hundreds) of data points, then you might want to hide the category labels. If you expand the Category labels section of the Formatting pane, you can also modify the color, font, and size of the category labels.

Title

As is the case with most visuals, you can choose to show or hide the title, as well as alter its text, font size, and background color.

Background

You can apply a colored background to the kind of visuals that you can see in this chapter, too.

Lock Aspect

If you set Lock Aspect to On, then you can resize the visual while keeping it proportionally sized.

Border

As is the case with just about any visual, you can add or remove a border to tree maps, too.

Gauges

One extremely useful visual that is available out of the box is the gauge. These kinds of visuals are particularly effective when you want to compare actuals to targets or see how a metric compares to a key performance indicator (KPI), for instance. In this example, you will use a gauge to see how the total cost of purchases and spares compares to the threshold set by the finance director:

1. Open the `C:\PowerBiDesktopSamples\CarSalesDataForReports.pbix` file, or click an empty part of the dashboard canvas.

2. Click the Gauge icon in the Visualizations pane. A blank gauge visual will appear.

3. Expand the InvoiceLines table and drag the Cost Plus Spares
    Margin field into the Value box in the field well. Alternatively, drag
    this field directly into the gauge that you just created.

4. Drag the Cost Plus Spares Maximum field from the InvoiceLines
    table into the Maximum value box in the field well.

5. Drag the Cost Plus Spares Target field (also from the InvoiceLines
    table) into the Target value box in the field well.

The gauge will look like Figure 18-5.

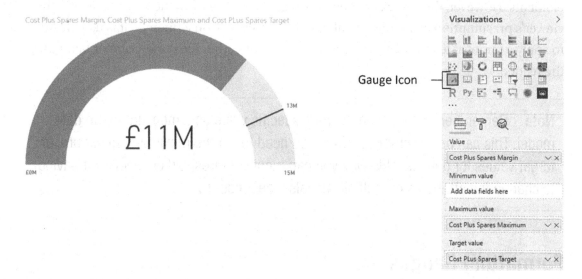

Figure 18-5. *A gauge in Power BI Desktop*

Gauges are designed to show progress against a target or a total. Consequently, you
can set the elements described in Table 18-1 for a gauge.

Table 18-1. *The Specific Data Requirements for Gauges*

Element	Description
Value	The element that appears as a colored bar in the gauge.
Minimum value	The minimum value to alter the perceptual effect of the gauge.
Maximum value	The maximum value to alter the perceptual effect of the gauge.
Target value	A metric that is defined as something to be attained.

In fact, all that a gauge needs is a value. It will work without any of the other three elements. However, the real visual power of a gauge comes from the way that it uses the viewer's presumption of a target or value to be achieved. Consequently, it is usually best to apply a target at least and a maximum value to convey an idea of success or failure for the reader.

Note   Remember that you can define a specific value as a measure in the data model. This can be extremely useful if you need to set the maximum, minimum, or target values for gauges. This way you can modify a threshold once without having to change the attributes of multiple visuals independently.

Formatting Gauges

Many of the gauge formatting options are highly specific to gauge visuals. So here is a quick trip through the available presentation techniques that you need to know to enhance this type of visual:

1. Click the gauge that you created previously.

2. In the Visualizations pane, remove the Target value (the CostPlusSpares field).

3. Remove the Maximum value (the SalePrice field).

4. In the Visualizations pane, click the Format icon.

5. Expand the Gauge axis section.

6. Enter **2000000** as the minimum value.

7. Enter **30000000** as the maximum value.

8. Enter **10000000** as the target.

9. Expand the Data labels section.

10. Ensure that the Data labels switch is set to On and expand the Data labels section.

11. Choose a color from the popup palette for colors for the data labels and set a larger font size.

12. Ensure that the Target switch is set to On and expand the Target section.

13. Choose a color from the popup palette for colors for the target.

14. Expand the Callout Value section.

15. Ensure that the Callout Value switch is set to On and expand the Callout Value section.

16. Choose a color from the popup palette for colors for the callout value.

17. Expand the Data colors section and select a color for the fill and the target. The gauge will look something like Figure 18-6.

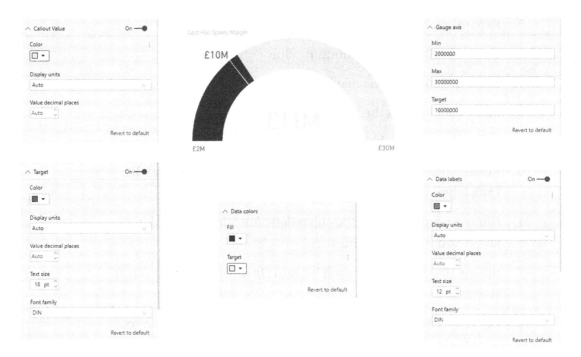

Figure 18-6. *A formatted gauge*

If you wish, you can also alter the background data labels, border, and title just as you did previously for other visuals. You can also choose not to display the data labels or the callout value (the value of the gauge) if you prefer. All you have to do is to set their respective switches to the Off position.

Note   When entering figures in the Formatting pane (referenced earlier in the chapter) of the Visualizations pane, you must not add any numeric formatting, such as thousands separators. If you do, the formatting will not work and Power BI will wait until you have entered the numbers in their raw form.

Gauges are a simple yet effective visual. A set of gauges can also be a truly effective way of displaying high-level key metrics on a dashboard.

The remaining gauge formatting options are common to most of the visuals that you have already seen:

- Title

- Background

- Lock aspect

- Border

KPIs

Power BI Desktop can also create key performance indicator visuals that illustrate how a data element is trending compared to a target value. Here is one example of this:

1. Still using the CarSalesDataForReports.pbix file click the KPI icon to add a clustered column chart visual to the dashboard. Leave the blank KPI visual selected. You can see this icon in Figure 18-7.

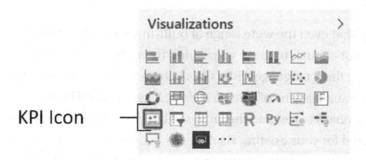

KPI Icon

Figure 18-7. The KPI icon

2. Add the Gross Margin field (from the InvoiceLines table) as well as the MonthAndYearAbbr field (from the DateDimension table).

3. Add the Gross Margin Target field from the InvoiceLines table to the target goals well of the Visualizations pane.

4. Click the Format icon in the Visualizations pane.

5. Expand the Goals section. Ensure that Distance (which shows any percentage shortfall or excess) and Goal (which displays the cumulative figure for the goal) are set to On.

6. Expand the Indicator section and select Thousands as the display unit. Reduce the text size.

7. Expand Color coding and select another color for the Good Color. The KPI will look like the one shown in Figure 18-8.

Figure 18-8. *A KPI visual*

R Visuals

Should you find that even the wide range of built-in visuals that Power BI Desktop has to offer are just not enough to make your point, then you can take visuals to another, higher level using the R language. "R" as it is known is a language that is used to analyze data and create visualizations of statistical data. It can be used inside Power BI Desktop reports and dashboards to extend the analysis that you are delivering using the data that you have prepared for your existing visuals.

R is not an intuitive language, but it is extremely powerful. So here is an example of how you can add an R visual to a dashboard using the CarSales data that you have already loaded:

Note   Creating R visuals implies installing an R engine on the PC that hosts Power BI Desktop. You can find one of the available R downloads at `https://mran.revolutionanalytics.com/download/`.

---

1. Open the Power BI Desktop file `C:\PowerBiDesktopSamples\CarSalesDataForReports.pbix` (unless it is already open).

2. Click the R visuals icon in the Visualizations pane; the Enable script visuals dialog will be displayed, like the one shown in Figure 18-9.

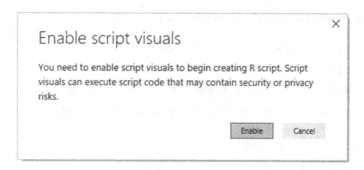

Figure 18-9. *The Enable script visuals dialog*

3. Click Enable. An empty R visual will be added to the desktop canvas, and a pane containing the R script editor will appear under the report. You can see this in Figure 18-10.

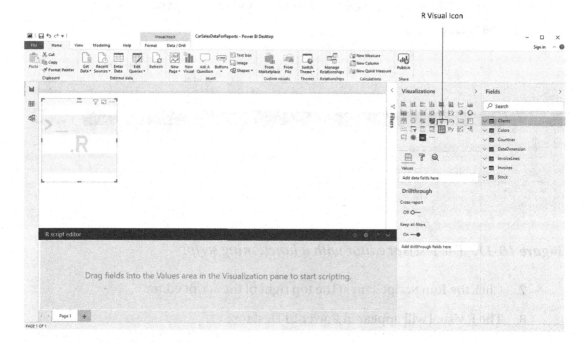

Figure 18-10. *Adding an R visual*

4. Drag the following fields into the R visual (both are from the Stock table):

    a. Make

    b. CostPrice

5. Resize the R visual so that it is wider than it is tall.

6. Add the following script under the header lines in the R script editor (this script is available in the file C:\PowerBiDesktopSamples\Rscript.txt). Once you have done this, the script editor will look like Figure 18-11.

```
rdata <- table(dataset)
barplot(rdata
,axes=F
,main="Make"
,xlab="Cost Price"
,ylab = "Number Sold per Price Point"
,legend = rownames(rdata)
,col=c("darkblue","red", "green", "yellow", "pink", "orange",
"darkgreen") )
```

Figure 18-11. *The R script editor with a functioning script*

7. Click the Run Script icon at the top right of the script editor.

8. The R visual will appear in Power BI Desktop.

9. Resize the R visual as necessary. The visual could end up looking like the one shown in Figure 18-12.

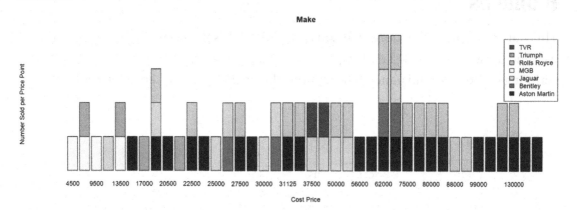

Figure 18-12. *An R visual*

You can, of course, only create R visuals if you are prepared to learn the R language. As this is the subject of entire tomes, I will not be describing the language here. Instead I suggest that you refer to the many excellent resources that are already available on this subject.

Note   If you resize the R visual, you may have to rerun the R script (by clicking the Run Script icon in the R script editor) to force the visual to display correctly.

The R script editor icons are described in Table 18-2.

Table 18-2. *The R Script Editor Icons*

Icons	Description
Run Script	Runs—or reruns—the R script and re-creates the R visual in Power BI Desktop.
R script options	Display the dialog with available R script options.
Edit script in external R IDE	Runs an external R script editor, using the script from the Power BI Desktop R visual.
Minimize the script pane	Hides (or redisplays) the R script pane.

R Options

There are a couple of R options that you can adjust if this proves really necessary. You can find these by choosing File ➤ Options and Settings ➤ Options and then clicking R scripting in the left-hand pane of the Options dialog that you can see in Figure 18-13.

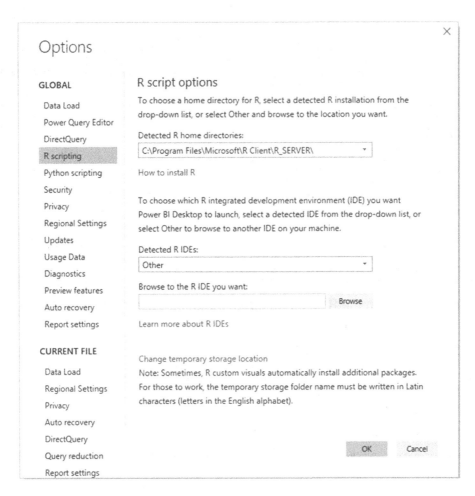

Figure 18-13. *R options*

There are, essentially, only a couple of possible tweaks that you could have to make:

- *R scripting engine*: Power BI Desktop should detect the R scripting engine that you have previously installed. Should it not do this, then you can browse to the directory containing the R scripting engine. Simply select Other in the popup list and click the Browse button.

- *IDE*: If you prefer to use a different external R integrated development environment (IDE), then simply click the Browse button to select a preferred R IDE. This will then be invoked the next time that you click the External Editor icon at the top right of the R script editor.

Note   The vast majority of formatting for an R visual is done inside the R script itself. You can, however, format the background, border, and title of the visual using the Power BI formatting options.

Python Visuals

A fairly recent extension to Power BI Desktop is the possibility of creating your own visuals scripted in Python. While this is pretty similar to the approach that you just saw for R visuals, there are a few minor differences.

Firstly, you will need to install Python on your PC. There are several available approaches to doing this, and a quick search on the Web should provide you with the path to an up-to-date version of Python.

Secondly, you will probably need to install the pandas and possibly matplotlib libraries on your PC—unless they are already installed—as both these libraries are needed in the majority of cases when scripting Python charts as Power BI visuals.

To save you researching the techniques, all you have to do is to run the two following lines of code:

```
pip install pandas
pip install matplotlib
```

in the python script directory (on my machine this is C:\Users\Adam\AppData\Local\Programs\Python\Python37-32\Scripts).

To create a Python chart as a Power BI visual:

1. Open (or leave open) the Power BI Desktop file C:\PowerBiDesktopSamples\CarSalesDataForReports.pbix.

2. Click the Python visual icon in the Visualizations pane. You can see this in Figure 18-14. A pane containing the Python script editor will appear under the report.

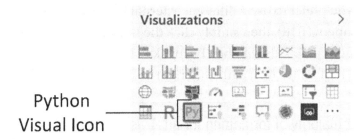

Figure 18-14. *The Python visual icon*

3. Drag the following fields into the Python visual (both are from the
    Stock table); a dataframe is created automatically from the fields
    added to the field well.

    a. Make

    b. CostPrice

4. Add the following script under the header lines in the Python
    script editor:

```
import matplotlib.pyplot as plt
dataset.plot(kind='bar', x='Make', y='SalePrice')
plt.show()
```

5. Once you have done this, the script editor will look like the one in
    Figure 18-15.

```
Python script editor                                                    ⏵  ⚙  ↗  ⌄
1 # The following code to create a dataframe and remove duplicated rows is always executed and acts as a preamble for
  your script:
2
3 # dataset = pandas.DataFrame(Make, SalePrice)
4 # dataset = dataset.drop_duplicates()
5
6 # Paste or type your script code here:
7 import matplotlib.pyplot as plt
8 dataset.plot(kind='bar', x='Make', y='SalePrice')
9 plt.show()
```

Figure 18-15. *The Python script editor*

6. Click the Run Script icon at the top right of the script editor. The Python visual will appear in Power BI Desktop.

7. Resize the Python visual as necessary. The visual could end up looking like the one shown in Figure 18-16.

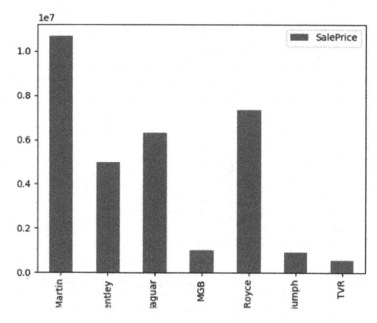

Figure 18-16. *A simple Python visual*

Note   The vast majority of formatting for a Python visual is done inside the R script itself. You can, however, format the background, border, and title of the visual using the Power BI formatting options.

This is quite possibly the simplest Python visual that you could make. However, the point is not to blind you with swathes of Python code, but rather to show you how easy it is to capitalize on your Python skills if you are moving to Power BI Desktop. Alternatively, you can use Power BI Desktop as an excellent training ground to learn Python for data visualization as you perfect your Python coding skills.

Python Options

As was the case with R visuals, you can tweak a couple of options to specify Python script options for Power BI Desktop. As these are essentially identical to those described previously for R, I will not repeat these elements here. You can, however, see the available options in Figure 18-17.

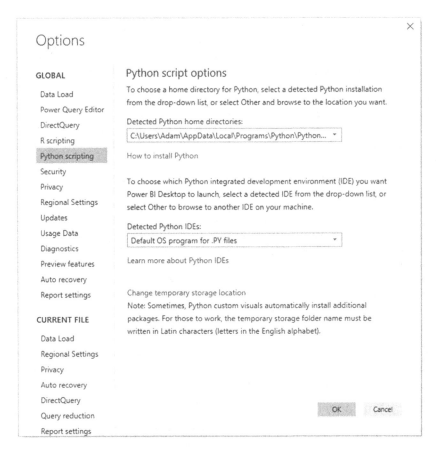

Figure 18-17. *Python options*

Decomposition Tree

One visual that has recently been added to the panoply of built-in visuals (accompanied by a huge cheer of welcome from the Power BI community) is the Decomposition Tree. This visual lets you drill down through multiple elements (that it calls dimensions) to see the path down to the lowest level of your analysis.

1. In the `CarSalesDataForReports.pbix` file click the Decomposition Tree icon in the Visualizations pane. You can see this icon in Figure 18-18.

2. Resize the blank visual that appears to make it larger.

3. Add the CostPrice field to the Analyze well.

4. Add the following elements to the Explain by well:

    a. Make (from the Stock table)

    b. Model (from the Stock table)

    c. Color (from the Colors table)

    d. CountryName (from the Countries table)

5. The resulting visual looks like the one in Figure 18-18.

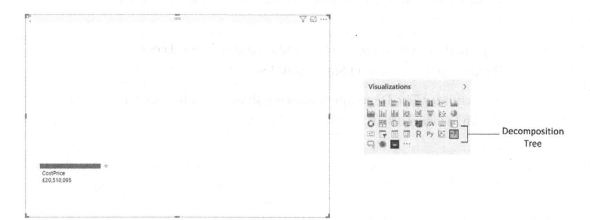

Figure 18-18. *An initial Decomposition Tree*

6. Click the cross to the right of the initial element in the Decomposition Tree (CostPrice). The popup menu displays the elements that you added previously to the Explain by well.

7. Click CountryName. Each country appears as a sublevel in the Decomposition Tree showing the relative values of the value that you initially selected.

8. Click the cross to the right of one of the countries. The popup menu displays the remaining elements that you added previously.

9. Select Color.

10. Click the cross to the right of one of the colors and select a Make.

11. Activate the Formatting pane for the visual that you have created.

12. Expand the Tree section and set

    a. The Primary color to Blue (this indicates the drillthrough path that you selected)

    b. The Connector color to light gray (this shows nonselected paths)

13. Expand the Data bars section and choose a different color for the positive bar from the color palette.

14. Expand the Category labels section and alter the Font family, size, and color.

15. Expand the Data labels section and alter the Font family, size, and color.

16. Expand the Level header section and set a Background color from the color palette, then set Show subtitles to Off.

17. Add a border. The Decomposition Tree should look like the one shown in Figure 18-19.

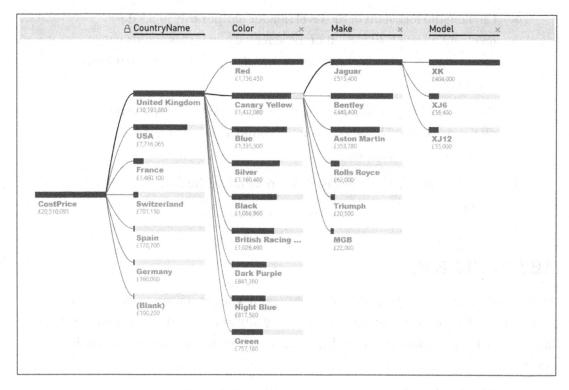

Figure 18-19. *A Decomposition Tree*

Once a basic Decomposition Tree is set up, you can interact with it by clicking any element at any level to see, instantly, the composition of values at all the levels of the hierarchy that you have established.

There are several things that you need to know to get the best out of a Decomposition Tree:

- You can extend the hierarchy by adding further levels to the Explain by well at any time. These levels then appear in the popup menu.

- You remove a level from the hierarchy simply by clicking the cross at the top right of the element name. This does not remove the level from the Explain by well.

- To alter the drill path down through the levels, simply remove any sublevels and then add them back in a different order.

- Clicking the lock icon in the level header temporarily locks the level and all levels to the left of the selected level. This avoids you removing it by mistake. Clicking a second time the lock icon unlocks the level.

- Double-clicking a value (say the color Blue in this example) will hide all the sublevels. This allows you to rebuild a path down through the hierarchy in a few clicks.

- Selecting a node from the last level cross-filters the data in other visuals.

Key Influencers

The Key Influencers visual can be extremely useful when you want to examine the factors that influence a metric that you are analyzing and compare and contrast these factors. As with all visuals, it is probably easier to see it in action in order to understand it better.

1. Click the Key Influencers icon in the Visualizations pane.

2. Add the Weeks in Stock field (from the Stock table) to the Analyze well.

3. Add the following fields to the Explain by well:

   a. CostPrice

   b. TotalDiscount

   c. Mileage

The Key Influencers visual should look like the one shown in Figure 18-20.

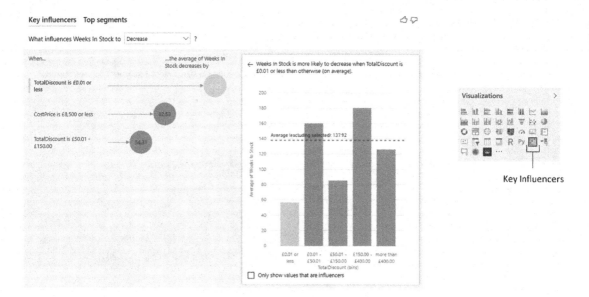

Figure 18-20. *A Key Influencers visual*

4. Expand the Data bars section and choose a different color for the Primary color and Secondary colors from the color palettes.

5. Expand the Drill visual colors section and alter the Default and Reference line colors.

You can now see which factors are considered to influence the time that a vehicle stays in stock.

There are, perhaps inevitably, several things that you need to know to use a Key Influencers visual efficiently:

- Clicking any of the influencers on the left of the visual shows the detail of the influencer.

- You can choose from the popup at the top of the visual whether to select influencers that potentially increase or decrease the element that you are analyzing.

- Clicking the Segments pane at the top of the visual switches to displaying a segmented population of the element that you are analyzing. You can see this in Figure 18-21.

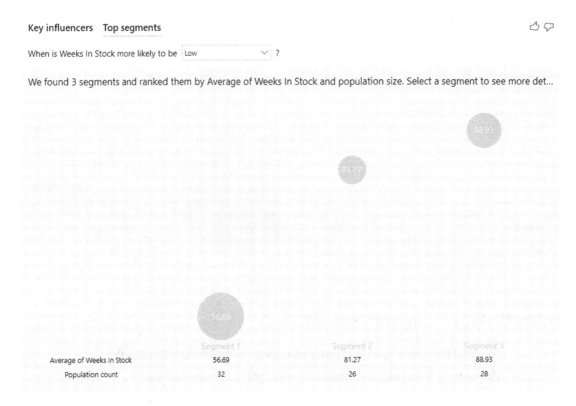

Figure 18-21. *Key Influencers segments*

Conclusion

Over the course of the previous five chapters, you have met a wide range of visuals that let you express the trends hidden in your data. This chapter built on the previous chapters, by adding tree maps, gauges, and R- and Python-based visuals to the mix as well as Decomposition Trees and Key Influencers visuals. In the next chapter, you will see how to extend the already considerable range of visuals available "out of the box" with an extensive choice of third-party visuals that are currently available to download and use in Power BI Desktop.

CHAPTER 19

Third-Party Visuals

By now, you must surely have come to appreciate the sheer range of visual possibilities that Power BI Desktop has to offer. From a range of chart types to gauges, tables, and cards, it delivers a wealth of easy-to-use ways of delivering insight into your data clearly and effectively.

Yet Power BI Desktop does not stop with the built-in visualizations that you have seen so far. It has been designed to be a completely open and extensible business intelligence application that will allow third parties (and even Microsoft) to add other visuals. This means that the core elements that you have met so far are only a starting point. There are many other chart, text, and map visuals that you can add to Power BI Desktop in a few clicks—and then literally stun your audience with an eye-catching variety of dashboard elements.

As a freely extensible platform, Power BI Desktop also hosts a wide and growing variety of visuals developed by both Microsoft and third parties. This gallery of visual extensions is continually growing and incredibly easy to access and use. The final part of this chapter shows you some of the current visuals and how to find, add, and use them in your Power BI Desktop dashboards. This chapter will use the file `C:\PowerBiDesktopSamples\CarSalesDataForReportsWithVisuals.pbix` as the basis for the visuals that you will create.

Adding and using these enhancements are both quick and easy. This is because nearly all Power BI visualizations use the same interface, and they are based on the underlying data model in exactly the same way. Consequently, learning to use a new visual will most likely only take a couple of minutes, as you are always building on the knowledge and techniques that you have already acquired.

Note You need to be aware that not all the custom visuals that are available are entirely bug-free. Also, they might not have all the formatting attributes or interactive capabilities available that you might wish for. However, this does not make them any less useful—or any less fun to use. In any case, we can reasonably expect them to be enhanced and improved over time.

© Adam Aspin 2020
A. Aspin, *Pro Power BI Desktop*, https://doi.org/10.1007/978-1-4842-5763-0_19

The Power BI Visuals Gallery

The first thing to do is become acquainted with the Power BI visuals gallery. This is a central hub where you can find a range of free visuals, developed either by Microsoft or by third parties, that are ready to be added to your Power BI dashboards.

The following explains how to connect to the Power BI visuals gallery:

1. In the Insert ribbon, click the More visuals button, then select FromAppSource in the popup menu. If you are not logged in to a Power BI account, you will see a dialog like the one shown in Figure 19-1, where you can log in.

Figure 19-1. *The Power BI login dialog*

2. Enter your password and sign in. You will see the dialog from Figure 19-2.

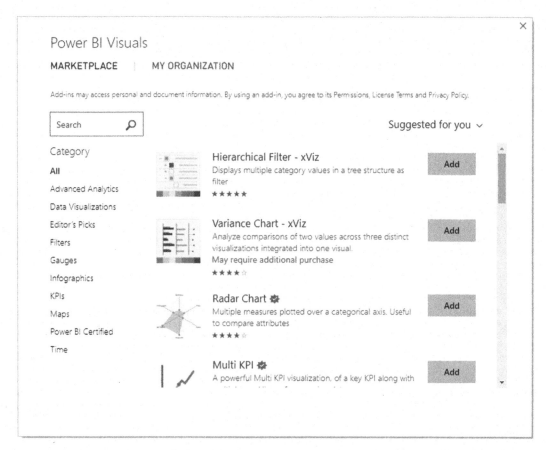

Figure 19-2. *The custom visuals gallery*

3. Click one of the visuals from among those available (you can
    search for a specific visual by entering a search term in the Search
    box or see them grouped and filtered by type if you click a type of
    visual on the left of the dialog). You will see a dialog like the one in
    Figure 19-3.

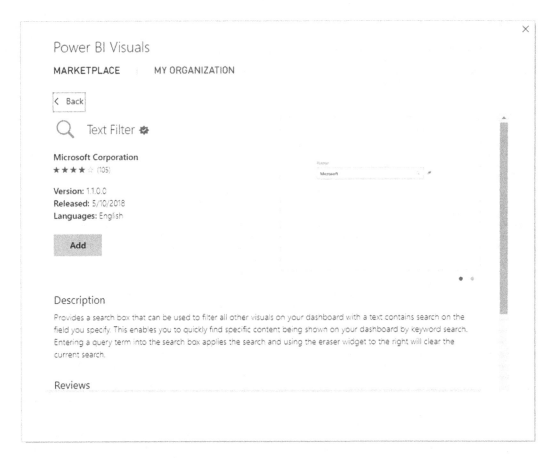

Figure 19-3. *Selecting a third-party visual*

4. Click Add. The visual will be added to the palette of available visualizations, and the dialog that you can see in Figure 19-4 will be displayed.

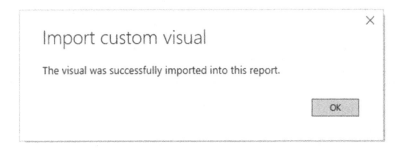

Figure 19-4. *Confirmation dialog for visual import*

5. Click OK. You can now use the visual in the current Power BI Desktop report.

This selection of third-party visuals has undoubtedly evolved considerably since this book went to print, and so I imagine that what you are looking at now is very different. Hopefully, though, you should be excited to see lots of new and amazing types of data visualization that will allow you to add unparalleled pizzazz to your dashboards.

Note   If you are certain that you have found the visual that you want from the initial marketplace dialog (shown in Figure 19-2), then you can import it directly by clicking the Add button.

Loading Custom Visuals from Disk

Another way to access this treasure trove of extra presentation elements for your reports is to download them to your PC and then add them to Power BI Desktop as and when you need them. Here is how to do this:

1. In your web browser, navigate to `https://appsource.microsoft.com/en-us/marketplace/apps?product=power-bi-visuals`. You will see the custom visuals for Power BI web page. As things stand, it looks like Figure 19-5.

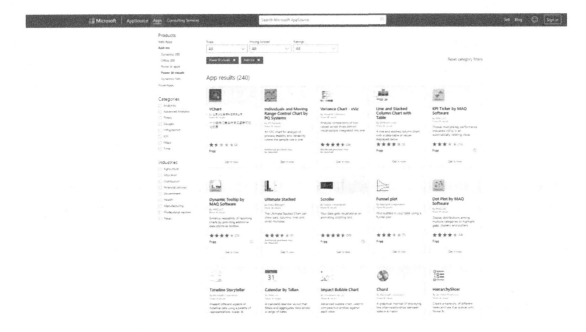

Figure 19-5. *The custom visuals for Power BI web page*

2. Click the visual that you want to download. A second web page
    devoted to this specific visual will be displayed. It will look
    something like Figure 19-6.

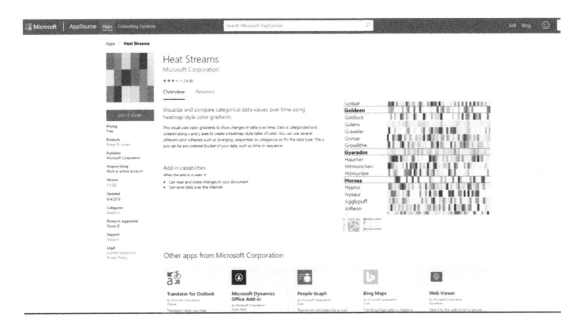

Figure 19-6. *The visuals download dialog*

3. Click the GET IT NOW button.

4. Click Select to Download. The visual will be downloaded.
   Depending on your browser (and any machine-specific
   configuration), it will be placed in a specific folder or give you the
   choice of a folder.

5. In Power BI Desktop, click More visuals ➤ From my files in the
   Home ribbon. A cautionary dialog will appear.

6. Click Import. The Windows File Open dialog will appear.

7. Navigate to the folder where you downloaded the visual file in
   step 4. Click the visual file.

8. Click Open. The confirmation dialog will appear, as shown
   previously in Figure 19-4.

The icon for the visual will appear at the bottom of the visuals gallery in the
Visualizations pane. You can then use this visual just like any other Power BI visual.

Tip   Visuals are added as required to each individual Power BI Desktop file. So
while you only download the visuals once, you have to load them into each Power
BI Desktop (.pbix) file that you want to use them in. If you find yourself frequently
using the same third-party visuals, you should create a Power BI Desktop file that
contains all the visuals that you use and then save it as a template for your future
dashboard development. This was explained in Chapter 9.

Another way to import custom visuals that you have already downloaded is to click
the ellipses in the gallery of visuals in the Visualizations pane. This will display a popup
menu with the option to import visuals—either from the Power BI Store or from your
collection of downloaded visuals.

Once you have added custom visuals to Power BI Desktop, you will see icons
representing them in the Visualizations pane. As you can see in Figure 19-7, they are
grouped underneath the built-in visuals.

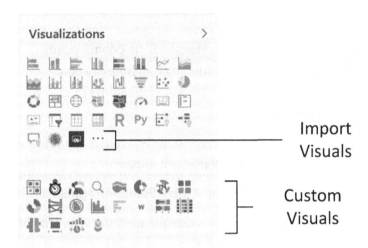

Figure 19-7. *Custom visuals in the Visualizations pane*

Removing Custom Visuals

If you wish to remove a third-party visual from the Visualizations pane

1. Click the ellipses in the gallery of visuals in the Visualizations pane.

2. Select Delete a Custom Visual. The dialog that you can see in Figure 19-8 will appear.

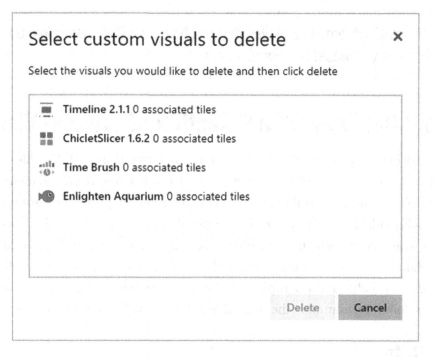

Figure 19-8. *Deleting a custom visual*

3. Select the visual(s) to remove from the current report. You can Ctrl-click several visuals in the dialog to select multiple visuals.

4. Click Delete. The dialog shown in Figure 19-9 will be displayed.

Figure 19-9. *The custom visuals delete dialog*

5. Click Yes, delete.

Note   This will not remove any files that you have previously downloaded. You delete those as you would any standard file.

A Rapid Overview of a Selection of Custom Visuals

As the gallery of custom visuals is in a state of permanent flux, it is impossible to discuss all the currently available extensions to Power BI. However, to give you an idea of some of the possible enhancements that are available, the next few pages show *some* of the added visuals made available by Microsoft. Since there is no guarantee that these visuals will still be available in their current state by the time that you are reading this book, I do not explain how to create them, but merely show some examples of other chart types using the data available in the sample data that you have been using in this book.

In all the following examples, the visual title indicates the fields used to create the visual.

Aster Plots

An *aster plot* is derived from the standard donut chart. However, it uses an extra data value to provide the "sweep" that you see in Figure 19-10.

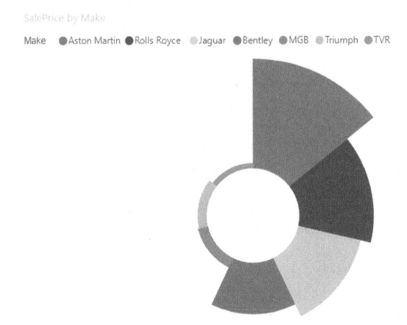

Figure 19-10. *An aster plot*

Radar Charts

Radar charts are often used in performance analyses to display metrics and how they compare. They allow you to show multiple values relative to a shared axis, as you can see in Figure 19-11.

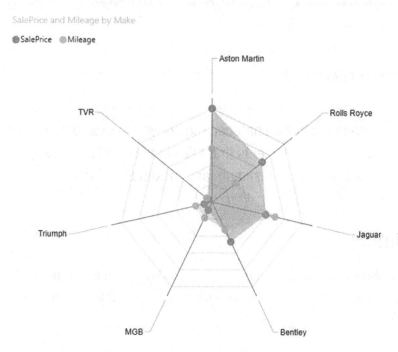

Figure 19-11. *A radar chart*

Bullet Charts

Bullet charts are extremely useful for tracking KPIs against targets. They frequently require you to add data that provides the thresholds against which performance is measured, either as absolute values or as percentages. However, they can be extremely effective at displaying how results compare to targets, as Figure 19-12 shows.

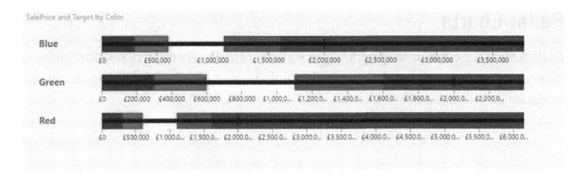

Figure 19-12. *A bullet chart*

Note   Be aware that a bullet chart can require you to extend and prepare the source data to add all the elements that this kind of chart requires—such as the various thresholds as well as minimum and maximum values.

Word Clouds

A *word cloud* shows the number of times that words in a dataset appear relative to each other. It can be a uniquely visual way to show relative weights of values, as you can see in Figure 19-13.

Figure 19-13. *A word cloud*

Streamgraphs

A *streamgraph* is a smoothed, stacked, area chart. As you can see in Figure 19-14, a streamgraph is good at showing how values change over time.

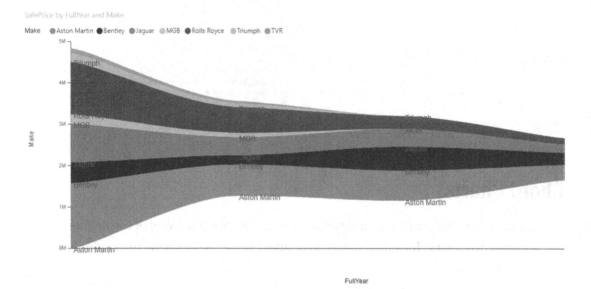

Figure 19-14. *A streamgraph*

Interestingly, a streamgraph has many more formatting options available than is the case for some other imported visuals.

Tornado Charts

A *tornado chart* is a variation of a bar chart, only the separation between two sets of values is made clearer by the vertical separation, as you can see in Figure 19-15. As was the case with bar charts, you can sort tornado charts by any of the data elements in the chart.

LaborCost and SpareParts by Color

Red	£55,281	£85,735
Canary Yellow	£52,794	£98,725
Blue	£35,940	£52,015
Silver	£35,750	£40,620
Black	£31,563	£40,815
Green	£29,921	£37,805
Dark Purple	£25,305	£49,480
British Racing Green	£25,284	£59,880
Night Blue	£20,121	£33,755

Figure 19-15. *A tornado chart*

Chord Charts

A *chord chart* is an interesting—and somewhat less traditional—way of displaying the relationship between values in a matrix structure. Figure 19-16 shows how colors and countries relate by sales.

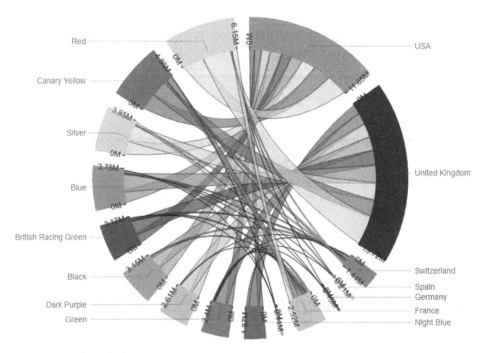

Figure 19-16. *A chord chart*

Sankey Diagrams

The *Sankey diagram* in Figure 19-17 also displays how colors and country sales relate. This chart has been filtered so that it only displays data for four countries.

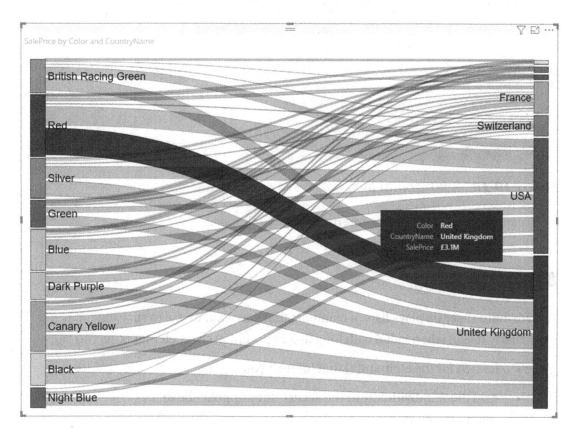

Figure 19-17. *A Sankey diagram*

Horizontal Bar Chart

The horizontal bar chart places the text for each bar inside the bars. This is essentially a space-saving technique. You can see this in Figure 19-18.

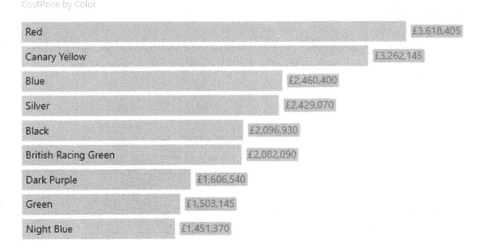

Figure 19-18. *A horizontal bar chart*

It can also display lines, hammerheads, and lollipops.

Attribute Slicer

The attribute slicer displays lists of elements that you want to use to slice data. It is particularly useful when faced with long lists of potential slicer elements, as you can

- Search for the element(s) that interest you.

- Add them individually to the slicer—they appear above the remaining elements.

- See the actual values of each element when you hover over a bar.

You can see an example of this in Figure 19-19.

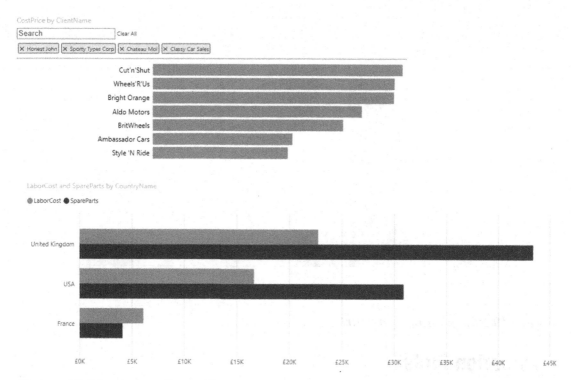

Figure 19-19. An attribute slicer

Histogram Chart

A histogram chart shows data grouped into bins and is an estimate of the probability distribution of a continuous variable. You can see an example of this in Figure 19-20.

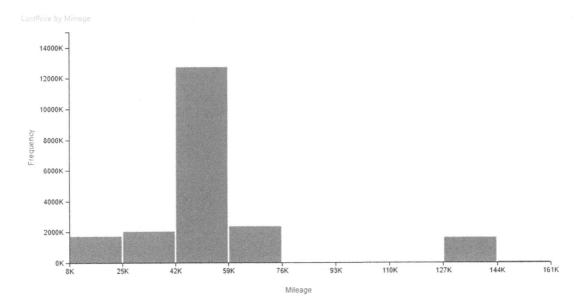

Figure 19-20. *A histogram chart*

Correlation Plots

The correlation plot in Figure 19-21 shows how spare parts and labor costs relate.

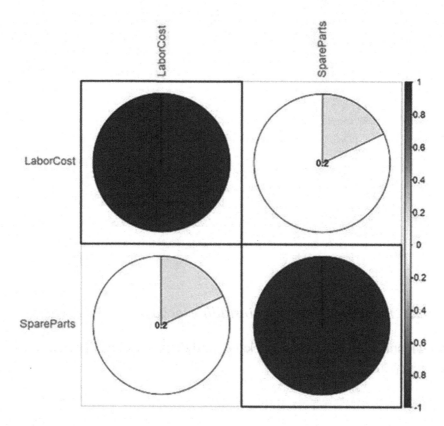

Figure 19-21. *A correlation plot*

It is worth remarking that this visual (like many of the third-party visuals available) uses the R language. This kind of visual will require you to have one or more R packages installed on your computer. If these packages are not already installed, you will see a dialog like the one shown in Figure 19-22.

Figure 19-22. *R packages that need installing locally*

Clicking Install will install the R packages and then cause the dialog that you can see in Figure 19-23 to be displayed.

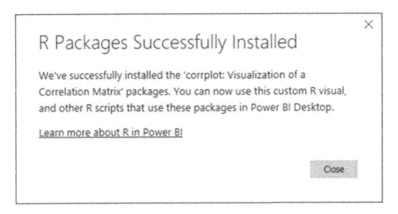

Figure 19-23. *Successfully installed R packages for a custom visual*

Countdown Timer

The countdown shows the number of days, hours, minutes, and seconds in a "clock" that decrements in real time in any report. You can see an example in Figure 19-24.

15 : 21 : 19 : 23
Days Hours Minutes Seconds

Figure 19-24. *The countdown*

Infographic Designer

One addition to the collection of Microsoft-sourced third-party visuals that can add real pizzazz to your dashboards is the Infographic Designer. This visual allows you to create charts that use images for the chart elements. Moreover, it can layer multiple images to create extremely compelling infographics. The only initial drawback is that it uses a highly idiosyncratic interface that can take a while to master—and that is not at all intuitive, in my opinion. In any case it is certainly worth a look.

1. Add the Infographic Designer to the Visualizations pane (unless you have already done this).

2. Click the Infographic Designer icon in the Visualizations pane.

3. Add the following fields:

   a. Make to the Category well.

   b. LaborCost to the Measure well.

4. A fairly standard-looking column chart will appear.

5. Hover the pointer over the visual. The Edit Mark will appear at the top right. You can see an example in Figure 19-25.

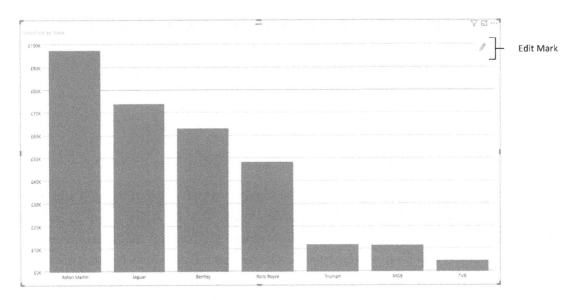

Figure 19-25. *Infographic Designer with Edit Mark*

6. Click the Edit Mark. The Mark Designer—that you can see in Figure 19-26—will appear. This is where you carry out virtually all your modifications to an infographic visual.

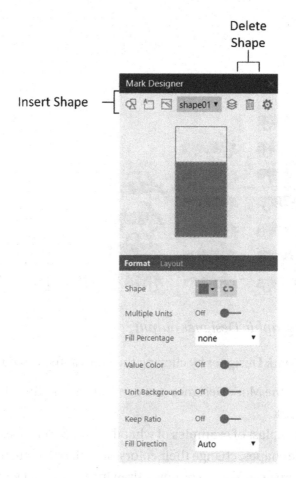

Figure 19-26. *Infographic Designer*

7. Click the Delete Element icon.

8. Click the Insert Shape icon and choose a shape type. I am selecting Transportation in this example.

9. Select a shape. I am selecting the Car shape in this example.

10. In the lower part of the Mark Designer, set Multiple Units to On. You can see an example of the output in Figure 19-27.

Figure 19-27. *Infographic Designer output*

11.   Close the Mark Designer by clicking the cross at the top right.

You can redisplay the Mark Designer and continue formatting visuals simply by reclicking the Edit Mark.

This is only the simplest of examples of what the Infographic Designer can deliver. You can add multiple shapes, change their colors, stretch or isolate them, and so much more. You can even create and add your own drawings. So, when you need a visual that breaks with the more traditional charts and tables that you are using, I suggest that you try it out. Just be aware that it requires a small investment in time to understand its myriad possibilities—and how its interface works.

Custom Slicers

There are also several excellent custom slicers available in the Microsoft App Store. I will introduce a few of these in Chapter 22.

Conclusion

In this chapter, just as you thought that it could not get any better, you discovered the jewel in the crown of Power BI Desktop: an extensive range of freely available extensions that you can add to your dashboards to deliver your insights in ways that leave other analytics tools in the dust. You have met some of the additional visuals that are available for download that let you express the trends hidden in your data.

You can now give free rein to your creativity and astound your audiences with a variety of ways of presenting your insights that will surely impress even the most jaded users.

CHAPTER 20

Maps in Power BI Desktop

Another powerful technique that you can use to both analyze and present your insights is to display the data in map form. All that this requires is that your source data contains information that can be used for geographical representation. So if you have country, state, town, postal (or ZIP) code, or even latitude and longitude in the dataset, then you can get Power BI Desktop to add a map to your report and show the selected data using the map as a background.

Better yet, a Power BI Desktop map behaves just like any other visual. This means that you can filter the data that is displayed in a map, as well as highlight it, just as you can do for charts, tables, and matrices. Not only that, but a map is an integral part of a Power BI Desktop report. So if you highlight data in a chart, a map in the same report will also be highlighted. However, you will have to wait for the next chapter to discover all this in detail.

Power BI Desktop provides you with four types of map visuals:

- Maps
- Filled maps
- Shape maps
- ArcGIS maps

The first three map types are simple and expressive. The fourth type (ArcGIS maps) requires a little more effort to master, but is capable of delivering some truly stunning output.

The aim of this chapter is to show you some of the ways in which you can add real spice to your reports by using maps. Then, when presenting your analyses, you can interact with the maps and *really* impress your audience.

This chapter will use the file `C:\PowerBiDesktopSamples\CarSalesDataForReports.pbix` as the basis for the visuals that you will create.

© Adam Aspin 2020

A. Aspin, *Pro Power BI Desktop*, https://doi.org/10.1007/978-1-4842-5763-0_20

Working with Bing Maps

Before adding the first map, I want to explain how mapping works in Power BI Desktop. The geographical component is based on Bing Maps. So, in order to add a map, you need to be able to connect to the Internet and use the Bing Maps service. Secondly, the underlying dataset must contain fields that are recognized by Bing Maps as geographical data. In other words, you need country, state, town, or other information that Bing Maps can use to generate the plot of the map. Fortunately, Power BI Desktop will indicate if it recognizes a field as containing data that it can use (hopefully) to create a map, as it will display a tiny icon of a globe in the field well for every field in the underlying dataset that apparently contains geographical data.

To avoid the risk of misinterpreting data, you can add metadata to the underlying data model, which defines geographical field types. By applying data categories to fields, Power BI Desktop maps will then use these categories to interpret geographical data for mapping. Preparing data so that any fields used by Bing Maps are not only recognizable as containing geographic data but also uniquely recognizable is vital. You must help Bing Maps so that if you are mapping data for a city named Paris, Bing can see whether you mean Paris, France, or Paris, Texas. Chapter 13 explains some of the ways in which you can prepare your data for use by Bing Maps and, consequently, use it to add map visuals to Power BI Desktop.

Note   There are some areas of the world that cannot use Bing Maps. So if you attempt to use Power BI Desktop mapping in these geographical zones, you will not see any map appear when you attempt to create a map.

Creating Maps in Power BI Desktop

Let's begin by creating a map of Sales by Country. Fortunately, the sample dataset contains the country where the sale was made. This means that we can use this data to make Power BI Desktop display a map of our worldwide sales. Here is how to create an initial map:

1. Open the `C:\PowerBiDesktopSamples\CarSalesDataForReports.pbix` file.

2. Click the Map icon in the Visualizations pane (this is the largely empty globe that you can see in Figure 20-1). A blank map will appear (even if it looks a little peculiar, it is meant to be a map).

3. Expand the Countries table and drag the CountryName field into the map visual. The visual will display a map showing points in all the countries for which there are values.

4. Expand the InvoiceLines table and drag the SalePrice field into the map visual. The visual will change the size of each data point to reflect the sales value.

5. Place the cursor over the map and drag Europe to the center of the map.

6. Using the mouse wheel, zoom in to fit the countries with sales in the center of the visual. It will look something like Figure 20-1.

Figure 20-1. *A map of sales*

It is probably worth clarifying a few points about maps in Power BI Desktop before we go any further. The following are the essential points to note:

- A map is a visual like any other. You can resize and move it anywhere on the Power BI Desktop canvas.

- The map will apply any filters that have been set for the report (you will learn more about filters in the next chapter).

- Each data point (or bubble) in a map is proportional to the relative size of the underlying data.

You can hover the mouse pointer over a data "bubble" to display a popup showing the exact data that is represented. An example of this is shown in Figure 20-2.

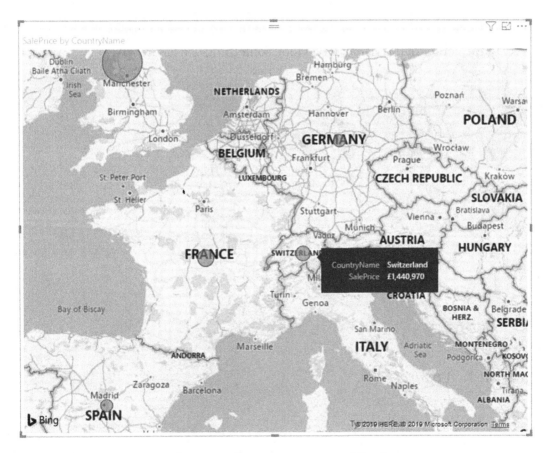

Figure 20-2. *Displaying the exact data in a Power BI Desktop map*

Using Geographical Data

While it might seem obvious, you need geographical data if Power BI Desktop is to display your insights overlaid upon a map. So you really, absolutely must ensure that your underlying dataset contains columns of data that can be interpreted as geographical information. In the examples so far, you have seen how Power BI Desktop is capable of interpreting country names and using these to display data in maps. However, it is not limited to displaying only countries. You can use any of the following to generate map visuals:

- Country

- Zip (postal) code

- State

- County

- Town

- Latitude and longitude

As an example, take a look at Figure 20-3, where the Town field in the Clients table was used in the Location box in the field well. The map was then adjusted to display only the United Kingdom using the techniques described in steps 5 and 6 of the initial example.

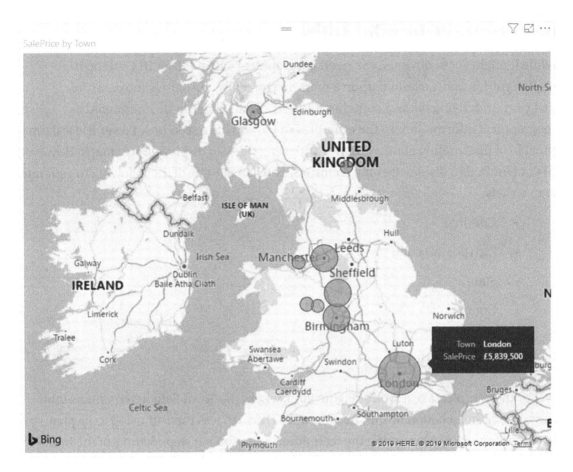

Figure 20-3. *Displaying relative sales per town*

Geographical Data Types

Power BI Desktop really is exceptionally helpful and forgiving when it comes to creating maps. If the data that you have can be interpreted geographically, then Power BI Desktop will do its best to display a map. However, you will almost certainly have to mold the dataset into a coherent data model before you start using Power BI Desktop.

In the first Power BI Desktop example, we added a single geographical data field. What is more, this field was recognized instantly for what it was—country names. In the real world of mapping data, however, you may have to not only add several fields but also specify which type of geographical data each field represents. Put simply, Power BI Desktop needs to know what the data you are supplying represents. Not only that, it needs to know what it is looking at without ambiguity. Consequently, it is up to you to define the source data as clearly and unambiguously as possible. This can involve one or more of several possible approaches.

Define the Data Category in the Data Model

As you saw in Chapter 13, you can define a data category for each column of data in Power Pivot. Although this is not an absolute prerequisite for accurate mapping with Power BI Desktop, it can help reduce the number of potential anomalies.

Add Multiple Levels of Geographical Information

The Power BI Desktop data model lets you add several levels of geographical information to a table. For instance, you can add not just a country but also a county and a town to a record in a table. The advantage of adding as many relevant source data fields as possible is that by working in this way, you are helping Power BI Desktop dispel possibly ambiguous references. For instance, if you only had a Town field, Power BI Desktop might not know if you are referring to Birmingham, Alabama, or England's second city. If the data source has a Country field *and* a Town field, however, then Power BI Desktop has a much better chance of detecting the correct geographical location. This principle can be extended to adding states, counties, and other geographical references.

Drilling Down in Maps

Power BI Desktop lets you drill into geographical data just as you can drill into other data hierarchies in other types of visualization. To see this, you can carry out the following steps:

1. Create a new map visual, using the following fields (and in this order):

    a. CountryName (from the Countries table)

    b. Town (from the Clients table)

    c. SalePrice (from the InvoiceLines table)

2. Click the Drill Mode icon at the top right of the map visual to activate drill down.

3. Click the bubble for the United Kingdom. The map visual will
   display data at the next level (town) for the selected country.
   You can see this in Figure 20-4, which shows both levels of
   data.

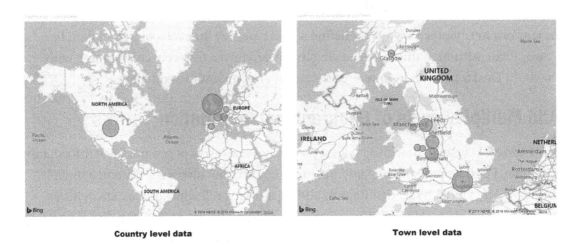

      Country level data   Town level data

Figure 20-4. *Drilling down into a geographical hierarchy*

Fortunately, the techniques that you use to drill down and up in maps are identical
to those that you have already seen for matrices and charts. To resume, briefly

- Click the Drill Up icon at the top left to go up one level.

- Click the "Go to the next level in the hierarchy" icon to see data from
  the next level down.

Note   As you might expect, Power BI Desktop will zoom into a country to show
the detail at the town level if you are drilling down from the country. The map will
stay at its original resolution if you decide to show all data from a lower level.

Adjusting the Map Display in Power BI Desktop

As you have seen, creating a map is extremely easy. However, the initial map is not necessarily the finalized version that you wish to show to your audience. You may wish to

- Position the map elements more precisely inside the visual

- Zoom in or out of the map

In the next few sections, we will look at the various modifications that you can make to Power BI Desktop maps. Hopefully, you will find these tweaks both intuitive and easy to implement. In any case, with a little practice, you should find that these modifications take only a few seconds to accomplish.

Positioning the Map Elements

If the area displayed in a map is not quite as perfect as you would prefer, then you can alter the area (whether it is a country or a region) that appears in the map visual. You can do this as follows:

1. Place the mouse pointer over the map. The pointer icon will become a hand icon.

2. Click and drag the pointer around to move the map elements.

Zooming In or Out

It is conceivable that the map that is displayed is not at a scale, which you would prefer. Fortunately, this is extremely easy to fix. All you have to do is the following:

1. Place the mouse pointer over the map.

2. Roll the mouse scroll wheel forward to zoom in to see a part of the map in greater detail. Alternatively, roll the mouse scroll wheel backward to zoom out of the map.

Note   There are currently no keyboard shortcuts for moving around in maps or zooming in and out of maps.

Multivalue Series

So far, you have seen how you can add a single data series to a map and have the data represented as a data point. Power BI Desktop can extend this paradigm by allowing you to display the data bubble as a pie that contains a second data series—and consequently display the data broken down by a specific dataset per geographical entity.

As an example of this (and to revise some of the map creation techniques that we have seen so far), let's try to analyze European car sales by age range:

1. Keep the map that you created in the previous section (or create it if you have not yet done so).

2. Expand the Colors table and drag the Color field into the Legend field well.

3. Resize the map visual.

The map now contains a legend for the colors of vehicles sold. Each bubble is now a pie of data. The overall size of the pie represents, proportionally, the sum total data for each country compared to the other pies. The map should now look like Figure 20-5.

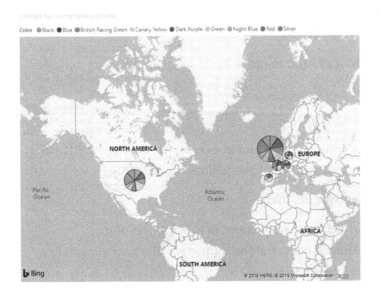

Figure 20-5. *Displaying pie charts in a Power BI Desktop map*

It is worth remarking that if you hover the mouse pointer over the data representation (the pie) for a country, as you pass the pointer over each pie segment, you will see a tooltip giving the details of the data, including which car color it refers to.

Note   When displaying maps, you nearly always need to filter data in some way. You will discover all the details about filtering data in the next chapter.

Highlighting Map Data

If you have added data to the Legend box of the field well, and a legend is displayed, you can highlight segments of data in a map. This allows you to draw the audience's attention to specific trends in your data.

Using the map that you created previously and can see in Figure 20-5, click Blue (the second element) in the legend. The pie segments that correspond to blue cars sold are highlighted, as shown in Figure 20-6.

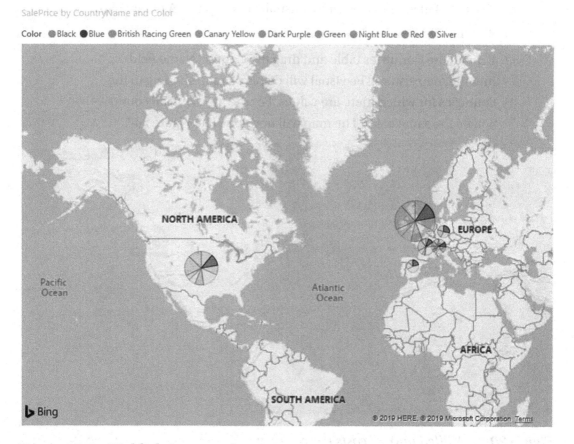

Figure 20-6. *Highlighting map data*

To remove highlighting from a map, all you have to do is click the legend element that you are using to highlight data or simply click the title of the legend. Alternatively, click any of the highlighted elements on the map.

This is just a preview of how Power BI Desktop applies highlighting to visuals. You will learn more about this technique in Chapter 22.

Filled Maps

Another way to display data is to fill a geographical area with color rather than to display a bubble. Power BI Desktop lets you do this, too.

1. Click an empty part of the dashboard canvas in the
   `C:\PowerBiDesktopSamples\CarSalesDataForReports.pbix` file.

2. Click the Filled Map icon in the Visualizations pane. A blank map
   will appear.

3. Expand the Countries table and drag the CountryName field
   into the map visual. The visual will display a map shading in the
   countries for which there are values. For the moment, all countries
   will be the same color. The map will now look like Figure 20-7.

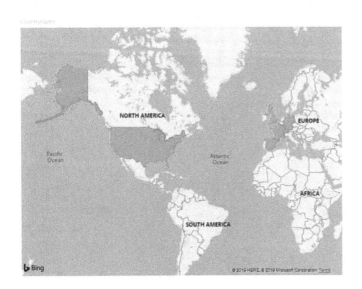
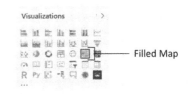

Figure 20-7. *A filled map of costs per country*

4. Select the Format icon and expand the Data colors section.

5. Hover the pointer over the default color. The vertical ellipses (three dots) will appear to the top right of this section of the Formatting pane.

6. Click the ellipses. The Conditional formatting popup will appear. Click this, and the Default Color – Data colors dialog will appear.

7. In the Based on field popup, expand the Stock table and select the CostPrice. Select different colors for the Minimum and Maximum values. The Default Color – Data colors dialog will look like the one in Figure 20-8.

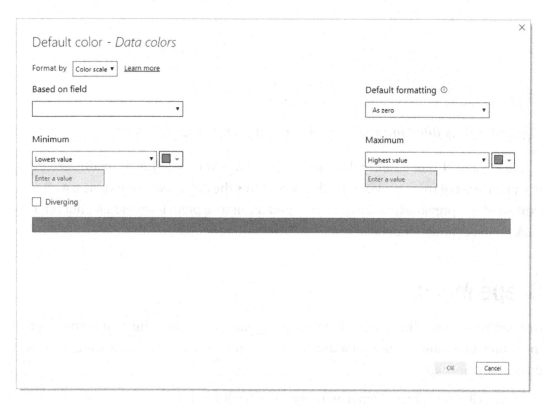

Figure 20-8. *Setting the fill colors for a map*

8. Click OK. The map will change the color of the shading for each country to reflect the sales value. A darker shade indicates a higher value. The map will now look like Figure 20-9.

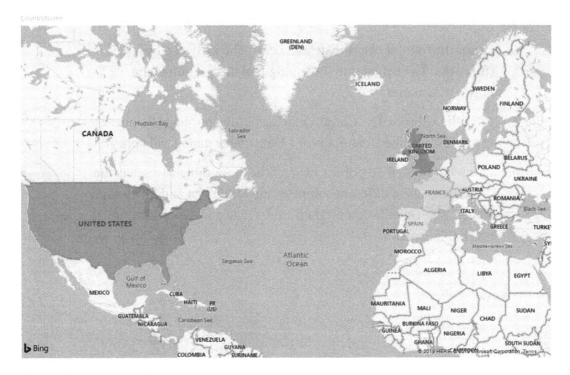

Figure 20-9. *A filled map of costs per country with custom shading*

The Default Color – Data colors dialog also allows you to define the colors according to a precise set of rules or even a field that contains the color reference values. As I explained this previously in Chapter 14, I prefer not to explain it again here, but refer you back to that chapter for details.

Shape Maps

Another way to visualize geographical data is by state or region. This option implies that the source data contains the standard codes that are used to define states and regions. To create a shape map:

1. Click the Shape Map icon in the Visualizations pane.

2. Drag the OuterPostcode field (from the Clients table) into the Location well (or into the map).

3. Drag the SalePrice field (from the InvoiceLines table) into the
    Color saturation well (or into the map). The shape map will look
    like the one in Figure 20-10.

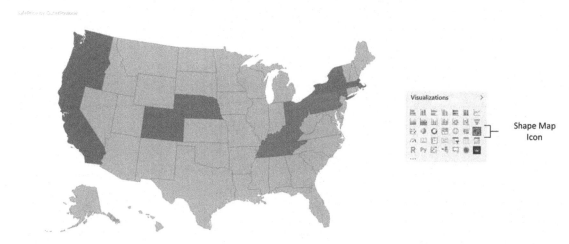

Figure 20-10. *A shape map*

Map Keys

You will probably need to find the map keys (the region codes) that Power BI Desktop
uses to display data in a shape map. This way you can add them to your source data or
tweak the source data to include the appropriate geographical codes.

1. Select the shape map that you created in Figure 20-10.

2. Click the Format icon in the Visualizations pane.

3. Expand the Shape section.

4. Select the map (the country) whose codes you want to display.

5. Click View Map Keys. A dialog containing the map keys will be
    displayed, as you can see in Figure 20-11.

Figure 20-11. *Map keys for a specific country*

This is the list of the data elements that Power BI Desktop will use to allocate data to a geographical area. It follows that you will need to have this data—or to be prepared to add it—in your source data. So at least one column in the source data must correspond to one of the values shown in Figure 20-11.

Adding Shape Maps

If you have specific map shapes (and this can include everything from towns to floor plans), then you can load these by clicking the Add Map button in the Shape section of the Formatting pane for shape maps.

Shape map definitions must be created in a specific .json format. Unfortunately, looking at creating these is outside the scope of this book.

Formatting Maps

As you would probably expect, there are numerous formatting options that you can apply to maps. Indeed, the way that you can format maps is virtually identical to the way that you apply formatting to other visuals. Given that the five previous chapters covered many of these options in detail, I will only explain the possibilities in this section and refer you back to Chapters 14 through 18 if you want all the details.

As far as maps and filled maps are concerned, you can modify the following:

- *Title*: This includes displaying or hiding the title, as well as setting the title text, font color, and background color.

- *Background*: This covers applying a background, setting its color, and defining its transparency.

- *Lock aspect*: If you set Lock Aspect to On, then you can resize the map while keeping it sized proportionally.

- *Border*: You can add or remove a border for a map just as you can with just about any Power BI Desktop visual.

All map types allow you to adjust the data colors. However, the way that the colors are modified is slightly different, depending on the map type. We will now look at the individual formatting options by map type.

Maps

Map visuals allow you to adjust the following aspects of their formatting:

- Data colors
- Category labels
- Bubbles
- Map controls
- Map styles

Some of these elements are similar to formatting options that you have seen before, so I will not re-explain them here. However, other elements of formatting are handled either in completely new ways or in a manner so different from how a similar format option is dealt with in other types of visual that they need a fresh explanation.

Data Colors

Selecting a data color for a map allows you to select the color that will be used for the data bubble.

Note   You cannot apply different colors to the various data points in a map.

Category Labels

If you need to supply the name of the geographical element that is currently displayed in a map (the town or the country, say), then you can set the Category labels button to On. If you expand the Category labels section, then you can also choose the font family, size, and color for the category labels.

Bubbles

Expanding the Bubbles section allows you to adjust the Size slider to set the relative size of the bubbles. You can see an example of this in Figure 20-12.

Map Controls

There is currently only one map control that can be tweaked, and that is the auto zoom function. The default (Auto Zoom set to On) means that filtering the map data will cause only relevant geographical areas to appear in the map. If you switch this option to Off, then the map will display the same area until you alter this manually.

Map Styles

There are currently five map styles in the version of Power BI Desktop that was available as this book went to press:

- Road (the default)
- Aerial

- Dark

- Light

- Grayscale

You can see the difference that selecting an aerial view makes in Figure 20-12 (where you can also see the effect of tweaking the bubble size and adding category labels).

Figure 20-12. *A formatted map*

Tooltips

Just as was the case for charts, you can add extra data fields to the Tooltips well in the Visualizations pane. Then, when you hover the pointer over a map data point (which could be a country in a shaded map like the one in Figure 20-12), you will see the extra data information for the map point in the tooltip.

Shape Maps

The essential thing that you can change in a shape map is the color—or colors—of the actual shapes. Apart from this—which you have already seen—you have one main option:

- Set a color range for each geographical area for which there is data.

As well, you can select a color for any parts of the map for which there is no data.

Defining a Color Range for Data

If a shape map contains numeric data, then you can set the colors for each geographical zone using a diverging color range—much as you did in the case of a filled map. Here is how:

1. Create a shape map by adding Outer Postcode field (from the Clients table) to the Location well in the Visualizations pane and the SalePrice field (from the InvoiceLines table) to the Color saturation well.

2. Click the Format icon and expand the Data colors section (in the middle of the Formatting pane).

3. Set Diverging to On.

4. Select a color for the Minimum, Center, and Maximum.

5. Expand the Default color section.

6. Set Show to On.

7. Select a default color from the Color palette.

8. Select a border color from the Border color palette. The map will now look like the one in Figure 20-13.

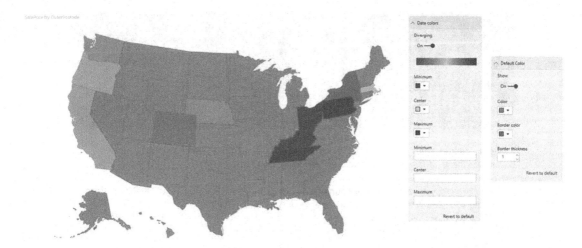

Figure 20-13. *A shaded filled map*

ArcGIS Maps

Microsoft has collaborated with ESRI (an international supplier of geographic information system [GIS] software) to include ArcGIS mapping in Power BI Desktop. Quite simply, this feature allows you to take geospatial representation of data to a whole new level. Using ArcGIS maps, you can

- Perform spatial analysis by adding heat maps and aggregating data

- Add demographic and reference data

- Make any map look great

Creating an ArcGIS Map

In this section you will see a couple of examples of how using ArcGIS maps can add real pizzazz to your dashboards.

1. Open the file C:\PowerBiDesktopSamples\
   CarSalesDataForReports.pbix.

2. In the Visualizations pane, click the ArcGIS maps for Power BI
   icon. The Welcome dialog will appear, as shown in Figure 20-14.

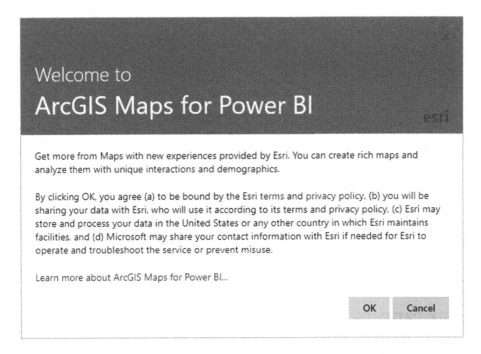

Figure 20-14. *The ArcGIS Welcome dialog*

    3.   A blank ArcGIS map will be added to the report canvas. You can see this in Figure 20-15.

Figure 20-15. *The ArcGIS map visual placeholder*

    4.   Add the following fields to the ArcGIS map:

       a. Town (from the Clients table)

       b. SalePrice (from the InvoiceLines table)

5. Enlarge the visual to get a clearer view. The ArcGIS map will look like the one in Figure 20-16.

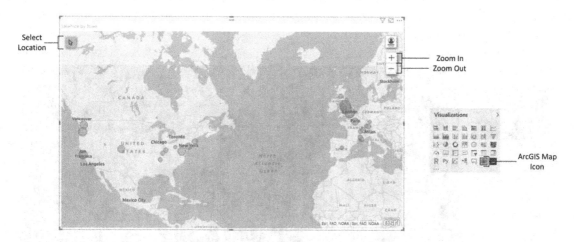

Figure 20-16. *An initial ArcGIS map*

So far so easy—and in all honesty, this is not so very different from what you have done already using the traditional Power BI Desktop mapping tools. However, things are about to get much more interesting as you learn to use the added options in ArcGIS maps.

Note   You can move the display area in an ArcGIS map or zoom in and out just as you can for any other map in Power BI Desktop.

Selecting a Basemap Type

Once you have created an ArcGIS map, you can extend it with some powerful effects. One option is to change the appearance of the map itself:

1. In the ArcGIS map, click the popup menu at the top right (the ellipses).

2. Select Edit from the context menu. The map will expand to full screen and add the mapping toolbar at the top of the map.

3. Click Basemap at the left of the toolbar.

4. Select a basemap from the palette of available types. The map
    display will change to reflect your choice, as you can see in
    Figure 20-17.

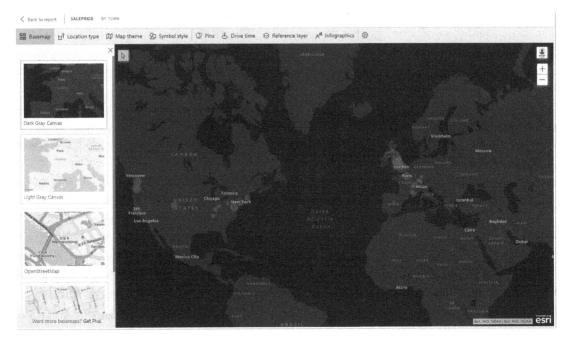

Figure 20-17.   *Changing the basemap type of an ArcGIS map*

5. Click Back to Report at the top left of the ArcGIS map to return to
    the report canvas.

Note   To close the palette of basemaps and display only the map itself, simply
click the small cross at the top right of the basemap type palette. This will, of
course, only apply to ArcGIS editing mode.

Selecting a Location Type

You can choose how map data is displayed using the Location type option. This lets you
decide between displaying

- Data as points

- Data as boundaries (areas)

If you select that locations will be represented as boundaries, you can then select exactly which boundaries will be displayed. The type of boundary will depend on the selected country. Table 20-1 shows a few of the boundary definitions that are available.

Table 20-1. *Boundary Types*

Location Type	Country	Description
Entire country	USA	Takes the entire USA as the map boundary.
States	USA	Uses each state as a geographical element.
DMAs	USA	Uses each DMA as a geographical element.
Congressional districts	USA	Uses each congressional district as a geographical element.
CBSAs	USA	Uses each core-based statistical area as a geographical element.
Counties	USA	Uses each county as a geographical element.
County subdivisions	USA	Uses each part of a county as a geographical element.
ZIP codes	USA	Uses each ZIP (postal) code as a geographical point.
Cities and towns	USA	Uses individual towns and cities as a geographical point.
Census tracts	USA	Uses each census area as a geographical element.
Block Groups	USA	Uses each Census Block Group as a geographical boundary.
Country	UK	Uses each of the four countries of the UK as a geographical boundary.
Regions	UK	Uses each region as a geographical element.
Postcode areas	UK	Uses each postcode area as a geographical element.
Counties	UK	Uses each county as a geographical boundary.
Districts	UK	Uses each district as a geographical element.
Postcode districts	UK	Uses each postcode district (outer postcode) as a geographical element.
Postcode sectors	UK	Uses each postcode sector (inner postcode) as a geographical element.
Census areas	UK	Uses each census area as a geographical element.

Note   For boundary display to be effective, the underlying data must contain the data that allows ArcGIS maps to identify the boundary.

Adding a Map Theme

Map themes let you change the way that geographical data is displayed to powerful effect. As an example, suppose that you want to display the sales data as a heat map:

1. Edit the ArcGIS map that you created previously.

2. Select Map theme from the menu buttons. A palette of available options appears on the left.

3. Select Heat Map.

You can see the results of selecting this option in Figure 20-18.

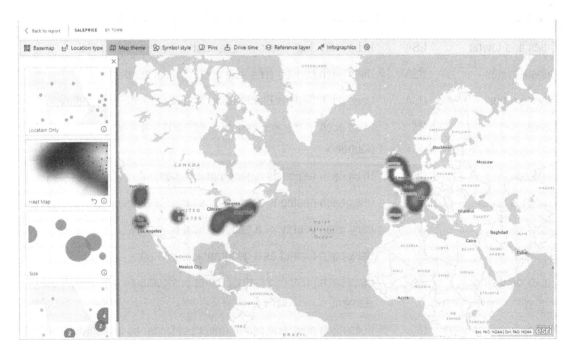

Figure 20-18. *A heat map applied to an ArcGIS map*

Choosing a Symbol Type

ArcGIS maps also give you a variety of ways of displaying data points on a map. You can see this in the following example:

1. Re-create the ArcGIS map that you first saw in Figure 20-16 at the start of this section.

2. Edit the map.

3. Ensure that the Map theme is Location Only.

4. Select Symbol style from the menu buttons.

5. Under Symbol style on the left, select the diamond symbol.

6. Increase the symbol size by dragging the Symbol size slider to the right.

7. Select a symbol fill color from the palette of available colors.

8. Tweak the outline color and thickness (and the various transparency settings) if you wish. You will see something like the map shown in Figure 20-19.

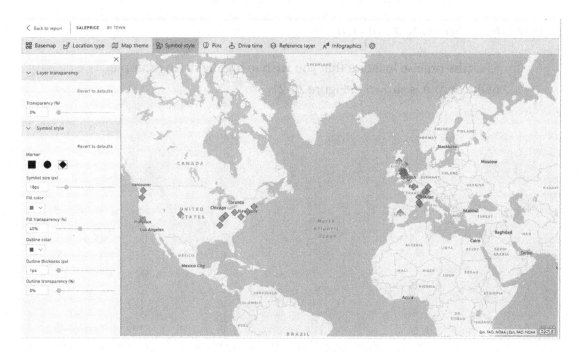

Figure 20-19. *An ArcGIS map with formatted symbols*

Adding Pins

An original way to highlight specific points on a map is to add a pin. This is used to highlight a specific geographical location independently of the underlying data. You do this using the Pins menu button of the ArcGIS Maps toolbar as follows:

1. In an existing ArcGIS map visual, click the Pins menu button of the ArcGIS Maps toolbar. The Locations pane will appear on the left.

2. Enter the location to search for in the search field. A list of possible locations will appear, as shown in Figure 20-20.

Figure 20-20. *Selecting a pin location*

3. Click the precise location that you wish to highlight. An example of the output is shown in Figure 20-21.

Figure 20-21. *A pin added to an ArcGIS map*

To remove a pin, simply click Delete for the pin that you want to remove from the map in the Locations pane.

Tip   You can add multiple individual pins to an ArcGIS map.

Adding a Reference Layer

ArcGIS maps allow you to access certain statistical geographical datasets and add them to maps. You could, for instance, add the median American home value data to a map and see how (if at all) that relates to car sales:

1. Re-create the initial ArcGIS map that you used at the start of this section.

2. Edit the ArcGIS map.

3. Click the Reference layer button on the ArcGIS Maps toolbar.

4. Select the 2016 USA Median Home Value reference layer from the Reference layer pane. You can see this in Figure 20-22.

Figure 20-22. *Some of the available reference layers in ArcGIS maps*

5. Adjust the map display to zoom in on the United States. You can
    see the resulting map with reference data in Figure 20-23.

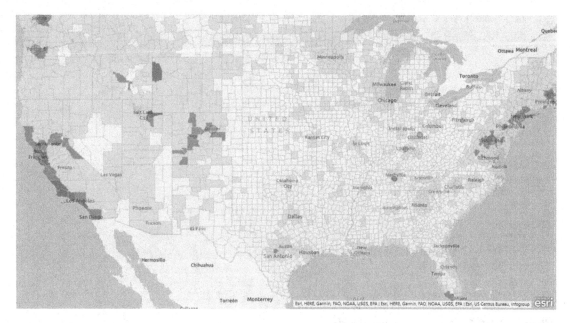

Figure 20-23. *A USA map with reference data added*

Tip   You can only add one layer of reference data at a time.

Adding Infographics

ArcGIS maps also come with access to data relating to demographics. This data is limited to North America for the moment. You can add reference data like this:

1. Re-create and then edit the initial ArcGIS map that you used at the start of this section.

2. Click the Infographics button on the ArcGIS Maps toolbar.

3. Select the following options:

    a. Total population

    b. Household income

4. Zoom in to the San Francisco area on the map. The reference data is adjusted to correspond to the area that is displayed. You can see this in Figure 20-24.

Figure 20-24. *ArcGIS reference data*

Conclusion

In this chapter, you saw how to display geographical data in a variety of map types, from filled maps, where the data is represented by the intensity of an area's shading, to bubble maps, where the size of data points on a map lets the data speak for itself. You also saw how to add truly expressive ArcGIS map visuals to your reports, where you were able to add extra geographical data to enhance your analysis.

Over the course of seven chapters, you have met a wide range of visuals that let you express the trends hidden in your data. This chapter built on the six previous chapters, where you learned all about text-based visuals, charts, tree maps, gauges, and custom visuals, by adding maps to the mix. Now it is time to learn how to filter and slice the data in your dashboards.

CHAPTER 21

Filtering Data

Power BI Desktop is built from the ground up to enable you, the user, to sift through mounds of facts and figures so that you can deliver meaningful insights. Consequently, what matters is being able to delve into data and highlight the information it contains quickly and accurately. This way, you can always explore a new idea or simply follow your intuitions without needing either to apply complex processes or to struggle with an impenetrable interface. After all, Power BI Desktop is there to help you come up with new analyses that could give your business an edge on the competition.

Power BI Desktop provides three main approaches to assist you in focusing on the key elements of your data:

- *Filters*: Restrict the data displayed in a report, page, or visual. This is the subject of the current chapter.

- *Slicers*: Allow users to filter data interactively inside a dashboard— and to see the results instantly.

- *Cross-filtering*: Allows you to highlight key information instantly and visually for an audience.

We will look at filters in this chapter, and slicers and cross-filtering in the next chapter.

Filters

The people who developed Power BI Desktop recognize that your data is the key to delivering accurate analysis. This is why you can filter on any field or set of fields in the underlying data model to extract its real value. This approach is not only intuitive and easy, it is also extremely fast, which ensures that you almost never have to wait for results to be returned.

© Adam Aspin 2020
A. Aspin, *Pro Power BI Desktop*, https://doi.org/10.1007/978-1-4842-5763-0_21

Filters apply to the data that underlies reports and visuals. They are not necessarily made visible to the user. They are, nevertheless, immensely powerful in restricting the data that appears in a dashboard.

You can add filters before, after, or during the creation of a Power BI Desktop report. If you add filters before creating a table, then your table will only display the data that the filter allows through. If you add a filter to an existing report, then the data visualization will alter before your eyes to reflect the new filter. If you modify a filter when you have visualizations on a Power BI Desktop report, then (as you probably guessed by now) all the visualizations affected by the filter will also be updated to reflect the new filter criteria—instantaneously.

You can filter any type of data:

- Text

- Numeric values

- Dates

- Logical values

Each data type has its own ways of selecting elements and setting (where possible) ranges of values that can be included—or excluded. This chapter will explain the various techniques for isolating only the data that you want to display. You will then be able to create Power BI Desktop reports based only on the data that you want them to show.

We will see all how these approaches work in detail in the rest of this chapter. In any case—and as is so often the case with Power BI Desktop—it is easier to grasp these ideas by seeing them in practice than by talking about them, so let's see how filters work. This chapter uses the `C:\PowerBiDesktopSamples\CarSalesDataForReports.pbix` sample file as the basis for all the filters that you will learn to apply.

Filter Hierarchy

Subsetting data in Power BI Desktop is based on the correct application of filters. Consequently, the first thing that you need to know about filters is that they work at three levels. You have

- Report-level filters

- Page-level filters

- Visualization-level filters

The characteristics of these three kinds of filter are described in Table 21-1.

Table 21-1. *Power BI Desktop Filters*

Filter Type	Application	Comments
Report-level	Applies to every visualization in the current report.	Filters data for every visual in the current file.
Page-level	Applies to every visualization in the active page.	Filters data for every visual in the current page.
Visual-level	Only applies to the selected visualization.	Applies only to the selected visual (table, chart, etc.).

Filters are always applied in exactly the same way. What matters is the extent that they affect the visuals in a Power BI Desktop presentation. In practice, this makes your life much easier because you only have to learn how to apply a filter once, and then you can use it in the same way at different levels in separate files.

Let's now look at how to use filters, beginning at the lowest level of the filter hierarchy: visual-level filters.

Visual-Level Filters

Saying that there are three types of filter available in Power BI Desktop is a purely descriptive distinction. For Power BI Desktop, any filter is a filter, and all filters work in the same way. However, as there is a clear hierarchy in their application, I will begin with visual-level filters and then move on to their ascendants—page-level filters and report-level filters. Given the general similarity between the three, it is probably worth noting that it is important you ensure that you are creating or modifying the appropriate filter. As this is not always obvious, not least when you are starting out with Power BI Desktop, I will try to make it clear as we proceed how exactly you can distinguish at what level you are applying a filter, as the effects can have wide-ranging consequences for the message that you are trying to convey.

The Filters Pane

The first thing to note is that all filters are applied in the Filters Pane. This is a collapsible pane immediately to the right of the report canvas and looks (for a selected sample visual) like Figure 21-1.

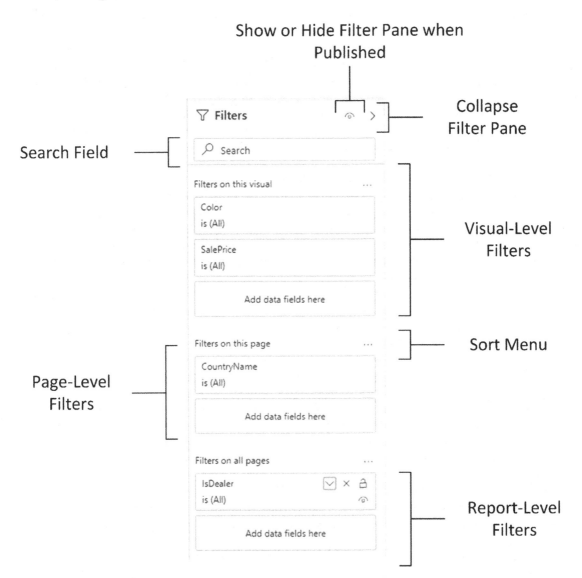

Figure 21-1. *The Filters Pane*

As you can see in this figure, different filters have been applied at all the possible levels of the filter hierarchy. If you look closely, you can also see that each filter gives an indication of how (if at all) the filter is applied. Since no filtering has been applied here, each filter shows *All* as the current selection. This tells you that all data is allowed through for the filter. You will learn how to add and adjust filters in the following few pages.

Note   The Filters Pane only shows visual-level filters if a visual is selected.

Collapsing and Expanding the Filters Pane

The Filters Pane takes up a significant amount of screen real estate. This can be mitigated by collapsing the Filters Pane when you do not need it and expanding it when you need either to add filters or modify existing filters.

To collapse the Filters Pane, simply click the collapse button (the right-facing chevron) at the top right of the Filters Pane. The pane will become a thin vertical bar on the right of the screen. To make the Filters Pane reappear, click once again the same button (which is now a left-facing chevron). You can see the collapse/expand button in Figure 21-1.

Adding Filters

The Filters Pane automatically adds any fields that you use as the basis for a visualization. To see this, create the following visual:

1. Open the C:\PowerBiDesktopSamples\CarSalesDataForReports. pbix file.

2. Create a clustered bar chart using these fields:

   a. Make (from the Stock table)

   b. SalePrice (from the InvoiceLines table)

The Filters Pane will look like Figure 21-2.

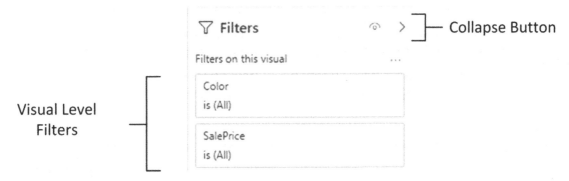

Figure 21-2. *Automatic creation of visual-level filters*

Figure 21-2 shows that adding a data field to a visual automatically adds the same field to the Visual-Level Filters Pane.

Applying Filters

To see the filter working, let's limit the chart to displaying only a few makes of vehicle:

1. Select the clustered bar chart that you created previously.

2. In the Filters Pane, hover the pointer over the Make filter. A downward-facing chevron will appear at the right of the field that is being used as a filter. This will be a visual-level filter.

3. Expand the Make filter by clicking the chevron. The Filters Pane will display all the makes that appear in the visual.

4. Select the following makes in the Filters Pane by selecting the check box to the left of each of the following elements:

    a. Jaguar

    b. Rolls Royce

    c. Triumph

You will see that data is only displayed for the makes of car that were selected in the filter. The resulting chart should look like Figure 21-3.

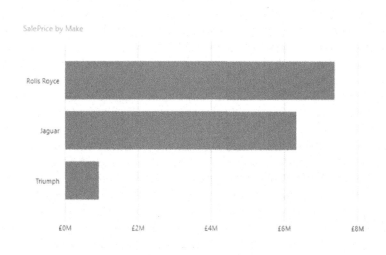

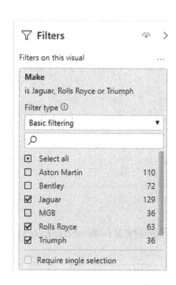

Figure 21-3. *A simple filtered chart*

You will have noticed that when the filter was first applied, every check box was empty, including the Select all check box. The default is (fairly logically) to set up a filter ready for tweaking, but not actually to filter any data until the user has decided what filters to apply. Once you start adding filter elements, they will be displayed in the Filters Pane just below the name of the field that is being used to filter data. Another point to note is that once a filter has been modified, it will normally be displayed in a different color in the Filters Pane.

You modify filters the same way you apply them. All you have to do to remove a selected filter element is to click the check box with a check mark to clear it. Conversely, to add a supplementary filter element, just click a blank check box.

One final thing to note is that if you subsequently minimize the filter for a field (by clicking the upward-facing chevron that has replaced the downward-facing chevron to the right of the field name), you will now see not only the field name in the Filters Pane but also a succinct description of the filter that has been applied. You can see an example of this in Figure 21-4.

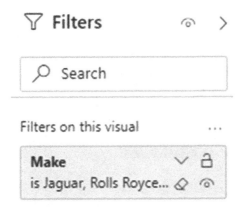

Figure 21-4. *Filter description*

Note   You can also add fields to the Filters Pane before adding data fields to the visual. Simply create a blank visual and then leave it selected while you add the filter fields to the Filters Pane.

The Select All Filter

The only subtlety concerning simple filters is that you also have the Select all check box. This acts as a global on/off switch to select, or deselect, all the available filter elements for a given filter field. The Select all filter field has three states:

- *Blank*: No filters are selected for this field.

- *Checked*: All filters are selected for this field.

- *Dotted*: Some filters are selected for this field.

Checking or unchecking the Select all filter field will select or deselect all filter elements for this field, in effect rendering the filter inactive. The Select all filter field is particularly useful when you want not only to remove multiple filter selections in order to start over but also want to select all elements in order to deselect certain elements individually (and avoid manually selecting reams of elements).

Note   When selecting multiple elements in filter lists, you may be tempted to apply the classic Windows keyboard shortcuts that you may be in the habit of using in, for instance, Excel or other Windows applications. Unfortunately, Ctrl- or Shift-clicking

---

to select a subset of elements does not work. Neither can you select and deselect a check box using the space bar. It is not possible to use the cursor keys to pass from one element to another in a filter list either.

Clearing Filters

Setting up a finely honed filter so that you are drilling through the noise in your data to the core information can take some practice. Fortunately, the virtually instantaneous application of filters means that you can see almost immediately if you are heading down the right path in your analysis. However, there are frequent occasions when you want to start over and remove any settings for a particular filter. This can be done in one of two ways. The first is a single step:

1. With the filter contents expanded, click the small eraser icon to the right of the filter, as shown in Figure 21-5.

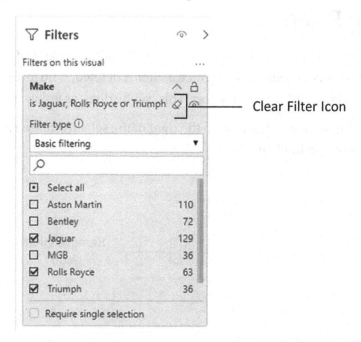

Figure 21-5. *The Clear Filter icon*

Alternatively, you can do the following, but *only* for basic filters:

1. Expand the filter in the Filters Pane by clicking the downward-facing chevron.

2. Click the Select all option to remove all filter selections.

3. Minimize the filter.

Once a filter has been cleared, the only way to get it back to its previous state is to press Ctrl+Z immediately. Otherwise, you will have to reapply the requisite criteria.

Adding Filters

You are not restricted to filtering visuals on the data fields that you used to create the visual. You can, in fact, filter a visual on any field in the data model. To do this:

1. Drag the field you want to filter on into the Add data fields here well in the Filters on this visual section of the Filters Pane.

2. Apply the filter as you saw in previous sections.

Removing Filters

When working with filters, at times you may want to clear the decks and start over. The fastest way to do this is to delete a filter; once a filter is deleted, it no longer has any effect on the data in the Power BI Desktop report. This can be done as follows:

1. Click the Remove Filter icon to the right of the selected filter. This icon is shown in Figure 21-6.

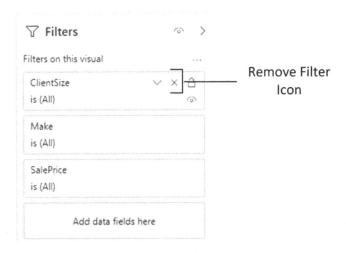

Figure 21-6. Removing a filter

The art here is to ensure that you have selected the correct filter to remove. The technique, however, is the same for all report- and page-level filters, as well as for visual-level filters that are not used to display data.

Once a filter has been removed, the only way to get it back is to click Undo (or press Ctrl+Z) immediately; otherwise, you will have to rebuild it from scratch. Interestingly, although you can add filters by dragging elements into the Filters Pane, you cannot drag them out of the Filters Pane to remove them.

However, you can remove visualization-level fields (that are not used as data for the visual) from the Filters Pane by clicking the cross at the right of the field name.

Note   Visual-level filters cannot be removed, only reset to empty so that no filters are applied.

Filtering Different Data Types

So far, you have only seen how Power BI Desktop can filter text elements. Although text-based elements are a major part of many data filters, they are far from the only available type of data. There are also

- Numeric data

- Date and time data

- Logical (true/false) data

Filtering Numeric Data

You can filter on numeric elements just as you can filter on text-based elements in Power BI Desktop. However, when filtering on numbers, you likely want to select ranges of numbers as precise figures.

Range Filter Mode

The first trick worth knowing is that, when filtering on numeric data, the default option is to use a *threshold selector*, which is the only filter for numeric filters. The threshold selector allows you to set the lower and/or upper limits of the range of numbers that you want to display in a Power BI Desktop report, page, or visual.

The following explains how to set the range of figures for which data is displayed:

1. Select the chart that you created previously.

2. Clear any existing filters.

3. In the Filters Pane, hover the pointer over the SalePrice filter. A downward-facing chevron will appear at the right of the field that is being used as a filter.

4. Expand the SalesPrice filter by clicking the chevron. The Filters Pane will display two popups that will enable you to set thresholds.

5. Click the upper popup and select the "is greater than or equal to" option.

6. In the box under the upper popup, enter the value **1000000** (without any thousands separators or currency units).

7. Ensure that the And radio button is selected under the popup.

8. Click the lower popup and select the "is less than or equal to" option.

9. In the box under the lower popup, enter the value **8000000** (without any thousands separators or currency units).

10. Click Apply filter. The chart will change to show only values in the range that you set in the filter.

That is it. You have set a range for all data in the Power BI Desktop report corresponding to the selected field. It should look like Figure 21-7. It is worth noting that in this figure I have widened the Filters Pane so that you can see the entire text that Power BI Desktop adds to a range filter to explain what the filter does. If you leave the Filters Pane at its default width, you will only see an abbreviated version of the filter definition.

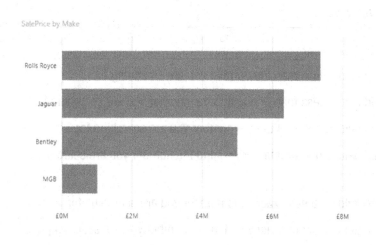

Figure 21-7. *A filter range*

When selecting a range of numeric data, you do not have to set both upper and lower bounds. You may set either one or both.

Note   Should you want to select a precise number from those available in a dataset, you can switch a numeric filter's filter type to basic filtering. This will show all the individual numbers in the selected field, as well as the number of times that each value occurs.

Numeric Filter Options

Numbers cannot be filtered exactly the same ways as text; the filtering options are slightly different. These filter options are described in Table 21-2.

Table 21-2. *Numeric Filter Options*

Filter Option	Description
Is less than	The selected field is less than the number you are searching for.
Is less than or equal to	The selected field is less than or equal to the number you are searching for.
Is greater than	The selected field is greater than the number you are searching for.
Is greater than or equal to	The selected field is greater than or equal to the number you are searching for.
Is	The selected field matches exactly the number you are searching for.
Is not	The selected field does not exactly match the number you are searching for.
Is blank	The selected field is blank.
Is not blank	The selected field is not blank.

If you are using both threshold levels to define a range of values to include or exclude, or even specific values to include or exclude, then you need to apply one of the logical filter options. These are shown in Table 21-3.

Table 21-3. *Logical Filter Options*

Filter Type	Description
And	Applies both filter elements to *reduce* the amount of data allowed through the filter.
Or	Applies either of the filter elements separately to *increase* the amount of data allowed through the filter.

When applying a numeric filter, you must—not altogether surprisingly—enter a numeric value. If you enter text by mistake, you will see a yellow lozenge appear at the right of the box to alert you to the fact that you entered a text by mistake, and the Apply filter text will remain grayed out.

In this case, you have to delete the characters that you entered and enter a numeric value in the place of the text.

Filtering Date and Time Data

At its simplest, date and time data is merely a list of elements or a range of numeric data. Consequently, dragging a field from a date dimension into the Filters Pane allows you to select one or more elements (such as years or months) or to define a range (of weeks, for instance). Take the following steps to see this in action:

1. Select the chart that you created earlier using the Make and SalePrice fields.

2. Clear any existing filters.

3. Expand the DateDimension table in the Fields list.

4. Drag the FullYear field into the Add data fields here well in the Filters on this visual section of the Filters Pane. Since Power BI Desktop assumes that the years are numbers, it switches to advanced filtering.

5. Select Basic filtering from the Filter type popup list to revert to a list of years.

6. Click one or two years in the filter list. Figure 21-8 demonstrates this. The chart will be updated to show only data for the chosen years.

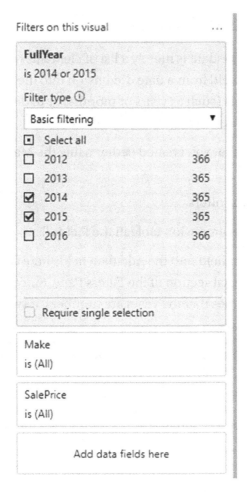

Figure 21-8. *A date filter*

One of the reasons that I created a date dimension is to allow you to filter on date elements easily. So you can now use any of the fields in the DateDimension table to restrict the data that is in a visualization. In my opinion, the following are very useful fields in this dimension:

- FullYear

- MonthAndYearAbbr

- QuarterAndYear

- YearAndWeek

However, you need to remember that you can combine multiple elements in a filter to get the correct result. So there is nothing to stop you from filtering on a specific year and then adding the day of the week and calculating all the sales for the Saturdays in the year, for instance. By combining different filter elements from a properly constructed data dimension, you can look at how data varies over time incredibly easily.

This means that, when filtering by dates, you could need to apply multiple filters, where you can select elements from each of the different filters: Year, Quarter, and/or Month. Alternatively, if you will be filtering on successive elements in a date hierarchy (Year, followed by Month, for instance), you may find it more intuitive to drag the filter elements from the date hierarchy to the Filters Pane in the temporal order in which you will be using them (i.e., Year followed by Month). This way, you can proceed in a logical manner, from top to bottom in the Filters Pane, to apply the date criteria that interest you.

Note   Whatever the data type, you cannot add hierarchies to a filter. Instead, you must expand the hierarchy in the Fields list and drag each element of a hierarchy into the required Filters Pane.

Date and Time Filters

If you are filtering on a Date or DateTime field, then you quickly notice that Power BI Desktop adapts the filter to help you select dates and times more easily. In essence, Power BI Desktop lets you select from four ways of filtering date and time data:

- Select one or more exact dates or times (basic filtering)

- Define a range of dates or times (advanced filtering)

- Specify a range of dates relative to the current day (relative date filtering)

- Select a top few dates (top N filtering)

Moreover, the filter well for a date adds

- A calendar popup that lets you click a day of the month (and scroll through the months of the year, forward and backward)

- A time series scroll filter that lets you select times to every minute throughout the day

To see this in action, imagine that you want to see all sales for a range of dates:

1. Select the chart that you created previously.

2. Delete the FullYear filter from it, as described earlier.

3. Leaving the chart selected, expand the DateDimension table and drag the DateKey field into the Add data fields here well in the Filters on this visual section of the Filters Pane. You will see a list of all the dates in the DateDimension table in the filter.

4. Click Advanced filtering.

5. From the "Show items when the value" popup list, select "is on or after."

6. Click the calendar icon beneath the popup. The calendar popup is shown in Figure 21-9.

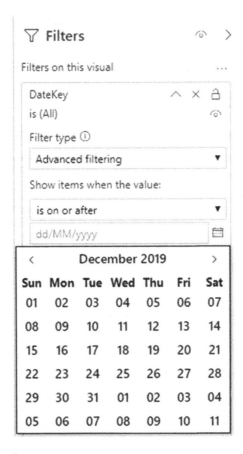

Figure 21-9. *The calendar popup*

7. Select a date from the calendar. This date will appear in the box under the calendar icon.

8. Click the And radio button.

9. In the second popup, select "is on or before."

10. Click the calendar icon beneath the popup and select a date from the calendar. This date will appear in the box under the second popup.

11. Click Apply filter. The Filters Pane will look like Figure 21-10.

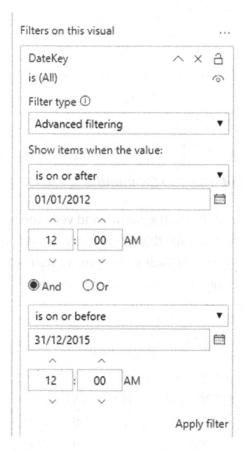

Figure 21-10. *A date range filter*

There are a couple of tricks that may save you time when you are selecting dates from the calendar popup (you may be familiar with these techniques in other desktop packages):

- When using the calendar popup, clicking the right-facing chevron to the right of the month and year displays the following month.

- When using the calendar popup, clicking the left-facing chevron to the left of the month and year displays the previous month.

- When using the calendar popup, clicking the month and year displays a Year popup, in which you can click the right-facing chevron to the right of the year to display the following year (or click the left-facing chevron to the left of the year to display the previous year), and then you can select the month from those displayed. You can see this in Figure 21-11.

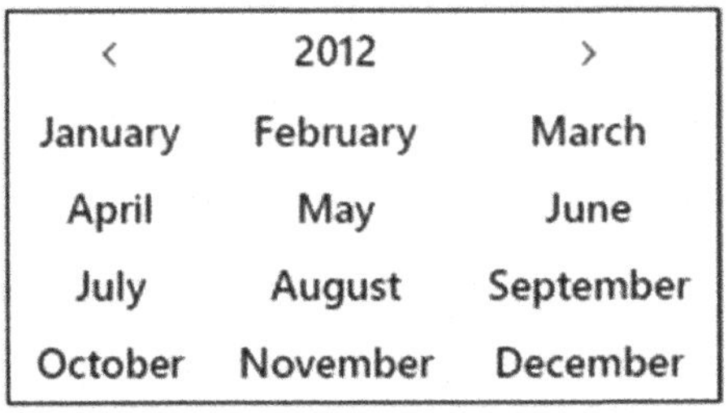

‹	2012	›
January	February	March
April	May	June
July	August	September
October	November	December

Figure 21-11. *The calendar popup for months*

- If you have already clicked the month and year and are looking at the months for a year, you can click the year to see ranges of years. You can use the left- and right-facing chevrons to scroll through previous and successive ranges of years, then select the year that you want to filter on. You can see this in Figure 21-12.

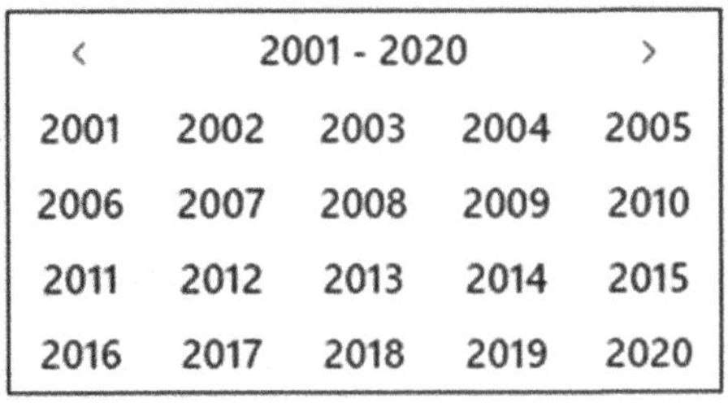

‹	2001 - 2020			›
2001	2002	2003	2004	2005
2006	2007	2008	2009	2010
2011	2012	2013	2014	2015
2016	2017	2018	2019	2020

Figure 21-12. *The calendar popup for years*

- When using the time popup, clicking inside any constituent part of the time (hour, minute, or second) and then clicking the up and down scroll triangles above and below the time field allows you to scroll rapidly through the available options.

- Clicking AM or PM to the right of the time box lets you switch from AM to PM.

If you do not want to select a date using the calendar popup, then you can enter a date directly in the date box of the advanced filter for a Date (or DateTime) field. Just remember that you must enter the date in the date format corresponding to the environment that you are using and that can be understood by Power BI Desktop.

Note   If you enter a date where the format does not correspond to the system format, or if the date is purely and simply invalid (the 30th of February, for instance), then Power BI Desktop will not let you apply the filter. To correct this, simply select a correct date using the calendar popup. Similarly, if you enter a nonexistent time, then Power BI Desktop will refuse to accept it and will revert to the previous (acceptable) time that was chosen.

Date Filter Options

Dates cannot be filtered in exactly the same ways as text or numbers. Consequently, the advanced filtering options for date filters are slightly different from those used when filtering other data types. They are described in Table 21-4.

Table 21-4. *Advanced Date Filter Options*

Filter Option	Description
Is	The selected field contains the date that you are searching for.
Is not	The selected field does not contain the date that you are searching for.
Is after	The selected field contains dates after the date that you entered, that is, later dates that do not include the date you entered.
Is on or after	The selected field contains dates beginning with the date that you entered or later.

(continued)

Table 21-4. (*continued*)

Filter Option	Description
Is before	The selected field contains dates before the date that you entered, that is, earlier dates, not including the date you entered.
Is on or before	The selected field contains dates on or before the date that you entered, that is, earlier dates up to and including the date you entered.
Is blank	The selected field is blank.
Is not blank	The selected field is not blank.

Relative Date Filtering

Another way of finding data for a range of dates applies specifically to the current date. Power BI Desktop can help you find, for instance, sales in the past days, weeks, months, or even years. Here is how:

1. Select the chart that you created previously.

2. Clear all filters from it, as described earlier.

3. Leaving the chart selected, expand the DateDimension table and add the DateKey field to the Filters Pane for the visual.

4. In the Filter type popup list, select Relative date filtering.

5. In the popup for "Show items when the value," select "is in this."

6. In the second popup for "Show items when the value," select year. The Filters Pane will look like the one in Figure 21-13.

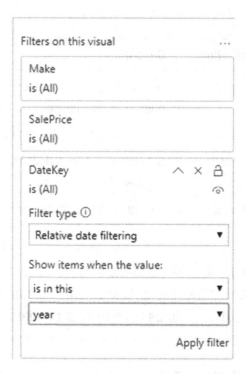

Figure 21-13. *Applying a relative date filter*

7.   Click Apply filter to filter the data in the visual.

There are several options available for relative date filtering. These are described in Table 21-5.

Table 21-5. *Relative Date Filter Options*

Filter Option	Filter Definition	Description
Is in the last	Relative positioning	Takes a range of dates before the current date.
Is in this	Relative positioning	Specifies the current time period to be used.
Is in the next	Relative positioning	Takes a range of dates after the current date.
Days	Time element	Sets days as the number of time periods.
Weeks	Time element	Sets weeks (rolling seven-day periods) as the number of time periods.
Calendar weeks	Time element	Sets full calendar weeks as the number of time periods.

(continued)

Table 21-5. (*continued*)

Filter Option	Filter Definition	Description
Months	Time element	Sets months (rolling periods from date to date) as the number of time periods.
Calendar months	Time element	Sets full months as the number of time periods.
Years	Time element	Sets years (rolling periods from date to date) as the number of time periods.
Calendar years	Time element	Sets full years as the number of time periods.

Note   Selecting "Is in the last" or "Is in the next" relative date filter options will display an additional field in the Filters Pane where you can enter the number of days, weeks, months, and so on to be used to filter the data.

Filtering True or False Data

There are other data types in the source data that you are likely to be handling. You might have Boolean (true or false) data, for instance. However, for Power BI Desktop, this is considered, for all intents and purposes, to be a text-based filter. On the other hand, there are data types that you cannot filter on and that do not ever appear in the Filters Pane. Binary data (such as images) is a case in point.

So if you filter on Boolean data, Power BI Desktop displays True and False in the expanded filter for this data type. The following explains how to see this:

1. Create a clustered bar chart using the following fields:

    a. IsCreditWorthy (from the Clients table)

    b. SalePrice (from the InvoiceLines table)

2. Expand the IsCreditWorthy field in the Filters Pane.

3. Select True and Blank. The chart and Filters Pane will look like they do in Figure 21-14.

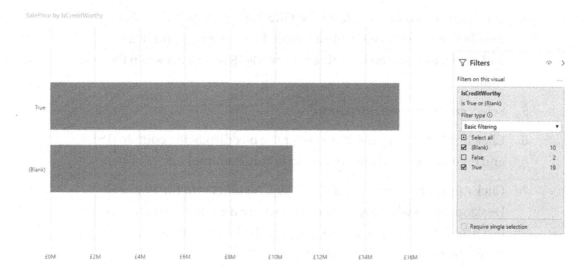

Figure 21-14. *Applying a Boolean filter*

Advanced Text Filters

In many cases, when you are delving into your data, merely selecting a "simple" filter will be enough to highlight the information that interests both you and your audience. There will inevitably be cases when you need to filter your data more finely in order to return the kinds of results that sort the wheat from the chaff. This is where Power BI Desktop's advanced filtering capabilities come to the fore. Advanced filtering lets you search inside field data with much greater precision, and it is of particular use when you need to include, or exclude, data based on parts of a field if it is text.

Applying an Advanced Text Filter

Let's begin with a simple example of how to apply an advanced filter to a text field:

1. Click the visual that you want to filter. Once again, we will use the chart that you created earlier in this chapter using Make and SalePrice as the data fields.

2. Clear any existing filters.

3. Expand the Make field in the Filters Pane (unless it has already been done).

761

4. Select Advanced filtering from the Filter type popup. The body of the filter switches to show the advanced filter popups and boxes, and the text under the filter title now reads "Show items when the value."

5. Select contains from the popup.

6. Click inside the filter text box (under the box displaying contains) and enter the text to filter on (**aston** in this example).

7. Click Apply filter or press the Enter key. All objects in the Power BI Desktop report will only display data where the client contains the text *aston*. The result is shown in Figure 21-15; the advanced filter used to produce it is also shown.

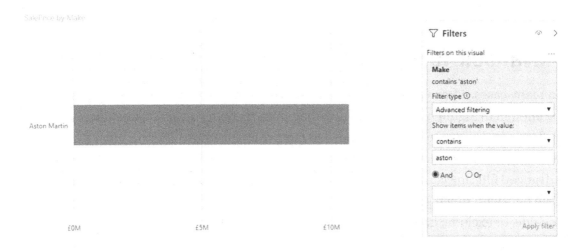

Figure 21-15. *The results of applying an advanced filter*

Here are several comments that it is important to make at this stage:

- Advanced filtering is *not* case-sensitive. You can enter uppercase or lowercase characters in the filter box; the result is the same.

- Spaces and punctuation are important, as they are taken literally. For instance, if you enter *A* (with a space after the A), then you only find elements containing an A (uppercase or lowercase) followed by a space.

- Advanced filters, just like standard filters, are cumulative in their effect. So, if you have applied a filter and do not get the results you were expecting, be sure to check that no other filter at another level is active that might be narrowing the data returned beyond what you want.

- If your filter excludes all data from the result set, then any tables in the Power BI Desktop report displays "This table contains no rows."

- Similarly, if your filter excludes all data, charts will be empty.

In any case, if you end up displaying no data, or data that does not correspond to what you wanted to show, just clear the filter and start over.

Clearing an Advanced Filter

Inevitably, you will also need to know how to remove an advanced filter. The process is the same as for a standard filter; all you have to do is click the Clear Filter icon at the top of the filter for this field (just under the chevron for the field in the field well). The filter elements are removed for this filter.

Reverting to Basic Filtering

If you decide that you no longer wish to define and use a complex filter, but you wish to revert to basic filtering, then all you have to do is select Basic filtering from the Filter type popup list for the selected filter. The Filters Pane will switch to basic filtering for the selected field.

Text Filter Options

When filtering on the text contained in a data field, you can apply the string you are filtering on to the underlying data in several ways. These are the same for both the upper and lower of the two advanced filter options for a text field. They are described in Table 21-6.

Table 21-6. *Advanced Text Filter Options*

Filter Option	Description
Contains	The selected field contains the search text anywhere in the field data.
Does not contain	The selected field does not contain the search text anywhere in the field data.
Starts with	The selected field begins with the search text, followed by any data.
Does not start with	The selected field does not begin with the search text, followed by any data.
Is	The selected field matches the search text exactly.
Is not	The selected field does not match the search text exactly.
Is blank	The selected field is blank.
Is not blank	The selected field is not blank.

You are not limited to setting a single advanced text filter. Just as was the case for numeric values, you can set two filters and apply either of them (by setting the logical operator to Or). Alternatively, you can set two complementary text filters by setting the logical operator to And.

Top N Filtering

One of the reasons to filter data is to extract meaning from the mass of available information. One easy way to deliver meaningful analysis to isolate the best-performing (or worst-performing) elements. Suppose, for instance, that you want to see the top three best-selling makes of car:

1. Click the visual that you want to filter. Once again, we will use the chart that you created earlier in this chapter using Make and SalePrice as the data fields.

2. In the Filters Pane, expand the Make section of the Visual-Level Filters Pane.

3. Select Top N from the Filter type popup list.

4. Ensure that Top is selected from the available elements in the Show items popup list.

5. Enter 3 in the field to the right of the Show items popup list.

6. Drag the SalePrice field into the By value field.

7. Click Apply filter. You will see the chart and filter looking like they
    do in Figure 21-16.

Figure 21-16. *Applying a top N filter*

What has happened here is that the SalePrice field has been aggregated for each
make in the background. Then the highest three values have been used to filter the data.

Note   Filtering on the bottom N elements merely means selecting Bottom in the
Show items list.

Specific Visualization-Level Filters

So far in this chapter, we have looked at filters where the fields that were used to filter
a visual were *also* visible in the actual visual—be it a chart, map, or table. Inevitably,
there will be times when you will want to filter on a field that is *not* displayed in a visual.
Although we touched on this earlier, it is worth explaining the concept in greater detail.

The following example explains how to apply a visualization-level filter:

1. Create a clustered bar chart of SalePrice by ClientName using the
    file CarSalesDataForReports.pbix.

2. Display the Filters Pane (unless it is already visible).

3. Expand the Colors table and drag the Color field into the Filters
    Pane in the Add data fields here well for the visual. The list of
    colors will be expanded automatically in the Filters Pane. The
    Color field will *not* be displayed in the visual, however.

4. Select a couple of colors, such as Night Blue and Silver. The result
    is shown in Figure 21-17.

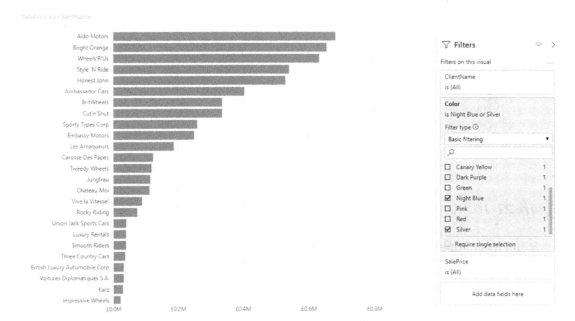

Figure 21-17. *A visualization-level filter without using the data field*

You will notice right away that the filters that you have applied only affect the
selected visualization (the chart in this example). When you create complex reports that
contain several visualizations, you will see that no other visualizations in the report have
their underlying data modified in any way.

You can clear any filter at the visualization level by clicking the Clear icon at the top
right of the filter name. Moreover, you can add multiple fields to the Filters Pane for a
visual *and* you can add them in any order.

Note   Removing a field from the field well will not remove this field from the Filters Pane if the filter is active. This can be deceptive because the field is no longer displayed in the visual; however, its effects can still be seen.

Multiple Filters

So far, we have treated filters as if only one was ever going to be applied at a time. Believe me, when dealing with large and intricate datasets, it is unlikely that this will be the case. As a matter of course, Power BI Desktop will let you add multiple filters to a report. This entails some careful consideration of the following possible repercussions:

- All filters are active at once (unless you have cleared a filter), and their effect is cumulative. That is, data will only be returned if the data matches *all* the criteria set by all the active filters. So, for example, if you have requested data between a specified date range and above a certain sales figure, you will *not* get any data in which the sales figure is lower than the figure that you specified or with a sales date before or after the dates that you set.

- If you are dealing with multiple filters (be they visual level, page level, or report level), you can choose to display only a subset of the active filters by entering a few characters of the fields that are used in a filter in the Search box at the top of the Filters pane. This will instantly display any filters that are based on any fields containing the characters you entered. To clear the Search box, simply click the cross icon at the right of the Search box.

- To sort filters at any level (visual level, page level, or report level), just click the ellipses at the right of the filter and select the sort order from the popup that appears. Refer back to Figure 21-1 if you want to see the sort menu.

- It is easy to forget that filters can be active. Remember that all active filters in the Filters Pane remain operational whether the Filters Pane itself is expanded or collapsed. If you are going to collapse filters to make better use of the available space on the screen, then it is worth getting into the habit of looking at the second line below any filter title that will give you a description of the current filter state. It will display something like Contains Rolls. Of course, the exact text varies according to the filter that you have applied.

Page-Level Filters

Now that you have seen what filters are and how you can apply them to visuals, it is time to extend the concept and see how filters can be applied to multiple visuals.

The good news is that all filters are configured in exactly the same way whatever the level at which they are applied. Consequently, applying filters at page level or report level is simply a question of choosing where in the Filters Pane to place a filter.

As an example, suppose that you want to filter all the visuals on a page to display data for a specific year:

1. In an open Power BI Desktop file (such as the one containing the chart that you can see in Figure 21-18), click the dashboard canvas outside any existing visuals.

2. Expand the DateDimension table.

3. Drag the FullYear field into the field well into the Page-Level Filters box. The advanced filtering options for this field will be displayed.

4. Select Basic filtering as the filter type.

5. Select 2014 from the list of available years. All visuals on the current page will be filtered to display only data for this year.

Figure 21-18 shows you the Filters Pane for this operation. You can see that a page-level filter looks identical to a visual-level filter. The only difference (apart from the effect that it produces) is the position in the Filters Pane.

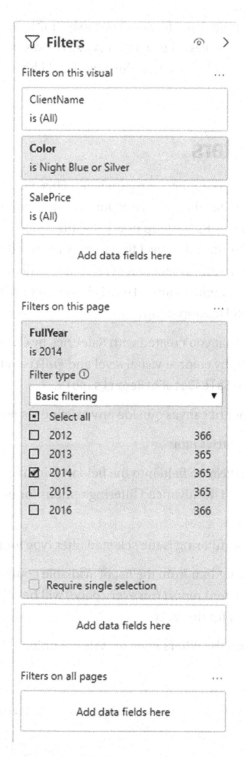

Figure 21-18. *Applying a page-level filter*

You can add multiple page-level filters if you wish simply by dragging further fields into the field well and into the Page-Level Filters box. The order in which the fields are added is unimportant. You will notice that the page-level filters remain visible whether you have selected a visual or not.

Report-Level Filters

The highest level of filtering is applied at report level. This means that any filter set here will apply to every page (or dashboard) in a report and consequently also to every visual in the file. I realize that Power BI Desktop now calls this concept "Filters on all pages," but I prefer to use the old terminology as I find it more expressive. Applying report-level filters is virtually identical to the application of page-level filters. So, let's suppose that your entire report covers a single country. Here is how to set a filter that will apply to every page in the Power BI Desktop report:

1. Take the report that you created with SalePrice by ClientName and then filtered by color at visual level and FullYear at page level using the file `CarSalesDataForReports.pbix`.

2. Click the dashboard canvas outside any existing visuals.

3. Expand the Countries table.

4. Drag the CountryName field into the field well into the Report-Level Filters box. The advanced filtering options for this field will be displayed.

5. Ensure that Basic filtering is the selected filter type for this filter.

6. Select United Kingdom from the list of available countries. All visuals in the current report (on every page) will be filtered to display only data for this year.

Figure 21-19 shows you the Filters Pane for this operation.

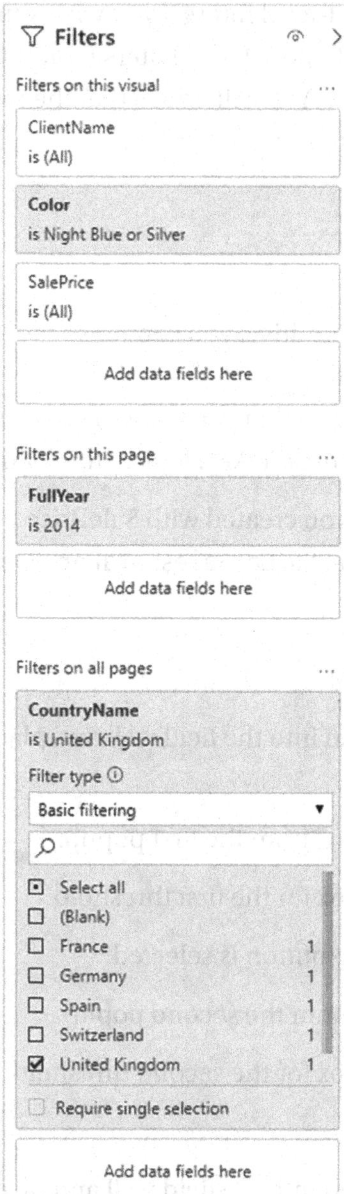

***Figure 21-19.** Applying a report-level filter*

You can add multiple report-level filters if you wish simply by dragging further fields into the field well and into the Report-Level Filters Pane. Once again, the order in which the fields are added is irrelevant. You will notice that the report-level filters remain visible whether you have selected a visual or not.

Filter Field Reuse

Although it may seem counterintuitive, you can reuse the same field at the same filter level to assist you in certain cases.

As an example of this, imagine that you want to see all the mileage for vehicles between clearly defined thresholds. Take a look at the following example:

1. Take the report that you created with SalePrice by ClientName and then filtered using the file CarSalesDataForReports.pbix.

2. Remove all filters.

3. Expand the Stock table.

4. Drag the Mileage field into the field well and place it in the Filters on all pages well.

5. Select "is greater than" from the first popup.

6. Enter **50000** in the box for the first threshold.

7. Ensure the And radio button is selected.

8. Select "is less than" from the second popup.

9. Enter **70000** in the box for the second threshold.

10. Click Apply filter.

11. Drag the Mileage field into the field well and place it in the Filters on all pages well under the filter that you just created.

12. Ensure that Basic filtering is selected for this filter. A list of available mileage for vehicles in stock (as well as the number of cars for each mileage figure) for the selected mileage range will appear. You can see this in Figure 21-20.

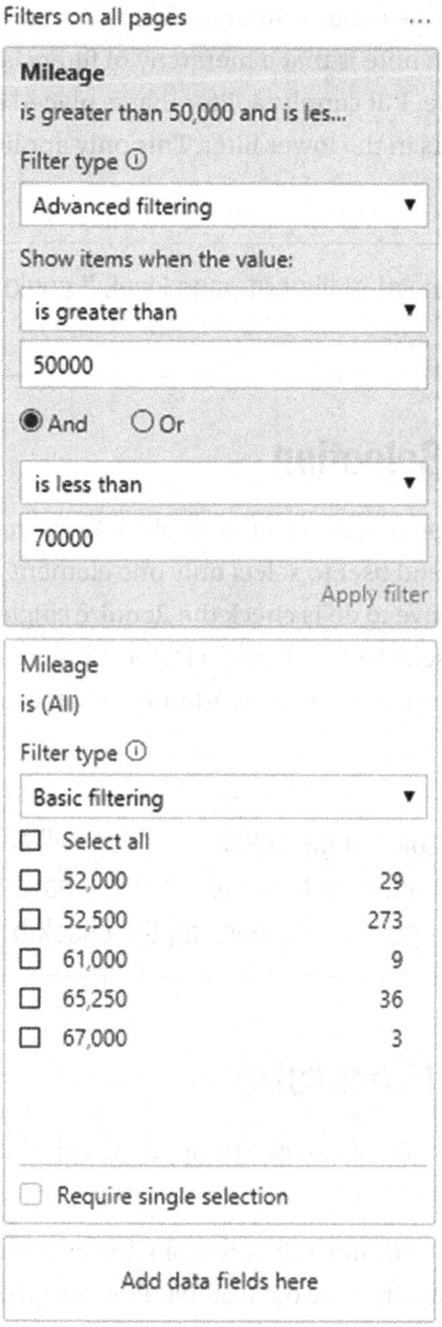

Filters on all pages   ...

Mileage

is greater than 50,000 and is les...

Filter type ⓘ

| Advanced filtering | ▼ |

Show items when the value:

| is greater than | ▼ |

| 50000 |

⦿ And   ◯ Or

| is less than | ▼ |

| 70000 |

Apply filter

Mileage

is (All)

Filter type ⓘ

| Basic filtering | ▼ |

☐   Select all

☐   52,000   29

☐   52,500   273

☐   61,000   9

☐   65,250   36

☐   67,000   3

☐   Require single selection

Add data fields here

Figure 21-20. *Combining multiple iterations of the same field in a filter*

You can now use the more detailed filter to filter the visuals on the current page.

The interesting thing to note is that a hierarchy of filters is applied, even inside a filter box in the Filters Pane. Put simply, a filter that is placed above another filter will filter the available elements in the lower filter. This only applies, however, to reuse of the same filter.

Note   This example was set to filter at page level. It could equally well have been applied at report level.

Requiring Single Selection

Some filter choices will allow you to select multiple options from a list. You may want to force either yourself or an end user to select only one element from this list.

In such cases, all you have to do is check the Require single selection check box under the list. This will deselect any existing selected elements from the list both once this option is active and (possibly more importantly) when a new selection is made in the filter.

Note   Choosing the Require single selection option will also hide the Filter type popup list. To switch to a different filter type, you will have to deactivate the Require single selection option by unchecking the check box.

Using the Filter Hierarchy

Given the multiple levels of filters that can be applied, a hierarchy of filters is applied in Power BI Desktop:

- First, at the data level, any selections or choices you apply to the underlying data restrict the dataset that Power BI Desktop can use to visualize your information.

- Second, at the report level, any report-level filters that you apply affect all visualizations in the report using the (possibly limited) available source data.

- Third, at the page level, any page-level filters that you apply will affect all visualizations on the view, using the (possibly limited) available source data filtered by any report-level filters.

- Finally, for each visualization, any visualization-level filters that you apply will further limit the data that is allowed through the report- and page-level filters—but only for the selected visualization.

It is worth noting the following points:

- You have no way to apply a completely different selection to a visualization filter if it has been filtered out at a higher (report or page) level. Clicking Select all will *only* select from the subset of previously filtered elements.

- If you apply a filter at visualization level and then reapply the same filter at report or page level, but with different elements selected, you will still be excluding all unselected elements from the filter at visualization level. I stress this because Power BI Desktop will remember the previously selected elements at visualization level and leave them visible even if they cannot be used in a filter, because they have already been excluded from the visualization-level filter by being ruled out at view level. In my opinion, this adds a certain visual confusion, even if the hierarchical selection logic is applied.

Hopefully, this shows you that Power BI Desktop is rigorous in applying its hierarchy of filters. Should you need to apply a filter at visualization level when the filter choice is excluded at report or page level, you have no choice but to remove the filter at the higher level and then reapply visualization-level filters to all necessary visualizations.

Filtering Tips

Power BI Desktop makes it incredibly easy to filter data and to exclude any data that you feel is not helpful in your data analysis. However, like many powerful tools, this ability to apply filters so quickly and easily can be something of a double-edged sword. So here are a few words of advice and caution when applying filters to your data.

Don't Filter Too Soon

As an initial point, I would say that a key ground rule is "Don't filter too soon." By this, I mean that if you are examining data for trends, anomalies, and insights, you have to be careful not to exclude data that could contain the very insights that can be game changing.

The problem is that when you first delve into a haystack of data in search of needles of informational value, you have no idea what you could be looking for. So I can only suggest the following approaches:

- Begin with no filters at all and see what the data has to say in its most elemental form.

- Apply filters one at a time and remember to delete a filter before trying out another one.

- Try to think in terms of "layers" of filters. So, once you have defined an initial set of filters, add further filters one by one.

- Go slowly. The temptation is to reach a discovery in order to shout about it from the rooftops. This can lead to excessive filtering and unreliable data.

- Always remove any filters that are not absolutely necessary.

- Be careful if you hide the Filters Pane. It is too easy to forget that there are active filters if they are not visible in some way.

- Remember that you can have filters specific to a visualization that might not be immediately visible in the Filters Pane without scrolling. So always check if any visualization filters are active for each table and chart in a report.

- Be aware that filters are part of the underlying "plumbing" of Power BI. They are not designed for interactivity. If you are looking for intuitive interaction with the data, then you should consider using slicers and cross-filtering (as explained in the next chapter).

- Filters can be hidden from report users (or report readers, as Power BI calls them). This will only take effect if your reports are published to the Power BI Service. To hide filters from users, click the Show or hide filter pane icon at the top right of the Filters Pane. This icon is called out in Figure 21-1.

Annotate, Annotate, Annotate

If you are presenting a key finding based on a dataset, then it can save a lot of embarrassment if you make it clear in every case what the data does and does not contain. For example, you could be so pleased with the revelatory sales trend that you have discovered that you forget to note an important exclusion in the underlying data. Now, no one is suggesting that you are doing anything other than making a point, but your audience needs to know what has been excluded and why—just in case it makes a difference. After all, you don't want a workplace rival pointing this out to invalidate your findings in the middle of a vital meeting, do you?

Annotation techniques are described in Chapter 22 if you need to jump ahead to check this out now.

Avoid Complex Filters

Power BI Desktop filters are designed to be intuitive and easy to use. A consequence of this is that they can prove to be a little limited when you need to apply very complex filters—be they text, numeric, or date filters.

If you need to create a complex filter, it's probably best *not* to create one in the report. Instead, consider trying to filter source data using Power BI Desktop Query. Should you need a more interactive way of switching between complex filter settings in a report, then use DAX to define columns that display a text as the result of a filter, then use the result of the filter as a selection. As a very simple example of this, consider the Mileage Range column. In effect, this groups vehicle mileage into certain bandings. It follows that selecting one or more bandings in a filter will restrict the display to data that matches the predefined data ranges. With a little practice, you can extend this technique to create quite complex filters in DAX at the data level.

Note   As DAX is a vast subject in its own right, this book will not provide an introduction to this language.

Conclusion

This chapter has shown you how to apply and fine-tune a series of techniques to enable you to restrict the underlying data that will be used in your Power BI Desktop reports. The main thing to take away is that you can filter data at three levels: the overall report, each page, and each visualization on a page.

You have also seen a variety of selection techniques that allow you to subset data. These range from the avowedly simple selection of a few elements to the specification of a more complex spread of dates or values. Finally, it is worth remembering that you can filter data using any of the fields in the underlying dataset, whether the field is displayed in a visual in a report or not.

Now that you have mastered filters, it is time to build on this knowledge and move on to the other techniques that Power BI Desktop uses to subset data: slicers and cross-filtering. These are the subject of the next chapter.

CHAPTER 22

Using Slicers

With your filters in place, you now have some extremely powerful and insightful dashboards ready to be paraded in front of your colleagues, bosses, and clients. Yet static illustrations can only tell a story in a certain way. What you need to clinch the deal or convince an audience is some truly telling interaction with your facts and figures. Once again, Power BI Desktop is the tool of choice, as it highlights the key metrics in your presentation with a single click—and makes your point, simply and elegantly.

Put less breathlessly, you can interact with your filtered data in Power BI Desktop reports to subset or isolate metrics. These elements have the following characteristics:

- Always visible in the Power BI Desktop report

- Instantly accessible

- Interactive

- Clearly indicate which selections are being applied

So what are the effects that you can add to a Power BI Desktop report to select and project your data? Essentially, they boil down to three main approaches:

- Slicers

- Cross-filtering

- Highlighting

These interactive elements can be considered to function as a supplementary level of filtering. That is, they take the current filters that are set in the Filters well (at any level) and then provide further fine-grained *interactive* selection on top of the dataset that has been allowed through the existing filters. Each approach has its advantages and limitations, but used appropriately, each gives you the ability not only to discover the essence of your data but also to make your point clearly and effectively.

© Adam Aspin 2020
A. Aspin, *Pro Power BI Desktop*, https://doi.org/10.1007/978-1-4842-5763-0_22

Moreover, you can specify which slicers and visuals are allowed to affect the other visuals on a dashboard page. This aspect of Power BI Desktop (called visual interaction) is another aspect of using slicers that you will learn in this chapter.

You will use the `C:\PowerBiDesktopSamples\CarSalesDataForReports.pbix` sample file as the basis for all the slicers that you create in this chapter.

Slicers

A key form of interactive filter in Power BI Desktop is the *slicer*. This is, to all intents and purposes, a standard multiselect filter, where you can choose one or more elements to filter data in a report. The essential difference is that a slicer remains visible on the Power BI Desktop report, whereas a filter is normally hidden. So this is an overt rather than a covert approach to data selection—and one that makes the selection criteria immediately visible. Moreover, you can add multiple different slicers to a Power BI Desktop report and consequently slice and dice the data instantaneously and interactively using multiple, cumulative, criteria. Slicers can be text based, or indeed, they can be simple charts, as you will soon see. You can even add third-party slicers to your dashboards if you require even more advanced—or visually interesting—ways to slice your data.

Adding a Slicer

To appreciate all that slicers can do, we need to see one in action. This means having at least one standard visual in a page so that you can see the result of applying a slicer. To test a slicer:

1. Open the Power BI Desktop file `C:\PowerBiDesktopSamples\ CarSalesDataForReports.pbix`.

2. Create a table (to show the effect of using a slicer) using the following fields:

    a. CountryName (from the Countries table)

    b. SalePrice (from the InvoiceLines table)

3. Resize the table so that it fits the data.

4. In the Fields list, expand the Colors table.

5. Drag the Color field to an empty part of the dashboard canvas. It will become a single-column table.

6. Click the Slicer icon in the Visualizations pane. The table of colors will become a slicer. The Slicer icon is shown in Figure 22-1.

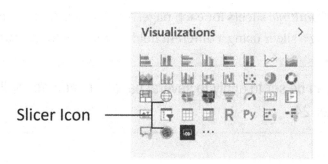

Slicer Icon

Figure 22-1. *The Slicer icon*

7. Adjust the size of the slicer to suit your requirements using the corner or lateral handles. If the slicer contains many elements, Power BI Desktop will add a vertical scroll bar to indicate that there are further elements available.

You can recognize a slicer by the small squares (or possibly circles) to the left of each element in the list. This way you know that it is not just a single-column table. Figure 22-2 shows a slicer using the Color field.

CountryName	SalePrice
	£141,250
France	£2,524,510
Germany	£145,750
Spain	£207,750
Switzerland	£1,440,970
United Kingdom	£15,725,000
USA	£11,653,960
Total	**£31,839,190**

Color
☐ Black
☐ Blue
☐ British Racing Green
☐ Canary Yellow
☐ Dark Purple
☐ Green
☐ Night Blue
☐ Pink
☐ Red
☐ Silver

Slicer

Figure 22-2. *A slicer*

Tip   If the Slicer icon is grayed out, then ensure that the table that you are trying to convert to a slicer has only *one* column (i.e., one field in the Values box of the field well for this visual).

You can create *multiple* slicers for each page. All you have to do is repeat steps 3 through 6 for adding a slicer using a different field as the data for the new slicer.

Note   Slicers can be set to apply to several pages at once. You will learn how to do this in Chapter 24.

Applying Slicers

To apply a slicer and use it to filter data on a page, click a single element in the slicer or Ctrl-click multiple elements.

All the objects in a Power BI Desktop page are filtered to reflect the currently selected slicer list. In addition, each element in the slicer list that is active (and consequently used to filter data by that element) now has a small rectangle to its left, indicating that this element is selected.

Figure 22-3 shows what happens when the slicer defined previously is applied to the visualization shown in Figure 22-2.

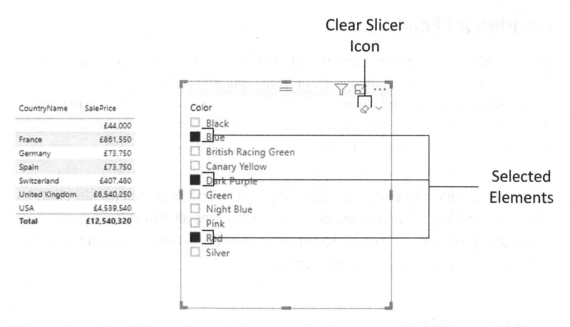

Figure 22-3. *Applying a slicer*

When you apply a slicer, think filter. That is, if you select a couple of elements from a slicer based on the CountryName field, as well as three elements in another slicer based on the Color fields, you are forcing the two slicers (filters) to limit all the data displayed in the page to two countries that have any of the three colors that you selected. The core difference between a slicer and a filter is that a slicer is always visible—and that you have to select or unselect elements, not ranges of values.

If you experiment, you will also see that you cannot create a slicer from numeric fields in the source data. A slicer has to be based on a text field. If you need slicers based on ranges of data, then you will need to prepare these ranges in the data model. The CarAgeBucket field is an example of this.

Tip   If you Ctrl-click all the selected elements in a slicer, you can unselect all the data it represents. This will not clear the Power BI Desktop report, however. Unselecting everything is the same as selecting everything—despite the fact that the selection squares are no longer visible to the left of each element in the slicer. Using Shift-click is no different from clicking a slicer element, however.

Clearing a Slicer

To clear a slicer and stop filtering on the selected data elements in a view, click the Clear Slicer icon at the top right of the slicer. This icon is pointed out in Figure 22-3.

Any filters applied by the slicer to the view are now removed. You will see that each element in the slicer list now has a small empty rectangle to its left, indicating that this element is not selected. No data is now filtered out of the report.

Tip   Another technique used to completely clear a slicer is to click (or Ctrl-click) the last remaining active element in a slicer. This leaves all elements inactive. Additionally, you can Ctrl-click to select every item. So, in effect, removing all slicer elements is the same as activating them all.

Deleting a Slicer

To delete a slicer and remove all filters that it applies for a view, select the slicer and press the Delete key. Alternatively, click the context menu button (the ellipses) that appears at the top right when you hover the mouse pointer over a slicer, and select Remove.

Any filters applied by the slicer to the view, as well as the slicer itself, are now removed.

You can even copy and paste slicers if you wish. This is very useful when you are copying slicers across different Power BI Desktop reports or between report pages.

Converting a Slicer to Another Visual Type

If you intend to use the field that was the basis for a slicer in a table or chart, you do not need to delete the slicer and re-create a table based on the same underlying field. You can merely

1. Select the slicer

2. Click the Table button in the Design ribbon, and select the type of table (table, matrix, or card) to which you want to convert the slicer

The instant that a slicer becomes a table, it ceases to subset the data in the Power BI Desktop report.

Modifying a Slicer

If all you want to do is replace the field that is used in a slicer with another field, then it is probably simplest to do this:

1. Select the slicer that you want to modify.

2. Drag the new field over the existing field in the field well.

The current slicer field is replaced by the new field, and the slicer updates to display the contents of the field that you added. Alternatively, you can delete the slicer and re-create it.

When you start applying slicers to your Power BI Desktop reports, you rapidly notice one important aspect of the Power BI Desktop filter hierarchy. A slicer can only display data that is not specifically excluded by a report- or page-level filter. For instance, if you add a Color filter at page level and select only certain colors in this filter, you are only able to create a slicer that also displays this subset of colors. The slicer is dynamic and reflects the elements that can be displayed once any report and page filters have been applied—just like any other visual. Consequently, adding or removing elements in a filter causes these elements to appear (or disappear) in a slicer that is based on the filtered field.

If you wish, you can apply a filter specifically to a slicer. This allows you to restrict the elements that appear in a slicer. If you want to do this, then you must apply the filter after step 3 in the previous example and *before* you convert the table to a slicer. However, be aware that the slicer itself does *not* give you any indication that it is being filtered; that is, there is no visual-level filter displayed in the Filters well.

Conversely, to remove a filter from a slicer, you need to switch it back to a table and remove the filter and then switch back to a slicer.

Tip   When you save a Power BI Desktop file containing Power BI Desktop reports with active slicers, the slicer is reopened in the state in which it was saved.

Date Slicers

Selecting ranges of dates can extend the appearance and usefulness of slicers. As this is probably easier to appreciate if you see it in action, I suggest that you try out the following:

1. Open the sample file `C:\PowerBiDesktopSamples\ CarSalesDataForReports.pbix`.

2. In the Visualizations pane, click the Slicer icon. An empty slicer will be added to the report canvas.

3. Expand the DateDimension table and check the FullYear field (or drag the FullYear field into the newly created slicer).

4. Drag the left-hand (lower) threshold to the right until the left year field shows 2013.

5. Drag the right-hand (upper) threshold to the left until the right year field shows 2015. The slicer will look like the one in Figure 22-4. Any data in the page will be filtered to exclude dates outside this range of years.

Figure 22-4. *Slicing on years*

You can, if you prefer, enter a year directly in one of the year fields in a slicer like this one. However, I feel that the usefulness of a slicer like this is precisely in its ability to alter the threshold values quickly and easily using the slider.

If you use a data field that is set as a *date type*, then the slicer can help you set dates quickly and easily, but in a slightly different way. Here's how:

1. In the Visualizations pane, click the Slicer icon. An empty slicer will be added to the report canvas.

2. Expand the DateDimension table and check the DateKey field.

3. Click inside one of the date fields. The slicer will look like the one in Figure 22-5.

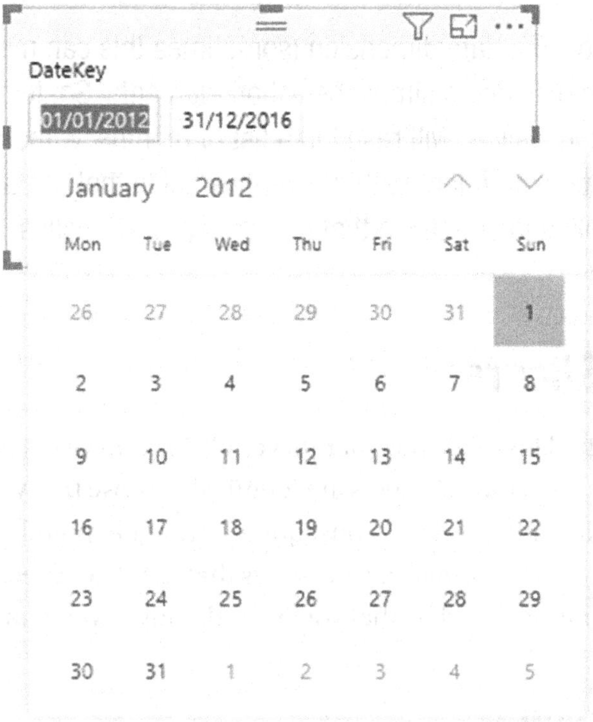

Figure 22-5. *A date slicer*

    4. Select the date that you want to set for the date threshold.

To make the most of this calendar, you need to know a few tricks:

- Clicking the up and down chevrons displays the following or preceding month.

- Clicking the year in the calendar popup displays a list of years. From here you can select the required year.

- Clicking the month in the calendar popup displays a list of months. From here you can select the required month.

- You cannot select an upper date that is less than the lower date.

- The calendar *will* allow you to select dates that are not included in the underlying table of dates. This, however, can cause some unexpected results to appear in your reports.

Note   Certain fields in a date dimension (sometimes this can mean most of them) are considered as being simple selection elements. So, for instance, using the MonthFull field in a slicer will result in a list of months, without sliders. The best thing to do is to experiment with the various fields that are available in the DateDimension table and use those that best suit your purposes.

Formatting Slicers

Slicers can be formatted just like any other Power BI Desktop visual. Indeed, many of the techniques that you use to format slicers are identical to those that you have already seen when formatting tables and matrices. Consequently, to avoid pointless repetition, this section concentrates on any formatting attributes that are slicer specific and only refers in passing to formatting approaches that you have already covered in previous chapters.

Slicer Orientation

To help you to make the best possible use of report real estate, slicers can be configured to appear vertically (as in Figure 22-2) or horizontally. To switch a slicer's orientation:

1. Select the slicer that you want to modify. (I selected the colors slicer that you created previously.)

2. In the Visualizations pane, click the Format icon.

3. Expand the General section.

4. In the Orientation popup, select Horizontal.

5. Resize the slicer to suit your dashboard. A horizontal slicer will look something like the one in Figure 22-6.

Figure 22-6. *A horizontal slicer*

As you can see in Figure 22-6, a horizontal slicer does not have the small check boxes that a vertical slicer does. Consequently, when a horizontal slicer element is selected, the entire element is in "reverse video."

You probably also noticed that Power BI Desktop alters the number of rows of text as well as the width of text elements when you resize the slicer. It follows that you are best advised to experiment when altering slicer height and width in order to get the effect that suits you best.

Slicer Responsiveness

In the previous section, you adjusted the size of the slicer in order to fit all the available options onto a single horizontal row. There is, however, another available option when displaying slicers, and that is to make all the option elements adjust to take up all the available space in the slicer. Here is an example of this approach:

1. Select the slicer that you want to modify. (I will carry on using the colors slicer that you created previously.)

2. In the Visualizations pane, click the Format icon.

3. Expand the General section.

4. Set the Responsive button to On.

5. Resize the slicer. You will see that the slicer elements alter to take up the available space provided that they can all fit. The slicer will now look something like the one in Figure 22-7.

Figure 22-7. *A horizontal slicer*

Note   If the slicer elements cannot fit into the slicer, you will see a chevron indicating that you can scroll through the available elements.

Modifying the Outline

For Power BI Desktop, the outline is the line that separates the title from the items in a slicer. The following discusses how you can format this particular element:

1. Select the slicer that you want to modify. (I used the horizontal colors slicer that you created earlier using the file CarSalesDataForReports.pbix.)

2. In the Visualizations pane, click the Format icon.

3. Expand the General section.

4. Use the Outline weight slider to set the weight of the outline to 3 points.

5. Click the Outline color popup and choose a color. The separator line will change to reflect the modifications that you have made.

Adjusting Selection Controls

If you are not happy with the way that Power BI Desktop lets you select items in a slicer, then you can adjust the way that you interact with this particular visual. While the Power BI default mode of interaction is probably sufficient in most cases, it certainly does no harm to know that there are other ways of selecting elements in slicers.

Adding or Removing the Select All Box

You can add the Select all box to slicer as follows:

1. Select the slicer that you want to modify. (I used the original, vertical colors slicer that you created earlier.)

2. In the Visualizations pane, click the Format icon.

3. Expand the Selection controls section.

4. Slide the Select all switch to the On position. This will add a Select all item to the top (or left) of the slicer.

Should you *not* want a Select all item in a slicer, all you have to do is ensure that the Select all switch is set to Off in step 4.

Enabling Multiselect

A slicer's default mode is to select only a single item. This does not preclude you from selecting multiple items in a slicer, provided Multiselect is active (which it is by default). Should you need to activate—or deactivate—Multiselect, follow these steps:

1. Select the slicer that you want to modify. (I used the original, vertical colors slicer that you created earlier.)

2. In the Visualizations pane, click the Format icon.

3. Expand the Selection controls section.

4. Slide the Multiselect with Ctrl switch to the On position. This will allow multiple slicer elements to be selected.

Enabling Single Select

A slicer's default mode is to select only a single item, unless the user Ctrl-clicks several items. If you prefer to add items one at a time—and deactivate them individually too—you can enable Single select to do just this. Simply follow these steps:

1. Select the slicer that you want to modify. (I used the original, vertical colors slicer that you created earlier.)

2. In the Visualizations pane, click the Format icon.

3. Expand the Selection controls section.

4. Slide the Single select switch to the On position. This will set the slicer interaction to single select. You can see the result of this operation in Figure 22-8, where the slicer check boxes have become radio buttons.

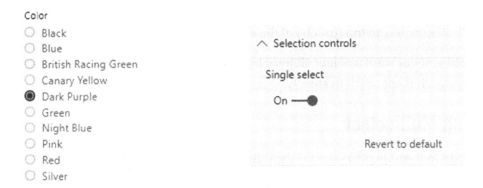

Figure 22-8. *Altering a slicer's selection controls*

Note   Setting Single select to On makes the Multiselect and Select all options disappear from the Formatting pane.

Setting the Exact Size and X and Y Coordinates of a Slicer

If you want to place a slicer with total accuracy on a dashboard canvas, then you can set the X and Y (horizontal and vertical) coordinates for the slicer. You can also specify its exact height and width. The following explains how:

1. Select the slicer that you want to modify.

2. In the Visualizations pane, click the Format icon.

3. Expand the General section.

4. Replace the X Position, Y Position, Width, and Height values with the pixel values that define the size and position of the slicer that you wish to apply.

Formatting the Slicer Header

Should you want to add some visual pizzazz to a slicer, you can tweak the display of the slicer header. This can be a useful visual cue to users to help them distinguish slicers from other visuals. Here is an example of how to do this:

1. Select the slicer that you want to modify. (I used the horizontal colors slicer that you created earlier.)

2. In the Visualizations pane, click the Format icon.

3. Expand the Slicer Header section.

4. Ensure that the Header switch is in the On position.

5. Click the Font color popup and choose a color for the header text.

6. Click the Background color popup and choose a color for the header background.

7. Adjust the Text size to tweak the size of the header text.

Formatting Slicer Items

Slicer items are the individual elements that make up the list of data that appear in a slicer, based on the underlying field. These, too, can be formatted to focus the attention of the reader. Here's an example:

1. Select the slicer that you want to modify (continuing with the colors slicer that you used in the previous section).

2. In the Visualizations pane, click the Format icon.

3. Expand the Items section.

4. Click the Font color popup and choose a color for the item text.

5. Click the Background color popup and choose a color for the background of each item.

6. Adjust the Text size for the text of the items.

7. Click the Outline popup and select Frame.

You can also format the following aspects of a slicer:

- Background

- Title

- Lock aspect ratio

However, since all of these are identical to formatting attributes that apply to tables and charts (and that you have seen in previous chapters), I will not repeat the description of them.

Finally, Figure 22-9 shows you a slicer with many of the formatting options that you just saw.

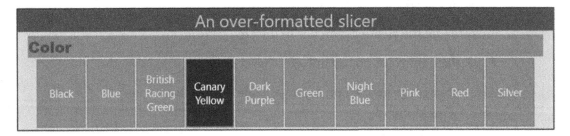

Figure 22-9. *A formatted slicer*

Sorting Slicer Elements

The elements in a slicer will be displayed in alphabetical order. If you wish, you can reverse this sort order, as follows:

1. Click the ellipses at the top right of the slicer.

2. Select Sort by color (or whatever the field name is).

The slicer elements will now be displayed in reverse alphabetical order.

Tip   You can add a Sort by column to any data field that you wish to display in another sort order.

Switching to Dropdown Slicers

Slicers are amazingly useful, but they do have one drawback: they can take up a lot of valuable screen space. So the development team at Microsoft has come up with an elegant solution. This is to use dropdown slicers, where the slicer elements only appear when you click a popup menu.

To convert an existing slicer to a dropdown slicer:

1. Select an existing slicer (or hover the mouse pointer over it). I will use the colors slicer that you have used so far in this chapter.

2. Click the chevron on the top right next to the Clear Selections icon. A popup menu will appear, as you can see in Figure 22-10.

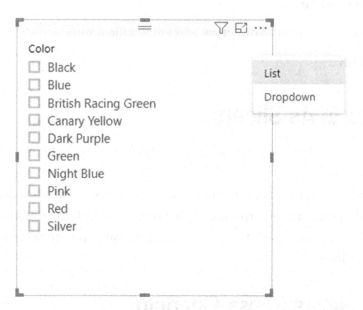

Figure 22-10.   *Switching to dropdown slicer*

3. Select Dropdown. The slicer will convert to a dropdown slicer. You can see what this now looks like in Figure 22-11.

Color

All

Figure 22-11. *A dropdown slicer*

4.   Click the chevron for the slicer popup list and select the element
that you want to slice the data on.

Tip   Dropdown slicers can be particularly useful when designing Power BI reports
for mobile phones.

Exporting Slicer Data

Slicer data can be exported just like the data in any other visual:

1.   Click the ellipses at the top right of the slicer.

2.   Select Export data.

3.   Browse to the desired directory and enter a file name.

4.   Click Save.

Using Charts As Slicers

You have seen how a table can become a slicer, which is a kind of filter. Well, charts can
also be used as slicers. Knowing how charts can affect the data in a Power BI Desktop
report can even influence the type of chart that you create or your decision to use a chart
to filter data rather than a standard slicer. Charts can be wonderful tools to grab and hold
your audience's attention—as I am sure you will agree once you have seen the effects
that they can produce.

Charts As Slicers (Cross-Filtering)

To begin with, let's see how a chart can be used to act as a slicer to filter data interactively
for any or all of the visualizations in a Power BI Desktop report. This technique is also
referred to as *cross-filtering*. Initially, let's assume that we are aiming to produce a report
using two objects:

- A cost plus spares by Color table

- A spare parts by Make column chart

Let's create a Net Margin by Color table. It is principally used to show the effect that using a chart as a slicer in a Power BI Desktop report has on other objects. As an added extra, you will apply a filter to the page to demonstrate that filters and slicers work together, as described.

1. Open the `C:\PowerBiDesktopSamples\CarSalesDataForReports.pbix` file and add a new blank page. You will need an entire uncluttered dashboard page for this example.

2. Add a table based on the following fields:

   a. Color (from the Colors table)

   b. CostPlusSpares (from the InvoiceLines table)

3. Add a bar chart based on the following fields:

   a. Make (from the Stock table)

   b. SpareParts (also from the Stock table)

4. Adjust the layout of the two visualizations so that it looks something like Figure 22-12.

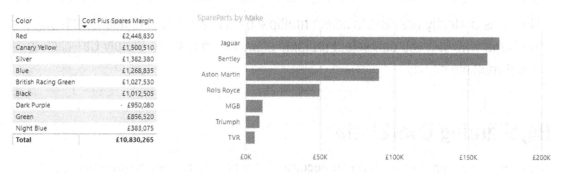

Color	Cost Plus Spares Margin
Red	£2,448,830
Canary Yellow	£1,500,510
Silver	£1,362,380
Blue	£1,268,835
British Racing Green	£1,027,530
Black	£1,012,505
Dark Purple	· £950,080
Green	£856,520
Night Blue	£383,075
Total	£10,830,265

Figure 22-12. *Preparing a chart for use as a slicer*

To see how to use a chart as a slicer, click any column in the chart of parts costs by make. I will choose Jaguar in this example.

The Power BI Desktop report will look something like Figure 22-13.

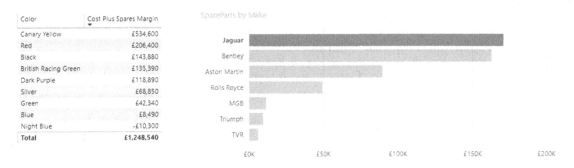

Figure 22-13. *Slicing data using a chart*

You will see that not only is the make that you selected highlighted in the chart (the bars for other makes are dimmed) but that the figures in the table also change. They, too, only display the cost plus spares (for each color) for the selected make.

To slice on another make, merely click the corresponding column in the column chart. To cancel the effect of the chart acting as a slicer, all you have to do is click for a *second time* the highlighted column.

Any bar chart, pie chart, or column chart can act like a slicer in this way, as can funnel charts, tree maps, scatter charts, bubble charts, and maps. The core factor is that for a simple slice effect, you need to use a chart that contains only one axis; that is, there will only be a single axis in the source data and no color or legend. What happens when you use more evolved charts to slice, filter, and highlight data is explained next.

Tip   It is perfectly possible to select multiple bars in a chart to highlight data in the same way that you can select multiple elements in a slicer. Simply Ctrl-click to select multiple items.

Highlighting Chart Data

So far, we have seen how a chart can become a slicer for all the visualizations in a dashboard page. However, you can also use another aspect of Power BI Desktop interactivity to make data series in charts stand out from the crowd when you are presenting your findings. This particular aspect of data presentation is called *highlighting*.

Once again, highlighting is probably best appreciated with a practical example. First, we will create a stacked bar chart of parts and labor costs by CountryName; and then we will use it to highlight the various costs inside the chart.

1. In a blank Power BI Desktop report (so you do not get distracted), create a clustered column chart based on the following fields:

    a. CountryName (from the Countries table)

    b. SpareParts (from the Stock table)

    c. LaborCost (from the Stock table)

2. Click SpareParts in the *legend*. All the sales costs will be highlighted (i.e., remain the original color) in the column for each country, whereas the other costs will be grayed out.

After highlighting has been applied, the chart will look like Figure 22-14.

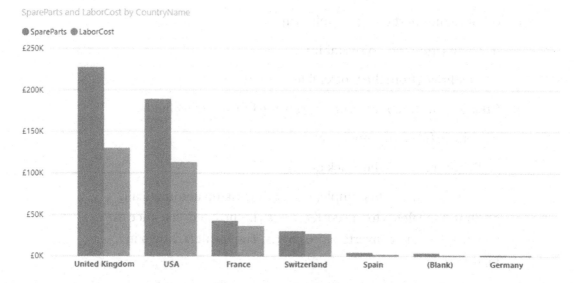

Figure 22-14. *Highlighting data inside a chart*

To remove the highlighting, all you have to do is click a second time the same element in the legend. Or, if you prefer, you can click another legend element to highlight this aspect of the visualization instead. Yet another way to remove highlighting is to click inside the chart, but not on any data element.

Highlighting data in this way should suit any type of bar or column chart as well as line charts. It can also be useful in pie charts where you have added data to both the Axis and Legend boxes, which, after all, means you have multiple elements in the chart just as you can have with bar, column, and line charts. You might find it less useful with scatter charts.

Cross-Chart Highlighting

Cross-chart highlighting adds an interesting extra aspect to chart highlighting and filtering. If you use one chart as a filter, the other chart is updated to reflect the effect of selecting this new filter not only by excluding any elements (slices, bars, or columns) that are filtered out but also by showing the proportion of data excluded by the filter.

As an example of this, create a pie chart of cost price by color and a column chart of direct costs by vehicle type using the file `CarSalesDataForReports.pbix`. We will then cross-filter the two charts and see the results. The steps to follow are

1. Create a pie chart using the following fields:

   a. Color (from the Colors table)

   b. CostPrice (from the Stock table)

2. Create a (clustered) column chart using the following fields:

   a. Vehicle (from the Stock table)

   b. CostPrice (from the Stock table)

   For charts that are this simple, Power BI Desktop automatically attributes the fields to the correct boxes in the Fields list once the source tables are converted into charts. The result is shown in Figure 22-15.

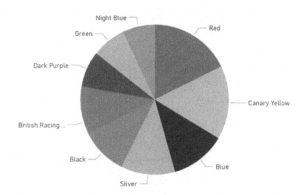

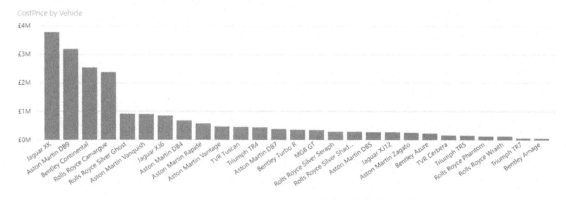

Figure 22-15. *Preparing charts for cross-chart highlighting*

3. Now click a slice in the pie chart (I have selected Red). You should see the result given in Figure 22-16. Not only have all the other segments of the pie chart been dimmed, but the bars in the bar chart have been highlighted to show the proportion of the selected color of the total sales cost per vehicle cost.

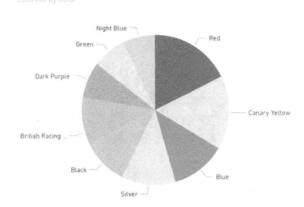

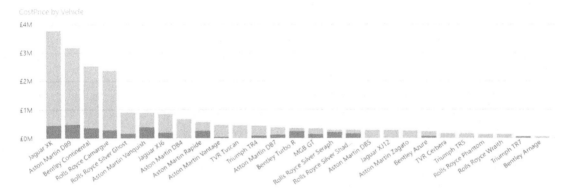

Figure 22-16. *Cross-chart highlighting*

4.   Now click the bar in the bar chart representing Aston Martin
DB9. You are now using the bar chart as a slicer. As you can see in
Figure 22-17, the pie chart displays the proportion of Aston Martin
DB9 sales for each color.

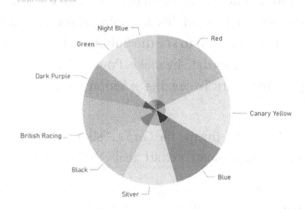

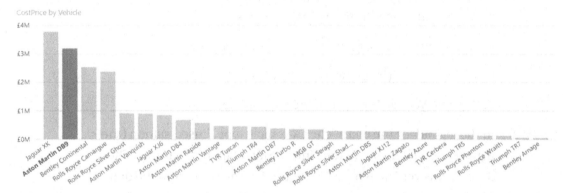

Figure 22-17. *Cross-chart highlighting applied to a pie chart*

Note   When you use a filter, you do not highlight a chart but actually filter the data that feeds into it; consequently, you remove elements from the chart. Highlighting leaves elements in a chart but accentuates certain aspects of the data relative to others.

Highlighting Data in Bubble Charts

Often when developing a visualization whose main objective, after all, is to help you to see through the fog of data into the sunlit highlands of comprehension, profit, or indeed, whatever is the focus of your analysis, you may feel that you cannot see the forest for the trees. This is where Power BI Desktop's ability to highlight data in a chart visualization can be so effective.

Let's take a visualization that contains a lot of information; in this example, it is a bubble chart of vehicle types. Indeed, in this example, an audience might think that there is so much data that it is difficult to see the bubbles for specific makes of car and so analyze the uniqueness for sales data by make. Power BI Desktop has a solution to isolate a data series in such a chart. To see this in action and to make the details clearer, you need to do as follows:

1. Create a bubble chart using the file `CarSalesDataForReports.pbix` (remember that this is a scatter chart, really) using the following elements:

   a. *X axis*: Average Parts Cost Ratio (from the Stock table)

   b. *Y axis*: SalePrice (from the InvoiceLines table)

   c. *Size*: Gross Margin (from the InvoiceLines table)

   d. *Details*: Color (from the Colors table)

   e. *Legend*: VehicleType (from the Stock table)

2. In the legend for the chart, click a vehicle type. I used saloon (the British word for sedan in the United States) in this example. The data for this vehicle type is highlighted in the chart, and the data for all the other vehicle types are dimmed, making one set of information stand out. This is shown in Figure 22-18.

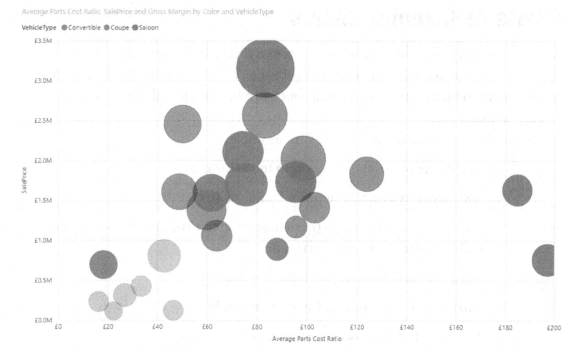

Figure 22-18. *Highlighting data in bubble charts*

This technique needs a few comments:

- To highlight another dataset, merely click another element in the legend.

- To revert to displaying all the data, click the selected element in the legend again.

- Highlighting data in this way also filters data in the entire page, as described previously.

Tip   You can add drill down to charts and still use chart highlighting in exactly the same way as you would use it normally, provided that you have disabled drill down using a chart element, as described in Chapter 16. In this case, you have to drill down (as well as up) using the Drill icons. The chart highlights an element at a drill-down level or sublevel, as well as applies filtering to the Power BI Desktop report.

Charts As Complex Slicers

Now that you have seen how charts can be used as slicers, let's take things one step further and see them used as more complex slicer elements. To show this, I build on the principles shown in the previous example, but add a bubble chart that will slice data on two elements at once.

Follow these steps for the purposes of this example:

1. Build a Power BI Desktop report with the following:

    a. A SalePrice by CountryName and Color matrix

    b. A Cost Plus Spares Margin (from the Stock table) by Make (from the Stock table) clustered column chart

2. Create a bubble chart using the following data:

    a. *X axis*: SalePrice (from the InvoiceLines table)

    b. *Y axis*: SpareParts (from the Stock table)

    c. *Size*: Weeks In Stock (from the Stock table)

    d. *Details*: CountryName (from the Countries table)

    e. *Legend*: Color (from the Colors table)

3. Resize and tweak the bubble chart so that it is displayed under the existing column chart and table.

4. Click the bubble next to the top-right bubble in the bubble chart. The Power BI Desktop report should look like Figure 22-19. The tooltip indicates which bubble has been used to filter the other visuals.

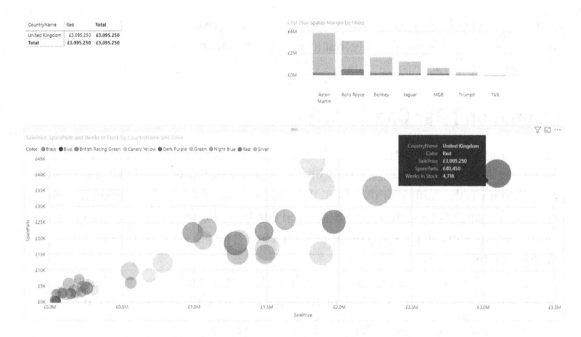

Figure 22-19. *Highlighting and filtering using a chart*

You can see that the other visualizations are filtered so that both the elements that make up the individual bubble (CountryName and Color) are used as filters (or double slicers if you prefer to think of them like that). This means that

- The table only shows colors where there are sales for this country and this color.

- The chart highlights data for this country and color only.

As was the case with simple chart slicers, you can cancel the filter effect merely by clicking for a second time the selected bubble. Or you can switch filters by clicking another bubble in the bubble chart. You will also see the chart itself has data highlighted, but this is explained a little further on.

Clearly, you do not have to display the fields on which you are filtering and highlighting in all the visualizations in a report. I chose to do it in this example to make the outcome clearer. In the real world, all other visualizations in a report are filtered on the elements in the Details and Legend boxes of the bubble chart.

Bubble charts are not the only chart type that lets you apply two simultaneous filters, however. All chart types that display multiple fields allow this. However, I am of the opinion that some charts are better suited than others to this particular technique. Specifically, I am not convinced that line charts are always suited to being used as filters for a Power BI Desktop report. Scatter charts may work—visually, that is—if you use cross-filtering, but it is just as likely that they will not. Stacked bar and stacked column charts can be ideal for cross-filtering, as you will see in the following sections.

Column and Bar Charts As Filters

Column charts and bar charts can also be used to filter a Power BI Desktop report on two elements simultaneously. The only limitation is that you can only have one set of numeric data as the values for the chart. If the bar or column chart is a stacked bar, then you can click any of the sections in the stacked bar. In addition, if the chart is a clustered bar or column, you can click any of the columns in a group to slice by the elements represented in that section.

If this limitation is not a problem, then this is how you can use bar or column charts (whether they are clustered, stacked, or 100% stacked) to apply double filters to a report:

1. Create a Power BI Desktop dashboard using the
   `C:\PowerBiDesktopSamples\CarSalesDataForReports.pbix`
   file with the following two elements:

   a. A matrix based on color and country name (as the rows), sales price, gross margin, and cost price (as the values). Once the matrix is created, click the Expand all down one level icon in the hierarchy to see all the levels of data.

   b. A clustered bar chart of sales price by country name.

2. Then create a stacked column chart using the following data:

   a. *Values*: Gross Margin (from the InvoiceLines table)

   b. *Axis*: CountryName (from the Countries table)

   c. *Legend*: VehicleAgeCategory (from the Stock table)

Once tweaked to clarify the appearance of the chart, the net result should look like Figure 22-20.

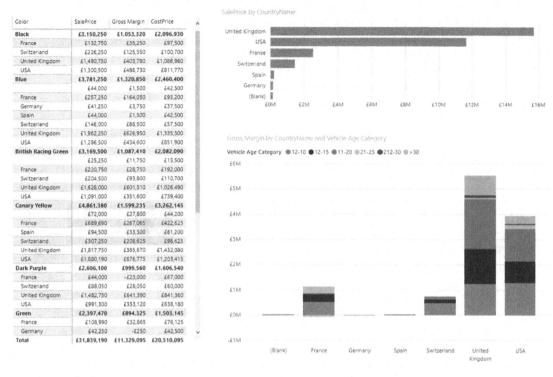

Figure 22-20. *A report ready for chart-based filtering and highlighting*

Clicking any segment of a column filters and highlights other visualizations on the same report for that country and car age range. An example of this is given in Figure 22-21, where the car age range of 11–20 has been selected for the USA column.

Color	SalePrice	Gross Margin	CostPrice
Black	**£574,250**	**£248,470**	**£325,780**
USA	£574,250	£248,470	£325,780
Blue	**£225,500**	**£115,500**	**£110,000**
USA	£225,500	£115,500	£110,000
British Racing Green	**£186,250**	**£33,750**	**£152,500**
USA	£186,250	£33,750	£152,500
Canary Yellow	**£445,690**	**£210,690**	**£235,000**
USA	£445,690	£210,690	£235,000
Dark Purple	**£407,750**	**£169,360**	**£238,390**
USA	£407,750	£169,360	£238,390
Green	**£286,750**	**£108,860**	**£177,890**
USA	£286,750	£108,860	£177,890
Red	**£652,250**	**£177,360**	**£474,890**
USA	£652,250	£177,360	£474,890
Silver	**£362,500**	**£228,500**	**£134,000**
USA	£362,500	£228,500	£134,000
Total	**£3,140,940**	**£1,292,490**	**£1,848,450**

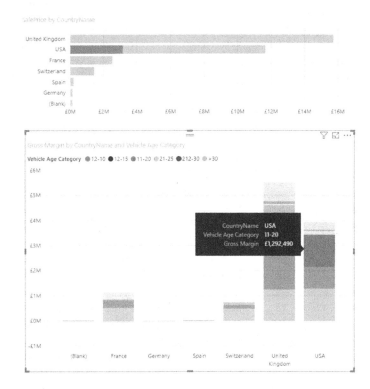

Figure 22-21. *Applying filters and highlights*

Clicking any car age range in the legend will filter by car age range only. You see this in Figure 22-22, where the legend item for 12-15 has been selected.

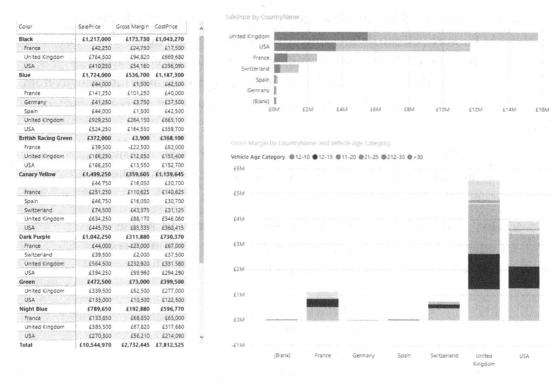

Figure 22-22. *Filtering using a legend element*

So in fact, you can choose to filter on a single element or multiple elements, depending on whether you use the chart or the legend as the filter source.

Note A line chart will not produce the same effect when you click only a data point. If you click a series in a line chart, you are highlighting that series, which is numeric data, and so it cannot be used as a slicer. Similarly, if you click an element in the legend of a column or bar chart, you are selecting a data series, and this, too, cannot serve as a slicer (even though it highlights the series in the chart).

Specifying Visual Interactions

In the previous few sections, you saw that the effects of selecting one or more items in a slicer are applied automatically to every visual on a page, as will the effects of using a chart as a slicer. This is indeed true and is the default behavior of Power BI Desktop unless you specifically configure a visual *not* to react when a chart or slicer on the page has items selected.

In effect, this means that you can attain a tremendous degree of subtlety in your dashboards, because you can define which visuals are to remain interactive—and which must not change when a slicer, chart, or multiple slicers and charts are used.

The following explains how to alter the default setting and remove interactivity from a visual. You need to be aware that you need at least two visuals in a report to carry out this modification.

1. Select the visual (this can be a text visual, a chart visual, or a slicer, for instance) that you want to prevent from having a highlighting effect on other visuals.

2. In the Format ribbon, click the Edit Interactions button. All the other visuals on the page will display the interaction icons that you can see in Figure 22-23 (a funnel in a chart and a "no entry" sign).

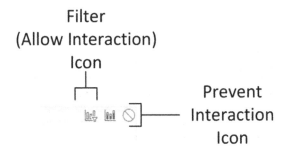

Figure 22-23. *The visual interaction icons for visuals*

3. Click the Stop Interaction icon (the "no entry" sign) in another visualization. I used the table of sales by country that you created previously. This icon will appear filled in, as shown in Figure 22-24.

CountryName	SalePrice
	£141,250
France	£2,524,510
Germany	£145,750
Spain	£207,750
Switzerland	£1,440,970
United Kingdom	£15,725,000
USA	£11,653,960
Total	**£31,839,190**

Figure 22-24. *The visual interaction icons set to prevent interaction*

4. Repeat steps 2 and 3 for all visuals that you want to "disconnect" from the selected visual.

5. In the Home ribbon, click the Edit Interactions button to stop the configuration of visual interaction. This will keep the existing interaction settings, but prevent the display of the interaction icons.

You can then iterate through all the charts and slicers on a page to set their dependency on another element.

Note   A slicer can also be linked to or dependent on another slicer on the page. Consequently, you can set the interaction for a slicer just as you can for any other visual.

What-If Slicers

A really interesting (and fairly new) feature in Power BI Desktop is the ability to interact with data using what-if slicers. These allow you to define variable values that are then applied to the data in the data model for any fields that you choose. You can then adjust the what-if value in a slider on screen and watch the calculated values change in real time.

This feature is best appreciated if you experiment with it. So here is one example of a what-if slicer. Let's suppose that you want to see what happens to gross margin if suppliers increase the cost of spare parts using the file CarSalesDataForReports.pbix.

1. In the Modeling ribbon, click the New Parameter button.

2. Enter **SparePartsVariation** in the Name box.

3. Select Decimal number as the data type from the Data type popup list.

4. Leave the Minimum value as 0, and enter **0.5** (50%) as the Maximum value.

5. Set the increment to **0.02** (2%). The dialog will look like the one in Figure 22-25.

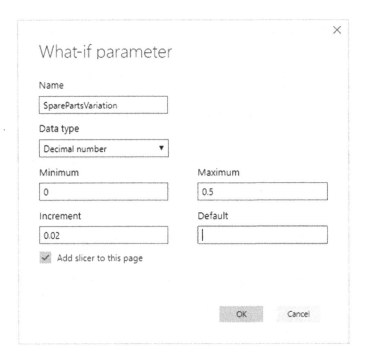

Figure 22-25. *The What-if parameter dialog*

6. Click OK. Power BI Desktop will add a new table to the data model named SparePartsVariation as well as a slicer to the desktop canvas. After resizing the slicer, you can see these, as well as the data in the new table (from the Data View), in Figure 22-26.

SparePartsVariation

0.12

What-If Slicer

SparePartsVariation

☐ 🗐 SparePartsVariation

☐ ▣ SparePartsVariation Value

New Table in Fields List

SparePartsVariation ▾
0
0.02
0.04
0.06
0.08
0.1
0.12
0.14
0.16
0.18
0.2
0.22
0.24
0.26
0.28
0.3
0.32
0.34
0.36
0.38
0.4
0.42
0.44
0.46
0.48

Table Values

Figure 22-26. *A what-if slicer*

7. Click the Stock table in the Fields list and then click New Measure
    in the Home or Modeling ribbons.

8. Enter the following formula in the formula bar (this will calculate
    a new spare parts cost using the multiplier from the what-if slicer):

    ```
    SparePartsNew = SUM(Stock[SpareParts]) + (SUM(Stock[SpareParts]) *
    'SparePartsVariation'[SparePartsVariation Value])
    ```

9. Click the check box on the formula bar to confirm the creation of
    the new column. You can see this column in the Data View if you
    select the SparePartsVariation table.

10. Create a clustered column chart using the following fields:

    a. Make (from the Stock table)

    b. SpareParts (from the Stock table)

    c. SparePartsNew (from the SparePartsVariation table)

11. Adjust the slider to apply a new percentage increase in the cost of spare parts. The resulting chart and slicer will look like those in Figure 22-27 (I have formatted the SparePartsVariation to appear as a percentage).

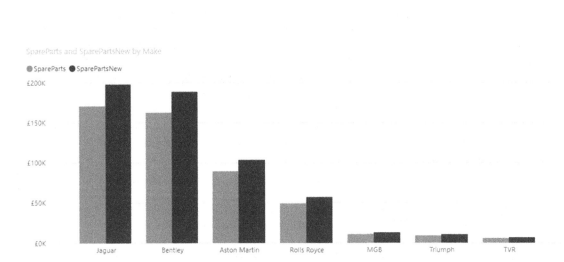

Figure 22-27. *A what-if slicer applied to a chart*

The values that you add in the table that underlies the what-if slicer can be fixed values, percentages—anything you like. Moreover, you can create as many new measures based on the what-if value as you want to.

Note   The code that you entered in step 8 was a short snippet of DAX. Unfortunately, an introduction to DAX is beyond the scope of this book.

Custom Visuals As Slicers

There are many excellent third-party visuals available that are designed to be slicers. This section provides a few pointers to some of the currently available third-party slicers. These are only a few of the slicers that you can find. Once again I have limited the selection to third-party visuals developed by Microsoft.

All the third-party slicers that are explained in the following sections can be added to a Power BI Desktop file using the techniques that you saw in Chapter 19.

Timeline Slicer

The timeline slicer lets you drag the upper and lower limits of a date range. You can also define the date element (year, quarter, month, week, or day) to use interactively. You can see this in Figure 22-28, where the timeline slicer is using the DateKey field from the DateDimension table.

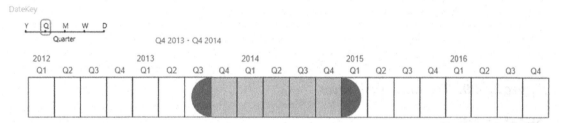

Figure 22-28.   *The timeline slicer*

The timeline slicer allows you to specify

- The depth of detail that you wish to display from a hierarchy of time (year level, quarter level, month level, week level, or day level)

- A visual data range that you specify by dragging the ends of the data range left and right

Timebrush Slicer

A timebrush slicer allows you to highlight a section of a time-ordered dataset. You can see this in Figure 22-29, where you can see that selecting a time range has filtered the table. This approach allows you to "home in" on potentially interesting data expressed in the slicer and see the detail displayed in other visuals.

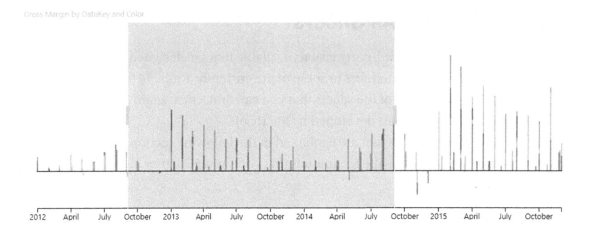

Gross Margin by DateKey and Color

Color	SalePrice	LaborCost	CostPrice	Gross Margin
Black	£935,250	£11,179	£605,490	£329,760
Blue	£1,900,250	£16,182	£1,135,100	£765,150
British Racing Green	£1,380,000	£11,093	£919,490	£460,510
Canary Yellow	£1,878,940	£21,410	£1,272,315	£606,625
Dark Purple	£944,500	£8,221	£564,180	£380,320
Green	£1,055,490	£13,943	£690,715	£364,775
Night Blue	£779,600	£8,545	£594,290	£185,310
Red	£2,623,990	£23,276	£1,492,295	£1,131,695
Silver	£1,233,690	£11,783	£813,770	£419,920
Total	£12,731,710	£125,632	£8,087,645	£4,644,065

Figure 22-29. *The timebrush slicer*

Chiclet Slicer

A chiclet slicer is a slicer that you can arrange and format in a multitude of ways. You can see a simple example in Figure 22-30.

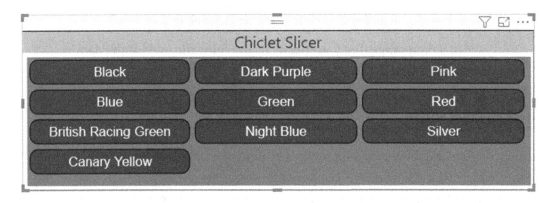

Figure 22-30. *The chiclet slicer*

This particular slicer really does add a multitude of options. I strongly recommend that you take a look at all that it can do. To whet your appetite, it is worth noting that you can

- Specify colors of selected and unselected elements

- Define the standard height and width of elements

- Add images to elements

Text Filter

The text filter is a kind of slicer in that it lets you enter a text—which need not be a complete word or even match any complete word in a field—to filter on the text interactively. You can see a text filter as well as the results of applying it (through clicking the magnifying glass icon) in Figure 22-31.

Model	LaborCost	CostPrice
Arnage	£2,500	£56,400
Camargue	£31,856	£2,379,105
Total	£34,356	£2,435,505

Figure 22-31. *A text filter in operation*

Choosing the Correct Approach to Interactive Data Selection

Now that you have taken a tour of the interactive options that Power BI Desktop offers, it is worth remembering that there is a fundamental difference between slicers and chart filters:

- Slicers and chart filters apply to all visuals on the Power BI Desktop page. Unless, that is, you have tweaked the visual interactions between selected slicers and the visuals that they should (not) affect.

- Highlighting only applies to the selected chart, although it filters data in other tables and highlights the percentage of this element in other charts.

Conclusion

In this chapter, you have seen how to use the interactive potential of Power BI Desktop to enhance the delivery of information to your audience. You saw how to add slicers to a report and then how to use them to filter out data from the visualizations it contains. Then, you learned how to highlight data in charts. Next, you saw how to use charts as interactive slicers to isolate specific elements in a presentation.

Then you saw how to control the way that slicers interact with other visuals on the page as well as how to apply what-if slicers. Finally, you took a peek at some of the third-party slicers that are available.

These techniques are powerful tools that can dramatically enhance the way that you present data to an audience. Used carefully, they will help your dashboards become more powerful and even more memorable. So all that remains is for you to start applying these techniques using your own data. Then you can see how you can impress your audiences using all the interactive possibilities of Power BI Desktop.

CHAPTER 23

Enhancing Dashboards

After spending a little time working with Power BI Desktop, I can assume that you have analyzed your data. In fact, I imagine that you have been able to tease out a few extremely interesting trends and telling facts from your deep dive into the figures—and you have created the tables, charts, maps, and gauges to prove your point. To finish the job, you now want to add the final tweaks to the look and feel of your work so that it will come across to your audience as polished and professional.

Fortunately, Power BI Desktop is on hand to help with all of these final touches, too. It can propel your effort onto a higher level of presentation—without you needing to be a graphic artist—so that your audience is captivated. With a few clicks, you can

- Align and distribute objects on the report canvas

- Add free-form text

- Add images to a report

- Apply a report background

- Add basic shapes to enhance your visuals

- Superpose objects and define how they are placed one on top of another

- Prepare reports ready for smartphone use

- Apply predefined themes (or stylesheets) to standardize the presentation of your reports

So, while not attempting to rival expensive drawing applications, Power BI Desktop can certainly add the necessary design flourishes that will help you to seize your audience's attention and convince them of the value of your analysis. Moreover, you can now apply a corporate standard presentation style using Power BI stylesheets to all your dashboards.

© Adam Aspin 2020
A. Aspin, *Pro Power BI Desktop*, https://doi.org/10.1007/978-1-4842-5763-0_23

This chapter takes you through these various techniques and explains how to use them to add the final touches to your analysis by enhancing the presentation of your dashboards. We will use the C:\PowerBiDesktopSamples\CarSalesDataForReports.pbix file as the source data and as an example of all the dashboards in this chapter. You will also have to download the image files to the C:\PowerBiDesktopSamples\Images folder from the Apress website, as described in Appendix A.

Formatting Ribbons

When enhancing dashboards, you will need to use three further ribbons:

- The View ribbon

- The Insert ribbon

- The Format ribbon

These three ribbons are described in the following sections.

The View Ribbon

The View ribbon options are illustrated in Figure 23-1 and explained in Table 23-1.

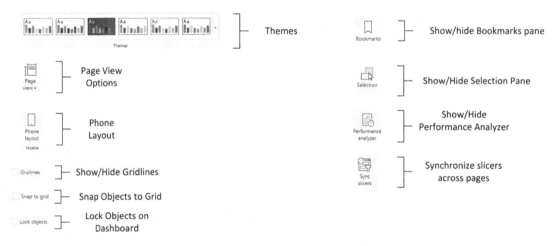

Figure 23-1. *The View ribbon*

Table 23-1. *View Ribbon Options*

Option	Description
Themes	Lets you choose a theme to apply to your entire dashboard.
Phone layout	Switches from desktop layout to phone layout and back.
Page view: fit to page	Scales the display to fit the available screen dimensions.
Page view: fit to width	Scales the display to fit the width of the screen.
Page view: actual size	Displays the page at its actual size.
Show or hide gridlines	Displays or hides the underlying grid.
Snap objects to grid	Forces visuals to align to the grid (hidden or visible) or leaves them free-floating.
Lock objects	Fixes all objects in place and prevents them from being resized or moved.
Bookmarks pane	Shows or hides the Bookmarks pane. You will learn about this in the next chapter.
Selection pane	Shows or hides the Selection pane. You will learn about this in the next chapter.
Sync slicers	Shows or hides the Sync slicers pane. This allows you to enable slicers to filter data on the pages that you select.
Performance analyzer	Shows or hides the Power BI Desktop Performance Analyzer. This tool can help you monitor the time taken by each visual in a report to query the data and render the result.

The Insert Ribbon

The Insert ribbon options are illustrated in Figure 23-2 and explained in Table 23-2.

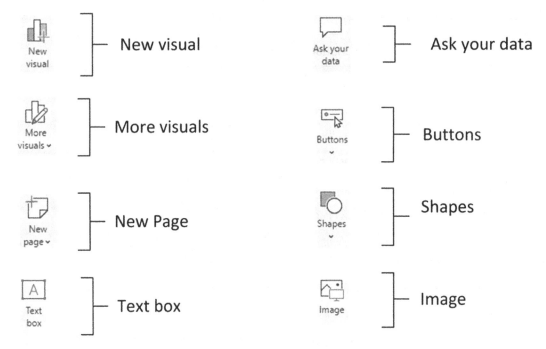

Figure 23-2. *The Insert ribbon*

Table 23-2. *Insert Ribbon Options*

Option	Description
New visual	Inserts a new blank visual into the current page.
More visuals	Lets you add third-party visuals from disk or the App Store.
New page	Lets you copy the current page or insert a blank page after the existing page.
Text box	Inserts an empty text box into the current page.
Ask your data	Lets you ask questions of the data using natural language.
Buttons	Adds a button to the current page.
Shapes	Adds a shape to the current page.
Image	Adds an image to the current page.

The Format Ribbon

The Format ribbon options are illustrated in Figure 23-3 and explained in Table 23-3.

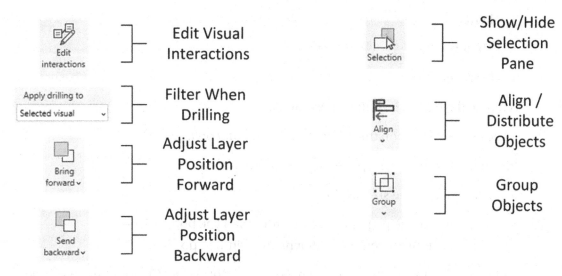

Figure 23-3. *The Format ribbon*

Table 23-3. *Format Ribbon Options*

Option	Description
Edit interactions	Changes how visuals react when data points in other visuals are selected.
Apply drilling to	Allows drill down to filter data in other visuals.
Bring forward	Brings a visual toward the top of a layer of objects.
Send backward	Sends a visual toward the bottom of a layer of objects.
Selection	Displays the Selection pane which allows you to show and hide (and set the tab order for) all the visuals on the page.
Align objects	Aligns and distributes selected visuals.
Group	Groups selected visuals.

Formatting the Page

Before you spend a certain amount of time and effort finalizing a presentation, it is vital to define one fundamental aspect of the output—the page format. Power BI Desktop lets you select from among the following output device formats:

- 16:9

- 4:3

- Letter

- Tooltip

- Custom

To change the page size, follow these steps:

1. Click anywhere on the report canvas (and *not* on a visual).

2. In the Visualizations pane, click the Format icon.

3. Expand the Page size section.

4. Select one of the page size presets from the Type popup list—or select Custom and enter the height and width in pixels.

Should you wish to specify your own page size, simply select Custom from the Type popup list and then enter the required page height or width in pixels. You can use the scroll arrows to set the required figure if you prefer. You can see the results of this in Figure 23-4.

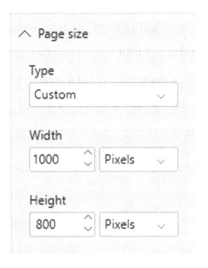

Figure 23-4. Custom page size settings

Note   Currently, the only available unit of measure is pixels.

Aligning and Distributing Visuals

There is one quick and easy tweak that is capable of adding a polished look to any dashboard. This is the simple decision to align visuals flawlessly so that you avoid giving an impression of ragged positioning. Like it or not, well-aligned visuals will help convince your audience that your analysis is valid.

To be clear, when I say *align visuals*, I include distributing visuals in the concept. So here is how you can apply both techniques to give a patina of professionalism to your dashboards.

Aligning Visuals

A set of neatly aligned elements on a page will always please an audience. What is more, it literally only takes a couple of seconds to take a set of existing visuals and to present them harmoniously. The following explains what you do:

1. Select the visuals that you want to align (Ctrl-click each one).

2. In the Format ribbon, click the Align button to display the popup menu. It will look like Figure 23-5.

Figure 23-5. *Alignment options*

3. Select the required option.

The selected elements will be aligned along their tops, bottoms, left or right sides, or centered, depending on the choice that you made. The available alignment options are outlined in Table 23-4.

Table 23-4. *Alignment Options*

Option	Description
Align left	Aligns all the selected visuals along their left sides.
Align center	Centers all the selected visuals.
Align right	Aligns all the selected visuals along their right sides.
Align top	Aligns all the selected visuals along their top edges.
Align middle	Aligns all the selected visuals in the middle of the elements.
Align bottom	Aligns all the selected visuals along their bottom edges.

Distributing Visuals

One way to add a final touch that implies "attention to detail" to a dashboard is to make sure that all visuals are neatly distributed horizontally and/or vertically. This will simply guarantee that there is always the same amount of space between each element.

1. Select the visuals that you want to distribute (Ctrl-click each one).

2. In the Format ribbon, click the Distribute button to display the popup menu. It will look like Figure 23-6.

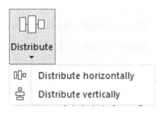

Figure 23-6. *Distribution options*

3. Select the required option.

4. The selected elements will be distributed horizontally or vertically, depending on the choice that you made. The available distribution options are outlined in Table 23-5.

Table 23-5. *Distribution Options*

Option	Description
Distribute horizontally	Distributes a selected series of visuals along a horizontal plane.
Distribute vertically	Distributes a selected series of visuals along a vertical axis.

Note   You may need to distribute a collection of visuals both horizontally and vertically to get the best effect. You will need to carry out the two alignment operations successively to obtain this result.

Aligning to the Grid

The Power BI Desktop canvas includes a grid (like a sheet of squared paper) that you can use to align visuals and other objects. This can help you create more polished-looking presentations. To align to the grid, simply

1. Activate the View menu

2. Select Snap objects to grid

Now, whenever you move or resize an object, it will align to the grid or increase/ decrease in size by one grid point (or pixel).

Displaying the Grid

If you prefer you can also display the grid to help you align objects:

1. Activate the View menu.

2. Select Show gridlines.

You will now see a pattern of dots (1 every 10 pixels) representing the hidden grid.

Note   The number of pixels in the Power BI Desktop report canvas will depend on the selected page size.

Specifying the Exact Position of a Visual

A final option that you can apply when placing visuals is to specify their exact position, height, and width. This feature is particularly useful when you want to make a series of visuals the same size. Follow these steps:

1. Select the visual that you want to resize and/or reposition.

2. In the Visualizations pane, click the Format icon.

3. Expand the General section.

4. Set the X (horizontal starting) position, Y (vertical starting) position, height, and width.

Power BI Desktop uses pixels as the unit of placement as it does for the underlying grid.

Adding Text Boxes to Annotate a Report

Let's begin at the start. You have spent quite a while digging into data and have found effective ways of drawing your audience's attention to the valuable information that it contains. However, you need the one, final, cherry on the cake—a title for the report. As a title is nothing other than a text box, this is your introduction to adding, formatting, and modifying text boxes.

A text box is a floating text entity that you can place anywhere on the Power BI Desktop report canvas. They are especially useful for annotating specific parts of a dashboard.

Adding a Text Box

Adding a text box is so easy that it takes longer to describe than to do, but nonetheless, this is how you do it:

1. In the Insert ribbon, click the Text box button. An empty text box will appear on the dashboard canvas.

2. Type in the text that you want to add; it will be a title. I entered **Sales for 2017**.

3. Place the mouse pointer over either the corner or lateral central indicators of the title box and drag the mouse to resize the title box.

4. Click the text box header bar (the gray area at the top of the text box) and drag the text box to the top center of the page.

5. Click outside the title anywhere in the blank report canvas.

Figure 23-7 shows you a text box in a report. Moreover, should you want to modify a text, it is as easy as clicking inside the text box and altering the existing text just as you would in, say, PowerPoint.

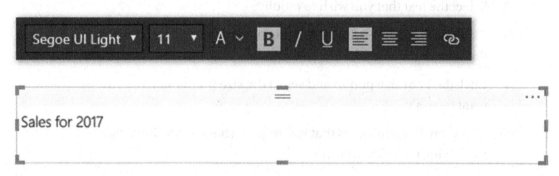

Figure 23-7. *Adding a text box to a report*

Note   If a text box is too small to hold the entire text, then scroll bars are added to the text box when you select it.

Moving Text Boxes

Text boxes are a Power BI Desktop visualization like any other, and consequently, they can be moved and resized just as if they were a table or a chart. So all you have to do to move a title is to

1. Hover the mouse pointer over the text box. A container will appear indicating the text box shape.

2. Click the top bar of the text box and drag the text box elsewhere on the dashboard canvas.

Alternatively, you can select the text box and then place the mouse pointer over the edges of the text box (but not on the corner or side handles) and drag the text box to a new position.

Formatting a Text Box

A text box can be formatted specifically so that you can give it the weight and power that you want. Even though this is completely intuitive, for the sake of completeness, here is a short example of what you can do:

1. Select the text box that you created previously. The Format palette will be displayed under or above the text box.

2. Select the text that you wish to modify.

3. Click the Font popup and select the font that you want to apply to the selected text.

4. Click the Font size popup and select the size (in points) that you want to apply.

5. Apply any font attributes that you require (bold, underline, italic) by clicking the relevant icons.

6. Align the text by clicking one of the three alignment icons. This will apply to all the text in the box.

Tip   Remember that you must highlight the text to format it. If you select the text box itself, then you can only alter the alignment of the text in the text box.

The formatting options for text boxes are explained in Table 23-6.

Table 23-6. *Formatting Options for Text Boxes*

Element	Icon	Description
Font	Segoe UI Light ▼	Lets you choose a font from those installed on the computer.
Font size	11 ▼	Lets you choose a font size.
Theme colors	A ⌄	Lets you choose a color.
Bold	B	Makes the text appear in boldface.
Italic	/	Makes the text appear in italics.
Underline	U	Underlines the text.
Left	☰	Aligns the text on the left of the text box.
Center	☰	Centers the text in the text box.
Right	☰	Places the text on the right of the text box.
Hyperlink	⚭	Adds a hyperlink for the selected text.

Adding a Hyperlink

Power BI Desktop dashboards certainly do not exist in isolation. It follows that you can use them as a starting point to link to other documents or web pages. Remember, however, that a hyperlink will *only* work once a Power BI Desktop file has been deployed to the Power BI Service in the cloud.

To add a hyperlink:

1. Select the text box that you created previously.

2. Select the text that will be the hyperlink.

3. Click the Hyperlink icon. The Format palette will expand to display the hyperlink box.

4.   Enter or paste in a URL.

5.   Click the Done button in the Format palette.

Removing a Hyperlink

To remove a hyperlink that you have already added:

1.   Select the text box containing a hyperlink that you created previously.

2.   Click inside the hyperlink. The Format palette will expand.

3.   Click the Remove button.

If you prefer, you can always simply remove the text that is the link.

Deleting Text Boxes

If you want to delete a text box, then be sure to

1.   Select the text box.

2.   Click the popup menu for the text box (the ellipses at the top right of the text box).

3.   Select Remove. The text box will be deleted.

An alternative way to delete a text box is to select the text box and press the Delete key.

Note   Merely selecting and deleting the text inside the text box will not remove the text box itself; so to be sure that you do not leave any unnecessary clutter in a report, delete any unwanted and empty text boxes.

Modifying the Page Background Color

Power BI Desktop does not condemn you to presenting every report with a white background. To avoid monotony you can add a different background color to each page in a report individually with a couple of clicks.

To apply a background to a report, all you have to do is

1. Click inside the dashboard canvas, but not on any existing visuals.

2. In the Visualizations pane, click the Format icon.

3. Expand the Page background section. The available options will look like they do in Figure 23-8.

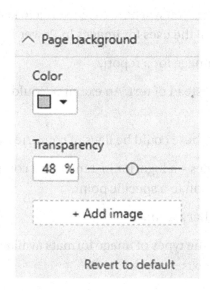

Figure 23-8. *Page background options*

4. Select a color from the palette of available colors.

5. Slide the Transparency button left or right to select a level of intensity for the chosen color.

Note   You have to format every page in a report individually. You cannot Ctrl-click to select multiple pages simultaneously.

Images

We all know what a picture is worth. Well, so does Power BI Desktop. Consequently, you can add pictures, or images, as they are generically known, to a Power BI Desktop report to replace words and enhance your presentation. The images that you insert into a Power BI Desktop report can come from the Web or from a file on a disk—either local or on an available network share. Once an image has been inserted, it is *not* linked to the source file. So if the source image changes, you will have to reinsert it to keep it up to date.

The following are some of the uses for images in Power BI Desktop:

- As a background image for a report.

- Images in tables instead of text. An example could be to use product images.

- Images in slicers. These could be flags of countries, for instance.

- Independent images—a logo, for instance, or a complement to draw the viewer's attention to a specific point.

- Images as a chart background.

Once we have looked at the types of image formats available, we will see how images can be used in all these contexts.

Image Sources

There are multitudes of image formats. Power BI Desktop accepts all of the following industry-standard image types:

- *JPEG*: This is a venerable standard image file format.

- *PNG*: This is a standard file format for Internet images.

- *BMP*: This is a standard image type produced by MS Paint, for instance.

- *GIF*: This is a venerable image format frequently used in web pages.

- *TIFF*: This is a standard format for scanned images.

- *RLE:* Run length encoding format.

- JPE: The 24-bit compressed JPEG graphic format.

- *JFIF*: A bitmap graphic that uses JPEG compression.

All of these formats (and their various descendant formats that Power BI Desktop can handle) can deliver reasonable quality images that should certainly suffice for Power BI Desktop reports. However, if you attempt to insert an image that is not in a format that Power BI Desktop can handle, you will get an alert and the image will *not* be inserted.

Note   When you attempt to insert an image from a file, the Open dialog filters the files so that only files with one of the acceptable extensions are visible. You can force the dialog to display other file formats, but Power BI Desktop may not be able to load them.

Adding an Image

You may still want to add completely free-form floating images to a report. However, before getting carried away with all that can be done with images, remember that Power BI Desktop is not designed as a high-end presentation package. If anything, it is there to help you analyze and present information quickly and cleanly. Inevitably, you will find that there are things that you cannot do in Power BI Desktop that you are used to doing in, say, PowerPoint. Consequently, there are many presentation tricks and techniques that you may be tempted to achieve in Power BI Desktop using images to get similar results. Indeed, you can achieve many things in a Power BI Desktop report by adding images. Yet the question that you must ask yourself is "Am I adding value to my report?" I am a firm believer that less is more in a good presentation. Consequently, although I will show you a few tricks using images, many of them go against the grain of fast and efficient Power BI Desktop report creation and can involve considerable adjustment whenever the data in a visualization changes. So I advise you not to go overboard using images to enhance your presentations unless it is really necessary.

Despite these caveats, let's add a floating, independent image to a Power BI Desktop report. In this example it is a company logo—that of Brilliant British Cars, the company whose metrics we are analyzing throughout the course of this book.

Adding an image is really simple. All you have to do is

1. In the Power BI Desktop Home ribbon, click the Image button. A
    classic Windows dialog will appear; it lets you choose the source
    image, as shown in Figure 23-9.

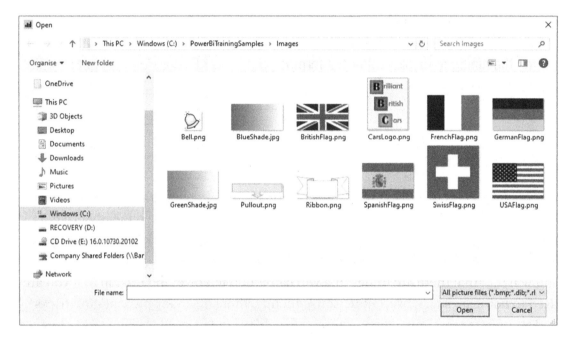

Figure 23-9. *Navigating to an image file*

2. Navigate to the directory containing the image that you wish to
    insert. There are several sample images in the
    `C:\PowerBiDesktopSamples\Images folder`, which you can
    install as described in Appendix A.

3. Click the image file. I use the example image CarsLogo.png in this
    example.

4. Click Open. The selected image will be loaded into the page.

5. Drag the image to the top left of the page and resize it. The
    dashboard will look like it does in Figure 23-10.

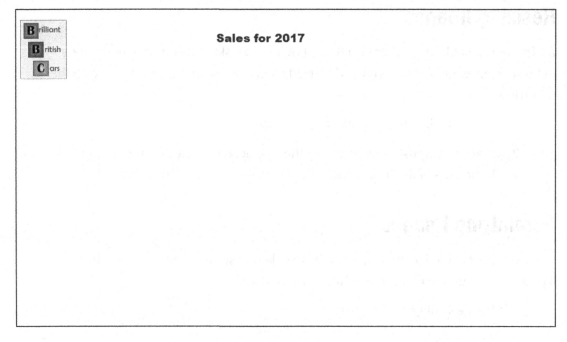

Figure 23-10. *An image added to a dashboard*

Removing an Image

To remove an image, all you have to do is

1. Select the image.

2. Click the popup menu for the image (the ellipses at the top right of the text box).

3. Select Remove. The image will be removed from the report. The original image file, of course, will not be affected in any way.

An alternative way to delete an image is to select the image and press the Delete key. The selected image will disappear from the report.

Resizing Images

An image is just like any other visual in a Power BI Desktop dashboard in that any of these elements can be moved and resized in exactly the same way. Simply do the following:

1. Select the image that you want to resize.

2. Place the mouse pointer over either the corner or lateral central indicators of the image and drag the mouse to resize the image.

Formatting Images

Once you have added an image, it can be tweaked to some extent in Power BI Desktop. The following are the parameters that you can modify:

- Image scaling

- Image title

- Image background

- Image border

- Aspect ratio

- Exact position and size

All of these modifications except for the first are common to most of the visualizations in Power BI Desktop. Indeed, you have come across some of them several times already. Consequently, I will not waste your time repeating things that you already know or can find elsewhere in this book.

Image *scaling* is completely new, however. Here is how you can alter the way that an image is altered if you resize it:

1. Select the image whose scaling you want to modify.

2. In the Visualizations pane (which has switched automatically to show only formatting options), expand the Scaling section.

3. In the Scaling popup, select Fill.

The image will adjust to take up all the available space in the image placeholder. The three available image scaling options are explained in Table 23-7.

Table 23-7. *Image Scaling Options*

Option	Description
Normal	The image maintains its height-to-width ratio (whatever the Lock Aspect setting) and resizes to fill the image placeholder as well as it can.
Fill	The image fills the image placeholder but distorts the image.
Fit	The image fills the image placeholder but cuts off parts of the image rather than distort the image.

Background Images

One major, and frequently very striking, use of images is as a background to a report—and possibly even to a whole series of reports. So, let's take a look at how to use images for report backgrounds.

Adding a Background Image

Before anything else, you need to add a background image. This is, once again, extremely simple:

1. Click the dashboard canvas for the page where you want to add a background image. Make sure that no visuals are selected.

2. In the Visualizations pane, click the Format icon.

3. Expand the Page background section.

4. Click Add image. A classic Windows dialog will appear; it lets you choose the source image.

5. Navigate to the directory containing the image that you wish to insert. In this example, it will be `C:\PowerBiDesktopSamples\Images`.

6. Click the image file. I will use the example image GreenShade.jpg in this example.

7. Click Open. The selected image will be loaded into the page.

8. In the Image fit popup list, select Fit.

The selected image will cover the entire page behind any visuals.

There are three possible ways of adjusting the size of an image. These are given in Table 23-8.

Table 23-8. *Background Image Sizing Options*

Option	Description
Normal	The image stays the size it was created.
Fit	The image expands (and may be deformed) to cover the entire dashboard area.
Fill	The image is expanded proportionally to cover as much of the dashboard area as possible.

Moreover, you can alter a background image's intensity once it has been added to a page. To do this:

1. With the Page background section of the Format panel expanded, slide the Transparency slider left or right.

Note   There is nothing that you can do to resize an image manually in Power BI Desktop. If you need an image to be a certain size, you have to create it at the exact required size in an image creation application.

Some Uses for Independent Images

The limits of what images can do to a report are only those of your imagination, so it is impossible to give a comprehensive list of suggestions. Nonetheless, the following are a few uses that I have found for free-form images:

- *Company logos*, as we have just seen.

- *Images added for a purely decorative effect.* I would hesitate before doing this at all, however, as it can distract from the analysis rather than enhance it. Nonetheless, at times, this may be precisely what you want to do (to turn attention away from some catastrophic sales figures, for instance). So add decoration if you must, but please use sparingly!

- *To enhance the text in a text box* by providing shading that is in clear relief to the underlying image or background.

- *As a background* to a specific column in a table. Be warned, however, that the image cannot be made to move with a column if it is resized.

Note   If you want to add an image that covers the entire dashboard page, then do *not* add an independent image to the page, but use the background image technique. Otherwise you risk making other visuals on the page inaccessible.

Adding Shapes

Sometimes your figures may need just a little help to stand out from the crowd. Maybe a small set of visuals (gauges or cards perhaps) are best grouped together. Whatever the need, Power BI Desktop can add a few final touches to your dashboards by adding one or more shapes to a page.

The following are built-in shapes that you can choose from:

- Rectangle (which means squares, too)

- Oval (including circles)

- Line

- Triangle

- Arrow

Let's suppose that you want to add a decorative arrow to a dashboard to draw the reader's attention to a specific figure. The following explains how you can do this:

1. In the Home ribbon, click the Shapes button to see a popup list of available shapes. You can see this in Figure 23-11.

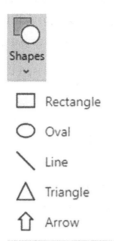

Figure 23-11. *The Shapes popup*

2. Select Rectangle. A square will be added to the dashboard canvas.

3. Resize the square in the same way that you would resize a chart or an image. If you use the top, bottom, or side handles, then the square will become a rectangle.

As the other available shapes can be inserted in exactly the same way, I will not explain them individually, but will let you have some fun by adding different shapes to a page to see how they can enhance a dashboard.

Formatting Shapes

You can tweak the following aspects of shapes:

- Lines

- Fill

- Rotation

- Title

- Background

- Aspect ratio

- Exact position and size (X and Y coordinates)

As it is only the first three that are new as far as formatting visuals is concerned, let's see them in action.

Lines and Fill Color in Shapes

When we say "lines" in shapes, we are really talking about the exterior boundary of the shape. Power BI Desktop lets you alter its

- Color

- Thickness (or weight, as it is known)

- Transparency

As well as you can set the fill color of the shape. Here is how you can alter basic characteristics for any of the available shapes:

1. Select the shape to format.

2. In the Visualizations pane (that now displays only the Format shape options), expand the Line section.

3. Select a color for the line from the popup palette of available colors. The exterior line of the shape will change color.

4. Adjust the Weight to set the line thickness. The exterior line of the shape will grow thicker.

5. Move the Transparency slider to the left to adjust the intensity of the color.

6. Expand the Fill section.

7. Select a color for the fill from the popup palette of available colors. The interior of the shape will change color.

8. Move the Transparency slider to the right to adjust the intensity of the color. The Visualizations pane and the shape will look like they do in Figure 23-12.

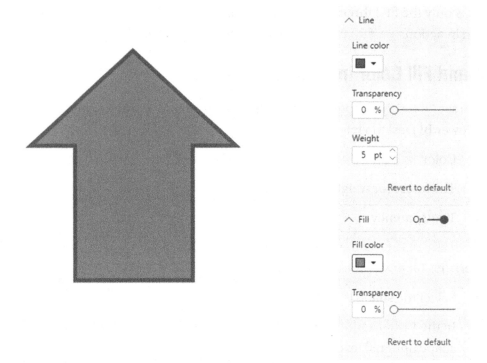

Figure 23-12. *Formatting a shape*

Shape Rotation

Some shapes need to be rotated to point in the right direction for the effect that you are trying to produce. The shapes that generally need adjusting in this way are arrows and triangles—though this technique can be applied to any shape. To rotate a shape:

1. Select the shape to rotate.

2. In the Visualizations pane (that now displays only the Format shape options), expand the Rotation section.

3. Drag the Rotation slider left and/or right to set the arrow to point in the direction that you want. Alternatively, you can enter the exact rotation value in the Rotation box to the left of the slider. The shape and Visualizations pane will look like they do in Figure 23-13.

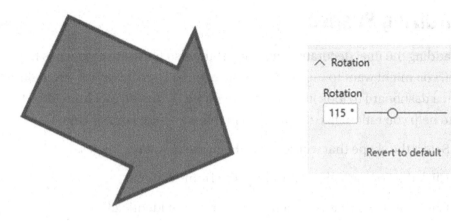

Figure 23-13. *Rotating a shape*

It is worth noting that you can enter a precise rotation value in the Rotation box if you prefer. This is particularly useful when swiveling a shape through multiples of 45 or 90 degrees.

Note   When adding an ellipse or a rectangle, you will discover that Power BI Desktop begins by creating these as, respectively, circles and squares. To ensure that they stay perfectly formed (if that is what you want), ensure that the Lock Aspect formatting option is set to On before you resize the shape.

Removing Shapes

To remove a shape, all you have to do is

1. Select the shape to remove.

2. Click the popup menu for the shape (the ellipses at the top right of the text box).

3. Select Remove. The shape will be deleted.

An alternative way to delete a shape is to select the shape and press the Delete key. The selected shape will disappear from the report.

Standardizing Shapes

If you are adding the final decorative (and hopefully also illustrative) touches to a dashboard, you might want to make a series of shapes all look identical. After all, you never want a dashboard to look like a patchwork quilt. A trusted tool from MS Office is available to help you rationalize dashboards in this way—the Format Painter.

1. Select the shape that will serve as the model for other shapes.

2. Click the Format Painter button in the Home ribbon.

3. Click the shape that you want to see formatted identically to the first shape.

Note   You cannot double-click the Format Painter to apply the same format several times to different shapes as you can when formatting in MS Word or Excel.

Organizing Visuals on the Page

A complex dashboard can consist of many elements (though hopefully not so many that you end up confusing your public). This is where some elementary polishing of the final appearance can help. Put simply:

- An audience gives more credence to a slickly organized dashboard.

- Clarity of layout is interpreted as clarity of thought—and so adds to the credibility of the facts and figures that you are presenting.

- Good aesthetics add to, rather than detract from, the points that you are making.

So to finish our tour of the ways that you can finalize and perfect your dashboards, you need to learn how to adjust the way that visuals (whether they are tables, charts, gauges, images, or shapes) relate to one another on the page; this essentially means layering visuals vertically.

Layering Visuals

As a report gets more complex, you will inevitably need to arrange the elements that it contains not only side by side but also one on top of the other. Power BI Desktop lets you do this simply and efficiently.

As an example of this, let's create a chart with another chart superposed on it:

1. Create a donut chart using the following two fields:

    a. Cost Plus Spares Margin (from the InvoiceLines table)

    b. CountryName (from the Countries table)

2. Create a (clustered) column chart using the following two fields:

    a. Make (from the Stock table)

    b. RatioNetMargin (from the InvoiceLines table)

3. In the donut chart, add a legend and set it to appear on the right. Also, set the Detail labels option to Off. Set the Donut background option to Off.

4. Place the donut chart in the top right-hand corner of the bar chart.

5. With the donut chart selected, choose Bring Forward ➤ Bring To Front from the Power BI Desktop Format ribbon.

Your composite chart should look like Figure 23-14. Bringing the donut chart to the front means that the gridlines for the column chart are now under the donut chart.

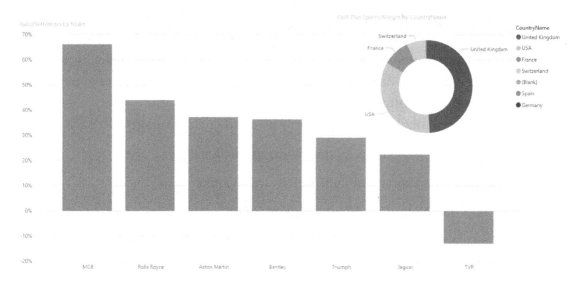

Figure 23-14. *Layering charts*

This technique is particularly useful when you are adding independent images as was described in the previous section. It is also handy when you are combining elements such as images and text boxes, as you will see in the next section.

Grouping Visuals

Power BI Desktop also lets you group multiple visuals into a single visual. This can be extremely practical when you want to copy or resize multiple objects.

To do this:

1. Create the two charts described in the previous section.

2. Select both charts.

3. In the Format menu, click Group ➤ Group.

4. Resize the (single) visual that the two (previously separate) visuals have become. You should see something like Figure 23-15.

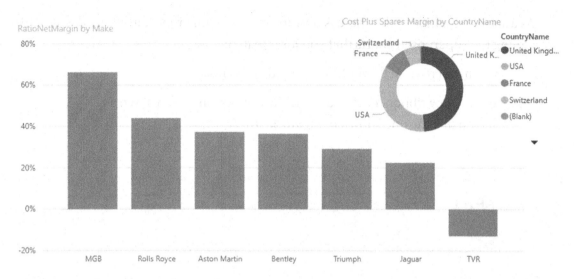

Figure 23-15. *Grouped visuals*

Phone Layout

More and more information workers need their data on the move. This means consulting Power BI dashboards on their mobile phones. To make this easier, the Power BI team at Microsoft has added a valuable feature to Power BI Desktop—phone layout.

This technique lets you take an existing report and define how each of the visuals that make up the dashboard is displayed on a smartphone. There are several advantages to this approach:

- Power BI detects the type of device being used and applies the appropriate presentation style automatically.

- You do not have to create duplicate reports, one for a computer screen and another for a phone, and then update them both.

- You do not have to include all the visuals in a dashboard on the phone version.

- Any changes in a visual for the dashboard are reflected in the corresponding phone layout.

As a simple example of this, here is how to create a phone report from the dashboard containing the superposed charts that you just created:

1. Open, or create, a Power BI Desktop dashboard.

2. In the View ribbon, click the Phone layout button. You will see a screen like the one shown in Figure 23-16.

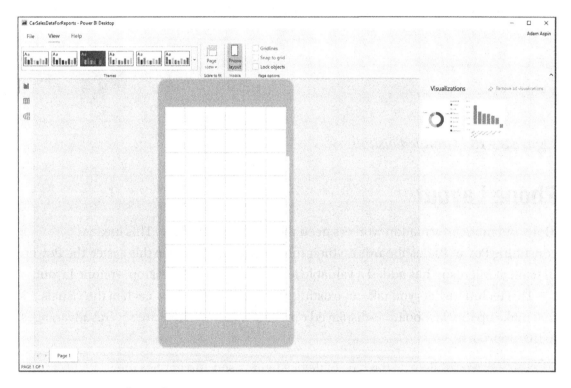

Figure 23-16. *Phone layout*

3. Drag the first visual that you want to use in a phone version of this report to the phone image.

4. Resize the visual so that it covers the required phone screen real estate.

5. Add any other visuals that you wish to use and position them to suit your requirements. The phone layout screen could look like Figure 23-17.

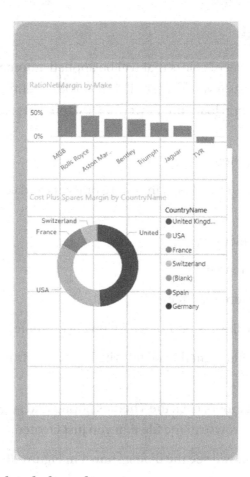

Figure 23-17. *A completed phone layout*

6. Switch back to desktop layout by clicking the Phone layout button once again.

Now, once this report is published to the Power BI Service (or an on-premises Power BI Report Server), any mobile users will see the phone layout on their smartphones. Unfortunately, setting up and using the Power BI Service is a large—and separate—topic that I cannot go into here.

Note   If a visual is not completely visible in phone layout, you will see ellipses and a small down-facing triangle in the visual to indicate that visibility may be an issue.

Report Themes

You can define your own set of colors that will be applied automatically to tables, matrices, and data in charts if you so wish. This involves creating a simple file in a specific format that you then load into Power BI Desktop. This file must contain the following elements:

- A name for the theme

- A set of data colors enclosed in square brackets and comma-separated

- A background element

- A foreground element

- An accent element for tables

You can see a sample file in step 1 of the following example:

1. Load the .json file named BrilliantBritishCars.json from the sample data.

2. In the Format ribbon, click the Themes popup and select Browse for theme and browse to the file that you just created.

3. Click Open. You will see the dialog shown in Figure 23-18.

Figure 23-18. *The Import theme dialog*

4. Click OK. The theme file will open and apply the theme to all the pages in the current file.

The background, foreground, and table accent colors will now apply to every table and matrix in the report. Moreover, the data colors will, by default, be those specified in the themes file. You can see this in Figure 23-19.

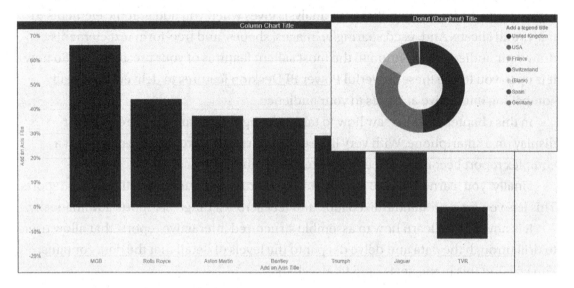

Figure 23-19. *Applying a theme to a report*

This theme file is also available in the folder `C:\PowerBiDesktopSamples` (assuming that you have downloaded the sample files from the Apress website).

Note   To remove the theme that you have just loaded and revert to the default theme, click Switch Theme ➤ Default Theme in the Home ribbon.

Report themes are very much a work in progress in Power BI Desktop and are currently in a constant state of flux. I imagine that the structure of the JSON file will have evolved considerably by the time that this book is published. It is such a complex subject that I can only refer you to the multitude of available resources on this subject that can be found on the Web. So I cannot, with any certainty, delve any deeper into the question of report branding and creating the underlying JSON files in this edition of this book. What I can do is suggest that you look at the file BrilliantBritishCars.json from the sample data to get an idea of what is required. Indeed, you should be able to use this file as the basis for your own style templates.

Conclusion

In this chapter, you saw how to push the envelope when using Power BI Desktop to deliver particularly compelling presentations. You saw how adding images can turbocharge the impression that your analysis gives when you add graphic elements to tables and slicers. And, used sparingly, images, shapes, and free-form text elements can draw your audience's attention to the most salient features of your presentation. So now it is up to you to use these powerful Power BI Desktop features to deliver some really compelling interactive analyses to your audience.

In this chapter you also saw how to take existing reports and prepare them for display on a smartphone. With very little extra effort, you were able to ensure that a complex report becomes perfectly adapted for a mobile device.

Finally, you learned how to apply your own "branding" for Power BI Desktop reports. This lets you create a standardized look and feel across a range of reports automatically.

It is now time to learn how to assemble structured interactive reports that allow users to drill through the data and delve deep into the levels of detail that the data contains. You will find this in the next—and final—chapter.

CHAPTER 24

Advanced Dashboarding Techniques

In the final chapter of this book, I want to finish by introducing a series of techniques that you can use to add real power and depth to your dashboards. The approaches that you will discover here are specifically designed to add structure to your reports. This means that you will be able to

- Guide your users in a path of data discovery from the highest to the lowest level of detail

- Add popup windows to explain specific aspects of the data in greater detail

- Provide navigation through multipage reports

- Use your data to tell a story

- Present your data narrative as an interactive slideshow

Taken individually, the techniques that you can use to achieve these objectives are all extremely useful and can drive insight and understanding. Used together, however, they can turbocharge your dashboard and wake up even the most jaded audience at your presentations.

In this chapter, then, you will learn how to

- Implement drillthrough between report pages—and even across reports

- Add popup visual tooltips

- Create bookmarks to memorize various aspects of the page display—and to move between pages

© Adam Aspin 2020
A. Aspin, *Pro Power BI Desktop*, https://doi.org/10.1007/978-1-4842-5763-0_24

- Set up buttons and images to control user interaction with a dashboard—including adding internal links between pages

- Apply slicers across some or all of the pages in a report

- Use templates to ensure a standardized look and feel for your dashboards across a department or enterprise

Drillthrough

One of the key techniques that you can apply to shape your data narrative is the ability to drill down through the data and display progressively more detailed levels of information. In simple terms, Power BI Desktop lets you jump to another page based on an interactive selection criterion quickly and easily. This enables you—and your users—to delve into the detail about your data in a progressive and structured way.

Drillthrough is a function that requires at least two pages in a report:

- The source page that contains data about many elements

- A destination (or detail) page that provides a different set of visuals that exist to provide a more detailed level of information on a single aspect of the data

Let's see this in action. To avoid pages of instructions, I will only ask that you create two very simple report pages. In practice, of course, your reports could be much more complicated than these.

The Source Page

The source page is the page that you will use for the high-level view of your data. For argument's sake, let's assume that this is the total sales for the company since it was founded, expressed as a chart:

1. Open the Power BI Desktop file `C:\PowerBiDesktopSamples\CarSalesDataForReports.pbix`.

2. Rename the blank page **Sales**.

3. On this page, create a bar chart using the following fields:

   a. Make

   b. SalePrice

You can see this chart in Figure 24-2.

The Destination Page

This page must be designed to show more detailed data that is relevant to the single element that you used as the basis for the drillthrough on the source page. In this example that means information about a *make* of vehicle. This page will also have a couple of specific tweaks added that specify that it is the destination for a drillthrough action.

1. Add a new page to the existing report.

2. Rename this page **Make Details**.

3. Add a card using the field Make. Don't worry about the actual make that is displayed at this stage.

4. In the Formatting pane for the card, set the Category label to Off.

5. Add a table using the following fields:

   a. FullYear

   b. CostPrice

   c. SalePrice

6. Add an area chart using the following fields:

   a. Color

   b. LaborCost

   c. SpareParts

   You can see these two visuals in Figure 24-3.

7. Click the report canvas (outside any visual) and drag the Make field into the Drillthrough area of the Visualizations pane. Place this field in the Drillthrough Filters well. A back button appears automatically at the top left of the current page.

8. Place the button where you prefer it to appear on the dashboard.

9. Click the report canvas and take a look at the Drillthrough area of the Visualizations pane. You can see the result in Figure 24-1.

Figure 24-1. *The Drillthrough Filters well*

The two pages—source and destination—are now linked and ready to drill down into the data.

Applying Drillthrough

You can now use your drillthrough report.

1. Go to the Sales page.

2. Right-click any bar in the chart. I am using *Rolls Royce* in this example. You will see the popup menu that is shown in Figure 24-2.

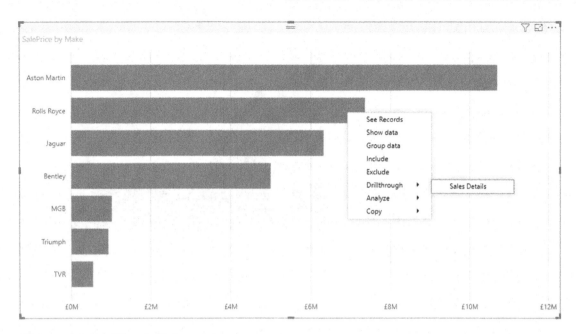

Figure 24-2. *The drillthrough context menu*

3. Select Drillthrough ➤ Sales Details. Power BI Desktop will
    display the Sales Details page—where you can see the make that
    you clicked in the source page displayed in the card visual. In
    Figure 24-3 you can see the destination page after applying the
    drillthrough.

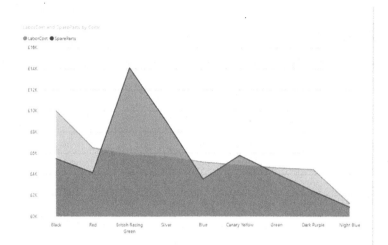

Figure 24-3. *The drillthrough destination page*

4. Ctrl-click the back button to return to the source report.

The Make Details report will be displayed and will filter the data to display the make of the row or data point that you right-clicked.

Power BI Desktop created a back button automatically on the drillthrough report (the "destination" report page). However, you do not have to use this button if you do not want to. In fact, any shape or image can become a back button. If you consider it superfluous, you can delete it.

Multiple Levels of Drillthrough

Drillthrough is not limited to a single level. Once you have drilled down into greater detail on a second page, there is nothing to prevent you drilling down yet again to an even deeper level of detail on a third page. All you have to do is to repeat the process that you learned in the previous section, only this time you use the "destination" page as the starting point—and create a third page as the new destination.

When drilling down to deeper and deeper levels of analysis, it is worth noting that you can choose to apply any existing filters that are in place when drilling down (which is a fairly standard approach)—or you can override any slicers and filters when drilling down except for the drillthrough filter itself (i.e., the element that you clicked in step 3 of the previous example).

If you wish to inhibit filter propagation when drilling down between pages, simply set the Keep all filters option in the Values pane to Off. You can see this in Figure 24-4.

Figure 24-4. *Inhibiting filter propagation during drillthrough*

Drillthrough Across Power BI Files

Drillthrough is not limited to a single report. You can also drill down across reports. However this will only happen with reports that you have deployed to the Power BI Service.

To enable drillthrough across reports, simply set the Cross-report button to On in the Values pane. You saw this button in Figure 24-4.

Popup Tooltips

Popup tooltips are among the most impressive capabilities that Power BI Desktop has to offer—at least in the opinion of most of the users that I have spoken to. Popup tooltips allow you to hover the cursor over, for example, a pie chart segment or a bar chart element (or indeed just about any metric in a dashboard) and immediately display a selected chart, table, or a combination of both that hovers over the existing dashboard visual. This allows you to add an immediate level of detail to a dashboard page without having to leave the page.

In essence, popup tooltips are a separate page that has been configured in a specific way to host a small number of visuals (anything above two or three generally defeats the object of the exercise). The main steps that are explained in the following are

- Add a new page

- Specify that the page is a tooltip

- Reduce the page size

- Add a tooltip filter

Before actually creating a tooltip page, it is important to know what metric you will be filtering on. This is because a tooltip filter is designed to provide a more granular level of detail for a specific element. Consequently, you need to know what the filter element will be when you are building the popup tooltip.

In the following example, you will be using the file `C:\PowerBIDesktopSamples\CarSalesDataForMultipages.Pbix`. This file contains a pie chart with sales by make. The aim is to add a tooltip filter that provides further details about each make. So the field *Make* is the tooltip filter field that we will use.

1. Open the file CarSalesDataForMultipages.Pbix.

2. Add a new page and name it **CostsTooltip**.

3. Click the Format icon for the page in the Visualizations pane.

4. Expand Page information and set Tooltip to On.

5. Expand Page size and select Tooltip from the popup list of available sizes.

6. Expand Page background and select a color for the page background (this will make the popup tooltip stand out more clearly from the underlying dashboard). The format options are shown in Figure 24-5.

Figure 24-5. *Tooltip formatting options*

7. Click the Fields icon in the Visualizations pane to switch back to the Fields information.

8. Drag the Make field into the "Drag tooltip fields here" well as shown in Figure 24-6.

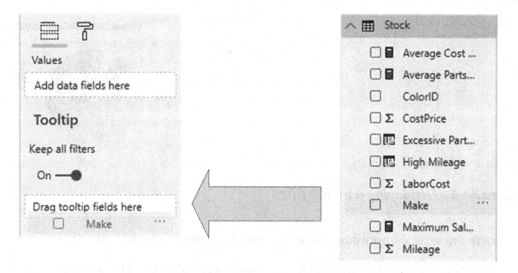

Figure 24-6. *Specifying a tooltip filter*

9. Create a clustered column chart of LaborCost and SpareParts by Model in the new tooltip page. You will see that the chart is much larger than is normally the case. This is because the final popup tooltip is shown with a smaller page size taking up the entire dashboard design surface in the tooltip page.

10. Resize the chart to take up all the available space in the tooltip page.

11. Format the chart to your liking.

Now, when you hover over any segment of the pie chart, the popup tooltip appears, as shown in Figure 24-7.

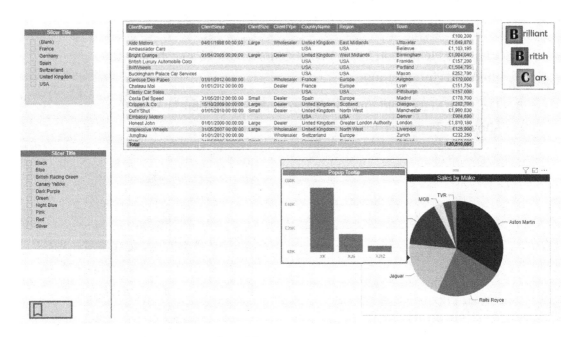

Figure 24-7. *Displaying a tooltip filter*

There are several important points to note when creating tooltip visuals:

- You may prefer to specify the exact size of the page used for a popup tooltip in pixels, rather than using the preset value "tooltip." To do this, first select Custom in the Type popup of the Page size section of the Page formatting options, then enter a height and width for the popup tooltip in pixels.

- You might want to hide the tooltip page once created to prevent users from clicking it and displaying it as a page, rather than a tooltip. To do this, all you have to do is to right-click the page table and select Hide page from the available options in the context menu.

- The tooltip popup will appear any time the filter metric is used. In other words, any visual that contains (in this example) the Make field will display the popup tooltip, whichever page the visual is on.

- You can format the tooltip visual(s) and the page that becomes a tooltip just as you would any standard visual or page.

- Tooltip visuals can contain several different visuals on the tooltip page if you wish.

- Tooltip visuals cannot, themselves, invoke other tooltip visuals.

Bookmarks

Bookmarks are one of the most powerful and useful features of Power BI. They help you to take analytics from the merely interactive to the totally meaningful by helping your data to tell its own story. Bookmarks are a method of memorizing selected aspects of a dashboard so that you can reset them quickly and easily. In practice, this means that you can remember the state of

- The current page.

- Any active filters.

- Slicers—this includes both the slicer type (dropdown or list) and the slicer state (the selected elements).

- Visual selection state (such as any cross-filtering applied).

- Any sort order that has been applied to some or all visuals.

- Drill state.

- Object visibility (using the Selection pane—as you will learn in a few pages' time).

- The focus or Spotlight modes of any visible object.

As with most Power BI Desktop features, bookmarks are best understood through seeing them in action. So here is an example of how to create two bookmarks and then apply them in turn:

1. Open the file CarSalesDataForMultipages.Pbix.

2. Remove any filter elements and slicer selections that are not necessary, and ensure that no cross-filtering is active.

3. In the View ribbon, click the Bookmarks icon. The Bookmarks pane will appear.

4. Click Add. A new bookmark (called Bookmark 1, probably) will appear in the list of bookmarks.

5. Click the ellipses to the right of the new bookmark to display the context menu (alternatively, you can right-click the bookmark name).

6. Select Rename.

7. Enter the new name and press Enter. I suggest **Baseline** in this example. The Bookmarks pane will look like the one in Figure 24-8. What you have done is to "memorize" the state of the page and all the visuals it contains before any slicers or filters are applied.

Figure 24-8. *The Bookmarks pane*

8. Apply one or two slicer choices and click one of the pie chart sections to cross-filter the data. Then click the ellipses on the top right of the table and select Spotlight. These modifications will alter the data displayed on this page.

9. Create a second bookmark (as described in steps 4–7) named **SlicedData**. You have now "memorized" the new, altered state of the page after the slicers and spotlight were applied.

Clicking either of the bookmarks will reapply the state of the slicers, filters, and cross-filters that were active when you created the bookmark.

Updating a Bookmark

A bookmark, once created, is never set in stone. You can update an existing bookmark at any time as your analytics requirements evolve.

1. Click the bookmark that you want to update.

2. Add or remove slicer elements, filters, and cross-filter selections to adjust the dashboard display.

3. Click the ellipses to the right of the new bookmark to display the context menu (alternatively, you can right-click the bookmark name) and select update.

The bookmark is updated (even if nothing is immediately visible to indicate this), and the new state of the page is now memorized.

Defining the Extent of a Bookmark's Application

As I mentioned earlier, bookmarks can be applied to several aspects of a dashboard. However, you do not have to apply a bookmark to every aspect of a dashboard. You can choose to have a bookmark apply to the range of options that are described in Table 24-1.

Table 24-1. *Bookmark Application*

Extent	Description
Data	This means that any filters, slicers, cross-filtering, or sorting that have been applied are memorized with the bookmark.
Display	This means essentially that any visuals that have had the spotlight option applied will have this attribute "remembered" with the bookmark.
Current page	The current page is included in the definition of the bookmark—and applying the bookmark will make display the page where the bookmark was applied.
Visuals	You can select one or more visuals to restrict the number of visuals that will be affected when the bookmark is used.

Essentially, this means that a bookmark has a variable scope and effect—and you decide how far-reaching this should be. Each individual bookmark can be tailored to suit your needs like this:

1. Click the bookmark that you want to update.

2. Click the ellipses to the right of the new bookmark to display the context menu (alternatively, you can right-click the bookmark name) and uncheck Display.

3. Select Display from the context menu.

4. Click the ellipses to the right of the new bookmark and select Update.

The bookmark will now cease to apply any spotlighting of visuals that were associated with the bookmark.

Note   At least one of the bookmark options (data, display, or current page) must be selected—or the bookmark becomes inactive.

Arranging Bookmarks

Once you have learned to appreciate just how useful bookmarks can be, you may find yourself creating quite a collection of them. So it is worth noting that there are a few techniques on offer to make managing bookmarks easier. They are

- Changing the order in which bookmarks appear in the Bookmarks pane

- Grouping bookmarks

- Deleting bookmarks

For example, to change the order in which bookmarks appear in the Bookmarks pane

1. In the Bookmarks pane, drag a bookmark vertically to a new position in the list of bookmarks.

Deleting bookmarks is as simple as right-clicking a bookmark and selecting Delete from the popup menu.

Slideshows Using Bookmarks

Power BI Desktop is not only a superb analytical tool. It can also help you in presenting data to tell a meaningful story—and bookmarks can be a valuable assistant when it comes to making the data speak for itself. This is because a series of bookmarks can be played back as a slideshow.

1. In the Bookmarks pane, organize the bookmarks from top to bottom in a meaningful sequence that represents the order of your data-driven narrative.

2. In the Bookmarks pane, click View. The first bookmark in the list will be activated. A new bar appears at the bottom of the report. You can see this in Figure 24-9.

Bookmark 1 of 2	SlicedData	‹ › ✕

Figure 24-9. *The SlideShow bar*

3. Click the right-facing chevron to activate the next bookmark in the list.

4. Once the slideshow is finished, click the Exit button at the top right of the Bookmarks pane.

It is probably self-evident, but clicking the left-facing chevron activates the previous bookmark in the list.

Buttons

Power BI is, above all, a reporting tool. However, this does not mean that it has to be static in any way. To allow you to develop more interactive reports, you can add buttons to any dashboard page. Once set up, buttons let users

- Jump to a specific page

- Return to the previously used page

- Open the Power BI Q&A dialog

- Open a web or intranet page

In this example you will see how to add a button that will display a selected page. This will mean creating a new "destination" page that you will "jump" to by clicking a button in a different page.

1. Open the Power BI Desktop file C:\PowerBIDesktopSamples\ CarSalesDataForMultipages.Pbix.

2. Insert a new page and rename it **DetailedAnalysis**.

3. Add a bar chart of SalePrice and CountryName.

4. Add a bookmark (as described previously) named **Destination**.

5. Return to Page 1.

6. In the Insert menu, click the popup chevron in the Buttons icon. You will see the selection of available buttons in the popup menu as shown in Figure 24-10.

Figure 24-10. *The Buttons popup menu*

7. Select Bookmark as the button type. A bookmark-style button will be added to the dashboard.

8. Place the button on an empty area of the dashboard, and leave the button selected.

9. In the Visualizations pane, set the Button Text to On.

10. Expand the Text section.

11. Enter **Click to Jump** as the button text.

12. Ensure the Action section is set to On and expand it.

13. Ensure that the button type is set to Bookmark.

14. Select Destination (the name of the bookmark that you created in step 4) as the bookmark to link to this button. The Action section of the Visualizations pane will look like Figure 24-11.

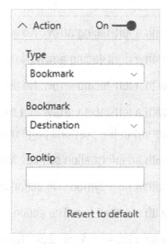

Figure 24-11. *Setting a button action to Bookmark*

If you now Ctrl-click the button, this will make the new page appear.

Note   It is only in Power BI Desktop that you have to use Ctrl-click to activate a button action. Once deployed to the Power BI Service in Azure, a simple click will suffice.

> **Warning**   If you leave a button selected and insert another button, the existing button will be converted to the new button type.

Button Options

Power BI Desktop gives you a series of button types that you can choose from. Choosing a button type that is appropriate to the interaction that you want to define will help you create interactive dashboards quickly and painlessly. It is worth noting, however, that you can change any button type once it has been created and that selecting the button type merely applies presets that you can override later if necessary.

Table 24-2 lists the built-in button types that you can choose from.

Table 24-2. *Button types*

Option	Description
Left arrow	Inserts a button with a left-facing arrow. No action is specified by default.
Right arrow	Inserts a button with a right-facing arrow. No action is specified by default.
Reset	Inserts a button with a left-facing arrow. No action is specified by default.
Back	Inserts a button with a left-facing arrow in a circle. The action is set automatically to return to the previous page used.
Information	Inserts a button with an information symbol. No action is specified by default.
Help	Inserts a button with a help symbol. No action is specified by default.
Q&A	Inserts a button with a callout box. The action is specified as active Q&A.
Bookmark	Inserts a button with a bookmark symbol. The action is set automatically to invoke a bookmark—you only have to specify which one to use.
Blank	Inserts a button without an icon. No action is specified by default.

Changing the Button Type

Fortunately, the button type that you originally choose is not set forever. You can switch between button types quickly and easily.

1.   Select the button you wish to modify.

2.   In the Visualizations pane, expand the Action section.

3.   Ensure the Action section is set to On and expand it.

4.   Select a different action from the list of available actions.

Button Actions

There are currently four predefined actions that you can "attach" to a Power BI dashboard button to add interactivity to your reports. Table 24-3 shows the actions that you can associate to a button.

Table 24-3. *Button actions*

Option	Description
Back	This adds a back button that is preset to return to the previously used page.
Bookmark	This type of button lets you select a bookmark to apply. This allows you either to modify page filters, slicers, and sort order or move to a different page—or a combination of both.
Q&A	Presents a Q&A Explorer window.
Web URL	Jumps to the URL that you enter in the Action section of the Visualizations pane once Web URL is selected.

Note   When you are using buttons merely to move between pages, it is often best to define the bookmark for the destination page that you will be using *without* the data and display options enabled for the bookmark (as described previously). This will ensure that you jump to the destination page without adding unexpected filters or slicers.

Formatting Buttons

As you might expect, Power BI allows you to format buttons much as you can format any visual in a dashboard. The elements that you can format are

- The button text—indeed, you can define three different button texts:

  - *Default state*: The standard appearance of the button text

  - *Hover state*: The text that is displayed when the cursor is placed over a button

  - *Pressed state*: The state of a button once pressed (assuming that any button action does not immediately display a new page)

- The outline

- The button fill

- The button background

You can also, technically, add a title and a border to a button, but in my opinion these are largely superfluous given the other available options.

1. Select the button you wish to modify.

2. In the Visualizations pane, expand the Button Text section.

3. Select On Hover from the popup list of possible button states.

4. Add a text for the hover state. I will simply add **Hovering**.

5. Modify the font, font color, alignment, and text size.

6. Expand the Icon section and select a different icon from the list of those available.

7. Expand the Outline section and modify the outline color and outline weight for the default state.

8. Select On Hover from the popup list of possible button states.

9. Modify the outline color and outline weight for the hover state.

10. Expand the Fill section and modify the fill color for the default state.

11. Select On Hover from the popup list of possible button states.

12. Modify the fill color for the hover state.

13. You can see the results of altering the formatting for two button states in Figure 24-12.

Figure 24-12. *Button formatting*

Note   Power BI Desktop does not yet allow you to apply your own images to buttons. However, as you can see in the next section, you can use images and shapes as buttons to produce the same effect.

Using Images and Shapes as Buttons

Quite possibly to compensate for the current inability to add your own images to buttons, Power BI Desktop nonetheless allows you to use images and shapes as buttons. This is mercifully easy—as it simply parallels the method that you just saw for setting actions for buttons.

As an example, here is how to jump to a page using the bookmark that you created previously:

1. Ensure that you have added a bookmark to the page that you wish to move to (the "destination" page).

2. On a different page, add—or select—the image you wish to use as the clickable element to jump to the destination page.

3. With the image selected, expand the Action section in the Visualizations pane.

4. Ensure the Action section is set to On and expand it.

5.   Select a bookmark from the list of available actions.

6.   Select the bookmark name from the list of available bookmarks.

Note   You can apply exactly the same technique to any of the shapes added from the Insert ribbon.

Applying Slicers Across Multiple Pages

Chapter 22 introduced you to the concept and application of slicers to Power BI dashboards. Yet slicers still have more secrets to reveal. Specifically, you can fine-tune the application of slicers across multipage reports and specify which slicers apply to which pages in a Power BI report. This means that you can, for instance, create a "home" page for a report that contains a series of slicers and then tweak Power BI Desktop to ensure that any or all of the slicers on this page will automatically apply to other selected pages. This guarantees a predictable and reassuring user experience for readers—as well as avoiding the necessity of having to copy and paste a set of slicers across multiple pages. Another non-negligible factor is this approach frees up considerable screen real estate across the pages in a report.

Suppose that you have a report with a first page named "Cover Page" that contains a couple of slicers and then three other pages. This is how you can apply a slicer from the initial page to other pages:

1.   Click the tab for the page containing the slicers.

2.   Select the slicer whose effect you want to extend to other pages.

3.   In the View pane, click Sync slicers. The Sync slicers pane appears, displaying the list of all the pages in the report. The third column of the page list (which indicates if a slicer is visible on the report page) is checked for the current page. You can see this in Figure 24-13.

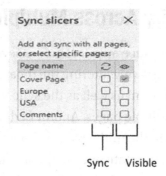

Figure 24-13. *The Sync slicers pane*

4. Check the second column (which specifies that the slicer is
    active on the page) for all the other pages. You can see this in
    Figure 24-14.

Figure 24-14. *The Sync slicers pane with slicers synchronised across several pages*

5. Close the Sync slicers pane by clicking the cross icon in the top-
    right corner of the pane.

Now, when you use the selected slicer to filter data interactively, the slicer's effect
will extend beyond the current page to all the selected pages

---

Note   It may seem counterintuitive, but you have to check the sync box for the
current page—or the slicer will have no effect on the other pages.

Setting Slicer Visibility Across Multiple Pages

If you want slicers not only to produce an effect across several pages but also to appear on the pages where they will be actively filtering the data, then all you have to do is to check the box in the visibility column as well as the sync box. This avoids you having to copy and paste slicers across multiple pages. Another advantage is that formatting or repositioning the source slicer on the initial page will result in the slicers that have been made visible on other pages to automatically be updated to reflect any changes.

Note   It is not currently possible to select multiple slicers and define their application and visibility together by Ctrl-clicking the source slicers.

Templates

To conclude this book, I want to draw your attention to one Power BI technique that can save you a considerable amount of time when mass-producing dashboards. This is the use of templates that contain

- Standard layouts (such as logos and graphic elements).

- Predefined styles (in a JSON stylesheet that you have attached to the template file). You saw this in Chapter 23.

- Selected third-party visuals.

A Power BI template is nothing more than a standard Power BI Desktop file that contains some or all of the preceding elements ready for you to use as a basis for a dashboard that will deliver a standardized corporate look and feel that will also save you time as you do not have to add the same graphic elements every time to a new dashboard.

To save a file as a dashboard:

1. Create a standard Power BI Desktop file that contains all the elements (logos, styles, decorative graphics, repeating elements such as the date of the last data update, etc.).

2. In the File menu, click Save As....

3. Select Power BI Template files (*.pbit) as the Save As type.

4. Give the file a name and click Save.

5. The Export a template dialog will appear, where you can enter a description for the template. You can see this dialog in Figure 24-15.

Figure 24-15. *The Export a template dialog*

6. Click OK.

Now, when you want to create a new dashboard based on the template

1. Click File ➤ Open and click the Browse button. The Windows Open dialog will appear.

2. On the bottom right of the dialog, select Power BI Template files (*.pbit).

3. Navigate to the template file that you created, select it, and click Open.

The template will open as a new file. This means that when you save the file, Power BI Desktop will prompt you for a file name—which prevents you from opening an existing file (to use as a model) and accidentally overwriting the original.

Conclusion

In this final chapter, you learned how to enhance dashboards and develop them into structured reports that guide the user to a progressively deeper understanding of the data that they are analyzing with Power BI. You saw how to create a data story by adding drillthrough paths into the data both inside a report and across separate reports.

You also discovered how to draw attention to specific data elements using popup tooltips as well as how to define specific paths through the pages of a report using buttons and bookmarks. You then learned how to control the effect of slicers across all or part of a multipage report.

As a final flourish, you saw how to create reusable templates that not only accelerate dashboard creation but also project a standardized corporate look and feel to users and audiences alike.

You have now reached the end of your journey through dashboard creation with Power BI Desktop. I sincerely hope that you have enjoyed this experience and will have amazing fun delivering analytics with this truly awesome tool.

APPENDIX A

Sample Data

Sample Data

If you wish to follow the examples used in this book—and I hope you will—you will need some sample data to work with. All the files referenced in this book are available for download and can easily be installed on your local PC. This appendix explains where to obtain the sample files, how to install them, and what they are used for.

Downloading the Sample Data

The sample files used in this book are currently available on the Apress site. You can access them as follows:

1. In your web browser, navigate to the following URL: `https://www.apress.com/gb/book/9781484257623`.

2. Click the button Download Source Code. This will take you to the GitHub page for the source code for this book.

3. Click Clone or Download ➤ Download Zip and download the file PowerBIDesktopSamples.zip.

You will then need to extract the files and directories from the zip file. How you do this will depend on which software you are using to handle zipped files. If you are not using any third-party software, then one way to do this is

1. Create a directory named `C:\PowerBIDesktopSamples`.

2. In the Windows Explorer navigation pane, click the file PowerBIDesktopSamples.zip.

© Adam Aspin 2020

A. Aspin, *Pro Power BI Desktop*, https://doi.org/10.1007/978-1-4842-5763-0_25

3. Select all the files and folders that it contains.

4. Copy them to the folder that you created in step 1.

Images

The images used in various chapters can be found in the directory `C:\PowerBIDesktop Samples\Images`.

Index

A

Add Column ribbon, 196–198
Advanced Editor, 285, 399
    core elements, 400, 401
    database connection, 402, 403
    expressions, 400
    let statement, 401
    modification, 402
    optional settings, 404
    syntax checking, 400, 403
Advanced text filters
    applying, 761
    clear icon, 763
    option, 764
    stage, 762
Aligning visuals, 827, 828
Analysis Services databases
    CarSalesOLAP, 69
    credentials, 70
    cube tools, 73–75
    SSAS cube, 71, 72
Application programming interface
    (API), 169
Applied Steps list, 191
ArcGIS maps
    adding pins, 732, 733
    adding theme, 730
    Basemap type, 727
    choosing symbol type, 731
    creation, 725

    infographics, 735
    location type, 728, 729
    reference data, 736
    reference layer, 733
    visual placeholder, 726
    welcome dialog, 726
Area charts, 636, 637
Aster plot, 688
Attribute slicer, 694, 695
Axis modification
    X axis, 630, 631
    Y axis, 632–634
Azure Blob Storage, 144–147
Azure security, 147
Azure SQL database
    on-premises server, connect, 138, 139
    PaaS, 134
    Power BI Desktop, connect, 135–137
Azure SQL data warehouse, 139–141
Azure Virtual Machine, 142–144

B

Bar/column charts
    double filters, 808
    highlighting/filtering, 809, 810
    legend element, 811
Bing maps, 706
Bookmarks
    application, 869, 870
    arrangement, 870

885

© Adam Aspin 2020
A. Aspin, *Pro Power BI Desktop*, https://doi.org/10.1007/978-1-4842-5763-0

Printed in the United States
by Bookmasters

Printed in the United States
By Bookmasters